THE ANALYSIS OF

HOUSEHOLD

SURVEYS

THE ANALYSIS OF HOUSEHOLD SURVEYS

A Microeconometric Approach

to Development Policy

Angus Deaton

Published for the World Bank
The Johns Hopkins University Press
Baltimore and London

©1997 The International Bank for Reconstruction
and Development / THE WORLD BANK
1818 H Street, N.W.
Washington, D.C. 20433, U.S.A.

The Johns Hopkins University Press
Baltimore, Maryland 21211-2190, U.S.A.

The findings, interpretations, and conclusions expressed n this study are entirely those of the authors and should not be attributed in any manner to the World Bank, to its affiliated organizations, or to its Board of Executive Directors or the countries they represent.

Photographs on the back cover: *top and bottom*, household interviews during the Kagera Health and Development Survey, 1991–94; *middle*, woman being weighed as part of the Côte d'lvoire Living Standards Survey, 1986 (top photo by T. Paul Schultz; middle and bottom photos by Martha Ainsworth).

Library of Congress Cataloging-in-Publication Data

Deaton, Angus.
    The analysis of household surveys : a microeconometric approach to
  development policy / Angus Deaton.
        p.   cm.
    Includes bibliographical references and index.
    ISBN 0-8018-5254-4
    1. Household surveys—Developing countries—Methodology.
  2. Developing countries—Economic conditions—Econometric models.
  I. Title.
  HB849.49.D43   1997
  339.4' 07'23—dc21   97-2905
                                                                  CIP

Contents

Introduction

The collection of household survey data in developing countries is hardly a new phenomenon. The National Sample Survey Organization in India has been collecting such data on a regular basis since the 1940s, and there are many other countries with long-running and well-established surveys. Until recently, however, the handling and processing of large microeconomic data sets was both cumbersome and expensive, so that survey data were not widely used beyond the production of the original survey reports. In the last ten or fifteen years, the availability of cheap and convenient microcomputers has changed both the collection and analysis of household survey data. Calculations that could be done only on multi-million-dollar mainframes in 1980—and then with some difficulty—are now routinely carried out on cheap laptop computers. These same machines can be carried into the field and used to record and edit data as they are provided by the respondents. As a result, survey data are becoming available in a more timely fashion, months rather than years after the end of the survey; freshly collected data are much more useful for policy exercises than are those that are many years old. At the same time, analysts have become more interested in exploring ways in which survey data can be used to inform and to improve the policy process. Such explorations run from the tabulations and graphical presentation of levels of living to more basic research on household behavior.

Purpose and intended audience

This book is about the analysis of household survey data from developing countries and about how such data can be used to cast light on a range of policy issues. Much of the analysis works with household budget data, collected from income and expenditure surveys, though I shall occasionally address topics that require wider information. I shall use data from several different economies to illustrate the analysis, drawing examples of policy issues from economies as diverse as Côte d'Ivoire, India, Pakistan, South Africa, Taiwan (China), and Thailand. I shall be concerned with methodology as well as substance, and one of the aims of the book is to bring together the relevant statistical and econometric methods that are useful for building the bridge between data and policy. The book is not intended as a manual for the analysis of survey data—it is hardly possible to reduce policy research to a formula—but it does provide a number of illustrations of what can be done, with fairly detailed explanations of how to do it. Nor can a "how-to" book provide a comprehensive review of all the development topics that have been addressed with household survey data; that purpose has already been largely met by the microeconomic survey papers in the three volumes of the *Handbook of Development Economics*. Instead, I have focused on topics on which I have worked myself, in the hope that the lack of coverage will be compensated for by the detailed knowledge that can only come from having carried out the empirical research. The restriction to my own work also enables me to provide the relevant computer code for almost all of the empirical results and graphics, something that could hardly be combined with the broad coverage of a genuine survey. The Appendix gives code and programs using STATA; in my experience, this is the most convenient package for working with data from household surveys. The programs are not a package; users will have to substitute their own data sets and will need sufficient basic knowledge of STATA to adapt the code. Nevertheless, the programs provide a template for generating results similar to those presented and discussed here. I have also tried to keep the programs simple, sometimes at the expense of efficiency or elegance, so that it should not be too difficult to translate the logic into other packages.

I hope that the material will be of interest to development practitioners, in the World Bank and elsewhere, as well as to a more academic audience of students of economic development. The material in the first two chapters is also designed to help readers interpret applied econometric work based on survey data. But the audience that I most want to reach is that of researchers in developing countries. Statistical offices, research institutes, and universities in developing countries are now much less constrained by computation than they were only a few years ago, and the calculations described here can be done on personal computers using readily available and relatively inexpensive software. I have also tried to keep the technical presentation at a relatively modest level. I take for granted most of what would be familiar from a basic course in econometrics, but I devote a good deal of space to expositions of useful techniques—such as nonparametric density and regression estimation, or the bootstrap—that are neither widely taught in elementary econometrics courses nor described in standard texts. Nevertheless, there are points where there is an inevitable conflict between simplicity, on the one hand, and clarity and precision, on the other. When necessary I have "starred" those sections or subsections in which the content is either necessarily technical or is of interest only to those who wish to try to replicate the analysis. Occasional "technical notes," usually starred, are shorter digressions that can readily be skipped at a first reading.

Policy and data: methodological issues

Household surveys provide a rich source of data on economic behavior and its links to policy. They provide information at the level of the individual household about many variables that are either set or influenced by policy, such as prices, transfers, or the provision of schools and clinics. They also collect data on outcomes that we care about and that are affected by the policy variables, such as levels of nutrition, expenditure patterns, educational attainments, earnings, and health. Many important research questions concern the link between the instruments of policy and the outcome variables: the rate of return to government-provided schooling, the effectiveness of various types of clinics, the equity and efficiency effects of transfers and taxes, and the nutritional benefits of food subsidies. Because household surveys document these links, they are the obvious data bases for this sort of policy research, for evaluating the welfare benefits of public programs. Of course, associations in the data establish neither causality nor the magnitude of the effects. The data from household surveys do not come from controlled experiments in which the effects of a "treatment" can be unambiguously and convincingly determined.

In recent years, there has been a great deal of interest in social experiments, including the use of household survey data to evaluate the results of social experiments. Nevertheless, experiments are not always possible, and real experiments usually deviate from the ideal in ways that present their own difficulties of interpretation. In some cases, good luck, inspiration, and hard work throw up circumstances or data that allow a clear evaluation of policy effects in the absence of controlled experiments; these "quasi" or "natural" experiments have been the source of important findings as well as of some controversy. Even without such solutions, it seems as if it ought to be possible to use standard survey data to say something about the policy effects in which we are interested. A good starting point is to recognize that this will not always be the case. Many policy questions are not readily answerable at all, often because they are not well or sharply enough posed, and even when an answer is available in principle, there is no reason to suppose that it can be inferred from the data that happen to be at hand. Only when this is appreciated is there much chance of progress, or even of a realistic evaluation of what can be accomplished by empirical analysis.

Much of the empirical microeconomic literature in development uses econometric and statistical methodology to overcome the nonexperimental nature of data. A typical study would begin with a structural model of the process at hand, for example, of the effects on individual health of opening a new clinic. Integral to the model are statistical assumptions that bridge the gap between theory and data and so permit both the estimation of the parameters of the model and the subsequent interpretation of the data in terms of the theory. I have no difficulty with this approach in principle, but often find it hard to defend in practice. The statistical and economic assumptions are often arbitrary and frequently implausible. The econometric technique can be complex, so that transparency and easy replicability are lost. It becomes difficult to tell whether the results are genuine features of the data or are consequences of the supporting assumptions. In spite of these problems, I shall spend a good deal of space in Chapter 2 discussing the variety of econometric technique that is available for dealing with nonexperimental data. An understanding of these matters is necessary in order to interpret the literature, and it is important to know the circumstances in which technical fixes are useful.

Most of the analysis in this book follows a different approach which recognizes that structural modeling is unlikely to give convincing and clean answers to the policy questions with which we are concerned. Rather than starting with the theory, I more often begin with the data and then try to find elementary procedures for describing them in a way that illuminates some aspect of theory or policy. Rather than use the theory to summarize the data through a set of structural parameters, it is sometimes more useful to present features of the data, often through simple descriptive statistics, or through graphical presentations of densities or regression functions, and then to think about whether these features tell us anything useful about the process whereby they were generated. There is no simple prescription for this kind of work. It requires a good deal of thought to try to tease out implications from the theory that can be readily checked against the data. It also requires creative data presentation and processing, so as to create useful and interesting stylized facts. But in the end, I believe that we make more progress, not by pretending to estimate structural parameters, but by asking whether our theories and their policy implications are consistent with well-chosen stylized facts. Such facts also provide convenient summaries of the data that serve as a background to discussions of policy. I hope that the examples in this book will make the case that such an approach can be useful, even if its aims are relatively modest.

Structure and outline

Household budget surveys collect information on who buys what goods and services and how much they spend on them. Information on how poor people spend their money has been used to describe poverty and to build the case for social reform since the end of the eighteenth century, and household surveys remain the basis for documenting poverty in developing countries today. When surveys are carried out on a regular basis, they can be used to monitor the welfare of various groups in society and to keep track of who benefits and who loses from development. Large-scale national surveys allow a good deal of disaggregation and allow us to look beyond means to other features of distributions, distinguishing households by occupational, regional, sectoral, and income groups.

In most poor countries, a large fraction of government revenue is raised by indirect taxes on goods and services, and many countries subsidize the prices of commodities such as basic foodstuffs. Household expenditure surveys, by revealing who buys each good and how much they spend, tell us who pays taxes and who benefits from subsidies. They thus yield a reckoning of the gainers and losers from a proposed changes in taxes and subsidies. When data are collected on the use of services provided by the state, such as health and education, we also discover who benefits from government expenditures, so that survey data can be used to assess policy reform and the effectiveness of government taxation and expenditure.

Data from household surveys are also a base for research, for testing theories about household behavior, and for discovering how people respond to changes in the economic environment in which they live. Some recent surveys, particularly the World Bank's Living Standards Measurement Surveys, have attempted to collect data on a wide range of household characteristics and activities, from fertility and physical measurement of weights and heights to all types of economic transactions. Such data allow us to examine all the activities of the household and to trace the behavioral links between economic events and individual welfare.

This book follows the progression of the previous three paragraphs, from data description through to behavioral analysis. Chapters 1 and 2 are preliminary to the main purpose and are concerned with the collection of household survey data, with survey design, and with its consequences for analysis. Chapter 1 is not meant to provide a guide to constructing surveys in developing countries, but rather to describe those features of survey design that need to be understood in order to undertake appropriate analysis. Chapter 2 discusses the general econometric and statistical issues that arise when using survey data for estimation and inference; the techniques discussed here are used throughout the rest of the book, but I also attempt to be more general, covering methods that are useful in applications not explicitly considered. This is not a textbook of econometrics; these two chapters are designed for readers with a basic knowledge of econometrics who want some preparation for working with household survey data particularly, but not exclusively, from developing countries.

Chapter 3 makes the move toward substantive analysis and discusses the use of survey data to measure welfare, poverty, and distribution. I review the theoretical underpinnings of the various measures of social welfare, inequality, and poverty and show how they can be given empirical content from survey data, with illustrations from the Ivorian and South African Living Standards Surveys. I highlight a number of techniques for data analysis that have proved useful in policy discussions, with particular emphasis on graphical methods for displaying large amounts of data. These methods can be used to investigate the distribution of income, inequality, and poverty and to examine changes in the levels of living of various groups over time. The chapter also shows how it is possible to use the data to examine the distributional consequences of price changes directly, without having to construct econometric models. These methods are applied to an analysis of the effects of rice price policy on the distribution of real income in Thailand.

Chapter 4 discusses the use of household budget data to explore patterns of household demand. I take up the traditional topic of Engel curve analysis in developing countries, looking in particular at the demand for food and nutrition. For many people, nutritional issues are at the heart of poverty questions in developing countries, and Engel curve analysis from survey data allows us to measure the relationship between the elimination of hunger and malnutrition and more general economic development, as captured by increases in real disposable income. This chapter also addresses the closely related question of how goods are allocated within the household and the extent to which it is possible to use *household* data to cast light on the topic. One of the main issues of interest is how different members of the household are treated, especially whether boys are favored over girls. Analyses of the effects of household composition on demand patterns can perhaps shed some light on this, as well as on the old but vexed question of measuring the "costs" of children. In most surveys, larger households have more income and more expenditure, but they also have less income or expenditure on a per capita basis. Does this mean that large households are poorer on average or that small households are poorer on average? The answer depends on whether there are economies of scale to large households—whether two people need twice as much as one—and whether children, who are relatively plentiful in larger households, need less money to meet their needs than do adults. This chapter discusses the extent to which the survey data can be used to approach these questions.

Chapter 5 is about price reform, its effects on equity and efficiency, and how to measure them. Because surveys provide direct information on how much is consumed of each taxed or subsidized good, it is straightforward to calculate the first-round effects of price changes, both on revenue and on the distribution of real income. What are much harder to assess are the behavioral responses to price changes, the degree to which the demand for the good is affected by the change in price, and the extent to which revenues and expenditures from taxes and subsidies on other goods are affected. The chapter discusses methods for estimating price responses using the spatial price variation that is typically quite pronounced in developing countries. These methods are sensitive enough to detect differences in price responses between goods and to establish important cross-price effects between goods, effects that are often large enough to substantially change the conclusions of a policy reform exercise. Reducing a subsidy on one staple food has very different consequences for revenue and for nutrition, depending on whether or not there is a closely substitutable food that is also subsidized or taxed.

Chapter 6 is concerned with the role of household consumption and saving in economic development. Household saving is a major component and determinant of saving in most developing countries, and many economists see saving as the wellspring of economic growth, so that encouraging saving becomes a crucial component of a policy for growth. Others take the view that saving rates respond passively to economic growth, the roots of which must be sought elsewhere. Survey data can be used to explore these alternative views of the relationship between saving and growth, as well as to examine the role that saving plays in protecting living standards against fluctuations in income. The analysis of survey evidence on household saving, although fraught with difficulty, is beginning to change the way that we think about household saving in poor economies.

I have benefited from the comments of many people who have given generously of their time to try to improve my exposition, to make substantive suggestions, and in a few cases, to persuade me of the error of my ways. In addition to the referees, I should like to thank—without implicating any of them—Martha Ainsworth, Harold Alderman, Tony Atkinson, Dwayne Benjamin, Tim Besley, Martin Browning, Kees Burger, Lisa Cameron, David Card, Anne Case, Ken Chay, John Dinardo, Jean Drèze, Eric Edmonds, Mark Gersovitz, Paul Glewwe, Margaret Grosh, Bo Honoré, Susan Horton, Hanan Jacoby, Emmanuel Jimenez, Alan Krueger, Doug Miller, Juan Muñoz, Meade Over, Anna Paulson, Menno Pradhan, Gillian Paull, James Powell, Martin Ravallion, Jeremy Rudd, Jim Smith, T. N. Srinivasan, David Strömberg, Duncan Thomas, and Galina Voronov. I owe special thanks to Julie Nelson, whose comments and corrections helped shape Chapter 5, and to Christina Paxson, who is the coauthor of much of the work reported here. Some of the work reported here was supported by grants from the National Institute of Aging and from the John D. and Catherine T. MacArthur Foundation. The book was written for the Policy Research Department of the World Bank.

1 *The design and content of household surveys*

In his splendid essay on early studies of consumer behavior, Stigler (1954, p. 95) tells how the first collectors of family budgets, the Englishmen Reverend David Davies (1795) and Sir Frederick Morton Eden (1797), were "stimulated to this task by the distress of the working classes at this time." Davies used his results to draw attention to the living conditions of the poor, and to argue in favor of a minimum wage. The spread of working-class socialism in Europe in the late 1840s also spawned several compilations of household budgets, including the one of 200 Belgian households by Edouard Ducpetiaux in 1855 that was used two years later by Ernst Engel, not only as the basis for his law that the fraction of the budget devoted to food is larger for poorer families, but also to estimate the aggregate consumption, not of Belgium, but of Saxony! The use of budget data to expose poverty and living standards, to argue for policy reform, and to estimate national aggregates are all topics that are as relevant today as they were two centuries ago. The themes of the research were set very early in the history of the subject.

The early investigators had to collect data where they could find it, and there was no attempt to construct representative samples of households. Indeed, the understanding that population totals can be estimated from randomly selected samples and the statistical theory to support such estimation were developed only in the first quarter of this century. Around the turn of the century, Kiaer in Norway and Wright in the United States were among the first to use large-scale representative samples, but the supporting statistical theory was not fully worked out until the 1920s, with Bowley, Ronald Fisher, and Neyman making important contributions. The acceptance of sampling is well illustrated by the case of Rowntree, who was unpersuaded by the reliability of sampling when he undertook his survey of poverty in the city of York in 1936. Having collected a full census, he was later convinced by being able to reproduce most of the results from samples drawn from his data (see the supplementary chapter in Rowntree 1985). One of the first large-scale scientific surveys was carried out by Mahalanobis in Calcutta, who estimated the size of the jute crop in Bengal in 1941 to within 2.8 percent of an independent census at less than 8 percent of the cost—see Mahalanobis (1944, 1946) for the classic early accounts, and Seng (1951) and Casley and Lury (1981, ch. 1) for more history and citations to the early literature.

Modern household surveys begin after World War II. Under the leadership of Mahalanobis at the Indian Statistical Institute in Calcutta, the Indian National Sample Survey (NSS) started the annual collection of household consumption data in 1950. Many other economies, both industrialized and developing, now have regular household consumption surveys, sometimes on an annual basis, as in India until 1973–74, or in Taiwan, The Republic of Korea, Britain, and the United States today, but more often less frequently, as for example in India after 1973–74 (quinquennially), the United States prior to 1980, and many other countries. These surveys were often intended to provide data on poverty and income distribution, for example in the form of frequency distributions of households by levels of living— usually defined by per capita income or consumption—but this was by no means their only purpose. In many cases, the surveys were designed to produce *aggregate* data, to help complete the national accounts, to provide weights for consumer price indexes, or to provide the basis for projecting demand patterns in planning exercises. Once begun, it was typically difficult to change the mode of operation or to use the data for purposes different from those in the original design. The former would generate incompatibilities and inconsistencies in the data, while the latter required a computational capacity and willingness to release household-level data that were rarely in evidence. There are, of course, genuine confidentiality issues with household information, but these can be met by removing some information from the publicly available data, and hardly justify their treatment as state secrets.

Recent years have seen a marked change in survey practice, in data collection, and in analysis. Although there are still laggard countries, many government statistical offices have become more open with their data and have given bona fide researchers and international organizations access to the individual household records. Reductions in the real cost of computation have led to more analysis, although it is only in the last few years that mass-storage devices and cheap memory have made it convenient to use microcomputers to analyze large data sets. Perhaps as important have been changes in the design of surveys, and there is now a much wider range of survey instruments in use than was the case a decade ago. Following a number of experimental and innovative surveys in the 1960s and 1970s—particularly the Malaysian Family Life Survey in 1976–77—the World Bank's Living Standards Surveys first collected data in Peru and Côte d'Ivoire in 1985 and incorporated important innovations in data collection and in content. Originally designed to improve the World Bank's ability to monitor poverty and to make international comparisons of living standards, poverty, and inequality, they evolved into vehicles for collecting comprehensive information on a wide range of household characteristics and activities. The rapid availability and ease of analysis of survey data has led to a productive feedback from analysis to design that was rare prior to 1980. In consequence, survey practice and questionnaire design are probably changing more rapidly now than ever before.

This chapter and the next, which are preliminary to the analytical studies in the rest of the book, are concerned with the design and content of household surveys (this chapter) and with its implications for statistical and econometric analysis (the final section of this chapter and Chapter 2). In line with the substantive studies later in the book, I give disproportionate attention to income and expenditure surveys, or to the income and expenditure sections of broader, integrated surveys such as the Living Standards Surveys. Even so, much of the discussion carries over to other types of household survey, for example to employment or fertility surveys, though I do not give explicit attention to those topics.

The four sections of this chapter are concerned with the design of surveys, with the type of data that they collect, and with the effect of design on the calculation of descriptive statistics such as means. Section 1.1 discusses the practical and statistical issues concerned with choosing households for inclusion into a survey. Section 1.2 is concerned with the types of data that are usually collected, and their likely quality. Section 1.3 focusses on the particular features of the Living Standards Surveys from which data are used in some of the later chapters. Many of the policy analyses that use household survey data were not contemplated when the surveys were designed, so that mechanical calculations that ignore the design of the survey can produce unpredictable results. For example, surveys that are designed to estimate means or population totals may be quite unsuitable for measuring dispersion. In most surveys some types of households are overrepresented relative to their share in the population, while others are underrepresented, so that corrections have to be made to calculate genuinely representative totals. It is also wise to be sensitive to the possibility—in most cases the certainty—of measurement errors, to their effects on the calculations, and to strategies that can be used to protect inference in their presence. These issues are further complicated when, as in some of the Living Standards Surveys, households are observed on more than one occasion, and we are interested in analyzing changes in behavior over time. Section 1.4, which is more technical than the others, presents some of the most useful formulas for estimating means and their sampling variability taking into account the survey design. The discussion is useful both for Chapter 2, where I move from descriptive statistics to a more econometric approach, and for Chapter 3, where I deal with poverty measures, which are a particular kind of descriptive statistic. This section also contains a brief introduction to the bootstrap, a technique that is often useful for calculating standard errors and confidence intervals.

1.1 Survey design

The simplest household survey would be one where there exists a reliable, up-to-date list of all households in the population, where the design assigns an equal probability to each household being selected from the list to participate in the survey and where, in the implementation stage, all households asked to participate actually do so. The sample would then be a simple random sample, with each household standing proxy for an equal number of households in the population. Such samples are easy to use and a few actual surveys approximate this simple structure. However, for a number of good and some not-so-good reasons, most surveys are a good deal more complex. I begin by discussing the list (or frame) from which households are selected and which defines the potential coverage of the survey, and then pass on to stratification and sampling issues.

Survey frames and coverage

A typical household survey collects data on a national sample of households, randomly selected from a "frame" or national list of households. Sample sizes vary widely depending on the purpose of the survey, on the size of the population in the country being surveyed, and on the degree to which regional or other special subsamples are required. Sample sizes of around 10,000 are frequently encountered, which would correspond to a sampling fraction of 1:500 in a population of 5 million households, or perhaps 25 million people. Since the accuracy of sample statistics increases less than proportionally with the sample size—usually in proportion to its square root—sampling fractions are typically smaller in larger populations, a tendency that is reinforced by limits on the size of survey that can be mounted by many data collection agencies. Nevertheless, there are some very large surveys such as the current Indian NSS, where a full national sample contains around a quarter of a million households.

The frame is often a census, which in principle provides a list of all households and household members, or at least of all dwellings. However, there are many countries where there is no up-to-date census, or no reliable recent census, so that other frames have to be constructed, usually from administrative records of some kind (see Casley and Lury 1981, ch. 6, who discuss some of the possibilities). Perhaps the most common method of selecting households from the frame uses a two-stage design. At the first stage, selection is from a list of "clusters" of households, with the households themselves selected at the second stage. In rural areas, the clusters are often villages but the choice will depend on the frame. Censuses have their own subunits that are suitable for first-stage sampling. Once the clusters are chosen, households can be selected directly if an up-to-date list is available, and if the list is detailed enough to allow identification in the field. Otherwise, all households in the selected clusters can be listed prior to the second stage. Since it is often possible to include some household information at the listing stage, the procedure allows the second-stage selection of individual households to be informed by prior knowledge, a possibility to which I shall return in the next subsection. Note finally that two-stage sampling is not inconsistent with each household in the population having an equal chance of selection into the sample. In particular, if clusters are randomly selected with probability proportional to the number of households they contain, and if the same number of households is selected from each cluster, we have a *self-weighting* design in which each household has the same chance of being included in the survey.

The use of outdated or otherwise inaccurate frames is an important source of error in survey estimates. It should also be noted that in some countries—including the United States—censuses are politically sensitive so that various interest groups can be expected to try to interfere with the count. Even when the frame is accurate in itself, its coverage of the population will typically not be complete. Homeless people are automatically excluded from surveys that start from *households*, and in many countries people living in various institutional settings—the armed forces or workers' dormitories—will be excluded.

One example of the differences between a sample and population is provided by the data in Figure 1.1, which shows age-sex pyramids for Taiwan for selected years between 1976 and 1990. There are two pyramids for each year; those on the left-hand side were calculated from household survey data, and were previously reported in Deaton and Paxson (1994a), while those on the right-hand side are calculated from the official population data in Republic of China (1992). The survey data, which are described in detail in Republic of China (1989), come from a set of surveys that have been carried out on a regular basis since 1976, and that are carefully and professionally conducted. The 1976 sample has data on some 50,000 individuals, while the later years cover approximately 75,000 persons; the population of Taiwan grew from 16.1 million in 1975 to 20.4 million in 1990.

The differences between the two sets of pyramids is partly due to sampling error—each year of age is shown in the graphs—but there are also a number of differences in coverage. The most obvious of these causes the notches in the sample pyramids for men aged 18 to 20. Taiwanese men serve in the military during those years and are typically not captured in the survey, and roughly two-thirds of the age group is missing. These notches tend to obscure what is one of the major common features of both population and sample, the baby boom of the early 1950s. In 1988 and 1990, there is some evidence that the survey is missing young women, although the feature is much less sharp than for men and is spread over a wider age range. The design feature in this case is that the survey does not include women attending college nor those living in factory dormitories away from home. As the

Figure 1.1. Age and sex pyramids for survey data and population, Taiwan (China), selected years, 1976–90

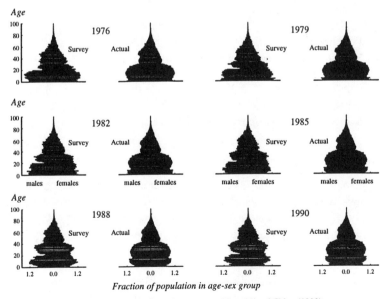

Fraction of population in age-sex group

Source: Author's calculations using survey data tapes, and Republic of China (1992).

population pyramids make clear, some of these women—together with the men in the same age group—are genuinely "missing" in the sense that the cohort of babies born around 1975 is substantially smaller than those immediately preceding or succeeding it. A number of other distinctive features of these graphs are not design effects, the most notable being the excess of men over women that is greatest at around age 45 in 1976, and moves up the age distribution, one year per year, until it peaks near age 60 in 1990. These men are the survivors of Chiang Kai-shek's army who came to Taiwan after their defeat by the communists in 1949.

The noncoverage of some of the population is typical of household surveys and clearly does not prevent us from using the data to make inferences. Nevertheless, it is always wise to be careful, since the missing people were not missed at random and will typically have different characteristics from the population as a whole. In the Taiwanese case, we should be careful not to infer anything about the behavior of young Taiwanese males. Another notable example comes from Britain, where the annual Family Expenditure Survey (FES) regularly underestimates aggregate alcohol consumption by nearly a half. Much of the error is attributed to coverage; there is high alcohol consumption among many who are excluded from the survey, primarily the military, but also innkeepers and publicans (see Kemsley and others 1980). To the effects of noncoverage by design can be added the effects of non-respondents, households that refuse to join the survey. Nonresponse is much less of a problem in developing countries than in (for example) the United States, where refusal to participate in surveys has been increasing over time. Although many surveys in developing countries report almost complete cooperation, there will always be specific cases of difficulty, as when wealthy households are asked about incomes or assets, or when households are approached when they are preoccupied with other activities. Once again, some of the low alcohol reports in the British data reflect the relatively low response rates around Christmas, when alcohol consumption is highest (see Crooks 1989, pp. 39–44). It is sometimes possible to study survey nonresponse patterns by tracing refusals in a contemporaneous census, using data from the census to assess the determinants of refusal in the survey (see Kemsley 1975 for such an exercise for the British FES using the 1971 census). Sometimes the survey itself will collect some information about nonrespondents, for example about housing. Groves (1989, ch. 4) discusses these and other techniques for assessing the consequences of nonresponse.

Strata and clusters

A two-stage sample design, first selecting clusters and then households, generates a sample in which sample households are not randomly distributed over space, but are geographically grouped. This arrangement has a number of advantages beyond the selection procedure. It is cost-effective for the survey team to travel from village to village, spending substantial time in each, instead of having to visit households that are widely dispersed from one another. Clustered samples also facilitate repeat visits to collect information from respondents who may not have been present at the first visit, to monitor the progress of record keeping, or to ask supplementary questions about previous responses that editing procedures have marked as suspect. That there are several households in each village also makes it worthwhile to collect village-level information, for example on schools, clinics, prices, or agroclimatic conditions such as rainfall or crop failures. (Though the clusters defined for statistical purposes will not always correspond to well-defined "communities.") For all these reasons, nearly all surveys in developing countries (and elsewhere, with telephone surveys the notable exception) use clustered samples.

The purposes of the survey sometimes dictate that some groups be more intensively sampled than others, and more often that coverage be guaranteed for some groups. There may be an interest in investigating a "target" group that is of particular concern, and, if members of the group are relatively rare in the population as a whole, a simple random sample is unlikely to include enough group members to permit analysis. Instead, the sample is designed so that households with the relevant characteristic have a high probability of being selected. For example, the World Bank used a Living Standards–type survey in the Kagera region of Tanzania to study the economic effects of AIDS. A random sample of the population would not produce very many households with an infected person, so that care was taken to find such households by confining the survey to areas where infection was known to be high and by including questions about sickness at the listing stage, so that households with a previous history of sickness could be oversampled.

More commonly, the survey is required to generate statistics for population subgroups defined (for example) by geographical area, by ethnic affiliation, or by levels of living. *Stratification* by these groups effectively converts a sample from one population into a sample from many populations, a single survey into several surveys, and guarantees in advance that there will be enough observations to permit estimates for each of the groups.

There are also statistical reasons for departing from simple random samples; quite apart from cost considerations, the precision of any given estimate can be enhanced by choosing an appropriate design. The fundamental idea is that the surveyor typically knows a great deal about the population under study prior to the survey, and the use of that prior information can improve the efficiency of statistical inference about quantities that are unknown. Stratification is the classic example.

Suppose that we are interested in estimating average income, that we know that average rural incomes are lower than average urban incomes, and we know the proportions of the population in each sector. A stratified survey would be two identical surveys, one rural and one urban, each of which estimates average income. (It would not necessarily be the case that the sampling fractions would be the same in each stratum.) The average income for the country as a whole, which is the quantity in which we are interested, is calculated by weighting together the urban and rural means using the proportions of the population in each as weights—which is where the prior information comes in. The precision of this combined estimate is assessed (inversely) from its variance over replications of the survey. Because the two components of the survey are independent, the variance of the overall mean is the sum of the variances of the estimates from each strata. Hence, variance depends only on *within*-sector variance, and not on *between*-sector variance. If instead of a stratified survey, we had collected a simple random sample, the variance of the overall mean would still have depended on the within-sector variances, but there would have been an additional component coming from the fact that in different surveys, there would have been different fractions of the sample in rural and urban. If rural and urban means are different, this variability in the composition of the sample will contribute to the variability of the estimate of the overall mean. In consequence, stratification will have the largest effect in reducing variance when the stratum means are different from one another, and when there is relatively little variation within strata. The formulas that make this intuition precise are discussed in Section 1.4 below.

In household income and expenditure surveys, rural and urban strata are nearly always distinguished, and sometimes there is additional geographic stratification, by regions or provinces, or by large and small towns. Ethnicity is another possible candidate for stratification, as is income or its correlates if, as is often the case, some indication of household living standards is included in the frame or in the listing of households—landholdings and housing indicators are the most frequent examples. Stratification can be done explicitly, as discussed above, or "implicitly." The latter arises using "systematic" sampling in which a list of households is sampled by selecting a random starting point and then sampling every jth household thereafter, with j set so as to give the desired sample size. Implicit stratification is introduced by choosing the order in which households appear on the list. An example is probably the best way to see how this works. In the 1993 South African Living Standards Survey, a list was made of clusters, in this case "census enumerator subdistricts" from the 1991 census. These clusters were split by statistical region and by urban and rural sectors—the *explicit* stratification—and then in order of percentage African—the *implicit* stratification. Given that the selection of clusters was randomized only by the random starting point, the implicit stratification guarantees the coverage of Africans and non-Africans, since it is impossible for a sample so selected not to contain clusters from high on the list, which are almost all African, and clusters low on the list, which are almost all non-African.

While stratification will typically enhance the precision of sampling estimates, the clustering of the sample will usually reduce it. The reason is that households living in the same cluster are usually more similar to one another in behavior and characteristics than are households living in different clusters. This similarity is likely to be more pronounced in rural areas, where people living in the same village share the same agroclimatic conditions, face similar prices, and may belong to the same ethnic or tribal group. As a result, when we sample several households from the same cluster, we do not get as much information as we would from sampling several households from different clusters. In the (absurd) limit, if everyone in the same cluster were replicas or clones of one another, the effective sample size of the survey would not be the number of households, but the number of clusters. More generally, the precision of an estimate will depend on the correlation within the cluster of the quantity being measured; once again, the formulas are given in Section 1.4 below.

A useful concept in assessing how the sample design affects precision is Kish's (1965) "design effect," often referred to as *deff*. *Deff* is defined as the ratio of the variance of an estimate to the variance that it would have had under simple random sampling; some explicit examples are included in Section 1.4. Stratification tends to reduce *deff* below one, while clustering tends to increase it above one. Estimates of the means of most variables in stratified clustered samples have *deffs* that are greater than one (Groves 1989, ch. 6), so that in survey design the practical convenience and cost considerations of clustering usually predominate over the search for variance-reduction.

Unequal selection probabilities, weights, and inflation factors

As we have seen, it is possible for a survey to be stratified and clustered, and for each household in the population to have an equal probability of inclusion in the sample. However, it is more common for probabilities of inclusion to differ, because it costs more to sample some households than others, because differential probabilities of inclusion can enhance precision, and because some types of households may be more likely to refuse to participate in the survey. Because noncooperation is rarely taken into account in design, even samples that are meant to have equal probabilities of selection often do not do so in practice.

Variation in costs is common, for example between rural and urban households. In consequence, the cost of any given level of precision is minimized by a sample in which urban households are overrepresented and rural households underrepresented. The use of differential selection probabilities to enhance precision is perhaps less obvious, but the general principle is the same as for stratification, that prior information can be used to tell us where to focus measurement. To fix ideas, suppose again that we are estimating mean income. The estimate will be more precise if households that contribute a large amount to the mean—high-income households—are overrepresented relative to low-income households, who contribute little. This is "probability proportional to size," or *p.p.s.,* sampling. Of course, we do not know household income, or we would not have to collect data, but we may have information on correlated variables, such as landholdings or household size. Overrepresentation of large households or large landholding households will typically lead to more precise estimates of mean income (see again Section 1.4 for formulas and justification).

When selection probabilities differ across households, each household in the survey stands proxy for or represents a different number of households in the population. In consequence, when the sample is used to calculate estimates for the population, it is necessary to weight the sample data to ensure that each group of households is properly represented. Sample means will not be unbiased estimates of population means and we must calculate weighted averages so as to "undo" the sample design and obtain estimates to match the population. The rule here is to weight according to the reciprocals of sampling probabilities because households with low (high) probabilities of selection stand proxy for large (small) numbers of households in the population. These weights are often referred to as "raising" or "inflation" factors because if we multiply each observation by its inflation factor we are estimating the total for all households represented by the sample household, and the sum of these products over all sample households is an estimate of the population total. Inflation factors are typically included in the data sets together with other variables.

Table 1.1 shows means and standard deviations by race of the inflation factors for the 1993 South African survey. This is an interesting case because the original design was a self-weighting one, in which there would be no variation in inflation factors across households. However, when the survey was implemented there were substantial differences by race in refusal rates, and there were a few clusters that could not be visited because of political violence. As a result, and in order to allow the calculation of unbiased estimates of means, inflation factors had to be introduced after the completion of the fieldwork. The mean weight for the 8,848 households in the survey is 964, corresponding to a population of households of 8,530,808 (= 8,848 × 964). Because whites were more likely to refuse to participate in the survey, they attract a higher weight than the other groups.

This South African case illustrates an important general point about survey weights. Differences in weights from one household to another can come from different probabilities of selection *by design*, or from different probabilities *by accident*, because the survey did not conform to the design, because of non-response, because households who cooperated in the past refused to do so again, or because some part of the survey was not in fact implemented. Whether by design or accident, there are ex post differences in sampling probabilities for different households, and weights are needed in order to obtain accurate measures of population quantities. But the design weights are, by construction, the reciprocals of the sampling probabilities, and are thus controlled in a way that accidental weights are not. Weights that are added to the survey ex post do not have the same pedigree, and are often determined by judgement and modeling. In South Africa, the response rate among White households was lower, so the weights for White households were adjusted upwards. But can we be sure that the response rate was truly determined by race, and not, for example, by some mixture of race, income, and location? Adoption of survey weights often involves the implicit acceptance of modeling decisions by survey staff, decisions that many investigators would prefer to keep to them-

Table 1.1. Inflation factors and race, South Africa, 1993

Race	Mean weight	Standard deviation	Households in sample
Blacks	933	79	6,533
Coloreds	955	55	690
Asians	885	22	258
Whites	1,135	219	1,367
All	964	133	8,848

Source: Author's calculations using the South African Living Standards Survey, 1993.

selves. At the least, survey reports should document the construction of such weights, so that other researchers can make different decisions if they wish.

Sample design in theory and practice

The *statistical* arguments for stratification and differential sampling probabilities are typically less compelling in developing-country surveys than are the *practical* arguments. Optimal design for precision works well when the aim of the survey is the measurement of a single magnitude—average consumption, average income, or whatever. Once this objective is set, all the tools of the sample survey statistician can be brought to bear to design a survey that will deliver the best estimate at the lowest possible cost. Such single-purpose surveys do indeed occur from time to time and more frequently there is a main purpose, such as the estimation of weights for a consumer price index, or the measurement of poverty and inequality. Even in these cases, however, it is recognized that there are other uses for the data, and in general-purpose household surveys there is a range of possible applications, each of which would mandate a different design. Precision for one variable is imprecision for another, and it makes no sense to design a survey for each. In addition, optimizing for one purpose can make it difficult to use the survey for other purposes. A good example is the Consumer Expenditure Survey in the United States, where the main aim is the calculation of weights for the consumer price index. That object is relentlessly pursued, with some expenditures obtained by interviewing some households, some expenditures obtained by diary from other households, and each household is visited five times over fifteen months but with different kinds of data collected at each visit. All of this allows a relatively small sample to deliver good estimates of the average American spending pattern, but the complexity of the design makes it difficult—sometimes even impossible—to make calculations that would have been possible under simpler designs.

Another problem with optimal schemes is that the selection of households according to efficiency criteria can compromise the usefulness of the data. For example, the use of public transport is efficiently estimated by interviewing travelers, and travelers are most easily and economically found by conducting "on-board" surveys on trains, on buses, or at stations. But if we are to study what determines the demand for travel, and who benefits from state subsidies to public transport, we need to know about nontravelers too, information that is better collected in standard household surveys. Indeed, if observations are selected into the sample according to characteristics that are correlated with the magnitude being studied—precisely the recipe in *p.p.s.* sampling—attempts to estimate models that explain that magnitude are likely to be compromised by the selection of the sample. This "choice-based sampling" problem has been studied in the literature (see Manski and Lerman 1977, Hausman and Wise 1977, 1981, and Cosslett 1993) and there exist techniques for overcoming the difficulties. But once again it is much easier to work with a simpler survey, and the results are likely to be more comprehensible and more convincing if they do not require complex corrections, especially when the corrections are supported by assumptions that are difficult or impossible to check.

There are also good practical reasons for straightforward designs. In their book on collecting data in developing countries, Casley and Lury (1981, p. 2) summarize their basic message in the words "keep it simple." As they point out:

> The sampling errors of any rational design involving at least a moderate sample size are likely to be substantially smaller than the nonsampling errors. Complications of design may create problems, resulting in larger nonsampling errors, which more than offset the theoretical benefits conferred.

As we shall see, the econometric analysis will have to deal with a great many problems, among which nonsampling errors are not the least important. Correction for complex designs is an additional task that is better avoided whenever possible.

Panel data

The standard cross-sectional household survey is a one-time affair and is designed to obtain a snapshot of a representative group of households at a given moment in time. Although such surveys take time to collect (frequently a year) so that the "moment in time" varies from household to household, and although households are sometimes visited more than once, for example to gather information on income during different agricultural seasons, the aim of the survey is to gather information from each household about a given year's income, or about consumption in the month previous to the interview, or about the names, sexes, and ages of the members of the household on the day of the interview.

By contrast, longitudinal or panel surveys track households over time, and collect multiple observations on the same household. For example, instead of gathering income for one year, a panel would collect data on income for a number of years, so that, using such data, it is possible to see how survey magnitudes change for individual households. Thus, the great attraction of panel data is that they can be used to study dynamics for individual households, including the dynamics of living standards. They can be used to address such issues as the persistence of poverty, and to see who benefits and who loses from general economic development, or who gains and loses from a specific shock or policy change, such as a devaluation, a structural adjustment package, or a reduction in the prices of commodity exports. However, as we shall see in Chapter 2, panel data are *not* required to track outcomes or behavior for *groups* of individuals—that can be done very well with repeated cross-sectional surveys—but they are the only data that can tell us about dynamics at the individual level. Panel surveys are relatively rare in general, and particularly so in developing countries. The panel that has attracted the greatest attention in the United States is the Michigan Panel Study of Income Dynamics (PSID), which has been following the members of about 4,800 original households since 1968. The most widely used panel data from a developing country come from the Institute for Crop Research in the Semi-Arid Tropics (ICRISAT) in Hyderabad, India, which followed some 40 agricultural households in each of six villages in southwestern India for five or ten years between 1975 and 1985.

These long-standing surveys are not the only way in which panel data can be collected; an alternative is a *rotating panel* design in which some fraction of households is held over to be revisited, with the rest dropped and replaced by new households. Several of the Living Standards Surveys—to be discussed in Section 1.3 below—have adopted such a design. For example, in Côte d'Ivoire, 1,600 households were selected into the 1985 survey, 800 of which were retained in 1986. To these original panelists 800 new households were added in 1986, and these were retained into 1987. By the pattern of rotation, no household is observed for more than two years, so that while we have two observations in successive years on each household (apart from half of the start-up households) we do not get the long-term observation of individual households that come from panel data.

A third way of collecting data is to supplement cross-sectional data. Occasionally this can be done by merging administrative and survey data. More often, an earlier cross-sectional survey is used as the basis for revisiting households some years after the original survey. If records have been adequately preserved, this can be done even when there was no intention in the original survey of collecting panel data; indeed, it is good practice to design any household survey so as to maximize the probability of recontacting the original respondents. Such methods have been successful in a number of instances. Although the Peruvian Living Standards Survey of 1985–86 was designed as a cross section, households living in Lima were revisited in 1990; of the 1,280 dwellings in the original survey, 1,052 were reinterviewed (some dwellings no longer existed, or the occupants refused to cooperate) and, of these, 745 were occupied by the same family (Glewwe and Hall 1995). In 1988–89, RAND carried out a successful reinterview of nearly three-quarters of the individuals in the original 1976–77 Malaysian Family Life Survey (Haaga, DaVanzo, Peterson, and Peng 1994). Bevan, Collier, and Gunning (1989, Appendix) also appear to have been successful in relocating a high fraction of households in East Africa; in Kenya a 1982 survey reinterviewed nearly 90 percent of survey households first seen in 1977–78, while in Tanzania, 73 percent of the households in a 1976–77 survey were reinterviewed in 1983.

In some cases, panel data can be constructed from a single interview by asking people to recall previous events. This works best for major events in people's lives, such as migration or the birth or death of a child; it is likely to be much more difficult to get an accurate recollection of earnings or expenditures in previous years. There is a substantial literature on the accuracy of recall data, and on the various biases that are induced by forgetting and selective memory (see Groves 1989, ch. 9.4). In the context of developing countries, Smith, Karoly, and Thomas (1992) and Smith and Thomas (1993) use their repeat of the Malaysian Family Life Survey to compare recollections about migrations in the first and second surveys.

As well as their unique advantages, panel data have a number of specific problems. One of the most serious is *attrition*, whereby for one reason or another, households are lost from the survey, so that as time goes on, fewer of the original households remain in the survey. The extent of attrition is affected by the design of the panel, whether or not the survey follows individuals who leave the original households or who move away from the original survey area. Another reason for attrition is refusal; households that have participated once are sometimes unwilling to do so again. Refusal rates are typically lower in surveys in developing countries, and presumably attrition is too. In industrial countries with long-running surveys such as the PSID, there can be a substantial loss of panel members in the first few years until the panel "settles down." Becketti and others (1988) show that although 12 to 15 percent of the individuals in the PSID do not reappear after the first interview, the subsequent attrition rate is much lower so that, for example, of the individuals in the first wave in 1968, 61.6 percent were still present fourteen years later.

Even when households are willing to cooperate, there may be difficulties in finding them at subsequent visits; individuals may move away, and the households may cease to exist if the head dies, or if children split off to form households of their own. Depending on whether the survey attempts to follow these migrants and "splits," as well as whether new births or immigrants are added to the sample, the process of household dissolution and formation can result in changes in the representativeness of the sample over time. (Or what appears to be a panel may not be, if enumerators substitute the new household for the old one without recognizing or recording the change.) There is therefore likely to be a tradeoff between, on the one hand, obtaining a representative sample, which is best done by drawing a new sample each year and, on the other hand, tracking individual dynamics, which requires that households be held over from year to year. Even so, Becketti and others (1988) found no serious problems of representativeness with the PSID when they compared the fourteen-year-old panel with the population of the United States.

Although the main attractions of panel data are for analytical work, for the measurement of dynamics and for controlling for individual histories in assessing behavior, panel designs can also enhance the precision of estimates of aggregate or average quantities. The standard example is estimating changes. Suppose that we compare the case of two independent cross sections with a panel, in which the same households appear in the two time periods. From both designs, the change in average income, say, would be estimated by the difference in average incomes in the two periods. The variance of the estimate from the two cross sections would be the sum of the variances in the two periods because each cross-sectional sample is drawn independently. In the panel survey, by contrast, the same households appear in both periods, so that the variance of the difference is the sum of the variances of the individual means *less* twice the covariance between the two estimates of mean income. If there is a tendency for the same households to have high (or low) incomes in both periods—which we should expect for incomes and will be true for many other quantities—the covariance will be positive and the variance of the estimated change will be less than the sum of the variances of the two means.

The greatest precision will be obtained from a panel, a rotating panel, or independent cross sections depending on the degree of temporal autocorrelation in the quantity being estimated. The higher the autocorrelation, the larger the fraction of households that should be retained from one period to the next. The formulas are given in Hansen, Hurwitz, and Madow (1953, pp. 268–72) and are discussed in the context of developing countries by Ashenfelter, Deaton, and Solon (1986). Provided precision is the main aim, a rotating panel is a good compromise; for example, retaining only half the households from one period to the next will give a standard error for the change that is at most 30 percent larger than the standard error from the complete panel that is the optimal design, and will do better than this when the autocorrelation is low. Given that most surveys are multipurpose, and that there is a need to measure levels as well as changes, there is a good argument for considering rotating panels.

When using panel data to measure differences, it is important to be alive to the possibility of measurement (nonsampling) error and to its consequences for various kinds of analysis; indeed, the detection and control of measurement error will be one of the main refrains of this book. Suppose, to fix ideas, that household i in period t reports, not the true value x_{it} but x_{it}^* defined by

$$(1.1) \qquad\qquad x_{it}^* = x_{it} + \epsilon_{it}$$

where ϵ_{it} is a mean zero measurement error with cross-sectional variance ω^2, and where I assume for convenience that the error variance is the same in both periods. If the reporting error is uncorrelated with the truth, then the variance of measured x is the variance of the true x—the signal—plus the variance of the measurement error—the noise. If the observations are differenced over time, we have

$$(1.2) \qquad \Delta x_{it}^* = \Delta x_{it} + \Delta \epsilon_{it}; \quad \mathrm{var}(\Delta x_{it}^*) = \mathrm{var}(\Delta x_{it}) + 2\omega^2(1-\rho)$$

where ρ is the correlation between the errors in the two periods.

There are several important consequences of (1.2). Note first that the presence of measurement error is likely to further enhance the advantages of panel data over independent cross sections for measuring changes in the means, at least if the same individuals tend to make the same reporting errors period after period. Second, the signal-to-noise ratio will be different for the changes in (1.2) than for the levels in (1.1). The prototypical example is where the underlying variable x changes only slowly over time, so that the variance of the true changes is smaller than the variance of the levels. By contrast, the variance of the measurement error in changes will be double that in levels if $\rho = 0$, and will be increased by the differencing unless $\rho > 0.5$. There is no general result here, but there will be many cases in household survey data where the variance of the measured changes will be dominated by measurement error, even when the measurement of the levels is relatively accurate.

The data in Table 1.2 are taken from the 1985–86 panel of the Living Standards Survey of Côte d'Ivoire and illustrate a number of these issues. The figures shown are summary statistics for consumption and income for 730 panel households who were in the survey in both years. Although the original design called for 800 panelists, not all households could be found in the second wave, nor yielded useful data. While there is no direct way of assessing the size of the measurement error, both magnitudes are hard to estimate, and for the reasons discussed in the next section, the individual data are likely to be very noisy. The upper part of the table shows that means and standard deviations of consumption and income are of similar size, so that with 730 households, the standard errors of the estimates of the mean levels

Table 1.2. Consumption and income for panel households, Côte d'Ivoire, 1985–86

(thousands of CFAs per month)

	Mean	Standard deviation	Median	Interquartile range
Levels				
Consumption, 1985	1,561	1,513	1,132	1,344
Consumption, 1986	1,455	1,236	1,070	1,090
Income, 1985	1,238	1,464	780	1,137
Income, 1986	1,332	1,525	871	1,052
Differences 1986–85				
Consumption	– 106	987	– 17	679
Income	94	1,128	92	723

Notes: The figures shown are for total consumption and disposable income, both including imputed rental values of housing and durable goods. Data from 730 panel households.

Source: Author's and World Bank calculations using the Côte d'Ivoire Living Standards Surveys, 1985–86.

are about 4 percent ($1/\sqrt{(730)} \approx 0.04$) of the means. The changes in the bottom two rows have much smaller means than do the levels, and although the standard deviations are also smaller—the correlation coefficients between the years are 0.76 for consumption and 0.72 for income—the standard errors of the estimates of mean change are now relatively much larger. The correlation between the variables is also affected by the differencing. In the micro data, the levels of consumption and income are strongly correlated in both years, 0.81 in 1985 and 0.78 in 1986, but the correlation is only 0.46 for the first differences. There is, of course, nothing in these figures that proves that measurement error is in fact present, let alone that it is determining the outcomes. As we shall see in Chapter 6, there is no difficulty in accounting for the results in Table 1.2 even under the implausible assumption that consumption and income are perfectly measured. However, the phenomena that we observe here are typical of what happens when measurement error is present and important.

1.2 The content and quality of survey data

One of the main reasons for collecting household survey data is the measurement and understanding of living standards. At the least, such measurement requires data on consumption, income, household size, and prices. For broader concepts of living standards, we also want information on health, nutrition, and life expectancy, and on levels of education, literacy, and housing. Moving from measurement to modeling extends the scope a good deal wider. To understand consumption, we need to know about income and assets, and about their determinants, saving behavior, inheritances, education, and the opportunities for working in the labor market, on a farm, or in small businesses of one kind or another. We also need information about public goods, such as schools and hospitals, and on individuals' access to them. In the past, different types of data often have been collected by different kinds of surveys. Budget surveys collected data on consumption and its components; income and employment surveys have collected data on sources of income, on occupations, and on unemployment; fertility surveys have collected data on children ever born, contraceptive practices, and attitudes towards fertility; and nutritional surveys have collected data on how much food people consume, how it is prepared and eaten, and its calorie, protein, and nutrient content. The Living Standards Surveys, described in Section 1.3, collect data on almost all of these topics from the same households in a single survey, sacrificing sample size for an integrated treatment of a relatively small number of households. This section is concerned with data quality issues that arise more or less independently whether we are dealing with multipurpose or more focussed surveys. Again, I make no attempt to be comprehensive; this section is not a list of what does or ought to appear in the ideal survey. My aim is rather to introduce a number of definitional and measurement issues that will recur throughout the book when using the data, and of which it is necessary to be aware in order to analyze them appropriately.

Individuals and households

The standard apparatus of welfare economics and welfare measurement concerns the well-being of individuals. Nevertheless, a good deal of our data have to be gathered from households, and while in some cases—earnings or hours worked—data are conceptually and practically available for both individuals and households, this is not the case for those measures such as consumption that are most immediately relevant for assessing living standards. Some goods are consumed privately by each member of the household, but many others are shared, and even for food, the most important nonshared good in developing countries, information about each person's consumption usually cannot be inferred from the data on household purchases of food that are typically observed. Chapter 4 will take up these questions in some detail, and review methods that have been proposed for inferring individual welfare from household-level data, as well as a broader avenue of research that uses household data to draw conclusions about allocations within the household. A prior question is the definition of the household in the data, why it is that some people are grouped together and others not. Broadly defined households, containing servants and distant relatives, will be larger and more likely to have a membership that responds to changes in the economic environment. While this will be inconvenient for some purposes, and will certainly make it difficult to impute living standards, it may still be the unit that is relevant for decisions like migration or the allocation of work.

There is no uniformity in definitions of the household across different surveys, although all are concerned with living together and eating together, and sometimes with the pooling of funds. A range of possibilities is reviewed by Casley and Lury (1981, pp. 186–88), who point out that different criteria are often in conflict, and emphasize that household arrangements are often not constant over time. Many of the problems are associated with the complex structure of living arrangements in developing countries, and the fact that households are often production as well as consumption units so that a definition that is sensible for one may be inappropriate for the other. When men have several wives, each wife often runs what is effectively a separate household within a larger compound presided over by the husband. Even without polyandry, several generations or the families of siblings may live in a single compound, sometimes eating together and sometimes not, and with the group breaking up and reforming in response to economic conditions. In some countries, there are lineages to which groups of households belong, and the head of the lineage may have power to command labor, to order migration, to tax and reward individuals, and to control communal assets. Even so, members of the lineage will typically live in separate households, which will nevertheless not be the appropriate units for the analysis of at least some decisions.

An example of the consequences of alternative definitions comes from Thailand, where compound living arrangements are common. The National Statistical Office changed its survey practice between the 1975–76 and 1981 surveys, and now counts subunits as separate households. Between the two surveys, average household size fell from 5.5 persons to 4.5 persons, and at least some of the difference can be attributed to the change in procedure. A decision to separate previously pooled households should not affect estimates of average consumption or income per head, but will increase measures of inequality, since the previous single estimate for the pooled household is replaced by multiple estimates for each of the subhouseholds, estimates that are not necessarily the same. Splitting households has the same effect on the distribution of income or consumption as an increase in dispersion with no change in mean, and so must increase measures of inequality (see Kanbur and Haddad 1987 and Chapter 3 below).

Reporting periods

When households are asked to report their income or consumption, a choice has to be made about the reference or reporting period. As with optimal sample design, the ideal reporting period depends on the purpose of the survey. For example, if the object of the exercise is to estimate average consumption over a year, one extreme is to approach a sample of households on January 1 and ask each to recall expenditures for the last year. The other extreme is to divide the sample over the days of the year, and to ask each to report consumption for the previous day. The first method would yield a good picture of each household's consumption, but runs the risk of measurement error because people cannot recall many purchases long after they have been made. The second method is likely to be more economical, because the survey effort is spread over the year, and will give a good estimate of mean consumption over all households. However, unless each household is visited repeatedly, the survey will yield estimates of individual expenditures that, while accurate on average, are only weakly related to the mean or normal expenditures that are appropriate measures of individual standards of living. Nor are short recall periods immune to recall errors, such as "boundary" or "start-up" bias whereby respondents report events that occurred just before the beginning of the reporting period, in an effort to be helpful and to ensure that the enumerator does not miss "relevant" events.

Scott and Amenuvegbe (1990) cite a number of studies showing that reported rates of consumption diminish with the length of the recall period, and their own experiments with households from the Ghanaian Living Standards Survey showed that for 13 frequently purchased items, reported expenditures fell at an average of 2.9 percent for every *day* added to the recall period. They found no evidence of start-up bias; rather their results confirm that recall deteriorates with time, even over a matter of days. If these conclusions are more generally valid, recall periods of even two weeks—as is often the case—will result in downward-biased estimates of consumption.

Even in the absence of reporting errors, so that sample means are unaffected by the choice of recall period, different designs applied to the same underlying population will give different estimates of inequality and of poverty. Many people receive no income on any given day, and many (albeit fewer) will spend nothing on any given day, but neither fact is a real indication that the individual is truly poor, nor that differences between individuals on a given day are indicative of the true extent of inequality. In practice, most surveys adopt sensible designs that tradeoff potential recall bias from long reporting periods against potential variance from short periods. For consumption, frequently purchased items like food have a recall period of between a week and a month, while larger or rarer items, like durable goods, are asked about on an annual recall basis. Even when the recall period is a day, households are revisited every day or two or, when practical, are asked to keep diaries for one or two weeks. Aggregate annual consumption can then be estimated for each household by multiplying monthly food expenditures by twelve and adding the durable and other items. Such a calculation will typically give a useful indication of household consumption, and the average over the households in the survey is likely to be a good estimate of average household consumption in the population.

However, good estimates of means do not imply good estimates of dispersion. For any given household, expenditures will vary from one reporting period to another, so that even in a "survey" that repeatedly interviewed the same household once a week for a year and used the weekly reports to calculate 52 annual estimates, not all would be the same. The measured dispersion of annualized expenditures will contain both intrahousehold and interhousehold components, the former from the within-year dispersion for each household, and the latter from the genuine inequality across households in annual expenditure. Since it is the latter in which we are usually interested, the use of reporting periods shorter than a year will overestimate dispersion. Some of the intrahousehold variation is seasonal, and seasonal patterns can be estimated from the data and used to make corrections. The same is not true for the random nonseasonal variation across weeks or months for each household. Scott (1992) makes calculations for this case and gives a plausible example in which the standard deviation of annual expenditures is overestimated by 36 percent from a survey that gathers consumption data on a monthly basis.

In several of the Living Standards Surveys (LSS), respondents were asked to report expenditures for more than one period. The standard LSS format calls for two visits, roughly two weeks apart, and the interviewer asks how much was spent on each food item "since my last visit." Respondents are also asked in how many months of each year they buy the item, and what they "normally" spend in each of those months. For some nonfoods, households report expenditures both "since the last visit" as well as "in the last year." Results of comparisons are reported in Grosh, Zhao, and Jeancard (1995) for the Living Standards Surveys of Ghana and Jamaica, and in Deaton and Edmonds (1996) for Côte d'Ivoire, Pakistan, and Viet Nam. Estimates of mean expenditure tend to be larger for shorter reporting periods, which is consistent both with recall failure over time, which would bias down the long-period data, but also with boundary effects, which would bias up the short-period data. It is unclear which (or if either) measure is correct. For total expenditures, the ratio of means (short-to-long) are 1.04, 1.08, 1.10, and 1.01 for Côte d'Ivoire, Ghana, Jamaica, and Viet Nam, respectively. There is also evidence, from Côte d'Ivoire and Pakistan, but not from Viet Nam, that when the time between visits is longer, reported expenditures do not increase proportionately, so that the *rate* of expenditure is lower the longer the recall period; once again, this is consistent with progressive amnesia about purchases. Measures of dispersion are also somewhat higher for shorter reporting periods; in Côte d'Ivoire for example, the standard deviations of monthly per capita consumption are 368 and 356 thousand CFAs for short and long periods, respectively. In general, "normal" expenditures on food are usually not very different from those reported "since the last visit," and while the discrepancies in both means and variances are larger for nonfoods, they account for a smaller share of the total budget. Given the other uncertainties associated with defining and measuring consumption—see the next subsection—we should perhaps not be too concerned with the discrepancies that are attributable to differences in reporting periods, at least over the practical range. Of course, such a conclusion does not provide reassurance that the measures of inequality and poverty from the surveys correspond to the measures of inequality and poverty that we should like.

Measuring consumption

If our main concern is to measure living standards, we are often more interested in estimating total consumption that its components. However, some individual items of expenditure are of interest in their own right because their consumption is of direct interest—health care, education, food, especially nutrient-rich foods such as milk—or because the items are subsidized or taxed at differential rates, so that the pattern of demand has implications for public expenditures and revenues. We also need a separate accounting of public goods and their contribution to welfare, and we need to separate expenditures on nondurables from durables, since the latter do not contribute to living standards in the same way as the former. Forecasts of demand patterns are often useful, and are essential for the sort of planning exercises that were once a routine part of development policy. The rate at which consumption switches from food to manufactures and services, and, in poorer economies, the rate at which a largely vegetarian and cereal-based diet is supplemented with meat, exert a powerful influence on the fraction of the population employed in agriculture and on the type and intensity of agricultural production.

Even when the survey is concerned only with the measurement of living standards, questions about total expenditure are unlikely to provoke accurate responses, and it is necessary to disaggregate to some extent in order to obtain satisfactory estimates. There are often other sources of information about components of consumption—crop surveys and trade data about cereals, for example—so that assessing the reliability of the survey typically requires disaggregation. Traditional household surveys in developing countries have surveyed consumption in great detail, and the Indian NSS, the Indonesian Survei Sosial Ekonomi Nasional (SUSE-NAS), and many other surveys collect information on around 200 separate food items alone, both in physical quantity and monetary units, together with several dozen more nonfood items. The World Bank's Living Standard Surveys have usually been less detailed, on the grounds that the detail and the data on physical quantities are necessary only for calculating calorie and nutrient intake, but not to obtain accurate estimates of total consumption and living standards.

There is mixed evidence on whether it is possible to obtain accurate estimates of total consumption from a small number of expenditure questions. A test survey in Indonesia (World Bank 1992, Appendix 4.2) subjected 8,000 households to both short and long questionnaires. In the former, the number of food items was reduced from 218 to 15, and the number of nonfood items from 102 to 8. Total measured food expenditures differed little between the questionnaires, either in mean or distribution, although the long questionnaire yielded about 15 percent more nonfood expenditure. But these encouraging results have not been replicated elsewhere. A similar experiment in El Salvador with 72 versus 18 food and 25 versus 6 nonfood items gave ratios (long-to-short) of 1.27 for food and 1.40 overall (Jolliffe and Scott 1995). A 1994 experiment in Jamaica produced similar results, with a long-to-short ratio of 1.26 for both food and nonfood (Statistical Institute and Planning Institute of Jamaica 1996, Appendix III). Although the shorter questionnaires can sometimes lead to dramatic reductions in survey costs and times —in Indonesia from eighty minutes to ten—it seems that such savings come at a cost in terms of accuracy.

The quality of consumption data has been subject to a good deal of debate. Minhas (1988) and Minhas and Kansal (1989) have compared various item totals from the Indian NSS consumption surveys with the independently obtained production-based totals of the amounts of various foods available for human consumption. While the results vary somewhat from food to food, and while it is important not to treat the production figures as necessarily correct, there is typically very close agreement between the two sets of estimates. The survey figures are, if anything, somewhat higher, for example by 4 percent for cereals in 1983. In Britain, the annual FES underestimates total consumption, although as we have already seen, some of the discrepancy is due to the downward bias in alcohol and tobacco expenditures, a part of which reflects the coverage of the survey. In the United States, the

Consumer Expenditure Survey also appears generally to underestimate consumption; again alcohol and tobacco are major offenders, underestimating the national accounts figures by a half and a third, respectively, but there are problems with other categories, and even food expenditures were some 15 percent lower than the estimates from the national income and product accounts (NIPA), with the discrepancy growing over time (see Gieseman 1987).

There are peculiar sampling problems associated with variables whose distribution in the population is extremely positively skewed. Assets—including land—are the most obvious example, but the same is true to a lesser extent of income, consumption, and many of its components. Consider the most extreme case, when one household owns all of the assets in the economy. Then surveys that do not include this household will yield an estimate of mean assets of zero, while those that do will yield an overestimate of the mean, by the ratio of population to sample size. Although the estimate of mean assets over all samples is unbiased, it will usually be zero. More generally, sample means will inherit some of the skewness of the distribution in the population, so that the modal survey estimate will be less than the population mean.

There are two other issues that tend to compromise the quality of consumption data in developing countries. Both are associated with the fact that most agricultural households are producers as well as consumers, and both reflect the difficulty of disentangling production and consumption accounts for people who have no reason to make the distinction. The first problem, which will arise again in Chapter 4, is that wealthy households hire workers, both domestic servants and agricultural workers, and in many cases supply them with food, explicitly or implicitly as part of their wages. Food expenditures for wealthy households will therefore usually include expenditures for items that are not consumed by the immediate family and for large agricultural households the discrepancy can be large.

The second problem relates to consumption of home-produced items, typically food grown or raised on the farm or in kitchen gardens. Such items, often referred to as *autoconsommation*, are properly recorded as both income and consumption, but are often difficult to value, especially in economies—as in much of West Africa —where some markets are not well developed, and where home production and hunting may account for a large share—perhaps more than a half—of total consumption. In cases where prices are available, and where the items being consumed are similar to those that are sold nearby, imputation is not difficult, although there are often difficulties over the choice between buying and seeling prices. Where there are differences in quality, or where the item is rarely sold, some price must be imputed, and the choice is nearly always difficult. In one extreme example, a comprehensive survey in West Africa went so far as to collect data on the amount of water that people fetched from local rivers and ponds and used for cooking and washing. Regarding this as an item of *autoconsommation*, its price was calculated using an algorithm applied to all such items, which was to select the price for a similar traded item in the geographically nearest market. In this case, river water was effectively valued at the current price of *L'Eau Perrier* in the nearest city, thus endowing rural households with immense (but alas illusory) riches.

Quite apart from being aware of the general measurement error that is likely to be introduced when imputations are responsible for a large fraction of total consumption, it is also important to recognize that such errors will be common to measures of both income and consumption, since imputations are added to both. As a result, if we are interested in the relationship between consumption and income, the same measurement error will be present in both dependent and independent variables, so that there is a spurious correlation between the two, something that needs to be taken into account in any analysis.

Measuring income

All of the difficulties of measuring consumption—imputations, recall bias, seasonality, long questionnaires—apply with greater force to the measurement of income, and a host of additional issues arise. Income is often a more sensitive topic than is consumption, especially since the latter is more obvious to friends and neighbors than the former. Accurate estimates of income also require knowledge of assets and their returns, a topic that is always likely to be difficult, and where respondents often have incentives to understate.

Perhaps most important of all is the fact that for the large number of households that are involved in agriculture or in family business, personal and business incomings and outgoings are likely to be confused. Such households do not need the concept of income, so that respondents will not know what is required when asked about profits from farms or own enterprises. The only way to obtain such measures is by imposing an accounting framework on the data, and painstakingly constructing estimates from myriad responses to questions about the specific components that contribute to the total. Even in the industrialized countries, the measurement of self-employed income is notoriously inaccurate; for example, Coder (1991) shows that estimates of nonfarm self-employment income from the March round of the Current Population Survey (CPS) in the United States are 21 percent lower than independent estimates from fiscal sources, while the estimates for farm self-employment income are 66 percent lower. Yet the ratio of the CPS estimate to the tax estimate for wages and salaries is 99.4 percent. A farmer in a developing country (or in the United States for that matter) who buys seeds and food in the same market on the same day has no reason to know that, when computing income, it is only expenditure on the former that should be deducted from his receipts. A street trader selling soft drinks may report that his profits are zero, when the fact is that at the end of each day, after buying food and giving some money to his wife and children, he has just enough left to finance the next day's inventory. Those close to subsistence, whose outgoings are close to incomings, are quite likely to report that income is zero. To get better estimates, the survey must collect detailed data on all transactions, purchases of inputs, sales of outputs, and asset transactions, and do so for the whole range of economic activities for wage earners as well as the self-employed. This is an enormous task, especially in countries where households are large and complex and where people are involved in a wide range of income-generating activities.

The practical and conceptual difficulties of collecting good income data are severe enough to raise doubts about the value of trying; the costs are large and the data may not always be of great value once collected. Apart from some early experiments, the Indian NSS has not attempted to collect income data in their consumer expenditure surveys. Very few households refuse to cooperate with the consumption surveys, and, as we have seen, their estimates of aggregate consumption cross-check with independent estimates. The belief is that the attempt to collect income could compromise this success, and would lead, not only to poor income figures, but also to a deterioration in the quality of the estimates of consumption. That said, the World Bank's experience with the various Living Standards Surveys as well as that of RAND with the Malaysian and Indonesian Family Life Surveys has been that it is possible to collect data on income components—accurately or inaccurately—without any effect on response rates. On the conceptual issues, anyone who has made the calculations necessary to assemble a household income estimate from a detailed integrated survey, such as the Living Standards Survey, with the hundreds of lines of computer code, with the arbitrary imputations, and with allowances for depreciation and appreciation of capital goods and livestock, will inevitably develop a lively skepticism about the behavioral relevance of such totals, even if the calculation is useful as a rough measure of the flow of resources into the household.

Survey-based estimates of income are often substantially less than survey-based estimates of consumption, even when national income estimates show that households as a whole are saving substantial fractions of their incomes, and even in industrialized countries where self-employment is less important and income easier to measure. Although there are often good reasons to doubt the absolute accuracy of the national income figures, the fact that surveys repeatedly show large fractions of poor people dissaving, and apparently doing so consistently, strongly suggests that the surveys underestimate saving. What little we know about the accuracy of the consumption estimates indicates that consumption is more likely to be underestimated than overestimated, so that it seems likely that most survey estimates of income are too low. Some of the underestimation may come from positive skewness in the distribution of income, so that survey estimates of the mean will also be skewed with a mode below the mean (see p. 28 above.) But underestimation of individual incomes is almost certainly important too. While this conclusion is far from well documented as a general characteristic of surveys in developing countries, many statisticians find it plausible, given the conceptual and practical difficulties of measuring income. Discovering more about the discrepancies between national income and survey-based estimates of saving should be given high priority in future research. Most theories of saving relate to individual or family behavior, and yet much of the concern about saving, growth, and macroeconomic performance relates to national aggregates. If household data cannot be matched to national data, it is very difficult to make progress in understanding saving behavior.

Table 1.3 presents data on income, expenditure, and saving from the Socioeconomic Survey of the Whole Kingdom of Thailand in 1986. The left-hand panel groups the households in the survey according to a comprehensive definition of

Table 1.3. Household saving by income and expenditure deciles, Thailand, 1986

(baht per month)

	By income decile			By expenditure decile	
Decile	*Income*	*Saving*	*Decile*	*Income*	*Saving*
1	690	-683	1	950	49
2	1,096	-737	2	1,409	-6
3	1,396	-741	3	1,768	-23
4	1,724	-775	4	2,119	-73
5	2,102	-746	5	2,523	-145
6	2,589	-593	6	3,005	-221
7	3,231	-503	7	3,649	-103
8	4,205	-358	8	4,579	-379
9	5,900	82	9	6,119	-308
10	13,176	2,761	10	12,283	-1079
All	3,612	-229	All	3,841	-229

Notes: Figures are averages over all households in each decile; there are 10,918 households in the survey. In the left-hand panel, households are grouped by deciles of total income, in the right-hand panel, by deciles of total expenditure.

Source: Author's calculations using the Social Survey of the Whole Kingdom of Thailand, 1986 (see Example 1.1 in the Code Appendix).

household total income, and shows the average saving figures for households in each decile group. According to these estimates, households dissave in total, while the National Income Accounts for Thailand (U.N. 1991) estimate that household saving was 12.2 percent of household income in 1986. Moreover, low-income households dissave more than higher-income households, and the bottom nine deciles each show negative saving on average. Although such behavior is not universal—see, for example, the results for Taiwan (China) in Chapter 6—it is common in surveys in developing countries (see, for example, Visaria and Pal 1980). Such evidence makes it easy to see why early observers of economic development inferred that saving was confined to rich households. However, the right-hand side of the table shows that such an explanation is not correct, at least not in any simple way. Households that are well-off in terms of income are also likely to be well-off in terms of consumption, so that if saving rates are higher for richer households, saving should also rise across consumption deciles. But the date show that the largest amount of dissaving is done by households in the top expenditure decile.

These findings probably owe a good deal to measurement error. If income and consumption are independently measured, at least to some extent, households who overstate their incomes will also, on average, overstate their savings, while households who overstate their consumption will correspondingly understate their saving. The top deciles of income contain a large fraction of households with overstated incomes and will thus show the highest saving rates, with the opposite effect for consumption. Of course, exactly the same story can be told with "transitory income" and "transitory consumption" replacing "measurement error" in income and consumption, respectively, and it is this analogy that lies at the heart of Friedman's (1957) permanent-income theory of consumption. Indeed, since Friedman defined transitory and permanent income as if they were measurement error and the unobserved "true" income, respectively, an explanation in terms of measurement error can always be recast as a permanent-income story. Even so, the results in Table 1.3 are consistent with the importance of measurement error in income, as is the discrepancy between the national accounts and survey results.

Paxson (1992) has argued that the presence of inflation also tends to overstate consumption relative to income given that surveys usually have different reference (reporting) periods for consumption and income. As we have seen, the reference period for consumption varies from item to item, but is often a week or two weeks for food—which may account for two-thirds or more of the budget—while the importance of seasonality in incomes means that reference periods for income are usually a year. Consumption is then denominated in more recent, higher prices than is income, imparting a downward bias to measures of saving. Since inflation in Thailand in 1986 was only 2 percent per annum, the appropriate correction makes little difference to the figures in Table 1.3, though Paxson shows that the corrections for Thailand in the previous 1980–81 survey, when inflation was 16 percent, increase saving by around 7 percent of income.

1.3 The Living Standards Surveys

The Living Standards Measurement Study (LSMS) was begun in the World Bank in 1979 in the last months of the McNamara presidency. The original aim was to develop the World Bank's ability to monitor levels of living, poverty, and inequality in developing countries, to allow more accurate statements about the number of people in poverty around the world, and to permit more useful comparisons between countries. In conjunction with host statistical offices, the project fielded its first surveys in Peru and in Côte d'Ivoire in 1985–86. Since then, there have been several dozen LSMS or LSMS-related surveys. These surveys are different from the typical earlier survey in developing countries, and the experience with them has been influential in shaping current survey practice. It is therefore useful to devote some space to a description of their special features, and to attempt some assessment of what has been learned from the LSMS experience.

A brief history

In the late 1970s, it became clear that it was impossible for the World Bank—or for anyone else—to make well-supported statements about world poverty, especially statements that required internationally comparable data. There was no firm basis assessing such fundamental topics as the extent of poverty in the world, which countries were the poorest, or whether the inequality within and between nations was expanding or contracting. Even within countries, the simplest statements about distributional outcomes were difficult. One particularly important case was that of

Brazil, where there was dispute as to the extent that poor people had benefited from the "economic miracle" of the 1960s. According to an analysis by Fields (1977), the poor had done much better than the nonpoor, but Ahluwalia and others (1980) showed that neither this result, *nor any other useful conclusion* could be supported by the available evidence. While national income data were not above criticism, then as now, statistical offices worldwide were generating useful, credible, and comparable data on average economic performance, but there were no corresponding data on distribution. At the same time, writers in the "basic needs" literature, for example Streeten and others (1981), were arguing for a reevaluation of the relationship between economic growth and poverty. While there was no lack of economists on either side of the issue, the data did not exist to settle what was largely a factual question. Even in India, the motherland of household surveys, evidence on poverty trends was controversial and hotly debated (see Bardhan 1971, Lal 1976, Ahluwalia 1978, and Griffin and Ghose 1979). Because data on consumer expenditures were collected only every five years, and because rural poverty in India is so sensitive to fluctuations in the harvest, it was impossible before the mid-1980s to separate trend from fluctuations, and be sure from the NSS data that poverty rates were indeed falling (see Ahluwalia 1985).

The original aim of the LSMS project was to remedy this situation, by collecting —or at least by helping others to collect—comparable survey data across countries, and so allowing comparisons of poverty and inequality over time and space. In retrospect, it is unclear how such an objective could have been achieved except by the establishment of international standards for surveys that were comparable, for example, to the U.N.'s system of national accounts (SNA); even then, it would have been much more difficult to establish a common set of protocols for estimating dispersion than for estimating means. However, by the time that the first full LSMS survey was ready for implementation in Côte d'Ivoire in 1985, attention had shifted from measurement towards a more ambitious program of gathering data to be used to understand the processes determining welfare at the household level. Although either set of objectives would have required a multipurpose household income and expenditure survey of some kind, the new aims were best served by an intensive, integrated survey in which each household was asked about every aspect of its economic and domestic activity. While the expense of such a design necessitated a smaller sample size, as well as less detail on individual topics than had been the case in traditional single-purpose surveys, such as agricultural or consumption surveys, these were accepted as the costs of the opportunity to model household behavior as a whole.

The shift in emphasis owed much to "Chicago" views of household and farm behavior, particularly Schultz's arguments that households respond rationally and purposively to prices and incentives and to the development by Becker of the "new household economics." These views first influenced survey practice in RAND's 1976–77 Malaysian Family Life Survey, the experience of which helped shape the first Living Standards Surveys. The latter have in turn influenced later RAND surveys, particularly the 1988–89 second Malaysian Family Life Survey and the 1993 Indonesian Family Life Survey. Behind these designs rests the belief that policy advances should rest on an enhanced empirical understanding of how such households respond to their economic and physical environments, and on the role of government policy in shaping those environments. Although such a perspective was different from the original one, the practical consequences were confined to the tradeoff between sample size and the amount of information from each individual. Nothing in the new design would prevent the data being used for its original purposes and indeed, in recent years, one of the main uses of LSMS surveys has once again been for the measurement of poverty.

Another theme in the original design was an emphasis on collecting at least some panel data. As shown above, a panel design is often an efficient way to collect information on changes over time, which was one of the aims of the LSMS project. Panel data also seemed to be well suited to the documentation of the losses and gains from economic development, or from structural adjustment. In the late 1970s and early 1980s, there was also a great deal of interest in academic circles in the econometric possibilities associated with panel data, so that the collection of such data, which was rare in developing countries, was an exciting and promising new endeavor.

The Ivorian Living Standards Survey collected data in 1985, 1986, 1987, and 1988, with an intended sample size of 1,600 households. There were three panels of 800 households each, which ran for two years each in 1985–86, 1986–87, and 1987–88; no household was retained for longer than two years, but in principle, all households would be interviewed at two visits a year apart, except for half of those in the first and last years. A larger (5,120-household) single-year survey was carried out in Peru in 1985–86, followed by a two-year panel survey with 3,200 households in Ghana in 1987–88 and 1988–89. Since then there have been LSMS or LSMS-related surveys in Mauritania (1988), Morocco (1990–91), Pakistan (1991), Venezuela (1991–93), Jamaica (1988 to date), Bolivia (1989 to date), the Kagera region of Tanzania (1991–93), Peru (1990, 1991, and 1994), Russia (1991–92), South Africa (1993), Viet Nam (1993), Kyrgyz Republic (1993), Nicaragua (1993), Guyana (1993), Ecuador (1994), Romania (1994–95), Bulgaria (1995), and the Hebie and Liaoning provinces of China (1995). At the time of writing, LSMS surveys are in the design or implementation stage for Brazil, Kazakhstan, Mongolia, Nepal, Paraguay, Tunisia, Turkmenistan, and Uzbekistan. These surveys are far from identical, although all have common design elements as described below. But the surveys have been adapted to different needs in different countries, so that, for example, the Jamaican survey is a compromise between a full LSMS survey and a previously existing and long-running labor force survey, while the survey in Kagera is concerned with monitoring economic responses to the AIDS epidemic. For further details, see Grosh and Glewwe (1995), from which the information in this paragraph is culled, or the LSMS homepage on the World Wide Web.

Design features of LSMS surveys

The design and implementation of the Ivorian survey is described in Ainsworth and Muñoz (1986) and their description remains a good account of a prototypical LSMS survey. The implementation manual by Grosh and Muñoz (1995) provides a fuller and more recent account, incorporating the lessons of past experience, and is essential reading for anyone designing an LSMS or LSMS-related survey.

There are three separate questionnaires in the "standard" LSMS survey; a household questionnaire, a community questionnaire, and a price questionnaire. The first is long by previous standards, and comprises (up to) seventeen sections or modules, some of which are technical, such as the section that identifies suitable respondents for subsequent modules, or the section that links individuals across years for panel households. Most modules are substantive and cover a long list of topics: household composition, housing and its characteristics, education, health, economic activities and time use, migration, agricultural and pastoral activities, nonfarm self-employment activities, food expenditures, durable-goods expenditures and inventories, fertility, other sources of income including remittances, saving, assets, and credit markets, and anthropometric measurement of household members. The community questionnaire, which is sometimes used only in rural areas, gathers data from knowledgeable local people (such as chiefs, village headmen or elders, medical personnel, or teachers) about local demographics (population, ethnicity, religion, and migration), and about local economic and service infrastructure, such as transportation, marketing, extension services, primary and secondary schools, and health and hospital facilities. The price questionnaire, administered country wide, was collected by enumerators visiting local markets and observing prices, mostly of foods.

The surveys are designed to produce high-quality data, and to deliver the results quickly; to this end, use is made of microcomputers both for the design of questionnaires and for data entry and editing. The use of computer software to turn questions into a printed questionnaire, with appropriate pagination and skip patterns, not only cuts down on error, but also permits rapid redesign and reprinting after field tests. Many responses are precoded on the questionnaire, so that there is no coding by keyboard operators at the data entry stage. In each round, households are visited twice with an interval of two weeks, and roughly half the questionnaire administered at each visit. Between the two visits, the first data are entered into the computers and are automatically subject to editing and consistency checks by the software as they are entered. Such procedures not only minimize data entry errors, but permit the enumerators to correct some response errors during the second visit. They also mean that much less time is required to edit the data after the survey, so that instead of the several years that are common in some countries, the preliminary data and tabulations are available in three to six months after the completion of the fieldwork.

What have we learned?

It is too early for any final verdict on the contribution of LSMS surveys to data collection in developing countries in general, let alone to their ultimate aim, of improving policymaking and the understanding of economic behavior in developing countries. At the time of writing it is only eleven years since the first household was interviewed. New data are continuously becoming available and new uses in policy and analysis are being developed. However, the LSMS surveys have taught us a great deal that we did not know in 1980, and the experience has certainly changed the way household data are—or at least ought to be—collected in developing countries.

The experiments with microcomputers have been successful. Computer-assisted questionnaire design works and the procedures for precoding, software-controlled data entry, and checking enhance data quality and speed delivery. Although local conditions typically preclude using computers during interviews, so that there are limits on the use of the computer-aided interview techniques that are rapidly developing in the United States and elsewhere, it is feasible to install microcomputers at local survey headquarters, and these are used to enter and check the data within a few days of capture. Given the cost and robustness of microcomputers, there is every reason for their use to be universal in household survey practice around the world. There is no good reason—except for entrenched bureaucracy and vested interests—why survey results and tabulations should be delayed until years after fieldwork is completed.

We also know now that long and complex household questionnaires are practical. Because there are two visits separated by two weeks, and because different members of the household are interviewed for different parts of the questionnaire, no one person is subjected to an impossibly long interview. At the beginning of the LSMS project, opinions were sharply divided on the feasibility of long questionnaires, with experienced surveyors arguing both for and against. In practice, and although each round of the LSMS survey was two to three hours long, depending on the number of household members, there were no refusals based on length, and no appearance of declining cooperation as the interviews progressed. Of course, at any given cost, there is a tradeoff between length of the questionnaires and the number of households that can be covered in the sample. The fact that LSMS surveys favor the former has meant that survey results are less useful than traditional, larger surveys for disaggregated measurement of living standards, by region, occupation, or other target group. As a result, and as interest has turned back to the use of survey data to assess poverty, the later surveys have tended to be simpler and to have larger sample sizes, and there has been some reversion towards the original aims of measurement rather than analysis.

While it is difficult to assess data quality without some sort of controlled experiment, the feedback from users has usually been positive, and there is no evidence to suggest that the timeliness of the data has been bought at the price of lower quality compared with data sets where the cleaning and editing process has taken a great deal longer. To be sure, there are difficulties with the LSMS data, but these appear to be the sort of problems that can and do arise in any survey, irrespective of design. The community and price questionnaires are elements that are more experimental in the LSMS design and there currently appears to be little hard evidence on their usefulness. The community questionnaire can be regarded as an efficient way of collecting information that could, in principle, have been collected from individual households. The data on the provision of services has been routinely combined with the household data in various analyses, for example of the determinants of access to education and health facilities. One difficulty lies in the concept of a community. The simplest idea is of a village, whose inhabitants share common health, educational, and other facilities, and who buy and sell goods in the same markets. But communities may not conform to this model; people may belong to different "communities" for different purposes, and in some parts of the world, there are no well-defined villages at all. Nor is there any guarantee that the primary sampling units or clusters in the survey necessarily correspond to units that have any unified social or administrative structure. In consequence, even when the community questionnaire yields data on schools, clinics, or transportation, we do not always have a clear delineation of the population served by those facilities, or on its relationship to the survey households in the cluster.

Information about prices is not easy to collect. Enumerators are given a list of well-defined items, and are required to price at three different sites in local markets. For obvious reasons, an enumerator is not given money to make actual purchases, but instead approaches the seller, explains that he or she is conducting a survey (which has nothing to do with taxes or law enforcement), and asks the price of an item. There is no haggling, but the enumerator is supplied with scales and asks the seller's permission to weigh the potential purchase. While it is easy to see the problems that might accompany such a procedure, it is harder to devise alternatives. "Market price" is a concept that is a good deal more complex in an African market than in an American supermarket or an economics textbook. Different people pay different amounts, there are quantity discounts, and many foods are presented for sale in discrete bundles (half a dozen yams, or a bunch of carrots) whose weights or volumes may vary even at the same price. There are also wide geographical differences in the range of items in local markets, so that it is difficult to collect the sort of price data that will permit reliable calculation of the cost-of-living indexes required to compare real living standards across different areas of the country, and between rural and urban households. Even so, in those LSMS surveys (for example Pakistan and Viet Nam) where consumers reported both expenditures and physical quantities, the unit values from these reports are well correlated across space with the prices from the price questionnaire (see Deaton and Edmonds 1996). An alternative procedure is recommended by Grootaert (1993) who suggests collecting prices using the standard price surveys that usually exist to gather cost-of-living data, although such a solution sacrifices the exact match between survey households and the prices that they face.

The experience of collecting panel data has been somewhat mixed. The original emphasis has been muted over time, and few of the recent surveys have been explicitly designed as panels. While the LSMS surveys should not be judged on their success (or lack of it) in collecting panel data, the experience has been useful, particularly given the rarity of such data from developing countries. Some critics had suggested that it would be difficult to locate many households for the second annual visit and these worst fears were not realized. Even so, there is a good deal of migration of household members, and there are occasional refusals, so that actual panels are smaller than the design. In Côte d'Ivoire, where the design called for 800 panel households out of a total sample of 1,600, there were 793 "panel-designate" households from whom valid data were collected in 1985; 730 of them (92 percent) provided valid data in 1986. In the second panel in 1986–87, 693 (87 percent) of the 800 designated households provided data, and in 1987–88, there were 701 (88 percent) out of 800. Since attrition is generally at its worst in the first year, and since the LSMS surveys make no attempt to follow households that have moved, these fractions are impressively high, comparing well with the attrition rates in the PSID.

Perhaps less satisfactory is the occasional difficulty of determining whether two so-called panel households in two years are in fact the same household. When panel households could not be located in the second year, replacement households were selected, and these were not always labeled as clearly as they should have been. The section of the questionnaire that links panel households and their members is a great help in this regard, and is a testament to the fact that the designers clearly anticipated the problems that arise with panel households, but there are cases where examination of this section, and the difficulty of matching individuals, raises questions about whether what is labeled as a panel household is not in fact a replacement. The underlying fear is that, in the absence of detailed supervision, enumerators may too readily substitute new households for the intended panelists, and that the fact that they have done so may not be easily detectable after the event. The "linking" section of the questionnaire is extremely important, and has to be a focus in any satisfactory panel survey. Linking is best done by having a list of the names of all household members, which can conflict with the usual promises of anonymity.

There are also questions about the general value of the data obtained from two-year rolling panels as in the Ghanaian and Ivorian surveys. One issue is measurement error, particularly in income and, to a lesser extent, in consumption. Given that we want to measure changes in levels of living at the individual level, and given that in much of Africa economic progress has been slow at best, measured changes over a single year will be dominated by a combination of measurement error and the normal fluctuations of agricultural income, neither of which is of primary interest. It is probably also true that attrition is at its worst between the first and second year of a panel, so that a two-year design suffers a larger proportional loss per household year than would a longer panel. Longer panels also offer greater opportunities for assessing and controlling for measurement error (see, for example, Griliches and Hausman 1986 and Pischke 1995).

What would be more useful is one of two things; first, estimates of change over much longer periods, five or ten years say, and second, estimates of change over periods when there have been major policy changes, such as those induced by structural adjustment programs, or clearly defined outside shocks that have affected living standards. Obtaining either of these can be a matter of good fortune, of having a survey in place at just the right time, but will be guaranteed only when surveys are organized on a continuing basis by a permanent local survey organization. As I have already noted, it is also sometimes possible to revisit households from an earlier survey even when there was no original intention of constructing a panel. Such revisits can allow long observation periods without having to maintain a permanent survey, and can be designed on an ad hoc basis to examine some event of interest (see Bevan, Collier, and Gunning 1989, who looked at the consequences of booms in coffee prices in Kenya and Tanzania in the mid-1980s, or Glewwe and Hall 1995, who looked at the effects of macroeconomic shocks in Peru). Although the Ivorian and Ghanaian surveys were originally intended to be permanent, data collection has ceased in both. The timing was particularly unfortunate in Côte d'Ivoire because data collection ceased just before the decline in world prices forced the government to cut the procurement prices of cocoa and coffee, which are the major sources of agricultural income in much of the country. Studying the effects of this policy change, which terminated a thirty-year regime of approximately constant real prices, could have produced important insights about policy and welfare but the opportunity was lost. In general, it is unclear that, except by chance, there are major benefits to be expected from gathering short-term panel data in slowly growing or stagnant economies.

The usefulness of the LSMS data for policymaking and research is another question on which a verdict is premature, although there is certainly a strong demand by the countries themselves for such surveys. For several of the LSMS countries, the surveys have replaced an almost total absence of information with at least some information, and the tabulations are routinely used in policy operations, project evaluation, and poverty assessment inside the World Bank and in the countries themselves. The surveys have also produced large amounts of microeconomic data that are potentially available for the sort of research described in this book. The LSMS group within the World Bank has also produced an impressive (and impressively long) list of working papers, most of which are concerned with policy-related empirical analysis of the data. However, there is less evidence that the data are being used to capacity in the countries from which they originally came.

One of the aims of the LSMS project, from its first inception, was to provide an easily accessible data base for the analysis of policy on a daily basis. While no one supposed that cabinet ministers would sit in front of terminals displaying the LSMS data, there was hope that their assistants and advisors would, and that tabulations or graphics could be produced in hours, not months or years (or not at all) as is often the case. Questions about whether food subsidies are reaching their intended recipients, or who would be hurt by an increase in fertilizer prices, are examples of the sort of questions that arise regularly among policymakers and their advisors, and that can be quantified and clarified by survey data (see Chapter 3). Such distributional analyses are a regular feature of policymaking in the United States or Britain, for example, but for whatever reason—computing facilities, software, or personnel— similar analyses are rare in developing countries. Even so, there are signs of progress. Most notable is the case of Jamaica, where there was an unusually high degree of (powerful) local interest from the start, and where the LSMS data have been used in a wide range of domestic policy exercises, on poverty assessment, on the effectiveness of food stamps, and on health questions. The data are even used as part of the standard training in quantitative methods at the University of the West Indies (Grosh and Glewwe 1995).

In recent years there has also been a great deal of progress in the archiving of the data and in making them available to the research community, for example via the LSMS page on the World Wide Web. While there are real problems of ownership and confidentiality with all household survey data, arrangements can be—and in an increasing number of cases have been—worked out to give access to the individual household records (again see the LSMS homepage for up-to-date information). Finally, a note about survey costs. The Implementation Manual (Grosh and Muñoz 1996, Table 8.1) presents total costs for eight actual surveys. These vary from $78 per household for a 2,000-household survey in Jamaica to over $700 per household for a 4,480-household survey in Brazil; in several other cases, the per household cost lies between $150 and $250. Much of the variation is explained by whether or not vehicles had to be purchased. The high estimates are inflated by these costs—only a fraction of which are directly attributable to the one-year survey—but are understated by amount of technical assistance provided by the World Bank, which is not included in these estimates.

1.4 Descriptive statistics from survey data

One of the first calls on survey data is to calculate descriptive statistics, often for a survey report containing a standard set of tables. In this section, I discuss some of the issues that arise in calculating these statistics, and in particular how we make sure that statistics describe the *population* rather than the particular *sample* that is available for analysis. To do so, we need to know how the sample was designed and to understand its relationship to the population of interest. Different sample designs require the data to be processed in different ways to estimate the same magnitude. I present some useful formulas for calculating the standard error of estimated means, again taking the sample design into account. These formulas are useful in themselves, as well as for the descriptive material that appears later in the book, particularly in Chapter 3 on the measurement of poverty. They also provide a starting point for the analytic and econometric material in Chapter 2.

Common examples of descriptive statistics are measures of central tendency, such as means and medians, and of dispersion, such as variances and interpercentile ranges. Living standards are often measured by the means of income or consumption, inequality by their dispersion, and poverty by the fraction of the population whose income or consumption is below the poverty line. The quantities that are to be summarized are sometimes continuous, as with income or consumption, and sometimes discrete, as in poverty where the basic data are indicators of whether or not a household is in poverty. While the estimation of means and standard errors is familiar, it is worth recording the formulas that take account of differential weights (inflation factors) and that allow for stratification and clustering.

Finite populations and superpopulations

To make inferences using survey data we need a framework for thinking about how the data were generated, which means thinking about the population from which the data came and about how data collection induces randomness into our sample. There are two different approaches. In the first, which is standard among survey statisticians, the population is a finite one—for example all households in Côte d'Ivoire in calendar year 1985—and the sample households are randomly selected from that population just as, in the classic textbook example, balls are drawn from an urn. The survey data are random because replication of the survey would generate different samples so that the variability of an estimate, such as the mean of household income, is assessed by thinking about how it would vary from one sample to another. The quantity of interest—in the example the average reported household income of Ivorian households in 1985—is a fixed number that could be measured with perfect accuracy from a census, which is when the sample coincides with the population. No assumptions are made about the distribution of income in the population; what is being estimated is simply the average income in the population in the survey year, not the parameter of a distribution.

In the second approach, we are less interested in the actual population in the survey year, regarding it as only one of many possible populations that might have existed. The actual population is itself regarded as a sample from all possible such populations, the infinite *superpopulation*. The focus of attention is instead the statistical law or economic process that generated income in the superpopulation, in populations like the one under study, and the mean is of interest less for itself than as a parameter or a characteristic of that law or process.

The finite-population or survey-statistical approach is typically associated with *description*, while the superpopulation approach is associated with *modeling*. The distinction is made by Groves (1989, esp. ch. 6) and will be useful in this book in which I shall be concerned with both. The distinction between description and modeling is often of no more than philosophical interest—there is no dispute about the appropriate formula for a mean or standard deviation. But when we come to the econometric analysis in Chapter 2, where the tradition has been of modeling, there are sometimes sharp differences in the recommended calculation of apparently identical concepts. Recent trends in econometric practice have tended to emphasize description at the expense of modeling—an emphasis shared by this book—so that the traditional gulf between the practice of survey statisticians and econometricians is narrowing. In consequence, I shall sometimes follow one approach, and sometimes the other, whichever seems more appropriate to the problem at hand.

The example of the mean can be used to illustrate the two approaches and provides an opportunity to record the basic formulas. Suppose that we have a simple random sample of n observations from a population of size N, and that the quantity of interest is x, with observations x_i, i running from 1 to n. The sample mean $\bar{x}$ is the obvious estimator of the population mean, where

(1.3)
$$\bar{x} = n^{-1} \sum_{i=1}^{n} x_i.$$

The sample mean, (1.3), is a random variable that will vary from one sample to another from a given population and, in the superpopulation approach, from one population to another.

Suppose that we want to know the expectation of $\bar{x}$ over the different surveys. This seems like a complicated matter for the survey statistician, because there are a large number of different ways in which n objects can be selected from a population of N objects, and it is necessary to calculate the mean for each and its associated probability of occurrence. A simple shortcut (see Cochrane, 1977, p. 28) is to rewrite (1.3) as

$$(1.4) \qquad \bar{x} = n^{-1} \sum_{i=1}^{N} a_i x_i$$

where the sum now runs over the whole population, to N rather than n, and a_i is a random variable that indicates whether i is in the sample, taking the value 1 if so, and 0 otherwise. The x's on the right-hand side of (1.4) are no longer random variables, but simply the fixed x's in the (finite) population. Hence, when we take expectations of (1.4), we need only take expectations of the a's. Since we have a simple random sample, each i has an equal probability of being included, and that probability is simply the ratio of n to N. The expectation of each a_i is therefore 1 times the probability of its being 1, which is n/N, plus 0 times the probability of its being 0, which is $(1 - n/N)$, a total of n/N. We then have

$$(1.5) \qquad E(\bar{x}) = n^{-1} \sum_{i=1}^{N} (n/N) x_i = N^{-1} \sum_{i=1}^{N} x_i = \bar{X}$$

where $\bar{X}$ is the population average in which we are interested.

A superpopulation approach makes more assumptions, but is in some ways more straightforward. It might postulate that, in the superpopulation, x is distributed with mean μ, a parameter that is the same for all households. We then have immediately, from (1.3),

$$(1.6) \qquad E(\bar{x}) = n^{-1} \sum_{i=1}^{n} \mu = \mu$$

also as desired. The finite-population approach is more general, in that it makes no assumptions about the homogeneity of the observations in the sample, but it is also more limited, in that it is specifically concerned with one population only, and makes no claim to generality beyond that population.

The technical note at the end of this subsection shows that the variance of $\bar{x}$ is

$$(1.7) \qquad V(\bar{x}) = \frac{1-f}{n} S^2$$

where S^2 is given by

$$(1.8) \qquad S^2 = (N-1)^{-1} \sum_{i=1}^{N} (x_i - \bar{X})^2$$

and can be thought of as the population variance, and $1 - f$ is the "finite-population correction" (*fpc*),

$$(1.9) \qquad 1-f = (N-n)/N.$$

Except in the unusual situation where the sample is a large fraction of the population, the *fpc* is close enough to unity for the factor $1-f$ in (1.9) to be ignored. Indeed, in this book I shall typically assume that this is the case; sampling texts are more careful, and can be consulted for the more complex formulas where necessary.

The superpopulation approach to the variance would postulate that each x_i is independently and identically distributed with mean μ and variance σ^2, so that from (1.3),

$$(1.10) \qquad V(\bar{x}) = E(\bar{x}-\mu)^2 = n^{-1}\sigma^2.$$

Since both σ^2 and S^2 are estimated from the sample variance

$$(1.11) \qquad \hat{s}^2 = (n-1)^{-1}\sum_{i=1}^{n}(x_i-\bar{x})^2$$

and provided we ignore the *fpc*, there is no operational difference between the two approaches. Both use the same estimate of the mean, and both estimate its variance using the formula

$$(1.12) \qquad \hat{v}(\bar{x}) = n^{-1}\hat{s}^2 = n^{-1}(n-1)^{-1}\sum_{i=1}^{n}(x_i-\bar{x})^2.$$

Books on sampling often give separate treatment to the estimation of means and the estimation of proportions. However, a proportion is simply the mean of a binary (0,1) indicator that tells us whether the observation does or does not possess the attribute of interest. In consequence, the formulas above—as well as those in the next subsections—can also be used for estimating proportions and their sampling variability. To see how this works and to link up with the analysis of poverty in Chapter 3, suppose that x_i is 1 if household i is in poverty, and is 0 otherwise. The estimate of the proportion of households in poverty is then the mean of x

$$(1.13) \qquad \hat{p} = n^{-1}\sum_{i=1}^{n}x_i = n_1/n$$

where n_1 is the number of households with $x_i = 1$. If we have a simple random sample, the estimated variance of $\hat{p}$ is given by (1.12), which since x_i can only take on the two values 0 or 1, takes the simple form

$$(1.14) \qquad \hat{v}(\hat{p}) = n^{-1}(n-1)^{-1}[\sum_{i=1}^{n_1}(1-\hat{p})^2 + \sum_{i=n_1+1}^{n}\hat{p}^2] = (n-1)^{-1}\hat{p}(1-\hat{p}).$$

Formula (1.14) is useful because it is simple to remember and can be calculated on the back of an envelope. Even so, the same answer is given using the standard formulas and treating the x's as if they were continuous.

Technical note: the sampling variance of the mean

I follow the derivation in Cochrane (1977, p. 29) which starts from (1.4) and from its implication that

$$(1.15) \qquad V(\bar{x}) = n^{-2} [\sum_{i=1}^{N} x_i^2 \text{var}(a_i) + 2 \sum_{i=1}^{N} \sum_{j<i}^{N} x_i x_j \text{cov}(a_i a_j)].$$

Because a_i is binomial with parameter (n/N), its variance is $(n/N)(1-n/N)$. The random variable $a_i a_j$ is either 1, if both i and j are in the sample, or 0, if not. Since the sample is drawn without replacement, the probability of the former is (n/N) multiplied by $(n-1)/(N-1)$. Hence

$$
\begin{aligned}
(1.16) \qquad \text{cov}(a_i a_j) &= E(a_i a_j) - E(a_i)E(a_j) \\
&= \frac{n(n-1)}{N(N-1)} - \left(\frac{n}{N}\right)^2 = -\frac{n}{N(N-1)}\left(1 - \frac{n}{N}\right).
\end{aligned}
$$

If the variance and covariance formulas are substituted into (1.15), and rearranged, we obtain (1.7) and (1.8).

Using weights or inflation factors

In most surveys different households have different probabilities of being selected into the sample. Depending on the purpose of the survey, some types of households are overrepresented relative to others, either deliberately as part of the design, or accidentally, for example because of differential response. In both cases, if the different types of households are different, sample means will be biased estimators of population means. To undo this bias, the sample data are "reweighted" to make them representative of the population. In this subsection, I discuss some of the reasons for different probabilities of selection, and the procedures that can be used to calculate population statistics and to assess sampling variability.

Suppose that each of the N households in the population is assigned a sampling probability π_i. A sample of size n is chosen, and I assume that the selection is done with replacement, so that in principle a given household can appear more than once. Although samples are almost never selected this way in practice, the difference between sampling with and without replacement is only important when the sample size is large relative to the population. Pretending that the sample is drawn with replacement is akin to ignoring finite-population corrections, and has the advantage of simpler formulas and derivations. Note that π_i is not the probability that i is in the sample, but the probability that i is selected at each draw, the sample being constructed from n such identical draws. Sample households with low values of π_i have a low ex ante probability of being selected into the sample, and such households are underrepresented relative to those with high ex ante probabilities. In order to correct this imbalance between sample and population, the observations need to be reweighted, weighting up those that are underrepresented and weighting down those that are overrepresented.

The weights that we need are inversely proportional to π_i; in particular, define for each household the weight w_i

$$(1.17) \qquad w_i = (n\pi_i)^{-1}.$$

For a simple random sample with replacement, each household's probability of selection at each trial is $1/N$ so that, in this case, the weights w_i are the same for all observations and equal to N/n, which is the "inflation factor" that blows up the sample to the population. When the probabilities differ, the quantity $n\pi_i$ is the expected number of times that household i shows up in the survey. When the sample is small relative to the population, so that the probability of a household appearing more than once is small, $n\pi_i$ is also approximately equal to the probability of i being in the sample. As a result, w_i in (1.17) is approximately equal to the number of population households represented by the sample household i and can therefore be thought of as the household-specific inflation factor.

Consider first the sum of the weights which, since each is a household inflation factor, might be thought to be an estimate of the population size N; hence the notation

$$(1.18) \qquad \hat{N} = \sum_{i=1}^{n} w_i.$$

Define the random variable t_i as the number of times that household i shows up in the sample; this will usually take the values 1 or 0 but, since sampling is with replacement, could in principle be larger. Its expected value is $n\pi_i$, the number of trials multiplied by the probability of success at each. The sum of weights in (1.18) can then be rewritten as

$$(1.19) \qquad \hat{N} = \sum_{i=1}^{N} t_i w_i$$

with the sum running from 1 to N. Taking expectations,

$$(1.20) \qquad E(\hat{N}) = \sum_{i=1}^{N} E(t_i) w_i = \sum_{i=1}^{N} n\pi_i w_i = N$$

so that the sum of the weights is an unbiased estimator of the population size.

Suppose that x_i is the quantity of interest reported by household i. We estimate the *total* of x in the population by multiplying each x_i by its weight w_i and adding up, so that

$$(1.21) \qquad \hat{X}_{tot} = \sum_{i=1}^{n} w_i x_i.$$

By a precisely analogous argument to that for $\hat{N}$, we have

$$(1.22) \qquad E(\hat{X}_{tot}) = \sum_{i=1}^{N} E(t_i) w_i x_i = \sum_{i=1}^{N} x_i = X_{tot}$$

so that $\hat{X}_{tot}$ is unbiased for the population total. The sampling variance of (1.21) is

$$(1.23) \qquad V(\hat{X}_{tot}) = \frac{1}{n} \sum_{i=1}^{N} \pi_i \left(\frac{x_i}{\pi_i} - X_{tot} \right)^2 = \frac{1}{n} \left(\sum_{i=1}^{N} \frac{x_i^2}{\pi_i} - X_{tot}^2 \right)$$

(see the technical note on p. 49 below and Cochrane 1977, pp. 252–54). An un-biased estimate of (1.23) can be obtained from the sample by defining $z_i = w_i x_i$ and using the formula

$$(1.24) \qquad \hat{v}(\hat{X}_{tot}) = \frac{n}{n-1} \sum_{i=1}^{n} (z_i - \bar{z})^2.$$

The sampling variance (1.23) can be used to give a formal answer to the question of why different probabilities can enhance efficiency, and to tell us what the optimal probabilities should be. In particular, it is a simple matter to show that (1.23) is minimized subject to the constraint that the π's add to 1 by selecting the π's to be proportional to the x's. This is sampling with *probability proportional to size (p.p.s.)*; larger values of x contribute more to the mean so that efficiency is en-hanced when larger values are overrepresented. Of course, if we knew the x's, there would be no need to sample, so that in practice we can use only approximate *p.p.s.*, in which the π's are set proportional to some other variable that is thought to be correlated with x and that is known prior to sampling.

We are often interested, not in the total of x, but its mean, $\bar{X}$, which can be estimated from the ratio of the estimated total (1.21) to the estimated population, (1.19). This is the *probability-weighted mean*

$$(1.25) \qquad \bar{x}_w = \sum_{i=1}^{n} w_i x_i / \sum_{i=1}^{n} w_i = \sum_{i=1}^{n} v_i x_i$$

where the v_i are the w_i from (1.17) normalized to sum to unity,

$$(1.26) \qquad v_i = w_i / \sum_{k=1}^{n} w_k.$$

A simple example of the effects of weighting is given in Table 1.4, which pre-sents the weighted and unweighted means and medians—see (1.30) below for the definition of a weighted median—for total household expenditure by race in the South African Living Standards Survey. These calculations use the weights sum-marized in Table 1.1 and discussed on page 16 above. For the Blacks, Coloreds,

Table 1.4. Household total expenditures, weighted and unweighted means, South Africa, 1993
(rand per month)

	Means		Medians	
Race	*Weighted*	*Unweighted*	*Weighted*	*Unweighted*
Blacks	1,053	1,045	806	803
Coloreds	1,783	1,790	1,527	1,547
Asians	3,202	3,185	2,533	2,533
Whites	4,610	4,621	4,085	4,083
All races	1,809	1,715	1,071	1,029

Source: Author's calculations using the South African Living Standards Survey, 1993.

and Asians, the weights do not vary much within each group, so that there is little difference between the weighted and unweighted estimates. For Whites, there is more within-group variance in weights, but it has little effect on either estimate because there is little or no correlation between the weights and the level of income within the group. However, as we saw in Table 1.1, lower participation by Whites made the weights higher for Whites than for the other groups, so that when we calculate estimates for the whole country, their higher incomes result in weighted estimates that are larger than the unweighted estimates. This result illustrates the general point that, whenever there is an association between the sampling probabilities and the quantity being measured, unweighted estimates are biased.

Because $\bar{x}_w$ is the ratio of two random variables, it is not an unbiased estimator. However, because the variances of its numerator and denominator, (1.21) and (1.19), both converge to zero as n tends to infinity, it will converge to the population mean. The sampling variance of $\bar{x}_w$ can be evaluated using standard approximation techniques for ratio estimators; in the technical note on p. 49 below, I sketch the argument that leads to

$$(1.27) \qquad V(\bar{x}_w) \approx N^{-2} \sum_{i=1}^{N} w_i (x_i - \bar{X})^2$$

which can be estimated from the sample data using

$$(1.28) \qquad \hat{v}(\bar{x}_w) = \frac{n}{n-1} \sum_{i=1}^{n} v_i^2 (x_i - \bar{x}_w)^2.$$

Note that the estimated variance will usually need to be specially coded. In particular and except for simple random sampling, (1.28) is *not* equal to the sample estimate of the population variance—equation (1.29) below—divided by the sample size (compare (1.11) and (1.12)). Formula (1.27) can also be used to find the probabilities that maximize the precision of the probability-weighted mean (1.25). Recalling that $w_i = (n\pi_i)^{-1}$ and choosing the π's to minimize (1.27) subject to the constraint that their sum be 1, it is easily shown that the optimal selection probabilities should be proportional to the absolute value of the deviation from the mean $|x_i - \bar{X}|$. It is information on the exceptional cases that adds most to the precision of the estimated mean.

It is worth noting that the probability-weighted mean (1.25) is not the only possible estimate. In particular, if the population size N is known, an estimate of the mean can be obtained by dividing $\hat{X}_{tot}$ by N. But there are a number of reasons why the weighted mean is frequently more useful. First, the population size is often not known, but is estimated from the survey itself, for example by randomly selecting a set of villages, enumerating all households in each, and using the totals to estimate the number of households in the population. Second, when we come to use the survey data to calculate means or other statistics, some data are unusable, because they are missing, because of transcription errors, or because they take on clearly implausible values. There is then little option but to average over the "good" observations, renormalizing the weights to sum to unity. Third, in many applications we are not interested in means per household, but in means per person.

We want to know the fraction of *people* in poverty, not the fraction of *households* in poverty. Or we may want to know the fraction of elderly, or women, or children who have some characteristic. In such cases, we weight the data, not by the number of *households* represented by the sample household, but by the number of *people* it represents. To get statistics about persons in the population, the quantity surveyed, say household per capita consumption, should be weighted not by the w_i themselves, but by the w_i multiplied by the number of people in household i. The total of these weights is (in expectation) the number of people in the population, not the number of households; as before, this population total may or may not be known in advance, but we often encounter cases where the relevant population total is estimated by summing weights from the survey estimate. Fourth and finally, we often want to calculate means for subgroups, and to do so in a way that is representative of the relevant subpopulations. Once again, $\bar{x}_w$ is the relevant estimator unless we know the size of each subpopulation.

The weights can be used to estimate other population statistics analogously to the mean in (1.25). For example, the population variance S^2 is estimated from the sample by weighting the individual squared deviations from the mean so that

$$(1.29) \qquad \hat{s}_w^2 = \frac{n}{n-1} \sum_{i=1}^{n} v_i (x_i - \bar{x}_w)^2 = \frac{n}{n-1} \sum_{i=1}^{n} w_i (x_i - \bar{x}_w)^2 / \sum_{i=1}^{n} w_i$$

where the adjustment factor $n/(n-1)$ is of no practical significance, but matches (1.29) to the standard unbiased estimator (1.11) in the case where $w_i = N/n$. Expression (1.29) would be used, for example, when using the variance of income or of the logarithm of income to measure inequality. Weights must also be used when ranking households, for example when calculating medians, quartiles, or other percentiles in the population. In the sample, median household income (for example) is that level of income below which (and above which) lie half the sample observations. When estimating the median for the population, we must find instead the level of income such that, when we take all sample households with lower income, the sum of their weights is half the total sum of weights. Formally, the median $\bar{x}_w$ is defined by

$$(1.30) \qquad \sum_{i=1}^{n} 1(x_i \le \bar{x}_w) v_i = 0.5$$

where the v_i are the normalized weights in (1.26) and the function $1(e)$ is an indicator that takes the value 1 if the statement e is true and is 0 otherwise. Other percentiles are calculated by replacing the 0.5 in (1.30) by the appropriate fraction. In practice, the easiest way to work is to sort the data in order of increasing x_i, and then to calculate a running sum of the normalized weights. The percentiles are then read off from this running sum. Example 1.1 in the Code Appendix gives the STATA program used to calculate the results in Table 1.3; this shows how to label households by their deciles of total household income and expenditure, and to summarize variables by those deciles.

In principle, formulas can be derived for sampling variances for medians, variances, and functions of these statistics. But the calculations are in some cases quite complex, and the approximations and assumptions required are not always palatable. As we shall see below, the bootstrap often offers a more convenient way to assess sampling variability in these cases.

*Technical note: sampling variation of probability-weighted estimates

The probability-weighted mean is the ratio of two estimates, $\hat{X}_{tot}$ and $\hat{N}$. The variance of such a ratio can be approximated by

$$(1.31) \qquad \mathrm{var}(\bar{x}_w) \approx N^{-2}[\mathrm{var}(\hat{X}_{tot}) - 2\bar{X}\mathrm{cov}(\hat{X}_{tot}\hat{N}) + \bar{X}^2\mathrm{var}(\hat{N})].$$

I illustrate only the derivation of the first term in square brackets; the other variance and the covariance are readily obtained in the same manner. From (1.21),

$$(1.32) \qquad \hat{X}_{tot} = \sum_{i=1}^{N} t_i w_i x_i.$$

The only random variables in (1.32) are the t's, so that

$$(1.33) \qquad \mathrm{var}(\hat{X}_{tot}) = \sum_{i=1}^{N} w_i^2 x_i^2 \mathrm{var}(t_i) + \sum_{j \neq i}^{N} \sum_{i=1}^{N} w_i w_j x_i x_j \mathrm{cov}(t_i t_j).$$

The t's follow a multinomial distribution, so that the variance of t_i is $n\pi_i(1-\pi_i)$ and the covariance between t_i and t_j is $-n\pi_i\pi_j$. Substituting in (1.33) and rearranging gives (1.23) above. That (1.24) is unbiased for (1.23) is shown by inserting t's, and changing the summation from n to N, and taking expectations (see also Cochrane). Substitution of (1.33) into (1.31) together with the comparable formulas for $\mathrm{var}(\hat{N})$ and $\mathrm{cov}(\hat{X}_{tot},\hat{N})$ gives (1.27). The sample estimate (1.28) is constructed by replacing the square of N in the denominator by the square of its estimate $\hat{N}$, replacing $\bar{X}$ by its estimate $\bar{x}_w$, and replacing the population sum of squares by its sample equivalent, remembering that for every household in the sample, there are w_i in the population. The scaling factor $n/(n-1)$ is conventional and clearly has little effect if n is large (see also (1.29)).

Stratification

The effect of stratification is to break up a single survey into multiple independent surveys, one for each stratum. When we think of the different samples that might be drawn in replications of the survey, the strata will be held fixed while the particular households selected from each will vary from sample to sample. Without stratification, the fraction of the sample in each stratum is left to chance. In consequence, estimates of population parameters vary across samples because each sample has different fractions of observations in each stratum so that, when the means differ across strata, their weighted average will also differ. As a result, stratification can reduce sampling variability whenever the means differ across strata.

Suppose that there are S strata, labeled by s, that we know the total population N as well as the population in each stratum N_s, and that the mean for stratum s is $\bar{X}_s$. The population mean, or "grand" mean, is then

(1.34)
$$\bar{X} = \sum_{s=1}^{S} (N_s/N)\bar{X}_s$$

which can be estimated from

(1.35)
$$\bar{x} = \sum_{s=1}^{S} (N_s/N)\bar{x}_s$$

where $\bar{x}_s$ is the estimated mean for stratum s. Note that the calculation of these means will typically involve weights, as in (1.25) above. The population shares may or may not be the same as the sample shares; stratification is about breaking up the sample into subsamples, not about weighting. Nevertheless, it is often the case that the sampling fractions are different in different strata. In such cases, as I shall show below, it is possible to incorporate the stratum weights into the weights for each observation.

Because the strata are independent, the variance of the estimate of the population mean (1.35) takes the simple form, ignoring the *fpc*,

(1.36)
$$V(\bar{x}) = \sum_{s=1}^{S} (N_s/N)^2 V(\bar{x}_s),$$

where $V(\bar{x}_s)$ is the variance of the estimate of the stratum mean. If instead of the stratified survey, we had used a simple random sample, the numbers in each stratum, n_s, would be random variables within the total sample size n. Hence, if we write the sample mean for the simple random sample design analogously to (1.35),

(1.37)
$$\bar{x}_{srs} = \sum_{s=1}^{S} (n_s/n)\bar{x}_s$$

which looks very similar to (1.35), especially since the expectations of the sample ratios (n_s/n) are the population ratios (N_s/N). However, in the unstratified design, the fractions of the sample in each stratum will vary from sample to sample, so that the variability of the estimate will not only have a component from the variability of the stratum means, as in the stratified sample, but also a component from the variability of the fractions in each stratum. With some algebra, it can be shown that the variances of the two estimates are linked by the approximation

(1.38)
$$V(\bar{x}_{srs}) \approx V(\bar{x}) + n^{-1}\sum_{s=1}^{S} (N_s/N)(\bar{x}_s - \bar{x})^2.$$

As would be expected, the variance is larger in the simple random sample than in the stratified sample, and will be the more so the larger is the heterogeneity across strata. When the strata means coincide with the grand mean, there is no increase in efficiency from stratification.

In practice, estimation in stratified samples is usually done using simple adaptations of the formulas for the weighted estimates in the previous subsection. Suppose that we think of each stratum as a separate survey, and write the inflation factors for households in stratum s as w_{is}, where, corresponding to (1.17),

(1.39)
$$w_{is} = (n_s \pi_{is})^{-1}$$

where n_s is the sample size from stratum s, and π_{is} is the probability that i is drawn at each trial. The within-stratum sum of these weights is an unbiased estimator of the stratum population, N_s, and the grand sum over all observations is an unbiased estimator of the total population. Hence, we can define a probability-weighted estimate of the grand mean corresponding to (1.35)

$$(1.40) \qquad \bar{x}_w = \sum_{s=1}^{S} (\hat{N}_s/\hat{N}) \, \bar{x}_{sw}$$

where $\bar{x}_{sw}$ is the probability-weighted mean (1.25) computed for stratum s. Note that in (1.40), unlike (1.35), the fractions of the population in each stratum are estimated, and are therefore random variables. As a result, (1.40) loses what might be expected from stratification, that without variation within strata, there is no variance in an estimate from a stratified sample (see (1.36). That this is not the case is because there are differential weights within strata, so that different samples will give different weights to each stratum mean. Of course, if the ratios N_s/N are available, they can be used to replace the estimates in (1.40), with a gain in precision.

If we substitute the appropriate sums of weights for $\hat{N}_s$ and $\hat{N}$ in (1.40), we get

$$(1.41) \qquad \bar{x}_w = \left(\sum_{s=1}^{S} \sum_{i=1}^{n_s} x_{is} w_{is} \right) \Big/ \left(\sum_{s=1}^{S} \sum_{i=1}^{n_s} w_{is} \right)$$

where x_{is} is the observation from household i in stratum s. Note that (1.41) is simply the probability-weighted mean without any explicit allowance for the stratification; each observation is weighted by its inflation factor and the total divided by the total of the inflation factors for the survey. Like (1.25), it is also a ratio estimator; the mean is estimated by the ratio of the estimated total—in the numerator—to the estimated population size—in the denominator. In consequence, we can use the variance formula (1.31) to approximate the variance of (1.41) in terms of the variances and covariance of the totals which, in turn, are sums of stratum-specific terms because sampling is independent within each stratum. The algebra is similar to that used to derive (1.23) and (1.27), and yields

$$(1.42) \qquad V(\bar{x}_w) = \frac{1}{N^2} \sum_{s=1}^{S} \frac{1}{n_s} \sum_{i=1}^{N_s} \pi_{is} \left[\left(\frac{x_{is}}{\pi_{is}} - N_s \bar{X}_s \right) - \bar{X} \left(\frac{1}{\pi_{is}} - N_s \right) \right]^2 .$$

As was the case for (1.23) and (1.24), a feasible sample-based estimator of (1.42) starts from defining $z_{is} = x_{is} w_{is}$, and using the formula

$$(1.43) \qquad \hat{v}(\bar{x}_w) = \sum_{s=1}^{S} \frac{n_s}{n_s - 1} \sum_{i=1}^{n_s} [(z_{is} - \bar{z}_s) - \bar{x}_w (w_{is} - \bar{w}_s)]^2$$

where $\bar{z}_s$ and $\bar{w}_s$ are the stratum means of the z's and the weights, respectively.

Two-stage sampling and clusters

Within strata, most household surveys collect their data in two stages, first sampling clusters, or primary sampling units (PSUs), and then selecting households from within each cluster; this is the standard two-stage stratified design. Clustered samples raise different statistical issues from stratified samples. When we imagine replicating a survey, which is how we think about sampling variability, the strata are held constant from sample to sample, but new clusters are drawn every time. For example, each potential survey might select an equal number of households from all of the provinces of the country (the strata), but would always select a new set of villages within provinces (the clusters). Probabilities of selection can differ at either or both stages of the survey, between clusters, or between households within clusters. The formulas for weighted and unweighted means are not affected by the two-stage design any more than they were affected by stratification. But the sampling variability of these estimates *is* affected by the design. Because households within clusters are often similar to one another in their relevant characteristics, it is frequently the case that clustering will *increase* variability compared with simple random sampling. In this subsection, I introduce some notation, record the formulas for the means and their sampling variation, and explain how it is that clustering reduces precision, and the consequences of ignoring the clustering in calculating variability. This is perhaps the most important message of this subsection, that it can be a serious mistake to treat a two-stage sample as if it were a simple random sample; the use of standard formulas can seriously overstate the precision of the estimates.

I start by supposing that there is no stratification, or equivalently, that there is only a single stratum. Because separate strata can be thought of as separate surveys, a simple way to deal with a stratified sample is to work with one stratum at a time, and then to reassemble the survey as a whole from its components. I shall do so, and record the relevant formulas, at the end of the subsection.

We need notation for the numbers of clusters and households in the sample and in the population. Suppose that there are N clusters in the population from which n are selected into the survey; this preserves the previous notation for the case where each observation is a cluster. I use the suffix c to denote a cluster or PSU, and m_c and M_c to denote the number of sample and population households in cluster c. I shall use T for the total number of households in the population

$$(1.44) \qquad\qquad T = \sum_{c=1}^{N} M_c.$$

Suppose that sampling is with replacement, but with unequal probabilities at both stages. I use π_c to denote the probability of selection for cluster c in the first stage, and π_{ic} for the probability that i is selected at the second stage, conditional on c having been selected at the first. The unconditional probability that household i in cluster c is selected at a single two-stage draw is therefore $\pi_{ic}\pi_c$. Proceeding as before, we can define inflation factors for each stage of the survey. To differentiate these stage-specific inflation factors from the overall inflation factors, I use different notations for each. Define h_c and h_{ic} by

$$(1.45) \qquad\qquad h_c = (n\pi_c)^{-1}, \quad h_{ic} = (m_c\pi_{ic})^{-1}$$

so that h_c is the number of population *clusters* represented by cluster c, and h_{ic} is the number of cluster-c households represented by household i in cluster c. The overall inflation factor, the number of households in the population represented by household i, is the product of h_c and h_{ic}, which corresponds to our previous survey weight w_{ic},

$$(1.46) \qquad w_{ic} = h_c h_{ic} = (\pi_c \pi_{ic} m_c n)^{-1}.$$

Note that the sum of these weights over cluster c,

$$(1.47) \qquad w_c = \sum_{i=1}^{m_c} w_{ic} = h_c \sum_{i=1}^{m_c} h_{ic}$$

is an inflation factor that tells us how many population households are represented by the collectivity of sample households in cluster c.

The probability-weighted mean is defined in the standard way; adapting (1.25) to recognize the clusters,

$$(1.48) \qquad \bar{x}_w = \frac{\sum\limits_{c=1}^{n} \sum\limits_{i=1}^{m_c} w_{ic} x_{ic}}{\sum\limits_{c=1}^{n} \sum\limits_{i=1}^{m_c} w_{ic}} = \frac{\sum\limits_{c=1}^{n} w_c \bar{x}_{cw}}{\sum\limits_{c=1}^{n} w_c} = \sum_{c=1}^{n} v_c \bar{x}_{cw}$$

where $\bar{x}_{cw}$ is the probability-weighted mean for cluster c and the v's are the cluster weights (1.47) normalized to sum to 1. The evaluation of the variance of (1.48) is complicated by the randomness in the cluster means, as well as in the selection of clusters themselves. The algebra is simplified if we follow Cochrane (1977, pp. 275–76) and calculate expectations and variances in two stages, so that, for the mean $\bar{x}_w$

$$(1.49) \qquad E(\bar{x}_w) = E_1[E_2(\bar{x}_w)]$$

where the expectation E_2 is taken with respect to the second-stage sampling, treating the choice of clusters as fixed, and where E_1 is taken with respect to the choice of clusters. The corresponding variance formulas are

$$(1.50) \qquad V(\bar{x}_w) = V_1[E_2(\bar{x}_w)] + E_1[V_2(\bar{x}_w)].$$

The application of (1.49) and (1.50) is relatively straightforward using previous results, and after a good deal of algebra, we reach

$$(1.51) \qquad V(\bar{x}_w) = n^{-1} \sum_{c=1}^{N} \pi_c \phi_c^2 (\bar{X}_c - \bar{X})^2 + T^{-2} \sum_{c=1}^{N} \sum_{j=1}^{M_c} w_{jc} (X_{jc} - \bar{X}_c)^2$$

where ϕ_c is the fraction of the population in cluster c, and $\bar{X}_c$ and $\bar{X}$ are the true means for the cluster and the population, respectively. (For comparison, note that (1.51) reduces to (1.27) when each cluster contains a single household and the weights satisfy $n^{-1} \pi_c = w_c$ and $\phi_c = N^{-1}$). A consistent estimate of (1.51) can be obtained from

$$(1.52) \qquad \hat{v}(\bar{x}_w) = \frac{n}{n-1} \sum_{c=1}^{n} v_c^2 (\bar{x}_{cw} - \bar{x}_w)^2$$

which is identical to (1.28), with households replaced by clusters, and individual data points replaced by cluster means.

It should be emphasized that, in spite of its formal similarity, the variance (1.52) is quite different from the corresponding formula when there is no clustering, and that the use of the incorrect formula can be seriously misleading. While it is sometimes the case that estimated variances are not much altered by allowing for stratification or differential weights, clustering is ignored at one's peril. I illustrate for the simplest case, where there are M households in each of the N clusters, and at the first stage, clusters are selected by simple random sampling. Each cluster is then equally weighted, so that when we estimate the variance from (1.52) we get

$$(1.53) \qquad \hat{v}(\bar{x}) = \frac{1}{n(n-1)} \sum_{c=1}^{n} (\bar{x}_c - \bar{x})^2.$$

If we were mistakenly to ignore the clustering and treat each observation as an independent draw in a simple random sample of size mn, we would use (1.12) to give

$$(1.54) \qquad \hat{v}_{srs}(\bar{x}) = \frac{1}{mn(mn-1)} \sum_{c=1}^{n} \sum_{i=1}^{m} (x_{ic} - \bar{x})^2 = \frac{1}{mn} \hat{s}^2.$$

If we substitute for the cluster means in (1.53) and rearrange, we get

$$(1.55) \qquad \hat{v}(\bar{x}) \approx \hat{v}_{srs}(\bar{x})[1 + (m-1)\hat{\rho}]$$

where $\hat{\rho}$ is defined by

$$(1.56) \qquad \hat{\rho} = \frac{\sum_{c=1}^{n} \sum_{j=1}^{m} \sum_{k \neq j}^{m} (x_{jc} - \bar{x})(x_{kc} - \bar{x})}{mn(m-1)\hat{s}^2}.$$

The quantity in (1.56) is a sample estimate of the *intracluster correlation coefficient*. Like any correlation coefficient, ρ measures the similarity of values, in this case within the clusters. When all the x's are the same in the same cluster, $\rho = 1$, when they are unrelated, $\rho = 0$. In practice, for quantities like income and consumption in rural areas of developing countries, ρ is often substantially larger than zero and values of 0.3 to 0.4 are frequently encountered.

Equation (1.55) shows how the magnitude of ρ affects the variability of sample estimates, at least in this simple case. When $\rho = 0$, the variance of the estimate from the clustered sample coincides with the variance of the estimate from the simple random sample. At the other extreme, when $\rho = 1$, the factor in square brackets in (1.55) is m, so that $\hat{v}(\bar{x}) = \hat{s}^2/n$ and the effective sample size is not the number of sample *observations*, mn, but the number of sample *clusters*, n. When the observations are the same within each cluster, sampling more than one from each does nothing to increase the precision of the estimate. In the next subsection, I shall give some practical examples of the way in which assumptions about sample design affect calculations of standard errors, and of the potential for being misled by the wrong assumption.

Two-stage samples often use a "self-weighting" design. At the first stage, clusters are selected with probability proportional to the number of households they contain while, at the second stage, an equal number of households is drawn from each cluster using simple random sampling. This has the effect of making the overall, surveywide, inflation factors w_{ic} the same for all households. To see how this works, set

$$(1.57) \qquad \pi_c = \frac{M_c}{\sum\limits_{c=1}^{N} M_c} = \frac{M_c}{T}, \quad \pi_{ic} = \frac{1}{M_c}, \quad m_c = m$$

so that, substituting into (1.46), we have

$$(1.58) \qquad w_{ic} = T/(mn)$$

which is the same as in a simple random sample. (Of course, this only applies to the weights and the computation of sampling variability must still allow for the two-stage design. A two-stage self-weighting sample is *not* the same thing as a simple random sample.)

Self-weighting is simple and elegant. It also had practical utility when computation was so difficult that the additional complexity of weights was best avoided if possible. However, self-weighting designs are rarely self-weighting in practice because adjustments are often made to the weights after the survey, for example to compensate for unanticipated nonresponse by some set of households, and weights have to be used in any case. An example is the South African Living Standards Survey, which had a self-weighting design, but which had to be weighted ex post (see Table 1.1). Since computation is hardly an issue today, it is unclear why the design remains so popular.

In practice, it is necessary to combine the formulas for the clustered case with those that allow for multiple strata. This is conceptually straightforward, although the notation makes the formulas look forbidding. I denote the strata by the subscript s, and rewrite the mean for stratum s from (1.48) as

$$(1.59) \qquad \bar{x}_{sw} = \sum_{c=1}^{n_s} w_{cs} \bar{x}_{csw} / \sum_{c=1}^{n_s} w_{cs}$$

where the only change is to add a suffix s to indicate the stratum. From (1.35), we can compute the grand mean over all the strata using

$$(1.60) \qquad \bar{x}_w = \sum_{s=1}^{S} \hat{N}_s \bar{x}_{sw} / \hat{N}$$

where the hats denote the usual estimates from the sums of the weights. Substituting (1.59) into (1.60) gives the probability-weighted estimate of the grand mean in the familiar form of a ratio between the estimated total of X, and the estimated population size,

$$(1.61) \qquad \bar{x}_{sw} = \frac{\displaystyle\sum_{s=1}^{S}\sum_{c=1}^{n_s} w_{cs}\bar{x}_{csw}}{\displaystyle\sum_{s=1}^{S}\sum_{c=1}^{n_s} w_{cs}} = \frac{\displaystyle\sum_{s=1}^{S}\sum_{c=1}^{n_s}\sum_{i=1}^{m_c} w_{ics} x_{ics}}{\displaystyle\sum_{s=1}^{S}\sum_{c=1}^{n_s}\sum_{i=1}^{m_c} w_{ics}} = \frac{\hat{X}_{tot}}{\hat{N}}$$

which is simply the weighted mean using all the observations and all the weights in the survey. An estimate of the variance of (1.59) and (1.61) is obtained following the same general procedures as for the ratio estimator (1.41) in the stratified case, but making the adaptions for clustering for the variances within each stratum. The formulas are simplified if we define the cluster level variable

$$(1.62) \qquad z_{cs} = \sum_{i=1}^{m_c} w_{ics} x_{ics}.$$

If z_s is the mean of z_{cs} over clusters in stratum s, the variance of (1.61) can be estimated from (compare (1.43))

$$(1.63) \qquad \hat{v}(\bar{x}_{sw}) = \frac{1}{\hat{N}^2}\sum_{s=1}^{S}\frac{n_s}{n_s-1}\sum_{c=1}^{n_s}[(z_{cs}-z_s)-\bar{x}_{sw}(w_{cs}-\bar{w}_s)]^2$$

where w_{cs} is the total weight in cluster c of stratum s, and $\bar{w}_s$ is the stratum-s mean of w_{cs}. Sample code for equation (1.63) is given in Example 1.2 of the Code Appendix; it is also available as a special case of the more general formulas available in Version 5.0 of STATA.

A superpopulation approach to clustering

It is also possible to take a superpopulation approach to clustering, and as was the case with simple random sampling, the results are in many ways simpler. They also provide a useful bridge to the discussion of clustering and regression in Section 1 of Chapter 2. Suppose that there are no weights and that

$$(1.64) \qquad x_{ic} = \mu + \alpha_c + \epsilon_{ic}$$

where μ is the mean, α_c is a cluster effect, and ϵ_{ic} is a random variable with mean 0 and variance σ_ϵ^2 that is independently and identically distributed for all i and c. The cluster effects α_c are also random with mean 0 and variance σ_α^2, are independently and identically distributed across clusters, and are independent of the ϵ's. These independence assumptions are the counterpart of the independence of the two stages of the sampling in the finite-population approach and the presence of the α's allows cluster means to differ from the overall mean.

As before, the obvious estimator of μ is the sample mean $\bar{x}$, and straightforward calculation gives

$$(1.65) \qquad E(\bar{x}) = \mu; \quad V(\bar{x}) = n^{-1}\sigma_\alpha^2 + (nm)^{-1}\sigma_\epsilon^2.$$

The variance in (1.65) is the counterpart of (1.51) when both stages are by simple random sampling. It is also instructive to write it in the form

$$(1.66) \qquad V(\bar{x}) = \frac{\sigma_\epsilon^2 + \sigma_\alpha^2}{nm}\left(1 + (m-1)\frac{\sigma_\alpha^2}{\sigma_\epsilon^2 + \sigma_\alpha^2}\right) = \frac{\sigma^2}{nm}[1 + (m-1)\rho],$$

where $\sigma^2 = \sigma_\epsilon^2 + \sigma_\epsilon^2$ is the variance of x_{ic} and ρ, the ratio of σ_α^2 to σ^2 is the intra-cluster correlation coefficient (compare (1.55) above).

An unbiased estimator of $V(\bar{x})$ is given by

$$(1.67) \qquad \hat{v}(\bar{x}) = n^{-1}\hat{s}_1^2 = n^{-1}(n-1)^{-1}\sum_{c=1}^{n}(\bar{x}_c - \bar{x})^2$$

which corresponds to (1.52). In both cases the variance can be computed by considering only the variation of the estimated cluster means, ignoring within cluster variability.

Illustrative calculations for Pakistan

For poverty and welfare calculations, we often use household per capita expenditure (PCE)—total expenditure on goods and services divided by household size—as a measure of living standards. I use measurements of PCE from the Pakistan Living Standards Survey—formally the Pakistan Integrated Household Survey, or PIHS—to illustrate the sort of design that is encountered in practice, as well as the consequences of the design for the calculation of statistics and their standard errors.

The survey documentation will usually explain how the stratification was done and the primary sampling units selected. Identifiers for the stratum and cluster of each household are sometimes included as data in one of the household files, but are more usually incorporated into the household identifiers. This is the case for the PIHS, where the first three digits of the household code gives the stratum, the next three the cluster, and the last three the household within the cluster. Example 1.2 in the Code Appendix shows how the household identifiers are broken down to give stratum and cluster identifiers. In the PIHS there are 22 strata; the four provinces—Punjab, Sindh, North-West Frontier (NWFP), and Baluchistan—which are further stratified by urban and rural and by income level. There are 280 PSUs, or clusters, between 2 and 37 in each of the strata, and there are between 13 and 32 households in each cluster. The probability weights are sufficiently correlated with PCE for the weighting to make a difference; the unweighted average of household PCE is 730 rupees a month, whereas the weighted mean is only 617 rupees a month.

Table 1.5 shows these estimates for the country as a whole and for its four provinces together with various calculated standard errors. The first two columns are doubly incorrect; the estimated means ignore the probability weights, and the standard errors ignore the sample design. The weights are negatively correlated with PCE—in this case, better-off households are oversampled—so that the unweighted means are biased up, which makes the standard errors of little interest. The third column shows the (correct) weighted means, and the other columns show various possible standard errors, each calculated under different assumptions about

Table 1.5. Estimates of mean household per capita expenditure and calculated standard errors, Pakistan, 1991

(rupees per capita per month)

Province	$\bar{x}$	$\hat{s}/\sqrt{n}$	$\bar{x}_w$	$\hat{s}_w/\sqrt{n}$	Weight	Weight, strata	Weight, strata, PSU
Punjab	660	16.0	584	13.5	17.4	17.5	22.6
Sindh	754	21.9	693	18.3	17.4	17.4	35.1
NWFP	963	66.8	647	30.8	24.6	24.6	37.6
Baluchistan	682	30.6	609	31.0	41.0	41.1	96.2
Pakistan	730	14.1	617	9.9	12.0	12.0	17.0

Note: $\bar{x}$ is the unweighted mean, and $\hat{s}/\sqrt{n}$ a standard error calculated according to (1.12). $\bar{x}_w$ is the probability-weighted mean and $\hat{s}_w/\sqrt{n}$ is computed from the weighted sample variance (1.29). The column headed "weight" takes the probability weights into account using (1.28), but ignores stratification and clustering. The column headed "weight, strata" uses (1.28) for each stratum and then adds the stratum variances using (1.36). The final column is the appropriate standard error calculated from (1.60).

Source: Author's calculations using the Pakistan Integrated Household Survey, 1991 (see Example 1.2 in the Code Appendix).

the sample design. The column headed $\hat{s}_w/\sqrt{n}$ is what might be calculated if the weights were used to estimate the standard deviation, using (1.28) rather than (1.11), but the sample was incorrectly assumed to have been drawn as a simple random sample for which (1.10) would be the true variance. The next column recognizes the probability weights explicitly and comes from (1.28), but takes no account of stratification nor clustering. Allowing for the stratification in the next column has very little effect on the calculations because most of the variation is within the strata rather than between them (see equation (1.38) above). The largest changes come in the last column, where the cluster structure is recognized and the standard error calculated from (1.62). Because PCE is correlated within the clusters —the intracluster correlation coefficient for the whole sample is 0.346—the effective sample size is a good deal smaller than 4,800, and the standard errors that recognize the fact are a good deal larger. For the country as a whole, the correctly calculated standard error in the last column is almost twice that in column 4, and for the province of Baluchistan, the ratio is more than three.

The bootstrap

The more complex is the survey design, the more difficult it becomes to assess the variability of estimates based on the results. In the previous subsections, I have discussed only a few of the most important designs, and have provided formulas for variances only for estimates of the mean. There are other designs, some of truly bewildering complexity, and there are other statistics in which we are interested. Books on sampling techniques provide many more results than can be discussed here, but even the full range of formulas often falls short of what we need. For example, it is more difficult to obtain good estimates of the sampling variability of a median than of a mean, and yet in many situations, the median is the more useful measure of central tendency, if only because it is less influenced by the sort of outliers that often occur in real data. It should also be noted that for ratios of random variables, such as the probability-weighted mean, the variance formulas are approximate, not exact, and the accuracy of the approximation is not always apparent in practice. Yet means, medians, and ratios are among the simplest quantities that we want to calculate from survey data. The econometric analyses in later chapters often involve more elaborate calculations and the derivation of sampling distributions in these cases can present formidable difficulties, especially when we want to allow for the survey design.

The bootstrap is an alternative method of assessing sampling variability. It is no panacea, and it will not always give better results than the variance formulas, even approximate formulas. But it offers a mechanical procedure that can be applied in a wide variety of "difficult" situations, it works in much the same way whether we are estimating something straightforward, like a mean or a median, or something more complex, and it substitutes computer power for statistical analysis and algebra, a substitution that is welcome to all who do not enjoy the contemplation of balls and urns. The bootstrap, which was invented by Efron (1979), samples repeatedly, not from the population, which is of course not available for the purpose, but from the sample. For each resampling, we make whatever calculation we are interested in, and we keep track of the results over the replications. The variability of these resampled estimates is then used to assess the variability of the estimator over different samples from the population. An excellent, readable, and clear introduction to the bootstrap is provided by Efron and Tibshirani (1993).

As always, the simplest case is where we have a simple random sample of (say) n households. The bootstrap works by repeatedly drawing samples of size n from the sample *with replacement*. At each replication, the statistic of interest—mean, median, variance, or whatever—is calculated and stored. After K replications, the K values of the statistic are used to compute a measure of dispersion, for example the standard deviation as a measure of standard error, or—and necessarily in cases where the moments may not exist—percentiles used to estimate percentiles of the sampling distribution. The value of K will vary from application to application. Small values (around 100, say) will typically give a good idea of variance, when the variance exists, but when we need to calculate the fractions of occurrences in the tails of the distributions—as will often be the case for percentiles—much larger numbers of replications may be required. Given a desired level of precision and some idea of the sampling distribution, the required number of replications can be calculated in the usual way.

In simple cases, bootstrapping can be shown to lead back to the usual statistics. For example, suppose that we have a simple random sample $(x_1, x_2, \ldots, x_n)$ from which we draw bootstrap samples, always with replication and of the same size as the original. A typical replication might be denoted $(x_1^b, x_2^b, \ldots, x_n^b)$, with the superscripted b standing for "bootstrap." If we wished to bootstrap the mean, or the weighted mean, we would at each replication calculate the quantities $\bar{x}^b = n^{-1}\sum x_i^b$ or $\bar{x}_w^b = \sum w_i^b x_i^b / \sum w_i^b$, where the w's are drawn simultaneously with the x's.

Finding the means and variances of these expressions over the bootstrap replications can be done in exactly the same way as we found the means and variances for estimators using samples from the population rather than samples from the sample. The calculations are particularly straightforward because the bootstrap sample is drawn by simple random sampling and is the same size as the "population" so that t_i, the number of times each sample x_i appears in the bootstrap sample, is a random variable with mean 1, variance $(1-n^{-1})$, and covariance with t_j of $-n^{-1}$. Using these facts, it is straightforward to show that the mean across replications of the bootstrapped mean converges to the mean in the original sample, and that the variances are given by, for the unweighted mean:

$$(1.68) \qquad V(\bar{x}^b) = n^{-2} \sum_{i=1}^{n} (x_i - \bar{x})^2$$

and for the weighted mean:

$$(1.69) \qquad V(\bar{x}_w^b) = \sum_{i=1}^{n} v_i^2 (x_i - \bar{x})^2.$$

Up to the ratio $n/(n-1)$, the inclusion of which is a matter of convention in any case, these are identical to the variance formulas presented above (see (1.12) and (1.28), respectively). Hence, for both the weighted and unweighted mean, we get the same estimate of sampling variance either by direct calculation, or by simulation using the bootstrap, provided we have enough replications. Of course, it would be absurd to use the bootstrap in this case; the simulation is expensive and adds nothing to the direct and straightforward calculations. But there are many other cases where analytical formulas are not available, but where the bootstrap can be used in exactly the same way. And if the bootstrap did not give the right answer in these familiar settings, there would be no reason to trust it in more complex cases.

It should be noted that the formulas (1.68) and (1.69) do not contain any finite-population corrections. More generally, the fact that the bootstrap uses sampling with replacement will prevent it from giving good results when the original sample is large relative to the population (see Rao and Wu 1988 and Sitter 1992 for a discussion of methods of dealing with these cases). Care must also be taken in applying the bootstrap to dependent observations, and it cannot be applied without modification to data that were collected using a two-stage clustered design. Attempts to do so will usually understate sampling variability just as the use of formulas that ignore clustering will usually understate variability. However, the bootstrap can still be applied to a stratified clustered sample if we treat the strata separately, each its own survey, and if we resample, not the basic underlying units—the households—but rather the primary sample units—the clusters. This is straightforward to implement; a list of the n sample clusters is made, a bootstrap sample of size n is drawn with replacement, and the individual cluster-level data merged in (see Example 1.3 in the Code Appendix). Following this procedure for the PIHS and using 100 bootstrap replications gives a bootstrapped standard error for PCE of 16.5, compared with 17.0 from the formula (see the last column of Table 1.5). The median PCE is much lower than mean PCE, 461 as opposed to 617 rupees per month, and its bootstrapped standard error is only 7.7, less than half the estimated standard error of the mean. Because the median is relatively unaffected by outliers, and because the distribution of PCE is so positively skewed, the median varies much less from one sample to another than does the mean.

These calculations illustrate only the most basic use of the bootstrap although other, more complex, examples will be seen in later chapters. However, the replication of the quantity of interest—the mean, median, or whatever—is not always the best way to use the bootstrap. In particular, when we wish to calculate a confidence interval, the recommended procedure is not to bootstrap the estimate itself, but rather to bootstrap the distribution of the t-value. This is feasible in the frequently occurring situation where we have an approximate or large-sample version of the standard error, but are skeptical about its accuracy in the application at hand. The method works as follows. Start out as usual, drawing repeated samples from the base sample, taking into account the design, and calculating the estimate for each bootstrap replication. But instead of recording the estimate itself, subtract from it the estimate from the original full sample, and divide the difference by the approximate standard error $\hat{\sigma}$, say. The result is a bootstrapped t- or z-value whose distribution would be $N(0,1)$ if the estimates were normally distributed and the approximate standard were correct. But we do not need to assume either normality or accuracy of the approximation. Instead we carry out enough replications of the bootstrap to obtain an idea of the actual distribution of the bootstrapped t-values. In particular, if we want a 90 percent confidence interval for the sample mean, we calculate the fifth and ninety-fifth percentiles of the distribution of the t's, t_{05} and t_{95}, and use them to construct the confidence interval $[\hat{x} - t_{05}\hat{\sigma}, \hat{x} + t_{95}\hat{\sigma}]$. Note that the accurate calculation of the tails of the distribution is likely to require large numbers of bootstrap replications. The benefit is that the procedure will provide more accurate estimates of confidence intervals than either the simple descriptive bootstrap or the approximate standard errors. An explanation of why this should be so is beyond the scope of this book; the interested reader is referred to Hall (1995) for a review.

1.5 Guide to further reading

There are several good texts on survey design, notably Cochrane (1977), Hansen, Hurwitz, and Madow (1953), Kish (1965), Som (1973), Levy and Lemenshow (1991), and Wolter (1985). Much the same ground is covered by Murthy (1977), who also gives a description of the design of the Indian National Sample Survey. The discussion of sample design and sampling variation in Section 1.4 makes most use of Cochrane's treatment; I have also been influenced by the discussion of sample design and poverty measurement by Howes and Lanjouw (1995). Casley and Lury (1981) discuss sample surveys in developing countries, covering sample and questionnaire design and a host of practical matters. Much the same territory for developed countries is covered by Groves (1989), who discusses many of the issues of this chapter, including a much more systematic treatment of the various sources of measurement error. He also, like Casley and Lury, discusses questionnaire design, a major omission from this chapter. Sample design issues in the LSMS surveys are dealt with in Grosh and Muñoz (1996); see also Ainsworth and Muñoz (1986) and Grootaert (1993). The LSMS group is currently preparing a monograph that will deal with the experience to date and make recommendations about the design of similar surveys in the future. Data quality in a broader perspective is covered in the special June 1994 issue of the *Journal of Development Economics.* Pudney (1989) and Skinner, Holt, and Smith (1989) both contain chapters on survey design and its implications for analysis, Pudney from an econometric perspective, and Skinner et al. from a statistical perspective. Both bridge the material in this chapter and the next. An excellent introduction to the bootstrap is provided by Efron and Tishbirani (1993), and Wolter (1985) discusses a number of alternative computation-intensive methods for calculating variance. Version 5 of STATA (which was released in the fall of 1996, and thus too late for the applications in this book) contains a set of commands for dealing with complex survey designs; as often, the documentation is a good introduction to the theory. Among many other things, these commands implement the formulas in Section 1.4. A review of econometric applications of the bootstrap is Jeong and Maddala (1993).

2 Econometric issues for survey data

This chapter, like the previous one, lays groundwork for the analysis to follow. The approach is that of a standard econometric text, emphasizing regression analysis and regression "diseases" but with a specific focus on the use of survey data. The techniques that I discuss are familiar, but I focus on the methods and variants that recognize that the data come from surveys, not experimental data nor time series of macroeconomic aggregates, that they are collected according to specific designs, and that they are typically subject to measurement error. The topics are the familiar ones; dependency and heterogeneity in regression residuals, and possible dependence between regressors and residuals. But the reasons for these problems and the contexts in which they arise are often specific to survey data. For example, the weighting and clustering issues with which I begin do not occur except in survey data, although the methodology has straightforward parallels elsewhere in econometrics.

What might be referred to as the "econometric" approach is not the only way of thinking about regressions. In Chapter 3 and at several other points in this book, I shall emphasize a more statistical and descriptive methodology. Since the distinction is an important one in general, and since it separates the material in this chapter from that in the next, I start with an explanation. The statistical approach comes first, followed by the econometric approach. The latter is developed in this chapter, the former in Chapter 3 in the context of substantive applications.

From the statistical perspective, a regression or "regression function" is defined as an expectation of one variable, conventionally written y, conditional on another variable, or vector of variables, conventionally written x. I write this in the standard form

$$(2.1) \qquad m(x) = E(y|x) = \int_{-\infty}^{\infty} y \, dF_c(y|x)$$

where F_c is the distribution function of y conditional on x. This definition of a regression is descriptive and carries no behavioral connotation. Given a set of variables (y,x) that are jointly distributed, we can pick out one that is of interest, in this case y, compute its distribution conditional on the others, and calculate the associated regression function. From a household survey, we might examine the regression of per capita expenditure (y) on household size (x), which would be equivalent to a tabulation of mean per capita expenditure for each household size. But we might just as well examine the reverse regression, of household size on per capita expenditure, which would tell us the average household size at different levels of resources per capita. In such a context, the estimation of a regression is precisely analogous to the estimation of a mean, albeit with the complication that the mean is conditioned on the prespecified values of the x-variables. When we think of the regression this way, it is natural to consider not only the conditional mean, but other conditional measures, such as the median or other percentiles, and these different kinds of regression are also useful, as we shall see below. Thinking of a regression as a set of means also makes it clear how to incorporate into regressions the survey design issues that I discussed at the end of Chapter 1.

When the conditioning variables in the regression are continuous, or when there is a large number of discrete variables, the calculations are simplified if we are prepared to make assumptions about the functional form of $m(x)$. The most obvious and most widely used assumption is that the regression function is linear in x,

$$(2.2) \qquad m(x) = \beta'x$$

where β is a scalar or vector as x is a scalar or vector, and where, by defining one of the elements of x to be a constant, we can allow for an intercept term. In this case, the β-parameters can be estimated by ordinary least squares (OLS), and the estimates used to estimate the regression function according to (2.2).

The econometric approach to regression is different, in rhetoric if not in reality. The starting point is usually the linear regression model

$$(2.3) \qquad y = \beta'x + u$$

where u is a "residual," "disturbance," or "error" term representing omitted determinants of y, including measurement error, and satisfying

$$(2.4) \qquad E(u|x) = 0.$$

The combination of (2.3) and (2.4) implies that $\beta'x$ is the expectation of y conditional on x, so that (2.3) and (2.4) imply the combination of (2.1) and (2.2). Similarly, because a variable can always be written as its expectation plus a residual with zero expectation, the combination of (2.1) and (2.2) imply the combination of (2.3) and (2.4). As a result, the statistical and econometric approaches are formally identical. The difference lies in the rhetoric, and particularly in the contrast between "model" and "description." The linear regression as written in (2.3) and (2.4) is often thought of as a model of determination, of how the "independent" variables x determine the "dependent" variable y. By contrast, the regression function (2.1) is more akin to a cross-tabulation, devoid of causal significance, a descriptive device that is (at best) a preliminary to more "serious," or model-based, analysis.

A good example of the difference comes from the analysis of poverty, where regression methods have been applied for a very long time (see Yule 1899). Suppose that the variable y_i is 1 if household i is in poverty and is 0 if not. Suppose that the conditioning variables x are a set of dummy variables representing regions of a country. The coefficients of a linear regression of y on x are then a "poverty profile," the fractions of households in poverty in each of the regions. These results could also have been represented by a table of means by region, or a regression function. A poverty profile can incorporate more than regional information, and might include local variables, such as whether or not the community has a sealed road or an irrigation system, or household variables, such as the education of the household head. Such regressions answer questions about differences in poverty rates between irrigated and unirrigated villages, or the extent to which poverty is predicted by low education. They are also useful for targeting antipoverty policies, as when transfers are conditioned on geography or on landholding (see, for example, Grosh 1994 or Lipton and Ravallion 1995.) Of course, such descriptions are not informative about the *determinants* of poverty. Households in communities with sealed roads may be well-off because of the trade brought by the road, or the road may be there because the inhabitants have the economic wherewithal to pay for it, or the political power to have someone else do so. Correlation is not causation, and while poverty regressions are excellent tools for constructing poverty profiles, they do not measure up to the more rigorous demands of project evaluation.

Much of the theory and practice of econometrics consists of the development and use of tools that permit causal inference in nonexperimental data. Although the regression of individual poverty on roads cannot tell us whether or by how much the construction of roads will reduce poverty, there exist techniques that hold out the promise of being able to do so, if not from an OLS regression, at least from an appropriate modification. Econometric theorists have constructed a catalog of regression "diseases," the presence of any of which can prevent or distort correct inference of causality. For each disease or combination of diseases, there exist techniques that, at least under ideal conditions, can repair the situation. Econometrics texts are largely concerned with these techniques, and their application to survey data is the main topic of this chapter.

Nevertheless, it pays to be skeptical and, in recent years, many economists and statisticians have become increasingly dissatisfied with technical fixes, and in particular, with the strong assumptions that are required for them to work. In at least some cases, the conditions under which a procedure will deliver the right answer are almost as implausible, and as difficult to validate, as those required for the original regression. Readers are referred to the fine skeptical review by Freedman (1991), who concludes "that statistical technique can seldom be an adequate substitute for good design, relevant data, and testing predictions against reality in a variety of settings." One of my aims in this chapter is to clarify the often rather limited conditions under which the various econometric techniques work, and to indicate some more realistic alternatives, even if they promise less. A good starting point for all econometric work is the (obvious) realization that it is not always possible to make the desired inferences with the data to hand. Nevertheless, even if we must sometimes give up on causal inference, much can be learned from careful inspection and description of data, and in the next chapter, I shall discuss techniques that are useful and informative for this more modest endeavor.

This chapter is organized as follows. There are nine sections, the last of which is a guide to further reading. The first two pick up from the material at the end of Chapter 1 and look at the role of survey weights (Section 2.1) and clustering (Section 2.2) in regression analysis. Section 2.3 deals with the fact that regression functions estimated from survey data are rarely homoskedastic, and I present briefly the standard methods for dealing with the fact. Quantile regressions are useful for exploring heteroskedasticity (as well as for many other purposes), and this section contains a brief presentation. Although the consequences of heteroskedasticity are readily dealt with in the context of regression analysis, the same is not true when we attempt to use the various econometric methods designed to deal with limited dependent variables. Section 2.4 recognizes that survey data are very different from the controlled experimental data that would ideally be required to answer many of the questions in which we are interested. I review the various econometric problems associated with nonexperimental data, including the effects of omitted variables, measurement error, simultaneity, and selectivity. Sections 2.5 and 2.6 review the uses of panel data and of instrumental variables (IV), respectively, as a means to recover structure from nonexperimental data. Section 2.7 shows how a time series of cross-sectional surveys can be used to explore changes over time, not only for national aggregates, but also for socioeconomic groups, especially age cohorts of people. Indeed, such data can be used in ways that are similar to panel data, but without some of the disadvantages—particularly attrition and measurement error. I present some examples, and discuss some of the associated econometric issues. Finally, section 2.8 discusses two topics in statistical inference that will arise in the empirical work in later chapters.

2.1 Survey design and regressions

As we have already seen in Section 1.1, there are both statistical and practical reasons for household surveys to use complex designs in which different households have different probabilities of being selected into the sample. We have also seen that such designs have to be taken into account when calculating means and other statistics, usually by weighting, and that the calculation of standard errors for the estimates should depend on the sample design. We also saw that, standard errors can be seriously misleading if the sample design is not taken into account in their calculation, particularly in the case of clustered samples. In this section, I take up the same questions in the context of regressions. I start with the use of weights, and with the old and still controversial issue of whether or not the survey weights should be used in regression. As we shall see, the answer depends on what one thinks about and expects from a regression, and on whether one takes an econometric or statistical view. I then consider the effects of clustering, and show that there is no ambiguity about what to do in this case; standard errors should be corrected for the design. I conclude the section with a brief overview of regression standard errors and sample design, going beyond clustering to the effects of stratification and probability weighting.

Weighting in regressions

Consider a sample in which households belong to one of S "sectors," and where the probability of selection into the sample varies from sector to sector. In the simplest possible case, there are two sectors, for example, rural and urban, the sample consists of rural and urban households, and the probability of selection is higher in the urban sector. The sectors will often be sample strata, but my concern here is with variation in weights across sectors—however defined—and not directly with stratification. If the means are different by sector, we know that the unweighted sample mean is a biased and inconsistent estimator of the population mean, and that a consistent estimator can be constructed by weighting the individual observations by inflation factors, or equivalently, by computing the means for each sector, and weighting them by the fractions of the population in each. The question is whether and how this procedure extends from the estimation of means to the estimation of regressions.

Suppose that there are N_s population households and n_s sample households in sector s. With simple random sampling within sectors, the inflation factor for a household i in s is $w_{is} = N_s/n_s$, so that the weighted mean (1.25) is

$$(2.5) \qquad \bar{x}_w = \frac{\displaystyle\sum_{s=1}^{S}\sum_{i=1}^{n_s} w_{is}x_{is}}{\displaystyle\sum_{s=1}^{S}\sum_{i=1}^{n_s} w_{is}} = \frac{\displaystyle\sum_{s=1}^{S} N_s\bar{x}_s}{\displaystyle\sum_{s=1}^{S} N_s} = \sum_{s=1}^{S}\frac{N_s}{N}\bar{x}_s = \bar{x}.$$

Hence, provided that the sample means for each sector are unbiased for the corresponding population means, so is the weighted mean for the overall population mean. Equation (2.5) also shows that it makes no difference whether we take a weighted mean of individual observations with inflation factors as weights, or whether we compute the sector means first, and then weight by population shares.

Let us now move to the case where the parameters of interest are no longer population totals or means, but the parameters of a linear regression model. Within each sector $s = 1, \ldots, S$,

$$(2.6) \qquad y_s = X_s\beta_s + u_s$$

and, in general, the parameter vectors β_s differ across sectors. In such a case, we might decide, by analogy with the estimation of means, that the parameter of interest is the population-weighted average

$$(2.7) \qquad \beta = N^{-1}\sum_{s=1}^{S} N_s\beta_s.$$

Consider the only slightly artificial example where the regressions are Engel curves for a subsidized food, such as rice, and we are interested in the effects of a general increase in income on the aggregate demand for rice, and thus on the total cost of the subsidy. If the marginal propensity to spend on rice varies from one sectors to another, then (2.7) gives the population average, which is the quantity that we need to know.

Again by analogy with the estimation of means, we might proceed by estimating a separate regression for each sector, and weighting them together using the population weights. Hence,

$$(2.8) \qquad \hat{\beta} = \sum_{s=1}^{S} \frac{N_s}{N} \hat{\beta}_s, \quad \hat{\beta}_s = (X_s' X_s)^{-1} X_s' y_s.$$

Such regressions are routinely calculated when the sectors are broad, such as in the urban versus rural example, and where there are good prior reasons for supposing that the parameters differ across sectors. Such a procedure is perhaps less attractive when there is little interest in the individual sectoral parameter estimates, or when there are many sectors with few households in each, so that the parameters for each are estimated imprecisely. But such cases arise in practice; some sample designs have hundreds of strata, chosen for statistical or administrative rather than substantive reasons, and we may not be sure that the parameters are the same in each stratum. If so, the estimator (2.8) is worth consideration, and should not be rejected simply because there are few observations per stratum. If the strata are independent, the variance of $\hat{\beta}$ is

$$(2.9) \qquad V(\hat{\beta}) = \sum_{s=1}^{S} \left(\frac{N_s}{N} \right)^2 V(\hat{\beta}_s) = \sum_{s=1}^{S} \left(\frac{N_s}{N} \right)^2 \sigma_s^2 (X_s' X_s)^{-1}$$

where σ_s^2 is the residual variance in stratum s. Because the population fractions in (2.9) are squared, $\hat{\beta}$ will be more precisely estimated than are the individual $\hat{\beta}_s$.

Instead of estimating parameters sector by sector, it is more common to estimate a regression from all the observations at once, either using the inflation factors to calculate a weighted least squares estimate, or ignoring them, and estimating by unweighted OLS. The latter can be written

$$(2.10) \qquad \hat{\beta} = \left(\sum_{s=1}^{S} X_s' X_s \right)^{-1} \left(\sum_{s=1}^{S} X_s' y_s \right).$$

In general, the OLS estimator will not yield any parameters of interest. Suppose that, as the sample size grows, the moment matrices in each stratum tend to finite limits, so that we can write

$$(2.11) \qquad \plim_{n_s \to \infty} n_s^{-1} X_s' X_s = M_s; \quad \plim_{n_s \to \infty} n_s^{-1} X_s' y_s = c_s = M_s \beta_s$$

where M_s and c_s are nonrandom and the former is positive definite. (Note that, as in Chapter 1, I am assuming sampling with replacement, so that it is possible to sample an infinite number from a finite population.) By (2.11), the probability limit of the OLS estimator (2.10) is

$$(2.12) \qquad \text{plim}\,\beta = \left(\sum_{s=1}^{S} (n_s/n) M_s \right)^{-1} \sum_{s=1}^{S} (n_s/n) c_s$$

where I have assumed that, as the sample size grows, the proportions in each sector are held fixed. If all the β_s are the same, so that $c_s = M_s\beta$ for all s, then the OLS estimator will be consistent for the common β. However, even if the structure of the explanatory variables is the same in each of the sectors, so that $M_s = M$ for all s and $c_s = M\beta_s$, equation (2.12) gives the *sample-weighted* average of the β_s, which is inconsistent unless the sample is a simple random sample with equal probabilities of selection in all sectors.

The inconsistency of the OLS estimator for the population parameters mirrors the inconsistency of the unweighted mean for the population mean. Consider then the regression counterpart of the weighted mean, in which each household's contribution to the moment matrices is inflated using the weights,

$$(2.13) \qquad \beta_w = \left(\sum_{s=1}^{S} \sum_{i=1}^{n_s} w_{is} x_{is} x_{is}' \right)^{-1} \left(\sum_{s=1}^{S} \sum_{i=1}^{n_s} w_{is} x_{is} y_{is} \right)$$

where x_{is} is the vector of explanatory variables for household i in sector s, and y_{is} is the corresponding value of the dependent variable. In this case, the weights are N_s/n_s and vary only across sectors, so that the estimator can also be written as

$$(2.14) \qquad \beta_w = \left(\sum_{s=1}^{S} \frac{N_s}{n_s} X_s' X_s \right)^{-1} \left(\sum_{s=1}^{S} \frac{N_s}{n_s} X_s' y_s \right) = (X'WX)^{-1} X'Wy$$

where X and y have their usual regression connotations—the X_s and y_s matrices from each sector stacked vertically—and W is an $n \times n$ matrix with the weights N_s/n_s on the diagonal and zeros elsewhere. This is the weighted regression that is calculated by regression packages, including STATA.

If we calculate the probability limits as before, we get instead of (2.12)

$$(2.15) \qquad \text{plim}\,\beta_w = \left(\sum_{s=1}^{S} \frac{N_s}{N} M_s \right)^{-1} \sum_{s=1}^{S} \frac{N_s}{N} M_s \beta_s$$

so that, where we previously had *sample* shares as weights, we now have *population* shares. The weighted estimator thus has the (perhaps limited) advantage over the OLS estimator of being independent of sample design; the right-hand side of (2.15) contains only population magnitudes. Like the OLS estimator it is consistent if all the β_s are identical, and unlike it, will also be consistent if the M_s matrices are identical across sectors. We have already seen one such case; when there is only a constant in the regression, $M_s = 1$ for all s, and we are estimating the population mean, where weighting gives the right answer. But it is hard to think of other realistic examples in which the M_s are common and the c_s differ. In general, the weighted estimator will not be consistent for the weighted sum of the parameter vectors because

$$(2.16) \quad \left(\sum_{s=1}^{S} (N_s/N) M_s \right)^{-1} \sum_{s=1}^{S} (N_s/N) c_s \neq \sum_{s=1}^{S} (N_s/N) M_s^{-1} c_s = \sum_{s=1}^{S} (N_s/N) \beta_s = \beta.$$

In this case, which is probably the typical one, there is no straightforward analogy between the estimation of means and the estimation of regression parameters. The weighted estimator, like the OLS estimator, is inconsistent.

As emphasized by Dumouchel and Duncan (1983), the weighted OLS estimator will be consistent for the parameters that would have been estimated using census data; as usual, the weighting makes the sample look like the population and removes the dependence of the estimates on the sample design, at least when samples are large enough. However, the difference in parameter values across strata is a feature of the population, not of the sample design, so that running a regression on census data is no less problematic than running it on sample data. In neither case can we expect to recover parameters of interest. The issue is not sample design, but population heterogeneity. Of course, if the population is homogeneous, so that the regression coefficients are identical in each stratum, both weighted and unweighted estimators will be consistent. In such a case, and in the absence of other problems, the unweighted OLS estimator is to be preferred since, by the Gauss-Markov theorem, least squares is more efficient than the weighted estimator. This is the classic econometric argument against the weighted estimator: when the sectors are homogeneous, OLS is more efficient, and when they are not, both estimators are inconsistent. In neither case is there an argument for weighting.

Even so, it is possible to defend the weighted estimator. I present one argument that is consistent with the modeling point of view, and one that is not. Suppose that there are many sectors, that we suspect heterogeneity, but the heterogeneity is not systematically linked to the other variables. Consider again the probability limit of the weighted estimator, (2.15), substitute $c_c = M_s \beta_s$, and write $\beta_s = \beta + (\beta_s - \beta)$ to reach

$$(2.17) \quad \text{plim} \beta_w = \beta + \left(\sum_{s=1}^{S} (N_s/N) M_s \right)^{-1} \sum_{s=1}^{S} (N_s/N) M_s (\beta_s - \beta).$$

The weighted estimate will therefore be consistent for β if

$$(2.18) \quad \sum_{s=1}^{S} (N_s/N) M_s (\beta_s - \beta) = 0.$$

This will be the case if the variation in the parameters across sectors is random and is unrelated to the moment matrices M_s in each, and if the number of sectors is large enough for the weighted mean to be zero. The same kind of argument is much harder to make for the unweighted (OLS) estimator. The orthogonality condition (2.18) is a condition on the *population*, while the corresponding condition for the OLS estimator would have to hold for the *sample*, so that the estimator would (at best) be consistent for only some sampling schemes. Even then, its probability limit would not be β but the sample-weighted mean of the sector-specific β_s, a quantity that is unlikely to be of interest.

Perhaps the strongest argument for weighted regression comes from those who regard regression as descriptive, not structural. The case has been put forcefully by Kish and Frankel (1974), who argue that regression should be thought of as a device for summarizing characteristics of the population, heterogeneity and all, so that samples ought to be weighted and regressions calculated according to (2.13) or (2.14). A weighted regression provides a consistent estimate of the population regression function—provided of course that the assumption about functional form (in this case that it is linear) is correct. The argument is effectively that the regression function itself is the object of interest. I shall argue in the next chapter that this is frequently the case, both for the light that the regression function sometimes sheds on policy, and when not, as a preliminary description of the data. Of course, if we are trying to estimate behavioral models, and if those models are different in different parts of the population, the classic econometric argument is correct, and weighting is at best useless.

Recommendations for practice

How then should we proceed? Should the weights be ignored, or should we use them in the regressions? What about standard errors? If regressions are primarily descriptive, exploring association by looking at the mean of one variable conditional on others, the answer is straightforward: use the weights and correct the standard errors for the design. For modelers who are concerned about heterogeneity and its interaction with sample design, matters are somewhat more complicated.

For descriptive purposes, the only issue that I have not dealt with is the computation of standard errors. In principle, the techniques of Section 1.4 can be used to give explicit formulas that take into account the effect of survey design on the variance-covariance matrices of parameter estimates. At the time of writing, such formulas are being incorporated into STATA. Alternatively, the bootstrap provides a computationally intensive but essentially mechanical way of calculating standard errors, or at least for checking that the standard errors given by the conventional formulas are not misleading. As in Section 1.4, the bootstrap should be programmed so as to reflect the sample design: different strata should be bootstrapped separately and, for two-stage samples, bootstrap draws should be made of clusters or primary sampling units (PSUs), not of the households within them. Because hypothetical replications of the survey throw up new households at each replication, with new values of x's as well as y's, the bootstrap should do the same. In this context, it makes no sense to condition on the original x's, holding them fixed in repeated samples. Instead, each bootstrap sample will contain a resampling of households, with their associated x's, y's, and weights w's, and these are used to compute each bootstrap regression.

In practice, the design feature that usually has the largest effect on standard errors is clustering, and the most serious problem with the conventional formulas is that they overstate precision by ignoring the dependence of observations within the same PSU. We have already seen this phenomenon for estimation of the mean in Section 1.4, and it is sufficiently important that I shall return to it in Section 2.2 below. It is as much an issue for structural estimation as it is for the use of regressions as descriptive tools.

The regression modeler has a number of different strategies for dealing with heterogeneity and design. At one extreme is what might be called the standard approach. Behavior is assumed to be homogeneous across (statistical or substantive) subunits, the data are pooled, and the weights ignored. The other extreme is to break up the sample into cells whenever behavior is thought likely to differ or where the sampling weights differ across groups. Separate regressions are then estimated for each cell and the results combined using population weights according to (2.8). When the distinctions between groups are of substantive interest—as will often be the case, since regions, sectors, or ethnic characteristics are often used for stratification—it makes sense to test for differences between them using covariance analysis, as described, for example, by Johnston (1972, pp. 192–207).

When adopting the standard approach, it is also wise to adopt Dumouchel and Duncan's suggestion of calculating both weighted and unweighted estimators and comparing them. Under the null that the regressions are homogeneous across strata, both estimators are unbiased, so that the difference between them has an expectation of zero. By contrast, when heterogeneity and design effects are important, the two expectations will differ. The difference between the weighted estimator (2.13) and the OLS estimator can be written as

$$
\begin{aligned}
\hat{\beta}_w - \hat{\beta}_{OLS} &= (X'WX)^{-1}X'Wy - (X'X)^{-1}X'y \\
&= (X'WX)^{-1}X'W(I - X(X'X)^{-1}X')y \\
&= (X'WX)^{-1}X'WM_X y
\end{aligned}
$$

(2.19)

where M_X is the matrix $I - X(X'X)^{-1}X'$. By (2.19) the difference between the two estimators is the vector of parameter estimates from a weighted regression of the unweighted OLS residuals on the x's. Its variance-covariance matrix can readily be calculated in order to form a test statistic, but the easiest way to test whether (2.19) is zero is to run the "auxiliary" regression

$$
(2.20) \qquad y = Xb + WXg + v
$$

and to use an F-statistic to test $g = 0$ (see also Davidson and MacKinnon 1993. pp. 237–42, who discuss Hausman (1978) tests, of which this is a special case).

In the case of many sectors, when we rely on the interpretation that the intersectoral heterogeneity is random variation in the parameters as in (2.17) above, note that the residuals of the regressions, whether weighted or unweighted, will be both heteroskedastic and dependent. Rewrite the regressions (2.6) as

$$
(2.21) \qquad y_s = X_s\beta + X_s(\beta_s - \beta) + u_s = X_s\beta + \xi_s
$$

where β is defined in (2.7) and where the compound residual ξ_s is defined by the second equality. If the intrasectoral variance-covariance matrix of the β_s is Ω_β, the variances and covariances of the new residuals are zero between residuals in different sectors, while within each sector we have

(2.22) $$E(\xi_s \xi_s') = X_s \Omega_\beta X_s' + \sigma^2 I_{n_s}$$

where I_{n_s} is the $n_s \times n_s$ identity matrix. Hence, if the different sectors in (2.21) are combined, or "stacked," into a single regression, the variance-covariance matrix of the residuals will have a block diagonal structure, displaying both heteroskedasticity and intercorrelation. In such circumstances, neither the weighted nor unweighted regressions will be efficient, and perhaps more seriously, the standard formulas for the estimated standard errors will be incorrect. In the next two sections, we shall see how to detect and deal with these problems in a slightly different but mathematically identical context.

2.2 The econometrics of clustered samples

In Chapter 1, we saw that most household surveys in developing countries use a two-stage design, in which clusters or PSUs are drawn first, followed by a selection of households from within each PSU. In Section 1.4, I explored the consequences of clustered designs for the estimation of means and their standard errors. Here I discuss the use of clusters in empirical work more broadly. When the survey data are gathered from rural areas in developing countries, the clustering is often of substantive interest in its own right. I begin with some of these positive aspects of clustered sampling, and then discuss its effects on inference in regression analysis.

The economics of clusters in developing countries

In surveys of rural areas in developing countries, clusters are often villages, so that households in a single cluster live near one another, and are interviewed at much the same time during the period that the survey team is in the village. In many countries, these arrangements will produce household data where observations from the same cluster are much more like one another than are observations from different clusters. At the simplest, there may be neighborhood effects, so that local eccentricities are copied by those who live near one another and become more or less uniform within a village. Sample villages are often widely separated geographically, their inhabitants may belong to different ethnic and religious groups, they may have distinct occupational structures as well as different crops and cropping patterns. Where agriculture is important—as it is in most poor countries—there will usually be more homogeneity within villages than between them. This applies not only to the types of crops and livestock, but also to the effects of weather, pests, and natural hazards. If the rains fail for a particular village, everyone engaged in rainfed agriculture will suffer, as will those in occupations that depend on rainfed agriculture. If the harvest is good, prices will be low for everyone in the village, and although the effects will spread out to other villages through the market, poor transport networks and high transport costs may limit the spread of low prices to other survey villages. Indeed, there is often only one market in each village, so that everyone in the village will be paying the same prices for what they buy, and will be facing the same prices for their wage labor, their produce, and their livestock. This fact alone is likely to induce a good deal of similarity between households within a given sample cluster.

Cluster similarity has both costs and benefits. The cost is that inference is simplest when all the observations in the sample are independent, and that a positive correlation between observations not only makes calculations more complex, but also inflates variance above what it would have been in the independent case. In the extreme case, when all villagers are clones of one another, we need sample only one of them, and if the sample contains more than one person from each village, the effective sample size is the number of *villages* not the number of *villagers*. This argument applies just as much to regressions, and to other types of inference, as it does to the estimation of means.

The benefit of cluster sampling comes from the fact that the clusters are villages, and as such are often economically interesting in their own right. For many purposes it makes sense to examine what happens within each village in a different way from what happens between villages. In addition, cluster sampling gives us multiple observations from the same environment, so that we can sometimes control for unobservables in ways that would not otherwise be possible. One important example is the effects of prices, a topic to which I shall return in Chapter 5. Often, we do not observe prices directly, and since prices in each village will typically be correlated with other village variables such as incomes or agricultural production, it is impossible to estimate the effects of these observables uncontaminated by the effects of the unobservable prices. However, if we are prepared to maintain that prices have additive effects on the variable in which we are interested, differences between households within a village are unaffected by prices, and can be used to make inferences that are robust to the lack of price data. In this way the village structure of samples can be turned to advantage.

Estimating regressions from clustered samples

If the cluster design of the data is ignored, standard formulas for variances of estimated means are too small, a result which applies in essentially the same way to the formulas for the variance-covariance matrices of regression parameters estimated by OLS. At the very least then, we require some procedure for correcting the estimated standard errors of the least squares regression. There is also an efficiency issue; because the error terms in the regressions are correlated across observations, OLS regression is not efficient even within the class of linear estimators and it might be possible to do better with some other linear estimator. (Efficiency is also a potential issue for the sample mean, though I did not discuss it in Section 1.4.)

The simplest example with which to begin is where the cluster design is balanced, so that there are *m* households in each cluster, and where the explanatory variables vary only between clusters, and not within them. This will be the case, for example, when we are studying the effects of prices on behavior and there is only one market in each village, or when the explanatory variables are government services, like schools or clinics, where access is the same for everyone in the same village. I follow the discussion in Section 1.4 on the superpopulation approach to clustering and write the regression equation for household i in cluster c [compare (1.64)],

$$(2.23) \qquad y_{ic} = x_c'\beta + \alpha_c + \epsilon_{ic} = x_c'\beta + u_{ic}$$

so that the x's are common to all households in the cluster, and the regression error term u_{ic} is the sum of a cluster component α_c and an individual component ϵ_{ic}. Both components have mean 0, and their covariance structure can be derived from the assumption that the α's are uncorrelated across clusters, and the ϵ's both within and across clusters. Hence,

$$(2.24) \qquad \begin{aligned} E(u_{ic}^2) &= \sigma^2 = \sigma_\alpha^2 + \sigma_\epsilon^2 \\ E(u_{ic}u_{jc}) &= \sigma_\alpha^2 = \left(\frac{\sigma_\alpha^2}{\sigma_\alpha^2 + \sigma_\epsilon^2}\right)\sigma^2 = \rho\sigma^2, \quad i \neq j \\ E(u_{ic}u_{jc'}) &= 0, \quad c \neq c'. \end{aligned}$$

Within the cluster, the errors are equicorrelated with intracluster correlation coefficient ρ, but between clusters, they are uncorrelated.

This case has been analyzed by Kloek (1981), who shows that the special structure implies that the OLS estimator and the generalized least squares estimator are identical, so that OLS is fully efficient. Further, the true variance-covariance matrix of the OLS estimator—as well as of the generalized least squares (GLS) estimator—is given by

$$(2.25) \qquad V(\beta) = \sigma^2(X'X)^{-1}[1 + (m-1)\rho]$$

so that, just as in estimating the variance of the mean, the variance has to be scaled up by the design effect, a factor that varies from 1 to m, depending on the size of ρ.

As before, ignoring the cluster design will lead to standard errors that are too small, and t-values that are too large. There is also a (lesser) problem with estimating the regression standard error σ^2. If N is the sample size—the number of clusters n multiplied by m, the number of observations in each—and k is the number of regressors, the standard formula $(N-k)^{-1}e'e$ is no longer unbiased for σ^2, although it remains consistent provided the cluster size remains fixed as the sample size expands. Kloek shows that an unbiased estimator can be calculated from the design effect $d = 1 + (m-1)\rho$ using the formula

$$(2.26) \qquad \tilde\sigma^2 = e'e(N - kd)^{-1}.$$

Moulton (1986, 1990) provides a number of examples of potential underestimation of standard errors in this case, some of which are dramatic. For example, in an individual wage equation for the U.S. with only state-level explanatory variables, the design effect is more than 10; here a small but significant intrastate correlation coefficient, 0.028, is combined with very large cluster sizes, nearly 400 observations per state. In this case, ignoring the correction to (2.25) would understate standard errors by a factor of more than three.

That this is likely to be the worst case is shown in papers by Scott and Holt (1982) and Pfefferman and Smith (1985). They show that when the explanatory variables differ within clusters, (2.25)—or when there are unequal numbers of observations in each cluster, (2.25) with the size of the largest cluster replacing m—provides an *upper bound* for the true variance-covariance matrix, and that in most cases, the bound is not tight. They also show that, although the OLS estimator is inefficient when the explanatory variables are not constant within clusters, the efficiency losses are typically small. These results are comforting because they provide a justification for using OLS, and a means of assessing the maximal extent to which the design effects are biasing standard errors. Even so, the biases might still be large enough to worry about, and to warrant correction.

One obvious possibility is to estimate by OLS, use the residuals to estimate $\hat{\sigma}^2$ from (2.26)—or even from the standard formula—as well as an estimate of the intracluster correlation coefficient

$$(2.27) \qquad \hat{\rho} = \frac{\sum\limits_{c=1}^{n} \sum\limits_{j=1}^{m} \sum\limits_{k \neq j}^{m} e_{ic} e_{jc}}{nm(m-1)\hat{\sigma}^2}$$

and then to estimate the variance-covariance matrix using

$$(2.28) \qquad \tilde{V}(\hat{\beta}) = \hat{\sigma}^2 (X'X)^{-1} X' \tilde{\Lambda} X (X'X)^{-1}$$

where $\tilde{\Lambda}$ is a block-diagonal matrix with one block for each cluster, and where each block has a unit diagonal and a $\hat{\rho}$ in each off-diagonal position. An alternative and more robust procedure is to use the OLS residuals from each cluster e_c to form the cluster matrices $\tilde{\Sigma}_c$ according to

$$(2.29) \qquad \tilde{\Sigma}_c = e_c e_c'$$

and then to place these matrices on the diagonal of $\tilde{\Lambda}$ in (2.28). This is equivalent to calculating the variance-covariance matrix using

$$(2.30) \qquad \tilde{V}(\hat{\beta}) = (X'X)^{-1} (\sum\limits_{c=1}^{n} X_c' e_c e_c' X_c)(X'X)^{-1}.$$

Provided that the cluster size remains fixed as the sample size becomes large—which is usually the case in practice—(2.30) will provide a consistent estimate of the variance-covariance matrix of the OLS estimator, and will do so even if the error variances differ across clusters, and even in the face of arbitrary correlation patterns within clusters (see White 1984, pp. 134–42.) In consequence, it can also be applied to the case of heterogeneity within strata discussed in the previous section; the strata are simply thought of as clusters, and the same analysis applied. As we shall see in Section 2.4 below, the same procedures can also be applied to the analysis of panel data where there are repeat observations on the same individuals—the individuals play the role of the village, and successive observations play the role of the villagers (see also Arellano 1987).

Note that the consistency of (2.30) does not suppose (or require) that the $\tilde{\Sigma}_c$ matrices in (2.29) are consistent estimates of the cluster variance-covariance matrices; indeed it is clearly impossible to estimate these matrices consistently from a single realization of the cluster residuals. Nevertheless, (2.30) is consistent for the variance-covariance matrix of the parameters, and will presumably be more accurate in finite samples the more clusters there are, and the smaller is the cluster size relative to the number of clusters. Although (2.30) will typically require special coding or software, it is implemented in STATA as the option "group" in the "huber" or "hreg" command.

Table 2.1 shows the effects of correcting the standard errors of "quality choice" regressions using data on the unit values—expenditures divided by quantities bought—of consumer purchases from the Pakistan Household Income and Expenditure Survey of 1984–85. The substantive issue here is that, because different households buy different qualities of goods, even within categories such as rice and wheat, unit values vary systematically over households, with richer households reporting higher values.

The OLS estimates of the expenditure elasticity of the unit values—what Prais and Houthakker (1955) christened "quality" elasticities—are given in the first column, and we see that there are quality elasticities of 0.13 for wheat and rice, while for the other two goods, which are relatively homogeneous and whose prices are supposedly controlled, the elasticities are small or even negative. Household size elasticities are the opposite sign to total expenditure elasticities, as would be the case (for example) if quality depended on household expenditure per head. Except for sugar, the size elasticities are all smaller in absolute value than the expenditure elasticities, so that, at constant per capita expenditure, unit values rise with household size, an effect that Prais and Houthakker attributed to economies of scale to household size. At the same level of per capita total ex-

Table 2.1. Effects of cluster design on regression t-values, rural Pakistan, 1984–85

Good	Expenditure elasticity	t-value Raw	t-value Robust	Size elasticity	t-value Raw	t-value Robust
Wheat	0.128	20.2	18.4	−0.070	−10.5	−9.0
Rice	0.129	12.2	8.7	−0.074	−6.9	−5.4
Sugar	0.005	3.1	1.5	−0.009	−5.2	−3.7
Edible oils	−0.004	−3.0	−1.9	0.002	1.6	1.2

Note: Underlying regression has the logarithm of unit value as the dependent variable, and the logarithms of household total expenditure and of household size as independent variables.
Source: Author's calculations using the Household Income and Expenditure Survey.

penditure, larger households are better-off than smaller households and, in consequence, buy better-quality foods. The robust *t*-values are smaller than the uncorrected values, although as suggested by the theoretical results, the ratios of the adjusted to unadjusted values are a good deal smaller than the (square roots of the) design effects. Even so, the reductions in the *t*-values for the estimated quality elasticities for sugar and edible oils are substantial. Without correction, we would almost certainly (mistakenly) reject the hypothesis that the quality elasticities for these two goods are zero; after correction, the *t*-values come within the range of acceptance.

2.3 Heteroskedasticity and quantile regressions

As we shall see in the next chapter, when we come to look at the distributions over households of the various components of living standards—income, consumption of various goods and their aggregate—it is rare to find variables that are normally distributed, even after standard transformations like taking logarithms or forming ratios. The large numbers of observations in many surveys permit us to look at the distributional assumptions that go into standard regression analysis, and even after transformation it is rarely possible to justify the textbook assumptions that, conditional on the independent variables, the dependent variables are independently, identically, and normally distributed. The previous section discussed how a cluster survey design is likely to lead to a violation of conditional independence. In this section, I turn to the "identically distributed" assumption, and consider the consequences of heteroskedasticity. Just as lack of independence appears to be the rule rather than the exception, so does heteroskedasticity seem to be almost always present in survey data.

The first subsection looks at linear regression models, at the reasons for heteroskedasticity, and at its consequences. I suggest that the computation of quantile regressions is useful, both in its own right, because quantile regression estimates will often have better properties than OLS, as a way of assessing the heteroskedasticity in the conditional distribution of the variable of interest, and as a stepping stone to the nonparametric methods discussed in the next two chapters. As was the case for clustering, a consequence of heteroskedasticity in regression analysis is to invalidate the usual formulas for the calculation of standard errors, and as with clustering, there exists a straightforward correction procedure.

Matters are much less simple when we move from regressions to models with limited dependent variables. In regression analysis, the estimation of scale parameters can be separated from the estimation of location parameters, but the separation breaks down in probits, logits, Tobits, and in sample selectivity models. I illustrate some of the difficulties using the Tobit model, and provide a simple but realistic example of censoring at zero where the application of maximum-likelihood Tobit techniques—something that is nowadays quite routine in the development literature—can lead to estimates that are no better than OLS. There are currently no straightforward solutions to these difficulties, but I review some of the options and make some suggestions for practice.

Heteroskedasticity in regression analysis

It is a fact that regression functions estimated from survey data are typically not homoskedastic. Why this should be is of secondary importance; indeed it is just as reasonable to ask why it should be supposed that conditional expectations should be homoskedastic. Nevertheless, we have already seen in Section 2.1 above that even when individual behavior generates homoskedastic regression functions within strata or villages, but there is heterogeneity between villages, there will be heteroskedasticity in the overall regression function. Similar results apply to heterogeneity at the individual level. If the response coefficients β differ by household, and we treat them as random, we may write

$$(2.31) \qquad E(y_i|x_i,\beta_i) = \beta_i'x_i; \quad V(y_i|x_i,\beta_i) = \sigma^2.$$

Suppose that the β_i have mean β and variance-covariance matrix Ω, then (2.31) generates the heteroskedastic regression model

$$(2.32) \qquad E(y_i|x_i) = \beta'x_i; \quad V(y_i|x_i) = \sigma^2 + x_i'\Omega x_i.$$

Models like (2.32) motivate the standard test procedures for heteroskedasticity such as the Breusch-Pagan (1979) test, or White's (1980) information matrix test (see also Chesher 1984 for the link with individual heterogeneity.) The Breusch-Pagan test is particularly straightforward to implement. The OLS residuals from the regression with suspected heteroskedasticity are first normalized by division by the estimated standard error of the equation. Their squares are then regressed on the variables thought to be generating the heteroskedasticity—if (2.32) is correct, these should include the original x-variables, their squares, and cross-products—and half the explained sum of squares tested against the χ^2 distribution with degrees of freedom equal to the number of variables in this supplementary regression.

In the presence of heteroskedasticity, OLS is inefficient and the usual formulas for standard errors are incorrect. In cases where efficiency is not a prime concern, we may nevertheless want to use the OLS estimates, but to correct the standard errors. This can be done exactly as in (2.30) above, a formula that is robust to the presence of *both* heteroskedasticity and cluster effects. If there are no clusters, (2.30) can be applied by treating each household as its own cluster so that there are no cross-effects within clusters and the formula can be written

$$(2.33) \qquad \tilde{V}(\beta) = (X'X)^{-1}(\sum_i e_i^2 x_i x_i')(X'X)^{-1}$$

where x_i is the column vector of explanatory variables for household i and e_i^2 is the squared residual from the OLS regression. This formula, which comes originally from Eicker (1967) and Huber (1967), was introduced into econometrics by White (1980). Its performance in finite samples can be improved by a number of possible corrections; the simplest requires that e_i^2 in (2.33) be multiplied by

$(n-k)^{-1}n$, where k is the number of regressors and n the sample size, see David-son and MacKinnon (1993, 552–56.) In practice, the heteroskedasticity correction to the variance-covariance matrix (2.33) is usually quantitatively less important than the correction for intracluster correlations, (2.30).

Quantile regressions

The presence of heteroskedasticity can be conveniently analyzed and displayed by estimating *quantile regressions* following the original proposals by Koenker and Bassett (1978, 1982). To see how these work, it is convenient to start from the standard *homoskedastic* regression model.

Figure 2.1 illustrates quantiles in the (standard) case where heteroskedasticity is absent. The regression line $\alpha + \beta x$ is the expectation of y conditional on x, and the three "humped" curves schematically illustrate the conditional densities of the errors given x; in principle, these densities should rise perpendicularly from the page. For each value of x, consider a process whereby we mark the percentiles of the conditional distribution, and then connect up the same percentiles for different values of x. If the distribution of errors is symmetrical, as shown in Figure 2.1, the conditional mean, or regression function, will be at the 50th percentile or median, so that joining up the conditional medians simply reproduces the regression. When the distribution of errors is also homoskedastic, the percentiles will always be at the same distance from the median, no matter what the value of x. Figure 2.1 shows the lines formed by joining the points corresponding to the 10th and 90th

Figure 2.1. Schematic figure of a homoskedastic linear regression function

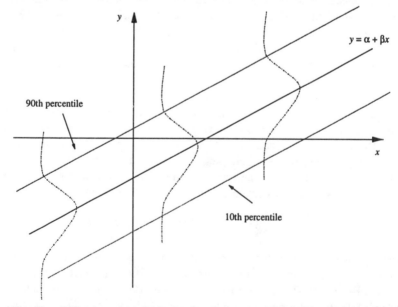

Note: The solid line shows the regression function of y on x, assumed to be linear. The broken lines show the 10th and 90th percentiles of the distribution of y conditional on x.

percentiles of the conditional distributions. Because the regression is homoske-dastic, these are straight lines that are parallel to, and equidistant from, the regression line.

When regressions are heteroskedastic, or when the errors are asymmetric, marking and joining up percentiles will give quite different results. If the residuals are symmetric but heteroskedastic, the distance of each percentile from the regression line will be different at different values of x. Joining up the percentiles for different values of x will not necessarily lead to straight lines or to any other simple curve. However, we can still *fit* straight lines to the percentiles, and it is this that is accomplished by quantile regression. If the heteroskedasticity is linked to the value of x, with the distribution of residuals becoming more or less dispersed as x becomes larger, then the quantile regressions for percentiles other than the median will no longer be parallel to the regression line, but will diverge from it (or converge to it) for larger values of x.

Figure 2.2 illustrates using a food Engel curve for the rural data from the 1984–85 Household Income and Expenditure Survey of Pakistan. Previous experience has shown that the budget share devoted to food can often be well approximated as a linear function of the logarithm of household expenditure per capita, as first proposed by Working (1943). The points in the figure are a 10 percent random sample of the 9,119 households in the survey whose logarithm of per capita expenditure lies between 3 and 8; a small number of households at the extremes of the distribution are thereby excluded from the figure, but not from the calcula-

Figure 2.2. Scatter diagram and quantile regressions for food share and total expenditure, Pakistan, 1984–85

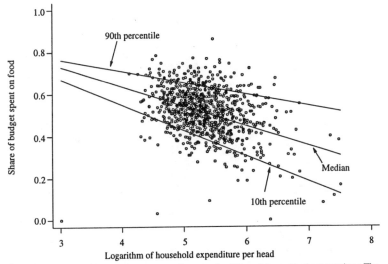

Note: The scatter as shown is a ten percent random sample of the points used in the regressions. The regression lines shown were obtained using the "qreg" command in STATA and correspond to the 10th, 50th, and 90th percentiles.

Source: Author's calculations based on Household Income and Expenditure Survey.

tions. The three lines in the figure are the quantile regressions corresponding to the 10th, 50th, and 90th percentiles of the distribution of the food share conditional on the logarithm of household expenditure per head; these were calculated using all 9,119 households. The procedures for estimating these regressions, calculated using the "qreg" command in STATA, are discussed in the technical note that follows, but the principle should be clear from the foregoing discussion.

The slopes of the three lines differ; the median regression (50th percentile) has a slope of –0.094 (the OLS slope is –0.091), while the lower line has slope –0.121, and the upper –0.054. These differences and the widening spread between the lines as we move to the right show the increase in the conditional variance of the regression among better-off households; the 10th and 90th percentiles of the conditional distribution are much further apart among richer than poorer households. Those with more to spend in total devote a good deal less of their budgets to food, but there is also more dispersion of tastes among them.

Quantile regressions are not only useful for discovering heteroskedasticity. By calculating regressions for different quantiles, it is possible to explore the shape of the conditional distribution, something that is often of interest in its own right, even when heteroskedasticity is not the immediate cause for concern. A very simple example is shown in Figure 2.3, which illustrates age profiles of earnings for black and white workers from the 1993 South African Living Standards Survey. Earnings are monthly earnings in the "regular" sector, and the graphs use

Figure 2.3. Quantile regressions of the logarithm of earnings on age by race, South Africa, 1993
(log of rand per month)

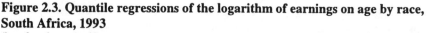

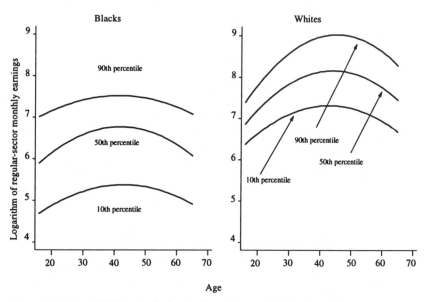

Source: Author's calculations using the South African Living Standards Survey, 1993.

only data for those workers who report such earnings. The two panels show the quantile regressions of the logarithm of earnings on age and age squared for the 10th, 50th, and 90th percentiles for Black and White workers separately. The use of a quadratic in age restricts the shapes of the profiles, but allows them to differ by race and by percentile, as in fact they do. The curves show not only the vast differences in earnings between Blacks and Whites—a difference in logarithms of 1 is a ratio difference of more than 2.7—but also that the shapes of the age profiles are different. Those whose earnings are at the top within their age group are the more highly-educated workers in more highly-skilled jobs, and because the human capital required for these jobs takes time to accumulate, the profile at the 90th percentile for whites has a stronger hump-shape than do the profiles for the 50th and 10th percentiles. There is no corresponding phenomenon for Blacks, presumably because, in South Africa in 1993, even the most able Blacks are restricted in their access to education and to high-skill jobs. These graphs and the underlying regressions do not tell us anything about the causal processes that generate the differences, but they present the data in an interesting way that can be suggestive of ideas for a deeper investigation (see Mwabu and Schultz 1995 for more formal analysis of earnings in South Africa, Mwabu and Schultz 1996 for a use of quantile regression in the same context, and Buchinsky 1994 for the use of quantile regressions to describe the wage structure in the U.S.)

There are also arguments for preferring the parameters of the median regression to those from the OLS regression. Even given the Gauss-Markov assumptions of homoskedasticity and independence, least squares is only efficient within the (restrictive) class of linear, unbiased estimators, although if the conditional distribution is normal, OLS will be minimum variance among the broader class of all unbiased estimators. When the distribution of residuals is not normal, there will usually exist nonlinear (and/or biased) estimators that are more efficient than OLS, and quantile regressions will sometimes be among them. In particular, the median regression is more resistant to outliers than is OLS, a major advantage in working with large-scale survey data.

Technical note: calculating quantile regressions

In the past, the applicability of quantile regression techniques has been limited, not because they are inherently unattractive, but by computational difficulties. These have now been resolved. Just as in calculating the median itself, median regression can be defined by minimizing the absolute sum of the errors rather than, as in least squares, by minimizing the sum of their squares. It is thus also known as the LAD estimator, for Least Absolute Deviations. Hence, the median regression coefficients can be obtained by minimizing ϕ given by

$$(2.34) \qquad \phi = \sum_{i=1}^{n} |y_i - x_i'\beta| = \sum_{i=1}^{n} (y_i - x_i'\beta) \operatorname{sgn}(y_i - x_i'\beta)$$

where $\operatorname{sgn}(a)$ is the sign of a, 1 if a is positive, and -1 if a is negative or zero. (I have reverted to the standard use of n for the sample size, since there is no longer a need to separate the number of clusters from the total number of observations.) The intuition for why (2.34) works comes from thinking about the first-order condition that is satisfied by the parameters that minimize (2.34), which is, for $j = 1, \ldots, k$,

$$(2.35) \qquad \sum_{i=1}^{n} x_{ij} \text{sgn}(y_i - x_i'\beta) = 0.$$

Note first that if there is only a constant in the regression, (2.35) says that the constant should be chosen so that there are an equal number of points on either side of it, which defines the median. Second, note the similarity between (2.35) and the OLS first-order conditions, which are identical except for the "sgn" function; in median regression, it is only the sign of each residual that counts, whereas in OLS it is its magnitude.

Quantile regressions other than median can be defined by minimizing, not (2.34), but

$$\begin{aligned}(2.36) \qquad \phi_q &= -(1-q) \sum_{y \leq x'\beta} (y_i - x_i'\beta) + q \sum_{y > x'\beta} (y_i - x_i'\beta) \\ &= \sum_{i=1}^{n} [q - 1(y_i \leq x_i'\beta)](y_i - x_i'\beta)\end{aligned}$$

where $0 < q < 1$ is the quantile of interest, and the value of the function $1(z)$ signals the truth (1) or otherwise (0) of the statement z. The minimization condition corresponding to (2.35) is now

$$(2.37) \qquad \sum_i x_{ij}[q - 1(y_i \leq x_i'\beta)] = 0$$

which is clearly equivalent to (2.35) when q is a half. Once again, note that if the regression contains only a constant term, the constant is set so that $100q$ percent of the sample points are below it, and $100(1-q)$ percent above.

The computation of quantile estimators is eased by the recognition that the minimization of (2.36) can be accomplished by linear programming, so that even for large data sets, the calculations are not burdensome. The same cannot be said for the estimation of the variance-covariance matrix of the parameter estimates. When the residuals are homoskedastic, there is an asymptotic formula provided by Koenker and Bassett (1982) that gives the variance-covariance matrix of the parameters as the usual $(X'X)^{-1}$ matrix scaled by a quantity that depends (inversely) on the density of the errors at the quantiles of interest. Estimation of this density is not straightforward, but more seriously, the formula appears to give very poor results—typically gross underestimation of standard errors—in the presence of heteroskedasticity, which is often the reason for using quantile regression in the first place!

It is therefore important to use some other method for estimating standard errors, such as the bootstrap, a version of which is implemented in the "bsqreg" command in STATA, whose manual, Stata Corporation (1993, Vol. 3, 96–106) provides a useful description of quantile regressions in general. (Note that the STATA version does not allow for clustering but it is straightforward, if time-consuming, to bootstrap quantile regressions using the clustered bootstrap illustrated in Example 1.3 in the Code Appendix.)

Heteroskedasticity and limited dependent variable models

In regression analysis, the presence of heteroskedasticity and nonnormality is problematic because of potential efficiency losses, and because of the need to correct the usual formulas for standard errors. However, regression analysis is somewhat of a special case because the estimation of parameters of location—the conditional mean or conditional median—is independent of the estimation of scale—the dispersion around the conditional location. In limited dependent variable models, scale and location are intimately bound together, and as a result, misspecification of scale can lead to inconsistency in estimates of location.

Probit and logit models provide perhaps the clearest examples of the difficulties that arise. There is a dependent variable y_i which is either 1 or 0 according to whether or not an unobserved or latent variable y_i^* is positive or nonpositive. The latent variable is defined by analogy to a regression model,

$$(2.38) \qquad y_i^* = f(x_i) + u_i, \quad E(u_i) = 0, \quad E(u_i^2) = \sigma^2[g(z_i)]^2$$

where x and z are vectors of variables controlling the "regression" and the "heteroskedasticity" respectively, and $f(.)$ and $g(.)$ are functions, the former usually assumed to be known, the latter unknown. Suppose that $F(.)$ is the cumulative distribution function (CDF) of the standardized residual $u_i / \sigma g(z_i)$, and that $F(.)$ is symmetric around 0 so that $F(a) = 1 - F(-a)$, then

$$(2.39) \qquad p_i = Prob(y_i = 1) = F[f(x_i)/\sigma g(z_i)].$$

If we know the function $F(.)$, which is in itself assuming a great deal, then given data on y, x, and z, the model gives no more information on which to base estimation than is contained in the probabilities (2.39). But by inspection of (2.39) it is immediately clear that it is not possible to separate the "heteroskedasticity" function $g(z)$ from the "regression" function $f(x)$. For example, suppose that $f(x)$ has the standard linear specification $x'\beta$, that the elements of z are the same as those of x, and that it so happens that $g(z) = g(x) = x'\beta / x'\gamma$. Then the application of maximum-likelihood estimation (MLE) will yield estimates that are consistent, not for β, but for γ! The latent-variable or regression approach to dichotomous models can be misleading if we treat it too seriously; we observe 1's or 0's, and we can use them to model the probabilities, but that is all.

The point of the previous paragraph is so obvious and so well understood that it is hardly of practical importance; the confounding of heteroskedasticity and "structure" is unlikely to lead to problems of interpretation. It is standard procedure in estimating dichotomous models to set the variance in (2.38) to be unity, and since it is clear that all that can be estimated is the effects of the covariates on the probability, it will usually be of no importance whether the mechanism works through the mean or the variance of the latent "regression" (2.38). While it is correct to say that probit or logit is inconsistent under heteroskedasticity, the inconsistency would only be a problem if the parameters of the function f were the parameters of interest. These parameters are identified only by the homoskedasticity assumption, so that the inconsistency result is both trivial and obvious. (It is perhaps worth noting that STATA has "hlogit" and "hprobit" commands for logit and probit that match the "hreg" command for regression. But these should not be used to correct standard errors in logit and probit; rather they should be used to correct standard errors for clustering, so that the analogy is with (2.30), not (2.33).)

Related but more serious difficulties occur with heteroskedasticity when analyzing censored regression models, truncated regressions, or regressions with selectivity, where the inconsistencies are a good deal more troublesome. I illustrate using the censored regression model, or Tobit—after Tobin's (1958) probit—because the model is directly relevant to the analysis in later chapters, and because the technique is widely used in the development literature. Consider in particular the demand for a good, which can be purchased only in positive quantities. If there were no such restriction, we might postulate a linear regression of the form

$$(2.40) \qquad y_i^* = x_i'\beta + u_i.$$

When y_i^* is positive, everything is as usual and actual demand y_i is equal to y_i^*. But negative values of y_i^* are "censored" and replaced by zero, the minimum allowed. The model for the observed y_i can thus be written as

$$(2.41) \qquad y_i = \max(0, x_i'\beta + u_i).$$

I note in passing that the model can be derived more elegantly as in Heckman (1974), who considers a labor supply example, and shows that (2.41) is consistent with choice theory when hours worked cannot be negative.

The left-hand panel of Figure 2.4 shows a simulation of an example of a standard Tobit model. The latent variable is given by $x_i - 40 + u_i$ with the x's taking the 100 values from 1 to 100, and the u's randomly and independently drawn from a normal distribution with mean zero and standard deviation 20. The small circles on the graph show the resulting scatter of y_i against x_i. Because of the censoring, which is more severe for low values of the explanatory variable, the OLS regression line has a slope less than one; in 100 replications the OLS estimator had a mean of 0.637 with a standard deviation of 0.055, so that the bias shown in the figure for one particular realization is typical of this situation. A better method is to follow Tobin, and maximize the log-likelihood function

$$(2.42) \qquad \begin{aligned} \ln L = {} & -\frac{n_+}{2}(\ln \sigma + \ln 2\pi) - \frac{1}{2\sigma^2} \sum_{i_+} (y_i - x_i'\beta)^2 \\ & + \sum_{i_0} \ln\left[1 - \Phi\left(\frac{x_i'\beta}{\sigma}\right)\right] \end{aligned}$$

where n_+ is the number of strictly positive observations, i_+ and i_0 indicate that the respective sums are taken over positive and zero observations, respectively, and Φ is the c.d.f. of the standard normal distribution. The first two terms on the right-hand side of (2.42) are exactly those that would appear in the likelihood function of a standard normal regression, and would be the only terms to appear in the absence of censoring. The final term comes from the observations that are censored to zero; for each such observation we do not observe the exact value of the latent variable, only that it is zero or less, so that the contribution to the log likelihood is the logarithm of the probability of that event. Estimates of β and σ are obtained by maximizing (2.42), a nonlinear problem whose solution is guaranteed by the fact the log-likelihood function is convex in the parameters, and so has a unique maximum. This maximum-likelihood technique works well for the left-hand panel of the figure; in the 100 replications, the Tobit estimates of the slope averaged 1.009 with a standard deviation of 0.100. In this case, where the normality assumption is correct, and the disturbances homoskedastic, maximum likelihood overcomes the inconsistency of OLS.

That all will not be as well in the presence of heteroskedasticity can be seen from the likelihood function (2.42) where the last term, which is the contribution to the likelihood of the censored observations, contains both the scale and location parameters. The standard noncensored likelihood function, which is (2.42) without the last term, has the property that the derivatives of the log-likelihood function with respect to the β's are independent of σ, at least in expectation, and *vice versa*, something that is not true for (2.42). This gives a precise meaning to the notion that scale and location are independent in the regression model, but

Figure 2.4. Tobit models with and without heteroskedasticity

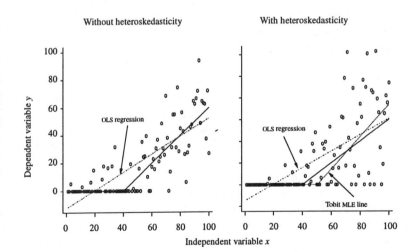

Note: See text for model definition and estimation procedures.
Source: Author's calculations.

dependent in these models with limited dependent variables. As a result of the dependence, misspecification of scale will cause the β's that maximize (2.42) to be inconsistent for the true parameters, a result first noted by Hurd (1979), Nelson (1981), and Arabmazar and Schmidt (1981).

The right-hand side of Figure 2.4 gives an illustration of the kind of problems that can occur with heteroskedasticity. Instead of being homoskedastic as in the left-hand panel, the u_i are drawn from independent normal distributions with zero means and standard deviations σ_i given by

$$(2.43) \qquad \sigma_i = 20\left(1 + 0.2\sqrt{\max(0, x_i - 40)}\right).$$

According to this specification there is homoskedasticity to the left of the cutoff point (40), but heteroskedasicity to its right, and the conditional variance grows with the mean of the dependent variable beyond the cutoff. Although (2.43) does not pretend to be based on any actual data, it mimics reasonable models of behavior. Richer households have more scope for idiosyncracies of behavior than do the poor, and as we see in the right-hand panel, we now get zero observations among the rich as well as the poor, something that cannot occur in the homoskedastic model. This is what happens in practice; if we look at the demand for tobacco, alcohol, fee-paying schools or clinics, there are more nonconsumers among the poor, but there are also many better-off households who choose not to purchase. Not purchasing is partly a matter of income, and partly a matter of taste.

The figure shows three lines. The dots-and-dashes line to the left is the OLS regression which is still biased downward; although the heteroskedasticity has generated more very high y's at high levels of x, the censoring at low values of x keeps the OLS slope down. In the replications the OLS slope averaged 0.699 with a standard deviation of 0.100; there is more variability than before, but the bias is much the same. The second, middle (solid) line is the kinked line $\max(0, x - 40)$ which is (2.41) when all the u_i are zero. (Note that this line is not the regression function, which is *defined* as the expectation of y conditional on x.) The third line, on the right of the picture, comes from maximizing the likelihood (2.42) under the (false) assumption that the u's are homoskedastic. Because the Tobit procedure allows it to deal with censoring at low values of x, but provides it with no explanation for censoring at high values of x, the line is biased upward in order to pass through the center of the distribution on the right of the picture. The average MLE (Tobit) estimate of the slope in the replications was 1.345 with a standard error of 0.175, so that in the face of the heteroskedasticity, the Tobit procedure yields estimates that are as biased up as OLS is biased down. It is certainly possible to construct examples where the Tobit estimators are better than least squares, even in the presence of heteroskedasticity. But there is nothing odd about the current example; heteroskedasticity will usually be present in practical applications, and there is no general guarantee that the attempt to deal with censoring by replacing OLS with the Tobit MLE will give estimates that reduce the bias. This is *not* a defense of OLS, but a warning against the supposition that Tobit guarantees any improvement.

In practice, the situation is worse than in this example. Even when there is no heteroskedasticity, the consistency of the Tobit estimates requires that the distribution of errors be normal, and biases can occur when it is not (see Goldberger 1983 and Arabmazar and Schmidt 1982). And since the distribution of the u's is almost always unknown, it is unclear how one might respecify the likelihood function in order to do better. Even so, censored data occur frequently in practice, and we need some method for estimating sensible models. There are two very different approaches; the first is to look for estimation strategies that are robust against heteroskedasticity of the u's in (2.41) and that require only weak assumptions about their distribution, while the second is more radical, and essentially abandons the Tobit approach altogether. I begin with the former.

*Robust estimation of censored regression models

There are a number of different estimators that implement the first approach, yielding nonparametric Tobit estimators—nonparametric referring to the distribution of the u's, not to the functional form of the latent variable which remains linear. None of these has yet passed into standard usage, and I review only one, Powell's (1984) censored LAD estimator. It is relatively easily implemented and appears to work in practice. (An alternative is Powell's (1986) symmetrically trimmed least squares estimator.)

One of the most useful properties of quantiles is that they are preserved under monotone transformations; for example, if we have a set of positive observations, and we take logarithms, the median of the logarithms will be the logarithm of the median of the untransformed data. Since $\max(0, z)$ is monotone nondecreasing in z, we can take medians of (2.41) conditional on x_i to get

$$(2.44) \qquad q_{50}(y_i | x_i) = \max[0, q_{50}(x_i'\beta + u_i | x_i)] = \max(0, x_i'\beta)$$

where $q_{50}(.|x)$ denotes the median of the distribution conditional on x and the median of u_i is assumed to be 0. But as we have already seen, LAD regression estimates the conditional median regression, so that β can be consistently estimated by the parameter vector that minimizes

$$(2.45) \qquad \sum_{i=1}^{n} |y_i - \max(0, x_i'\beta)|$$

which is what Powell suggests. The consistency of this estimator does not require knowledge of the distribution of the u's, nor is it assumed that the distribution is homoskedastic, only that it has median 0.

Although Powell's estimator is not available in standard software, it can be calculated from repeated application of median regression following a suggestion of Buchinsky (1994, p. 412). The first regression is run on all the observations, and the predicted values $x_i'\beta$ calculated; these are used to discard sample observations where the predicted values are negative. The median regression is then repeated on the truncated sample, the parameter estimates used to recalculate $x_i'\beta$

for the whole sample, the negative values discarded, and so on until convergence. In (occasional) cases where the procedure does not converge, but cycles through a finite set of parameters, the parameters with the highest value of the criterion function should be chosen. Standard errors can be taken from the final iteration though, as before, bootstrapped estimates should be used.

Such a procedure is easily coded in STATA, and was applied to the heteroskedastic example given above and shown in Figure 2.4 (see Example 2.1 in the Code Appendix). To simplify the coding, the procedure was terminated after 10 median regressions, so that to the extent that convergence had not been attained, the results will be biased against Powell's estimator. On average, the method does well, and the mean of the censored LAD estimator over the 100 replications was 0.946. However, there is a price to be paid in variance, and the standard deviation of 0.305 is three times that of the OLS estimator and more than one and a half times larger than that of the Tobit. As a result, and although both Tobit and OLS are inconsistent, in only 55 out of 100 of the replications is the censored LAD closer to the truth than both OLS and Tobit. Of course, the bias to variance trade-off turns in favor of Powell's estimator as the sample size becomes larger. With 1,000 observations instead of 100, and with the new x values again equally spaced but 10 times closer, the censored LAD estimator is closer to the truth than either OLS or Tobit in 96 percent of the cases. Since most household surveys will have sample sizes at least this large, Powell's estimator is worth serious consideration. At the very least, comparing it with the Tobit estimates will provide a useful guide to failure of homoskedasticity or normality (see Newey 1987 for an exercise of this kind).

Even so, the censored LAD estimator is designed for the censored regression model, and does not apply to other cases, such as truncation, where the observations that would have been negative do not appear in the sample instead of being replaced by zeros, nor to more general models of sample selectivity. In these, the censoring or truncation of one variable is determined by the behavior of a second latent variable regression, so that

$$(2.46) \qquad \begin{aligned} y_{1i}^* &= x_i'\beta + u_{1i} \\ y_{2i}^* &= z_i'\gamma + u_{2i} \end{aligned}$$

where u_1 and u_2 are typically allowed to be correlated, y_{2i} is observed as a dichotomous variable indicating whether or not y_{2i}^* is positive, and y_{1i} is observed as y_{1i}^* when y_{2i} is 1, and is zero otherwise. Equations (2.46) are a generalization of Tobit, whereby the censoring is controlled by variables that are different from the variables that control the magnitude of the variable of interest. If the two sets of u's are assumed to be jointly normally distributed, (2.46) can be estimated by maximum likelihood, or by Heckman's (1976) two-step estimator—the "Heckit" procedure (see the next section for further discussion). As with Tobit, which is a special case, these methods do not yield consistent estimates in the presence of heteroskedasticity or nonnormality, and as with Tobit, the provision of nonparametric estimators is a lively topic of current research in econometrics. I shall return to these topics in more detail in the next section.

Radical approaches to censored regressions

Serious attention must also be given to a second, more radical, approach that questions the usefulness of these models in general. There are conceptual issues as well as practical ones. In the first place, these models are typically presented as elaborations of linear regression, in which a standard regression equation is extended to deal with censoring, truncation, selectivity, or whatever is the issue at hand. However, in so doing they make a major break from the standard situation presented in the introduction where the regression *function*, the expectation of the dependent variable conditional on the covariates, coincides with the deterministic part of the regression *model*. In the Tobit and its generalizations, the regression functions are no longer simple linear functions of the x's, but are more complex expressions that involve the distribution of the u's. For example, in the censored regression model (2.41), the regression function is given by

$$E(y_i|x_i) = x_i'\beta + E(u\,|\,x_i'\beta + u \geq 0)$$

(2.47)
$$= x_i'\beta + [1 - F(-x_i'\beta)]^{-1} \int_{-x_i'\beta}^{\infty} u\,dF(u)$$

where $F(u)$ is the CDF of the u's. Absent knowledge of F, this regression function does not even identify the β's—see Powell (1989)—but more fundamentally, we should ask how it has come about that we have to deal with such an awkward, difficult, and nonrobust object.

Regressions are routinely assumed to be linear, not because linearity is thought to be exactly true, but because it is convenient. A linear model is often a sensible first approximation, and linear regressions are easy to estimate, to replicate, and to interpret. But once we move into models with censoring or selection, it is much less convenient to start with linearity, since it buys us no simplification. It is therefore worth considering alternative possibilities, such as starting by specifying a suitable functional form for the regression function itself, rather than for the part of the model that would have been the regression function had we been dealing with a linear model. Linearity will often not be appropriate for the regression function, but there are many other possibilities, and as we shall see in the next chapter, it is often possible to finesse the functional form issue altogether. Such an approach goes beyond partially nonparametric treatments that allow arbitrary distributional assumptions for the disturbances while maintaining linearity for the functional form of the model itself, and recognizes that the functional form is as much an unknown as is the error distribution. It also explicitly abandons the attempt to estimate the structure of selectivity or censoring, and focusses on features of the data—such as regression functions—that are clearly and uncontroversially observable. There will sometimes be a cost to abandoning the structure, but there are many policy problems for which the structure is irrelevant, and which can be addressed through the regression function.

A good example is the effect of a change in tax rates on tax revenue. A government is considering a reduction in the subsidy on wheat (say), and needs to know the extent to which demand will be reduced at the higher price. The quantity of interest is the effect of price on average demand. Suppose that we have survey data on wheat purchases, together with regional or temporal price variation as well as other relevant explanatory variables. Some households buy positive quantities of wheat, and some buy none, a situation that would seem to call for a Tobit Estimation of the model yields an estimate of the response of quantity to price for those who buy wheat. But the policymaker is interested not only in this effect, but also in the loss of demand from those who previously purchased, but who will drop out of the market at the higher price. These effects will have to be modeled separately and added into the calculation. But this is an artificial and unnecessarily elaborate approach to the problem. The policy question is about the effect of price on average demand, averaged over consumers and nonconsumers alike. But this is exactly what we would estimate if we simply regressed quantity on price, with zeros and nonzeros included in the regression. In this case, not only is the regression function more convenient to deal with from an econometric perspective, it is also what we need to know for policy.

2.4 Structure and regression in nonexperimental data

The regression model is the standard workhorse for the analysis of survey data, and the parameters estimated by regression analysis frequently provide useful summaries of the data. Even so, they do not always give us what we want. This is particularly so when the survey data are a poor substitute for unobtainable experimental data. For example, if we want to know the effect of constructing health clinics, or of expanding schools, or what will happen if a minimum wage or health coverage is mandated, we should ideally like to conduct an experiment, in which some randomly chosen group is given the "treatment," and the results compared with a randomly selected group of controls from whom the treatment is withheld. The randomization guarantees that there are no differences—observable or unobservable—between the two groups. In consequence, if there is a significant difference in outcomes, it can only be the effect of the treatment. Although the role of policy experiments has been greatly expanded in recent years (see Grossman 1994 and Newman, Rawlings, and Gertler 1994), there are many cases where experiments are difficult or even impossible, sometimes because of the cost, and sometimes because of the moral and political implications. Instead, we have to use nonexperimental survey data to look at the differences in behavior between different people, and to try to relate the degree of exposure to the treatment to variation in the outcomes in which we are interested. Only under ideal conditions will regression analysis give the right answers. In this section, I explore the various difficulties; in the next two sections, I look at two of the most important of the econometric solutions, panel data and the technique of instrumental variables.

The starting point for a nonexperimental study is often a regression model, in which the outcome variable y is related to a set of explanatory variables x. At least one of the x-variables is the treatment variable, while others are "control" variables, included so as to allow for differences in outcomes that are not caused by the treatment and to allow the treatment effect to be isolated. These variables play the same role as the control group in an experiment. The error term in the regression captures omitted controls, as well as measurement error in the outcome y, and is assumed to satisfy (2.4), that its expectation conditional on the x's is 0. In this setup, the expectation of y conditional on x is $\beta'x$, and the effects of the treatment and controls can be recovered by estimating β. The most common problem with this procedure is the failure—or at least implausibility—of the assumption that the conditional mean of the error term is zero. If a relevant variable is omitted, perhaps because it is unobservable or because data are unavailable, and if that variable is correlated with any of the included x's, the error will not be orthogonal to the x's, and the conditional expectation of y will not be $\beta'x$. The regression function no longer coincides with the structure that we are trying to recover, and estimation of the regression function will not yield the parameters of interest. The failure of the structure and the regression function to coincide happens for many different reasons, some more obvious than others. In this section, I consider a number of cases that are important in the analysis of household survey data from developing countries.

Simultaneity, feedback, and unobserved heterogeneity

Simultaneity is a classic argument for a correlation between error terms and explanatory variables. If we supplement the regression model (2.3) with another equation or equations by which some of the explanatory variables are determined by factors that include y, then the error term in (2.3) will be correlated with one or more of the x's and OLS estimates will be biased and inconsistent. The classic textbook examples of simultaneity, the interdependence of supply or demand and price, and the feedbacks through national income from expenditures to income, are usually thought not to be important for microeconomic data, where the purchases of individuals are too small to affect price or to influence their own incomes through macroeconomic feedbacks. As we shall see, this is not necessarily the case, especially when there are local village markets. Other forms of simultaneity are also important in micro data, although the underlying causes often have more to do with omitted or unobservable variables than with feedbacks through time. Four examples illustrate.

Example 1. Price and quantities in local markets

In the analysis of demand using microeconomic data, it is usually assumed that individual purchases are too small to affect price, so that the simultaneity between price and aggregate demand can be ignored in the analysis of the microeconomic data. Examples where this is not the case have been provided by Kennan (1989), and local markets in developing countries provide a related case. Suppose that the demand function for each individual in each village contains an unobservable village-level component, and that, because of poor transportation and lack of an integrated market, supply and demand are equilibriated at the village level. Although the village-level component in individual demands may contribute little to the total variance of demand, the other components will cancel out over the village as a whole, so that the variation in price across villages is correlated with village-level taste for the good. Villages that have a relatively high taste for wheat will tend to have a relatively high price for wheat, and the correlation can be important even when regressions are run using data from individuals or households.

To illustrate, write the demand function in the form

$$(2.48) \qquad y_{ic} = \alpha_0 + \beta x_{ic} - \gamma p_c + u_{ic} = \alpha_0 + \beta x_{ic} - \gamma p_c + \alpha_c + \epsilon_{ic}$$

where y_{ic} is demand by household i in cluster c, x_{ic} is income or some other individual variable, p_c is the common village price, and u_{ic} is the error term. As in previous modeling of clusters, I assume that u_{ic} is the sum of a village term α_c and an idiosyncratic term ϵ_{ic}, both of which are mean-zero random variables. Suppose that aggregate supply for the village is z_c per household, which comes from a weather-affected harvest but is unresponsive to price (or to income). Market clearing implies that

$$(2.49) \qquad z_c = \bar{y}_c = \alpha_0 + \beta \bar{x}_c - \gamma p_c + \alpha_c$$

which determines price in terms of the village taste effect, supply, and average village income. Because markets have to clear at the village level, the price is higher in villages with a higher taste for the commodity. In consequence, the price on the right-hand side of (2.48) is correlated with the α_c component of the error term, and OLS estimates will be inconsistent. The inconsistency arises even if the village contains many households, each of which has a negligible effect on price.

The bias can be large in this case. To make things simple, assume that $\beta = 0$, so that income does not appear in (2.48) nor average income in (2.49). According to the latter, price in village c is

$$(2.50) \qquad p_c = \gamma^{-1}(\alpha_0 + \alpha_c - z_c).$$

Write $\hat{\gamma}$ for the OLS estimate of γ obtained by regressing individual household demands on the price in the village in which the household lives. Provided that tastes are uncorrelated with harvests, it is straightforward to show that

$$(2.51) \qquad \text{plim}\,\hat{\gamma} = \frac{\gamma \sigma_z^2}{\sigma_\alpha^2 + \sigma_z^2}.$$

The price response is biased downwards; in addition to the negative effect of price on demand, there is a *positive* effect from demand to price that comes from the effect on both of village-level tastes. The bias will only vanish when the village taste effects α_c are absent, and will be large if the variance of tastes is large relative to the variance of the harvest.

Example 2. Farm size and farm productivity

Consider a model of the determinants of agricultural productivity, and in particular the old question of whether larger or smaller farms are more productive; the observation of an inverse relationship between farm size and productivity goes back to Chayanov (1925), and has acquired the status of a stylized fact; see Sen (1962) for India and Berry and Cline (1979) for reviews.

To examine the proposition, we might use survey data to regress output per hectare on farm size and on other variables not shown, *viz.*

$$(2.52) \qquad \ln(Q_i / A_i) = \alpha + \beta \ln A_i + u_i$$

where Q_i is farm output, A_i is farm size, and the common finding is that $\beta < 0$, so that small farms are "more productive" than large farms. This might be interpreted to mean that, compared with hired labor, family labor is of better quality, more safely entrusted with valuable animals or machinery, and needs less monitoring (see Feder 1985; Otsuka, Chuma, and Hayami 1992; and Johnson and Ruttan 1994), or as an optimal response by small farmers to uncertainty (see Srinivasan 1972). It has also sometimes been interpreted as a sign of *inefficiency*, and of dualistic labor markets, because in the absence of smoothly operating labor markets farmers may be forced to work too much on their own farms, pushing their marginal productivity below the market wage (see particularly Sen 1966, 1975). However, if a relationship like (2.52) is estimated on a cross section of farms, and even if the amount of land is outside the control of the farmer, (2.52) is likely to suffer from what are effectively simultaneity problems. Such issues have the distinction of being among the very first topics studied in the early days of econometrics (see Marschak and Andrews 1944).

Although it may be reasonable to suppose that the farmer treats his farm size as fixed when deciding what to plant and how hard·to work, this does not mean that A_i is uncorrelated with u_i in (2.52). Farm size may not be controlled by the farmer, but farms do not get to be the size they are at random. The mechanism determining farm size will differ from place to place and time to time, but it is unlikely to be independent of the *quality* of the land. "Desert" farms that are used for low-intensity animal grazing are typically larger than "garden" farms, where the land is rich and output per hectare is high. Such a correlation will be present whether farms are allocated by the market—low-quality land is cheaper per hectare so that it is easier for an owner-occupier to buy a large farm—or by state-mandated land schemes—each farmer is given a plot large enough to make a living. In consequence, the right-hand side of (2.52) is at least partly determined by the left-hand side, and regression estimates of β will be biased downward.

We can also give this simultaneity an omitted variable interpretation where land quality is the missing variable; if quality could be included in the regression instead of in the residual, the new residual could more plausibly be treated as orthogonal to farm size. At the same time, the coefficient β would more nearly measure the effect of land size, and not as in (2.52) the effect of land size contaminated by the (negative) projection of land quality on farm size. Indeed, when data are available on land quality—Bhalla and Roy (1988)—or when quality is controlled by IV methods—Benjamin (1993)—there is little or no evidence of a negative relationship between farm size and productivity.

The effect of an omitted variable is worth recording explicitly, since the formula is one of the most useful in the econometrician's toolbox, and is routinely used to assess results and to calculate the direction of bias caused by the omission. Suppose that the correct model is

$$(2.53) \qquad y_i = \alpha + \beta x_i + \gamma z_i + u_i$$

and that we have data on y and x, but not on z. In the current example, y is yield, and z is land quality. If we run the regression of y on x, the probability limit of the OLS estimate of β is

$$(2.54) \qquad \mathrm{plim}\,\beta = \beta + \gamma\,\frac{\mathrm{cov}(x,z)}{\mathrm{var}\,x}.$$

In the example, it might be the case that $\beta = 0$, so that farm size has no effect on yields conditional on land quality. But $\gamma > 0$, because better land has higher yields, and the probability limit of β will be negative because farm size and land quality are negatively correlated.

The land quality problem arises in a similar form if we attempt to use equations like (2.52) to measure the effects on output of extension services or "modern" inputs such as chemical fertilizer. Several studies, Bevan, Collier and Gunning (1989) for Kenya and Tanzania, and Deaton and Benjamin (1988) for Côte d'Ivoire, find that a regression of output on fertilizer input shows extremely high returns, estimates that, if correct, imply considerable inefficiency and scope for government intervention.

Deaton and Benjamin use the 1985 Living Standards Survey of Côte d'Ivoire to estimate the following regression between cocoa output, the structure of the orchard, and the use of fertilizer and insecticide,

$$(2.55) \qquad \begin{aligned} \ln(Q/LM) = {}&5.621 + 0.526\,(LO/LM) + 0.054\,Insect \\ &(68.5) \quad (4.3) \qquad\qquad\quad (2.5) \\ &+ 0.158\,Fert \\ &(2.8) \end{aligned}$$

where Q is kilos of cocoa produced on the farm, LM and LO are the numbers of hectares of "mature" and "old" trees, respectively, and $Insect$ and $Fert$ are expenditures in thousands of Central African francs per cocoa hectare on insecticide and fertilizer, respectively. According to (2.55), an additional 1,000 francs spent on fertilizer will increase the logarithm of output per hectare by 0.158, which at a sample mean log yield of 5.64 implies an additional 48 kilos of cocoa at 400 francs per kilo, or an additional 19,200 francs. However, only slightly more than a half of the cocoa stands are fully mature, and the farmers pay the *mettayeurs* who harvest the crop between a half and a third of the total. But even after these adjustments, the farmer will be left with a return of 5,400 for an outlay of 1,000 francs. Insecticide is estimated to be somewhat less profitable, and the same calculation gives a return of only 1,800 for each 1,000 francs outlay. Yet only 1 in 14 farmers uses fertilizer, and 1 in 5 uses insecticide.

On the surface, these results seem to indicate very large inefficiencies. However, there are other interpretations. It is likely that highly productive farms are more likely to adopt fertilizer, particularly if the use of fertilizer is an indicator of farmer quality and the general willingness to adopt modern methods, high-yielding varieties, and so on. Credit for fertilizer purchases may only be available to better, or to better-off farmers. Suppose also that some farmers cannot use fertilizer because of local climatic or soil conditions or because the type of trees in their stand, while others have the conditions to make good use of it. When we compare these different farms, we shall find what we have found, that farmers that use fertilizer are more productive, but there is no implication that more fertilizer should be used. Expenditure on fertilizer in (2.55) may do no more than indicate that the orchard contains new hybrid varieties of cocoa trees, something on which the survey did not collect data.

Example 3. The evaluation of projects

Analysis of the effectiveness of government programs and projects has always been a central topic in development economics. Regression analysis seems like a helpful tool in this endeavor, because it enables us to link outcomes—incomes, consumption, employment, health, fertility—to the presence or extent of programs designed to influence them. The econometric problems of such analyses are similar to those we encountered when linking farm outputs to farm inputs. In particular, it is usually impossible to maintain that the explanatory variables—in this case the programs—are uncorrelated with the regression residuals. Government programs are not typically run as experiments, in which some randomly selected groups are treated and others are left alone.

A regression analysis may show that health outcomes are better in areas where the government has put clinics, but such an analysis takes no account of the process whereby sites are chosen. Clinics may be put where health outcomes were previously very poor, so that the cross-section regression will tend to underestimate their effects, or they may be allocated to relatively wealthy districts that are politically powerful, in which case regression analysis will tend to overstate their true impact. Rosenzweig and Wolpin (1986) found evidence of underestimation in the Philippines, where the positive effect of clinics on children's health did not show up in a cross section of children because clinics were allocated first to the areas where they were most needed. The clinics were being allocated in a desirable way, and that fact caused regression analysis to fail to detect the benefits. In the next section, I shall follow Rosenzweig and Wolpin and show how panel data can sometimes be used to circumvent these difficulties. I shall return to the issue of project evaluation later in this section when I come to discuss selection bias, and again in Section 2.6 on IV estimation.

Example 4. Simultaneity and lags: nutrition and productivity

It is important to realize that in cross-section data, simultaneity cannot usually be avoided by using lags to ensure that the right-hand side variables are prior in time to the left-hand side variables. If x precedes y, then it is reasonable to suppose that y cannot affect x directly. However, there is often a third variable that affects y today as well as x yesterday, and if this variable is omitted from the regression, today's y will contain information that is correlated with yesterday's x. The land quality issue in the previous example can be thought about this way; although farm size is determined before the farmer's input and effort decisions, and before they and the weather determine farm output, both output and inputs are affected by land quality, so that there remains a correlation between output and the predetermined variables. As a final example, consider one of the more intractable cases of simultaneity, between nourishment and productivity. If poor people cannot work because they are malnourished, and they cannot eat because they do not earn enough, poor people are excluded from the labor market and there is persistent unemployment and destitution. The theory of this interaction was developed by Mirrlees (1975) and Stiglitz (1976), and it has been argued that such a mechanism helps account for destitution in India (Dasgupta 1993) and for the slow pace of premodern development in Europe (Fogel 1994).

People who eat better may be more productive, because they have more energy and work more efficiently, but people who work more efficiently also earn more, out of which they will spend more on food. Disentangling the effect of nutrition on wages from the Engel curve for food is difficult, and as emphasized by Bliss and Stern (1981), it is far from clear that the two effects can ever be - disentangled. One possibility, given suitable data, is to suppose that productivity depends on nutrition with a lag—sustained nutrition is needed for work—while consumption depends on current income. Hence, if y_{it} is the productivity of individual i at time t, and c_{it} is consumption of calories, we might write

$$(2.56) \qquad \begin{aligned} y_{it} &= \alpha_1 + \beta_1 c_{it-1} + \gamma_1 z_{1it} + u_{1it} \\ c_{it} &= \alpha_2 + \beta_2 y_{it} + \gamma_2 z_{2it} + u_{2it} \end{aligned}$$

where z_1 and z_2 are other variables needed to identify the system. Provided equation (2.56) is correct and the two error terms are serially independent, both equations can consistently be estimated by least squares in a cross section with information on lagged consumption. However, any form of serial dependence in the residuals u_{1it} will make OLS estimates of the first equation inconsistent. But there is a good reason to suppose that these residuals will be serially correlated, since permanent productivity differences across people that are not attributable to nutrition or the other variables will add a constant "individual" component to the error. Individuals who are more productive in one period are likely to be more productive in the next, even when we have controlled for their nutrition and other observable covariates. More productive individuals will have higher incomes and higher levels of nutrition, not only today but also yesterday, so that the lag in the equation no longer removes the correlation between the error term and the-right-hand-side variable. In a cross section, predetermined variables can rarely be legitimately treated as exogenous.

Measurement error

Measurement error in survey data is a fact of life, and while it is not always possible to counter its effects, it is always important to realize what those effects are likely to be, and to beware of inferences that are possibly attributable to, or contaminated by, measurement error.

The textbook case is the univariate regression model where both the explanatory and dependent variables are subject to mean-zero errors of measurement. Hence, for the correctly measured variables y and x, we have the linear relationship

(2.57) $$y_i = \alpha + \beta x_i + u_i$$

together with the measurement equations

(2.58) $$\tilde{x}_i = x_i + \epsilon_{1i}, \quad \tilde{y}_i = y_i + \epsilon_{2i}$$

where the measurement error is assumed to be orthogonal to the true variables. *Faute de mieux*, $\tilde{y}$ is regressed on $\tilde{x}$, and the OLS parameter estimate of β has the probability limit

(2.59) $$\text{plim}\,\hat{\beta} = \frac{\beta m_{xx}}{m_{xx} + \sigma_1^2} = \beta \lambda_0$$

where m_{xx} is the variance of the unobservable, correctly measured x, and σ_1^2 is the variance of the measurement error in x. Equation (2.59) is the "iron law of econometrics," that the OLS estimate of β is biased towards zero, or "attenuated." The degree of attenuation is the ratio of signal to combined signal and noise, λ_0, the *reliability ratio*. The presence of measurement error in the *dependent* variable does not bias the regression coefficients, because it simply adds to the variance of the equation as a whole. Of course, this measurement error, like the measurement error in x, will decrease the precision with which the parameters are estimated.

Attenuation bias is amplified by the addition of correctly measured explanatory variables to the bivariate regression (2.57). Suppose we add a vector z to the right-hand side of (2.57), and assume that z is uncorrelated with the measurement error in $\tilde{x}$ and with the original residuals. Then the probability limit of the OLS estimate of β, the coefficient of $\tilde{x}$, is now $\beta \lambda_1$, where the new reliability ratio λ_1 is

(2.60) $$\lambda_1 = \frac{\lambda_0 - R_{xz}^2}{1 - R_{xz}^2} \leq \lambda_0$$

and R_{xz}^2 is the R^2 from the regression of $\tilde{x}$ on z. The new explanatory variables z "soak up" some of the signal from the noisy regressor $\tilde{x}$, so that the reliability ratio for β is reduced, and the "iron law" more severely enforced.

More generally, consider a multivariate regression where all regressors may be noisy and where the measurement error in the independent variables may be correlated with the measurement error in the dependent variable. Suppose that the correctly measured variables satisfy

$$(2.61) \qquad\qquad y = X\beta + u.$$

Then the OLS parameter estimates have probability limits given by

$$(2.62) \qquad \mathrm{plim}\hat{\beta} = (M+\Omega)^{-1}M\beta + (M+\Omega)^{-1}\gamma$$

where M is the moment matrix of the true x's, Ω is the variance-covariance matrix of the measurement error in the $\tilde{x}$'s, and γ is the vector of covariances between the measurement errors in the $\tilde{x}$'s and the measurement error in $\tilde{y}$. The first term in (2.62) is the matrix generalization of the attenuation effect in the univariate regression—the vector of parameters is subject to a matrix rather than scalar shrinkage factor—while the second term captures any additional bias from a correlation between the measurement errors in dependent and independent variables. The latter effects can be important; for example, if consumption is being regressed on income, and if there is a common and noisily measured imputation term in both—home-produced food, or the imputed value of owner-occupied housing—then there will be an additional source of bias beyond attenuation effects. Even in the absence of this second term on the right-hand side of (2.62) and, in spite of the obvious generalization from scalar to matrix attenuation, the result does not yield any simple result on the direction of bias in any one coefficient (unless, of course, Ω is diagonal).

One useful general lesson is to be specific about the structure of measurement error, and to use a richer and more appropriate specification than the standard one of mean-zero, independent noise. The analysis is rarely complex, is frequently worthwhile, and will not always lead to the standard attenuation result. One specific example is worth a brief discussion. It arises frequently and is simple, but is nevertheless sometimes misunderstood. Consider the model

$$(2.63) \qquad\qquad y_{ic} = \alpha + \beta x_{ic} + \gamma z_c + u_{ic}$$

where i is an individual who lives in village c, y_{ic} is an outcome variable, x_{ic} and z_c are individual and village-level explanatory variables. In a typical example, y might be a measure of educational attainment, x a set of family background variables, and z a measure of educational provision or school quality in the village. The effect of health provision on health status might be another example. What - often happens in practice is that the z-variables are obtained from administrative, not survey data, so that we do not have village-level data on z, but only broader measures, perhaps at a district or provincial level. These measures are error-ridden proxies for the ideal measures, and it might seem that the iron law would apply. But this is not so.

To see why, write z_p for the broad measure—p is for province—so that

$$(2.64) \qquad z_p = n_p^{-1} \sum_{c \in p} z_c$$

where n_p is the number of villages in the province. Hence, instead of the measurement equation (2.58) where the observable is the unobservable plus an unrelated measurement error, we have

$$(2.65) \qquad z_c = z_p + \epsilon_c$$

and it is now the observable z_p that is orthogonal to the measurement error. Because the measurement error in (2.65) is the deviation of the village-level z from its provincial mean, it is orthogonal to the observed z_p by construction. As a result, when we run the regression (2.63) with provincial data replacing village data, there is no correlation between the explanatory variables and the error term, and the OLS estimates are unbiased and consistent. Of course, the loss of the village-level information is not without cost. By (2.65), the averages are less variable than the individuals, so that the precision of the estimates will be reduced. And we must always be careful in these cases to correct standard errors for group effects as discussed in Section 2.2 above. But there is no errors-in-variables attenuation bias.

In Section 2.6 below, I review how, in favorable circumstances, IV techniques can be used to obtain consistent estimates of the parameters even in the presence of measurement error. Note, however, that if it is possible to obtain estimates of measurement error variances and covariances, σ_1^2 in (2.59) or Ω and γ in (2.62), then the biases can be corrected and consistent estimates obtained by substituting the OLS estimate on the left-hand side of (2.62), replacing Ω, γ, and M on the right-hand side by their estimates, and solving for β. For (2.62), this leads to the estimator

$$(2.66) \qquad b = (\tilde{X}'\tilde{X} - n\Omega)^{-1}(\tilde{X}'\tilde{y} - n\gamma)$$

where n is the sample size, and the tildes denote variables measured with error. The estimator (2.66) is consistent if Ω and γ are known or are replaced by consistent estimates. This option will not always be available, but is sometimes possible, for example, when there are several mismeasured estimates of the same quantity, and we shall see practical examples in Section 5.3 and 5.4 below.

Selectivity issues

In Chapter 1 and the first sections of this chapter, I discussed the construction of samples, and the fact that the sample design frequently needs to be taken into account when estimating characteristics of the underlying population. This is particularly important when the selection of the sample is related to the quantity under study; average travel time in a sample of travelers is likely to be quite unrepresentative of average travel time among the population as a whole: if wages influence the decision to work, average wages among workers—which are often the only wages observed—will be an upward-biased estimator of actual and potential wages. Sample selection also affects behavioral relationships. In one of the first and most famous examples, Gronau (1973) found that women's wages were higher when they had small children, a result whose inherent implausibility prompted the search for an alternative explanation, and which led to the selection story. Women with children have higher reservation wages, fewer of them work, and the wages of those who do are higher. As with the other cases in this section, the econometric problem is the induced correlation between the error terms and the regressors. In the Gronau example, the more valuable is a woman's time at home, the larger will have to be the unobserved component in her wages in order to induce her to work, so that among working women, there is a positive correlation between the number of children and the error term in the wage equation.

A useful and quite general model of selectivity is given in Heckman (1990); according to this there are two different regressions or regimes, and the model switches between them according to a dichotomous "switch" that is itself explained. The model is written:

$$(2.67) \qquad y_{0i} = x'_{0i}\beta_0 + u_{0i}, \quad y_{1i} = x'_{1i}\beta_1 + u_{1i}$$

together with the $\{1,0\}$ variable d_i which satisfies

$$(2.68) \qquad d_i = 1(z'_i\gamma + u_{2i} > 0)$$

where the indicator function $1(.)$ takes the value 1 when the statement it contains is true, and is zero otherwise. The observed variable y_i is determined according to

$$(2.69) \qquad y_i = d_i y_{0i} + (1 - d_i)y_{1i}.$$

The model is sometimes used in almost exactly this form; for example, the two equations in (2.67) could be wage equations in the formal and informal sectors respectively, while (2.68) models the decision about which sector to join (see, for example, van der Gaag, Stelcner and Vijverberg 1989 for a model of this sort applied to LSMS data from Peru and Côte d'Ivoire). However, it also covers several special cases, many of them useful in their own right.

If the right-hand side of the second equation in (2.67) were zero, as it would be if $\beta_1 = 0$ and the variance of u_1 were zero, we would have the censored regression model or generalized Tobit. This further specializes to the Tobit model if the argument of (2.68) and the right-hand side of the first equation coincide, so that the switching behavior and the size of the response are controlled by the same factors. However, the generalized Tobit model is also useful; for example, it is often argued that the factors that determine whether or not people smoke tobacco are different from the factors that determine how much smokers smoke. In this case, (2.69) implies that for those values of y that are positive, the regression function is

(2.70) $$E(y_i|x_i, z_i, y_i>0) = x_i'\beta + \lambda(z_i'\gamma)$$

where, since there is only one x and one β, I have dropped the zero suffix, and where the last term is defined by

(2.71) $$\lambda(z_i'\gamma) = E(u_{0i}|u_{2i} \geq -z_i'\gamma).$$

(Compare this with the Tobit in (2.47) above.) This version of the model can also be used to think about the case where the data are truncated, rather than censored as in the Tobit and generalized Tobit. Censoring refers to the case where observations that fall outside limits—in this case below zero—are replaced by the limit points, hence the term "censoring." With truncation, observations beyond the limit are discarded and do not appear in our data. Censoring is easier to deal with because, although we do not observe the underlying latent variable, individual observations are either censored or not censored, and for both we observe the covariates x and z, so that it is possible to estimate the switching equation (2.68) as well as (2.70). With truncation, we know nothing about the truncated observations, so that we cannot estimate the switching process, and we are restricted to (2.70). The missing information in the truncated regression makes it difficult to handle convincingly, and it should be avoided when possible.

A second important special case of the general model is the "treatment" or "policy evaluation" case. In the standard version, the right-hand sides of the two switching regressions in (2.67) are taken to be identical apart from their constant terms, so that (2.69) takes the special form

(2.72) $$y_i = \alpha + \theta d_i + x_i'\beta + u_i$$

so that the parameter θ is the effect on the outcome variable of whether or not the "treatment" is applied. If this were a controlled and randomized experiment, the randomization would guarantee that d_i would be orthogonal to u_i. However, since u_2 in (2.68) is correlated with the error terms in the regressions in (2.67), least squares will not yield consistent estimates of (2.72) because d_i is correlated with u_i. This model is the standard one for examining union wage differentials, for example, but it also applies to many important applications in development where d_i indicates the presence of some policy or project. The siting of health clinics and schools are the perhaps the most obvious examples. As we have already seen above, this version of the model can also be thought of in terms of simultaneity bias.

There are various methods of estimating the general model and its variants. One possibility is to specify some distribution for the three sets of disturbances in (2.67) and (2.68), typically joint normality, and then to estimate by maximum likelihood. Given normality, the γ-parameters in (2.68) can be estimated (up to scale) by probit, and again given normality, the λ-function in (2.71) has a specific form—the (inverse) Mills' ratio—and as Heckman (1976) showed in a famous paper, the results from the probit can be substituted into (2.70) in such a way that the remaining unknown parameters can be estimated by least squares. Since I shall refer to this again, it is worth briefly reviewing the mechanics.

When u_0 and u_2 are jointly normally distributed, the expectation of each conditional on the other is linear, so that we can write

$$(2.73) \qquad u_{0i} = \sigma_0 \rho (u_{2i} / \sigma_2) + \epsilon_i$$

where ϵ_i is orthogonal to u_{2i}, σ_0 and σ_2 are the two standard deviations, and ρ is the correlation coefficient. (Note that $\rho \sigma_0 / \sigma_2 = \sigma_{02} / \sigma_2^2$ is the large-sample regression coefficient of u_0 on u_2, the ratio of the covariance to variance.) Given (2.73), we can rewrite (2.71) as

$$(2.74) \qquad \lambda(z_i'\gamma) = \rho\sigma_0 E\left(\frac{u_{2i}}{\sigma_2} \Big| \frac{u_{2i}}{\sigma_2} > -\frac{z_i'\gamma}{\sigma_2} \right) = \rho\sigma_0 \frac{\phi(z_i'\gamma/\sigma_2)}{\Phi(z_i'\gamma/\sigma_2)}$$

where $\phi(.)$ and $\Phi(.)$ are the density and distribution functions of the standard normal distribution, and where the final formula relies on the special properties of the normal distribution. The regression function (2.70) can then be written as

$$(2.75) \qquad y_i = x_i'\beta + \rho\sigma_0 \frac{\phi(z_i'\gamma/\sigma_2)}{\Phi(z_i'\gamma/\sigma_2)}.$$

The vector of ratios γ/σ_2 can be estimated by running a probit on the dichotomous d_i from (2.68), the estimates used to compute the inverse Mills' ratio on the right-hand side of (2.75), and consistent estimates of β and $\rho\sigma_0$ obtained by OLS regression.

This "Heckit" (Heckman's probit) procedure is widely used in the empirical development literature, to the extent that it is almost routinely applied as a method of dealing with selectivity bias. In recent years, however, it has been increasingly realized that the normality assumptions in these and similar procedures are far from incidental, and that the results—and even the identification of the models—may be compromised if we are not prepared to maintain normality. Even when normality holds, there will be the difficulties with heteroskedasticity that we have already seen. Recent work has been concerned with the logically prior question as to whether and under what conditions the parameters of these models are identified without further parametric distributional assumptions, and with how identified models can be estimated in a way that is consistent and at least reasonably efficient under the sort of assumptions that make sense in practice.

The identification of the general model turns out to be a delicate matter, and is discussed in Chamberlain (1986), Manski (1988), and Heckman (1990). Given data on which observations are in which regime, the switching equation (2.68) is identified without further distributional assumptions; at least if we make the (essentially normalizing) assumption that the variance of u_2 is unity. The identification of the other equations requires that there be at least one variable in the switching equation that does not appear in the substantive equations, and even then there can be difficulties; for example, identification requires that the variables unique to the switching equation be continuous. In many practical applications, these conditions will not be met, or at best be controversial. In particular, it is often difficult to exclude any of the selection variables from the substantive equations. Gronau's example, in which children clearly do not belong in the wage equation, seems to be the exception rather than the rule, and unless it is clear how the selection mechanism is working, there seems little point in pursuing these sorts of models, as opposed to a standard investigation of appropriate conditioning variables and how they enter the regression function.

The robust estimation of the parameters of selection models is a live research topic, although the methods are still experimental, and there is far from general agreement on which are best. In the censoring model (2.70), there exist distribution-free methods that generalize Heckman's two stage procedure (see, for example, Newey, Powell, and Walker 1990, who make use of the kernel estimation methods that are discussed in Chapters 3 and 4 below.

One possible move in this direction is to retain a probit—or even linear probability model, regressing d_i on z_i—for the first-stage estimation of (2.68), and to use the estimates to form the index $z'\gamma$, which is entered in the second-stage regression (2.70), not through the Mills' ratio as in (2.75), but in polynomial form, with the polynomial regarded as an approximation to whatever the true λ-function should be. This is perhaps an unusual mixture of parametric and nonparametric techniques, but the probit model or linear probability model (if the probabilities are typically far from either zero or one) are typically acceptable as functional forms, and it makes most sense to focus on removing the normality assumptions.

The "policy evaluation" or "treatment" model (2.72) is most obviously estimated using IV techniques as described in Section 2.6 below. Note that the classic experimental case corresponds to the case where treatment is randomly assigned, or is randomly assigned to certain groups, so that in either case the u_{2i} in (2.68) is uncorrelated with the errors in the outcome equations (2.67). In most economic applications, the "treatment" has at least some element of self-selection, so that d_i in (2.72) will be correlated with the errors, and instrumentation is required. The obvious instruments are the z-variables, although in practice there will often be difficulties in finding instruments that can be plausibly excluded from the substantive equation. Good instruments in this case can sometimes be provided by "natural experiments," where some feature of the policy design allows the construction of "treatments" and "controls" that are not self-selected. I shall discuss these in more detail below.

2.5 Panel data

When our data contain repeated observations on each individual, the resulting panel data open up a number of possibilities that are not available in the single cross section. In particular, the opportunity to compare the same individual under different circumstances permits the possibility of using that individual as his or her own control, so that we can come closer to the ideal experimental situation. In the farm example of the previous section, the quality of the farm—or indeed of the farmer—can be controlled for, and indeed, the first use of panel data in econometrics was by Mundlak (1961)—see also Hoch (1955)—who estimated farm production functions controlling for the quality of farm management. Similarly, we have seen that the use of regression for project evaluation is often invalidated by the purposeful allocation of projects to regions or villages, so that the explanatory variable—the presence or absence of the project—is correlated with unobserved characteristics of the village. Rosenzweig and Wolpin (1986) and Pitt, Rosenzweig, and Gibbons (1993) have made good use of panel data to test for such effects in educational, health, and family planning programs in the Philippines and Indonesia.

Several different kinds of panel data are sometimes available in developing countries (see also the discussion in Section 1.1 above). A very few surveys—most notably the ICRISAT survey in India—have followed the same households over a substantial period of time. In some of the LSMS surveys, households were visited twice, a year apart, and there are several cases of opportunistic surveys returning to households for repeat interviews, often with a gap of several years. Since many important changes take time to occur, and projects and policies take time to have their effect, the longer gap often produces more useful data. It is also possible to "create" panel data from cross-sectional data, usually by aggregation. For example, while it is not usually possible to match individuals from one census to another, it is frequently possible to match locations, so as to create a panel at the location level. A good example is Pitt, Rosenzweig, and Gibbons (1993), who use several different cross-sectional surveys to construct data on facilities for 1980 and 1985 for 3,302 *kecamatan* (subdistricts) in Indonesia. In Section 2.7 below, I discuss another important example in some detail, the use of repeated but independent cross sections to construct panel data on birth cohorts of individuals. For all of these kinds of data, there are opportunities that are not available with a single cross-sectional survey.

Dealing with heterogeneity: difference- and within-estimation

To see the main advantage of panel data, start from the linear regression model

$$(2.76) \qquad y_{it} = \beta'x_{it} + \theta_i + \mu_t + u_{it}$$

where the index i runs from 1 to n, the sample size, and t from 1 to T, where T is usually small, often just two. The quantity μ_t is a time (or macro) effect, that applies to all individuals in the sample at time t. The parameter θ_i is a fixed effect for observation i; in the farm size example above it would be unobservable land quality, in the nutritional wage example, it would be the unobservable personal productivity characteristic of the individual, and in the project evaluation case, it would be some unmeasured characteristic of the individual (or of the individual's region) that affects program allocation. These fixed effects are designed to capture the heterogeneity that causes the inconsistency in the OLS cross-sectional regression, and are set up in such a way as to allow their control using panel data. Note that there is nothing to prevent us from thinking of the θ's as randomly distributed over the population—so that in this sense the term "fixed effects" is an unfortunate one—but we are not prepared to assume that they are uncorrelated with the observed x's in the regression. Indeed, it is precisely this correlation that is the source of the difficulty in the farm, project evaluation, and nutrition examples.

The fact that we have more than one observation on each of the sample points allows us to remove the θ's by taking differences, or when there are more than two observations, by subtracting (or "sweeping out") the individual means. Suppose that $T = 2$, so that from (2.76), we can write

$$(2.77) \qquad y_{i2} - y_{i1} = (\mu_2 - \mu_1) + \beta'(x_{i2} - x_{i1}) + u_{i2} - u_{i1}$$

an equation that can be consistently and efficiently estimated by OLS. When T is greater than two, use (2.76) to give

$$(2.78) \qquad y_{it} - \bar{y}_{i.} = (\mu_t - \bar{\mu}) + \beta'(x_{i2} - \bar{x}_{i.}) + u_{it} - \bar{u}_{i.}$$

where the notation $\bar{y}_{i.}$ denotes the time mean for individual i. Equation (2.78) can be estimated as a pooled regression by OLS, although it should be noted (a) that there are $n(T-1)$ independent observations, not nT. Neither (2.77) nor (2.78) contains the individual fixed effects θ_i, so that these regressions are free of any correlation between the explanatory variables and the unobserved fixed effects, and the parameters can be estimated consistently by OLS. Of course, the fixed effect must indeed be fixed over time—which there is often little reason to suppose—and it must enter the equation additively and linearly. But given these assumptions, OLS estimation of the suitably transformed regression will yield consistent estimates in the presence of unobserved heterogeneity—or omitted variables—even when that heterogeneity is correlated with one or more of the included right-hand side variables.

In the example from the Philippines studied by Rosenzweig and Wolpin (1986), there are data on 274 children from 85 households in 20 *barrios*. The cross-section regression of child nutritional status (age-standardized height) on exposure to rural health units and family planning programs gives negative (and insignificant) coefficients on both. Because the children were observed in two years, 1975 and 1979, it is also possible to run (2.77), where changes in height are regressed on changes in exposure, in which regression both coefficients become positive. Such a result is plausible if the programs were indeed effective, but were allocated first to those who needed them the most.

The benefit of eliminating unobserved heterogeneity does not come without cost, and a number of points should be noted. Note first that the regression (2.77) has exactly half as many observations as the regression (2.76), so that, in order to remove the inconsistency, precision has been sacrificed. More generally, with T periods, one is sacrificed to control for the fixed effects, so that the proportional loss of efficiency is greatest when there are only two observations. Of course, it can be argued that there are limited attractions to the precise estimation of something that we do not wish to know, but a consistent but imprecise estimate can be further from the truth than an inconsistent estimator. The tradeoff between bias and efficiency has to be made on a case-by-case basis. We must also beware of misinterpreting a decrease in efficiency as a change in parameter estimates between the differenced and undifferenced equations. If the cross-section estimate shows that β is positive and significant, and if the differenced data yield an estimate that is insignificantly different from both zero and the cross-section estimate, it is not persuasive to claim that the cross-section result is an artifact of not "treating" the heterogeneity. Second, the differencing will not only sweep out *the* fixed effects, it will sweep out *all* fixed effects, including any regressor that does not change over the period of observation. In some cases, this removes the attraction of the procedure, and will limit it in short panels. In the Ivorian cocoa farming example in the previous section, most of the farmers who used fertilizer reported the same amount in both periods, so that, although the panel data allows us to control for farm fixed effects, it still does not allow us to estimate how much additional production comes from the application of additional fertilizer.

Panel data and measurement error

Perhaps the greatest difficulties for difference- and within-estimators occur in the presence of measurement error. Indeed, when regressors are measured with error, within- or difference-estimators will no longer be consistent in the presence of unobserved individual fixed effects, nor need their biases be less than that of the uncorrected OLS estimator.

Consider the univariate versions of the regressions (2.76) and (2.77), and compare the probability limits of the OLS estimators in the two cases when, in addition to the fixed effects, there is white noise measurement error in x. Again, for simplicity, I compare the results from estimation on a single cross section with those from a two-period panel. The probability limit of the OLS estimator in the cross section (2.76) is given by

$$(2.79) \qquad \text{plim}\beta \ = \ \frac{\beta m_{xx} + c_{x\theta}}{m_{xx} + \sigma_1^2}$$

where $c_{x\theta}$ is the covariance of the fixed effect and the true x, σ_1^2 is the variance of the measurement error, and I have assumed that the measurement errors and fixed effects are uncorrelated. The formula (2.79) is a combination of omitted variable bias, (2.54), and measurement error bias, (2.59). The probability limit of the difference-estimator in (2.77) is

$$(2.80) \qquad \text{plim}\tilde{\beta} \ = \ \frac{\beta m_{\Delta}}{m_{\Delta} + \sigma_{\Delta}^2}$$

where m_{Δ} is the variance of the difference of the true x, and σ_{Δ}^2 is the variance of the difference of measurement error in x.

That the estimate in the levels suffers from *two* biases—attenuation bias and omitted variable bias—while the difference-estimate suffers from only attenuation bias is clearly no basis for preferring the latter! The relevant question is not the number of biases but whether the differencing reduces the variance in the signal relative to the variance of the noise so that the attenuation bias in the difference-estimator is more severe than the combined attenuation and omitted variable biases in the cross-section regression. We have seen one extreme case already; when the true x does not change between the two periods, the estimator will be dominated by the measurement error and will converge to zero. Although the extreme case would often be apparent in advance, there are many cases where the cross-section variance is much larger than the variance in the changes over time, especially when the panel observations are not very far apart in time. Although measurement error may also be serially correlated, with the same individual misreporting in the same way at different times, there will be other cases where errors are uncorrelated over time, in which case the error difference will have twice the variance of the errors in levels.

Consider again the two examples of farm productivity and nutritional wages, where individual fixed effects are arguably important. In the first case, m_{xx} is the cross-sectional variance of farm size, while m_Δ is the cross-sectional variance of the change in farm size from one period to another, something that will usually be small or even zero. In the nutritional wage example, there is probably much greater variation in eating habits between people than there is for the same person over time, so that once again, the potential for measurement error to do harm is much enhanced. One rather different case is worth recording since it is a rare example of direct evidence on measurement error. Bound and Krueger (1991) matched earnings data from the U.S. Current Population Survey with Social Security records, and were thus able to calculate the measurement error in the former. They found that measurement error was serially correlated and negatively related to actual earnings. The reliability ratios—the ratios of signal variance to total variance—which are also the multipliers of β in (2.79) and (2.80), fall from 0.82 in levels to 0.65 in differences for men, and from 0.92 to 0.81 for women.

Since measurement error is omnipresent, and because of the relative inefficiency of difference- and within-estimators, we must be careful never to assume that the use of panel data will automatically improve our inference, or to treat the estimate from panel data as a gold standard for judging other estimates. Nevertheless, it is clear that there is more information in a panel than in a single cross section, and that this information can be used to improve inference. Much can be learned from comparing different estimates. If the difference-estimate has a different sign from the cross-sectional estimate, inspection of (2.79) and (2.80) shows that the covariance between x and the heterogeneity must be nonzero; measurement error alone cannot change the signs. When there are several periods of panel data, the difference-estimator (2.77) and the within-estimator (2.78) are mathematically distinct, and in the presence of measurement error will have different probability limits. Griliches and Hausman (1986) show how the comparison of these two estimators can identify the variance of the measurement error when the errors are independent over time—so that consistent estimators can be constructed using (2.66). When errors are correlated over time—as will be the case if households persistently make errors in the same direction—information on measurement error can be obtained by comparing parameters from regressions computed using alternative differences, one period apart, two periods apart, and so on.

Lagged dependent variables and exogeneity in panel data

Although it will not be of great concern for this book, I should also note that there are a number of specific difficulties that arise when panel data are used to estimate regressions containing lagged dependent variables. In ordinary linear regressions, serial correlation in the residuals makes OLS inconsistent in the presence of a lagged dependent variable. In panel data, the presence of unobserved individual heterogeneity will have the same effect; if farm output is affected by unobserved farm quality, so must be last period's output on the same farm, so that this period's residual will be correlated with the lagged dependent variable. Nor can the heterogeneity be dealt with by using the standard within- or difference-estimators. When there is a lagged dependent variable together with unobserved fixed effects, and we difference, the right-hand side of the equation will have the lagged difference $y_{it-1} - y_{it-12}$, and although the fixed effects have been removed by the differencing, there is a differenced error term $u_{it} - u_{it-1}$, which is correlated with the lagged difference because u_{it-1} is correlated with y_{it-1}. Similarly, the within-estimator is inconsistent because the deviation of lagged y_{it-1} from its mean over time is correlated, with the deviation of u_{it} from its mean, not because u_{it} is correlated with y_{it-1}, but because the two means are correlated. These inconsistencies vanish as the number of time periods in the panel increases but, in practice, most panels are short.

Nor are the problems confined to lagged-dependent variables. Even if all the right-hand side variables are uncorrelated with the contemporaneous regression error u_{it}, the deviations from their means can be correlated with the average over time, $u_{i.}$. For this not to be the case, we require that explanatory variables be uncorrelated with the errors at all lags and leads, a requirement that is much more stringent than the usual assumption in time-series work that a variable is predetermined. It is also a requirement that is unlikely to be met in several of the examples I have been discussing. For example, farm yields may depend on farm size, on the weather, on farm inputs such as fertilizer and insecticide, and on (unobserved) quality. The inputs are chosen before the farmer knows output, but a good output in one year may make the farmer more willing, or more able, to use more inputs in a subsequent year. In such circumstances, the within-regression will eliminate the unobservable quality variable, but it will induce a correlation between inputs and the error term, so that the within-estimator will be inconsistent.

These problems are extremely difficult to deal with in a convincing and robust way, although there exist a number of techniques (see in particular Nickell 1981; Chamberlain 1984; Holtz-Eakin, Newey, and Rosen 1988; and particularly the series of papers, Arellano and Bond 1991, Arellano and Bover 1993, and Alonso-Borrego and Arellano 1996). But too much should not be expected from these methods; attempts to disentangle heterogeneity, on the one hand, and dynamics, on the other, have a long and difficult history in various branches of statistics and econometrics.

2.6 Instrumental variables

In all of the cases discussed in Section 2.4, the regression function differs from the structural model because of correlation between the error terms and the explanatory variables. The reasons differ from case to case, but it is the correlation that produces the inconsistency in OLS estimation. The technique of IV is the standard prescription for correcting such cases, and for recovering the structural parameters. Provided it is possible to find instrumental variables that are correlated with the explanatory variables but uncorrelated with the error terms, then IV regression will yield consistent estimates.

For reference, it is useful to record the formulas. If X is the $n \times k$ matrix of explanatory variables, and if W is an $n \times k$ matrix of instruments, then the IV estimator of β is given by

$$(2.81) \qquad \beta_{IV} = (W'X)^{-1}W'y.$$

Since $y = X\beta + u$ and W is orthogonal to u by assumption, (2.81) yields consistent estimators if the premultiplying matrix $W'X$ is of full rank. If there are fewer instruments than explanatory variables—and some explanatory variables will often be suitable to serve as their own instruments—the IV estimate does not exist, and the model is underidentified. When there are exactly as many instruments as explanatory variables, the model is said to be exactly identified. In practice, it is desirable to have more instruments than strictly needed, because the additional instruments can be used either to increase precision or to construct tests. In this overidentified case, suppose that Z is an $n \times k'$ matrix of potential instruments, with $k' > k$. Then all the instruments are used in the construction of the set W by using two-stage least squares, so that at the first stage, each X is regressed on all the instruments Z, with the predicted values used to construct W. If we define the "projection" matrix $P_Z = Z(Z'Z)^{-1}Z'$, the IV estimator is written

$$(2.82) \qquad \beta_{IV} = (X'Z(Z'Z)^{-1}Z'X)^{-1}X'Z(Z'Z)^{-1}Z'y = (X'P_ZX)^{-1}X'P_Zy.$$

Under standard assumptions, β_{IV} is asymptotically normally distributed with mean β and a variance-covariance matrix that can be estimated by

$$(2.83) \qquad V = (XP_ZX)^{-1}(X'P_ZDP_ZX)(XP_ZX)^{-1}.$$

The choice of D depends on the treatment of the variance-covariance matrix of the residuals, and is handled as with OLS, replaced by $\hat{\sigma}^2 I$ under homoskedasticity, or by a diagonal matrix of squared residuals if heteroskedasticity is suspected, or by the appropriate matrix of cluster residuals if the survey is clustered (see (2.30) above). (Note that the residuals must be calculated as $y - X\beta_{IV}$, which is not the vector of residuals from the second stage of two-stage least squares. However, this is hardly ever an issue in practice, since econometric packages make the correction automatically.)

When the model is overidentified, and $k' > k$, the (partial) validity of the instruments is usually assessed by computing an *overidentification* (OID) test statistic. The simplest—and most intuitive—way to calculate the statistic is to regress the IV residuals $y - X\beta_{IV}$ on the matrix of instruments Z and to multiply the resulting (uncentered) R^2 statistic by the sample size n (see Davidson and MacKinnon 1993, pp. 232–37). (The uncentered R^2 is 1 minus the ratio of the sum of squared residuals to the sum of squared dependent variables.) Under the null hypothesis that the instruments are valid, this test statistic is distributed as a χ^2 statistic with $k'-k$ degrees of freedom. This procedure tests whether, contrary to the hypothesis, the instruments play a direct role in determining y, not just an indirect role, through predicting the x's. If the test fails, one or more of the instruments are invalid, and ought to be included in the explanation of y. Put differently, the OID test tells us whether we would get (significantly) different answers if we used different instruments or different combinations of instruments in the regression. This interpretation also clarifies the limitations of the test. It is a test of *over*identification, not of *all* the instruments. If we have only k instruments and k regressors, the model is exactly identified, the residuals of the IV regression are orthogonal to the instruments by construction, so that the OID test is mechanically equal to zero, there is only one way of using the instruments, and no alternative estimates to compare. So the OID test, useful though it is, is only informative when there are more instruments than strictly necessary.

Although estimation by IV is one of the most useful and most used tools of modern econometrics, it does not offer a routine solution for the problems diagnosed in Section 2.4. Just as it is almost always possible to find reasons—measurement error, omitted heterogeneity, selection, or omitted variables—why the structural variables are correlated with the error terms, so is it almost always difficult to find instruments that do not have these problems, while at the same time being related to the structural variables. It is easy to generate estimates that are different from the OLS estimates. What is much harder is to make the case that these estimates are necessarily to be preferred. Credible identification and estimation of structural equations almost always requires real creativity, and creativity cannot be produced to a formula.

Policy evaluation and natural experiments

One promising approach to the selection of instruments, especially for the treatment model, is to look for "natural experiments," cases where different sets of individuals are treated differently in a way that, if not random by design, was effectively so in practice.

One of the best, and certainly earliest, examples is Snow's (1855) analysis of deaths in the London cholera epidemic of 1853–54, work that is cited by Freedman (1991) as a leading example of convincing statistical work in the social sciences. The following is based on Freedman's account. Snow's hypothesis—which was not widely accepted at the time—was that cholera was waterborne. He discovered that households were supplied with water by two different water companies, the Lambeth water company, which in 1849 had moved its water intake to a point in the Thames above the main sewage discharge, and the Southwark and Vauxhall company, whose intake remained below the discharge. There was no sharp separation between houses supplied by the two companies, instead "the mixing of the supply is of the most intimate kind. The pipes of each Company go down all the streets, and into nearly all the courts and alleys. . . . The experiment, too, is on the grandest scale. No fewer than three hundred thousand people of both sexes, of every age and occupation, and of every rank and station, from gentlefolks down to the very poor, were divided into two groups without their choice, and in most cases, without their knowledge; one group supplied with water containing the sewage of London, and amongst it, whatever might have come from the cholera patients, the other group having water quite free from such impurity." Snow collected data on the addresses of cholera victims, and found that there were 8.5 times as many deaths per thousand among households supplied by the Southwark and Vauxhall company.

Snow's analysis can be thought of in terms of instrumental variables. Cholera is not directly caused by the position of a water intake, but by contamination of drinking water. Had it then been possible to do so, an alternative analysis might have linked the probability of contracting cholera to a measure of water purity. But even if such an analysis had shown significant results, it would not have been very convincing. The people who drank impure water were also more likely to be poor, and to live in an environment contaminated in many ways, not least by the "poison miasmas" that were then thought to be the cause of cholera. In terms of the discussion of Section 2.4, the explanatory variable, water purity, is correlated with omitted variables or with omitted individual heterogeneity. The identity of the water supplier is an ideal IV for this analysis. It is correlated with the explanatory variable (water purity) for well-understood reasons, and it is uncorrelated with other explanatory variables because of the "intimate" mixing of supplies and the fact that most people did not even know the identity of their supplier.

There are a number of good examples of natural experiments in the economics literature. Card (1989) shows that the Mariel boatlift, where political events in Cuba led to the arrival of 125,000 Cubans in Miami between May and September 1980, had little apparent effect on wages in Miami, for either Cubans or non-Cubans. Card and Krueger (1994) study fast-food outlets on either side of the border between New Jersey and Pennsylvania around the time of an increase in New Jersey's minimum wage, and find that employment rose in New Jersey relative to Pennsylvania. Another example comes from the studies by Angrist (1990) and Angrist and Krueger (1994) into earnings differences of American males by veteran status. The "treatment" variable is spending time in the military, and the outcome is the effect on wages. The data present somewhat of a puzzle because veterans of World War II appear to enjoy a substantial wage premium over other workers, while veterans of the Vietnam War are typically paid less than other similar workers. The suspicion is that selectivity is important, the argument being that the majority of those who served in Vietnam had relatively low unobservable labor market skills, while in World War II, where the majority served, only those with relatively low skills were excluded from service.

Angrist and Krueger (1994) point out that in the late years of World War II, the selection mechanism acted in such a way that those born early in the year had a (very slightly) higher chance of being selected than those born later in the year. They can then use birth dates as instruments, effectively averaging over all individuals born in the same quarter, so that to preserve variation in the averages, Angrist and Krueger require a very large sample, in this case 300,000 individuals from the 1980 census. (Large sample sizes will often be required by "natural experiments" since instruments that are convincingly uncorrelated with the residuals will often be only weakly correlated with the selection process.) In the IV estimates, the World War II premium is reversed, and earnings are lower for those cohorts who had a larger fraction of veterans. By contrast, Angrist (1990) finds that instrumenting earnings equations for Vietnam veterans using the draft lottery makes little difference to the negative earnings premium experienced by these workers, so that the two studies together suggest that time spent in the military lowers earnings compared with the earnings of those who did not serve.

Impressive as these studies are, natural experiments are not always available when we need them, and some cases yield better instruments than others. Because "natural" experiments are not genuine, randomized experiments, the fact that the experiment is effectively (or quasi-) randomized has to be argued on a case-by-case basis, and the argument is not always as persuasive as in Snow's case. For example, government policies only rarely generate convincing experiments (see Besley and Case 1994). Although two otherwise similar countries (towns, or provinces) may experience different policies, comparison of outcomes is always bedeviled by the concern that the differences are not random, but linked to some characteristic of the country (town or province) that caused the government to draw the distinction in the first place.

However, it may be possible to follow Angrist and Krueger's lead in looking, not at programs themselves, but at the details of their administration. The argument is that in any program with limited resources or limited reach, where some units are treated and some not, the administration of the project is likely to lead, at some level, to choices that are close to random. In the World War II example, it is not the draft that is random, but the fact that local draft boards had to fill quotas, and that the bureaucrats who selected draftees did so partially by order of birth. In other cases, one could imagine people being selected because they are higher in the alphabet than others, or because an administrator used a list constructed for other purposes. While the broad design of the program is likely to be politically and economically motivated, and so cannot be treated as an experiment, natural or otherwise, the details are handled by bureaucrats who are simply trying to get the job done, and who make selections that are effectively random. This is a recipe for project evaluation that calls for intimate knowledge and examination of detail, but it is one that has some prospect of yielding convincing results.

One feature of good natural experiments is their simplicity. Snow's study is a model in this regard. The argument is straightforward, and is easily explained to nonstatisticians or noneconometricians, to whom the concept of instrumental variables could not be readily communicated. Simplicity not only aids communication, but greatly adds to the persuasiveness of the results and increases the likelihood that the results will affect the policy debate. A case in point is the recent political firestorm in the United States over Card and Krueger's (1994) findings on the minimum wage.

Econometric issues for instrumental variables

IV estimators are invaluable tools for handling nonexperimental data. Even so, there are a number of difficulties of which it is necessary to be aware. As with other techniques for controlling for nonexperimental inconsistencies, there is a cost in terms of precision. The variance-covariance matrix (2.83) exceeds the corresponding OLS matrix by a positive definite matrix, so that, even when there is no inconsistency, the IV estimators—and all linear combinations of the IV estimates—will have larger standard errors than their OLS counterparts. Even when OLS is inconsistent, there is no guarantee that in individual cases, the IV estimates will be closer to the truth, and the larger the variance, the less likely it is that they will be so.

It must also be emphasized that the distributional theory for IV estimates is asymptotic, and that asymptotic approximations may be a poor guide to finite sample performance. Formulas exist for the finite sample distributions of IV estimators (see, for example, Anderson and Sawa 1979) but these are typically not sufficiently transparent to provide practical guidance. Nevertheless, a certain amount is known, and this knowledge provides some warnings for practice.

Finite sample distributions of IV estimators will typically be more dispersed with more mass in the tails than either OLS estimators or their own asymptotic distributions. Indeed, IV estimates possess moments only up to the degree of overidentification, so that when there is one instrument for one suspect structural variable, the IV estimate will be so dispersed that its mean does not exist (see Davidson and MacKinnon 1993, 220–4) for further discussion and references. As a result, there will always be the possibility of obtaining extreme estimates, whose presence is not taken into account in the calculation of the asymptotic standard errors. Given sufficient overidentification so that the requisite moments exist— and note that this rules out some of the most difficult cases—Nagar (1959) and Buse (1992) show that in finite samples, IV estimates are biased towards the OLS estimators. This gives support to many students' intuition when first confronted with IV estimation, that it is a clever trick designed to reproduce the OLS estimate as closely as possible while guaranteeing consistency in a (conveniently hypothetical) large sample. In the extreme case, where there are as many instruments as observations so that the first stage of two-stage least squares fits the data perfectly, the IV and OLS estimates are identical. More generally, there is a tradeoff between having too many instruments, overfitting at the first stage, and being biased towards OLS, or having too few instruments, and risking dispersion and extreme estimates. Either way, the asymptotic standard errors on which we routinely rely will not properly indicate the degree of bias or the dispersion.

Nelson and Startz (1990a, 1990b) and Maddala and Jeong (1992) have analyzed the case of a univariate regression where the options are OLS or IV estimation with a single instrument. Their results show that the central tendency of the finite-sample distribution of the IV estimator is biased away from the true value and towards the OLS value. Perhaps most seriously, the asymptotic distribution is a very poor approximation to the finite-sample distribution when the instrument is a poor one, in the sense that it is close to orthogonal to the explanatory variable. Additional evidence of poor performance comes from Bound, Jaeger, and Baker (1993), who show that the empirical results in Angrist and Krueger (1991), who used up to 180 instruments with 30,000 observations, can be closely reproduced with randomly generated instruments. Both sets of results show that poor instruments do not necessarily reveal themselves as large standard errors for the IV estimates. Instead it is easy to produce situations in which y is unrelated to x, and where z is a poor instrument for x, but where the IV estimate of the regression of y on x with z as instrument generates a parameter estimate whose "asymptotic t-value" shows an apparently significant effect. As a result, if IV results are to be credible, it is important to establish first that the instruments do indeed have predictive power for the contaminated right-hand-side variables. This means displaying the first-stage regressions—a practice that is far from routine—or at the least examining and presenting evidence on the explanatory power of the instruments. (Note that when calculating two-stage least squares, the exogenous x variables are also included on the right-hand-side with the instruments, and that it is the predictive power of the latter that must be established, for example, by using an F-test for those variables rather than the R^2 for the regression as a whole.)

In recent work, Staiger and Stock (1993) have proposed a new asymptotic theory for IV when the instruments are only weakly correlated with the regressors, and have produced evidence that their asymptotics provides a good approximation to the finite-sample distribution of IV estimators, even in difficult cases such as those examined by Nelson and Startz. These results may provide a better basis for IV inference in future work.

2.7 Using a time series of cross sections

Although long-running panels are rare in both developed and developing countries, independent cross-sectional household surveys are frequently conducted on a regular basis, sometimes annually, and sometimes less frequently. In Chapter 1, I have already referred to and illustrated from the Surveys of Personal Income Distribution in Taiwan (China), which have been running annually since 1976, and I shall use these data further in this section. Although such surveys select different households in each survey, so that there is no possibility of following *individuals* over time, it is still possible to follow *groups* of people from one survey to another. Obvious examples are the group of the whole population, where we use the surveys to track aggregate data over time, or regional, sectoral, or occupational groups, where we might track the differing fortunes over time of farmers versus government servants, or where we might ask whether poverty is diminishing more rapidly in one region than in another.

Perhaps somewhat less obvious is the use of survey data to follow *cohorts* of individuals over time, where cohorts are defined by date of birth. Provided the population is not much affected by immigration and emigration, and provided the cohort is not so old that its members are dying in significant numbers, we can use successive surveys to follow each cohort over time by looking at the members of the cohort who are randomly selected into each survey. For example, we can look at the average consumption of 30-year-olds in the 1976 survey, of 31-year-olds in the 1977 survey, and so on. These averages, because they relate to the same group of people, have many of the properties of panel data. Cohorts are frequently interesting in their own right, and questions about the gainers and losers from economic development are often conveniently addressed by following such groups over time. Because there are many cohorts alive at one time, cohort data are more diverse and richer than are aggregate data, but their semiaggregated structure provides a link between the microeconomic household-level data and the macroeconomic data from national accounts. The most important measures of living standards, income and consumption, have strong life-cycle age-related components, but the profiles themselves will move upward over time with economic growth as each generation becomes better-off than its predecessors. Tracking different cohorts through successive surveys allows us to disentangle the generational from life-cycle components in income and consumption profiles.

Cohort data: an example

The left-hand top panel of Figure 2.5 shows the averages of real earnings for various cohorts in Taiwan (China) observed from 1976 through to 1990. The data were constructed according to the principles outlined above. For example, for the cohort born in 1941, who were 35 years old in 1976, I used the 1976 survey to calculate the average earnings of all those aged 35, and the result is plotted as the first point in the third line from the left in the figure. The average earnings of 36-year-olds in the 1977 survey is calculated and forms the second point on the same segment. The rest of the line comes from the other surveys, tracking the cohort born in 1941 through the 15 surveys until they are last observed at age 49 in 1990. Table 2.2 shows that there were 699 members of the cohort in the 1976 survey, 624 in the 1977 survey, 879 in the 1978 survey (in which the sample size was increased), and so on until 691 in 1990. The figure illustrates the same process for seven cohorts, born in 1951, 1946, and so on backward at five-year intervals until the oldest, which was born in 1921, and the members of which were 69 years old when last seen in 1990. Although it is possible to make graphs for all

Figure 2.5. Earnings by cohort and their decomposition, Taiwan (China), 1976–90

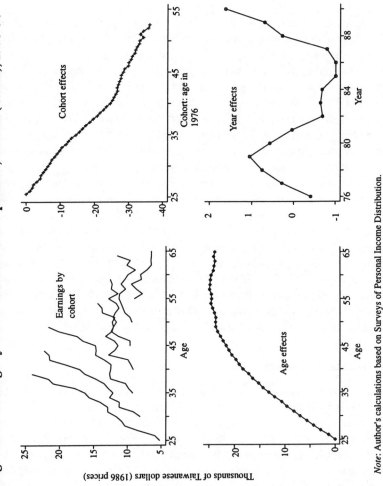

Note: Author's calculations based on Surveys of Personal Income Distribution.

118

Table 2.2. Number of persons in selected cohorts by survey year, Taiwan (China), 1976–90

Year	Cohort: age in 1976						
	25	*30*	*35*	*40*	*45*	*50*	*55*
1976	863	521	699	609	552	461	333
1977	902	604	624	535	585	427	308
1978	1,389	854	879	738	714	629	477
1979	1,351	796	846	708	714	574	462
1980	1,402	834	845	723	746	625	460
1981	1,460	794	807	720	750	624	426
1982	1,461	771	838	695	689	655	496
1983	1,426	737	846	718	702	597	463
1984	1,477	825	820	711	695	541	454
1985	1,396	766	775	651	617	596	442
1986	1,381	725	713	659	664	549	428
1987	1,309	634	775	632	675	513	0
1988	1,275	674	700	617	595	548	0
1989	1,225	672	652	600	609	519	0
1990	1,121	601	691	575	564	508	0

Note: The year is the year of the survey, and the numbers are the numbers of individuals in each cohort sampled in each survey year. 65 is used as an age cutoff, so the oldest cohort is not observed after 1986.
Source: Author's calculations from the Surveys of Personal Income Distribution.

birth years, I have shown only every fifth cohort so as to keep the diagram clear. Note that only members of the same cohort are joined up by connecting lines, and this construction makes it clear when we are following different groups of people or jumping from one cohort to another. (See also Figures 6.3 and 6.4 below for the corresponding graphs for consumption and for a comparison of cross-sectional and cohort plots.)

The top left-hand panel of the figure shows clear age and cohort effects in earnings; it is also possible to detect common macroeconomic patterns for all cohorts. With a very few exceptions at older ages, the lines for the younger cohorts are always above the lines for the older cohorts, even when they are observed at the same age. This is because rapid economic growth in Taiwan (China) is making younger generations better-off, so that, for example, those born in 1951—the youngest, left-most cohort in the figure—have average earnings at age 38 that are approximately twice as much as the earnings at age 38 of the cohort born 10 years earlier—the third cohort in the figure. There is also a pronounced life-cycle profile to earnings, and although the age profile is "broken up" by the cohort effects, it is clear that earnings tend to grow much more rapidly in the early years of the working life than they do after age 50. As a result, not only are the younger cohorts of workers in Taiwan (China) better-off than their predecessors, but they have also experienced much more rapid growth in earnings. The macroeconomic effects in the first panel of Figure 2.5 are perhaps the hardest to see, but note that each connected line segment corresponds to the same contemporaneous span of 15 years in "real" time, 1976–90. Each segment shows the impact of the slowdown in Taiwanese economic growth after the 1979 oil shock. Each cohort has very rapid growth from the second to third year observed, which is 1977–78, somewhat slower growth for the next two years, 1978–80, and then two years of slow or negative growth after the shock. This decomposition into cohort, age, and year effects can be formalized in a way that will work even when the data are not annual and not necessarily evenly spaced, a topic to which I return in the final subsection below. Before that, however, it is useful to use this example to highlight the advantages and disadvantages of cohort data more generally.

Cohort data versus panel data

A useful comparison is between the semiaggregated cohort data and genuine panel data in which individual households are tracked over time. In both cases, we have a time series of observations on a number of units, with units defined as either cohorts or individuals. The cohort data cannot tell us anything about dynamics within the cohorts; each survey tells us about the distribution of the characteristic in the cohort in each period, but two adjacent surveys tell us nothing about the joint distribution of the characteristic in the two periods. In the earnings example, the time series of cross sections can tell us about average earnings for the cohort over time, and it can tell us about inequality of earnings within the cohort and how it is changing over time, but it cannot tell us how long individuals are poor, or whether the people who are rich now were rich or poor at some earlier date. But apart from dynamics, the cohort data can do most of what would be expected of panel data. In particular, and as we shall see in the next subsection, the cohort data can be used to control for unobservable fixed effects just as with panel data, a feature that is often thought to be the main econometric attraction of the latter.

Cohort data also have a number of advantages over most panels. As we have seen in Chapter 1, many panels suffer from attrition, especially in the early years, and so run the risk of becoming increasingly unrepresentative over time. Because the cohort data are constructed from fresh samples every year, there is no attrition. There will be (related) problems with the cohort data if the sampling design changes over time, or if the probabilities of selection into the sample depend on age as, for example, for young men undergoing military training. The way in which the cohort data are used will often be less susceptible to measurement error than is the case with panels. The quantity that is being tracked over time is typically an average (or some other statistic such as the median or other percentile) and the averaging will nearly always reduce the effects of measurement error and enhance the signal-to-noise ratio. In this sense, cohort methods can be regarded as IV methods, where the instruments are grouping variables, whose application averages away the measurement error. Working with aggregated data at a level that is intermediate between micro and macro also brings out the relationship between household behavior and the national aggregates and helps bridge the gap between them; in Figure 2.5, for example, the behavior of the aggregate economy is clearly apparent in the averages of the household data.

It should be emphasized that cohort data can be constructed for any character-istic of the distribution of interest; we are not confined to means. As we shall see in Chapter 6, it can be interesting and useful to study how inequality changes within cohorts over time, and since we have the micro data for each cohort in each year, it is as straightforward to work with measures of dispersion as it is to work with measures of central tendency. Medians can be used instead of means—a technique that is often useful in the presence of outliers—and if the theory sug-gests working with some transform of the data, the transform can be made prior to averaging. When working with aggregate data, theoretical considerations often suggest working with the mean of a logarithm, for example, rather than with the logarithm of the mean. The former is not available from aggregate data, but can be routinely computed from the micro data when calculating the semiaggregated cohort averages.

A final advantage of cohort methods is that they allow the combination of data from different surveys on different households. The means of cohort consumption from an expenditure survey can be combined with the means of cohort income from a labor force survey, and the hybrid data set used to study saving. It is not necessary that all variables are collected from the same households in one survey.

Against the use of cohort data, it should be noted that there are sometimes problems with the assumption that the cohort population is constant, an assump-tion that is needed if the successive surveys are to generate random samples from the same underlying population. I have already noted potential problems with military service, migration, aging, and death. But the more serious difficulties come when we are forced to work, not with individuals, but with households, and to define cohorts of households by the age of the head. If households once formed are indissoluble, there would be no difficulty, but divorce and remarriage reorga-nize households, as does the process whereby older people go to live with their children, so that previously "old" households become "young" households in sub-sequent years. It is usually clear when these problems are serious, and they affect some segments of the population more than others, so that we know which data to trust and which to suspect.

Panel data from successive cross sections

It is useful to consider briefly the issues that arise when using cohort data as if they were repeated observations on individual units. I show first how fixed effects at the individual level carry through to the cohort data, and what steps have to be taken if they are to be eliminated. Consider the simplest univariate model with fixed effects, so that at the level of the individual household, we have (2.76) with a single variable

$$(2.84) \qquad\qquad y_{it} = \alpha + \beta x_{it} + \mu_t + \theta_i + u_{it}$$

where the μ_t are year dummies and θ_i is an individual-specific fixed effect. If there were no fixed effects, it would be possible to average (2.84) over all the households in each cohort in each year to give a corresponding equation for the cohort averages. When there are fixed effects, (2.84) still holds for the cohort population means, with cohort fixed effects replacing the individual fixed effects. However, if we average (2.84) over the members of the cohorts who appear in the survey, and who will be different from year to year, the "fixed effect" will not be fixed, because it is the average of the fixed effects of different households in each year. Because of this sampling effect, we cannot remove the cohort fixed effects by differencing or using within-estimators.

Consider an alternative approach based on the unobservable population means for each cohort. Start from the cohort version of (2.84), and denote population means in cohorts by the subscripts c, so that, simply changing the subscript i to c, we have

$$(2.85) \qquad y_{ct} = \alpha + \beta x_{ct} + \mu_t + \theta_c + u_{ct}$$

and take first differences—the comparable analysis for the within-estimator is left as an exercise—to eliminate the fixed effects so that

$$(2.86) \qquad \Delta y_{ct} = \Delta \mu_t + \beta \Delta x_{ct} + \Delta u_{ct}$$

where the first term is a constant in any given year. This procedure has eliminated the fixed effects, but we are left with the unobservable changes in the population cohort means in place of the sample cohort means, which is what we observe. If we replace Δy and Δx in (2.84) by the observed changes in the sample means, we generate an error-in-variables problem, and the estimates will be attenuated.

There are at least two ways of dealing with this problem. The first is to note that, just as the sample was used to provide an estimate of the cohort mean, it can also be used to provide an estimate of the standard error of the estimate, which in this context is the variance of the measurement error. For the example (2.86), we can use overbars to denote sample means and write

$$(2.87) \qquad \begin{aligned} \Delta \bar{y}_{ct} &= \Delta y_{ct} + \epsilon_{1ct} - \epsilon_{1ct-1} \\ \Delta \bar{x}_{ct} &= \Delta x_{ct} + \epsilon_{2ct} - \epsilon_{2ct-1} \end{aligned}$$

where ϵ_{1ct} and ϵ_{2ct} are sampling errors in the cohort means. Because they come from different surveys with independently selected samples, they are independent over time, and their variances and covariance, σ_1^2, σ_2^2, and σ_{12} are calculated in the usual way, from the variances and covariance in the sample divided by the cohort size (with correction for cluster effects as necessary.) From (2.87), we see that the variances and covariances of the sample cohort means are inflated by the variances and covariances of the sampling errors, but that, if these are subtracted out, we can obtain consistent estimates of β in (2.86) from—cf. also (2.62) above,

$$(2.88) \qquad \tilde{\beta} = \frac{\text{cov}(\Delta \bar{x}_{ct} \Delta \bar{y}_{ct}) - \sigma_{12t} - \sigma_{12t-1}}{\text{var}(\Delta \bar{x}_{ct}) - \sigma_{2t}^2 - \sigma_{2t-1}^2}$$

and where, for illustrative purposes, I have assumed that there are only two time periods t and $t-1$. The standard error for (2.88) can be calculated using the bootstrap or the delta method—discussed in the next section—which can also take into account the fact that the variance and covariances of the sampling errors are estimated (see Deaton 1985, who also discusses the multivariate case, and Fuller 1987, who gives a general treatment for a range of similar models).

Another possible estimation strategy is to use IV, with changes from earlier years used as instruments. Since the successive samples are independently drawn, changes in cohort means from $t-2$ to $t-1$ are measured independently of the change from t to $t+1$. In some cases, the cohort samples may be large enough and the means precisely enough estimated so that these corrections are small enough to ignore. In any case, it is a good idea to check the standard errors of the cohort means, to make sure that regression results are not being dominated by sampling effects, and if so, to increase the cohort sizes, for example, by working with five-year age bands instead of single years. In some applications, this might be desirable on other grounds; in some countries, people do not know their dates of birth well enough to be able to report age accurately, and reported ages "heap" at numbers ending in 5 and 0.

Decompositions by age, cohort, and year

A number of the quantities most closely associated with welfare, including family size, earnings, income, and consumption, have distinct and characteristic life-cycle profiles. Wage rates, earnings, and saving usually have hump-shaped age profiles, rising to their maximum in the middle years of life, and declining somewhat thereafter. The natural process of bearing and raising children induces a similar profile in average family size. Moreover, all of these quantities are subject to secular variation; consumption, earnings, and incomes rise over time with economic development, and family size decreases as countries pass through the demographic transition. In consequence, even if the shape of the age profiles remains the same for successive generations, their position will shift from one to the next. The age profile from a single cross section confounds the age profile with the generational or cohort effects. For example, a cross-sectional earnings profile will tend to exaggerate the downturn in earnings at the highest age because, as we look at older and older individuals, we are not just moving along a given age-earnings profile, but we are also moving to ever lower lifetime profiles. The cohort data described in this section allow us to track the same cohort over several years and thus to avoid the difficulty; indeed, the Taiwanese earnings example in Figure 2.5 provides a clear example of the differences between the age profiles of different cohorts. In many cases, diagrams like Figure 2.5 will tell us all that we need to know. However, since each cohort is only observed for a limited period of time, it is useful to have a technique for linking together the age profiles from different cohorts to generate a single complete life-cycle age profile. This is particularly true when there is only a limited number of surveys, and the intervals between them are more than one year. In such cases, diagrams like Figure 2.5 are harder to draw, and a good deal less informative.

In this subsection, I discuss how the cohort data can be decomposed into age effects, cohort effects, and year effects, the first to give the typical age profile, the second the secular trends that lead to differences in the positions of age profiles for different cohorts, and the third the aggregate effects that synchronously but temporarily move all cohorts off their profiles. These decompositions are based on models and are certainly not free of structural assumptions; they assume away interaction effects between age, cohort, and years, so that, for example, the shape of age profiles is unaffected by changes in their position, and the appropriateness and usefulness of the assumption has to be judged on a case-by-case basis.

To make the analysis concrete, consider the case of the lifetime consumption profile. If the growth in living standards acts so as to move up the consumption-age profiles proportionately, it makes sense to work in logarithms, and to write the logarithm of consumption as

$$(2.89) \qquad\qquad \ln c_{ct} = \beta + \alpha_a + \gamma_c + \psi_t + u_{ct}$$

where the superscripts c and t (as usual) refer to cohort and time (year), and a refers to age, defined here as the age of cohort c in year t. In this particular case, (2.89) can be given a theoretical interpretation, since according to life-cycle theory under certainty, consumption is the product of lifetime wealth, the cohort aggregate of which is constant over time, and an age effect, which is determined by preferences (see Section 6.1 below). In other contexts where there is no such theory, the decomposition is often a useful descriptive device, as for earnings in Taiwan (China), where it is hard to look at the top left-hand panel of Figure 2.5 without thinking about an age and cohort decomposition.

In order to implement a model like (2.89), we need to decide how to label cohorts. A convenient way to do so is to choose c as the age in year $t=0$. By this, c is just a number like a and t. We can then choose to restrict the age, cohort, and year effects in (2.89) in various different ways. In particular, we can choose polynomials or dummies. For the year effects, where there is no obvious pattern *a priori*, dummy variables would seem to be necessary, but age effects could reasonably be modeled as a cubic, quartic, or quintic polynomial in age, and cohort effects, which are likely to be trend-like, might even be adequately handled as linear in c. Given the way in which we have defined cohorts, with bigger values of c corresponding to older cohorts, we would expect γ_c to be declining with c. When data are plentiful, as in the Taiwanese case, there is no reason not to use dummy variables for all three sets of effects, and thus to allow the data to choose any pattern.

Suppose that A is a matrix of age dummies, C a matrix of cohort dummies, and Y a matrix of year dummies. The cohort data are arranged as cohort-year pairs, with each "observation" corresponding to a single cohort in a specific year. If there are m such cohort-year pairs, the three matrices will each have m rows; the number of columns will be the number of ages (or age groups), the number of cohorts, and the number of years, respectively. The model (2.89) can then be written in the form

$$(2.90) \qquad\qquad y = \beta + A\alpha + C\gamma + Y\psi + u$$

where y is the stacked vector of cohort-year observations—each row corresponds to a single observation on a cohort—on the cohort means of the logarithm of consumption. As usual, we must drop one column from each of the three matrices, since for the full matrices, the sum of the columns is a column of ones, which is already included as the constant term.

However, even having dropped these columns, it is still impossible to estimate (2.90) because there is an additional linear relationship across the three matrices. The problem lies in the fact that if we know the date, and we know when a cohort was born, then we can infer the cohort's age. Indeed, since c is the age of the cohort in year 0, we have

$$(2.91) \qquad\qquad a_{ct} = c + t$$

which implies that the matrices of dummies satisfy

$$(2.92) \qquad\qquad A s_a = C s_c + Y s_y$$

where the s vectors are arithmetic sequences $\{0,1,2,3,\ldots,\}$ of the length given by the number of columns of the matrix that premultiplies them. Equation (2.92) is a single identity, so that to estimate the model it is necessary to drop one more column from any one of the three matrices.

The normalization of age, cohort, and year effects has been discussed in different contexts by a number of authors, particularly Hall (1971), who provides an admirably clear account in the context of embodied and disembodied technical progress for different vintages of pickup trucks, and by Weiss and Lillard (1978), who are concerned with age, vintage, and time effects in the earnings of scientists. The treatment here is similar to Hall's, but is based on that given in Deaton and Paxson (1994a). Note first that in (2.90), we can replace the parameter vectors α, γ, and ψ by

$$(2.93) \qquad\qquad \tilde{\alpha} = \alpha + \kappa s_a, \quad \tilde{\gamma} = \gamma - \kappa s_c, \quad \tilde{\psi} = \psi - \kappa s_y$$

for any scalar constant κ, and by (2.92) there will be no change in the predicted value of y in (2.87). According to (2.90), a time-trend can be added to the age dummies, and the effects offset by subtracting time-trends from the cohort dummies and the year dummies.

Since these transformations are a little hard to visualize, and a good deal more complicated than more familiar dummy-variable normalizations, it is worth considering examples. Suppose first that consumption is constant over cohorts, ages, and years, so that the curves in Figure 2.5 degenerate to a single straight line with slope 0. Then we could "decompose" this into a positive age effect, with consumption growing at (say) five percent for each year of age, and offset this by a negative year effect of five percent a year. According to this, each cohort would get a five percent age bonus each year, but would lose it to a macroeconomic effect whereby everyone gets five percent less than in the previous year. If this were all, younger cohorts would get less than older cohorts at the same age, because they come along later in time. To offset this, we need to give each cohort five percent more than the cohort born the year previously which, since the older cohorts have higher cohort numbers, means a negative trend in the cohort effects. More realistically, suppose that when we draw Figure 2.5, we find that the consumption of each cohort is growing at three percent a year, and that each successive cohort's profile is three percent higher than that of its predecessor. Everyone gets three percent more a year as they age, and starting consumption rises by three percent a year. This situation can be represented (exactly) by age effects that rise linearly with age added to cohort effects that fall linearly with age by the same amount each year; note that cohorts are labeled by age at a fixed date, so that older cohorts (larger *c*) are poorer, not richer. But the same data can be represented by a time-trend of three percent a year in the age effects, without either cohort or year effects.

In practice, we choose a normalization that is most suitable for the problem at hand, attributing time-trends to year effects, or to matching age and cohort effects. In the example here, where consumption or earnings is the variable to be decomposed, a simple method of presentation is to attribute growth to age and cohort effects, and to use the year effects to capture cyclical fluctuations or business-cycle effects that average to zero over the long run. A normalization that accomplishes this makes the year effects orthogonal to a time-trend, so that, using the same notation as above,

$$(2.94) \qquad\qquad s_y' \psi = 0.$$

The simplest way to estimate (2.90) subject to the normalization (2.94) is to regress y on (a) dummies for each cohort excluding (say) the first, (b) dummies for each age excluding the first, and (c) a set of $T-2$ year dummies defined as follows, from $t = 3, .., T$

$$(2.95) \qquad\qquad d_t^* = d_t - [(t-1)d_2 - (t-2)d_1]$$

where d_t is the usual year dummy, equal to 1 if the year is t and 0 otherwise. This procedure enforces the restriction (2.94) as well as the restriction that the year dummies add to zero. The coefficients of the d_i^* give the third through final year coefficients; the first and second can be recovered from the fact that all year effects add to zero and satisfy (2.94).

This procedure is dangerous when there are few surveys, where it is difficult to separate trends from transitory shocks. In the extreme case where there are only two years, the method would attribute any increase in consumption between the first and second years to an increasing age profile combined with growth from older to younger cohorts. Only when there are sufficient years for trend and cycle to be separated can we make the decomposition with any confidence.

The three remaining panels of Figure 2.5 show the decomposition of the earnings averages into age, cohort, and year dummies. The cohort effects in the top right-hand panel are declining with age; the earlier you are born, the older you are in 1976, and age in 1976 is the cohort measure. Although the picture is one that is close to steady growth from cohort to cohort, there has been a perceptible acceleration in the rate of growth for the younger cohorts. The bottom left-hand panel shows the estimated age effects; according to this, wages are a concave function of age, and although there is little wage increase after age 50, there is no clear turning down of the profile. Although the top left panel creates an impression of a hump-shaped age profile of earnings, much of the impression comes from the cohort effects, not the age effects, and although the oldest cohort shown has declining wages from ages 58 through 65, other cohorts observed at the same ages do not display the same pattern. (Note that only every fifth cohort is included in the top left panel, but all cohorts are included in the regressions, subject only to age lying being between 25 and 65 inclusive.) The final panel shows the year effects, which are estimated to be much smaller in magnitude than either the cohort or age effects; nevertheless they show a distinctive pattern, with the economy growing much faster than trend at the beginning and end of the period, and much more slowly in the middle after the 1979 oil shock.

Age and cohort profiles such as those in Figure 2.5 provide the material for examining the structural consequences of changes in the rates of growth of population and real income. For example, if the age profiles of consumption and income are determined by tastes and technology, and are invariant to changes in the rate of economic growth, we can change the cohort effects holding the age effects constant and thus derive the effects of growth on aggregates of consumption, saving, and income. Changes in population growth rates redistribute the population over the various ages, so that, once again, we can use the age profiles as the basis for aggregating over different age distributions of the population. Much previous work has been forced to rely on single cross sections to estimate age profiles, and while this is sometimes the best that can be done, cross-sectional age profiles confuse the cohort and age effects, and will typically give much less reliable estimates than the methods discussed in this section. I return to these techniques in the final chapter when I come to examine household saving behavior.

2.8 Two issues in statistical inference

This final section deals briefly with two topics that will be required at various points in the rest of the book, but which do not fit easily into the rest of this chapter. The first deals with a situation that often arises in practice, when the parameters of interest are not the parameters that are estimated, but functions of them. I briefly explain the "delta" method which allows us to transform the variance-covariance matrix of the estimated parameters into the variance-covariance matrix of the parameters of interest, so that we can construct hypothesis tests for the latter. Even when we want to use the bootstrap to generate confidence intervals, asymptotic approximation to variances are useful starting points that can be improved using the bootstrap (see Section 1.4). The second topic is concerned with sample size, and its effects on statistical inference. Applied econometricians often express the view that rejecting a hypothesis using 100 observations does not have the same meaning as rejecting a hypothesis using 10,000 observations, and that null hypotheses are more often rejected the larger is the sample size. Household surveys vary in size from a few hundred to tens or even hundreds of thousands of observations, so that if inference is indeed the hostage of sample size, it is important to be aware of exactly what is going on, and how to deal with it in practice.

Parameter transformations: the delta method

Suppose that we have estimates of a parameter vector β, but that the parameters of interest are not β, but some possibly nonlinear transformation α, where

$$(2.96) \qquad\qquad \alpha = h(\beta)$$

for some known vector of differentiable functions h. In general, this function will also depend on the data, or on some characteristics of the data such as sample means. It will also usually be the case that α and β will have different numbers of elements, k for β and q for α, with $q \le k$. Our estimation method has yielded an estimate $\hat{\beta}$ for β and an associated variance-covariance matrix V_β for which an estimate is also available. The delta method is a means of transforming V_β into V_α; a good formal account is contained in Fuller (1987, pp. 85–88). Here I confine myself to a simple intuitive outline.

Start by substituting the estimate of β to obtain the obvious estimate of α, $\hat{\alpha} = h(\hat{\beta})$. If we then take a Taylor series approximation of $\hat{\alpha} = h(\hat{\beta})$ around the true value of β, we have for $i = 1 \ldots q$,

$$(2.97) \qquad\qquad \hat{\alpha}_i \approx \alpha_i + \sum_{j=1}^{k} \frac{\partial h_i}{\partial \beta_j} (\hat{\beta}_j - \beta_j)$$

or in an obvious matrix notation

$$(2.98) \qquad\qquad \hat{\alpha} - \alpha \approx H(\hat{\beta} - \beta).$$

The matrix H is the $q \times k$ Jacobian matrix of the transformation. If we then post-multiply (2.98) by its transpose and take expectations, we have

$$(2.99) \qquad\qquad V_\alpha \approx H V_\beta H'.$$

In practice (2.99) is evaluated by replacing the three terms on the right-hand side by their estimates calculated from the estimated parameters. The estimate of the matrix H can either be programmed directly once the differentiation has been done analytically, or the computer can be left to do it, either using the analytical differentiation software that is increasingly incorporated into some econometric packages, or by numerical differentiation around the estimates of β.

Variance-covariance matrices from the delta method are often employed to calculate Wald test statistics for hypotheses that place nonlinear restrictions on the parameters. The procedure follows immediately from the analysis above by writing the null hypothesis in the form:

(2.100) $$H_0: \alpha = h(\beta) = 0$$

for which we can compute the Wald statistic

(2.101) $$W = \hat{\alpha}' V_\alpha^{-1} \hat{\alpha}.$$

Under the null hypothesis, W is asymptotically distributed as χ^2 with q degrees of freedom. For this to work, the matrix V_α has to be nonsingular, for which a necessary condition is that q be no larger than k; clearly we must not try to test the same restriction more than once.

As usual, some warnings are in order. These results are valid only as large-sample approximations, and may be seriously misleading in finite samples. For example, the ratio of two normally distributed variables has a Cauchy distribution which does not possess any moments, yet the delta method will routinely provide a "variance" for this case. In the context of the Wald tests of nonlinear restrictions, there are typically many different ways of writing the restrictions, and unless the sample size is large and the hypothesis correct, these will all lead to different values of the Wald test (see Gregory and Veall 1985 and Davidson and MacKinnon 1993, pp. 463–71, for further discussion).

Sample size and hypothesis tests

Consider the frequently encountered situation where we wish to test a simple null hypothesis against a compound alternative, that $\beta = \beta_0$ for some known β_0 against the alternative $\beta \neq \beta_0$. A typical method for conducting such a test would be to calculate some statistic from the data and to see how far it is from the value that it would assume under the null, with the size of the discrepancy acting as evidence against the null hypothesis. Most obviously, we might estimate β itself without imposing the restriction, and compare its value with β_0. Likelihood-ratio tests—or other measures based on fit—compare how well the model fits the data at unrestricted and restricted estimates of β. Score—or Lagrange multiplier—tests calculate the derivative of the criterion function at β_0, on the grounds that non-zero values indicate that there are better-fitting alternatives nearby, so casting doubt on the null. All of these supply a measure of the failure of the null, and our acceptance and rejection of the hypothesis can be based on how big is the measure.

The real differences between different methods of hypothesis testing come, not in the selection of the measure, but in the setting of a critical value, above which we reject the hypothesis on the grounds that there is too much evidence against it, and below which we accept it, on the grounds that the evidence is not strong enough to reject. Classical statistical procedures—which dominate econometric practice—set the critical value in such a way that the probability of rejecting the null when it is correct, the probability of Type I error, or the *size* of the test, is fixed at some preassigned level, for example, five or one percent. In the ideal situation, it is possible under the null hypothesis to derive the sampling distribution of the quantity that is being used as evidence against the null, so that critical values can be calculated that will lead to exactly five (one) percent of rejections when the null is true. Even when this cannot be done, the asymptotic distribution of the test statistic can usually be derived, and if this is used to select critical values, the null will be rejected five percent of the time when the sample size is sufficiently large. These procedures take no explicit account of the *power* of the test, the probability that the null hypothesis will be rejected when it is false, or its complement, the Type II error, the probability of *not* rejecting the null when it is false. Indeed, it is hard to see how these errors can be controlled because the power depends on the unknown true values of the parameter, and tests will typically be more powerful the further is the truth from the null.

That classical procedures can generate uncomfortable results as the sample size increases is something that is often expressed informally by practitioners, and the phenomenon has been given an excellent treatment by Leamer (1978, pp. 100– 120), and it is on his discussion that the following is based.

The effect most noted by empirical researchers is that the null hypothesis seems to be more frequently rejected in large samples than in small. Since it is hard to believe that the truth depends on the sample size, something else must be going on. If the critical values are exact, and if the null hypothesis is exactly true, then by construction the null hypothesis will be rejected the same fraction of times in all sample sizes; there is nothing wrong with the logic of the classical tests. But consider what happens when the null is not exactly true, or alternatively, that what we mean when we say that the null is true is that the parameters are "close" to the null, "close" referring to some economic or substantive meaning that is not formally incorporated into the statistical procedure. As the sample size increases, and provided we are using a consistent estimation procedure, our estimates will be closer and closer to the truth, and less dispersed around it, so that discrepancies that were undetectable with small sample sizes will lead to rejections in large samples. Larger sample sizes are like greater resolving power on a telescope; features that are not visible from a distance become more and more sharply delineated as the magnification is turned up.

Over-rejection in large samples can also be thought about in terms of Type I and Type II errors. When we hold Type I error fixed and increase the sample size, all the benefits of increased precision are implicitly devoted to the reduction of Type II error. If there are equal probabilities of rejecting the null when it is true and not rejecting it when it is false at a sample size of 100, say, then at 10,000, we will have essentially no chance of accepting it when it is false, even though we are still rejecting it five percent of the time when it is true. For economists, who are used to making tradeoffs and allocating resources efficiently, this is a very strange thing to do. As Leamer points out, the standard defense of the fixed size for classical tests is to protect the null, controlling the probability of rejecting it when it is true. But such a defense is clearly inconsistent with a procedure that devotes none of the benefit of increased sample size to lowering the probability that it will be so rejected.

Repairing these difficulties requires that the critical values of test statistics be raised with the sample size, so that the benefits of increased precision are more equally allocated between reduction in Type I and Type II errors. That said, it is a good deal more difficult to decide exactly how to do so, and to derive the rule from basic principles. Since classical procedures cannot provide such a basis, Bayesian alternatives are the obvious place to look. Bayesian hypothesis testing is based on the comparison of posterior probabilities, and so does not suffer from the fundamental asymmetry between null and alternative that is the source of the difficulty in classical tests. Nevertheless, there are difficulties with the Bayesian methods too, perhaps most seriously the fact that the ratio of posterior probabilities of two hypotheses is affected by their prior probabilities, no matter what the sample size. Nevertheless, the Bayesian approach has produced a number of procedures that seem attractive in practice, several of which are reviewed by Leamer.

It is beyond the scope of this section to discuss the Bayesian testing procedures in any detail. However, one of Leamer's suggestions, independently proposed by Schwarz (1978) in a slightly different form, and whose derivation is also insightfully discussed by Chow (1983, pp. 300–2), is to adjust the critical values for F and χ^2 tests. Instead of using the standard tabulated values, the null is rejected when the calculated F-value exceeds the logarithm of the sample size, $\ln n$, or when a χ^2 statistic for q restrictions exceeds $q \ln n$. To illustrate, when the sample size is 100, the null hypothesis would be rejected only if calculated F-statistics are larger than 4.6, a value that would be doubled to 9.2 when working with sample sizes of 10,000.

In my own work, some of which is discussed in the subsequent chapters of this book, I have often found these Leamer-Schwarz critical values to be useful. This is especially true in those cases where the theory applies most closely, when we are trying to choose between a restricted and unrestricted model, and when we have no particular predisposition either way except perhaps simplicity, and we want to know whether it is safe to work with the simpler restricted model. If the Leamer- Schwarz criterion is too large, experience suggests that such simplifications are indeed dangerous, something that is not true for classical tests, where large-sample rejections can often be ignored with impunity.

2.9 Guide to further reading

The aim of this chapter has been to extract from the recent theoretical and applied econometric literature material that is useful for the analysis of household-level data. The source of the material was referenced as it was introduced, and in most cases, there is little to consult apart from these original papers. I have assumed that the reader has a good working knowledge of econometrics at the level of an advanced undergraduate, masters', or first-year graduate course in econometrics covering material such as that presented in Pindyck and Rubinfeld (1991). At the same level, the text by Johnston and DiNardo (1996) is also an excellent starting point and, on many topics, adopts an approach that is sympathetic to that taken here. A more advanced text that covers a good deal of the modern theoretical material is Davidson and MacKinnon (1993), but like other texts it is not written from an applied perspective. Cramer (1969), although now dated, is one of the few genuine applied econometrics texts, and contains a great deal that is still worth reading, much of it concerned with the analysis of survey data. Some of the material on clustering is discussed in Chapter 2 of Skinner, Holt, and Smith (1989). Groves (1989, ch. 6) contains an excellent discussion of weighting in the context of modeling versus description. The STATA manuals, Stata Corporation (1993), are in many cases well ahead of the textbooks, and provide brief discussions and references on each of the topics with which they deal.

3 Welfare, poverty, and distribution

One of the main reasons for collecting survey data on household consumption and income is to provide information on living standards, on their evolution over time, and on their distribution over households. Living standards of the poorest parts of the population are of particular concern, and survey data provide the principal means for estimating the extent and severity of poverty. Consumption data on specific commodities tell us who consumes how much of what, and can be used to examine the distributional consequences of price changes, whether induced by deliberate policy decisions or as a result of weather, world prices, or other exogenous forces. In this chapter, I provide a brief overview of the theory and practice of welfare measurement, including summary measures of living standards, of poverty, and of inequality, with illustrations from the Living Standards Surveys of Côte d'Ivoire from 1985 through 1988 and of South Africa in 1993. I also discuss the use of survey data to examine the welfare effects of pricing and of transfer policies using as examples pricing policy for rice in Thailand and pensions in South Africa.

The use of survey data to investigate living standards is often straightforward, requiring little statistical technique beyond the calculation of measures of central tendency and dispersion. Although there are deep and still-controversial conceptual issues in deciding how to measure welfare, poverty, and inequality, the measurement itself is direct in that there is no need to estimate behavioral responses nor to construct the econometric models required to do so. Instead, the focus is on the data themselves, and on the best way to present reliable and robust measures of welfare. Graphical techniques are particularly useful and can be used to describe the whole distribution of living standards, rather than focussing on a few summary statistics. For example, the Lorenz curve is a standard tool for charting inequality, and in recent work, good use has been made of the cumulative distribution function to explore the robustness of poverty measures. For other questions it is useful to be able to display (univariate and bivariate) density functions, for example when looking at two measures of living standards such as expenditures and nutritional status, or when investigating the incidence of price changes in relation to the distribution of real incomes. While cross-tabulations and histograms are the traditional tools for charting densities, it is often more informative to calculate nonparametric estimates of densities using one of the smoothing methods that have recently been developed in the statistical literature. One of the purposes of this chapter is to explain these methods in simple terms, and to illustrate their usefulness for the measurement of welfare and the evaluation of policy.

The chapter consists of three sections. Section 3.1 is concerned with welfare measurement, and Section 3.3 with the distributional effects of price changes and cash transfers. Each section begins with a brief theoretical overview and continues with empirical examples. The techniques of nonparametric density estimation are introduced in the context of living standards in Section 3.2 and are used extensively in Section 3.3 This last section shows how regression functions—conditional expectations—can often provide direct answers to questions about distributional effects of policy changes, and I discuss the use of nonparametric regression as a simple tool for calculating and presenting these regression functions.

3.1 Living standards, inequality, and poverty

Perhaps the most straightforward way to think about measuring living standards and their distribution is a purely statistical one, with the mean, median, or mode representing the central tendency and various measures of dispersion—such as the variance or interquartile range—used to measure inequality. However, greater conceptual clarity comes from a more theoretical approach, and specifically from the use of social welfare functions as pioneered by Atkinson (1970). This is the approach that I follow here, beginning with social welfare functions, and then using them to interpret measures of inequality and poverty.

Social welfare

Suppose that we have decided on a suitable measure of living standards, denoted by x; this is typically a measure of per capita household real income or consumption, but there are other possibilities, and the choices are discussed below. We denote the value of social welfare by W and write it as a nondecreasing function of all the x's in the population, so that

$$(3.1) \qquad W = V(x_1, x_2, \ldots, x_N)$$

where N is the population size. Although our data often come at the level of the household, it is hard to give meaning to household or family welfare without starting from the welfare of its members. In consequence, the x's in (3.1) should be thought of as relating to individuals, and N to the number of persons in the population. The issue of how to move from household data to individual welfare is an important and difficult one, and I shall return to it.

It is important not to misinterpret a social welfare function in this context. In particular, it should definitely not be thought of as the objective function of a government or policymaking agency. There are few if any countries for which the maximization of (3.1) subject to constraints would provide an adequate description of the political economy of decisionmaking. Instead, (3.1) should be seen as a statistical "aggregator" that turns a distribution into a single number that provides an overall judgment on that distribution and that forces us to think coherently about welfare and its distribution. Whatever our view of the policymaking process, it is always useful to think about policy in terms of its effects on efficiency and on equity, and (3.1) should be thought of as a tool for organizing our thoughts in a coherent way.

What is the nature of the function V, and how is it related to the usual concepts? When V is increasing in each of its arguments, social welfare is greater whenever any one individual is better-off and no one is worse-off, so that Pareto improvements are always improvements in social welfare. For judging the effects of any policy, we shall almost always want this *Pareto condition* to be satisfied. However, as we shall see, it is often useful to think about poverty measurement in terms of social welfare, and this typically requires a social welfare function that is unresponsive to increases in welfare among the nonpoor. This case can be accommodated by weakening the Pareto condition to the requirement that V be *nondecreasing* in each of its arguments.

Social welfare functions are nearly always assumed to have a *symmetry* or *anonymity* property, whereby social welfare depends only on the list of welfare levels in society, and not on who has which welfare level. This makes sense only if the welfare levels are appropriately defined. Money income does not translate into the same level of living at different price levels, and a large household can hardly be as well-off as a smaller one unless it has more money to spend. I shall return to this issue below, when I discuss the definition of x, and in Chapter 4, when I discuss the effects of household composition on welfare.

Finally, and perhaps most importantly, social welfare functions are usually assumed to prefer more equal distributions to less equal ones. If we believe that inequality is undesirable, or equivalently that a gift to an individual should increase social welfare in (3.1) by more when the recipient is poorer, then for any given total of x—and ignoring any constraints on feasible allocations—social welfare will be maximized when all x's are equal. (Note that policies that seek to promote equality will often have incentive effects, so that a preference for equality is not the same as a claim that equality is desirable once the practical constraints are taken into account.) Equity preference will be guaranteed if the function V has the same properties as a standard utility function, with diminishing marginal utility to each x, or more formally, when it is quasi-concave, so that when we draw social indifference curves over the different x's, they are convex to the origin. Quasi-concavity of V means that if x^1 and x^2 are two lists of x's, with one element for each person, and if $V(x^1) = V(x^2)$ so that the two allocations are equally socially valuable, then any weighted average, $\lambda x^1 + (1-\lambda)x^2$ for λ between 0 and 1, will have as high or higher social welfare. A weighted average of any two equally good allocations is at least as good as either. In particular, quasi-concavity implies that social welfare will be increased by any transfer of x from a richer to a poorer person, provided only that the transfer is not sufficiently large to reverse their relative positions. This is the "principle of transfers," originally proposed by Dalton (1920). It should be noted that the principle of transfers does not require quasi-concavity, but a weaker condition called "s-concavity" (see Atkinson 1992 for a survey and more detailed discussion).

Inequality and social welfare

For the purposes of passing from social welfare to measures of inequality, it is convenient that social welfare be measured in the same units as individual welfare, so that proportional changes in all x's have the same proportional effect on the aggregate. This will happen if the function V is homogeneous of degree one, or has been transformed by a monotone increasing transform to make it so. Provided the transform has been made, we can rewrite (3.1) as

$$(3.2) \qquad W = \mu V(\frac{x_1}{\mu}, \ldots, \frac{x_N}{\mu})$$

where μ is the mean of the x's. Equation (3.2) gives a separation between the mean value of x and its distribution, and will allow us to decompose changes in social welfare into changes in the mean and changes in a suitably defined measure of inequality. Finally, we choose units so that $V(1,1,\ldots,1) = 1$, so that when there is perfect equality, and everyone has the mean level of welfare, social welfare is also equal to that value.

Since social welfare is equal to μ when the distribution of x's is perfectly equal, then, by the principle of transfers, social welfare for any unequal allocation cannot be greater than the mean of the distribution μ. Hence we can write (3.2) as

$$(3.3) \qquad W = \mu (1-I)$$

where I is defined by the comparison of (3.2) and (3.3), and represents the cost of inequality, or the amount by which social welfare falls short of the maximum that would be attained under perfect equality. I is a measure of inequality, taking the value zero when the x's are equally distributed, and increasing with disequalizing transfers. Since the inequality measure is a scaled version of the function V with a sign change, it satisfies the principle of transfers in reverse, so that any change in distribution that involves a transfer from rich to poor will decrease I as defined by (3.2) and (3.3).

Figure 3.1 illustrates social welfare and inequality measures for the case of a two-person economy. The axes show the amount of x for each of the two consumers, and the point S marks the actual allocation or status quo. Since the social welfare function is symmetric, the point S', which is the reflection of S in the 45-degree line, must lie on the same social welfare contour, which is shown as the line SBS'. Allocations along the straight line SCS' (which will not generally be feasible) correspond to the same total x, and those between S and S' have higher values of social welfare. The point B is the point on the 45-degree line that has the same social welfare as does S; although there is less x per capita at B than at S, the equality of distribution makes up for the loss in total. The amount of x at B is

Figure 3.1. Measuring inequality from social welfare

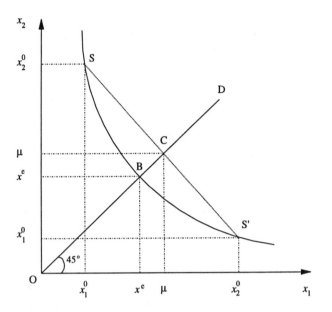

denoted x^e, and is referred to by Atkinson as "equally distributed equivalent x." *Equality* is measured by the ratio OB/OC, or by x^e/μ, a quantity that will be unity if everyone has the same, or if the social welfare contours are straight lines perpendicular to the 45-degree line. This is the case where "a dollar is a dollar" whoever receives it so that there is no perceived inequality. Atkinson's measure of inequality, defined by (3.3), is shown in the diagram as the ratio BC/OC.

One of the advantages of the social welfare approach to inequality measurement, as embodied in (3.3), is that it precludes us from making the error of interpreting measures of inequality *by themselves* as measures of welfare. It will sometimes be the case that inequality will increase at the same time that social welfare is increasing. For example, if everyone gets better-off, but the rich get more than the poor, inequality will rise, but there has been a Pareto improvement, and most observers would see the new situation as an improvement on the original one. When inequality is seen as a component of social welfare, together with mean levels of living, we also defuse those critics who point out that a focus on inequality misdirects attention away from the living standards of the poorest (see in particular Streeten et al 1981). Atkinson's formulation is entirely consistent with an approach that pays attention only to the needs of the poor or of the poorest groups, provided of course that we measure welfare through (3.3), and not through (negative) I alone. Just to reinforce the point, we might define a "basic-needs" social welfare function to be the average consumption of the poorest five percent of society, μ^p say. This measure can be rewritten as $\mu(1 - I)$, where I is the inequality measure $1 - \mu^p/\mu$.

Measures of inequality

Given this basic framework, we can generate measures of inequality by specifying a social welfare function and solving for the inequality measure, or we can start from a standard statistical measure of inequality, and enquire into its consistency with the principle of transfers and with a social welfare function. The first approach is exemplified by Atkinson's own inequality measure. This starts from the additive social welfare function

$$(3.4a) \qquad W = \frac{1}{N} \sum_{i=1}^{N} \frac{x_i^{1-\epsilon}}{1-\epsilon}, \quad \epsilon \neq 1$$

$$(3.4b) \qquad \ln W = \frac{1}{N} \sum_{i=1}^{N} \ln x_i, \quad \epsilon = 1.$$

The parameter $\epsilon \geq 0$ controls the degree of "inequality aversion" or the degree to which social welfare trades off mean living standards on the one hand for equality of the distribution on the other. In Figure 3.1, social welfare indifference curves are flatter when ϵ is small, so that, for the same initial distribution S, the point B moves closer to the origin as ϵ increases.

Atkinson's social welfare function, which will also prove useful in the tax reform analysis of Chapter 5, has the property that the ratio of marginal social utilities of two individuals is given by the reciprocal of the ratio of their x's raised to the power of ϵ:

$$(3.5) \qquad \frac{\partial W/\partial x_i}{\partial W/\partial x_j} = (x_j/x_i)^{\epsilon}.$$

Hence, if ϵ is zero so that there is no aversion to inequality, marginal utility is the same for everyone, and social welfare is simply μ, the mean of the x's. If ϵ is 2, for example, and i is twice as well-off as j, then the marginal social utility of additional x to i is one-fourth the marginal social utility of additional x to j. As ϵ tends to infinity, the marginal social utility of the poorest dominates over all other marginal utilities, and policy is concerned only with the poorest. When social welfare is the welfare of the poorest, which is what (3.4) becomes as ϵ tends to infinity, social preferences are sometimes said to be maximin (the object of policy is to maximize the minimum level of welfare) or Rawlsian, after Rawls (1972). Thinking about relative marginal utilities according to (3.5) is sometimes a convenient way of operationalizing the extent to which one would want poor people to be favored by policies or projects.

The inequality measure associated with (3.4) are, when $\epsilon \neq 1$,

$$(3.6a) \qquad I = 1 - \left(\frac{1}{N} \sum_{i=1}^{N} (x_i/\mu)^{1-\epsilon} \right)^{1/(1-\epsilon)}$$

and, when $\epsilon = 1$, the multiplicative form

$$(3.6b) \qquad I = 1 - \prod_{i=1}^{N} (x_i/\mu)^{1/N}.$$

These expressions are obtained by raising social welfare to the power of $1/(1-\epsilon)$, which makes the function homogeneous of the first degree, and then following through the procedures of the previous subsection. In line with the interpretation of ϵ as an aversion or perception parameter, there is no (perceived) inequality when ϵ is zero, no matter what the distribution of the x's. Conversely, if $\epsilon > 0$ and one person has all but a small amount α, say, with α spread equally over the others, then I tends to one as the number of people becomes large. Values of ϵ above 0 but below 2 appear to be useful, although in applications, it is often wise to look at results for a range of different values.

We may also choose to start from the standard measures of inequality. Provided these satisfy the principle of transfers, they will be consistent with Atkinson's approach, and will each have an associated social welfare function that can be recovered by applying (3.3). Some statistical measures of inequality do not satisfy the principle of transfers. The interquartile ratio—the 75th percentile less the 25th percentile divided by the median—is one such. Transferring x from a richer to a poorer person in the same quartile group will have no effect on inequality, and a transfer from someone at the bottom quartile to someone poorer will lower the bottom quartile and so will actually increase inequality. Less obviously, it is also possible to construct cases where a transfer from a better-off to a poorer person will increase the variance of logarithms. However, this can only happen when both people are far above the mean—which may not be relevant in some applications—and the other conveniences of the log variance may render it a competitive inequality measure in spite of this deficiency.

Other standard measures that *do* satisfy the principle of transfers are the Gini coefficient, the coefficient of variation, and Theil's "entropy" measure of inequality. The Gini coefficient if often defined from the Lorenz curve (see below), but can also be defined directly. One definition is the ratio to the mean of half the average over all pairs of the absolute deviations between people; there are $N(N-1)/2$ distinct pairs in all, so that the Gini is

$$(3.7a) \qquad \gamma = \frac{1}{\mu N(N-1)} \sum_{i>j} \sum_{j} |x_i - x_j|.$$

Note that when everyone has the same, μ, the Gini coefficient is zero, while if one person has $N\mu$, and everyone else zero, there are $N-1$ distinct nonzero absolute differences, each of which is $N\mu$, so that the Gini is 1. The double sum in (3.7a) can be expensive to calculate if N is large, and an equivalent but computationally more convenient form is

$$(3.7b) \qquad \gamma = \frac{N+1}{N-1} - \frac{2}{N(N-1)\mu} \sum_{i=1}^{N} \rho_i x_i$$

where ρ_i is the rank of individual i in the x-distribution, counting from the top so that the richest has rank 1. Using (3.7b), the Gini can straightforwardly and rapidly be calculated from microeconomic data after sorting the observations. I shall give examples below, together with discussion of how to incorporate sample weights, and how to calculate the individual-level Gini from household-level data.

Not surprisingly in view of (3.7b), the social welfare function associated with the Gini coefficient is one in which the x's are weighted by the ranks of each individual in the distribution, with the weights larger for the poor. Since the Gini lies between zero and one, the value of social welfare in an economy with mean μ and Gini coefficient γ is $\mu(1-\gamma)$, a measure advocated by Sen (1976a) who used it to rank of Indian states. The same measure has been generalized by Graaff (1977) to $\mu(1-\gamma)^\sigma$, for σ between 1 and 0; Graaff suggests that equity and efficiency are separate components of welfare, and that by varying σ we can give different weights to each (see also Atkinson 1992 for examples).

The coefficient of variation is the standard deviation divided by the mean, while Theil's entropy measure is given by

$$(3.8) \qquad I_T = \frac{1}{N} \sum_{i=1}^{N} \frac{x_i}{\mu} \ln\left(\frac{x_i}{\mu}\right).$$

I_T lies between 0, when all x's are identical, and $\ln N$, when one person has everything. This and other measures are discussed at much greater length in a number of texts, for example, Cowell (1995) or Kakwani (1980).

The choice between the various inequality measures is sometimes made on grounds of practical convenience, and sometimes on grounds of theoretical preference. On the former, it is frequently useful to be able to decompose inequality into "between" and "within" components, for example, between and within regions, sectors, or occupational groups. Variances can be so decomposed, as can Theil's entropy measure, while the Gini coefficient is not decomposable, or at least not without hard-to-interpret residual terms (see, for example, Pyatt 1976). It is also sometimes necessary to compute inequality measures for magnitudes—such as incomes or wealth—that can be negative, which is possible with the Gini or the coefficient of variation, but not with the Theil measure, the variance of logarithms, or the Atkinson measure. Further theoretical refinements can also be used to narrow down the choice. For example, we might require that inequality be more sensitive to differences between the poor than among the rich (see Cowell 1995), or that inequality aversion be stronger the further we are away from an equal allocation (see Blackorby and Donaldson 1978). All of these restrictions have appeal, but none has acquired the universal assent that is accorded to the principle of transfers.

Poverty and social welfare

In developing countries, attention is often focussed less on social welfare and inequality than on poverty. Indeed, poverty is frequently seen as the defining characteristic of underdevelopment, and its elimination as the main purpose of economic development. In such a context, it is natural for welfare economics to have a poverty focus. Even so, and although the poverty measurement literature has developed in a somewhat different direction, the social welfare function approach of this section is quite general, and as we have already seen, can readily accommodate a preference and measurement structure that is focusses attention exclusively towards the poor.

The social welfare function (3.1) transforms the distribution of x's into a single number that can be interpreted as a summary welfare measure that takes into account both the mean of the distribution and its dispersion. However, we are free to choose a function that gives little or no weight to the welfare of people who are well-off, so that social welfare becomes a measure of the welfare of the poor, in other words, a (negative) measure of poverty. In this sense, poverty measures are special cases of social welfare measures. However, in practical work, they serve rather different purposes. Poverty measures are designed to count the poor and to diagnose the extent and distribution of poverty, while social welfare functions are guides to policy. Just as the measurement of social welfare can be a inadequate guide to poverty, so are poverty measures likely to be an inadequate guide to policy.

As far as measurement is concerned, what separates the social welfare from the poverty literatures is that, in the latter, there is a *poverty line*, below which people are defined as poor, and above which they are not poor. In the language of social welfare, this effectively assigns zero social welfare to marginal benefits that accrue to the nonpoor, whereas the inequality literature, while typically assigning greater weight to benefits that reach lower in the distribution, rarely goes as far as assigning zero weight to the nonpoor. While the simplicity of a poverty line concept has much to recommend it, and is perhaps necessary to focus attention on poverty, it is a crude device. Many writers have expressed grave doubts about the idea that there is some discontinuity in the distribution of welfare, with poverty on one side and lack of it on the other, and certainly there is no empirical indicator—income, consumption, calories, or the consumption of individual commodities—where there is any perceptible break in the distribution or in behavior that would provide an empirical basis for the construction of a poverty line.

Even when there exists an acceptable, readily comprehensible, and uncontroversial line, so that we know what we mean when we say that α percent of the population is poor, we should never minimize this measure as an object of policy. The poverty count is an obviously useful statistic, it is widely understood, and it is hard to imagine discussions of poverty without it. However, there are policies that reduce the number of people in poverty, but which just as clearly decrease social welfare, such as taxes on very poor people that are used to lift the just-poor out of poverty. Similarly, a Pareto-improving project is surely socially desirable even when it fails to reduce poverty, and it makes no sense to ignore policies that would improve the lot of those who are poor by many definitions, but whose incomes place them just above some arbitrary poverty line.

The construction of poverty lines

Without an empirical basis such as a discontinuity in some measure, the construction of poverty lines always involves arbitrariness. In developed countries where most people do not consider themselves to be poor, a poverty line must be below the median, but different people will have different views about exactly how much money is needed to keep them out of poverty. Almost any figure that is reasonably central within the distribution of these views will make an acceptable poverty line. The official poverty line in the United States evolved from work in the early 1960s by Orshansky (1963, 1965) who took the cost of the U.S. Department of Agriculture's "low-cost food plan" and multiplied it by three, which was the reciprocal of the average food share in the Agriculture Department's 1955 household survey of food consumption.

While such a procedure might seem to be empirically well-grounded—and the perception that it is so has been important in the wide and continuing acceptance of the line—it is arbitrary to a considerable extent. The food plan itself was only one of several that were adapted by nutritional "experts" from the food consumption patterns of those in the lowest third of the income range in the 1955 survey, while the factor of three was based on food shares at the mean, not at the median, or at the 40th or the 25th percentile, for all of which a case could be mounted. In fact, Orshansky's line of a little over $3,000 for a nonfarm family of four was adopted, not because of its scientific foundations, but because her procedure yielded an answer that was acceptably close to another arbitrary figure that was already in informal use within the federal government (see Fisher 1992 for more on the history and development of the U.S. poverty line).

In India, poverty lines and poverty counts have an even more venerable history stretching back to 1938 and the National Planning Committee of the Indian National Congress. The more recent history is detailed in Government of India (1993), from which the following account is drawn. In 1962, "a Working Group of eminent economists and social thinkers" recommended that people be counted as poor if they lived in a household whose per capita monthly expenditure was less than 20 rupees at 1960–61 prices in rural areas, or 25 rupees in urban areas. These "bare minimum" amounts excluded expenditure on health and education, both of which were "expected to be provided by the State according to the Constitution and in the light of its other commitments." The precise economic and statistical basis for these calculations is not known, although the cost of obtaining minimally adequate nutrition was clearly taken into account, and the difference between urban and rural lines made an allowance for higher prices in the former.

Dandekar and Rath (1971a, 1971b) refined these poverty lines using a method that is still in widespread use. They started from an explicit calorie norm, 2,250 calories per person per day in both urban and rural areas. Using detailed food data from the National Sample Surveys (NSS), they calculated calorie consumption per capita as a function of total household expenditure per capita—the calorie Engel curve—and found that the norms were reached on average at 14.20 rupees per capita per month in rural areas, and 22.60 rupees per capita in urban areas, again at 1960–61 prices. These estimates were further refined by a "Task Force" of the Planning Commission in 1979, who revised the calorie norms to 2,400 in rural areas, and 2,100 in urban areas; the difference comes from the lower rates of physical activity in urban areas. The 28th round (1973–74) of the NSS was then used to estimate regression functions of calories on expenditure, and to convert these numbers to 49.09 rupees (rural) and 56.64 rupees (urban) at 1973–74 prices. These lines—updated for all-India price inflation—have been the basis for Indian poverty counts since 1979, although the "Expert Group" that reported in 1993 has recommended that allowance be made for interstate variation in price levels.

In poor countries such as India, where food makes up a large share of the budget, and where the concern with poverty is closely associated with concerns about undernutrition, it makes more sense to use food and nutritional requirements to derive poverty lines than it does in the United States The "low-cost food plan" in the United States can be replaced by something closer to the minimum adequate diet for the country and type of occupation, and because food is closer to three-quarters than a third of the budget, the "multiplier" needed to allow for nonfood consumption is smaller, less important, and so inherently less controversial.

Even so, the calorie-based procedure of setting a poverty line is subject to a number of serious difficulties. First, the minimum adequate calorie levels are themselves subject to uncertainty and controversy, and some would argue that resolving the arbitrariness about the poverty line with a calorie requirement simply replaces one arbitrary decision with another. Second, the concept of a behavioral Engel curve does not sit well with the notion that there is a subsistence level of calories. Suppose, for example, that a household is poor in that its expected calorie intake conditional on its income is inadequate, but has more than enough to buy the subsistence number of calories if it spent more of its budget on food. It seems that the subsistence number of calories is not really "required" in any absolute sense, or at least that the household is prepared to make tradeoffs between food and other goods, tradeoffs that are not taken into account in setting the line. Third, it is always dangerous to measure welfare using only a part of consumption, even when the part of consumption is as important as is food. When food is relatively cheap, people will consume more—even if only marginally so—and poverty lines will be higher where the relative price of food is higher, even though consumers may be compensated by lower prices elsewhere in the budget.

Bidani and Ravallion (1994) have examined this phenomenon in Indonesia. They show that higher food prices in the cities, together with the lower caloric requirements of more sedentary urban jobs, imply that the urban calorie Engel curve is lower than the rural calorie Engel curve. At the same level of PCE, urban consumers consume less calories than do rural consumers. In consequence, a common nutritional standard requires a higher level of PCE in the cities. In the Indonesian case, this results in a poverty line so much higher in urban than rural areas that there appears to be more poverty in the former, even though real incomes and real levels of consumption are much higher in the cities.

Once poverty lines are established they often remain fixed in real terms. In the United States, the current poverty line is simply Orshansky's 1961 poverty line updated for increases in the cost of living. In India, as detailed above, there have been revisions to methodology, but the lines have changed very little in real terms, and a number of studies, such as Bardhan (1973) and Ahluwalia (1978, 1985), have used poverty lines close to those proposed by Dandekar and Rath in 1971. This constancy reflects a view of poverty as an absolute; poverty is defined by the ability to purchase a *given* bundle of goods so that the poverty line should remain fixed in real terms. However, not everyone accepts this position, and it can be argued that poverty lines should move with the general standard of living, although perhaps not at the same rate. Some would argue that poverty is a purely relative phenomenon, defined by current social customs, and that the poor are simply those in the bottom percentiles of the distribution of welfare.

An intermediate view comes from Sen's (1985, 1992) view of welfare in terms of the capability to function in society. If economic growth means that food is sold with an increased amount of packaging and service built in, if city center stores relocate to suburban areas that cannot be reached on foot, and if urban growth increases the cost and time to travel to work, then a fixed absolute poverty line makes no sense. There is also some relevant empirical evidence that comes from asking people whether they are poor and what the poverty line ought to be (see Mangahas 1979, 1982, 1985, who makes good use of such surveys to assess poverty in the Philippines). In the United States, Gallup polls have regularly asked respondents how much money they would need "to get along," and more occasionally what they think would be an adequate poverty line. In the 1960s, the mean responses about the latter were close to the official (Orshansky) line, but have since increased in real terms, although not always as fast as has average real disposable income (see Rainwater 1974 and Vaughan 1992). Ravallion (1993) has also examined the cross-country relationship between real gross domestic product (GDP) and poverty lines, and found that the elasticity is close to unity. While many people—including this author—are uncomfortable with an entirely relative concept of poverty, it is surely right that there should be some movement of the line in response to changes in mean levels of living.

The conceptual and practical difficulties over the choice of a poverty line mean that all measures of poverty should be treated with skepticism. For policy evaluation, the social welfare function is all that is required to measure welfare, including an appropriate treatment of poverty. While it is possible—and in my view desirable—to give greater weight to the needs of the poorest, I see few advantages in trying to set a sharp line, below which people count and above which they do not. Poverty lines and poverty counts make good headlines, and are an inevitable part of the policy debate, but they should not be used in policy evaluation. Perhaps the best poverty line is an infinite one; everyone is poor, but some a good deal more so than others, and the poorer they are the greater weight they should get in measuring welfare and in policy evaluation.

The concept of a poverty line is deeply embedded in the poverty literature, and measures of poverty are typically based on it. Even so, a good deal of the recent literature on poverty has followed Atkinson (1987) in recognizing that the poverty line is unlikely to be very precisely measured, and trying to explore situations in which poverty measures are robust to this uncertainty. I shall return to this approach below once I have introduced some of the standard measures.

Measures of poverty

There are a number of good reviews of alternative poverty measures and their properties, see in particular Foster (1984) and Ravallion (1993), so that I can confine myself here to a brief discussion of the most important measures. The obvious starting point—and the measure most often quoted—is the *headcount ratio*, defined as the fraction of the population below the poverty line. If the line is denoted by z, and the welfare measure is x, then the headcount ratio is

$$(3.9) \qquad P_0 = \frac{1}{N} \sum_{i=1}^{N} 1(x_i \leq z)$$

where $1(.)$ is an indicator function that is 1 if its argument is true and 0 otherwise. The sum of the indicators on the right-hand side of (3.9) is the number of people in poverty, so that P_0 is simply the fraction of people in poverty.

It is worth noting that with a change of sign, (3.9) could conceivably be regarded as a social welfare function. It is the average value of a rather strange valuation function in which x counts as -1 when it is below the poverty line z, and as 0 when it is above z. This function is illustrated as the heavy line labeled P_0 in Figure 3.2; it is nondecreasing in x, so it has some of the characteristics of a utility function, but its discontinuity at the poverty line means that it is not concave. It is this lack of concavity that violates the principle of transfers, and makes it possible to increase social welfare by taking money from the very poor to lift some better-off poor out of poverty.

Even if the poverty line were correctly set, and even if it were acceptable to view poverty as a discrete state, the headcount ratio would be at best a limited measure of poverty. In particular, it takes no account of the degree of poverty, and would, for example, be unaffected by a policy that made the poor even poorer. The

Figure 3.2. Alternative poverty measures and social welfare

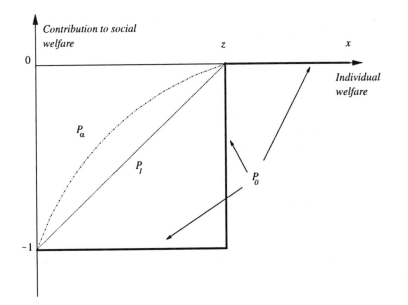

headcount ratio gives the same measure of poverty whether all the poor are just below a generous poverty line, or whether they are just above an ungenerous level of subsistence. One way of doing better is to use the *poverty gap* measure

(3.10)
$$P_1 = \frac{1}{N} \sum_{i=1}^{N} \left(1 - \frac{x_i}{z}\right) 1(x_i \leq z).$$

According to (3.10), the contribution of individual i to aggregate poverty is larger the poorer is i. P_1 can also be interpreted as a per capita measure of the total shortfall of individual welfare levels below the poverty line; it is the sum of all the shortfalls divided by the population and expressed as a ratio of the poverty line itself. Hence if, for example, P_1 were 0.25, the total amount that the poor are below the poverty line is equal to the population multiplied by a quarter of the poverty line.

It is tempting to think of P_1 (or at least $P_1 z$) as a measure of the per capita "cost" of eliminating poverty, but this is far from being so except in the impractical case where lump-sum taxes and subsidies are possible. Even when tax and subsidy administration is efficient and is not corrupt, redistributive taxes have incentive effects that may render the elimination of poverty neither possible nor desirable given the actual range of feasible policies. This is clearly the case in an economy where everyone is poor, but applies much more widely. Once again, the appropriate way to think about tax systems for poverty alleviation is to go back to the social welfare function (3.1), to make sure that it incorporates the appropriate degree of weighting towards the poor, and to apply the general theory of tax design (see Newbery and Stern 1987 for a general discussion of such problems in the contexts of developing countries, and Chapter 5 below for some of the empirical issues).

The poverty gap measure (3.10) has a number of advantages over the headcount ratio (3.9). In particular, the summand is now a continuous function of x, so that there is no longer a discontinuity in the contribution of an individual to the poverty measure as that individual's x passes through the poverty line. When x is just below z, the contribution to poverty is very small, it is zero when x equals z, and remains at zero above z. Furthermore the function $(1 - x/z) 1(x \leq z)$ is convex in x—although not strictly so—so that the principle of transfers holds—at least in a weak form. As a result, the social welfare interpretation of the poverty gap measure also makes more sense than that of the headcount ratio. The behavior of each individual's contribution to $-P_1$ is illustrated in Figure 3.2 by the piecewise linear function rising from −1 to 0, a value which it retains above z. This function is increasing in x, and is (just) concave, so that while social welfare is not altered by transfers among the poor or among the nonpoor, it is no longer possible to increase social welfare by acting as an anti–Robin Hood, taking resources from the poor to give to the rich.

The poverty gap measure will be increased by transfers from poor to nonpoor, or from poor to less poor who thereby become nonpoor. But transfers among the poor have no effect on the measure of poverty, and on this account we may wish to consider other poverty measures. Sen's (1976b) measure of poverty remedies the defect by incorporating the inequality among the poor. The definition is

$$(3.11) \qquad P_S = P_0\left(1 - (1 - \gamma^p)\frac{\mu^p}{z}\right)$$

where μ^p is the mean of x among the poor, and γ^p is the Gini coefficient of inequality among the poor, calculated by treating the poor as the whole population. Note that when there is no inequality among the poor, P_S reduces to the poverty gap measure P_1. Conversely, when all but one of the poor has nothing, $P_S = P_0$ and the Sen measure coincides with the headcount ratio. More generally, the Sen measure is the average of the headcount and poverty gap measures weighted by the Gini coefficient of the poor,

$$(3.12) \qquad P_S = P_0\gamma^p + P_1(1 - \gamma^p).$$

Because Sen's measure depends on the Gini coefficient, it shares two of its inconveniences. First, the Gini—and thus the Sen index—is not differentiable. Although there is no economic reason to require differentiability, the inability to differentiate is sometimes a nuisance. More seriously, Sen's measure cannot be used to decompose poverty into contributions from different subgroups, something that is often informative when monitoring changes in poverty. If the aggregate poverty measure can be written as a weighted average of the poverty measures for the rural and urban sectors, or for households by age, or by occupation of the head, then changes over time can be similarly decomposed thus helping to identify groups that are particularly at risk, as well as sometimes pointing to the underlying mechanisms. While decomposability is hardly as fundamental a property as (say) the principle of transfers, it is extremely useful.

Our final poverty measure, or set of measures, comes from Foster, Greer, and Thorbecke (1984). Their measures are direct generalizations of the poverty gap (3.10) and are written, for some positive parameter α,

$$(3.13) \qquad P_\alpha = N^{-1} \sum_{i=1}^{N} (1 - x_i/z)^\alpha 1(x_i \le z)$$

so that P_0 and P_1 are special cases corresponding to values for α of 0 and 1, respectively. The larger the value of α, the more does the measure penalize the poverty gaps. Most frequently used is $\alpha = 2$, which yields a poverty measure like the Sen index that is sensitive to distribution among the poor. The decomposability property of (3.13) follows immediately from its additive structure. In particular, if sectors are denoted by s, and there are S of them, we can write

$$(3.14) \qquad P_\alpha = N^{-1} \sum_{s=1}^{S} \sum_{j \in s} (1 - x_j/z)^\alpha 1(x_j \le z) = \sum_s (n_s/N) P_\alpha^s$$

where n_s is the number of people in sector s and P_α^s is the Foster, Greer, and Thorbecke index for poverty within the sector. Using (3.14), changes in aggregate poverty can be assigned to changes in sectoral poverty measures or to changes in the proportion of people in each sector.

Figure 3.2 shows how P_α measures up as a social welfare function. The third line, shown as dots and dashes, is the contribution of individual welfare to social welfare defined as $-P_\alpha$ in the case where α is greater than unity; as with P_1, this line continues along the x-axis to the right of z. Because the function is strictly concave below z, it is sensitive to the degree of inequality among the poor. It is also continuously differentiable, even at the poverty line, so that the implicit marginal social utility declines continuously from its maximum among the poorest to zero at and above the poverty line.

The choice of the individual welfare measure

Apart from a brief reference in the context of choosing a poverty line, I have so far avoided discussion of exactly how welfare is to be measured, and what practical concept should replace the x's in the various poverty and inequality formulas. Ideally, we should like a survey based measure that approaches as closely as possible the individual welfare measures of economic theory. Particularly useful here is the concept of money metric utility—see Deaton and Muellbauer (1980a, ch. 7) for an overview—whereby the indifference curves of individual preference orderings are labeled by the amount of money needed to reach them at some fixed set of prices. In order to avoid the specification of a parametric utility function, money metric utility can be approximated by real income or real expenditure, the two leading candidates for practical welfare measures. However, there are other possibilities, indicators of nutritional status being perhaps the most important, and even if we settle on income or expenditures, there are many other questions that have to be settled before going on to compute the measures. In this subsection, I discuss a few of the most important: the choice between consumption and income or other concepts, the choice between individual and household measures, the choice of time period, as well as some data issues, particularly the effects of measurement error and reporting periods.

In the context of measuring welfare in developing countries, there is a very strong case in favor of using measures based on consumption not income. The standard argument—that by the permanent income hypothesis, consumption is a better measure of lifetime welfare than is current income—is much weaker than arguments based on practicality and data. It is unwise to condition a welfare measure on the validity of a hypothesis whose empirical support is at best mixed. In particular and as we shall see in Chapter 6, there is very little evidence from developing countries—or anywhere else—that lifetime consumption profiles are detached from lifetime income profiles as is required if consumption is to be superior to income as an indicator of lifetime welfare. Of course, there is no doubt that households smooth their consumption over shorter periods, certainly days, months, and seasons, and to some extent over runs of years. Income, especially agricultural income, can be extremely variable, and a farmer's income in any month is a poor indicator of living standards in that month. A better case can be made for annual income, but if farmers can even partially smooth out good years and bad, consumption will be the better measure.

At the practical level, and as discussed in Section 1.2, the difficulties of measuring income are much more severe than those of measuring consumption, especially for rural households whose income comes largely from self-employment in agriculture. Given also that annual income is required for a satisfactory estimate of living standards, an income-based measure requires multiple visits or the use of recall data, whereas a consumption measure can rely on consumption over the previous few weeks. Note that these arguments are likely reversed if we were dealing with, for example, the United States, where individual consumption surveys are much less developed than income surveys, where a much smaller fraction of the population is self-employed, where seasonality is much less of an issue, and where it is both feasible and economical to obtain accurate estimates of income for most people.

The conversion of nominal measures of consumption to real measures requires a price index. In most cases, there will exist an adequate consumer price index or cost-of-living estimate that can be used to compare data collected in different time periods. In countries with rapid inflation, this may even have to be done within each survey year, since different households are interviewed at different times. What is often more difficult is the comparison of living costs across regions at a given time, for example, when we are trying to compare living standards or poverty rates across different regions. In some surveys—but not typically in the Living Standards Surveys—households are asked to report both quantities and expenditures on a range of goods, particularly foods, and these data can be used to calculate unit values. Although unit values are not the same as prices—an issue that will be discussed in some detail in Chapter 5—accurate price indexes for each region can nevertheless be obtained from the unit values by averaging within regions and calculating a Laspeyres index for each, that is by pricing out a fixed bundle of goods at the average unit values for each region. The Living Standards Surveys have usually collected price data, not from households, but from observations on prices in markets used by the households in the survey, and these data can also be used to construct regional price indexes.

Although consumption and income are the standard measures of economic welfare, we will often want to supplement them with other measures of well-being, such as nutritional and health status, life expectancy, and education. While it is possible to consider methods for combining these indicators into a single measure, there is no adequate theory underlying such an aggregate so that weighting schemes are inevitably arbitrary, and it is more informative—as well as honest—to keep the different indicators separate. This is not to downplay the importance of these other indicators, nor to deny that public goods such as hospitals and schools contribute an important part of individual welfare. However, it is important not to confuse the components of economic welfare with their aggregate. We have already seen how the definition of a poverty line in terms of calories can give misleading results when relative prices differ. The same argument applies to attempts to shortcut welfare measurement using indicators such as housing, or the ownership of durable goods. Immigrants to big cities often live in very poor-quality housing in order to have access to employment. In such cases, their poor housing reflects the high price of housing in urban areas, but may tell us little about their living standards.

Because surveys collect data at the level of the household, and not the individual, poverty and welfare measures must be based on consumption and income totals for the household, not for the individual. Although some surveys collect data on individual earnings, and even on individual income from assets, there is typically a component of household income—a large component in the case of family farms—that is not readily attributable to individual household members. For consumption, the position is even worse. Data on purchases are inevitably purchases for the household as a whole, and although some items—such as food—are conceptually assignable to particular individuals, the cost of observing who eats what is too large for all but specialist nutritional surveys. Even then there are questions about contamination of behavior by the presence of the enumerator during food preparation and family meals. There are also public goods in most households— goods and services the consumption of which by one member of the household does not exclude consumption by others. The consumption of these goods cannot be assigned to specific individuals.

As a result, we can either treat households as the units whose welfare is being measured, or we can use some rule to divide household total expenditure between its members, usually equally or in proportion to some measure of needs, and then treat each individual as the unit in the poverty and welfare calculations. Since it is hard to think of households as repositories for well-being, even in the best case where their membership does not change, an individual basis for measurement is conceptually clearer and is the recommendation carried throughout this book. One difficulty is that the assumption of equal division, or of each according to her or his needs, is bound to understate the true dispersion of consumption among individuals, and thus understate inequality and poverty. As pointed out by Haddad and Kanbur (1990), who have also investigated the magnitude of the biases, the assumed equal distribution within the household could be reached from the unknown true one by a system of equalizing transfers, so that any welfare measure that respects the principle of transfers will be overstated (or understated if a poverty measure) using household data.

It is also necessary to recognize that children do not have the same needs as adults. Assigning household PCE to each person gives too little to adults—especially those who do heavy manual work—and too much to children. If there are economies of scale, PCE will understate individual welfare levels, even if all household members are adults. Attempts to do better than PCE measures for individuals are discussed in Chapter 4, where I take up the question of allocation within the household, and the construction of "equivalence scales," numbers that are the theoretically appropriate deflators to move from household to individual welfare. However, I should point out in advance that the equivalence scale literature is still very far from providing satisfactory answers to these questions, and that the use of household PCE assigned to individuals is still best practice. Even so, it is wise to remain skeptical of estimates that appear to be purely statistical but rely heavily on arbitrary assignments, such as the number of children in poverty, or the average living standards of the elderly. The elderly rarely live by themselves in poor countries, and children do not do so anywhere, so that estimates of their welfare are determined as much by assumption as by measurement and should be treated as such. Measures of the fraction of children in poverty, or of women in poverty, are particularly fragile and international comparisons of such concepts cannot be treated seriously.

The choice of time period, like all of these issues, is partly one of theory and partly one of practicality. In theory, we need to decide the reference period for welfare measurement, whether someone is poor if they go without adequate consumption or income for a week, a month, or a year. The reference period can be shorter for consumption than for income, and if we use income, the choice of reference period will depend on what mechanisms—credit markets, familial support—are available to help people ride out fluctuations in income. In practice, long reference periods require either multiple visits or recall questions; the former are expensive and the latter risk measurement error. Note also that, if poverty and welfare measures are to be comparable across countries or over time, the reference periods must be the same. Because the dispersion of both consumption and income decrease the longer is the reference period, both the extent of inequality and poverty will be larger at short than at long reference periods.

One of the most difficult practical issues in estimating poverty and inequality is to separate genuine dispersion from measurement error. If we start from any distribution of welfare and add measurement errors that have zero mean and are uncorrelated with the true values, the new distribution is a spread-out version of the original one, so that if our measures respect the principle of transfers, measured inequality will be higher and social welfare lower. Poverty measures that satisfy the principle of transfers will also be higher. For the headcount, which does not satisfy the principle, matters are more complicated and measurement error can bias the count in either direction. If the country is wealthy enough for the poverty line to be below the mode, the addition of mean-zero measurement error will cause the measured headcount to overstate the number in poverty, and vice versa. Similarly if we try to assess the persistence of poverty using panel data by seeing who remains in poverty and who escapes it, measurement error will exaggerate the extent of mobility, and make poverty seem less persistent than is truly the case. In most cases, we have little idea of the magnitude of measurement error, or how much of the variance of consumption or income changes is noise as opposed to signal. However, and bearing in mind the problems of estimating consumption and income in surveys in developing countries, it is always wise to consider the robustness of conclusions to the presence of substantial measurement error.

Example 1. Inequality and poverty over time in Côte d'Ivoire

This subsection applies some of the foregoing concepts to Living Standards data from Côte d'Ivoire for the four years 1985 through 1988, focussing on change over time, while the next subsection uses data from South Africa in 1993 to look at differences by race. The translation of the formulas into numbers is essentially straightforward, but it is nevertheless useful to work through the exercise, partly to see how the theory can be used to help interpret the numbers, and partly to see some of the practical problems that are not dealt with by the theory.

As always, a good place to start is with standard summary statistics, some of which are shown in Table 3.1. In fact there is a good deal of work prior to this, checking out the data, and looking for and investigating outliers, to which measures of dispersion can be very sensitive. This sort of preliminary work is greatly aided by suitable methods of graphing the data; for example, the "oneway" command in STATA plots a small vertical bar for each observation so that it is easy to see outliers in relation to the main body of the data. In line with the foregoing arguments, I have chosen consumption rather than income as the welfare measure, and I use the estimate of total monthly household expenditure calculated by the World Bank and provided on the diskettes of the Côte d'Ivoire LSS.

I have also used the "corrective weights" provided by the Bank. These were calculated after the surveys were complete, and are designed to correct some known deficiencies in the design that led to over- or undersampling. The most controversial component of the weight "corrects" the surveys' estimates of household size. In the raw data, average household size declines over time at an implausible rate, something that could happen if large households were oversampled in the first survey, (see Coulombe and Demery 1993 and Demery and Grootaert 1993), or through progressive quality deterioration if enumerators became better at avoiding the very large households that can take many hours to interview (see Coulombe, McKay, and Pyatt 1993). The weights are based on the former hypothesis, and are controversial because they depend on its correctness; it is far from clear that they can be interpreted as inverse sampling probabilities. Unfortunately, inferences about per capita expenditures in Côte d'Ivoire are sensitive to these corrections (see again Coulombe, McKay, and Pyatt).

The first column in the table shows the weighted average over the households in each survey of total annual expenditures in real terms. The units are thousands of Central African francs, with 1,000 CFAF worth between three and four U.S. dollars at purchasing power parity, and the prices are those of Abidjan in 1985. I

Table 3.1. Consumption measures, Côte d'Ivoire, 1985–88
(thousands of CFAF per month)

Year	Total house-hold expenditure	Household size	PCE Household basis	Individual basis	Standard error
1985	1,548	6.51	292.2	237.8	8.75
1986	1,400	6.25	269.9	223.9	8.16
1987	1,345	6.20	264.3	217.0	9.13
1988	1,067	6.16	202.3	173.1	6.09

Note: There are 1,588 households in the 1985 sample, and 1,600 in 1986–88. Prices are those of Abidjan in 1985, and nominal amounts are converted to real terms using the regional price indexes for each year from Grootaert and Kanbur (1992). Standard errors are computed from the "svymean" command in STATA, with the regions as strata and the clusters as PSUs.
Source: Author's calculations based on CILSS, 1985–88.

have used Grootaert and Kanbur's (1992) price indexes for the four years and five regions—Abidjan, Other Cities, East Forest, West Forest, and Savannah—to convert the nominal survey measures to constant prices. Mean household total expenditure declines over the four years; indeed real per capita GDP declined in Côte d'Ivoire over these years in line with the experience of many other African economies during a period of falling world prices for their exports of primary commodities, mainly cocoa and coffee in the case of Côte d'Ivoire. The second column shows average household size; even after the correction there is some decline over time. The third column shows the (weighted) average over households of PCE which also shows a decline in every year, so that the decline in household size is not sufficient to offset the decline in the total.

The average of household PCE, although often used as a welfare measure, is not what we want here; welfare resides in individuals, not households, and we need to recompute the averages on an individual basis. This is done in Table 3.1 by assigning the household levels of PCE to each individual and then averaging over the individuals. Of course, this is just a reweighting of the household data, so that if household h has n_h members and PCE is x_h, then the average of PCE on an individual basis is

$$(3.15) \qquad \bar{x} = \sum_{h=1}^{H} w_h n_h x_h \Big/ \sum_{h=1}^{H} w_h n_h$$

where H is the total number of households and w_h is the household inflation factor or weight. Note that the weights and household size appear symmetrically in (3.15), so that is often convenient for calculation to redefine the weights by multiplying by household size, or household size by multiplying by the weights. Since $x_h n_h$ is simply total household expenditure, (3.15) implies that the individual average of PCE is the ratio of (weighted) average total household expenditure to (weighted) average household size, so that column 4 in Table 3.1 is the ratio of column 3 to column 2. Estimated standard errors for mean individual-level PCE are given in the final column; there are calculated using the "svymean" or "svyratio" commands in STATA, and take the regions as strata—although the CILSS was only implicitly stratified by region—and the clusters as PSUs.

In the unlikely event that we are unconcerned with distributional issues, the averages of individual PCE would be adequate welfare indicators. But to move from mean consumption levels to social welfare, we must also calculate inequality measures, and these are shown in Table 3.2. Once again, these estimates are estimates of inequality between individuals, not between households. The conceptually most straightforward way of going from one to the other is to "replicate" the observations in the data set, with one replication of the household PCE level for each individual in the household, and then to use the inequality formulas given above. In practice, this is both clumsy and inefficient compared with simple weighted estimates. Only in the case of the Gini coefficient is the calculation less than obvious. For example, to use household data to calculate the Atkinson inequality measure on an individual basis, we calculate the level of social welfare according to the appropriately modified version of (3.4). Each sample household with n_h members represents $w_h n_h$ individuals n the population, so that

$$(3.16) \qquad \tilde{x} = \left(\frac{\sum_{h=1}^{H} w_h n_h x_h^{1-\epsilon}}{\sum_{h=1}^{H} w_h n_h} \right)^{1/(1-\epsilon)}$$

where N is the total number of people. (When ϵ is 1, the calculation in (3.16) is replaced by exponentiating the weighted averages of the logarithms.) The Atkinson inequality index is then calculated by dividing (3.16) by the (weighted) mean and subtracting the result from one.

Calculation of the Gini coefficient from equation (3.7b) is only slightly more complicated by the need to convert household ranks to individual ranks. Since everyone in each household is assumed to have the same PCE, we can order them within the household in any way we choose. The first person in the best-off household is then given rank 1, the first person in the second household rank $1 + n_1$, where n_1 is the number of people in the first household, and so on. As before, if there are nonzero survey weights, the simplest treatment is to pretend that there are, not n_h, but $w_h n_h$ people in household h. Hence, and starting from $\rho_1 = 1$, the rank of the first person in household $h + 1$ can be defined recursively by

$$(3.17) \qquad \rho_{h+1} = \rho_h + n_h w_h.$$

The *average* rank of all the persons in household h is therefore

$$(3.18) \qquad \bar{\rho}_h = \rho_h + 0.5(w_h n_h - 1)$$

so that the Gini coefficient for individual-level PCE is given from (3.7b) by

$$(3.19) \qquad \gamma = \frac{N+1}{N-1} - \frac{2}{N(N-1)x_{\bar{w}}} \sum_{h=1}^{H} w_h n_h x_h [\rho_h + 0.5(n_h - 1)]$$

with the best-off household coming first and the ranks calculated from (3.17).

Since these inequality measures are independent of the scale of x, they will not be changed by deflation by the price index, provided that the price index does not vary from one household to another. Note too that, because the Gini coefficient is

Table 3.2. Inequality measures between individuals, Côte d'Ivoire, 1985–88

Year	Gini coefficient	S.d. of logs	Coeff. variation	Atkinson measures		
				$\epsilon = 0.5$	$\epsilon = 1.0$	$\epsilon = 2.0$
1985	0.383	0.716	0.807	0.118	0.223	0.394
1986	0.358	0.627	0.786	0.103	0.190	0.382
1987	0.381	0.665	0.894	0.119	0.215	0.444
1988	0.345	0.615	0.745	0.091	0.180	0.357

Note: Measures of inequality use household PCE attributed to individuals and are calculated on an individual basis using corrective weights. S.d. is standard deviation and Coeff. variation the coefficient of variation.
Source: Author's calculations based on CILSS, 1985–88.

invariant to scaling of population size—doubling the number of people with each x has no effect on the index—the calculations are unaffected by any rescaling of the survey weights.

The different measures are in broad agreement; all show that inequality is lowest in 1988, next lowest in 1986, and highest in 1985 and 1986. The Gini, the standard deviation of logs, and the Atkinson measure with $\epsilon = 1$ rank 1987 as more equal than 1985, while the reverse judgement is made by the coefficient of variation, and the Atkinson measures with ϵ set at either 0 or 2. The Atkinson measures show more inequality the larger is the inequality aversion parameter ϵ but, like the other measures, all rank 1988, 1986, and either 1985 or 1987 in the same way. Note that there is no simple relationship between the value of ϵ and the rankings; the distribution in 1985 is more equal than that in 1987 when ϵ is 0.5 or 2, but the reverse is true when ϵ is 1. Recall that inequality should always be interpreted jointly with the mean in order to assess changes in aggregate well-being. Even so, the decline in inequality from 1985 to 1988, although substantial by some of the measures, is not enough to have raised equality by the amount required to offset the decline in PCE and maintain the level of social welfare.

Table 3.3 reports four poverty measures based on individual PCE, the headcount, the poverty gap ratio, the Foster-Greer-Thorbecke measure with α set at 2, and Sen's poverty measure. There are no new difficulties of calculation here; the headcount is simply the fraction of people who live in households whose household PCE is less than equal to the poverty line, while P_1 and P_2 are calculated as weighted averages in the usual way. The Sen index is calculated according to (3.12) with the Gini for the poor calculated as described above but for the limited population of those in poverty. I have chosen a poverty line to match some arbitrary but reasonable percentile in the base year and then held it fixed in real terms in the other years. In 1985, (just over) 30 percent of people were in households whose PCE was below 128,600 CFAF—an amount that is close to the useful (if arbitrary) guideline of one U.S. dollar per head per day—and I use this figure as the poverty line. Table 3.3 also shows bootstrapped standard errors for these poverty measures. These come from 100 bootstrap replications and take into account the clustered structure of the CILSS (see the Code Appendix for the STATA code for the bootstrap and for the inequality and poverty measures.)

Table 3.3. Measures of individual poverty, Côte d'Ivoire, 1985–88
(bootstrapped standard errors in brackets)

Year	Headcount ratio, P_0	Poverty-gap ratio, P_1	FGT index, P_2	Sen poverty index, P_S
1985	0.300 (.030)	0.098 (.013)	0.045 (.007)	0.134 (.017)
1986	0.300 (.019)	0.082 (.007)	0.032 (.043)	0.112 (.009)
1987	0.348 (.025)	0.101 (.013)	0.043 (.008)	0.140 (.017)
1988	0.459 (.030)	0.142 (.016)	0.063 (.010)	0.196 (.021)

Note: Measures of poverty are based on household PCE attributed to individuals, and are calculated on an individual basis.
Source: Author's calculations based on CILSS, 1985–88.

These Ivorian estimates provide a good example of the fact that poverty does not always move in the same direction as average PCE. Although average PCE fell in every year from 1985 to 1988, the poverty measures decline from 1985 to 1986, only rising thereafter. The headcount ratio hardly changes from 1985 to 1986, but the decline is clear in the other measures. Although the mean of PCE fell between the two years, the fraction of people below the poverty line remained virtually unchanged and, as shown by the behavior of P_1, the average PCE among the poor rose in spite of the fall in the overall average PCE. That people at the bottom of the distribution did better than the average presumably also contributed to the declines in inequality in Table 3.2. Note also the sensitivity of the poverty rankings of 1985 relative to 1987. The latter year has a large fraction of poor than the former, but once we take into account the average of PCE among the poor and its distribution between them, the increase in poverty is less, and as measured by P_2, poverty declines.

It should be emphasized once again that these results on poverty, and the poverty rankings of the years are in accord with the Atkinson social welfare approach, provided enough weight is given to the poor. As argued in the theoretical section, there is little conceptual difference between social welfare measurement and poverty measurement, provided always that inequality indexes are interpreted jointly with means, and not on their own. The main difference between the two approaches is in the way the weighting is done, with everyone getting some weight in the social welfare function, although the poor get relatively more, while the nonpoor get no weight in the poverty indices.

Example 2. Inequality and poverty by race in South Africa

The South African Living Standards Survey collected data at the end of 1993, shortly before the elections that established the government of President Nelson Mandela. The survey was intended to establish a picture of living standards and poverty on the eve of the elections, and to serve as a baseline against which future progress could be assessed. Because there have been no subsequent LSMS surveys in South Africa, these data cannot be used to track living standards over time, but they provide a snapshot of living standards by race at the end of the apartheid era.

Table 3.4 brings together all of the statistics on the four racial groups. The top panel shows very large differences in levels of living, particularly between Blacks and Whites; the mean of individual PCE is almost seven times larger for Whites than for Blacks. The second panel shows that the ranking of groups by inequality is precisely the reverse of the ranking by average. Blacks are not only poorer than Whites, but their living standards are more unequally distributed. Indeed the Gini coefficient of 0.34 for Whites is low by any standards. As a result, even the seven-fold difference in mean PCE understates the difference in average welfare between Blacks and Whites. For example, if we measure social welfare as mean PCE multiplied by one minus the Gini, Whites are 8.4 times better-off than Blacks. The differences between the groups also gives very high measures of inequality for the country as a whole so that, for example, the overall Gini coefficient is 0.59.

Table 3.4. Welfare measures by race, South Africa, 1993

Measure	Blacks	Coloreds	Indians	Whites	All
Means					
Total household exp.	1,053	1,783	3,202	4,615	1,089
Household size	4.78	4.67	4.38	3.01	4.44
PCE (household)	325	483	828	1,793	615
PCE (individual)	220	378	732	1,531	406
Standard error	8.0	32.8	88.4	80.8	26.4
Inequality					
Gini	0.449	0.412	0.377	0.336	0.586
S. d. of logarithms	0.798	0.734	0.647	0.594	1.042
Coefficient of variation	1.062	0.994	0.924	0.733	1.563
Atkinson, $\epsilon = 0.5$	0.162	0.136	0.118	0.089	0.276
Atkinson, $\epsilon = 1.0$	0.289	0.247	0.210	0.166	0.460
Atkinson, $\epsilon = 2.0$	0.530	0.497	0.460	0.349	0.710
Poverty					
Headcount ratio P_0	0.317	0.080	0.0	0.0	0.250
Poverty gap ratio P_1	0.106	0.019	0.0	0.0	0.083
FGT P_2	0.049	0.008	0.0	0.0	0.039
Sen measure P_S	0.144	0.029	0.0	0.0	0.113

Notes: Inequality and poverty are based on imputing household PCE to individuals. The poverty line is set at a PCE of 105 rand per month. Numbers of observations vary across statistics because of missing values; there are approximately 6,500 African, 700 Colored, 250 Indian, and 1,350 White households in the survey.
Source: Author's calculations from South African Living Standards Survey, 1993.

The poverty measures in the third panel use a poverty line of 105 rand per month per person. This is much lower than poverty lines commonly discussed in South Africa, but is approximately equal to $1 (U.S.) per person per day, the same line I used for Côte d'Ivoire. More than 30 percent of Africans have less than even this very low cutoff; there are no Whites or Indians in poverty. As has often been noted, apartheid was a successful welfare state for the Whites, keeping incomes high, inequality low, and minimizing poverty. The majority of South Africa's citizens were less fortunate.

Exploring the welfare distribution: inequality

The welfare and poverty measures of the previous subsections are designed to aggregate the detailed distribution of welfare to a single number; provided that we know exactly the measure that we prefer, and provided that there is uncertainty neither about how to weight people at different income levels, nor about the level of the poverty line, then the summary measures are all we need. However, there is often substantial uncertainty about how much weight to give to the poor relative to the rich, and there is always a good deal of uncertainty about the poverty line. In consequence, it is often a good idea to explore the robustness of social welfare measures to parameters about which we are unsure. At the same time, the reduction of a distribution to a single number may be more aggregation than we want, and more fundamental insights into levels of living can often be obtained from graphical representations of either the whole distribution or of some part of it. I begin with inequality.

The most familiar graphical tool for examining the distribution of income or consumption is the Lorenz curve, which is a plot of cumulative fraction of population—starting from the poorest—on the x-axis against cumulative fraction of resources on the y-axis. Three (imaginary) distributions are sketched in Figure 3.3. If resources were equally distributed, with everyone receiving the same, the Lorenz curve would be the 45-degree line, thus labeled the line of complete equality, whereas the case of complete inequality, with the richest person having everything, would generate a Lorenz curve running along the x-axis with a right angle at (100,0) to terminate at (100,100). Lorenz curves have positive slopes and positive second derivatives. At point p on the horizontal axis, the slope of the curve is the ratio to mean x of the value of x below which lie fraction p of the population; formally, if the distribution function of x is $F(x)$ with mean μ, the slope of the Lorenz curve at p is $F^{-1}(p)/\mu$. This implies that the curves attain their maximum distance from the 45-degree line where the cumulative proportion of people is equal to the fraction of people with x below the mean (see Kakwani 1980, ch. 3, for this and further results).

The Gini coefficient is also closely associated with the Lorenz curve. It is the area between the curve and the 45-degree line as a fraction of 0.5, which is the total area under the 45-degree line. The Lorenz curve is unaffected by multiplying

Figure 3.3. Lorenz curves illustrating Lorenz dominance

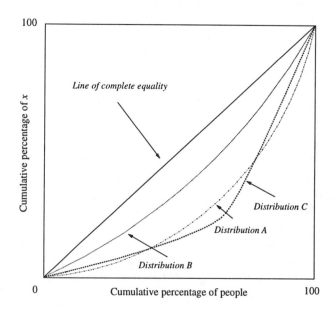

everyone's allocation by a positive number, and so can tell us nothing about the mean of the distribution. Apart from this, all the information in the distribution is contained in the Lorenz curve so that, provided we know the mean, it is possible, for example, to recover the density or distribution function from the Lorenz curve.

As first shown by Atkinson (1970), Lorenz curves play a very important role in characterizing the robustness of inequality measures. If two different Lorenz curves do not cross, as is the case for distributions *B* and either *A* or *C* in Figure 3.3, the lower curve can always be transformed into the upper curve by a series of equalizing transfers, by each of which welfare is transferred from a richer to a poorer individual. In consequence, when two Lorenz curves do not cross, the upper one represents an unambiguously more egalitarian distribution, one that will show a lower level of inequality using *any* measure of inequality that respects the principle of transfers. In Figure 3.3, the two distributions *A* and *C* cross one another (twice as shown), so that there is no unambiguous ranking of inequality without committing to more specific inequality measures. Distribution *C* is more equal among both the poorest and the richest, but is more unequal in the middle of the distribution than is distribution *A*. When one Lorenz curve is everywhere above another, we say that the distribution corresponding to the upper curve *Lorenz dominates* the distribution represented by the lower curve. Lorenz domination does not give a complete ordering of distributions; when Lorenz curves cross, neither distribution dominates the other.

Because the Lorenz curves are unaffected by the mean of the distribution, they cannot be used to rank distributions in terms of social welfare, only in terms of inequality. This deficiency is easily repaired by looking at "generalized" Lorenz curves—a concept introduced by Shorrocks (1983). The horizontal axis for the generalized Lorenz curve is the same as that for the Lorenz curve, the cumulative fraction of the population, but the vertical axis, instead of showing the cumulative *share* of income, wealth, or consumption, shows the cumulative share multiplied by the mean, so that a Lorenz curve can be converted into a generalized Lorenz curve by multiplying by mean welfare. Clearly, for any single Lorenz curve, this is only a change of scale, and has no effect on its shape; generalized Lorenz curves are used for comparing different distributions with different means and thus with different aggregates. If the generalized Lorenz curve in one period lies above the generalized Lorenz curve in another period, it implies that for all *p* from 0 to 100, the poorest *p* percent of the population have more resources in total in the first period's distribution which will therefore be preferred by any equity respecting social welfare function. The poorest person has more, there is more in aggregate, and more generally, each quantile of the distribution is higher. Hence an equity respecting social welfare function will always prefer a distribution whose generalized Lorenz curve lies above another.

The generalized Lorenz curves corresponding to the three distributions in Figure 3.3 are shown in Figure 3.4, where I have assumed that *A* and *B* have the same mean, but that mean *x* in distribution *C* is higher. As drawn, the effect is to "lift" the distribution *C* clear of distribution *A*, so that *C* now dominates *A* by the generalized Lorenz criterion, although not by the Lorenz criterion. As a result,

Figure 3.4. Generalized Lorenz curves for Lorenz curves in Figure 3.3

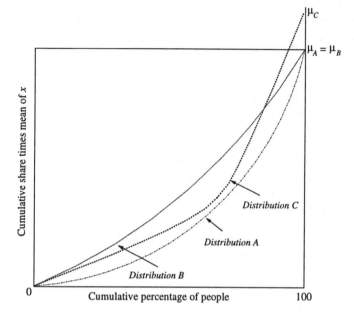

distribution C will be preferred to A by any equality-preferring social welfare function. The generalized Lorenz curve of C now crosses that of B, so that the social welfare ranking of the two will depend on the precise social welfare function used, on the tradeoff between more equality in B and the more mean in C. These examples should make it clear once again that inequality by itself is not a measure of welfare. If the mean of distribution C were further increased so that the generalized Lorenz curve for C were everywhere above that of B, we would have a situation where one distribution is preferred to another by all equity respecting social welfare functions, even though it is more unequal according to all measures of inequality that satisfy the transfer principle.

Lorenz curves and inequality in South Africa and Côte d'Ivoire

Figure 3.5 shows three Lorenz curves for the individual PCE distributions in South Africa in 1993 for the whole population—the outer curve—for Blacks—the broken line—and for Whites—the innermost line. These curves show, for example, that the poorest 20 (50) percent of South Africans receive only 3 (13) percent of all of PCE, that the poorest 20 (50) percent of Blacks receive 5 (20) percent of all PCE received by Blacks, while the poorest 20 (50) percent of Whites receive 7.5 (28) percent of all PCE received by Whites. Also important to note is that the Lorenz curve for Blacks lies everywhere outside the Lorenz curve for Whites. As a result, the unanimous ranking in Table 3.4, where the distribution of PCE among Whites is shown as more equal than that among Blacks by all the measures, is not a special

Figure 3.5. Lorenz curves for individual PCE by race, South Africa, 1993

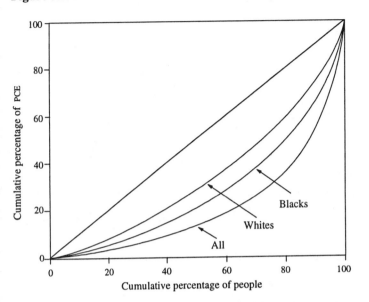

Source: Author's calculations based on South African Living Standards Survey, 1993.

feature of those particular measures but will be repeated for any other inequality measure that satisfies the principle of transfers. Put differently, provided we respect the principle of transfers, there can be no dispute that there is more inequality among Blacks than Whites.

A second example comes from Côte d'Ivoire. Figure 3.6 shows Lorenz curves for the four years of CILSS data, but in a slightly different way from usual. It is frequently the case with empirical Lorenz curves—as opposed to the theoretical curves in Figure 3.3—that different curves are very close to one another and are not easily told apart by inspection. That this was not the case for South Africa is because of that country's extreme differences in inequality between the races; Whites and Blacks are not only far apart in average living standards, but also in the dispersion of their living standards. Changes in inequality over time are likely to be less marked, and in Côte d'Ivoire from 1985–88, the Lorenz curves do not move much. Differences are more easily seen if we plot, not the Lorenz curve itself, but the distance of the Lorenz curve from the 45-degree line, and these curves are plotted in Figure 3.6. Because signs are changed, the higher curves are now those with the greatest inequality.

The figure shows why the results in Table 3.2 come out as they do and they tell us what would happen if we were to work with alternative measures of inequality. The curve for 1988 lies entirely below the curve for 1986, and both lie below the curves for 1985 and 1987; these last cannot be ranked relative to one another, but cross at around the 70th percentile of the population. Below the 70th percentile, the 1985 curve is higher because the poorest part of the distribution was poorer in

Figure 3.6. Transformed Lorenz curves, Côte d'Ivoire, 1985–88

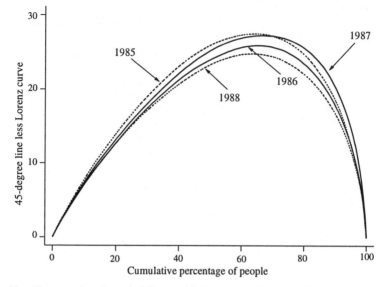

Note: The curves show the vertical distance of the Lorenz curve from the 45-degree line.
Source: Author's calculations using CILSS

1985 than in 1987. Above the 70th percentile, which is a part of the distribution about which we may be less concerned, the curve for 1985 is lower because the share of PCE in the hands of the best-off people is less. As we saw in Table 3.2, all the measures agreed that 1988 was more equal than 1986, and that both were more equal than either 1985 or 1987, while disagreeing on the relative ranking of those two years. This is exactly what must happen given the shapes of the Lorenz curves.

Table 3.1 shows that the average level of PCE is falling over time, so that a graph of generalized Lorenz curves over time will be one in which the standard Lorenz curves are progressively rotated clockwise from the origin. Because the changes in the mean are large relative to the changes in inequality, the generalized Lorenz curves move downward over time, with 1986 below 1985, 1987 below 1986, and 1988 below 1987. A small exception is that the generalized Lorenz curve for 1986 is slightly higher than that for 1985 at the very bottom of the distribution; the poorest people had absolutely more in 1986 than a year earlier, not just a larger share. This apart, social welfare fell in Côte d'Ivoire from 1985 to 1988, and the conclusion does not depend on how we measure inequality nor on our degree of aversion to it.

*Stochastic dominance

The mechanics of ranking welfare distributions are clarified by reference to the concept of stochastic dominance. While it is possible to read discussions of inequality and of poverty without knowing anything about stochastic dominance, a deeper understanding can be obtained with the aid of the few straightforward definitions and results given in this subsection. For those who wish to skip this material, I shall label the stochastic dominance results when I come to them, so that it is possible to move directly to the next subsection without loss of continuity.

Stochastic dominance is about ranking distributions, and the Lorenz dominance discussed above is only one of a set of definitions and results. All work by treating consumers as a continuum, so that instead of dealing with concepts such as the fraction of people whose consumption (say) is less than x, we think of x as being continuously distributed in the population with CDF $F(x)$. We shall typically be concerned with the comparison of two such (welfare) distributions, whose CDFs I write as $F_1(x)$ and $F_2(x)$, and we want to know whether we can say that one is "better" than the other, in some sense to be defined.

The first definition is *first-order stochastic dominance*. We say that distribution with CDF $F_1(x)$ first-order stochastically dominates distribution $F_2(x)$ if and only if, for *all* monotone nondecreasing functions $\alpha(x)$

$$(3.20) \qquad \int \alpha(x)dF_1(x) \geq \int \alpha(x)dF_2(x)$$

where the integral is taken over the whole range of x. The way to appreciate this definition is to think of $\alpha(x)$ as a valuation function, and monotonicity as meaning that more is better (or at least no worse.) According to (3.20), the average value of α is at least as large in distribution 1 as in distribution 2 no matter how we value x, so long as more is better. In consequence, distribution 1 is "better," in the sense that it has more of x, and it stochastically dominates distribution 2.

There is a useful result that provides an alternative characterization of first-order stochastic dominance. The condition (3.20) is equivalent to the condition that, for all x,

$$(3.21) \qquad F_2(x) \geq F_1(x)$$

so that the CDF of distribution 2 is always at least as large as that of distribution 1. (The proof of the equivalence of (3.20) and (3.21) is straightforward, and is left as an exercise. But we can go from (3.20) to (3.21) by choosing $\alpha(x)$ to be the function that is zero for $x \leq a$ and 1 thereafter, and we can go from (3.21) to (3.20) by first integrating the latter by parts.)

Note that distribution 1, which is the dominating distribution, is on the left-hand side of (3.20), but on the right-hand side of (3.21). Intuitively, (3.21) says that distribution 2 always has more mass in the lower part of the distribution, which is why any monotone increasing function ranks distribution 1 ahead of distribution 2.

The second definition is of *second-order stochastic dominance*, a concept that is weaker than first-order stochastic dominance in that first-order dominance implies second-order dominance, but not vice versa. We say that distribution $F_1(x)$ second-order stochastically dominates distribution $F_2(x)$ if and only if, for all monotone nondecreasing and *concave* functions $\alpha(x)$, the inequality (3.20) holds. Since monotone nondecreasing concave functions are members of the class of monotone nondecreasing functions, first-order stochastic dominance implies second-order stochastic dominance. In first-order stochastic dominance, the function $\alpha(x)$ has a positive first derivative; in second-order stochastic dominance, it has a positive first derivative and a negative second derivative.

When $\alpha(x)$ is concave, we can interpret the integrals in (3.20) as additive social welfare functions with $\alpha(x)$ the social valuation (utility) function for individual x. Given this interpretation, second-order stochastic dominance is equivalent to social welfare dominance for any concave utility function. As we have already seen, social welfare dominance is equivalent to generalized Lorenz dominance, so we also have the result that generalized Lorenz dominance and second-order stochastic dominance are equivalent. For distributions whose means are the same, second-order stochastic dominance, welfare dominance, and (standard) Lorenz dominance are the same.

Second-order stochastic dominance, like first-order stochastic dominance, can be expressed in more than one way. In particular, second-order stochastic dominance of $F_1(x)$ over $F_2(x)$ implies, and is implied by, the statement that, for all x,

$$(3.22) \qquad D_2(x) = \int^x F_2(t)\,dt \geq \int^x F_1(t)\,dt = D_1(x)$$

so that second-order stochastic dominance is checked, not by comparing the CDFs themselves, but by comparing the integrals beneath them. We shall see examples of both comparisons in the next subsection. As we might expect, the fact that first-order stochastic dominance implies second-order stochastic dominance is also apparent from the alternative characterizations (3.21) and (3.22). Clearly, if (3.21) holds for all x, (3.22) must also hold for all x. However, when discussing poverty, we will sometimes want a restricted form of stochastic dominance in which (3.21) is true, not for all x, but over some limited range $z_0 \leq x \leq z_1$. But when (3.21) holds in this restricted form it no longer implies (3.22) except in the special case when z_0 is the lowest possible value of x (see (3.27) and (3.28) below).

Further orders of stochastic dominance can be defined by continuing the sequence. For first-order dominance, distributions are ranked according to the inequality (3.20) where $\alpha(x)$ has a nonnegative first derivative. For second-order dominance, the $\alpha(x)$ function has nonnegative first derivative and nonpositive second derivative. Distribution $F_1(x)$ *third-order stochastically dominates* distribution $F_2(x)$ when (3.20) holds for all functions $\alpha(x)$ with nonnegative first derivative, nonpositive second derivative, and nonnegative third derivative. And so on in the sequence. Just as second-order dominance can be tested from (3.22) by comparing $D_1(x)$ and $D_2(x)$, themselves the integrals of $F_1(x)$ and $F_2(x)$, whose relative rankings tells us about first-order dominance, so can third-order dominance be tested using the integrals of $D_1(x)$ and $D_2(x)$.

Exploring the welfare distribution: poverty

If robustness analysis is desirable for social welfare and inequality comparisons, it is even more so for the measurement of poverty if we are not to be hostage to an ill-defined and arbitrarily selected poverty line. At the least, we need to explore the sensitivity of the various poverty measures to the choice of z, although when we do so, it should not be a surprise that we are thereby led back to something closely akin to the social welfare approach. If we have literally no idea where the poverty line is, and it is even possible that everyone is poor, poverty measures have to give at least some weight to everyone, although as always, poorer individuals will get more weight than richer ones. But this is exactly what a standard social welfare function does, so that the social welfare approach will only differ from the poverty approach when we can set some limits on permissible poverty lines.

Start from the headcount ratio, and consider what happens as we vary the poverty line z. Since P_0 is the fraction of the population whose welfare level is below z, we have

(3.23) $$P_0(z;F) = F(z)$$

where the notation on the left-hand side emphasizes not only that the headcount is a function of the poverty line z, but also that it is a function (technically a *functional*) of the distribution F. If we have two different distributions F_1 and F_2, relating to different years, sectors, or countries, and we want to know which shows more poverty and the extent to which the comparison depends on the choice of poverty line z, then (3.23) tells us that if, for all poverty lines z

(3.24) $$F_1(z) > F_2(z)$$

the headcount will always be higher for the first distribution than the second. Hence, all we have to do to test the robustness of the headcount ratio is to plot the CDFs of the two distributions that we are interested in comparing, and if one lies above the other over the range of relevant poverty lines, then the choice of poverty line within that range will make no difference to the outcome.

In the language of the previous subsection, the poverty ranking of two distributions according to the headcount ratio is robust to all possible choices of poverty line if, and only if, one distribution first-order stochastically dominates the other. In practice, we usually have some idea of the poverty line, or are at least able to rule out some as implausible, so that the more useful requirement is that (3.24) hold over some relevant range, which is a restricted form of stochastic dominance.

Figures 3.7 and 3.8 show part of the cumulative distributions for individual PCE in South Africa and in Côte d'Ivoire for 1985 through 1988. Since poverty lines at the very top of the distribution are usually implausible—even for a poor country— it is not necessary to show the complete range of PCE levels. In the South African case in Figure 3.7, the cutoff of 2,000 rand per capita per month excludes about 20 percent of Whites, but no one else. As was the case for the Lorenz curves, the extraordinary inequalities in South Africa produce an unusually clear picture. The four distribution functions are quite separate so that, no matter what poverty line we choose, there will be a higher fraction of people in poverty among Blacks than among Coloreds, a higher fraction among Coloreds than among Indians, and a higher fraction among Indians than among Whites.

Figure 3.7. Distribution functions of individual PCE by race, South Africa, 1993

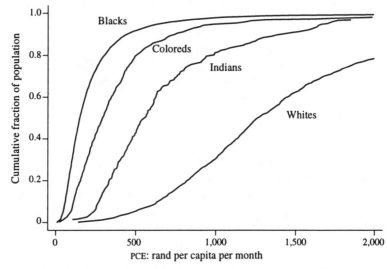

Source: Author's calculations based on South African Living Standards Survey, 1993.

The situation for Côte d'Ivoire is less clear because several of the distribution functions cross. Here I have excluded people living in households with per capita monthly expenditure of more than 300,000 CFAF, which is two and a half times the poverty line used in constructing Table 3.3. Given the declines in PCE over time, it is no surprise that, over most of the range, the curves are higher in the later years so that, for most poverty lines, the fraction of poor people will be increasing from 1985 through to 1988. However, around the poverty line of 128,600 CFAF used in Table 3.3, the distribution functions for the first three years are very close and, at the lowest values of PCE, the curve for 1985 lies above that for 1986 and 1987. As we have already seen in making inequality comparisons, the poorest did better in 1985 than in 1986, even though average PCE fell.

To examine the robustness of the other poverty measures, consider the "poverty deficit curve," defined as the area under the CDF up to some poverty line z

$$(3.25) \qquad D(z;F) = \int_0^z F(x)dx.$$

Why this measure is useful is revealed by integrating the right-hand side of (3.25) to give

$$(3.26) \qquad D(z;F) = zF(z) - \int_0^z f(x)x\,dx = zF(z)(1 - \frac{\mu^P}{z}) = zP_1(z;F)$$

where, as before, μ^P is the mean welfare among the poor and $P_1(z;F)$ is the poverty-gap measure of poverty. Equation (3.26) establishes that we can use the

Figure 3.8. Distribution functions of individual PCE, Côte d'Ivoire, 1985–88

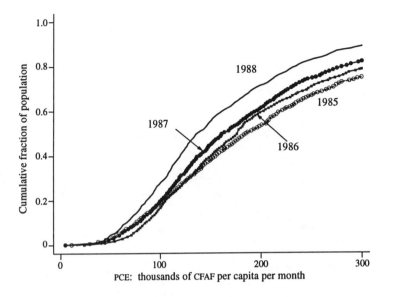

Source: Author's calculations based on CILSS.

poverty deficit curve to examine the robustness of the poverty-gap measure to different choices of the poverty line in exactly the same way that we used the CDF to examine the robustness of the headcount ratio. If the poverty deficit curve for one distribution lies above the poverty deficit curve of another, the first distribution will always have more poverty according to the poverty-gap measure.

Figure 3.9 shows the lower segments of the poverty deficit curves for the Ivorian data. These curves, which are marked in the same way as Figure 3.8, show that the poverty-gap ratio is higher in 1988 than in 1987 for a range of poverty lines, results that establish some robustness for the estimates in Table 3.3. The poverty deficit curve for 1987 is above that for 1986 and, except for low poverty lines, above that for 1985. Given previous results, the crossing of the 1985 and 1986 curves is to be expected; 1986 was better than 1985 at the bottom of the distribution, but worse on average.

It is possible to continue this type of robustness analysis beyond the headcount and poverty-gap ratios to the other poverty measures. However, it is better at this point to look at the pattern that is emerging, and once again to link the analysis of poverty back to the social welfare function. Note first that if, as happens in South Africa, or in Côte d'Ivoire for 1988 and 1987, one of the distribution functions had been higher than another from 0 up to some plausible upper limit for the poverty line z^+, say, then the same would automatically have been true for the poverty deficit curves. Formally, if for two distributions F_1 and F_2

$$(3.27) \qquad F_1(x) \geq F_2(x), \ 0 \leq x \leq z^+$$

Figure 3.9. Poverty deficit curves, Côte d'Ivoire, 1985–88

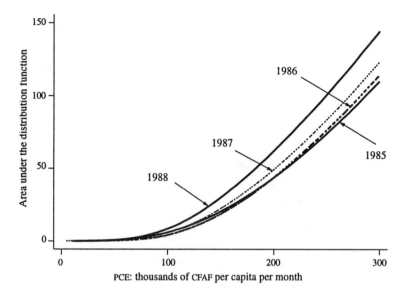

Source: Author's calculations based on CILSS.

then

$$(3.28) \qquad D(z;F_1) = \int_0^z F_1(x)dx \geq \int_0^z F_2(x)dx = D(z;F_2), \ 0 \leq z \leq z^+.$$

Hence if the distributions do not cross before the maximum possible poverty line, then not only are the headcount ratios robust to the choice of line, but so are the poverty-gap ratios. Indeed, if we were to push the analysis a stage further, and look at the area under the deficit curve, the resulting curves would not cross if the poverty deficit curves did not cross, so that measures like P_2 would also be robust to choice of the line. Of course, these results only work one way; it is possible for the distribution functions to cross and for the poverty deficit curves not to do so, as indeed is the case for 1987 versus 1986 in Côte d'Ivoire. But if we find that the distribution functions do not cross, we need look no further because all the poverty measures will be robust. If they do cross but the poverty deficit curves do not, then any measure that is sensitive to the depth of poverty will be robust, and so on.

While these results that take us from one type of robustness to another are useful, they are not always exactly what we need. As emphasized by Atkinson (1987), we may have a lower as well as an upper limit for the poverty line, and it may turn out that the distribution functions do not cross between the limits, so that (3.27) holds for $z^- \leq x \leq z^+$, say, so that the headcount ratio is robust to the choice of poverty line within the range of possibilities. Since the distribution functions may still cross below z^-, we no longer have the implication that (3.28) holds even over the restricted range.

It is also worth considering again what happens when the poverty line can be anything, from zero to infinity. This is the case where the robustness of the head-count ratio is equivalent to the distribution functions never crossing, which is (unrestricted) first-order stochastic dominance. If the poverty deficit curves never cross, we have second-order stochastic dominance; by definition, F_1 second-order stochastically dominates F_2 if the expectation of all monotone increasing concave functions is larger under F_1 than under F_2. If the social welfare function is additive over individual welfare levels, concavity is equivalent to diminishing marginal social utility, and thus to a preference for transfers from richer to the poorer people. Hence, noncrossing of the poverty deficit curves means that an additive equity-respecting social welfare function would prefer the distribution with the lower curve. Not surprisingly, the poverty deficit curve of one distribution is everywhere *above* that of another if and only if the generalized Lorenz curve of the former is everywhere *below* that of the former; generalized Lorenz curves and social welfare functions will rank distributions in the same way as one another and in the same way as poverty deficit curves when nothing is known about the poverty line.

If the poverty deficit curves cross or, equivalently, if the generalized Lorenz curves cross, we might want to consider one more order of integration or of dominance. If we draw the curves formed by integrating under the poverty deficit curves, and if these do not cross, then one distribution dominates the other at the third order. This means that it would be preferred by any additive social welfare function where social marginal utility is positive, diminishing, and diminishing at a decreasing rate. This last condition, sometimes referred to as the *principle of diminishing transfers* (see Kolm 1976), means that, not only does the social welfare function increase when transfers are made from rich to poor, but that a transfer from someone earning 300 rand to someone earning 200 rand is to be preferred to a transfer from someone with 500 rand to someone with 300 rand. These third-order connections were first recognized by Atkinson, who reviews them in more detail in Atkinson (1992).

Finally, it is worth emphasizing again the potential role of measurement error in household expenditures. The addition of random noise to a distribution spreads it out, and the contaminated distribution will be second-order stochastically dominated by the true distribution. If the contamination is similar across years, inter-temporal comparisons may be unaffected, but there is no reason to suppose that this is the case. Surveys often have start-up problems in their first year, and accuracy can be expected to improve over time in a well-run survey, or to deteriorate if enumerators are not carefully supervised.

3.2 Nonparametric methods for estimating density functions

All of the techniques discussed in the previous section relate to the distribution functions of welfare, to transformations like Lorenz curves or generalized Lorenz curves or to the integrals of areas beneath them. However, for many purposes, we are also interested in the density functions of income, consumption, or welfare.

Standard measures of central tendency and dispersion are often most easily visualized in terms of densities, and so it is useful to have techniques that provide estimates of densities. These techniques are the topic of this section which takes the form of a largely methodological digression between two more substantive discussions. It presents an introduction to the tools of nonparametric density estimation to be used in the next section, as well as in several subsequent chapters. These tools also help understand the nonparametric regressions that will be used in the next section. The distribution of welfare is only one of many examples where it is useful to calculate and display a density function. In the next section, where I consider the effects of pricing policies, I shall show how the joint density of the consumption or production of a commodity and levels of living can be used to describe the differential effects of price changes on the well-being of rich and poor.

Estimating univariate densities: histograms

A good place to start is with the distributions of PCE by race in South Africa that were discussed in the previous section. For each of the four groups, Figure 3.10 shows the standard histograms that are used to approximate densities. The histograms are drawn for the logarithm of real PCE at the individual level, not for the level; the distribution of the latter is so positively skewed as to preclude the drawing of informative histograms. The logarithmic transformation yields a distribution that is more symmetric and much closer to normal. Indeed, the curves drawn on each histogram show the normal densities with mean and variance equal to the

Figure 3.10. Histograms of log(PCE) by race, South Africa, 1993

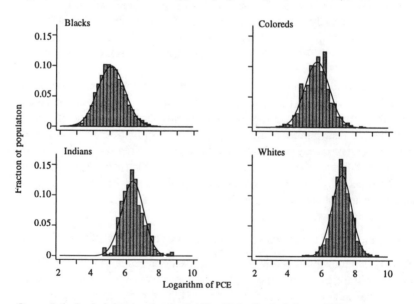

Source: Author's calculations based on South African Living Standards Survey, 1993.

means and variances of the underlying distributions of the logarithm of PCE; these appear to provide a reasonably good approximation to the empirical densities, at least as represented by the histograms.

The histograms and normal distributions of Figure 3.10 are all that we need for many purposes. They provide a visual impression of the position and spread of the data, and allow comparison with some convenient theoretical distribution, in this case the (log)normal. However, there are also a number of disadvantages of histograms. There is a degree of arbitrariness that comes from the choice of the number of "bins" and of their widths. Depending on the distribution of points, the choice of a bin boundary on one side or another of a cluster of points can change the shape of the histogram, so that the empirical distribution appears to be different. Perhaps more fundamental are the problems that arise from using histograms—which are tools for representing discrete distributions—to represent the continuously differentiable densities of variables that are inherently continuous. Such representations can obscure the genuine shape of the empirical distribution, and are inherently unsuited to providing information about the derivatives of density functions, quantities that are sometimes of interest in their own right, as we shall see in Chapters 4 and 5.

It is worth asking why these difficulties did not arise when graphing CDFs, or the areas beneath them as in Figures 3.7, 3.8, and 3.9 above. The answer is that they did, but because the data are cumulated and there are a large number of data points, the discontinuities are less apparent. The empirical distribution functions in Figures 3.7 and 3.8 are calculated from the formula

$$(3.29) \qquad \tilde{F}(x) = n^{-1} \sum_{i=1}^{n} 1(x_i \le x)$$

which is simply the fraction of the sample whose x's are less than or equal to the value x. $\tilde{F}(x)$ is a step function that jumps whenever x is equal to a data point, and that is flat between data points. Because there are many data points, the steps are all very small relative to the scale of the figure, and there are many steps, so that the eye does not perceive the jagged shape of the graph, at least away from the upper tail of the distribution where the points thin out. These considerations apply even more strongly to poverty deficit curves, which are the integrals of distribution functions; they are no longer discontinuous at the data points, but only have slopes that are discontinuous step functions. But changes in slopes are even harder to see, and the pictures give the impression of smooth and ever accelerating slopes. When we move from a CDF to a density, we are moving in the opposite direction, differentiating rather than integrating, so that the discontinuities in the empirical distribution function present serious difficulties in estimating densities, difficulties that are magnified even further if we try to estimate the derivatives of densities.

Estimating univariate densities: kernel estimators

The problems with histograms have prompted statisticians to consider alternative ways of estimating density functions, and techniques for doing so are the main topic of this subsection. One familiar method is to fit a parametric density to the data; the two-parameter lognormal is the simplest, but there are many other possibilities with more parameters to permit a better fit (see, for example, Cramer 1969 or Kakwani 1980.) Here I look at nonparametric techniques which, like the histogram, allow a more direct inspection of the data, but which do not share the histogram's deficiencies. Readers interested in following the topic further are encouraged to consult the splendid (and splendidly accessible) book by Silverman (1986), on whose treatment the following account is based.

Perhaps the simplest way to get away from the "bins" of the histogram is to try to estimate the density at every point along the x-axis. With a finite sample, there will only be empirical mass at a finite number of points, but we can get round this problem by using mass at nearby points as well as at the point itself. The essential idea is to estimate the density $f(x)$ from the fraction of the sample that is "near" to x. One way of doing this is to choose some interval or "band," and to count the number of points in the band around each x. Think of this as sliding the band (or window) along the x-axis, calculating the fraction of the sample per unit interval within it, and plotting the result as an estimate of the density at the mid-point of the band. If the "bandwidth" is h, say, the so-called naive estimator is

$$(3.30) \qquad \tilde{f}(x) = \frac{1}{nh} \sum_{i=1}^{n} 1\left(-\frac{h}{2} \le x - x_i \le \frac{h}{2} \right).$$

At each point x, we pass through the sample, giving a score of 1 to each point within $h/2$ of x, and zero otherwise; the density is estimated as the total score as a fraction of the sample size and divided by h to put it on a per unit basis.

The choice of the bandwidth h is something to which I shall return. For the moment, the point to note is that the bandwidth ought to be smaller the larger is the sample size. If we only have a few points, we need large bands in order to get any points in each, even if the wide bandwidth means that we risk biasing the estimate by bringing into the count data that come from a different part of the distribution. However, as the sample size grows, we can shrink the bandwidth so that, in the limit when we have an infinite amount of data, the bandwidth will be zero, and we will know the true density at each point. In fact, we have to do a little more than this. What has to happen in order to get a consistent estimate of the density at each point is that the bandwidth become smaller at a rate that is less fast than the rate at which the sample size is increasing. As a result, not only does the shrinking bandwidth guarantee that bias will eventually be eliminated by concentrating only on the mass at the point of interest, but it also ensures that variance will go to zero as the number of points within each band increases and the average within the band becomes more precise. In this way, the increase in the sample size is shared between more points per band, to increase the precision, and smaller bandwidths so as to ultimately eliminate bias. Of course, because some of the benefits of larger sample sizes have to be "diverted" from putting more observations into each band and devoted to shrinking the bandwidth, the rate of convergence to the density at each x is bound to be slower than the normal root-N convergence that is standard in sampling or regression analysis.

While the naive estimator captures the essential idea of nonparametric density estimation using the "kernel" method—the kernel is the band or indicator function in (3.30)—it does not solve one of the problems with which we began. In particular, there will be steps in $\tilde{f}(x)$ every time a data point enters or exits the band. But this can be dealt with by a simple modification. Instead of giving all the points inside the band equal weight, we give more weight to those near to x and less to those far away, so that points have a weight of zero both just outside and just inside the band. We can do this quite generally by replacing the indicator function in (3.30) by a "kernel" function $K(.)$, so that

$$(3.31) \qquad \tilde{f}(x) = \frac{1}{nh} \sum_{i=1}^{n} K\left(\frac{x-x_i}{h}\right)$$

which is the "kernel estimate" of the density $f(x)$.

There are many possible choices for the kernel function. Because it is a weighting function, it should be positive and integrate to unity over the band, it should be symmetric around zero, so that points below x get the same weight as those an equal distance above, and it should be decreasing in the absolute value of its argument. The "rectangular" kernel in (3.30)—so called because all observations in the band get equal weight—satisfies all these criteria except the last. A better choice is a kernel function that uses quadratic weights. This is the Epanechnikov kernel

$$(3.32) \qquad \begin{aligned} K(z) &= 0.75(1-z^2), \quad -1 \le z \le 1 \\ &= 0, \quad |z| > 1 \end{aligned}$$

whose weights have an inverted U–shape that decline to zero at the band's edges. Another obvious source of kernels is the class of symmetric density functions, the most popular of which is the Gaussian kernel

$$(3.33) \qquad K(z) = (2\pi)^{-0.5} \exp(-z^2/2).$$

The Gaussian kernel does not use a discrete band, within which observations have weight and outside of which they do not, but instead gives all observations some weight at each point in the estimated density. Of course, the normal density is very small beyond a few standard deviations from the mean, so that the Gaussian kernel will assign very little weight in the estimate of the density at x to observations that are further than (say) $3h$ from x. A third useful kernel is the quartic or "biweight"

$$(3.34) \qquad \begin{aligned} K(z) &= \tfrac{15}{16}(1-z^2)^2, \quad -1 \le z \le 1 \\ &= 0, \quad |z| > 1. \end{aligned}$$

The quartic kernel behaves similarly to the Epanechnikov kernel, declining to zero at the band's edges, but has the additional property that its derivative is continuous at the edge of the band, a property that is useful in a number of circumstances that we shall see as we proceed.

Although the choice of kernel function will influence the shape of the estimated density, especially when there are few points and the bandwidth is large, the literature suggests that this choice is not a critical one, at least among sensible alternatives such as those listed in the previous paragraph. As a result, a kernel can be chosen on other grounds, such as computational convenience or the requirement that it be continuously differentiable at the boundary.

More important is the choice of the bandwidth, and this is a practical problem that has to be faced in every application. As we have already seen, the bandwidth controls the trade-off between bias and variance; a large bandwidth will provide a smooth and not very variable estimate but risks bias by bringing in observations from other parts of the density, while a small bandwidth, although helping us pick up genuine features of the underlying density, risks producing an unnecessarily variable plot. Estimating densities by kernel methods is an exercise in "smoothing" the raw observations into an estimated density, and the bandwidth controls how much smoothing is done. Oversmoothed estimates are biased, and undersmoothed estimates too variable.

A formal theory of the trade-off between bias and variance provides helpful insights and is a useful guide to bandwidth selection. In standard parametric inference, optimal estimation is frequently based on minimizing mean-squared error between the estimated and true parameters. In the nonparametric case, we are attempting to estimate, not a parameter, but a function, and there will be a mean-squared error at each point on the estimated density. One natural procedure is to attempt to minimize the *mean integrated squared error*, defined as the expectation of the integral of the squared error over the whole density. Silverman (1986, pp. 38–40) shows how to approximate the mean integrated square error for a kernel estimate of a density, and shows that the (approximate) optimal bandwidth is

$$(3.35) \qquad h^* = \left[\int z^2 K(z) dz \right]^{-2/5} \left[\int K(z)^2 dz \right]^{1/5} \left[\int f''(x)^2 dx \right]^{-1/5} N^{-1/5}.$$

Since the evaluation of (3.35) requires knowledge of the very density that we are trying to estimate, it is not directly useful, but is nevertheless informative. It confirms that the bandwidth should shrink as the sample size increases, but that it should do so only very slowly, in (inverse) proportion to the fifth root of N. Note too the importance of the absolute size of the second derivative of the density. If there is a large amount of curvature, then estimates based on averaging in a band will be biased, so that the bandwidth ought to be small, and conversely on segments of the density that are approximately linear.

For most of the applications considered in this book, an adequate procedure is to consider a number of different bandwidths, to plot the associated density estimates, and to judge by eye whether the plots are undersmoothed or oversmoothed. This can perhaps be regarded as an informal version of an iterative procedure that computes a "pilot" estimate, calculates the optimal bandwidth from (3.35) assuming that the pilot is the truth, and then repeats. Applying the informal procedure usually leads to an easy separation of features in the density that are driven by random sampling from those that appear to be genuine characteristics of the underlying law from which the sample is drawn. There should also be some preference for undersmoothing when using graphical methods; the eye can readily ignore variability that it judged to be spurious, but it cannot discern features that have been covered up by oversmoothing.

It is very useful in these calculations to have a good bandwidth with which to start. If it is assumed that the density has some specific form, normal being the obvious possibility, then (3.35) yields an optimal bandwidth once a kernel is chosen. If the estimated density has the right shape, we have a good choice—indeed the best choice—and otherwise we can make informal adjustments by hand. If both the kernel and the density are Gaussian, (3.35) gives an optimal bandwidth of $1.06 \sigma N^{-1/5}$, where σ is the standard deviation of the density, which can be calculated prior to estimation. Silverman suggests that better results will typically be obtained by replacing σ by a robust measure of spread, in which case the optimal bandwidth is

$$(3.36) \qquad h^* = 1.06 \min(\sigma, 0.75 IQR) N^{-1/5}$$

where IQR is the interquartile range—the difference between the 75th and 25th percentiles. Similar expressions can easily be obtained from (3.35) using other kernels; for the Epanechnikov, the multiplying factor 1.06 should be replaced by 2.34, for the quartic by 2.42.

Estimating univariate densities: examples

The techniques of the previous subsection can be illustrated using the distributions of log (PCE) in Côte d'Ivoire and South Africa, as well as similar distributions from Thailand that I shall refer to again in the next section. Figure 3.11 shows the estimated density function for PCE in South Africa, with the data pooled by race. The calculations were done using the "kdensity" command in STATA, weighted using the sampling weights multiplied by household size, and with STATA's default choice of kernel—the Epanechnikov. The weighting is done using the obvious modification of (3.31)

$$(3.37) \qquad \tilde{f}_w(x) = h^{-1} \sum_{h=1}^{n} v_h K\left(\frac{x-x_i}{h}\right)$$

where v_h are the normalized weights, the sampling weights normalized by their sum (see equation 1.25). The top left panel uses STATA's default bandwidth, which comes from a formula similar to (3.36), while the other panels show what happens if the bandwidth is scaled up or down.

The South African expenditure distribution is a good illustration because the distributions for Africans and Whites are so far apart that the combined density has a distinct "bump," perhaps even a second mode, around the modal log (PCE) for Whites. With the default bandwidth, this can be clearly seen in the estimated density. It is a good deal less clear when the bandwidth is doubled, and is altogether smoothed away when the bandwidth is doubled again. Choosing too large a bandwidth runs the risk of smoothing out genuine, and genuinely important, features of the data. The figure in the bottom right panel uses a bandwidth that would usually be regarded as too small. Certainly, the graph is not very smooth, and the roughness is almost certainly a feature of the estimation, and not of the underlying true

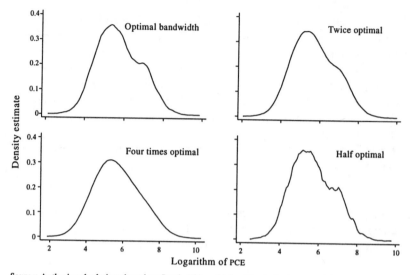

Source: Author's calculations based on South African Living Standards Survey, 1993.

density. Nevertheless, the mode for Whites is clear enough, and the eye is usually capable of smoothing away irrelevant roughness. In this sort of visual exercise, variance is less of a risk than bias, and some undersmoothing is often useful.

Figure 3.12 shows the results of estimating kernel densities for the logarithm of PCE for the four years of data from Côte d'Ivoire, and provides yet another representation of data that should by now be familiar. We see once again, although in a different form, the features displayed by the summary statistics in Table 3.1, and in the Lorenz, distribution, and deficit curves in Figures 3.6, 3.8, and 3.9. The densities generally move to the left over time, although 1986 moves to the right at the bottom, decreasing both poverty and inequality.

Extensions and alternatives

Although kernel estimators are the only nonparametric estimators of densities that I shall use in this book, there are several alternative techniques. Even within the kernel class, there are different ways of selecting the bandwidth, and there are several useful estimators based on other techniques. When the estimates are used for more than graphical presentation, for example as the input into further calculations, it is essential to have a method of bandwidth selection that is objective and replicable across investigators. Apart from the use of rules based on specific distributions, such as (3.36), the most commonly used technique is *cross-validation* (see again Silverman 1986, pp. 48–6, or Stoker 1991, pp. 123–24). The essential idea here is to compute alternative estimates of the density based on different

**Figure 3.12. Estimated density functions for log(PCE),
Côte d'Ivoire, 1985–88**

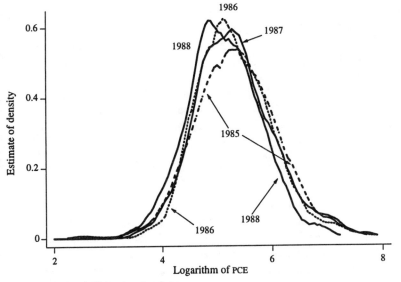

Source: Author's calculations based on CILSS.

bandwidths, to use the result to get some idea of the relationship between the band
width and mean-squared error, and thus to select a bandwidth that minimizes error.
Such calculations are computer-intensive, and are unnecessary for the types of applications considered in this book: when our main concern is the graphical inspection of data, it is usually sufficient to try several bandwidths, and to select a suitable one by inspection of the results.

Kernel methods can also be generalized to allow different bandwidths at different points of the distribution. One nonkernel approach that does so automatically
is the *nearest neighbor* method. Here the estimate of the density is obtained by calculating the distance from each point x to its kth nearest neighbor; k is a number
chosen by the investigator, equal perhaps to a fifth of the sample size, and which
plays the same role in nearest neighbor estimation as does the bandwidth in kernel
estimation. If $d_k(x)$ is the distance from x to the kth nearest of its neighbors, whether to the left or the right, the estimate of the density at x is given by

$$(3.38) \qquad \tilde{f}_k(x) = (k-1) / 2 d_k(x) n.$$

The logic is straightforward. Since the kth nearest neighbor is at distance $d_k(x)$,
there are $k - 1$ points, or a fraction $(k - 1)/N$ of the sample, to the left or right of
x, but in either case within an interval of width $2d_k(x)$ around it. The fraction of
the sample per unit of interval is therefore given by (3.38). The larger is k, the
smoother the estimate, and the larger the risk of bias, while small k avoids bias but

risks unnecessary variability; hence the analogy between k and the bandwidth. However, the nearest neighbor method, unlike the kernel method with fixed bandwidth, keeps the number of points in the band fixed, so that precision is more equally spread through the density.

One of the attractions of kernel methods is that they can be routinely extended to higher dimensional cases, at least in principle. Once again, the naive or rectangular kernel estimator is the most straightforward case to consider. Suppose that we have two variables x_1 and x_2, and that we have drawn a standard scatter diagram of one against the other. To construct the density at the point (x_1, x_2) we count the fraction of the sample in, not a band, but a box around the point. If the area around the point is a square with side h, which is the immediate generalization of an interval of width h in the unidimensional case, then the rectangular kernel estimator is

$$(3.39) \qquad \tilde{f}(x_1, x_2) = \frac{1}{Nh^2} \sum_{i=1}^{N} \left[1\left(-\frac{1}{2} \le \frac{x_{1i}-x_1}{h} \le \frac{1}{2} \right) 1\left(-\frac{1}{2} \le \frac{x_{2i}-x_2}{h} \le \frac{1}{2} \right) \right].$$

This is the immediate extension of (3.30) to the bivariate case, with the product of the two kernels indicating whether the point is or is not in the square around (x_1, x_2) and the division by h^2 instead of h required because we are now counting fraction of sample per unit *area* rather than interval, and the area of each square is h^2.

Of course the rectangular kernel is no better for bivariate than for univariate problems and the indicator functions in (3.39) need to be replaced by a bivariate kernel that gives greater weights to observations close to (x_1, x_2). There is also no need to use the square-contoured kernels that result from multiplying the univariate kernels and an obvious alternative is to count (and weight) points in a circle around each point where we want to estimate the density. However, there is a new issue that did not arise in the univariate case, and that is whether it makes sense to use the same bandwidth in both dimensions. For example, if the variance of x_1 is much larger than that of x_2 it makes more sense to use rectangles instead of squares, or ellipses instead of circles, and to make the axes larger in the direction of x_1. Similar considerations apply when the two variables are correlated, where we would want to align the ellipses in the direction of the correlation. In practice, these issues are dealt with by transforming the data prior to the calculations so that the transformed variables have equal variance and are orthogonal to one another. The transformation done, it is then appropriate to apply bivariate kernels that treat the two variables symmetrically, to estimate a density for the transformed observations, and then to transform back at a final stage.

These operations can all be done in one stage. I illustrate for the bivariate version of the Epanechnikov kernel; while it would be possible to use the product of two univariate Epanechnikov kernels in the bivariate context, we can also use the "circular" form

$$(3.40) \qquad K(z_1, z_2) = (2/\pi)(1 - z_1^2 - z_2^2) \, 1(z_1^2 + z_2^2 \le 1).$$

If the scatter of the data were approximately circular, which requires that the two variables be uncorrelated and have the same variance, we could apply (3.40) directly. More generally, we transform the data using its variance-covariance matrix before applying the kernel smoothing. This can be done in one step by writing the V for the 2×2 variance-covariance matrix of the sample, defining

$$(3.41) \qquad t_i^2 = (x_i - x)'V^{-1}(x_i - x)$$

and calculating the density estimate using the Epanechnikov kernel as

$$(3.42) \qquad \tilde{f}(x_1, x_2) = \frac{2(\det V)^{-1/2}}{\pi N h^2} \sum_{i=1}^{N} \left(1 - \frac{t_i^2}{h^2}\right) 1(t_i \le 1).$$

Corresponding formulas can be readily derived for the Gaussian and quartic kernels; for the former, (3.40) is replaced by the standardized bivariate normal, and for the latter, the $2/\pi$ is replaced by $3/\pi$ and the deviation of the squares from unity is itself squared.

The bivariate density estimates display the empirical structure underlying any statistical analysis of the relationship between two variables. Just as univariate densities are substitutes for histograms, bivariate densities can be used in place of cross-tabulation. In the context of welfare measurement, bivariate densities can illustrate the relationship between two different measures of welfare, calories and income, or income and expenditure, or between welfare measures in two periods. They can also be used to display the allocation of public services in relation to levels of living, and in the next section, I shall show how they can be put to good purpose to illuminate the distributional effects of pricing policies.

There is no difficulty in principle in extending these methods to the estimation of three- or higher-dimensional densities. Even so, there are a number of practical problems. One is computational cost: if there are k dimensions and N observations, the evaluation of the density on a k-dimensional grid of G points requires NG^k evaluations, a number that quickly becomes prohibitively large as k increases. A second difficulty is the "curse of dimensionality," the very large sample sizes required to give adequate estimates of multidimensional densities. An analogy with cross-tabulation is useful. For univariate and bivariate cross-tabulations, sample sizes of a few hundred can provide useful cell means, and so it is with density estimation provided we choose an appropriate bandwidth. In high-dimensional cross-tabulations, cells are frequently empty even when the underlying density is nonzero, and we need very large sample sizes to get an adequate match between the sample and the population.

The third difficulty is one of presentation. Univariate densities are straightforwardly shown as plots of $f(x)$ against x, and with two-dimensional densities, we can use the three-dimensional surface and contour plots that will be illustrated in Figures 3.13 through 3.16 below. Four dimensions can sometimes be dealt with by coloring three-dimensional plots, or if one of the variables is discrete, by reporting different three-dimensional plots for different discrete values. Perhaps the only current application of high-dimensional density estimation is where the estimated density is an intermediate input into another estimation problem, as in the average derivative estimates of Stoker (1991) and Härdle and Stoker (1989).

Estimating bivariate densities: examples

Figure 3.13 shows superimposed contour and scatter plots of the estimated joint density of the logarithm of PCE in the two years 1985 and 1986 on a household basis for the first set of panel households from the CILSS. The switch from an individual to a household basis is dictated by the fact that the panel structure is a household not an individual one, and since the people within households change from one year to the next, we cannot always track individuals over time. The plots make no use of weights; as in the univariate case, it is straightforward to incorporate the weights into the kernel estimation, but I have not done so in order to allow a clear comparison with the scatter plot.

The figure shows that PCE in 1986 is strongly positively correlated with PCE in 1985; as usual, we have no way of separating the differences that do exist into genuine changes in living standards on the one hand and measurement error on the other. The superimposed contour map is constructed using the bivariate Epanechnikov kernel, equations (3.41) and (3.42). Exactly as in the univariate case, I take a grid of equally spaced points from the minimum to maximum value, but now in two dimensions, so that with 99 points on each grid, the density is calculated according to (3.42) for each cell of a 99 by 99 matrix. (The choice of 99 rather than 100 reflects the fact that the surface drawing algorithm used here requires an odd number of points. A smaller grid, say 49 by 49, does not give such clear results; a fine grid is required to give smooth contours.) The calculations are again

Figure 3.13. Contour plot and scatter diagram of the joint density of ln(PCE) in 1985 and 1986 for panel households, Côte d'Ivoire

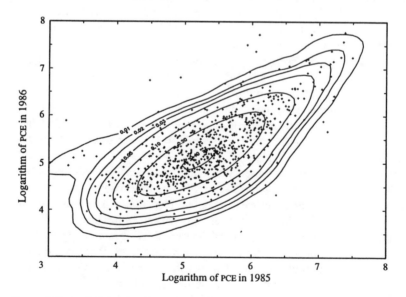

Source: Author's calculations based on CILSS.

Figure 3.14. Netmaps of the joint density of log(PCE) in 1985 and 1986 for panel households, Côte d'Ivoire

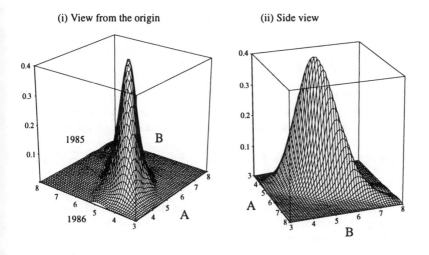

(i) View from the origin   (ii) Side view

Note: The same object is displayed in both figures; the letters A and B mark the same sides of the base.
Source: Author's calculations based on CILSS.

slow, and the time for the bivariate calculations approximately the square of that for the univariate calculations; even so, they are perfectly feasible on small personal computers. Unfortunately, while STATA can handle the univariate calculations, it does not currently have facilities for contour or surface plotting, so that it is necessary to turn to GAUSS or some other graphics program that is capable of plotting contours and surfaces (see the Code Appendix for the GAUSS code used for the figure.) A bandwidth of 1 was used for the contour map; note that the scaling in (3.41) means that the bandwidth refers to the standardized distribution rather than the original one, and so does not need to be scaled by a measure of dispersion.

Figure 3.14 shows the same estimated density in the form of a surface drawing or netmap, which is a projection of the three-dimensional object. While the contour maps are analogous to the usual topographical maps, the netmaps are more like aerial photographs. The two projections, both of which are of the same object plotted in the contour map in Figure 3.13, are shown from different perspectives. In the netmap on the left-hand side of the figure, the eye is (beyond) the bottom left corner of the contour in Figure 3.13, while in the netmap on the right-hand side, the eye position is beyond the lower right corner (see the matching letters A and B in the figure). The netmaps give a clearer overall visual impression than the contours, they do not overemphasize the tails of the distribution, and they can be calculated more cheaply since they do not require so fine a grid of points. However, netmaps also obscure information, and contour maps are recommended whenever we need an accurate and detailed picture of the structure of the density.

3.3 Analyzing the distributional effects of policy

Finding out who benefits and who loses from a policy change is a task to which household survey data are often well-suited. In this section, I look at two examples. The first, which comes from Deaton (1989a, 1991), considers policy on rice prices in Thailand, and uses the Socioeconomic Survey of 1981–82 to look at the effects of changes in prices on the distribution of income. Farm-households who are net producers of rice gain from higher prices, while net consumers will lose. Changes in rice prices therefore affect the distribution of real income between urban and rural sectors, as well as the distribution within sectors, depending on the relationship between levels of living and the net consumption and production of rice. I focus on this relationship, and discuss various techniques for estimating and displaying it.

My second example comes from South Africa and is drawn from Case and Deaton (1996). In recent years, the government in South Africa has paid a "social pension" to men aged 65 or over and women aged 60 or over. The monthly payments are conditioned on a means test—which excludes nearly all Whites—but the vast majority of age-qualified Africans receive payments. It is not immediately clear whether such a policy is effective in reaching poor people. Not everyone who is poor lives with a pensioner, and there are many unemployed adults who are unlikely to be reached by the scheme. However, we can use the South African Living Standards Survey to see who it is that lives in pensioner households, and to assess the distributional incidence of the scheme by calculating the average amount of pension income that is delivered to people at different levels of living.

In both the Thai and South African examples, I use the nonparametric methods discussed in the previous section. They provide simple and appealing graphics that tell us much of what we need to know, and do so in a way that is readily assimilable. Along the way, I also introduce techniques of nonparametric regression. Kernel regressions are a natural extension of the kernel density estimation methods of Section 3.2, and I use them in the analysis of rice prices in Thailand. I also discuss how to estimate nonparametric regressions using a locally weighted version of least squares. Recent work has shown that this method often works better than kernel regression, and this is the technique applied to the South African pension analysis.

Rice prices and distribution in Thailand

Although the Thai economy has become much more diversified in recent years, it was traditionally heavily dependent on exports of rice, and it remains (along with the United States) one of the world's two largest exporters. Since almost all rice is shipped down the Chao Phraya river and through the port of Bangkok, rice exports have always been a ready target for taxation, and until recently an export tax (the rice premium) has been a major contributor to government revenue in Thailand (see Siamwalla and Setboongsarng 1991 and Trairatvorakul 1984 for further discussion). If the world price can be taken as given—a matter of some dispute but a natural starting point—export taxes lower the domestic price of rice, favoring domestic consumers—rice is the basic staple in Thailand—and harming domestic producers. Export taxes thus favor urban at the expense of rural interests, but there are also distributional effects within the rural sector between rural consumers and producers; if net producers are typically much better-off than rural consumers, the tax may have favorable distributional effects within the rural sector.

The operation of these effects can be detailed using household survey data on consumption and production, and this section shows that nonparametric density estimation is a natural tool for the work. Nonparametric regressions are also useful, and I develop these methods as straightforward extensions of the tools introduced in Section 3.2. For other analyses of pricing that use the same techniques, see Budd (1993) and Benjamin and Deaton (1993); both studies use data from the CILSS to look at the pricing of food and cash crops, particularly cocoa and coffee.

The distributional effects of price changes: theory

Many rural households in Thailand are both producers and consumers of rice, so that when we work through the analysis of welfare, it is important to use a model that recognizes this dual role of households. The natural vehicle is the "farm-household" model (see, for example, Singh, Squire, and Strauss 1986). For my current purposes, I need only a utility function that can be used to examine the effect of price changes. As usual, the effects of price changes can most easily be seen by using an indirect utility function, in which the household's utility is written as a function of its income and prices. If we ignore saving—and the Thai surveys record little or no saving among rural households—the farm-household's utility can be written in the form

$$(3.43) \qquad u_h = \psi_h(x_h, p) = \psi_h(m_h + \pi_h, p)$$

where ψ is the indirect utility function, p is a vector of prices of consumption goods, including the price of rice, π_h is profits (net income) from farm activity, and m_h is income from nonfarm activities, such as wage-labor or transfers. Somewhat schizophrenically in view of the analysis to come in Chapter 5, I am assuming that prices are the same for all farmers, thus ignoring regional variation in prices. However, the survey data do not report household-specific prices, and provided all prices move with the export price—as seems to be the case— individual price variation will not affect the analysis.

Although the utility function in (3.43) is a standard one—given that goods' prices are p, it is the maximum utility that can be obtained from the efficient spending of all sources of income, whether from the farm or elsewhere—it rests on a number of important and by no means obviously correct assumptions. Most crucial is the "separation" property, that the only effect of the household having a farm is that it has farm income (see again Singh, Squire, and Strauss 1986 for further discussion). The validity of separation rests on the existence of efficient rural labor markets—a plausible assumption for Thailand—but also, and more dubiously, on the supposition that household and hired labor are perfect substitutes on the family farm. When these assumptions hold, the shadow price of family labor is its market price, which is the wage rate, and working on the household's farm is no different from any other job. As a result, workers in the household can be modeled as if they were wage earners at a fixed wage, and the ownership of the farm brings a rental income, as would the ownership of any other real or financial asset. There are good reasons to doubt the perfect substitutability of household and hired-in labor—differential monitoring costs or transport costs are two obvious examples—but the validity of the separation property as an adequate approximation is ultimately an empirical question. I am unaware of evidence from Thailand, but tests for Indonesia in Pitt and Rosenzweig (1986) and Benjamin (1992) have yielded reasonably favorable results.

The validity of (3.43) also requires a different sort of separability, that goods and leisure are separable in preferences, so that the direct utility function takes the form $u(l,v(q))$ for leisure l and vector of goods q. Given this, the indirect utility function in (3.43) corresponds to the utility of the goods that enter the direct subutility function $v(q)$. It is straightforward to relax this assumption in the present context, but only at the price of complicating the algebra. The same can be said for my ignoring intertemporal aspects and assuming that saving is zero.

Suppose now that there is a change in the ith price, in this case the price of rice. If we confine ourselves to small changes, the effects can be analyzed through the derivatives of the indirect utility function (3.43). In particular, using the chain rule

$$(3.44) \qquad \frac{\partial u_h}{\partial p_i} = \frac{\partial \psi_h}{\partial x_h} \frac{\partial \pi_h}{\partial p_i} + \frac{\partial \psi_h}{\partial p_i}$$

since, for households that are both producers and consumers, the price of rice affects both farm profits and the cost of living. For households, such as urban households, that produce nothing, the first term on the right-hand side of (3.44) will be zero, since there are no farm profits, and similarly for farmers who do not produce rice, whose profits are unaffected by the price of rice.

The two terms in (3.44) can be further elucidated using general results. The effects of prices on profits—often referred to as Hotelling's Lemma after Hotelling (1932)—are given by

$$(3.45) \qquad \frac{\partial \pi_h}{\partial p_i} = y_{hi}$$

where y_{hi} is the production of good i by h. The effect on utility of an increase in price is given by Roy's (1942) theorem,

$$(3.46) \qquad \frac{\partial \psi_h}{\partial p_i} = -q_{hi} \frac{\partial \psi_h}{\partial x_h}$$

where q_{hi} is the amount of good i consumed by household h, and the quantity $\partial \psi_h / \partial x_h$ is the marginal utility of money to household h, a nonoperational concept with which I shall dispense shortly. Producers benefit from a price change in proportion to the amount of their production and consumers lose in proportion to the amount of their consumption. For households that are both producers and consumers—farm-households—the gain or loss is proportional to the difference between production and consumption, which is $y_{hi} - q_{hi}$.

It is often more convenient to work with proportional changes in prices, and if we substitute (3.45) and (3.46) into (3.44) and multiply by p_i we obtain

$$(3.47) \qquad \frac{\partial u_h}{\partial \ln p_i} = \frac{\partial \psi_h}{\partial \ln x_h} \cdot \frac{p_i(y_{hi} - q_{hi})}{x_h}.$$

I shall refer to the last term on the right-hand side of (3.47) as the "net benefit ratio." It measures the elasticity with respect to price of money-equivalent utility, or consumers' surplus for those who prefer that much-abused concept. For policy work, we are concerned with the second of these two terms, but not the first. When considering a policy-induced price change, we need to know the money-equivalent losses and gains for different individuals, so that we can calculate the distributional effects as well as anticipate the likely political repercussions. The marginal utility of money to each individual, quite apart from being unobservable, will be subsumed in policy discussions by decisionmakers' views about the value of giving money to each individual, whether based on levels of living, region, caste, or political preference.

One simple way to summarize these effects is to write

$$(3.48) \qquad \frac{\partial W}{\partial \ln p_i} = \sum_h \zeta_h(x_h, z_h) p_i(y_{hi} - q_{hi})/x_h$$

where W is to be thought of as a social welfare function, and ζ_h captures, not the private marginal utility of money, but the social marginal utility of money. This is not something observable, but summarizes the attitudes of the policymaker towards giving resources to individual h, depending on that household's consumption level x_h as well as on other relevant characteristics z_h, such as perhaps region or ethnic characteristics. (For the remainder of this book, z will denote household characteristics, and not a poverty line.)

We still need to allow for the fact that the rice that is produced—paddy—is not the same commodity as the rice that is consumed—milled rice. Suppose that one kilogram of paddy generates $\lambda < 1$ kilograms of milled rice, and that p_i is the price of the latter, so that the price of paddy is λp_i. If we then rework the preceding analysis, the net benefit ratio is as before, but with λy_{hi} in place of y_{hi}. But this is still the ratio of the value of net sales of rice (or paddy) to total expenditure, so that provided everything is measured in money terms, the benefit ratio is correctly computed by subtracting the value of consumption from the value of sales.

There are a number of caveats that ought to be entered before going on to the empirical results. Note first that the use of the differential calculus, although convenient, limits the analysis to the effects of "small" price changes and may not give the correct answer for actual (finite) price changes. Of course, the result that producers gain and consumers lose from a price increase is a general one, not a local approximation. However, the magnitude of the welfare effects of finite price changes will depend, not just on the amounts produced and consumed, but also on the second-order effects, which involve the amounts by which consumption and

Table 3.5. Household PCE, rice production, and rice consumption in Thailand, 1981–82

	Whole Kingdom	Upper North	Lower North	Upper North East	Lower North East	Center	South	Bangkok
Municipal areas (urban)								
PCE	1,516	1,349	1,362	1,171	1,172	1,497	1,361	1,680
Value of rice sold	20	26	134	- 4	12	33	18	4
Value of rice bought	243	326	261	298	276	247	234	216
Budget share of rice	5.59	8.80	7.03	8.18	7.68	5.72	6.06	4.05
Villages (rural)								
PCE	675	560	647	472	441	862	712	1,021
Value of rice sold	909	426	1,471	580	711	1,183	366	1,515
Value of rice bought	388	377	377	469	468	374	324	285
Budget share of rice	18.70	21.77	19.44	24.64	26.78	14.21	14.38	8.59

Note: All figures are averages over all households in the sample. Amounts in the first three rows are baht per month. Production values are one-twelfth of the annual value of crops and are averaged over all households whether or not they produce rice. The budget shares of rice are the percentages of the nondurable expenditures devoted to rice derived for each household and averaged over households. Glutinous rice and nonglutinous rice are taken together.

Source: Deaton (1989a).

production respond to price changes. Since my main interest here is in the distributional effects of price changes, and in locating the benefits and costs of price changes in the distribution of living standards, these effects will change the conclusions only to the extent that the elasticities of supply and demand differ systematically between poor and rich. Although there is no reason to rule out such effects a priori, there is no reliable evidence on the topic; as I shall argue in Chapter 5, the measurement of the slopes of demand functions is difficult enough without trying to determine how the slopes vary with the level of living.

A more serious deficiency in the analysis is its neglect of repercussions in the labor market. Changes in the price of the basic staple will affect both supply and demand for labor, and these effects can cause first-order modifications to the results. Once again, although it is possible to write down models for how these effects might operate—see, for example, Sah and Stiglitz (1992) who work through several cases—there is little point in doing so here without more hard information about the structure and functioning of the rural labor market in Thailand.

Implementing the formulas: the production and consumption of rice

The empirical analysis starts from (3.48), and uses the 1981–82 Socioeconomic Survey of the Whole Kingdom of Thailand to provide the information. The general approach is to calculate net benefit ratios for each household, and to examine the distribution of these ratios in relation to living standards and regional variation. While it is evident without survey data that lower rice prices redistribute real resources from rural to urban areas, what is less obvious is how price changes redistribute real income between rich and poor people within the rural sector.

The Thai socioeconomic surveys collect data on households by three levels of urbanization, municipal areas (4,159 households in the 1981–82 survey), sanitary districts (1,898 households), and villages (5,836 households). The first corresponds to the urban sector, while the last is the rural area with which I am primarily concerned. (Sanitary districts are semiurban conglomerates of villages, and I shall typically ignore them.) Table 3.5 shows averages of household per capita expenditure as well as information on rice for the country as a whole and for seven major regions. Households in Bangkok are nearly half of urban households and their per capita expenditure is a good deal higher than elsewhere. The rural households that live on the fringes of Bangkok—an excellent rice growing region—are much better-off than other rural households, although substantially poorer than urban Bangkok households. Over the other regions, the average levels of per capita expenditure in the rural areas are a half to a third of the corresponding urban estimates. Once again, I do not have satisfactory price indices for rural versus urban, but there is little doubt that the urban households have a substantially higher standard of living. In consequence, there is no equity argument in favor of the redistribution from rural to urban that is brought about by export taxes on rice.

Not surprisingly, urban households produce little rice compared with rural households. Of the latter, those on the fringes of Bangkok, in the Center, and in the

Figure 3.15. Living standards and rice consumption in Thailand, 1981–82

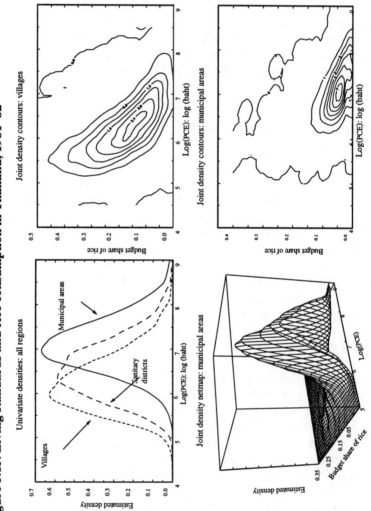

Source: Author's calculations based on Socioeconomic Survey of Thailand, 1981–82.

Lower North are the most productive; these are the regions in the alluvial river basin of central Thailand. In the North Eastern and Upper Northern regions, most production (and consumption) of rice is of the glutinous variety. Although there is little substitution in consumption between glutinous and nonglutinous rice, with distinct groups of people eating each, there is substitutability in production, and for the purpose of the current analysis I assume that the prices of the two kinds of rice move in parallel. Rice consumption is also higher in rural areas in spite of the higher levels of living among urban households. However, urban Thais spend substantial amounts on precooked meals—often good value for single-person households—and although the survey collects data on these expenditures, it cannot decompose these meals into their constituent commodities, so that urban consumption of rice is understated by reported purchases of rice. For this reason, and because rural households are poorer, their budget shares for rice are very high, around a quarter of all expenditures in the North East, which is the poorest region.

The four panels of Figure 3.15 provide a detailed graphical presentation of the data whose averages appear in Table 3.5. The top left-hand panel shows the estimated densities for the logarithm of PCE for the three regions, with the richer urban areas clearly separated from the rural areas with the sanitary districts in between. Note also that, unlike the traditional presumption that cities are more unequal, the Thai urban distribution shows the least dispersion of the three. Relative to a normal distribution, the densities have thick tails, particularly in the rural areas where there are a number of households with very high consumption levels. The other three panels show the relationship between the share of rice in household expenditures and the logarithm of per capita household expenditure. In the top right panel is the contour map of the bivariate distribution in the villages, while the bottom two panels show the netmap and contour map for the urban areas. All three diagrams show that the share of rice in the budget is lower for better-off households, but also that there is considerable dispersion at all levels of living. In line with the averages in the table, budget shares of rice are much lower in the urban than rural areas, and the netmap shows clearly that the urban density has finite mass at zero, presumably corresponding to those who get their rice by buying prepared meals.

While the relationship between rice purchases and living levels is of interest in its own right, and I shall return to these general questions in the next chapter, our main interest here is in net purchases of rice, or at least in the benefit ratio—net sales of rice as a ratio of total household expenditure. The bivariate density for the net benefit ratios and the logarithm of PCE is shown in Figure 3.16. The horizontal line corresponds to a net benefit of zero so that households who are self-sufficient in rice will be along that line at a position determined by their level of living. Households above the line—somewhat less than a half of all rural households—are net producers of rice (or at least were so in the survey year) while those below the line consume more than they grow. This majority of households includes non-farmers as well as those who are farmers but grow no rice.

The figure shows that those who benefit from higher rice prices, and among them those who benefit the most, tend to be located in the middle of the distribution of the logarithm of PCE. Among the best-off households, there are relatively few with positive benefit ratios, and none with large benefit ratios. The best-off rural households in Thailand are either nonfarmers (government employees or teachers, for example) or specialize in crops other than rice, which is usually a small-scale family enterprise unsuited for large-scale commercial agriculture. At the other end of the distribution, among the poorest families, there are many more rice growers, and a larger fraction of households who obtain a substantial fraction of their consumption by sales of rice. But on average, the poorest households, although they would be net beneficiaries from high rice prices, do not have benefit ratios as large as those for the households in the middle of the distribution. In consequence, higher prices for rice would benefit average rural households at all levels of living, but the greatest proportional benefits would be to the rural middle class, not to either rich or poor. Although higher rice prices would not be a very efficient way of helping the poor in rural Thailand—and bear in mind that I am ignoring any effects that work through the labor market—it is clearly not the case, as with plantation crops in some countries, that higher prices benefit only the richest and largest farmers.

Although Figure 3.16 contains essentially all the information that we need, the discussion in the previous paragraph rested, not so much on the detail of the density, but on an averaging over net benefit levels for different PCE groups. This conditional averaging is the essence of nonparametric (and indeed of parametric) regression, to which the next subsection provides an introduction.

Figure 3.16. Joint distribution of net benefit ratios and log(PCE), rural Thailand, 1981–82

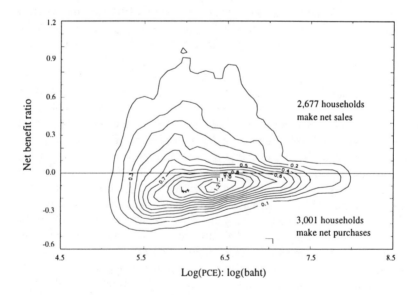

Source: Author's calculations based on Socioeconomic Survey of Thailand, 1981–82.

Nonparametric regression analysis

Economists often think of regression as linear regression, with one variable fitted by ordinary least squares on one or more explanatory variables. But recall from Chapter 2 that the definition of a regression is as a conditional expectation. For a variable y and a vector of covariates x, the expectation of y conditional on x is

$$(3.49) \qquad E(y|x) = m(x)$$

where the function $m(x)$, which in general will not be linear, is the regression function of y on x. Since y differs from its expectation by a residual that is, by construction, uncorrelated with the latter, the statistical definition coincides with the standard linear regression model when the regression function is linear. However, it should also be noted that, given a joint distribution for any set of variables, we can always calculate the regression function for any one variable conditional on the others, so that there can be no automatic association between regression and causality, or anything else that depends on an asymmetric treatment of the variables.

It is instructive to rehearse the standard links between a conditional expectation and the underlying distributions. In particular, we can write

$$(3.50) \qquad E(y|x) = \int y f_C(y|x) dy = \int y f_J(y, x) dy / f_M(x)$$

where the C, M, and J subscripts denote conditional, marginal, and joint distributions, respectively. Alternatively, the regression function can be written entirely in terms of the joint distribution,

$$(3.51) \qquad m(x) = E(y|x) = \int y f_J(y,x) dy / \int f_J(y,x) dy.$$

This equation suggests a nonparametric method for estimating the regression function; estimate the joint density using kernel (or other) methods, and use the results to calculate (3.51). In practice, there is a somewhat more direct approach through equation (3.50).

Perhaps the obvious way to calculate a regression function is to use the sample information to calculate the average of all y-values corresponding to each x or vector of x's. With an infinite sample, or with discrete explanatory variables, such an approach would be feasible. With finite samples and continuous x, we face the same problem as in density estimation, that there are no sample points exactly at each x, and we adopt the same solution, which is to average over the points near x, nearness being defined with reference to a bandwidth that will shrink to zero as the sample size increases. As with density estimation, weighting is desirable so as to avoid discontinuities in the regression function as individual observations move into and out of the bands, and this can be dealt with by calculating kernel regressions that are closely analogous to kernel estimates of densities. Indeed, the concept is perhaps already more familiar with regressions; the common practice of smoothing time series by calculating a moving average over a number of adjacent points is effectively a (rectangular) kernel regression.

The kernel regression estimator can be written as follows:

$$(3.52) \qquad \tilde{m}(x) = \sum_{i=1}^{n} y_i K\left(\frac{x-x_i}{h}\right) \bigg/ \sum_{i=1}^{n} K\left(\frac{x-x_i}{h}\right)$$

which, using $\tilde{f}(x)$ the kernel estimate of the density at x from (3.31) above, can be written as

$$(3.53) \qquad \tilde{m}(x) = (nh)^{-1} \sum_{i=1}^{n} y_i K\left(\frac{x-x_i}{h}\right) \bigg/ \tilde{f}(x).$$

This equation can be thought of as an implementation of (3.50) with the kernels acting to smooth out the discrete sample points. Using (3.52), the estimate of the regression function can also be written as a weighted average of the y's,

$$(3.54) \qquad \tilde{m}(x) = \sum_{i=1}^{n} w_i(x) y_i$$

where the weights are given from (3.52). According to (3.54), which makes clear the moving average analogy, the estimated regression function is a weighted average of all the y_i in the sample with the weights depending on how far away each corresponding x_i is from the point at which we are calculating the function.

As when estimating densities, bandwidths can be chosen by trying different values and by inspecting the plots of the resulting estimates, or by some more automatic and computationally intensive technique. The same kernels are available for regression analysis as for density estimation (see the formulas on p. 173). These matters, as well as other topics relating to nonparametric regression, are discussed in Härdle (1991) who also (p. 101) gives formulas for asymptotic confidence bands around the regression (3.54): if c_α is the $(1-\alpha)$ quantile of the t-distribution, the upper and lower $(1-\alpha)$ confidence bands for the regression are given by

$$(3.55) \qquad b_\alpha(x) = \tilde{m}(x) \pm c_\alpha \left[\int K(z)^2 dz\right]^{1/2} \tilde{\sigma}(x) \left[Nh\tilde{f}(x)\right]^{-1/2}$$

where $\tilde{\sigma}(x)$ is the estimate of the local regression standard error, and is calculated from

$$(3.56) \qquad \tilde{\sigma}^2(x) = N^{-1} \sum_{i=1}^{N} w_i(x) \left[y_i - \tilde{m}(x_i)\right]^2.$$

Although these bands are useful for assessing the relative precision of different points along the estimated regression function, they should not be treated very seriously. The asymptotic results are obtained by ignoring a number of terms—such as the bias of the regression—which tend to zero only very slowly. A better procedure is to use the bootstrap, and I shall give some substantive examples in Chapter 4. Even so, the routine presentation of confidence bands together with regressions is not always advisable, since it tends to clutter the diagrams and obscure more important features.

Nonparametric estimation of regression functions is a harder task than nonparametric estimation of densities. In particular, it is not possible to calculate a conditional expectation for values of x where the density is zero; if x cannot occur, it makes no sense to condition y on its occurrence, and the attempt to calculate the regression will involve dividing by zero; see (3.53). In practice, there will be difficulties whenever the estimated density is small or zero; while only the latter calls for division by zero, the former will make the regression function imprecise; see (3.55). Unlike linear regression, or regression with an assumed functional form, it is impossible to use nonparametric regression to calculate predictions for out-of-sample behavior. It is also necessary when calculating (3.52) to take care to calculate the regression only for values of x where the calculated density is reasonably large. This is not a problem for the density, since the estimated density is simply zero in places where there are no observations. In consequence, the regression can be calculated by evaluating the numerator and denominator of (3.53) for each value of x for which an estimate is desired, then calculating and presenting the ratio for only those values of x where $\tilde{f}(x)$ is above some critical value, set for example so as to exclude 5 percent of the sample observations.

The main strength of nonparametric over parametric regression is the fact that it assumes no functional form for the relationship, allowing the data to choose, not only the parameter estimates, but the shape of the curve itself. The price of the flexibility is the much greater data requirements to implement the nonparametric methods, the difficulties of handling high-dimensional problems, and to a lesser extent, computational costs. When data are scarce, the best that can be done is to focus on a few key parameters, and to make inferences conditional on plausible functional forms. But in many problems using household survey data—as in the Thai rice pricing example—there is enough information for it to make sense to ask the data to determine functional form, something that will be particularly attractive when functional form is an important issue, and when the dimension of the problem is low.

There are also many other regression techniques that bridge the gap between linear regression on the one hand and nonparametric kernel regression on the other. Polynomial regressions are a familiar tool, and are capable of modeling a wide range of functional forms provided the degree of the approximating polynomial is increased as the sample size increases. Fourier series offer an alternative way of approximating functional forms, an alternative that has been explored by Gallant and his colleagues, for example Gallant (1981). To regress y on x nonparametrically, run an OLS regression of y on a constant, x, x^2, and a series of terms of the form $\sin(jx)$ and $\cos(jx)$, for j running from 1 to J. For larger sample sizes, larger values of J are used, and increases in J correspond to reductions in bandwidth in kernel methods. In practice and with the usual sample sizes of a few thousand, setting J to 2 or 3 seems to work well.

Cleveland (1979) has proposed a local regression method, LOWESS, that can be thought of as a series of linear regressions at different points appropriately stitched together; I shall return to these locally weighted regressions below. There is also substantial experience in using spline functions for regression analysis (see, for example, Härdle 1991, pp. 56–65, and Engle et al 1986). There are also methods that allow some covariates to be treated nonparametrically, while others appear in the standard linear form (Robinson 1988 and Estes and Honoré 1996). Indeed, there is a rapidly growing literature on semiparametric estimation, well reviewed by Stoker (1991). All of these techniques have their strengths and weaknesses, and some are more appropriate for some problems than others. For example, polynomials tend not to work very well with household survey data, because their shapes can be very sensitive to the position of a few outliers. Some methods, such as kernels, are more readily generalizable to higher dimensions than others, such as splines. There are also important differences in computational costs, as well as in data requirements, topics that are still being actively researched, and on which it is currently difficult to give adequate practical guidance.

One important distinction between nonparametric and parametric econometrics is that the former lacks the menu of options that is available in the latter, for example for dealing with simultaneity, measurement error, selectivity, and so forth. In some cases, such as the selectivity models discussed in Chapter 2 where the models are identified by functional form assumptions, nonparametric alternatives are by definition impossible, which is only a dubious disadvantage. In other cases, such as simultaneity, it is because the techniques do not yet exist, although there will undoubtedly be further developments in this area. However, one problem for linear regression that is dealt with automatically by kernel estimation is when the dependent variable is discrete, as for example in the Thai case when we are interested in whether a given household is or is not a rice farmer. In the binary case where the dependent variable y_i takes the value 1 or 0, with the probability of the former given by some unknown function $\pi(x_i)$, the expectation of y_i conditional on x_i is simply the probability $\pi(x_i)$ which is therefore also the regression function. Hence, if we simply treat the 1's and 0's as we would any other values of a dependent variable, and mechanically apply the regression formulas (3.52) or (3.53), the results will converge to the probability function $\pi(x)$.

Nonparametric regressions for rice in Thailand

Nonparametric regression techniques can be used to complete the previous analysis, calculating the average benefit ratios at each level of living, and also to look behind the averages to the structures of rice farming that underlie them. Figure 3.17 starts with the latter and shows nonparametric regressions where the independent variable is—as usual—the logarithm of PCE, and the dependent variable is a dichotomous variable taking the value one if the household produces rice, and zero if not. Each panel shows this regression together with a similar regression for whether or not the household sells rice; the latter always lies below the former, since a household must be a producer to be a seller. The top left-hand panel shows the results for the whole rural sector, and indicates that the fraction of households growing rice diminishes with the level of living. Three-quarters of the poorest households are rice farmers, but less than one-quarter of the best-off households are so. However, conditional on being a rice farmer, the probability of being a

Figure 3.17. Proportions of households producing and selling rice, all rural and selected regions, Thailand, 1981–82

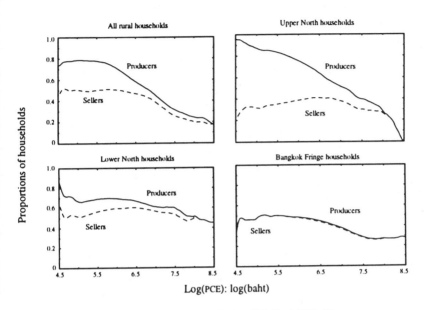

Source: Author's calculations based on Socioeconomic Survey of Thailand, 1981–82.

seller increases with log(PCE); the lower line draws closer to the upper line as we move from left to right. While most poor households in rural Thailand grow rice, many do so to meet their own food needs and have no surplus to sell on the market. And while better-off rice farmers are much more likely to be selling rice, the richer the household the less likely it is to farm rice at all.

The other three panels in the figure remind us that the top left panel is an average, and that there is considerable regional variation. The Upper North is a relatively poor area; nearly all its poor households grow rice, but only a fifth sell any. The Lower North in the next panel is a good deal better-off, and a higher fraction of rice farmers sell rice at all levels of living. In the extreme case of the Bangkok Fringe in the bottom right panel, only between 30 and 40 percent of households grow rice, but they do so extremely productively and almost all participate in the market.

These facts about rice production and rice sales help to interpret Figure 3.18, which shows the nonparametric regression of the net benefit ratio on the logarithm of household per capita expenditure. This regression is the conditional expectation corresponding to the joint density in Figure 3.16, and contains no new information. However, the regression provides the answer to the question of by how much the people at each level of living would benefit from an increase in the price of rice. Since the net benefit ratio expresses the benefit as a fraction of total household consumption, a flat line would show that all rural households benefit proportionately, so that the change would be neither regressive nor progressive. A positive

Figure 3.18. Net benefit ratios averaged by log(PCE), rural households, Thailand, 1981–82

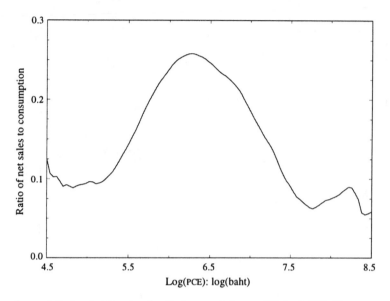

Source: Author's calculations based on Socioeconomic Survey of Thailand, 1981-82.

slope would indicate that the benefits are proportionately larger for those who are better-off, and vice versa for a negative slope. In fact, the graph shows none of those patterns; instead—and as we have already seen from Figure 3.16—it is the households in the middle of the distribution that benefit the most. The poor gain from a price increase, but not very much; although they grow rice, they sell relatively little on the market and many of them have to buy rice in addition to their own production, so that as a group they benefit only modestly from the price increase. Wealthy households also benefit modestly, but for precisely the opposite reasons. Wealthy rice farmers sell most of their crop on the market, but few wealthy households are rice farmers at all. In consequence, the regression function for the net benefit ratio has the inverted U–shape shown in Figure 3.18.

If we put this analysis together with the data on the sectoral expenditure distributions in Figure 3.15, we can conclude that the survey data do not support the argument that an export tax on rice is desirable on *distributional* grounds. The tax redistributes real resources from relatively poor rural growers to better-off urban consumers, while within the rural sector, all income groups lose, though the largest losses are born by those in the middle of the welfare distribution. Of course, these conclusions do not tell us everything that we would need to know in deciding on tax policy in Thailand. I have said nothing about the distortions caused by the tax, nor about the desirability or otherwise of alternative instruments for raising government revenue. Even so, the techniques of this section give information on who gets (or produces) what, and provide in a readily accessible form part of what

is required for making sensible decisions. Since the actual distributional consequences of policies are frequently misrepresented for political purposes, with mid-
dle-class benefits disguised as benefits for the poor, such analyses can play a
valuable role in policymaking.

Bias in kernel regression: locally weighted regression

Two potential sources of bias in kernel regression are illustrated in Figure 3.19.
The graph shows two highly simplified examples. On the x-axis, there are three
equally spaced data points, x_1, x_2, and x_3. Ignore the points x_A and x_B for the
moment. There are two regression functions shown; m_1 which is a straight line,
and m_2 which is curved. For each of these I have marked the y-points corresponding to the x's; y_1, y_2, and y_3 on m_1, and $y_1^*(=y_1)$, y_2^*, and y_3^* on m_2. Since
nothing depends on their being a scatter of points, I am going to suppose that the
y-values lie exactly on the respective regression lines. Consider what happens
when we try to estimate the two regression functions using kernel regression, and
focus on the point x_2, so that, for regression m_1, the right answer is y_2, while for
regression m_2, it is y_2^*.

Start with the concave regression function m_2. If the bandwidth is as shown,
only the points x_1, x_2, and x_3 will contribute, so that the estimate of the regression
at x_2 will be a weighted average of y_1, y_2^* and y_3^* in which y_2^* gets the most
weight, y_1 and y_3^* get equal weight, and the weights add up to 1. Because the
regression function is concave, such an average must be less than y_2^*, so that the
estimate is biased downward. If the regression function had been convex, the bias
would have been upward, and it is only in the linear case that there will be no bias.

Figure 3.19. Sources of bias in kernel regressions

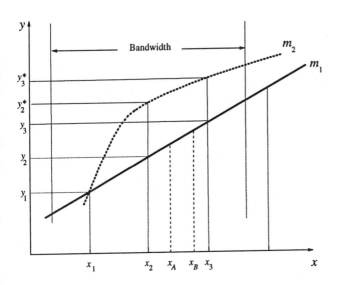

The bias will be gradually eliminated as the sample size gets larger because the bandwidth will get smaller, so that, in the limit, only the points at x_2 contribute to the estimate of the conditional mean. In practice, there is little comfort in the fact that there is no bias in some hypothetical situation, and we must always be careful when the bandwidth is large and there is curvature. Preliminary data transformations that induce approximate linearity are likely to be useful in reducing bias in kernel regression.

Even when the regression function is linear, there is another potential source of bias. Turn now to the linear regression function m_1, and consider once again estimating the regression function at x_2. When we use the points x_1, x_2, and x_3, everything works as it should, and the weighted average of y_1, y_2, and y_3 is y_2. But now introduce the two additional points x_A and x_B, so that there are now five points within the bandwidth, and they are no longer equally spaced. The kernel estimate of the regression at x_2 is now the weighted average of the five corresponding y-values. It is still the case that y_2 gets the most weight, and that y_1 and y_3 get equal weights, but the y-values corresponding to x_A and x_B also get positive weight, so that the estimate is biased upward. More generally, there will be bias of this kind when, at the point of estimation, both the regression function and the density of x have nonzero derivatives. In practice, this bias is likely to be most serious at the "ends" of the estimated regression. For example, suppose that x_1 is the smallest value of x in the sample. When we try to estimate a kernel regression at x_1, the average of nearby points can include only those to the right so that, if the regression function is positively (negatively) sloped, there will be an upward (downward) bias. There will be corresponding biases in the opposite direction for the largest x-values. These biases will diminish as we move from the extremes towards the center of the distribution but, if the bandwidth is large, they can seriously distort the estimated regression.

As shown by Fan (1992), the biases associated with unequally spaced x's can be eliminated by moving away from kernel regression. The idea, like its implementation, is straightforward. Note first that, in the example of the linear regression function in Figure 3.19, an OLS regression would not encounter the same difficulties as the kernel regression. Indeed, when the regression function is linear, OLS will be unbiased and consistent. The problem with OLS is that it cannot adapt to the shape of the regression function so that, no matter how large the sample, it can never estimate a nonlinear function such as m_2. But this can be dealt with by estimating a series of local regressions. Instead of averaging the y's around x_2, as in kernel regression, and instead of running a regression using all the data points as in OLS, we adopt the best of both procedures and run a regression using only the points "close" to x_2. As with kernel regression, we use a kernel to define "close," but instead of averaging, we run a weighted or GLS regression at x_2, where the weights are nonzero only within the band, and are larger the closer are the observations to x_2. We repeat this procedure for each point at which we want to estimate the regression function.

Fan's locally weighted regression smoother can be summarized as follows. As in the Thai example, suppose that we want to plot the estimated regression function for a range of values of x. As before, we divide up the range of x into a grid of points, usually 50 or 100 depending on how much detail we need to show. For each point x on the grid, calculate a series of weights for each data point using a kernel with a suitably chosen bandwidth. This can be done exactly as in kernel regression (3.52), so that we first define

$$(3.57) \qquad \theta_i(x) = \frac{1}{h} K\left(\frac{x - x_i}{h}\right).$$

We then estimate the locally weighted regression parameter estimates

$$(3.58) \qquad \hat{\beta}(x) = [X'\Theta(x)X]^{-1}X'\Theta(x)y$$

where $\Theta(x)$ is an $n \times n$ diagonal matrix with $\theta_i(x)$ in the ith position, and the $n \times 2$ matrix X has ones in its first column and the vector of x-values in its second. The predicted value of this regression at x is then the estimated value of the regression function at the grid point, i.e.,

$$(3.59) \qquad \hat{m}(x) = \hat{\beta}_1(x) + \hat{\beta}_2(x)x.$$

The predicted value in (3.59) is calculated for each point on the grid, and the results plotted as in Figures 3.17 and 3.18. As Fan notes, the value of $\hat{\beta}_1(x)$ from (3.58) is a natural estimator of the slope of the regression function at x and, as we shall see in the next chapter, plots of this function can also be informative.

The local regression in (3.58) can be extended to incorporate quadratic as well as linear terms in x, in which case the X matrix would have three columns, with x^2 in the third. The nonlinearity will generally help alleviate the first problem discussed above and illustrated in Figure 3.19, of forcing a linear structure on the data, even locally. The estimated regression will also provide a local estimate of the second derivative of the regression function. Presumably, higher-order polynomials could also be considered, and will yield estimates of higher-order derivatives.

The role of the bandwidth in (3.57) is the same for these locally weighted regressions as it is in kernel regressions. It controls the tradeoff between bias and variance and, for consistency of the estimates, it must tend to zero as the sample size tends to infinity and must do so slowly enough that the number of observations in each local regression also tends to infinity. As with kernel regressions, standard errors are best calculated using the bootstrap, and I shall give examples in the next chapter. The "ksm" command in STATA implements Cleveland's (1979) LOWESS estimation, which is closely related to Fan's locally weighted smoother; the difference is that LOWESS uses a nearest-neighbor definition of closeness in place of the kernel, but this should make little difference to the operating characteristics of the procedure. However, as implemented in STATA, "ksm" estimates the regression function at every observation, which is likely to be prohibitively expensive for large data sets. STATA code for a direct implementation of Fan's smoother is provided in the Code Appendix for the South African example in the next subsection.

The distributional effects of the social pension in South Africa

The following account is based on Case and Deaton (1996), which should be consulted for fuller details and documentation. The social security system in South Africa is unlike any other in the world. At the time of the Living Standards Survey of 1993, and well before the elections in the spring of 1994, the government paid a monthly "social" pension to age-qualified men and women whose (individual) income fell below a cutoff. In late 1993, the monthly payment was 370 rand, a little more than $100 at what was then the exchange rate. For comparison, 370 rand is around half of average household income in the survey, and is more than twice the median per capita household income of Blacks. That such comparatively enormous sums should be paid as pensions is a historical accident. In the apartheid era, most White workers were covered by privately funded occupational pension schemes, and the social pension was designed as a safety measure for those few Whites who reached retirement age without adequate coverage. During the transitional period, the social pension was gradually extended to non-Whites, first at lower rates, but ultimately uniformly subject to the means test. But because of the enormous disparity between the incomes of Whites and Blacks, a pension that is very small by White standards can be very large relative to the typical earnings of the majority population. We also have a situation where the means test rules out the vast majority of Whites while, at the same time, more than three-quarters of Black women over 59 and men over 64 are receiving payments.

In 1993 (and it remains true at the time of writing) the social pension accounted for most of social welfare expenditure in South Africa. Not only is there concern about the cost of the scheme (around seven billion rand), but there are also questions about whether a pension is the best way of spending the very limited social budget at the expense, for example, of payments to children or the unemployed. Nor is it clear that transferring cash to the elderly is an effective antipoverty strategy. In the United States, the elderly are somewhat less subject to poverty than the population as a whole, and because they usually live alone, or with other elderly, there is no automatic presumption that nonelderly benefit from pension payments. Much the same is true of White pensioners in South Africa but, by and large, they are not recipients of the social pension. In Black households, the elderly do not live alone, they live in households that are larger than average, and households with a pensioner actually have more children than households without a pensioner. Indeed, because of South African patterns of migrant labor, there are many "hollow" households, with elderly and children, but without working-age adults. In such circumstances, transfers in the form of a pension may be well-targeted towards poverty reduction, and the distributional effects are certainly worth serious investigation.

Figure 3.20 looks at the distributional incidence of pension income for White households and for Black households separately. The data from the Living Standards Survey are used to give, for each household, actual pension receipts, which are reported as a component of individual income, and "potential" pension receipts, defined as the number of age-qualified people—women aged 60 and over

Figure 3.20. Regressions of actual and potential pension receipts, by race, South Africa, 1993

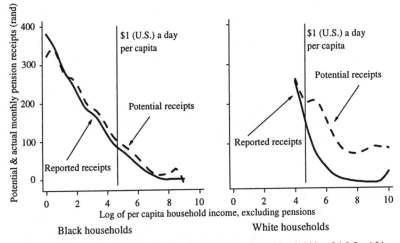

Note: Locally weighted regressions with quartic (biweight) kernels and bandwidths of 1.0 for African households and 1.5 for White households. The solid line is the regression function of household pension receipts conditional on the logarithm of household income (excluding pensions) per capita. The broken line is the corresponding regression for potential pension receipts, where potential receipts are 370 rand times the number of age-qualified people in the household.
Source: Case and Deaton (1996).

and men aged 65 and over—multiplied by the maximum monthly pension of 370 rand. Households would receive this potential amount if there were no means test—or if everyone qualified—and if everyone who was entitled to the pension actually received it in full. Locally weighted regressions are then used to calculate the conditional expectation of these actual and potential receipts as a function of household per capita income, excluding the pension.

In the left-hand panel, for Black households, the two lines are very close together, showing that the means test has little effect. At all levels of Black pre-pension income, most of those who are age-qualified receive the maximum payment. More importantly, both lines slope down from left to right, showing that the pension payments are progressive; households at the bottom of the per capita income distribution receive between 300 and 400 rand per month, while those at the top are entitled to—and receive—very little. Note that this is automatic targeting that owes nothing to the operation of the means test—potential receipts differ little from actual receipts—but works because the Black elderly live in households with low per capita income. The situation is very different for the White households shown in the right-hand panel. Although there are a few Whites with non-pension per capita household income below the dollar-a-day poverty line—though as we have seen there are no Whites with PCE below this level—and these people receive social pensions, very few of better-off White households receive pensions. At typical levels of per capita income among Whites, the means test rules out receipt of the social pension so that potential and actual receipts are far apart. That there is no similar discrepancy among Black households at the same level of per capita income suggests that the means test is not very consistently applied among Blacks—for which there is some independent if anecdotal evidence—but it should also be noted that there are very few Black households with incomes in this range.

As with the case of rice prices in Thailand, the nonparametric regressions provide a straightforward way of calculating and presenting the immediate distributional incidence of policy. But that this is only a starting point should be obvious. In the Thai case, I emphasized that such calculations take no account of behavioral consequences of price changes—particularly in the labor market—and there are similar caveats in the South African case. In particular, I have taken no account of changes in private transfers in response to the social transfers, nor of possible effects on the migration patterns that make them possible (see Jensen 1996 for evidence).

3.4 Guide to further reading

There are several good reviews of the material on inequality and distribution in Section 3.1. Atkinson (1970) remains the cornerstone of the inequality literature, and repays careful reading. Sen (1973), updated, with a review of the subsequent literature in Foster and Sen 1997) takes a somewhat different approach, starting from the statistical measures, and enquiring into their suitability for assessing economic inequality. This monograph should be read in conjunction with Sen (1992) which takes a much broader view of the meaning of inequality and its place in social arrangements more generally. Cowell (1995) is a useful review of alternative measures of inequality and of the practical problems of implementing them. Wolfson (1994) shows that the the polarization of incomes (as in the vanishing middle) is quite different from expanding inequality. Kakwani (1980) is recommended. His book focusses on inequality and poverty in developing countries, and covers a great deal of useful material not discussed in here, such as families of distributions for fitting to income distributions, and how to estimate inequality measures from the grouped data that are published in survey reports. He also provides a thorough treatment of inequality measures and of the Lorenz curve. The book also contains a useful discussion of poverty methods, but was written too early to cover the more recent developments. Sundrum (1990) is also a good discussion of inequality in developing countries. Shorrocks (1983) should be consulted for generalized Lorenz curves; the paper also contains empirical calculations for several countries. The literature on poverty measurement has grown rapidly in the last decade and has come into much closer alignment with the social welfare approach to welfare and inequality. Foster (1984) is a survey of the various different measures. Atkinson (1987, 1992) ties together the strands in the literature and his analysis and presentation strongly influenced the layout and ideas in this chapter. Ravallion's (1993) monograph is an excellent review that focusses on poverty in developing countries and together with Atkinson (1992) is strongly recommended as supplementary reading for this chapter. Anderson (1996) discusses possible methods for constructing statistical tests that can be used in conjunction with

stochastic dominanance comparisons, and provides references to the earlier literature. Nonparametric density and regression estimation is becoming more used in
economics, but much of the econometric literature remains (unnecessarily) obscure
and impenetrable, so that this useful material has found fewer applications than it
merits. A bright spot in this literature is the book by Silverman (1986), which is a
delight to read; it is focussed towards applications, with the level of technique
determined by what is strictly necessary to explain the ideas, and no more. Although Silverman is concerned only with density estimation, and not with regression analysis, the basic ideas are very similar, and this book remains the first stop
for anyone interested in pursuing these topics. The book by Härdle (1991) is about
nonparametric regression, and covers all of the important techniques, but it is not
as transparent as Silverman, nor is it as immediately useful for someone who wants
to use the techniques. Härdle and Linton (1994) is a useful summary review, and
although not all topics are covered, it is a better introduction than Härdle's book.
An excellent, up-to-date review of locally weighted regression is Hastie and
Loader (1993). Semi-parametric techniques are a live research area in econometrics. In many applications, especially those in high dimensions, a fully nonparametric approach requires too much data, so that there is a role for techniques that
blend parametric and nonparametric methods. Stoker (1991) is a good entry point
into this literature. For applications of nonparametric methods that are related to
those given in this chapter, see Bierens and Pott-Buter (1990) and Budd (1993).

4 Nutrition, children, and intrahousehold allocation

One of the traditional uses of household survey data has been the analysis of family budgets, starting with the descriptive work of the 18th and 19th centuries, and becoming more analytic and econometric in the 20th, with Prais and Houthakker's (1955) classic monograph perhaps still the best known. That literature has investigated the distribution of the budget over goods, how that allocation changes with levels of living—Engel curve analysis—and the relationship between the demographic structure of the household—the sexes and ages of its members—and the way in which it spends its resources. These studies have had a wide audience in the policy community. The early work came from social activists who hoped that documenting the living standards of the poor would generate a political demand to improve them. Engel curve analysis has been an important ingredient in understanding how the structure of economies changes in the process of economic growth (see in particular the classic work of Kuznets 1962, 1966). Much of the work on demographic structure has been motivated by attempts to derive "equivalence scales," numbers that tell us how much a child costs relative to an adult, and that might allow us to correct crude measures of living standards such as income or total expenditure for differences in household composition. Such corrections have a major impact on measures of poverty and inequality, on the identification of who is poor, and on the design of benefit programs. This chapter is concerned with these traditional topics in the context of surveys from developing countries.

In the eyes of many people, including many development economists, poverty is closely related to whether or not people get enough to eat, so that documenting the living standards of the poor becomes a question of counting calories and a major task of household surveys is to assess nutritional adequacy. Household survey data can also be used to examine how levels of nutrition change with the amount of money people have to spend. The topic is important in the debate over development strategy, between growth versus basic needs, and between less and more interventionist positions. If the elasticity of calories with respect to income is high, general economic development will eliminate hunger, while if the elasticity is low, we are faced with a choice, between a strategy for economic growth with hunger remaining a problem for a long time, perhaps indefinitely, or a more interventionist strategy that targets the nutrition of the poor while letting general economic development look after itself. This topic is addressed in Section 4.1 using survey data from India and Pakistan. I look at some of the theoretical as well as empirical issues, and argue that some of the questions in the debate can be approached using the nonparametric techniques discussed in Chapter 3.

Section 4.2 is about the demographic composition of the household, its effects on demand patterns, and about the use of such information to make inferences about the allocation within the household. Household surveys nearly always collect data on *household* consumption (or purchases), not on *individual* consumption, and so cannot give us direct information about who gets what. In the development literature, much attention has focussed on gender issues, particularly although not exclusively among children, and on the question of whether girls are treated as well as boys. I review some of this work, as well as recent theoretical developments on how to use household data to make inferences about intrahousehold allocation. I implement one specific methodology that tries to detect whether girls get more or less than boys, and look at evidence from India and Pakistan as well as from a number of other countries.

Section 4.3 turns from the relatively firm empirical territory of Sections 4.1 and 4.2 to the more controversial ground of equivalence scales. Although the construction of scales is of great importance for any enterprise that uses household survey data to draw conclusions about welfare, the state of knowledge and agreement in the area is not such as to allow incontrovertible conclusions or recommendations. Even so, it is important to understand clearly what the difficulties are in passing from the empirical evidence to the construction of scales, and to see the assumptions that underlie the methodologies that are used in practice. Clarification of assumptions is the main issue here; equivalence scales are not identified from empirical evidence alone although, once an identifying assumption has been made, the empirical evidence is relevant and useful. Nor is there any lack of practical empirically based scales once identifying assumptions have been made. The problem with much of the literature, both in the construction and use of equivalence scales, is that identifying assumptions are often implicit, and that the effects of the assumptions on the results can be hard to see. As a result, it is difficult to know whether different investigators are actually measuring the same thing, and those who use the scales run the risk of implicitly incorporating an assumption that they would have no hesitation in rejecting were it made explicit.

In most of this chapter, I adopt the standard convention of household budget analysis, that prices are the same for all households in the survey. The assumption of uniform prices is what has traditionally separated the fields of family budget analysis on the one hand from demand analysis on the other. The former investigates the nature of Engel curves and the effects of household composition, while the latter is mostly concerned with the measurement of price effects. Chapter 5 is about the effects of prices on demand in the context of tax and price reform, and while prices are typically not central to the questions of this chapter, there is no satisfactory justification for the uniform price assumption. Because transportation and distribution networks tend to develop along with economic growth, there is much greater scope for spatial price variation in less developed than more developed countries. In consequence, the uniform price assumption, while possibly defensible in the context of the United States or Great Britain, is certainly false in the countries analyzed in this book. I shall indicate places where I think that it is potentially hazardous to ignore price variation, but this is a poor substitute for the research that builds price variation into the analysis. That work is not straightforward. Price data are not always available, and when they are, they frequently come in a form that requires the special treatment that is one of the main issues in the next chapter.

4.1 The demand for food and nutrition

One attractive definition of poverty is that a person is poor when he or she does not have enough to eat, or in more explicitly economic terms, when they do not have enough money to buy the food that is required for basic subsistence. For the United States or other developed economies, where few people spend more than a third of their incomes on food, such a definition is clearly inadequate on its own, and must be supplemented by reference to commodities other than food. However, in countries such as India and Pakistan, where a substantial fraction of the population spend three-quarters or more of their budgets on food, a hunger-based definition of poverty makes sense. This section explores the relationship between measures of nutritional status, typically the number of calories consumed, and the standard economic measures of living standards, such as income or total expenditure. As usual, the analysis will be largely empirical, using data from India and Pakistan, but there are a number of theoretical issues that have to be given prior consideration.

Welfare measures: economic or nutritional?

If everyone spent all their income on food, and did so in the ways that are recommended by nutritionists, there would be no conflict between economic and nutritional views of living standards. However, people choose to buy goods other than food, some of which are obvious necessities like housing, shelter, and medical care, but others less obviously so, like entertainment or tobacco, and they buy such goods even when food intake is below the best estimates of subsistence. Furthermore, food purchases themselves are rarely organized according to purely nutritional considerations. As has been known (before and) since the first applications of linear programming—see Stigler (1945) and Dorfman, Samuelson, and Solow (1958, pp. 9–28) for an account—minimum nutritional requirements can usually be met for very small amounts of money, even by the standards of the very poorest. But minimum-cost diets are tedious and uninteresting, and they often bear no relation to what is actually eaten by poor people who presumably have interests beyond nutritional content. As a result, measures of welfare based on nutritional status will differ from the standard economic measures based on expenditures, income, or assets. There is, of course, no reason why we cannot have multidimensional measures of welfare—someone can be wealthy but hungry, or well-fed but poor—but we can run into difficulties if we do not keep the differences clear, especially when the two views have different implications for the design of policy.

The conflict between nutritional status and economic welfare is sharpest when we look at price changes, where it is possible for something that is desirable from the point of view of nutrition to be undesirable according to the standard economic criteria. In particular, economists tend to think that individuals with high substitution elasticities are in a good position to deal with price fluctuations, since they are well equipped both to avoid the consequences of price increases and to take advantage of price decreases. By contrast, nutritionists see high substitution elasticities as a cause for concern, at least among the poor, since nutritional status is thereby threatened by price increases. To clarify these issues, we need a simple formulation of welfare under the two alternative approaches.

For the economist, welfare is defined with reference to a preference ordering or utility function, which for these purposes we can write as $\upsilon(q_f, q_n)$, where the two components are food and non-food respectively. We can think of q_f and q_n as vectors, but nothing is lost here if we consider only two goods, one food and one nonfood. Corresponding to this utility function, there is an indirect utility function, written $\psi(x, p_f, p_n)$, whose value is the maximum utility that can be reached by someone who has x to spend and when the prices of food and nonfood are p_f and p_n, respectively. In practice, indirect utility would usually be approximated by real total expenditure, which is x deflated by a price index formed from p_f and p_n.

To consider the effect of price changes on welfare, it is convenient to follow the usual route of consumers' surplus and convert price changes into their money equivalents. For this, we use the cost or expenditure function $c(u, p_f, p_n)$, which is defined as the minimum expenditure needed to reach the welfare level u at prices p_f and p_n; see Deaton and Muellbauer (1980a, ch. 2) for a full discussion of the cost function and its properties. The partial derivatives of the cost function with respect to prices are the quantities consumed, while the matrix of second derivatives is the matrix of compensated price effects, the Slutsky matrix. The cost function is concave in the prices; holding utility constant, the response of cost to price is linear (and proportional to consumption) if consumption is held constant in face of the price increase, but will typically increase less rapidly because it is possible to substitute away from the more expensive good. In particular, if prices change by an amount Δp, the associated change in costs Δc satisfies the inequality

(4.1) $$\Delta c \leq q . \Delta p = q_f \Delta p_f + q_n \Delta p_n.$$

Equation (4.1) is illustrated for a single price change in Figure 4.1. The straight line through the origin is the case of no substitution, where the same is bought irrespective of price, and costs are proportional to price with slope given by the amount consumed. The other two cases show two different degrees of substitu-

Figure 4.1. Substitution and the costs of price change

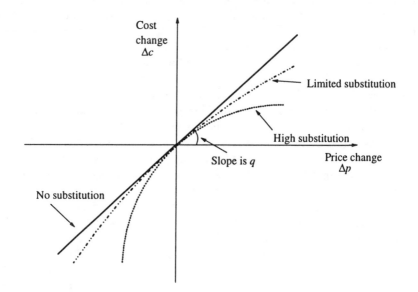

tion; because there is substitution away from the good as it becomes more expensive, as well as toward it when it becomes cheaper, consumers with more ability to substitute are hurt less by price increases and benefit more by price decreases.

Suppose now that only the price of food changes. A second-order Taylor approximation to the change in the cost of living can be obtained from the cost function using the fact that its first derivative is the quantity consumed and the second the substitution (Slutsky) term:

$$(4.2) \qquad \Delta c \approx q_f \Delta p_f + 0.5 s_{ff} \Delta p_f^2$$

where s_{ff} is the compensated derivative of demand with respect to price. Because the substitution effects of price must be nonpositive, so that $s_{ff} \le 0$, the second term in (4.2) is always zero or negative; the larger the opportunities for substitution, the more is the consumer able to offset the costs of the price increase. In Figure 4.1, s_{ff} is the curvature of each line at the origin, and thus (locally) determines how much consumers benefit from substitution. Clearly, substitution is a good thing; the higher the substitution, the less vulnerable is the consumer to increases in price, and the more he or she benefits from decreases. Further, any policy or other change that increases substitution possibilities (while preserving consumption levels) will make people better-off and is thus to be encouraged.

For the nutritionist, the costs of a price increase are measured in lost calories or other nutrients. If κ is the calorie content per unit of food, and k is total calorie intake (k for kilocalories,) the change in calories induced by the price change can be approximated by

$$(4.3) \qquad \Delta k \approx \kappa \frac{\partial q_f}{\partial p_f} \Delta p_f + 0.5\kappa \frac{\partial^2 q_f}{\partial p_f^2} \Delta p_f^2$$

where the derivatives are uncompensated. If we compare (4.2) and (4.3), both depend on the responsiveness of food consumption to prices, the latter through the uncompensated first and second derivatives, and the former through the compensated price derivative. We can perhaps be permitted to assume that the second term in (4.3) is negligible—it is the price derivative of the price derivative and certainly there is little or no empirical evidence about such a quantity—in which case the distinction between the two equations becomes quite sharp. In (4.2), the cost of a price increase is smaller the larger (absolutely) is the (compensated) price response, while in (4.3) the nutritional cost of the price increase is larger the larger (absolutely) is the (uncompensated) price response. The difference between the compensated and uncompensated price effects will be large when the good whose price is changing is a large share of the budget, which is true for food as a whole, but in practice we are usually concerned with the price of a particular food where the difference will be small.

The crux of the conflict between the two approaches can be seen by considering an example. Suppose that milk is being subsidized, that the poor receive a good deal of their nutrients from milk, and that the government is considering reducing the subsidy for budgetary reasons. Suppose also, for the purpose of the argument, that, according to the best empirical evidence, there is a large price elasticity among the poor, so that if the price is increased, the poor will reduce their consumption of milk and its associated nutrients. The nutritional advice is therefore to maintain the subsidy, while the economic advice is likely to be the reverse. By their high price elasticity, the poor have revealed that there are good substitutes for milk, in their own eyes if not in those of the nutritionists, so that the withdrawal of the subsidy is unlikely to hurt them much. For those who, like most economists, base welfare on people's purchasing power and leave the choice of individual goods up to people themselves, the large price elasticity is welcome since it is evidence that people are not vulnerable to increases in the price of milk.

This conflict between commodity-specific and money approaches to welfare occurs in many other situations; health care, education, and even telephones, are cases where policymakers and their constituents sometimes believe that consumption of a specific good is valuable independently of the general living standards of the consumer, and independently of whether people appear to value the good themselves. At the heart of the matter is whether or not we accept people's own judgments of what is good for them. While it is easy to find examples of people making poor choices, it is also difficult to find convincing cases where policymakers or other "experts" have done better on their behalf. One such case that is relevant for the current discussion is the history of food rationing in Britain during World War II; in spite of widespread shortages there was a marked improvement in general nutritional standards brought about by policies that simultaneously limited consumption (by rationing) while redirecting it towards commodities such as fresh milk that had not been widely consumed prior to the war and whose supply was guaranteed during it (see Hammond 1951). The policy seems also to have narrowed long-standing health and mortality inequalities, at least temporarily (see Wilkinson 1986). In any case, my quarrel is not with those who wish to change tastes, or who wish to eliminate hunger even at the expense of more general economic well-being. Although many economists would disagree with such prescriptions, there is no logical flaw in the arguments.

What *is* both incorrect and logically flawed is to try to follow both the commodity-specific and economic approaches simultaneously. High substitution effects are either a good thing or a bad thing; they cannot be both. It is entirely legitimate to worry about the effects of food prices on nutrition or of user charges on consumption of hospital services or education by the poor—and such has been a major research topic in the World Bank in recent years (see Jimenez 1987 or Gertler and van der Gaag 1990)—but it is necessary to take a view about what high price elasticities mean. If our goal is to provide these services to the poor even when their behavior suggests that they do not value them, then that fact should be explicitly recognized and its implications—for education, for example—taken into account. Alternatively, if we accept that the decisions of the poor have a reasonable basis—perhaps because the services are of poor quality and worth very little—then it is necessary to think hard about the justification for the subsidy, and whether or not the funds could not be better employed elsewhere, perhaps in improving quality and delivery. Spending scarce resources to subsidize facilities that are not valued by the poor will not do much to reduce poverty, and the true beneficiaries of such policies are often to be found elsewhere.

Nutrition and productivity

An important issue is the direction of causation, whether the link runs, not only from income to nutrition, but also from nutrition to income. One possibility is that those who do heavy manual labor require more calories than those who do not—see for example Pitt, Rosenzweig, and Hassan (1990), who also consider the implications for intrahousehold allocation. This possibility can be dealt with by controlling for the appropriate occupational variables in the nutrition demand function. However, it is also possible that not getting enough to eat impairs productivity to the point where poverty and malnutrition become a trap; it is impossible to work because of malnourishment, and impossible to escape from malnourishment without working.

Following Leibenstein (1957), the theory of nutritional wages has been worked out by Mirrlees (1975) and Stiglitz (1976) in some of the finest theoretical work in economic development. These models can account for the existence of unemployment; attempts by workers without jobs to underbid those with jobs will only succeed in reducing their productivity, so that the employer gains nothing by hiring them. By the same token, the theory can explain the existence of high wages in modern sector jobs. It is also consistent with unequal allocations within the family because equal shares may leave no one with enough energy to work the farm or to be productive enough to get a job. This model has been used to account for destitution in India by Dasgupta (1993, pt. IV see also Dasgupta and Ray 1986, 1987) as well as by Fogel (1994), who sees the mechanism as the major impediment to historical growth in Europe.

While there has been some empirical work that looks for such effects—most notably by Strauss (1986) for Sierra Leone—there are formidable difficulties in the way of constructing a convincing test. If we use data on self-employed workers, and find a relationship between income and nutrition, we need some means of knowing whether what we see is the common-or-garden consumption function, by which higher income generates more spending and more nutrition, or is instead what we are looking for, the hypothesized effect of nutrition on productivity, output, and income. In principle, such identification problems can be solved by the application of instrumental variables, but it is doubtful whether there are any variables that can convincingly be included in one relationship and excluded from the other. These points were argued by Bliss and Stern (1981), who also identified the corresponding difficulties in looking for nutritional effects among employed workers. Since employers will only hire well-nourished workers—which is the source of the model's predictions about unemployment—nutritional effects will only be found among the employees of those employers who are unaware of the effects of nutrition on productivity! The Mirrlees-Stiglitz theory hinges on non-linearities in the effects of nutrition on productivity, and requires that productivity be a convex function of nutrition at low levels, becoming concave as nutritional status improves. These nonlinearities would have to provide the basis for identification in the econometric analysis, which is likely to be both controversial and unconvincing.

There is one final point on which the empirical evidence is directly relevant. For the nutritional wage theory to be a serious contender to explain the phenomena for which it was invented, the calories required to maintain productivity must be costly. If it is possible to obtain enough calories to do a day's work for a very small fraction of the daily wage, then low productivity rooted in malnutrition is an implausible explanation for unemployment. In the empirical analysis below, we shall use Indian data to make these calculations.

The expenditure elasticity of nutrition: background

The relationship between nutritional intake and total expenditure (or income) in poor countries is the link between economic development and the elimination of hunger. In the simplest of worlds, one might imagine that food is the "first necessity," and that people whose incomes do not permit them to buy enough food would spend almost everything on food. Even admitting the existence of other necessities, such as clothing and shelter, it is still the case that the poorest households in India (for example) spend more than three-quarters of their budget on food, and that this share does not fall by much until the top quartile of the PCE distribution. For such people, the demand for food is elastic with respect to PCE, so that it might be supposed that the elasticity of nutrient intake would also be high, perhaps even close to unity as in the simplest case.

However, it has been recognized for many years that this view is too simple. Even if the expenditure elasticity of food were unity, the elasticity of calories need not be, since the composition of foods will change as income rises. This can happen through substitution between broad groups of goods, as when meats are substituted for cereals, or when "fine" cereals such as rice and wheat are substituted for roots (e.g., cassava) or coarse cereals such as sorghum or millet, or it can happen within food groups, as people substitute quality, variety, and taste for quantity and calories. As a result, the nutrient elasticity will be lower than the food elasticity, perhaps by as much as a half. Indeed, Reutlinger and Selowsky (1976), in one of the most cited studies of malnutrition and development, assumed that calorie intake and total expenditure were linked by a semilogarithmic relationship—with the implication that the elasticity falls as calorie consumption rises—but that even among households just meeting their caloric need, the elasticity was between 0.15 and 0.30.

The empirical evidence has produced a wide range of estimates of the elasticity, from close to unity to close to zero (see Bouis and Haddad 1992 and Strauss and Thomas 1995 for reviews of the literature) but, at least until recently, there would have been assent for the range suggested by Reutlinger and Selowsky, as well as for their assumption that the elasticity is higher among the poor than the rich. To paraphrase Alfred Marshall's dictum on the demand for food, the size of the elasticity is ultimately limited by the capacity of the human stomach, elastic though that may be. However, a number of recent studies have claimed that the true elasticity is very low, perhaps even zero, and that the earlier presumptions are based on studies that are flawed by inadequate data as well as by econometric and theoretical flaws. Bouis and Haddad (1992), using data from the Philippines, investigate a wide range of reporting and econometric biases, and conclude that the true estimate, although significantly positive, is in the range of 0.08 to 0.14. Behrman and Deolalikar (1987) use data from the ICRISAT villages in south India, and although their preferred point estimate is 0.37, it has an estimated standard error that is also 0.37, leading Behrman and Deolalikar to conclude that "for communities like the one under study, increases in income will *not* result in substantial improvements in nutrient intakes." (p. 505, italics in the original).

If we were to accept this extreme revisionist opinion, the conflict between basic needs and economic development is stark indeed. Even if structural adjustment or other policy reform were to succeed in accelerating (or in some countries just starting) economic growth, the poor will still not have enough to eat, and we will be left with the problems of endemic hunger and malnutrition, albeit in a richer world. Much of the applied economics of development policy would have to be rethought; the standard prescriptions of project evaluation, price reform, tax policy, and trade policy are all derived under the assumption that what we want to promote is people's general economic well-being, not their intake of nutrients, or if we are concerned with the latter, it is assumed that it will follow from the former. One can ultimately imagine a pricing policy that is designed, not to target the poor, to avoid distortion, nor to raise revenue, but to induce people to eat the recommended foods.

Evidence from India and Pakistan

The main results reported in this subsection are taken from Subramanian and Deaton (1996), which should be consulted for the details of the calculations. We use Indian NSS data for the state of Maharashtra in 1983 (38th round) to construct household calorie availabilities from the consumption data. Household surveys (including the NSS) typically collect data on consumption levels, not on nutrition, so that data on calorie intake have to be calculated ex post from the data on consumption of food. Because of substitution between foods as incomes rise, the multiplication of total food expenditures by an average "calorie per rupee" factor will systematically understate the calories of the poor and overstate those of the rich, so that the elasticity of nutrition with respect to income will be overstated. Since substitution can take place both between broad groups and within broad groups, it is good practice to evaluate calories using as much detail as possible.

In the Maharashtran data, 5,630 rural households report consumption during the last 30 days on each of more than 300 items, of which 149 are food items for which there are data on both expenditures and quantities. The latter are converted to calories using the tables on the nutritive values of Indian foods in Gopalan et al. (1971). In Indian households, a substantial amount of food is not consumed by household members, but is given to employees and guests, and conversely, many members of poorer households receive a fraction of their calories in the form of meals provided by employers. Although the data do not provide direct estimates of the calories involved in these transactions, the 38th round of the NSS asked respondents to report the number of meals taken by family members, provided to employees and by employers, and served to guests at both ceremonial and other occasions. These figures can be used to estimate the average calorie content of each type of meal by regressing the total calorie content of the food bought by the household on the numbers of meals provided by the household in each of the categories. Doing so suggests that each person-meal at home provides 727 calories, each meal to a servant 608 calories, while meals to guests have 1,550 calories at ceremonies and 1,379 at less formal occasions. These numbers can be used to correct the total calories, to exclude food not consumed by family members, and to include food received by family members as employees.

Table 4.1 shows how rural Maharashtran households obtained their calories in 1983, what foods they consumed and how much they spent on each. The top half of the table shows the allocations over broad groups of foods, while the bottom half looks at cereals alone. On the left side, I show the allocation of expenditure between the goods, in the middle the allocation of calories, and on the right, the prices that people paid for 1,000 calories obtained by purchases of each of the various foods or groups of foods. In each case, the table shows the mean for all rural households in the sample together with means for the bottom and top deciles of the PCE distribution. (Tabulations of means by decile is a special case of the method of fractile analysis introduced by Mahalanobis (1960), and can be thought of as a crude but often useful form of nonparametric regression, just as histograms are crude but useful nonparametric estimators of densities.)

Table 4.1. Expenditure patterns, calorie consumption, and prices per calorie, rural Maharashtra, 1983

Food	Expenditure shares (percent)			Calorie shares (percent)			Price per 1,000 calories (rupees)		
	Mean	Bottom 10%	Top 10%	Mean	Bottom 10%	Top 10%	Mean	Bottom 10%	Top 10%
Food groups									
Cereals	40.7	46.0	31.0	70.8	77.3	57.3	0.64	0.51	0.79
Pulses	8.9	10.2	7.8	6.6	6.2	7.2	1.51	1.44	1.60
Dairy	8.1	4.9	11.8	2.8	1.3	4.9	3.69	3.59	3.92
Oils & fats	9.0	9.2	9.2	5.9	4.8	7.6	1.74	1.67	1.81
Meat	5.1	3.4	6.4	0.7	0.4	1.0	11.7	11.0	12.2
Fruit & vegetables	10.5	8.5	12.0	3.5	2.3	5.4	3.90	3.83	3.85
Sugar	6.5	7.4	5.9	7.2	7.0	8.0	1.01	0.94	1.09
Other food	11.3	10.4	16.1	2.5	0.8	8.6	17.4	16.8	15.9
Cereals									
Rice	11.6	9.0	10.9	15.2	10.1	16.5	0.95	0.89	1.02
Wheat	5.6	3.8	7.9	8.5	4.7	14.4	0.79	0.73	0.82
Jowar	18.2	27.4	9.3	37.8	52.9	21.6	0.50	0.43	0.55
Bajra	3.0	2.7	1.3	6.6	4.9	3.2	0.48	0.48	0.50
Other coarse cereals	1.2	2.8	0.3	2.2	4.5	0.6	0.66	0.58	0.99
Cereal substitutes	1.1	0.5	1.3	0.6	0.2	0.8	2.23	2.22	2.22
Total food	67.4	73.4	54.1	2,120	1385	3382	1.14	0.88	1.50
Calories adjusted				2,098	1429	3167			

Note: Mean refers to the mean of the whole sample and bottom (top) 10 percent to the mean of households in the bottom (top) decile of PCE. Shares of calories and of expenditures are calculated on an individual-household basis and are averaged over all appropriate households. Calorie prices are averages over consuming households.
Source: Subramanian and Deaton (1996, table 1).

On average, rural Maharashtran households spent more than two-thirds (67.4 percent) of their budget on food; the corresponding figure is near three-quarters for the bottom decile (73.4 percent) and is still above a half (54.1 percent) among households in the top decile. From this they obtained 2,120 calories on average. More than 40 percent of expenditures were on cereals, with the poor buying mostly coarse cereals, mainly *jowar* (*sorghum vulgare*) while better-off households spent more on wheat and rice. Cereals provide calories more cheaply than do other foods. On average each 1,000 calories from cereals cost only 64 paise in 1983, and a large share of total calories—more than three-quarters in the bottom decile—came from this source. The coarse cereals provided calories even more cheaply, *jowar* and *bajra* (millet) at 50 paise per 1,000 calories, and the focus of poor households' consumption on these goods means that poor households spent 88 paise per 1,000 calories compared with 1.50 rupees for households in the top decile and 1.14 rupees on average. For comparison, the wage rate in rural Maharashtra in 1983 was around 15 rupees per day, so it is hard to believe that the inadequate nutrition is a bar to employment or productive labor for the individuals in this sample. Given that a substantial fraction of calories are required to maintain the body even at rest, and that an additional 2,000 calories can be purchased for one rupee, malnutrition alone is surely an insufficient force to keep people in destitution.

There are two other important points in the table. First, the increase in the cost per calorie from poor to rich is a consequence of the substitution between the broad groups of foods, at least provided that the different types of cereals are distinguished from one another. There is not much evidence of higher prices being paid within categories, so that, for example, the best-off households pay about the same per kilo for their dairy products or their wheat as do households in the bottom decile. Secondly, the correction for meals given and taken, which is shown in the last row of the table, works as expected, increasing the calories of the poorest households, decreasing the calories of the better-off, and leaving the mean relatively unchanged. If the correction is not made, we run the risk of overestimating the responsiveness of calories to income.

Table 4.1 also gives a rough idea of the various elasticities, and how the increase of food expenditure with income is divided between additional calories on the one hand and additional expenditure per calorie on the other. Since the budget share of a good is identically equal to the price multiplied by quantity (per capita) divided by total expenditure (per capita), the logarithm of the budget share is the logarithm of price plus the logarithm of quantity less the logarithm of total expenditure. The average of the logarithm of PCE among households in the top decile is 5.6, and that among those in the bottom decile is 3.8. If this is compared with the change in the logarithm of the budget share, from (the logarithm of) 73.4 to 54.1, we get a total elasticity of food expenditure per head of about 0.8, matching the slow decline of the food share with PCE. The corresponding rise in expenditure per calorie, from 0.88 to 1.50 rupees per 1,000, translates into an elasticity of around 0.3, so that the residual, which is the elasticity of calories with respect to PCE, is around 0.5. As we shall see, this estimate is on the high side, but the general picture is not; the food expenditure elasticity is large with substantial fractions accounted for by each of its two components, the elasticity of calories and the elasticity of the price of calories.

The general relationship between calories and PCE can also be illustrated using the bivariate density estimation techniques of Section 3.2. Figure 4.2 shows the estimated contours of the joint density of the logarithm of calories per head per day and the logarithm of monthly PCE. For comparative purposes, and using the same vertical scale (for calorie intake), Figure 4.3 shows the same plot for the Pakistani province of Sindh in 1984–85 based on data from the National Income and Expenditure Survey. I will not use the Pakistani data further in this section, but the general similarity between the two graphs is worthy of note. In both cases, the contours are approximately elliptical, as would happen if the joint density were in fact normal. The implicit regression functions are close to being both linear and homoskedastic, and the slope in each case is approximately one-half. Although both surveys come from the subcontinent, the dietary habits of the two regions are different, with rice the staple in the Sindh Province of Pakistan, while in Maharashtra the hierarchy of basic foods starts with *jowar* and progresses to rice, and eventually to wheat. Other similarities and differences between these two surveys will be further explored in Chapter 5 when I consider the response of food demand to prices.

Regression functions and regression slopes for Maharashtra

Given the results in Figure 4.2, it is hardly surprising that the associated regression function is close to linear. Figure 4.4 shows the estimated regression using a locally weighted smoother with a quartic kernel and a bandwidth of 0.50. The graphs also show confidence bands for the regression line. These were obtained by bootstrapping the locally weighted regressions 50 times, so that, at each point along the 100-point grid used for the regressions, there are 50 bootstrapped replications. These are used to calculate a standard error at each point, and then to plot lines that are two standard errors above and below the estimated regression function. The graph shows two such pairs of lines; the inner pair ignores the clustered structure of the sample and the outer pair takes it into account in the bootstrapping. In this case, the cluster structure makes little difference, and the confidence bands are tight around the regression line.

The graph suggests that the slope falls with PCE but is close to linear with slope 0.5. Given the economic plausibility of a slope that is higher among the poor, it is worth calculating and plotting a nonparametric estimate of the slope itself, allowing it to be different at different levels of PCE. Such estimates are a natural by-product of the locally weighted regressions, since each local regression delivers a slope parameter, and are shown in Figure 4.5, once again with two sets of estimated confidence bands. The graph shows an elasticity that declines gently with the level of PCE, from about 0.7 at the bottom to 0.3 at the top. These data do not show any evidence of a sharp change in the elasticity at some critical level of calorie intake as found by Strauss and Thomas (1995) for Brazil.

Figure 4.2. Calories per head and log(PCE), rural Maharashtra, 1983

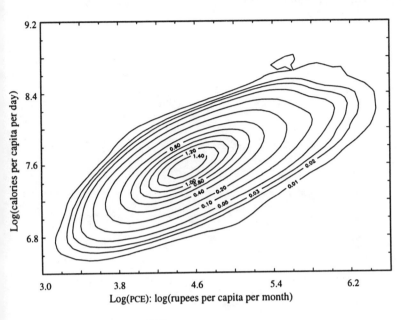

Source: Subramanian and Deaton (1996).

Figure 4.3. Calories per head and log(PCE), rural Sindh, 1984–85

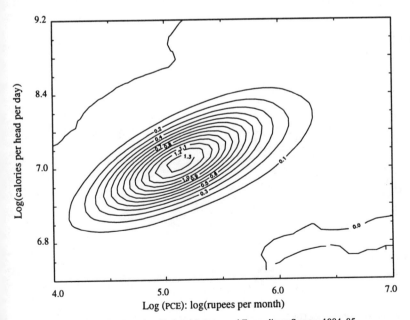

Source: Author's calculations based on National Income and Expenditure Survey, 1984–85.

Figure 4.4. Estimated regression function for log of calories per head and log(PCE), rural Maharashtra, 1983

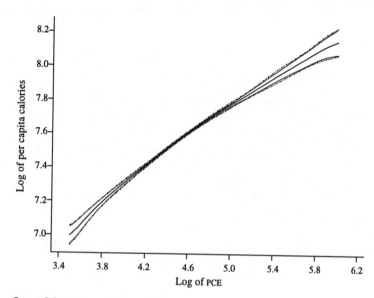

Source: Subramanian and Deaton (1996).

Figure 4.5. Elasticity of calories per head to PCE, Maharashtra, 1983

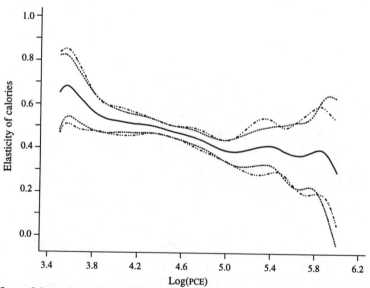

Source: Subramanian and Deaton (1996).

Allowing for household structure

One serious problem with the regressions and regression slopes in Figures 4.4 and 4.5 is that they portray only the bivariate relationship between calories per head and total household expenditure per head. While the latter is certainly the most important variable determining calorie consumption, it is by no means the only one, and even if we are less interested in other covariates than in the total budget, the calorie expenditure relationship will not be consistently estimated if the omitted variables are correlated with PCE. The most important omitted variables are those representing the size and composition of the household. While a relationship between calories per head and total expenditure per head is a natural starting point, and allows for household size in a rough way, it makes no concession to the fact that children consume fewer calories than do their parents, so that, controlling for PCE, households with more children will typically consume fewer calories per head. Even among all-adult households, we might expect the presence of economies of scale to imply that larger households with the same PCE are better-off than smaller households (but see Section 4.3 below) so that food consumption per capita will be a function of both PCE and household size. The same will be true if there are economies of scale in food consumption itself, for example if wastage is reduced when more people share the same kitchen and take meals together.

As always, nonparametric techniques are much better at handling bivariate than multivariate relationships, but it is possible to look at the calorie expenditure relationship nonparametrically for a range of household sizes. Figure 4.6 illustrates this, reproducing the nonparametric regression functions between the logarithm of calories per head and the logarithm of PCE, but now separately for households of different sizes. There are 10 curves, for household sizes 1 through 10, and each curve is based on a different number of households. The curve for five-person households uses 1,100 observations and is the most precisely estimated; the number of households in each category rises from 283 single-person households to 1,100 with 5 persons, and falls to only 96 households with 10 persons. There are several important points to note.

First, the curves are lower for larger households, so that, conditional on PCE, calorie consumption per capita falls with household size, an effect that is at least partly due to the fact that larger households have a larger proportion of children. Second, the elasticity of calories with respect to expenditure is not much affected by the size of the household. The different regression lines are approximately parallel to one another. Third, because per capita calorie consumption is negatively related to household size at constant PCE, and because in rural Maharashtra PCE is negatively related to household size—as it is in most household surveys—the omission of household size from the regression of per capita calorie consumption on PCE will have the effect of biasing upward the estimate of the calorie expenditure elasticity. As PCE rises, household size falls, which will have an independent positive effect on calories per head, and this effect will be attributed to—or projected on—PCE if household size is not included in the regression. A careful examination of Figures 4.6 and 4.4 shows that the slopes in the former are

Figure 4.6. Calorie-outlay regression functions by household size

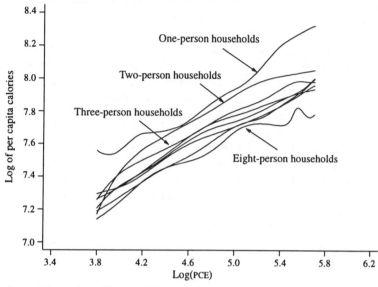

Source: Subramanian and Deaton (1996).

indeed lower. In Figure 4.4, a difference in the logarithm of PCE from 3.8 to 5.8 is associated with a change from 7.2 to 8.0 in the logarithm of per capita calories, a difference of 0.8, compared with a corresponding difference of about 0.7 in Figure 4.6. Controlling for household size will therefore tend to reduce the calorie expenditure elasticity, from about 0.40 to about 0.35, figures that are much more like the conventional than the revisionist wisdom.

Since the nonparametric regressions suggest that the relationship between the logarithm of calories per head and the logarithm of PCE is close to linear and that household size has an effect that is additive without interactions with log(PCE), the nonparametric results can be closely approximated by a linear regression of the logarithm of calories per head on the logarithms of PCE and of household size. This regression can then be used as a basis for examining the role of other covariates, since the completely nonparametric approach cannot handle any further increase in dimension. In fact, apart from household size, the inclusion of other variables—even including dummy variables for each of the 563 villages in the survey—has little effect on the estimates of the elasticity, which remains close to 0.35. Several of the other variables are important—see Subramanian and Deaton (1996, Table 2) for details—but unlike household size, they are sufficiently orthogonal to the logarithm of PCE to have little effect on the key coefficient.

One objection to the use of household size and household composition variables to "explain" calorie consumption is that these variables are themselves endogenous, so that their coefficients—as well as that on the total expenditure variable—are not readily interpreted. This is partly an argument about the endogeneity of fertility—families do not have children by random and unanticipated delivery (perhaps by storks!)—but more generally recognizes that family size is adjusted in many ways, by migration, by younger adults splitting off to form their own households, by marriage, and in some parts of the world, by large-scale fostering. All of these processes are (arguably) influenced by the economic position of the household. As usual, the fundamental problem is a possible correlation between the regression errors and the explanatory variables, so that the calorie expenditure elasticity will be biased if households who consume more calories than predicted are also those that are more fertile, more likely to absorb members than to shed them, and so forth, possibilities that can hardly be excluded on theoretical grounds.

In principle, the calorie expenditure relationship could be reestimated using instrumental variables, although in practice, our understanding of fertility or the adaptation of household size to economic change is far from sufficiently precise to provide instruments that are well-correlated with household size, let alone that are credibly excluded from the calorie expenditure relationship itself. Even so, it is useful to consider interpreting the relationships with and without household size as short-run versus long-run relationships, so that the reduced-form relationship, between calories and income (or total outlay), is taken as revealing the long-run influence of higher incomes on calorie consumption, taking into account those effects that operate indirectly through the adjustment of household size through fertility or other mechanisms. For some purposes, this is what we want to know; the effect of increasing per capita income on levels of nutrition once all the offsetting and reinforcing second-order effects have worked themselves out. If so, the appropriate elasticity would be at the upper end of the range, closer to 0.40 than 0.30.

The effect of measurement errors

The estimates of the calorie expenditure elasticity for Maharashtra—and the results are very similar for the 1984–85 Pakistani survey—are close to what I have characterized as the conventional wisdom, and are very much higher than the revisionist estimates of Behrman and Deolalikar (1987) and Bouis and Haddad (1992). Bouis and Haddad (see also Bouis 1994) note that their low estimates—as well as those of Behrman and Deolalikar—are obtained using data obtained by the direct observation by nutritionists of calorie consumption, and not, as in the Indian and Pakistani data and in most other studies, by using consumption data that has been converted to calories using tables of conversion ratios. Bouis and Haddad provide evidence from both the Philippines and from Kenya, where the data allow implementation of both methodologies, that the estimates from the direct nutritional data are lower. (Behrman and Deolalikar's estimates, which also come from Maharashtran villages, are not lower, but are insignificantly different from zero; their point estimate of 0.37 is essentially the same as that discussed above.) There can be no automatic presumption that the direct nutrition surveys provide the superior data, since the increased accuracy from observing what people actually eat could well be offset by the artificial and intrusive nature of the survey.

However, as Bouis and Haddad argue, there is one very good reason for suspecting that standard methods lead to upwardly biased estimates; because calories are counted by multiplying consumption quantities by positive factors (calorie conversion factors) and adding, and because total expenditure is obtained by multiplying those same quantities by other positive factors (prices) and adding, measurement error in the quantities will be transmitted to both totals, thus leading to a spurious positive correlation between total expenditure and total calories. Although the mismeasurement of total expenditure will typically bias downward the estimate of the elasticity—the standard attenuation effect of measurement error in an explanatory variable—there is here the additional effect of the common measurement error which will bias the elasticity upwards, and as shown in the paper by Bouis and Haddad, this effect will typically dominate. By contrast, the direct observation of calories, even if subject to measurement error, will yield estimates whose errors are independent of the measurement of total expenditure, so that the calorie elasticity, even if measured imprecisely because of the measurement errors, will not be biased in either direction.

The standard procedure for dealing with measurement error is to reestimate using an instrument for total expenditure, the obvious choice being the sum of the nonimputed components of income. This quantity is measured independently of expenditure, is well-correlated with expenditure, and is plausibly excluded from the calorie equation, conditional on expenditure. Unfortunately, the NSS consumption surveys do not collect income data. However, Subramanian and Deaton show that, just as the OLS estimator is biased up, the (inconsistent) estimator obtained by using nonfood expenditure as an instrument is biased down. But this estimate of the elasticity is still much larger than zero, 0.3 as opposed to 0.4, and is quite precisely estimated. This result is certainly consistent with the result that the calorie to PCE elasticity is biased upward by the standard method of imputing calories by converting quantities purchased, but it is not consistent with a true elasticity that is much less than 0.3, and certainly not with one that is 0.10 or even zero. If the difference between direct calorie measurement and imputed calorie measurement is correlated measurement error, we cannot sustain an argument that direct calorie estimation in Maharashtra would lead to very low estimates of the expenditure elasticity of calories.

It remains possible that the calorie data from the NSS are compromised in other ways. Bouis and Haddad observe in their Filipino data that meals given to servants by rich households tend to be understated as are meals received by servants and employees. If this is true in the Indian data, even our lowest estimates will be biased upward, although it is worth noting that the nonparametric estimates of regression functions and slopes at any given point depend only on data within the bandwidth around that point, so that estimates of the slope in the middle of the range of PCE, for example, are unaffected by measurement errors that affect only the richest and poorest.

4.2 Intrahousehold allocation and gender bias

Welfare, living standards, and poverty are all characteristics of individuals, not households, and although households are often the primary income recipients and are nearly always the units for which we observe consumption, we cannot be indifferent to the allocations to individual members of the household. If women systematically get less than men, or if children and old people are systematically worse-off than other members of the household, social welfare will be overstated when we use measures that assume that everyone in the household is equally treated. When people are treated differently but we assume the opposite, the true distribution of welfare among family members can be obtained from the supposed equal distribution by a set of mean-preserving but disequalizing transfers. In consequence, the supposed distribution always understates true inequality and overstates true social welfare. Measures of poverty are also usually evaluated by attributing household per capita income or consumption to each member of the household, a practice that is used even when we are counting the number of women, children, or old people in poverty. Without some idea of how resources are allocated within households, these measures are little more than guesses.

Even in cases where welfare is the same for all household members, per capita consumption measures will generally not provide a correct ranking of the living standards of different households or of the members within them. Children will often require less than adults to obtain the same level of living, while old people may need more of some things—health services or warmth in cold countries— and less of others—food or work-related consumption. Members of large families may therefore be better-off than members of smaller families with the same level of resources per capita, although we have no means of making the correction unless we understand enough about intrahousehold allocation to know how much money is needed to attain equal welfare levels for different types of household members.

There are two separate issues. The first is the positive question of whether and to what extent allocations within the household differ according to the gender and age of the recipient. The second is whether we can find a theoretical framework that will allow us to use the empirical evidence on the effects of household composition on household demand patterns to say enough about individual welfare to improve our measures of social welfare and poverty.

The issues also differ depending on whether we are dealing with gender issues, with children versus adults, or with the elderly. For issues of men versus women, or boys versus girls, we are most often concerned with whether differences exist, with their magnitude, and under what circumstances allocations depend on gender. For children versus adults, there are at least two questions. The first is the welfare of children as separate entities from their parents. Since the allocation of resources within the household is controlled by adults, and since children are not voluntary members of the families to which they belong, there can be no general presupposition that their interests are fully taken into account. The second question concerning children is about "equivalence scales," which is how much it costs to support children, whether and under what assumptions such calculations make sense, and how they can be used—if at all—to make comparisons of welfare levels between members of households of different compositions.

For the elderly, there are other issues that are only now coming into focus for developing countries. In much of Asia, the demographic transition that is either underway or recently completed is "aging" the population; reductions in mortality are leading to more elderly people, while reductions in mortality combined with reductions in fertility are increasing the ratio of the old to the young. There is much concern, although so far little hard knowledge, about the economic consequences of this change, about changes in living arrangements of the elderly, about support mechanisms both inside and outside the extended family, about the economic burdens for working-age people, and about the effects on saving and investment (see Cowgill 1986, Deaton and Paxson 1992, and Chapter 6 for further discussion and some empirical evidence).

In this section, I shall be concerned with the positive, empirical issues of how to use household survey data to look for patterns of discrimination between individuals by gender, and particularly between boys and girls. In the next, I turn to the issue of equivalence scales.

Gender bias in intrahousehold allocation

There is a large literature documenting that, at least in some areas of the world, the allocation of household resources favors males over females. Much of this work, which is reviewed for example by Drèze and Sen (1989), Harriss (1990), Dasgupta (1993), and Strauss and Thomas (1995), is not concerned with the allocation of consumption within the family, but with the direct comparison by gender of nutrition, health, or education. Perhaps best known are the findings on excess infant mortality among girls, particularly (but not exclusively) in China, Northern India, Pakistan, and Bangladesh (see among others Government of India 1988, Sen 1989, Drèze and Sen 1989, pp. 50–54, Rosenzweig and Schultz 1982, and Coale 1991). The mechanisms underlying these differences are not fully understood, but it is widely believed that female children are given less medical attention when they are sick, and it is certainly possible that they are provided with fewer resources in general. Other research has found more complex gender-related differences in nutrition; for example, Thomas (1994) used surveys from the United States, Ghana, and Brazil to document a positive association between a mother's education and her daughters' heights and between father's education and his sons' heights, an association that is attenuated or absent between mothers and sons and between fathers and daughters.

At first sight, household survey data on consumption do not appear to be useful for sorting out who gets what; data on consumption are for the household as a whole, not for its individual members. Even so, the surveys tell us about household composition, the numbers of household members, and the age and sex of each, so that it is certainly possible to study the relationship between household composition and household consumption patterns. Indeed, if the consumption of (say) food relative to nonfood depends on the ratio of males to females in the household, then we have established that allocations depend on gender, although we are very far from having understood what determines the differences, and in particular, whether they are the result of tastes or of discrimination. It is sometimes the case that we directly observe the consumption of individual members of the household, at least for some goods, or that there are goods that, by their very nature, are only consumed by a subset of family members. An example of the former would be surveys where each member of the household is asked to record each expenditure, some of which are directly assignable to that person's consumption. More common is the second case, where there are goods (adult clothing, women's clothing, alcohol, tobacco, or baby formula) that are exclusively used by some members or some groups and not others, such as men versus women or adults versus children. Given a suitable theoretical structure, these features of the data can be used as a lever to pry open the black box and to observe the internal workings of the household.

A theoretical digression

There are many different theories of how resources are allocated within the household. The simplest, which has dominated empirical research until recently, is one in which households are treated as monolithic entities, endowed with preferences as if the household were an individual. This can be thought of as a dictatorial model, in which (presumably) the *paterfamilias* decides on behalf of everyone so that the consumption behavior of the household will look very much like the behavior of the individual consumer of the textbook. At the other extreme, the household can be thought of as a group of individuals who bargain with each other over resources. Such models provide a richer structure to behavior than does the dictatorial model. For example, the allocation between a husband and wife will depend on what each would get should the marriage be dissolved, so that such models predict differences in household consumption patterns according to the relative earnings of each partner, unlike the dictatorial model in which all resources are pooled. It also makes sense to suppose that people in the family care for each other, and get pleasure from each other's consumption as well as from their own, or get pleasure from each other's pleasure. The consequences of these different assumptions have been explored in the literature, most notably by Manser and Brown (1980), McElroy and Horney (1981), Becker (1981), McElroy (1990), and Lundberg and Pollak (1993).

In a series of papers, Chiappori (1988, 1992), Bourguignon and Chiappori (1992), and Browning et al. (1994) have developed a methodology that is consistent with a number of these models and that permits empirical testing of their different predictions. Under appropriate, although not always uncontroversial assumptions, these methods allow recovery of the rules for resource allocation within the household. Their procedures are also useful for thinking about the empirical results later in this chapter and for discussing equivalence scales, so that it is useful to provide a brief introduction here.

The simplest case is where the household consists of two members A and B whose private consumption vectors are denoted q^A and q^B, respectively. Suppose also that there is a vector of public goods z, that are available to each, so that the two utility functions can be written $v^A(q^A, z)$ and $v^B(q^B, z)$. Chiappori and his coauthors remain agnostic about exactly how the allocative conflict between the two people is resolved, but instead focus on the assumption that the allocation is *efficient*, so that, given whatever each member gets, each individual's utility function is maximized subject to the effective budget of each. Given efficiency, the optimal choice for A can be written as the solution to the problem

$$(4.4) \qquad \max \; v^A(q, \bar{z}) \quad \text{s.t.} \quad p^A.q = \theta^A(p, p_z, y)$$

where $\bar{z}$ is the optimal choice of the public good, p is the price vector for all goods, p^A is the price of goods consumed by A, p_z is the price vector of public goods, and $\theta^A(p, p_z, y)$ is the *sharing rule*, the function that determines the total amount that A gets conditional on the prices of goods, including the prices of public goods, and total household resources y. The solution to (4.4) will be a set of demand functions

$$(4.5) \qquad q_i^A = g_i[\theta^A(p, p_z, y), p^A, \bar{z}].$$

If we hold fixed the allocation to A, $\theta^A(p, p_z, y)$, then because these demand functions are the result of the standard maximization problem (4.4), they have all the usual properties associated with well-behaved demand functions from the textbook. There is a precisely analogous maximization problem and set of demand functions for B, and the overall budget constraint implies that B's sharing rule satisfies

$$(4.6) \qquad \theta^B(p, p_z, y) = y - p_z.\bar{z} - p^A.q^A.$$

Although these results require the formal justification that is provided by Chiappori and his coauthors, the underlying intuition is quite straightforward. The efficiency criterion means that it is impossible to make one family member better-off without making the other worse-off, so that each person's utility must be maximized subject to whatever is spent on the goods and services entering that utility function, which is precisely the content of equation (4.4). The result clearly holds for the standard dictatorial or pooling model where the *paterfamilias* allocates resources to maximize a "family" social welfare function which has the individual utility functions—including his own—as arguments. But it holds much more widely, for example when the allocation is set by bargaining, or even when there is altruism, providing it is of the "caring" type, so that A and B care about each other's living standards, but not about the specific items of each partner's consumption. Different kinds of behavior will result in different sharing rules, but once the sharing rule is set, the individual demands will be characterized by equations (4.5) and (4.6).

What can this framework be used for, and how does it help us discover the allocation mechanisms within the household? Even without any further structure or assumptions, the results deliver testable predictions about behavior, so that it is possible to test whether efficiency holds, and to examine specific forms of efficiency, such as dictatorial behavior. Beyond this, and more importantly from the point of view of welfare analysis, we can ask what additional assumptions are required to identify the sharing rules.

Consider first the testing problem. Suppose that the household has two people, and three sources of income, one that accrues to A, one that goes to B, and one that is received collectively. We can think of these as individual earnings versus capital income from jointly owned assets, and they are denoted y^A, y^B, and y^O, with total household income y given by

$$(4.7) \qquad\qquad y = y^A + y^B + y^O.$$

The sharing rule will depend on all three types of income separately, so that suppressing the public goods and the prices to simplify the exposition, we can write the (observable) household demand for good i as

$$(4.8) \qquad q_i = g_i^A[\theta^A(y^A, y^B, y)] + g_i^B[y - \theta^A(y^A, y^B, y)]$$

where we have chosen to eliminate y^O so that we can consider the effects of varying the individual incomes y^A and y^B while holding total income constant, with collective income implicitly adjusted. If (4.8) is differentiated with respect to y^A and y^B in turn, and one derivative divided by the other, we obtain

$$(4.9) \qquad \frac{\partial q_i / \partial y^A}{\partial q_i / \partial y^B} = \frac{\partial \theta^A / \partial y^A}{\partial \theta^A / \partial y^B}.$$

The right-hand side of (4.9) is *independent of i* so that we can test for Pareto efficiency within the household by calculating the left-hand side for as many goods as we have data, computing the ratios, and testing that they are the same up to random variation. One attractive feature of (4.9) is that it is a generalization (i.e., a weaker version) of the condition that holds under dictatorial preferences. When household income is pooled, the ownership of income makes no difference, and the ratios in (4.9) should all be unity. We therefore have two nested tests, first of efficiency, and then of the more restrictive hypothesis of income pooling.

The evidence cited earlier is consistent with a failure of the dictatorial or pooling model. Moreover, using French data, Bourguignon et al. (1992) reject pooling but cannot reject the weaker restriction in (4.9). It would be a productive exercise to replicate these tests using data from developing countries, since they provide an obvious first step in an enquiry into the structure of household allocation. It should also be noted that the predictions underlying these tests, unlike the symmetry or homogeneity predictions of standard demand analysis literature, relate to income (or total expenditure) derivatives, and not to price effects. As a result, they require only a single cross section of survey data with no price variation. Even with time-series or panel data, where price effects can be identified, variation in relative prices is typically much less than variation in real incomes, so that tests based on the latter are both more powerful and easier to implement. On the negative side, a good deal of work remains to be done in interpreting findings that different types of income are spent in different ways. Some income sources are more regular than others, and some income flows are better measured than others. In either case, the different types of income will have different effects, whether real or apparent, and these differences would occur even if household resource are allocated according to the standard model of a unitary household.

Equation (4.9) is suggestive in another way. Since the ratios on the left-hand side are observable from the data, the right-hand side is econometrically identified, so that although this equation does not identify the sharing rule itself, it tells us something about it that we want to know, which is how the allocation to A is differentially affected by increments to the earnings of A and B, respectively. Is it possible to do even better than this, and to develop procedures that identify the rule itself? Without further assumptions, the answer is no. The demand equation (4.8) contains not only the sharing rule, but also the two sets of demand functions, and observation of household demand on the left-hand side is not sufficient to allow recovery of all three. However, for some goods we do indeed have additional information. In particular, and adopting Bourguignon and Chiappori's terminology, goods may be *assignable* in that the consumption of each person may be separately observed, or *exclusive*, in that consumption is known to be confined to one person. When one particular good, say good i, is assignable, we observe q_i^A and q_i^B separately, so that we can also observe (or at least estimate) the derivatives of each with respect to the three kinds of income. These derivatives are given by differentiating each of the two terms on the right hand side of (4.8) with respect to y^A and y in turn and computing ratios, so that

$$(4.10) \qquad \frac{\partial q_i^A / \partial y^A}{\partial q_i^A / \partial y} = \frac{\partial \theta^A / \partial y^A}{\partial \theta^A / \partial y}, \quad \frac{\partial q_i^B / \partial y^A}{\partial q_i^B / \partial y} = \frac{-\partial \theta^A / \partial y^A}{1 + \partial \theta^A / \partial y}.$$

Since the left-hand sides of both equations are observable, we can solve the two equations for the two unknowns, which are the derivatives of the sharing rule with respect to y and y^A. If the A and B superscripts in (4.10) are reversed, we can derive two more relationships that determine the derivatives of θ^A with respect to y (again) and y^B, so that all the derivatives of the rule are identified or overidentified, and the rule itself is identified up to a constant.

The role of assignable goods in this calculation can be taken by exclusive goods, as long as there are at least two of them, so that once again we have four ratios of derivatives corresponding to (4.10) that can be used to identify the rule. These remarkable results, although they are not (quite) sufficient to identify the allocation of resources to each family member, allow us to map out how the allocation changes in response to the distribution of earnings between household members, so that, for example, we can compare the change in the allocation to the husband of a change in the earnings of the wife compared with a change in the wife's allocation in response to a change in her husband's earnings. And as we shall see in the next subsection, the same techniques can be used to investigate the allocative effects of changes in variables other than the earnings of individual family members.

It is often difficult in practice to find commodities that are either assignable or exclusive, although in the longer run, survey practice can be adapted to collect better information. However, the likely candidates for exclusivity are items like men's clothing and women's clothing, and the most obvious of the assignable goods is leisure, since surveys routinely collect data on hours worked by various household members. But such commodities can only be thought of as exclusive or assignable in the narrowest sense. Most people are not indifferent to how their partner dresses or to the amount and disposition of their partner's leisure, so that, in terms of the formal model q^B appears in A's utility function and vice versa. Browning et al. (1994) provide estimates of Canadian sharing rules based on the assumption that clothing is assignable, or equivalently, that men's and women's clothing is exclusive. As they note, this "implies that wives care only about their husband's clothing insomuch as it contributes to the welfare of their husband (and vice versa). Many readers will be thoroughly skeptical of this implication." Whether it is possible to do better than this remains to be seen.

Adults, children, and gender

In the analysis so far, we have looked at the effects of different income sources on household allocations. However, a parallel analysis can be carried out for any other variables that exert income effects on demand. One such is household composition, where the needs that come with additional household members act so as to reduce the income available to each. Thinking about household composition in this way builds a bridge between the sharing rule approach and earlier treatments of the effects of household composition.

Instead of two individuals A and B, imagine the household divided into two groups, adults and children. In this context, the decisionmaking surely rests with the adults, but we can nevertheless think of a procedure that shares total resources between the children's needs, the adults' needs, and public goods that are available to both groups. This model has only one type of income, which accrues to the adults, but the role of the different types of income is now taken by the characteristics of children, their numbers and genders, which affect the consumption of the adults through the share of total income that they receive, Hence, if A stands for adult consumption, and C for the consumption of children, we might write the demand for adult goods

$$(4.11) \qquad q_i^A = g_i^A(x^A, p, z^C, z^A)$$

where z^C and z^A are the characteristics of the children and adults respectively. The argument x^A is the total expenditure that is allocated to the adults by the sharing rule

(4.12)
$$x^A = \theta(y, p, z^C, z^A).$$

There is a corresponding demand function for the children, and the observable household demand for each good is the sum of the two components.

Note that the child characteristics affect adult demand in two separate ways in (4.11), through the amount that adults get through the sharing rule—income effects—as well as directly through the demand functions—substitution effects. If we consider one particular change in child characteristics, namely the addition of a child to the household, the income effect is the reduction in adult consumption that is required to feed and clothe the child, while the substitution effects are the rearrangements in adult consumption that are desired (or required) in the new situation. These substitution effects are appropriately described as such because they would exist even if the adults were compensated for the income effects of the child by holding the value of the sharing function unchanged.

Paralleling the previous analysis, the identification of the sharing rule requires additional assumptions. Again, a good deal of progress can be made by working with goods that are exclusive, in this case goods or services that are consumed by adults and not by children. The standard choice for such commodities is adult clothing, alcohol, and tobacco, although in any given survey there may be other candidates. Because of the exclusivity, household consumption of these items is adult consumption, which helps identify the sharing rule in (4.12). Suppose also that there are no substitution effects for at least some of these goods, so that the only effects of children on the consumption of adult goods is through income effects. As a result the effect of an additional child on the expenditure on each adult good ought to be proportional to the effect of income on the expenditure on that adult good. The formal result is obtained by differentiating (4.11) and (4.12) when z^C is absent from the demand function (4.11), but not from the sharing rule (4.12), so that, in a manner precisely analogous to (4.9), the ratio

(4.13)
$$\frac{\partial q_i^A / \partial z^C}{\partial q_i^A / \partial y} = \frac{\partial \theta / \partial z^C}{\partial \theta / \partial y}$$

is the same for all such goods, and identifies part of the sharing rule. In particular, it allows us to measure in income units the effects of children (or child characteristics) on the adult's share of income. For example, if the characteristic is the number of children, and the ratio (4.13) is 100 rupees per child (say), then the effect of an additional child on the consumption of adult goods is equivalent to a reduction of 100 rupees in the budget. Although we must have at least one good that is known to be exclusively adult, when there is more than one, that (4.13) is the same for all goods can be used to construct a test.

This methodology is essentially that proposed by Rothbarth (1943) for measuring the costs of children, and applied in many subsequent studies, for example Henderson (1949–50a, 1949–50b), Nicholson (1949), Cramer (1969), Espenshade (1973), and Lazear and Michael (1988). Rothbarth chose a very broad group of adult goods (including saving), calculated how much the total was reduced by the presence of an additional child, and calculated the cost of the children to the adults by the amount that income would have to rise to restore the original expenditures. I shall return to the topic of child costs in the next section, but for the moment I wish to note the link between Rothbarth's technique and Chiappori's sharing rule analysis.

In this section, I use these methods to investigate another question, which is whether all children are treated equally, or whether there are differences in the effects on adult consumption according to whether the child is a boy or a girl. That there might be such differences is at least possible given the empirical evidence on discrimination against girls in education and health, and if the sharing rule approach works at all, we should expect to find a greater negative effect on adult consumption of additional boys than of additional girls. If parents treat boys better than girls, one way is to make greater reductions in their own expenditures for boys than they would for girls.

Empirical evidence from India

The relationship between gender and the pattern of household demand has been studied by Subramanian and Deaton (1991) using the Maharashtran NSS 38th round data used for the calorie work in Section 4.1. This subsection reports a selection of their results. Maharashtra is perhaps not the best state of India in which to look for gender bias, because there is little evidence of excess infant mortality among girls in Maharashtra or in southern India in general (see Government of India 1988). However, there is no need to prejudge the issue; the Maharashtran data provide an excellent example of how the analysis works, and I shall discuss other evidence below.

The analysis is parametric and begins from the specification of a standard Engel curve linking expenditures on individual goods to total expenditure and to the socioeconomic and demographic characteristics of the household. There are many possible functional forms for such a relationship, and the one used here is based on that introduced by Working (1943), who postulated a linear relationship between the share of the budget on each good and the logarithm of total expenditure. Such a relationship has the theoretical advantage of being consistent with a utility function—see for example Deaton and Muellbauer (1980a, p. 75)—and its shape conforms well to the data in a wide range of circumstances. The transformation of expenditures to budget shares and of total outlay to its logarithm induces an approximate normality in the joint density of the transformed variables, so that the regression function is approximately linear.

Working's Engel curve can be extended to include household demographic composition by writing for good i, $i = 1,\ldots,m$,

$$(4.14) \qquad w_i = \alpha_i + \beta_i \ln(x/n) + \eta_i \ln n + \sum_{k=1}^{K-1} \gamma_{ik}(n_k/n) + \tau_i \cdot z + u_i$$

where w_i is the share of the budget devoted to good i, $p_i q_i/x$, x is (as usual) total expenditure, n is household size, n_j is the number of people in age-sex class j,

Table 4.2. Engel curves showing effects of household composition on selected food demands, rural Maharashtra, 1983

(t-values in brackets)

	Rice		Wheat		Coarse cereals		Pulses		Sugar		Fruit & vegetables	
$\ln(x/n)$	-0.70	(1.8)	0.54	(4.1)	-9.82	(34.2)	-2.08	(22.0)	-1.51	(23.8)	-0.23	(2.2)
$\ln n$	-0.02	(0.1)	0.79	(6.3)	-0.79	(2.9)	-0.84	(9.3)	-0.50	(8.3)	-0.31	(3.2)
Males aged												
0–4	-1.46	(0.7)	0.72	(1.0)	-4.35	(2.9)	0.10	(0.2)	-1.15	(3.4)	-0.19	(0.3)
5–9	-1.63	(0.8)	0.64	(1.0)	-1.07	(0.7)	-0.79	(1.7)	-1.01	(3.2)	-1.69	(3.2)
10–14	-4.78	(2.6)	-0.04	(0.1)	2.44	(1.8)	-0.54	(1.2)	-1.07	(3.6)	-1.54	(3.1)
15–54	-4.63	(3.3)	0.74	(1.5)	0.36	(0.3)	-0.33	(1.0)	-0.71	(3.0)	-2.02	(5.3)
55 +	-5.11	(2.6)	-0.11	(0.2)	0.24	(0.2)	-0.66	(1.4)	0.15	(0.5)	-2.37	(4.4)
Females aged												
0–4	-2.44	(1.2)	-0.42	(0.6)	-6.18	(4.0)	-0.70	(1.4)	-1.79	(5.3)	-0.99	(1.8)
5–9	-0.46	(0.2)	-0.21	(0.3)	0.27	(0.2)	-1.04	(2.1)	-1.11	(3.5)	-2.02	(3.7)
10–14	-0.38	(0.2)	0.00	(0.0)	1.06	(0.7)	-0.54	(1.1)	-0.80	(2.4)	-1.85	(3.4)
15–54	1.25	(0.9)	0.92	(2.0)	0.89	(0.9)	0.22	(0.7)	-0.39	(1.8)	0.51	(1.4)
F-tests of equality by sex												
0–4	0.20		2.28		1.26		2.22		3.14		1.82	
5–9	0.31		1.36		0.73		0.23		0.16		0.33	
10–14	4.80		0.00		0.86		0.00		0.65		0.31	
15–54	24.00		0.19		0.35		3.63		2.61		61.52	
55 +	6.62		0.03		0.03		1.83		0.22		19.54	
Children	1.77		1.19		0.97		0.81		1.31		0.81	
All	6.48		0.75		0.67		1.44		1.41		14.91	

Source: Subramanian and Deaton (1991).

where there are K such age-sex classes in total, z is a vector of other socioeconomic variables such as religion, caste, or occupation, and u_i is the error term for the ith good. Note that i denotes the good, not the observation number, and that when (4.14) is estimated as a regression, the observations are the individual households. In Working's formulation, the sign of the β-coefficients determines whether goods are necessities or luxuries. When $\beta_i > 0$, the share of the budget increases with total outlay, so that its total expenditure elasticity is greater than unity, and vice versa when $\beta_i < 0$.

The way in which the demographics are entered in (4.14) is pragmatic but convenient. To the extent that household size and total expenditure are sufficient to explain demand, the terms in the summation will not be required and the θ coefficients will be zero. Indeed, in some cases per capita outlay may be all that is required to explain the budget share, in which case both the γ's and η's will be zero. In general, however, household composition will matter, and the γ coefficients tell us what are the effects of changing composition while holding household size constant, for example by replacing a man by a woman, or a young child by an older child. The K demographic categories come from a disaggregation of the household by age and by sex, in the example here there are 10 categories, males and females aged 0–4 years, 5–9 years, 10–14 years, 15–54 years, and older than 54. Note that only $K - 1$ of the ratios can be entered in the regression since the sum of all K is identically equal to unity. In the empirical work, the omitted category is females aged 55 and over.

As was the case for demand curves for calories in Section 4.1, the variables for household size and structure cannot be assumed to be exogenous. But as usual, the important point is to consider the consequences of endogeneity, not simply its existence. Estimates of (4.14) allow us to examine the expectation of adult goods expenditures conditional on total outlay and the structure of the household. If it is the case that the coefficients on boys and girls are different, we have found that the regression function differs by gender, so that among households at the same level of outlay, and the same household size, and the same number of adults, expenditure on adult goods depends on the sex composition of the children. If the fact is established, its interpretation needs to be argued. Discrimination against girls is the most obvious story, and the one that I am interested in here. Other interpretations require a mechanism whereby expenditure on adult goods exerts an effect on the ratio of boys to girls. Perhaps parents with a strong taste for adult goods are also those who discriminate against girls, for example, if drunken fathers maltreat their daughters.

Table 4.2 shows the results of estimating equation (4.14) by OLS on the 5,630 rural households for cereals, pulses, and fruits and vegetables. These foods are clearly consumed exclusively neither by adults nor by children, so that the regressions are designed, not to test for gender bias, but to explore how the pattern of household demand is influenced by household composition in general and gender in particular. The first two rows of the table show the effects of (the logarithm of) PCE and of (the logarithm of) household size, and these are followed by the coefficients on the various demographic ratios. Not shown in the table, but included in the regressions, are four occupational dummies, two religion dummies, and a dummy indicating whether the household belongs to a scheduled caste or tribe.

For the five foods shown in the table, only wheat is a luxury good; as we saw in Section 4.1, coarse cereals and pulses are the basic foodstuffs, followed by rice, which here has a total expenditure elasticity insignificantly different from unity, and finally wheat. Conditional on PCE, increases in household size decrease the shares of coarse cereals, pulses, and fruits and vegetables, have little or no effect on the budget share of rice, and increase the share of wheat. I shall return to these and similar findings when I discuss economies of scale in the next section.

Although the detailed demographic effects are important in the regressions, the effects of gender are modest. The bottom panel of the table reports a series of F-tests, the first set testing the equality of the male and female coefficients for each of five age ranges, the sixth testing the joint hypothesis that there are no gender differences among children, i.e., among the first three groups, and the seventh that there are no differences among adults, the last two demographic categories. For these five goods, there are no gender differences among children that show up as significant F-ratios for the three child groups together. The only case where there is an individually significant F-test is for rice on the 10- to 14-year-old category, where boys get less than girls, but note that this is the only significant result of 15 such tests, and can reasonably be attributed to chance. Among the adults, there are no apparent differences for wheat, coarse cereals, or pulses, but altering household composition by replacing women by men is estimated to decrease the budget shares of both rice and fruit and vegetables. The compensating changes elsewhere in the budget—the male intensive goods—are in coarse cereals (although the coefficient is not significant in the regression) and in goods not shown here, notably in processed food, entertainment, alcohol, and tobacco.

These results by themselves tell us nothing about the cause of the gender differences, and certainly do not allow us to separate the effects of tastes from a possible gender bias in household sharing rules. Men may prefer to smoke and drink more, while women prefer to consume more high-quality food, although the difference between coarse cereals and wheat may also come from the fact that men do more heavy agricultural work, and that coarse cereals provide calories more cheaply than does wheat (see Table 4.1 above). It is also possible that men control household budgets, and do not permit women to have the same access to the "luxuries" of intoxicants, tobacco, and entertainment.

Boys versus girls in rural Maharashtra: methodology

Once we have identified adult goods, we can make inferences about the effects of gender on the allocation, at least for children. Perhaps the most direct way of doing so is to run regressions corresponding to (4.14) for adult goods, to compare the coefficients on the ratios for boys and girls, and to test the difference using an F- or t-test. If the coefficient for boys is significantly more negative than the coefficient for girls, adults are making bigger sacrifices for boys than girls, and we have evidence of discrimination.

I shall show the results of such calculations below, but it is also useful to measure the effects in a different way, and explicitly to calibrate the effects of an additional child in terms of the effects of changes in the size of the budget. In particular, I define "outlay-equivalent ratios" as the derivatives of expenditure on each adult good with respect to an additional child divided by the corresponding derivatives with respect to total expenditure, with the results expressed as a fraction of PCE. The outlay-equivalent ratio for a male child on tobacco, say, is the fraction by which PCE would have to be reduced to induce the same reduction in tobacco expenditure as would an additional male child. More formally, if π_{ij} is the outlay-equivalent ratio for good i and demographic category j, (4.14) implies that

$$(4.15) \qquad \pi_{ij} = \frac{\partial q_i / \partial n_j}{\partial q_i / \partial x} \div \frac{x}{n} = \frac{(\eta_i - \beta_i) + \gamma_{ij} - \Sigma_k \gamma_{ik}(n_k / n)}{\beta_i + w_i}$$

where, by convention, the γ_{ik} for the last demographic category K is zero. Given estimates of the parameters, the outlay-equivalent ratios can be calculated. By (4.15), they will vary according to the values of the budget share and the demographic composition of the household. Rather than track this from household to household, I follow the usual procedure and calculate the ratios at the mean values of the data.

The convenience of this procedure lies in the relationship between the outlay-equivalent ratios and (4.13); if good i is indeed an adult good, and if there are no substitution effects of children on its consumption, then the outlay-equivalent ratio measures the ratio of derivatives of the sharing rule, and should be identical for all such adult goods. We can therefore calculate the outlay-equivalent ratios for a number of possible goods, and use the estimates to guide our choice of adult goods, or given a selection, test the predictions that the ratios are equal using (4.15) to calculate the ratios and (4.18) for their variances and covariances (see Deaton, Ruiz-Castillo, and Thomas 1989 for further details).

*Technical note: standard errors for outlay-equivalent ratios

Estimates of the variances and covariances of the different π-ratios can be obtained by bootstrapping, or from the variance-covariance matrix of the regression coefficients using the delta method discussed in Section 2.8.

Suppose that the regression equation for the ith good has the vector of parameters b_i, whose elements are $\alpha_i, \beta_i, \eta_i$, and $\gamma_{ij}, j = 1, \ldots, K-1$, plus the parameters for any other included variables. Since all the right hand side variables are the same in the regressions for all goods, we have the classical multivariate regression model as described, for example, in Goldberger (1964, pp. 201–12). For this model, for which equation-by-equation OLS coincides with full information maximum likelihood, the variances and covariances of the OLS estimates of the b's both within and across equations is given by the formula

$$(4.16) \qquad E(\hat{b}_i - b_i)(\hat{b}_j - b_j)' = \omega_{ij}(X'X)^{-1}$$

Table 4.3. Outlay-equivalent ratios for adult goods and possible adult goods, Maharashtra, 1983

	Males: Age group					Females: Age group				
	0–4	5–9	10–14	15–54	55 +	0–4	5–9	10–14	15–54	55 +
Adult goods										
Tobacco and *pan*	-0.42	-0.12	-0.13	0.57	0.87	-0.04	-0.01	-0.17	-0.01	0.03
Alcohol	0.02	0.11	-0.89	0.37	0.10	-0.31	-0.02	-0.76	-0.30	-0.24
Possible adult goods										
Men's clothing	-0.39	-0.48	-0.14	-0.14	0.07	-0.56	-0.23	-0.45	-0.57	-0.52
Women's clothing	-0.21	-0.37	-0.39	-0.54	-0.53	-0.31	-0.27	-0.40	-0.22	-0.20
Leather footwear	-0.60	-0.77	-0.09	0.22	-0.03	-0.69	-0.12	-0.59	-0.64	-0.40
Amusements	-0.25	-0.22	-0.46	0.97	-0.32	-0.46	-0.33	-0.35	-0.46	-0.44
Personal care	0.00	0.02	-0.08	0.12	-0.42	0.19	-0.14	0.16	0.26	-0.13

Source: Subramanian and Deaton (1991, Table 5).

where X is the matrix of explanatory variables and ω_{ij} is the covariance between the residuals in the ith and jth equations. This residual variance-covariance matrix is estimated from the OLS residuals from each equation, so that

$$(4.17) \qquad \tilde{\omega}_{ij} = n^{-1}e_i'e_j$$

where e_i and e_j are the vectors of estimated residuals from the ith and jth equations, respectively.

The covariance of any two outlay-equivalent ratios can then be obtained from (4.16) and (4.17) by the delta method, viz.

$$(4.18) \qquad E(\tilde{\pi}_{ik}-\pi_{ik})(\tilde{\pi}_{jl}-\pi_{jl}) = \Sigma_r\Sigma_s \frac{\partial\pi_{ik}}{\partial b_{ir}}\frac{\partial\pi_{jl}}{\partial b_{is}} \omega_{ij}(X'X)_{rs}^{-1}$$

where the derivatives are calculated from (4.15).

Boys versus girls in rural Maharashtra: results

Table 4.3 shows the calculated outlay-equivalent ratios for a number of adult goods or potential adult goods from the 38th round of the NSS for rural Maharashtra. As is the case in many other surveys, there are relatively few adult goods to choose from. The two best candidates are tobacco and *pan*, and alcohol, and the usefulness of the latter is even compromised by the fact that only 12 percent of rural households record any purchases of alcohol. Even so, Subramanian and Deaton treat these as "safe" adult goods, and their outlay-equivalent ratios are shown in the first two rows of the table. The NSS survey does not separate clothing and footwear into adult and child categories, but rather into male and female categories, with children's clothing included in the categories. Nevertheless, the table treats these as "possible" adult goods, along with three others, leather footwear, amusements, and personal care and toiletries.

As is perhaps to be expected from the data problems, only the results from tobacco and *pan* are really satisfactory. In all cases, the outlay-equivalent ratios for children are negative, indicating that additional children act like income reductions for this category, while the ratios for adults are positive, at least for the two male adult categories. There is little association between adult females and the consumption of tobacco and *pan*. For alcohol, there are significant negative π-ratios only for children in the 10- to 14-year-old group, and once again the positive effects of adults are confined to males. For the "possibles," while it is indeed the case that most of the child ratios are negative, so are several of those for the adults. A case could perhaps be made for amusements as an adult good, although as with tobacco and *pan* and alcohol, the adult effects are primarily associated with males. If we ignore these other categories, and also alcohol on grounds of infrequency of purchase, we are left with expenditure on tobacco and *pan* to indicate possible gender effects in allocations to children. For the two youngest age groups of children, the effects are indeed larger negative for boys than for girls, although the difference is only significant for the youngest group, those aged less than 5 years. The *F*-test of the underlying regression coefficients—of the hypothesis that the appropriate two γ coefficients are the same in (4.14)—is 4.3, which is significant at conventional values, and which could be taken as evidence of discrimination against girls relative to boys. The fact that there are no such differences among the other age groups could perhaps be regarded as evidence in the other direction, but it should also be noted that the evidence on excess mortality of girls is of excess infant mortality, precisely the age category in which the current tests detect a difference. If the analysis is repeated using the urban Maharashtran sample, there is no perceptible difference in treatment in any age group, including the youngest, but again it can be argued that it is in the rural areas where discrimination is most likely to be found.

Subramanian and Deaton conclude

> the evidence, while suggestive of discrimination against young girls in rural areas, is by no means conclusive. It is unlikely to persuade someone whose priors are strongly against the existence of such discrimination. Nevertheless, the issue is of great importance, and the results here are sufficiently positive to make it seem worthwhile repeating this exercise for other states for which the NSS data are available.

Subramanian (1994) has repeated the analysis using the 43rd round of the NSS (1987–88) on rural households from Andhra Pradesh, Haryana, Maharashtra, Punjab, and Rajasthan. The three Northwestern states of Haryana, Punjab, and Rajasthan are places where there is strong evidence of discrimination against girls; excess mortality among girls is high, and female literacy is low. For example, the 1991 census showed that among women aged seven and over, only 12 percent were literate in Rajasthan, 24 percent in Andhra, 33 percent in Haryana, 41 percent in Maharashtra, and 44 percent in Punjab. The results on *pan* and tobacco from the 1983 survey reappear for the 5- to 9-year age group in the later data from Maharashtra, but not in any of the other states. Perhaps Maharashtra is different in some way, or perhaps the Maharashtran results should be attributed to chance.

Côte d'Ivoire, Thailand, Bangladesh, Pakistan, and Taiwan (China)

Additional evidence on expenditure patterns and gender comes from other countries. In the first application of the method in Deaton (1989b), I looked at the effects of boys and girls on adult expenditures in Côte d'Ivoire and Thailand using the 1985 Living Standards and 1980–81 Socioeconomic Surveys, respectively. In Côte d'Ivoire, it is impossible to reject the hypothesis that the outlay-equivalent ratios are equal for a set of seven adult goods consisting of adult clothing, adult clothing fabric, adult shoes, alcohol, tobacco, meals taken away from home, and entertainment. For these goods taken together, the outlay-equivalent ratios are –0.12 for boys aged 0–4, and –0.49 for boys aged 5–14, while the corresponding estimates for girls are −0.22 and −0.48. The two pairs of numbers are not significantly different; if anything, the numerical estimates are in favor of young girls. There is certainly no evidence of favoritism toward boys. (As in the Indian data, there are gender effects among adults, with expenditure on alcohol and tobacco again associated with men.)

For the Thai data, the results are similar. For a three-good collection of adult goods consisting of tobacco, alcohol, and meals eaten away from home the outlay-equivalent ratios are −0.47, −0.52, and −0.34 for boys aged 0–2, 3–4, and 5–14, whereas the corresponding ratios for girls are −0.30, −0.36, and −0.22, all slightly smaller than the boys' ratios, but only the last is significantly so, a result that comes from apparent gender differences in expenditures on meals taken away from home. However, the tests for the equality across goods of the outlay-equivalent ratios give strong rejections, so that it is not legitimate to combine tobacco, alcohol, and outside meals into a single adult group. Even if we ignore the problem, the differences between the boys' and girls' ratios are hardly impressive.

Of course, Thailand and Côte d'Ivoire, like the state of Maharashtra in India, are not the places where we would expect to find evidence of discrimination against girls in the allocation of household expenditure. In West Africa, as in Thailand, women are economically productive, and girls are not seen as a burden on their parents. Much better laboratories for these techniques are provided by Bangladesh and Pakistan, two countries where there is a great deal of other evidence on differential treatment by gender. Ahmad and Morduch (1993) have applied the same methodology to data from the 1988 Household Expenditure Survey from Bangladesh. Like Subramanian (1994), they find no evidence of bias in favor of boys even though the survey itself shows that the number of boys exceeds the number of girls by 11 percent overall and 13 percent in rural areas, and although calculations using the 1988–89 Child Nutrition Survey show that the nutritional status of boys responds more to increases in household income than does the nutritional status of girls. These results suggest that the consumption-based methodology fails to detect gender bias, even when it is well documented by other measures.

Ahmad and Morduch's results are confirmed for Pakistan by my own calculations using the 1984 Household Income and Expenditure Survey. Table 4.4 shows the coefficients for boys and girls in the regressions (4.14) for tobacco and *pan*, and for men's and women's footwear, both defined to exclude children's footwear. As in Maharashtra, the results suggest that tobacco and *pan* are consumed by adult males, but unlike the Maharashtran case, there is no clear pattern of decreases in consumption in response to the presence of children. Boys aged 3–4 and girls aged 5–14 are the only child categories with negative coefficients, but neither the coefficients themselves nor their differences by gender are significantly different from zero. The evidence for the two footwear categories are much clearer, but like Ahmad and Morduch's results for Bangladesh, they appear to indicate identical treatment for boys and girls. Expenditure on both men's and women's footwear decreases in response to small children in the household, and for the two youngest child groups, those aged 4 and under, the coefficients are

Table 4.4. Tests for gender effects in adult goods, Pakistan, 1984

	Tobacco and pan		Men's footwear		Women's footwear	
$\ln(x/n)$	0.20	(2.9)	−0.33	(21.5)	−0.17	(17.4)
$\ln n$	0.04	(0.6)	0.12	(7.7)	0.06	(5.9)
Males						
0–2	1.08	(2.4)	−0.35	(3.5)	−0.78	(12.3)
3–4	−0.58	(1.2)	−0.15	(1.4)	−0.80	(11.4)
5–14	0.03	(0.1)	0.11	(1.5)	−0.82	(17.8)
15–54	2.07	(6.1)	1.41	(18.8)	−0.71	(14.9)
55	0.50	(1.2)	1.20	(12.6)	−0.69	(11.3)
Females						
0–2	0.22	(0.5)	−0.33	(3.2)	−0.75	(11.8)
3–4	0.11	(0.2)	−0.30	(2.7)	−0.77	(10.9)
5–14	−0.21	(0.6)	−0.31	(4.2)	−0.62	(13.1)
15–54	−0.52	(1.8)	−0.00	(0.0)	0.15	(3.7)
F-tests						
0–2		3.24		0.05		0.25
3–4		1.67		1.48		0.16
5–14		0.74		47.50		27.17
All children		1.85		16.31		9.14
15–54		78.61		469.86		436.38
All adults		1.34		157.89		236.69

Note: All coefficients multiplied by 100, t–values in parentheses.
Source: Author's calculations based on 1984 Household Income and Expenditure Survey.

essentially the same for boys and girls. For the older children, aged 5–14, the results show that boys use men's footwear and girls use ladies' footwear, so that the F-tests show significant differences by gender, but this is no evidence of discrimination.

Similar results were obtained by Rudd (1993), who analyzed Taiwanese data from 1990. While the evidence on gender bias is less clear in Taiwan (China) than in Bangladesh and Pakistan, work by Greenhalgh (1985) and by Parrish and Willis (1992) is consistent with the traditional view that Chinese families prefer boys to girls. But as in the other studies, Rudd finds no evidence of discrimination against girls in the expenditure data.

What should be concluded from this now quite extensive evidence? It is a puzzle that expenditure patterns so consistently fails to show strong gender effects even when measures of outcomes show differences between boys and girls. One possibility is that the method is flawed, perhaps by pervasive substitution effects associated with children, so that the outlay-equivalent ratios are not revealing the income effects of children, but are contaminated by the rearrangement of the budget that follows a change in family composition. While such substitution effects are likely enough, they are hardly an adequate explanation for those cases where the estimated coefficients are so similar for boys and girls. If boys are treated better than girls, and the results do not show it because of substitution, then the substitution effects associated with girls should be different from those for boys, and of exactly the right size to offset the discriminatory income effects. Such an explanation is far-fetched compared with the simple message that comes from the data, that parents—and where adult goods are largely alcohol and tobacco, parents means fathers—make the same amount of room in their budgets for girls as they do for boys. Perhaps discrimination requires action by mothers, who do not have access to adult goods, which are the prerogative of men.

If so, the discrimination against girls in (northern) India, Pakistan, Bangladesh, and possibly Taiwan (China) must take forms that are not detectable in the expenditure data. Ahmad and Morduch put forward three possible explanations: that girls have greater needs than boys (at least at some point); that certain critical interventions—such as access to a doctor when sick—are made for boys but not for girls; and that the discrimination is too subtle to be detected in even the sizes of samples available in household survey data. They cite Das Gupta's (1987) work showing that discrimination against girls is confined to those with older sisters as an example of the latter, and it is certainly true that neither this effect nor the occasional medical expenditure on boys would likely be detected using the adult-good method. It may also be that where medical expenses require families to go into debt, parents may be willing to incur debt to preserve an asset—a boy—but not to preserve a liability—a girl. It is also possible that discrimination works through allocations of time, not money, with mothers taking less time away from farm or market work after the birth of a girl. Indeed, Ahmad and Morduch find in Bangladesh that total household expenditure, which is treated as a conditioning variable in regressions like (4.14), responds negatively to the presence of small children in the household, and does so by more when the small child is a boy. However, the much larger Pakistani and Indian data sets used here show no such effects.

There is clearly a good deal more work to be done in reconciling the evidence from different sources before the expenditure-based methods can be used as reliable tools for investigating the nature and extent of gender discrimination.

4.3 Equivalence scales: theory and practice

In Chapter 3, where I discussed the measurement of welfare and poverty, I made the conversion from a household to an individual basis by dividing total household expenditure by the number of people in the household, and then used total household expenditure per capita as the measure of welfare for each member of the household. Not only does this procedure assume that everyone in the household receives an equal allocation—an assumption that can perhaps be defended as the best that can be done given current knowledge—but it also fails to recognize the fact that not everyone in the household is the same and has the same needs. While it is true that children consume special goods, they surely require less of most things than do adults. It is also possible that there are economies of scale to living together, perhaps because family members benefit from each other's consumption, or because there are public goods that can be used by all family members at no additional cost. Since the variation of needs within the household and the existence of economies of scale are commonplace observations that can hardly be contested, it would seem that we ought to be able to do better than measure welfare by total household expenditure per capita.

The obvious solution is a system of weights, whereby children count as some fraction of an adult, with the fraction dependent on age, so that effective household size is the sum of these fractions, and is measured not in numbers of persons, but in numbers of *adult equivalents*. Economies of scale can be allowed for by transforming the number of adult equivalents into "effective" adult equivalents, so that if two cannot live as cheaply as one, four adult equivalents can perhaps live as cheaply as three single adults. How these adult equivalents should be calculated, and whether it even makes sense to try, have been (occasional) topics of discussion in the economics literature for more than a century, although they have never really attracted the attention that is merited by their practical importance. Perhaps as a result, there is no consensus on the matter, so that the views presented in this section are necessarily my own, although I shall attempt to present and discuss the difficulties and the alternative interpretations.

Before discussing equivalence scales, I note one important approach that allows us to finesse the issue, at least in some cases. In the discussion of poverty and social welfare in Section 3.1, we saw that under some circumstances it is possible to tell whether poverty is greater or less without specifying the poverty line, even though all poverty measures require a poverty line for their calculation. For example, when the distribution function for one distribution lies entirely above that for another, the former shows more poverty whatever the line (see pp. 164–69 above). This is one case of stochastic dominance, and Chapter 3 showed how an examination of the various kinds of stochastic dominance allows us to rank at least some distributions in terms of poverty, inequality, and social welfare.

In a series of papers, Atkinson and Bourguignon (1982, 1987, 1989) have laid out an approach based on bivariate stochastic dominance which allows some distributions to be ranked without specifying equivalence scales for different family types. Atkinson and Bourguignon require that family types be ranked according to need, something that is much less demanding than constructing equivalence scales. Although we might have some difficulty telling whether (for example) a couple or a single person with two children has greater needs, it is easy to agree (for example) that two adults and two children need more resources than two adults and one child. Having ranked the family types, and on the assumption that the two distributions contain the same fractions of the different types, the two distributions are compared in the following way. Starting with the neediest type only, we check whether there is first-order (poverty line), second-order (social welfare, poverty deficit), or Lorenz (inequality) dominance, whichever is the concept of interest. If the dominance test is passed, the test is then applied to the neediest and second-neediest types pooled. If dominance holds all the way up to the last test, when all family types are combined, then one distribution is preferred to the other for any set of equivalence scales consistent with the original ranking by need. As usual, dominance tests rank only some pairs of distributions, and there will be cases where the ranking is ambiguous, just as when Lorenz curves or distribution functions cross. Nor is the dominance approach designed to help in making comparisons between families with different compositions in a single distribution; it will not tell us whether, given their respective incomes, larger families are better-off than smaller families.

Equivalence scales, welfare, and poverty

Given the difficulties of definition and of measurement, it would be convenient if the calculation of equivalence scales were unimportant for the measurement of welfare and poverty. Unfortunately such is not the case. As emphasized by Kuznets (1979), and in all household survey data of which I am aware, total household expenditure rises with household size, but not as rapidly, so that PCE decreases with household size. For example, in the data from rural Pakistan, the regression coefficient of the logarithm of total expenditure on the logarithm of total household size is 0.61, so that the regression coefficient of the logarithm of PCE on the logarithm of household size is −0.39; the corresponding figures for rural Maharashtra are 0.70 and −0.30, and for the Ivorian Living Standards Surveys are 0.58 and −0.42 in 1985, 0.63 and −0.37 in 1986, and 0.65 and −0.35 in 1987 and 1988. Given these correlations, the relationship between household size and individual welfare will depend on just how the equivalences are calculated.

At one extreme, it might be argued that economies of scale and altruism are so strong that *total* household expenditure is the appropriate measure of *individual* welfare. At the other extreme, we might refuse to admit any variation of needs, arguing that all persons are equal whatever their age and sex, so that individual welfare should be measured by total household expenditure per capita. These two procedures would certainly seem to set bounds on the ideal correction. But given the correlations in the data, the use of total household expenditure is effectively an assumption that welfare rises with household size and that small households are overrepresented among the poor. Conversely, the procedures in Chapter 3, which use PCE as the welfare measure, assume the contrary, that large household sizes are automatically associated with lower welfare and with greater poverty. Either of these relationships between household size and welfare could be correct, but they need to be demonstrated, not assumed.

Equivalence scales are required to compare poverty across different groups. In most societies, the elderly live in households that are relatively small and contain few children while children, who never live by themselves, live in households with children. In consequence, if we use equivalence scales that attribute low needs to children, or that incorporate large economies of scale, we will find that there are relatively few children in poverty, but a relatively large number of the elderly. For example, the "fact" that there is less poverty among the elderly in the United States depends on the assumption in the official counts that the elderly need less than other adults (see Deaton and Paxson 1997). International comparisons of poverty and inequality are also sensitive to the choice of equivalence scale (see Buhmann et al. 1988), something that is often given inadequate advertisement when the performance of different countries is presented in popular discussion.

The relevance of household expenditure data

For many economists and demographers since Engel more than a century ago, it has seemed that survey data on household expenditures can tell us something about equivalence scales. As we have already seen in the previous section, such data can be used to study how demand patterns vary with the demographic composition of the household. Several authors, starting with Dublin and Lotka (1930) and perhaps most recently Lindert (1978, 1980), have used the data to associate particular expenditures with children, and thus to calculate the "cost" of a child on an annual basis at different ages, or as in Dublin and Lotka, to estimate the cost of bringing a child to maturity, an amount that they treat as an input cost in their calculation of the "money value of a man." Such costs can readily be translated into an equivalence scale by dividing by the total budget; in a household of two adults and a child where child costs are one-fifth of the budget, the adults get two-fifths each, so a child is "equivalent to" one-half of an adult.

As first sight, such procedures seem unobjectionable. There are certain child goods, like education, whose costs can be attributed to the children—although even here it is unclear how we are to deal with the fact that richer parents spend more on the children's education than poorer parents, and whether this expenditure is to be credited entirely to the children—and the other nonexclusive expenditures can be prorated in some essentially arbitrary but sensible way. As we have seen above in the discussion of sharing rules, such prorating is hardly a trivial exercise, and what may seem like obvious procedures are typically incorrect. For example, it is tempting to identify child costs by estimating Engel curves in which expenditures are regressed on income (or outlay) and the numbers of adults and children, with the coefficients on the latter estimating how much is spent on each good for each child at the margin. However, if such regressions are applied to all the goods in the budget, and if total expenditure is included as an explanatory variable, the sum of the child coefficients must be zero. Additional children do not enlarge the budget, they cause it to be rearranged. In consequence, the regression method will only yield a positive estimate of costs if the regressions are restricted to a subset of goods. The inclusion of goods into or exclusion of goods from this subset determines the value of the scale and thus needs clear justification. Of course, exactly the same criticisms apply to Dublin and Lotka's cruder methods; while their procedure has the advantage of transparency, it also rests on counting the positive effects of children on expenditures as child costs, while ignoring the negative effects.

While it is important to understand why the estimation of the cost of a child is not simply a matter of counting up child expenditures, it must be emphasized that the criticism is directed at one specific method, and does not demonstrate that it is impossible to estimate child costs from household budget data in general. Indeed, as we have already seen in the previous section, Bourguignon and Chiappori's work establishes that, given appropriate assumptions, it is possible to use household data to identify at least some aspects of the rules whereby resources are allocated to different groups of people within the household. There also exist a number of specific methods for calculating child costs from survey data, some of considerable antiquity, and each resting on its own set of more or less palatable assumptions. One of my purposes in this section is to clarify and discuss these assumptions, to rule out some clearly unacceptable methodologies, and to attach the appropriate "health warnings" to the others. But before I can undertake that task, it is necessary to review some of the general theory that underlies all of these measures. The theory of equivalence scales and the cost of children is based on an analogy with the theory of cost-of-living indices and consumers' surplus. Since that theory is useful in its own right in development applications, and since it generalizes the results used in Section 3.3 on the welfare effects of price changes, I begin with a brief survey.

Cost-of-living indices, consumer's surplus, and utility theory

In standard consumer choice theory, a consumer maximizes a utility function $v(q)$ by choosing a bundle of goods to satisfy the budget constraint $p.q = x$. If the utility-maximizing choice results in a utility value of u, expenditure x must be the minimum cost of attaining u at prices p, so that if this minimum cost is represented by the *cost function* (or expenditure function) $c(u,p)$, we can write

$$(4.19) \qquad c(u,p) = x.$$

The maximum attainable utility can also be written as a function of total expenditure x and prices p using the indirect utility function

$$(4.20) \qquad u = \psi(x,p)$$

which is (4.19) rewritten; both equations link total expenditure, utility, and prices and each can be obtained from the other by rearrangement.

The theory of cost-of-living numbers was developed by the Russian economist Konüs in the 1920s, and rests on a comparison of the costs of obtaining the same utility at two different sets of prices. Formally, we can write

$$(4.21) \qquad P(p^1,p^0;u^R) = c(u^R,p^1) \div c(u^R,p^0)$$

where u^R is a "reference" or base utility level, typically either utility in period 0 or in period 1, so that the scalar value P is the relative cost of maintaining the standard of living u^R at the two sets of prices p^1 and p^0. Instead of a ratio of costs, we might also compute the difference of costs, which is simply

$$(4.22) \qquad D(p^1,p^0;u^R) = c(u^R,p^1) - c(u^R,p^0).$$

The measure D is known as the *compensating variation* when reference utility is base-period utility's, and as the *equivalent variation* when period 1's utility is the reference. These consumer surplus measures are simply different ways of expressing the same information as the Konüs cost-of-living index numbers.

It is important to realize that, given knowledge of the demand functions, the index numbers (4.21) and cost differences (4.22) are known or at least can be calculated. Although utility values are not observable—any monotone increasing transform of a utility function will have the same behavioral consequences as the original—so that it might seem that (4.21) is unobservable, this is not in fact the case. The essential point is that the derivatives of the cost function are the quantities consumed, which are directly observable, so that given the value of the cost function at one set of prices, its value at another can be obtained by integration. Since the literature does not always adequately recognize the observability of cost-of-living indices and equivalent and compensating variations, I include a brief technical note detailing the calculations. It can be skipped without losing the thread of the main argument.

*Technical note: calculating the welfare effects of price

The quantity demanded of good i can be written

$$(4.23) \qquad q_i = \partial c(u,p)/\partial p_i = h_i(u,p)$$

where $h_i(u,p)$ is the Hicksian (or compensated) demand function for good i. However, we can use the indirect utility function (4.20) to rewrite (4.23) as

$$(4.24) \qquad q_i = h_i(u,p) = h_i(\psi(x,p),p) = g_i(x,p)$$

where $g_i(x,p)$ is the familiar Marshallian (or uncompensated) demand function that gives demands as a function of total outlay and prices. These Marshallian demands are what we can hope to estimate from the data, and we need a procedure for evaluating the cost-of-living numbers from knowledge of these functions alone.

To illustrate, suppose that we wish to use base-period utility u^0 as the reference. Since $c(u^0,p^0) = x^0$, outlay in the base period, the only quantity that needs to be calculated for (4.21) and (4.22) is the counterfactual $c(u^0,p^1)$, the minimum cost of obtaining base utility at the new prices. As a first stage, write this as

$$(4.25) \qquad c(u^0,p^1) = c(u^0,p^0) + \int_{p^0}^{p^1} \sum_k [\partial c(u^0,p)/\partial p_k]\,dp_k$$

which by (4.23) and (4.24) is

$$(4.26) \qquad c(u^0,p^1) = c(u^0,p^0) + \int_{p^0}^{p^1} \sum_k [g_k(c(u^0,p),p)]\,dp_k.$$

The principle of the calculation can now be seen. We start from the initial price vector p^0. For this value, the terms in the integral are known from the demand function, so we can use (4.26) to calculate the new value of $c(u^0,p)$, not for p^1, but for some other price close to p^0 in the direction of p^1. Given this new value, we can move to a new price, so that by dividing up the path from p^0 to p^1 into many small steps, we can calculate (4.26) as accurately as we want, with more steps giving greater accuracy. The details of how to do this in practice need not concern us here; elegant algorithms have been proposed by Vartia (1983) and Hausman (1981) for the case where the parametric form of the Marshallian demands is known, while Hausman and Newey (1995) show how to perform the calculations when demands are estimated by the nonparametric kernel techniques discussed in Chapter 3. For the purposes of this chapter, what is required is the demonstration of the principle, that because the derivatives of the cost function are known or can be estimated, the cost-of-living indexes and consumers' surplus measures are known or can be estimated.

Equivalence scales, the cost of children, and utility theory

Consider now the extension of cost-of-living theory to the theory of the cost of children. At first sight the analogy seems close to perfect, with children, or more generally household characteristics, playing the role of prices. In particular, it is supposed that the cost function depends on demographic characteristics z, so that, for a utility-maximizing household, total expenditure is the minimum cost of reaching their utility level, and (4.19) is replaced by

$$(4.27) \qquad\qquad c(u,p,z) = x.$$

This equation is not without its problems, and in particular it does not make clear whose utility level is referred to. We are no longer dealing with the single agent of the standard cost-of-living theory, and there is more than one possible interpretation of (4.27). For example, we might be dealing with parents' welfare, with the cost function calculating the minimum expenditure required to maintain parents' utility in the face of social conventions about what needs to be spent on their offspring. Alternatively, each person in the household might have a separate utility function, and the sharing rule between them is set so that all obtain the same welfare level, in which case (4.27) is the minimum cost of bringing each member to the utility level u. In the next section, I shall sometimes have to be more explicit, but for the moment I note only that (4.27) is consistent with a number of sensible models of intrahousehold allocation.

The equivalence scale compares two households with compositions z^0 and z^1, in exactly the same way that the cost-of-living index number compares two price levels. Hence, if u^R and p^R are the reference utility level and price vector, respectively, the equivalence scale is written, by analogy with (4.21),

$$(4.28) \qquad m(z^1,z^0;u^R,p^R) = c(u^R,p^R,z^1) \div c(u^R,p^R,z^0).$$

In the simplest case, z^0 would represent a family of two adults and z^1 a family with two adults and a newborn child, so that using the prechild utility level and current prices as base, the excess of (4.28) over unity would be the cost of the newborn as a ratio of total household expenditure. Alternatively, we can follow the consumers' surplus analogy, and measure not the equivalence scale—which is an index number—but the cost of children—which corresponds to a consumers' surplus measure. This last is the cost of the difference in household characteristics, *cf.* (4.22)

$$(4.29) \qquad D(z^1, z^0; u^R, p^R) = c(u^R, p^R, z^1) - c(u^R, p^R, z^0)$$

which, in the simple example above, would be the amount of money necessary to restore the original welfare level.

The underidentification of equivalence scales

The analogy between the cost of living and the cost of children runs into difficulty when we consider how the theoretical concepts are to be implemented. As before, I assume that we know the demand functions, which is more than before, since we must know not only how demands respond to incomes and to prices, but also how they respond to changes in household composition. Of course, these demand functions have to be estimated, but the survey data contain the information to do so. But that done, and in contrast to the cost-of-living case, knowledge of the demand functions is not sufficient to identify the equivalence scale (4.28) nor the cost measure (4.29), a result due to Pollak and Wales (1979). I first sketch their argument, then interpret the result, and finally consider possible remedies.

Suppose that we start from a consumer whose preferences are represented by a cost function augmented by compositional variables as in (4.27) and that we track through the relationship between the cost function and the observable demands as in (4.23) and (4.24). With the addition of the z-vector, (4.24) becomes

$$(4.30) \qquad q_i = h_i(u, p, z) = h_i[\psi(x, p, z), p, z] = g_i(x, p, z)$$

where the Hicksian demand functions h_i are the partial derivatives of the cost function as in (4.23). Now consider a new (and different) cost function that is constructed from the original one by means of

$$(4.31) \qquad \tilde{c}(u, p, z) = c[\xi(u, z), p, z]$$

where $\xi(u, z)$ is a function that is increasing in its first argument, utility, so that in the new cost function, as in the old, it costs more to be better-off. Since ξ can be any increasing function, the new cost function and the old can be quite different, and are capable of embodying quite different attitudes of parents to their children, and quite different sharing rules between them.

The new Hicksian demand functions are given by differentiating the new cost function, so that by (4.31) they are related to the old Hicksian demands by

(4.32) $$\tilde{q}_i = \tilde{h}_i(\tilde{u},p,z) = h_i[\xi(u,z),p,z]$$

where $\tilde{u}$ is the utility level associated with the new cost function and the original total outlay x. However, since (4.31) is equal to x, it must be true that

(4.33) $$\xi(\tilde{u},z) = \psi(x,p,z).$$

By the definition of the new cost function, the expression $\xi(\tilde{u},z)$ plays the same role as did u in the original cost function, and in particular both are equal to the value of the original indirect utility function. As a result, when we convert from the Hicksian to the Marshallian demand functions by substituting for utility, we obtain, from (4.32) and (4.33),

(4.34) $$\tilde{q}_i = h_i[\psi(x,p,z),p,z] = g_i(x,p,z)$$

so that the new demand functions are identical to the old.

The two cost functions, the new and the old, although representing different preferences and different costs of children (or other compositional variables) result in the same observable behavior. As a result, if all we observe is the behavior, it is impossible to discover which cost function generated the data. But the costs of children depend on which is correct, so neither the scale nor the cost measure can be calculated from knowledge of the demand functions alone. This is the essence of Pollak and Wales' argument.

Like all situations where there is a failure of identification, the result does not mean that measurement is impossible, only that additional information is required, and in the next subsections, where I discuss specific proposals for estimating equivalence scales, I shall be explicit about the source of that additional information. However, before going on to that analysis, there are several general issues of interpretation with which we have to deal.

It is sometimes argued that it makes no sense even to try to measure the cost of children. While fertility control is not perfect, parents generally have children as a result of conscious choice, and are presumably made better-off by the birth of a child. By this argument, the costs of a child—the benefits of losing a child—are negative, perhaps infinitely so, so that to consider the additional expenditures associated with the child as a welfare cost to the parents makes no more sense than to claim that the cost of a car is a welfare loss to its purchaser. While this argument admits the reality of the costs, it would deny their relevance for welfare calculations, and views the identification problem as a symptom of the absurdity of trying to measure the happiness that a child brings to its parents by counting the cost of clothing and feeding them. If we insist on trying to define equivalence scales simply by making cost functions depend on household characteristics, the argument is entirely valid. If welfare in these equations is taken to be that of the parents, then the choice of the function ξ affects the welfare that parents get from their children without affecting the household demand functions, so that it is perfectly legitimate to interpret Pollak and Wales' underidentification argument in terms of a story of endogenous fertility. Whatever additional information is used to make the identification, it must clarify exactly what costs and benefits are being considered, and somehow rule out the direct benefits that parents get from the existence of their children.

Even if we were to suppose that having children is involuntary, and that all births are unanticipated events over which parents have no control, then the equivalence scales would still not be identifiable from demand functions alone. The most obvious case is if children were simply smaller versions of their parents, with identical tastes, but needing less of everything. Suppose that for every unit of each good that the parent receives, the child gets an amount $\alpha < 1$, which in this simple model is the equivalence scale. It is obvious that no amount of household expenditure data can identify the parameter α; reallocations within the household have no effect on what the household buys, only on how it is shared when the purchases are taken home. Fortunately children are not *homunculi*; they have different needs from their parents, and there are goods that are consumed only by adults and goods that are consumed only by children. Even so, this example makes clear the potential dangers of attaching welfare significance to the relationship between demographic composition and household expenditure patterns; in this case, the distribution of welfare can be changed arbitrarily without observable consequences for household demand.

What happens if the identification problem is ignored, if a cost function like (4.27) is specified, the demand functions derived and estimated, and the equivalence scales calculated? Indeed, this is the precise counterpart of the standard practice in demand analysis without compositional variables. Because the cost function is so closely linked to the demand functions, it is convenient to specify utility-consistent demand functions, not by writing down a utility function, but by writing down a cost function, typically one that allows a general pattern of responses to price and income—a flexible functional form. Differentiation and substitution from the indirect utility function as in (4.23) and (4.24) yield the demand functions whose parameters (which are also the parameters of the cost function) are then estimated from the data.

It is also possible to write down flexible functional forms for the cost function augmented by compositional variables, for example by augmenting one of the standard flexible forms such as the translog (Christensen, Jorgenson, and Lau 1975) or the "almost ideal demand system" (Deaton and Muellbauer 1980b). The translog indirect utility function is a quadratic form in the logarithms of the ratios of price to total expenditure, so that a translog with demographics can be generated simply by extending the vector of price ratios to include the demographics (see Jorgenson and Slesnick 1984 and Jorgenson 1990). This methodology will give results in spite of Pollak and Wales' underidentification theorem, but because of that theorem, we know that the results on the equivalence scales can be altered by respecifying the cost function or indirect utility function in a way that will have no effect on the estimated demand equations, and which is therefore uncheckable on the data. Identification has been achieved by an arbitrary selection of one from an infinity of observationally equivalent utility functions, each of which will generate a different equivalence scale. But since this selection is not justified, the identifying assumptions remain implicit, and there is no straightforward way of judging whether or not they make sense. The lesson of the under-identification result is not that scales cannot be estimated, but that scales that are not supported by explicit assumptions are scales that cannot be treated seriously.

Engel's method

The oldest of all the methods for constructing equivalence scales dates back to Engel (1857). Although many other procedures have been invented since, Engel's is one of the most straightforward, and is still widely used in practice. It is based on the identifying assumption that the share of the budget devoted to food expenditure correctly indicates welfare between households of differing demographic composition. A large household and a small household are equally well-off if, and only if, they devote the same fraction of their budget to food. I shall discuss the theoretical basis of this assumption and its plausibility at the end of this subsection, but I begin with an explanation of how the assumption allows calculation of the scale, and with some illustrative calculations.

Figure 4.7 shows the standard diagram for the Engel method. On the vertical axis is plotted the food share and on the horizontal axis total household expenditure. For any given household composition, Engel's Law implies that there is a negative relationship between the food share and total expenditure, and the figure illustrates two curves, one for a small family, *AB*, and one for a large family,

Figure 4.7. Engel's method for measuring the cost of children

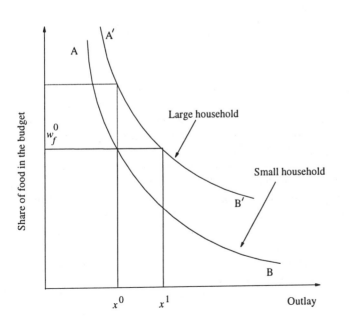

$A'B'$. At the same level of total outlay, the large family spends a larger share of its budget on food, so that its curve lies above and to the right of that for the small family. If we start from some reference point on the curve for the small family, say the combination x^0 and w_f^0 as illustrated, then we can use the identifying assumption to calculate the amount of total expenditure that the large household would require to be as well-off as the smaller family with x^0. In the diagram, the large family has budget share w_f^0 at x^1 so that, by the assumption, it requires x^1 to compensate it for its larger family size. If, for example, the larger family is two adults plus a child, and the smaller family is two adults, the cost of the child is $x^1 - x^0$, and the equivalence scale—the cost of a child relative to an adult couple—is $(x^1 - x^0)/x^0$.

In practice, the scale would be calculated using an estimated food Engel curve. Equation (4.14) above is one possible functional form and will serve to illustrate and provide concrete results. For a reference family of two adults, the food share is given by

$$(4.35) \qquad w_f^0 = \alpha + \beta \ln x^0 + (\eta - \beta) \ln 2 + \gamma_a . 1$$

where γ_a is the γ coefficient for adults, where I have suppressed any difference between males and females, and where the other γ coefficients are absent because the household is all adult, with ratio of number of adults to household size of unity. For a household with two adults and a child, the corresponding equation is

$$(4.36) \qquad w_f = \alpha + \beta \ln x + (\eta - \beta) \ln 3 + \gamma_a (2/3) + \gamma_c (1/3)$$

where γ_c is the coefficient for the ratio of the appropriate child category. The compensating level of expenditure x^1 is obtained by setting (4.36) equal to (4.35) and solving for x. Hence,

$$(4.37) \qquad \ln\left(\frac{x^1}{x^0}\right) = \left(1 - \frac{\eta}{\beta}\right) \ln\frac{3}{2} + \frac{\gamma_a - \gamma_c}{3\beta}.$$

If $\eta = 0$, so that the food share is independent of family size holding PCE constant, and if $\gamma_a = \gamma_c$, so that switching adults for children has no effect on food consumption, the ratio of x^1 to x^0 is simply the ratio of family sizes, here 3 to 2. But even if η is zero, this can be expected to overstate the compensation required because $\gamma_a > \gamma_c$, (adults eat more than children) and β is negative (Engel's Law) so that the last term in (4.37) will be negative.

Table 4.5 shows the coefficients from the food share regressions from the Indian and Pakistani data. The β-coefficients are both negative, as they must be for Engel's Law to hold, and so are the coefficients on the logarithm of household size, so that in both data sets, the food share decreases with household size when PCE is held constant. This result, which is a good deal stronger in the Indian than in the Pakistani data, means that, if were to accept Engel's contention that the food share indicates welfare, larger households behave as if they are better-off than smaller households with the same PCE. (Whether this is a sensible interpretation will be discussed below.) The coefficients on the demographic ratios show the

Table 4.5. Regression coefficients of food share in India and Pakistan

Coefficient of	Maharashtra, India	Pakistan
ln(x/n)	−0.1270	−0.1016
ln n	−0.0355	−0.0133
Ratio of adults		
15–54	0.0070	0.0128
Ratio of children		
0–4	−0.0231	−0.0205
5–9	−0.0116	−0.0020
10–14	−0.0049	0.0037

Source: India, Subramanian and Deaton (1991); Pakistan, author's calculations based on Household Income and Expenditure Survey, 1984–85.

expected pattern, increasing with the age of the group; small children consume less food than older children, who consume less than adults.

The calculations corresponding to (4.37) are shown in Table 4.6. The numbers show the estimated costs of a family of two adults plus one additional person of various ages all calculated relative to the costs of a childless couple. For the Indian data, a child aged between 0 and 4 years is equivalent to 0.24 of a couple, or 0.48 of an adult, a ratio that rises to 56 percent and 60 percent for children aged 5 to 9 and 10 to 14, respectively. The age groups for Pakistan are a little older, and the estimates a little higher; 56 percent of an adult for the youngest category, and 72 percent and 76 percent for the two older groups. However, these estimates must be compared with the last row of the table, which shows the equivalence scale when an additional adult is added to the household. The third adult is only 68 percent of each of the original pair in India and 84 percent in Pakistan, so that even in the latter, the method yields large economies of scale. But these economies of scale also operate for the child equivalence scales in the first three rows, so that when we say that a child is 48 percent of an adult, the effect is as much the consequence of the apparent economies of scale that operate for adults and children alike, as it is a consequence of children costing less than adults. One way of purging the child scales of the effects of the economies of scale is to look at the first three rows as ratios of the fourth row so as to measure the cost of an additional child relative to the cost of an additional adult. By this measure, children

Table 4.6. Equivalence scales using Engel's method, India and Pakistan

Age	Maharashtra, India	Pakistan
0–4	1.24	1.28
5–9	1.28	1.36
10–14	1.30	1.38
15–54	1.34	1.42

Note: The numbers shown are the estimated ratio of the costs of a couple with the child as shown to a couple without children.
Source: Table 4.5.

are very expensive indeed, with even the youngest child costing more than three-quarters of an adult.

Such results appear to be typical of the Engel method in developing countries; for example, Deaton and Muellbauer (1986) report even higher estimates from Sri Lanka and Indonesia. In their work as in the results reported here, the estimates are large because the coefficients of the demographic ratios do not differ very much between adults and children, so that the replacement of an adult by a child does not shrink the food share by much relative to the amount that the food share would be reduced by an increase in total outlay. By the Engel method and its identifying assumption, this finding translates into children being almost as expensive as adults.

Although we have no standard by which to judge these estimates other than crude observation and intuition, by these criteria they seem very high. However, we must be careful about the source of such intuition and in particular rule out other estimates obtained from different models. When another methodology is used, the identifying assumption is different from that in the Engel method, so that even though the results are called "child equivalence scales" or "child costs," we are in effect measuring different things. A comparison between scales from different models is not the same thing as a comparison of, say, the expenditure elasticity of food from different models. Models of child costs, unlike models of demand, not only provide estimates, they also provide the definition of what is being estimated. As a result, the validity of the Engel estimates can only be tested by considering the basic assumptions, and trying to decide whether or not they make sense. It is to that task I now turn.

Underlying the Engel methodology are two empirical regularities, and one assertion. The first regularity is Engel's Law itself, that the share of food in the budget declines as income or total outlay increases. The second regularity is that, with resources held constant, the food share increases with the number of children. The assertion, which was made by Engel himself, is that the food share is a good indicator of welfare. More precisely, if we rank households (inversely) according to their food shares, we have correctly ranked them in terms of well-being, and the procedure can be applied across households of different demographic compositions. It is important to note that this is indeed an assertion, and not an implication of the two empirical regularities. The truth of Engel's Law certainly implies that among households with the same demographic composition, those with higher food shares are generally those with the lower levels of income, and other things constant, with lower levels of welfare, but this is no more than a restatement of Engel's Law itself. Because the presence of additional children tends to increase the household's food share, it is true that additional children affect the budget in the same direction as does a reduction in income, but that is very different from a demonstration that an increase in income sufficient to restore the food share is the precise amount needed to compensate for the additional expenditures associated with the children.

Because food is so important in the budgets of poor households, the assertion that the food share indicates welfare has a superficial plausibility; food is the first necessity and, at least among the very poor, we can probably do a good job of assessing welfare by checking whether people have enough to eat. But the claim needs to be argued, and the primacy of food is not by itself enough to establish Engel's assertion. Even if our main concern is with food, and if we believe that food consumption is a rough but useful measure of welfare, why focus on the share of food in the budget in preference to more direct measures such as food consumption or nutrient intake?

That the share of the budget on food does *not* correctly indicate welfare over households of different compositions has been convincingly argued by Nicholson (1976). His argument runs as follows. Consider the standard case of a child born to a previously childless couple, and suppose that we know the true compensation, defined as the amount of money needed to provide for the child without cutting into the parents' consumption. If this compensation is paid, the parents are exactly as well-off as before, and will presumably consume much the same pattern of goods as before. However, the child's consumption patterns are different from those of its parents; in particular, they will be relatively biased towards food, which is one of the few goods consumed by small children. As a result, even when the correct compensation has been paid, the consumption pattern of the household will be tipped towards food in comparison with the pattern prior to the birth of the child. But according to Engel, the food share is an inverse indicator of welfare, so that the household is worse-off, and requires further compensation to reduce the food share to its original level. As a result, Engel compensation is overcompensation, and the estimates of child costs using the Engel methodology are too high.

Nicholson's argument has its weaknesses, for example in not being based on an explicit model of allocation, and in not allowing for the substitution in adult consumption that is likely to come about from the presence of the child. But it is nevertheless convincing. All that is required for its general validity is that the compensated household's food share is increased by the presence of a child, something that is hard to dispute. Note again that this is not a question that can be settled with respect to the empirical evidence; we are discussing the plausibility of an identifying assumption, whether or not we would find compelling a claim for compensation that cited as evidence an increase in the food share after the addition of a child to the household. The point of Nicholson's argument is to show that the "food share identifies welfare" assumption is unsupported, that it does not follow from the importance of food in the budget nor from the validity of Engel's Law, and that it is likely to lead to an overestimation of child costs and child equivalence scales. Because the argument is persuasive, it must be concluded that the identifying assumption of the Engel methodology is not an acceptable one. The method is unsound and should not be used.

Rothbarth's method

In Section 4.2 on sex bias, I used expenditure on adult goods to detect differential treatment of children by gender. This methodology is a simple extension of that suggested by Rothbarth in 1943 for measuring the costs of children. Rothbarth's idea was that expenditures on adult goods could be used to indicate the welfare of the adults, so that, if additional children reduce such expenditures, it is because of the resources that have been redirected towards the children. By calculating how much of a reduction in income would have produced the same drop in expenditures on adult goods, Rothbarth calculated the decrease in income that was equivalent to the additional children and used this as his measure of child costs. As I argued in the previous section, this method is effectively the same as the identification of a sharing rule on the assumption that there exist goods that are exclusively consumed by one group in the household, in this case adults. In his paper, Rothbarth used a very broad selection of adult goods, including virtually all luxuries and saving, but the subsequent literature has used much narrower definitions of adult goods, often confined to alcohol, tobacco, and adult clothing.

Although we are now using a different indicator of welfare—expenditure on adult goods rather than the food share—the procedure for calculating the Rothbarth measure is similar to that for calculating the Engel scale. Figure 4.8 corresponds to Figure 4.7, but instead of the food share we plot expenditure on adult goods against total outlay; the graph has a positive slope on the supposition that adults goods are normal goods. The larger household spends less on adult goods at the same level of total outlay, so that, if we pick the original x^0 as the reference outlay for the small household, the cost of children is once again $x^1 - x^0$.

Engel curves of the form (4.14) are not quite so convenient for the Rothbarth calculations as for the Engel method, although it is possible to follow through the

Figure 4.8. Rothbarth's method for measuring the cost of children

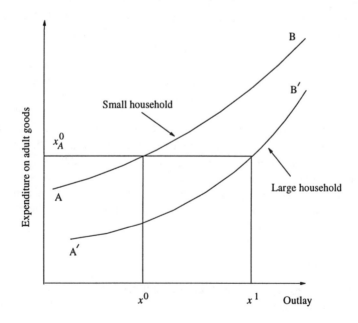

calculations that are parallel to (4.35) through (4.37). The equation for the share of adult goods in the budget is used to derive the expenditure on adult goods for both the reference family and the larger family, and equating the two defines the compensating value x^1. For this version of Working's Engel curve, the equation has no explicit analytical solution but can be readily solved iteratively. However, we need not take the trouble here since most of the calculations have already been done in the previous section.

Table 4.3 lists the outlay-equivalent ratios for boys and girls corresponding to various possible adult goods in the Maharashtran data. Up to a linear approximation, these ratios (with the sign changed) tell us how much total outlay would have to be increased in order to restore the adult expenditure to its level prior to addition of one more child. For tobacco and *pan*, which is the most reliable of the adult goods, the six child–gender combinations generate outlay-equivalent ratios of between 0.42 and 0.01, so that if we take 0.20 (say) as representative, the results suggest that an additional child costs rather less than half of an adult. For the Pakistani results in Table 4.4, the outlay-equivalent ratios are higher, a little less than a half for girls using men's footwear, and between a third and a half for boys using women's footwear, so that an additional child costs two-thirds or more of an adult. Deaton and Muellbauer (1986) used data from Sri Lanka and Indonesia together with the extreme assumption that all nonfoods are adult goods; they found that children cost between 20 and 40 percent of an adult.

The specific estimates are of less interest than the general point that the Rothbarth scales are a good deal smaller than the Engel scales, in these examples about half as much. There is no general result here; the relationship between the Rothbarth and Engel scales will depend on which goods are selected as adult goods, and on the empirical responses of food and adult goods to outlay and to demographic composition. However, in the special case where children consume only food, so that all nonfoods can be treated as adult goods, then Engel's Law implies that the Engel scale must be larger than the Rothbarth scale. The argument is from Deaton and Muellbauer (1986) and runs as follows. Suppose that, when a child is born, the parents are paid the Rothbarth compensation, so that expenditure on adult goods, here nonfood, is restored to its original level. But since positive compensation has been paid, total expenditure has risen with nonfood expenditure unchanged, so that the share of food in the budget has risen. According to Engel, this is a decrease in welfare, and insufficient compensation has been paid. The Engel scale is therefore larger than the Rothbarth scale.

What then are the problems with the Rothbarth methodology, and is its identifying assumption, that expenditure on adult goods is an indicator of adult welfare, any more reasonable than Engel's assertion about the food share? There are certainly a number of practical problems. As we saw in the previous section, it is not always easy to find convincing examples of adult goods, either because the survey does not collect such data—men's and women's clothing rather than adult or child clothing—or because adult goods are consumed by very few households—alcohol in Muslim societies. And while it is hard enough to find goods that are consumed only by adults, it can be even harder to find goods that are consumed only by adults and where it is plausible that children do not affect their consumption through substitution effects. Babies may not go to the movies, nor eat meals in restaurants, but their presence may alter their parents' consumption of movies and restaurant meals, even when they have been fully compensated for the costs of the children.

When we have a group of possible adult goods, so that it is possible to test the restriction that all give the same estimate of child costs, the restrictions are sometimes rejected, leaving the choice of adult goods controversial and arbitrary (see the discussion of the evidence from Thailand in Deaton 1989b or from Spain in Deaton, Ruiz-Castillo, and Thomas 1989). Another difficulty arises if adult goods as a group have an expenditure elasticity of zero or close to it, in which case it becomes impossible to calculate the compensating changes in total expenditure. If this happens, the theory is simply not working, since the children do not affect adult expenditures in the same way as do changes in income. If additional children cause changes in expenditure on alcohol and tobacco, and if income has no such effects, then children must be exerting substitution effects and the goods cannot be used as adult goods. However, this difficulty seems to occur only in developed countries when alcohol and tobacco are the adult goods (see Cramer 1969); in work on developing countries that I have seen, adult expenditures—including expenditures on alcohol and tobacco—respond strongly to changes in total outlay.

From a theoretical perspective, there are certainly problems with the Rothbarth identifying assumption, but they are less severe than those associated with that required for the Engel method. Nicholson's argument destroys the foundation of the Engel approach, but the arguments against the Rothbarth procedure are more about details, and with its failure to include some factors that might be important. And while we know that the Engel procedure biases upwards the estimates of the scales, it is much harder to sign any bias associated with Rothbarth's method.

The most serious arguments are concerned with the possible substitution effects of children, with the rearrangements in the budget that the children cause even when compensation has been paid. One model of substitution is that children exert price-like effects that cause substitution away from the goods in which they are most intensive. The idea here, first formalized by Barten (1964), is that goods that are consumed by both adults and children become more expensive to the adult than goods that are only consumed by adults. For example, on a visit to a restaurant, the father who prefers a soft drink and who would order it were he alone, finds that in the company of a child his soft drink is twice as expensive but that a beer costs the same, and so is encouraged to substitute towards the latter. If so, perfectly compensated adults will consume more adult goods in the presence of children than they would without, so that the Rothbarth compensation would be too small. Barten's analogy between children and price effects is both elegant and insightful, but it is hard to believe that this is the only way that substitution effects operate. Much of the budget reallocation in the presence of children is concerned with the need to allocate time differently, and it is just as likely that compensated adults will cut adult expenditures as increase them.

We must also question whether it is appropriate to measure adult welfare as indicated by their consumption of adult goods, and beyond that, whether the welfare of adults as indicated by expenditures on such goods can tell us anything useful about the welfare of other members of the household. Of course, the Rothbarth methodology does not claim that adults get no welfare from other goods, only that their welfare is a monotonic increasing function of adult goods' expenditures. But the demand function for adult goods will certainly also depend on the relative price of adult goods, and so we must be careful not to apply the method to compare welfare over situations where such price changes have taken place. More generally, and even in developing countries, the price of adult time is likely to be sensitive to the presence of children, and may affect purchases of adult goods, especially time-intensive adult goods. As far as the welfare of nonadults is concerned, it is certainly possible to imagine situations in which the welfare of the adults is monotonically related to the welfare of the children, as for example when the parents allocate resources so as to equalize welfare over all members of the family. If such an assumption makes sense in context, there is a justification for using Rothbarth scales to correct total household expenditure, and to attribute the results to each member of the household.

In the next subsection, I briefly discuss a number of other methods for calculating equivalence scales, but none of these is as readily implemented as are either the Engel or Rothbarth methods, and in none is the identifying assumption so transparent. As a result, the choice for practical policy applications is to do nothing—or at least to work with either total or PCE to use one of either Engel or Rothbarth. Since the Engel method is indefensible, and since the attribution of total household expenditure to each household member requires quite implausible economies of scale, the choice is between calculating equivalents according to Rothbarth, or using PCE as in Chapter 3. More realistically, since it would be cumbersome to calculate a set of equivalents on a case by case basis, a modified Rothbarth alternative would be to choose a set of scales in line with the results that are generally obtained by the method, for example a weight of 0.40 for young children aged from 0 to 4, and 0.50 for children aged 5 to 14. These numbers are obviously arbitrary to a degree, but there is no good evidence that can be marshaled against them, and they are broadly consistent with results from a procedure that has much to commend it.

In Chapter 3, I followed standard practice, using PCE for welfare and poverty calculations, rather than these equivalence scales. However, the decision was more for convenience of presentation than from intellectual conviction. Indeed, welfare measures based on PCE certainly overstate the costs of children, and understate the welfare levels of members of large families relative to those of small families. Whether or not the procedure of counting children at about half of adults is considered to be an improvement depends on the weights we give to the various arguments and compromises that underlie these estimates. The measurement of welfare and poverty would rest on a much firmer footing if there existed a solid empirical and theoretical basis for the construction of equivalence scales. But given current knowledge, numbers like a half are as good as we have, and in my view, it is better to use such estimates to construct welfare measures than to assume that everyone is equal as we do when we work with per capita measures.

Other models of equivalence scales

There are several other methods for estimating equivalence scales, and at least one of these, the method proposed by Prais and Houthakker (1955), has been used in the development literature. The basic idea behind this method, which traces back to earlier work by Sydenstricker and King (1921), is to write the household demand functions in the form

$$(4.38) \qquad\qquad p_i q_i / m_i = f_i(x/m_0)$$

where m_i and m_0 are commodity-specific and "general" scales that are functions of household composition, and are to be thought of as measuring the need for each good and for total outlay of different types of household. A household with children would have large commodity specific scales for child foods, children's clothing and education, and the overall scale would reflect each of these specific needs. Indeed, because the budget constraint must hold, the general scale in (4.38) can be defined as the solution to

$$(4.39) \qquad\qquad \Sigma m_i f_i(x/m_0) = x.$$

This model is estimated by specifying functional forms for each m_i in terms of the observable demographic characteristics, substituting into (4.38), and estimating (4.38) and (4.39) as a set of nonlinear demand equations. This apparently straightforward procedure is incomplete, at least conceptually if not numerically, because the model is not identified, a result first shown by Muellbauer (1980) (see also Deaton and Muellbauer 1980a, pp. 202–05 for further discussion). To make things worse, researchers sometimes select functional forms for the demand functions—such as double logarithmic demands—that do not permit the budget constraint (4.39) to be satisfied exactly. This failure of the model can result in the empirical version of the model being econometrically identified, essentially because of a failure of approximation to the theoretically underidentified true model, and there are examples in the literature where authors have thus succeeded in estimating a model that is theoretically unidentified. Parameters obtained in such a way are clearly of no practical value.

In order to obtain genuine identification, it is necessary to have prior information about at least one of the commodity scales, a result that should come as no surprise given the earlier discussion of identification in general. Note too the close relationship with Bourguignon and Chiappori's approach, where the identification of the sharing rule is obtained by finding goods that are exclusive or assignable, and with Rothbarth's, where we specify exclusively adult goods. In the Prais-Houthakker method, an obvious way to proceed would be to identify the model by assuming that the commodity-specific scale for adult goods is unity.

Having identified the model in this or some other way, estimation can proceed and scales be obtained. However, it is not clear what is gained over the much simpler Rothbarth methodology. The calculation of the Prais-Houthakker scales requires estimation of a potentially large system of nonlinear equations, a task that is a good deal easier than it once was, but the effort requires a justification that is not apparent, at least to this author.

I have already mentioned a second alternative, the model originally proposed by Barten (1964), and extended by Gorman (1976). Barten's procedure is even less suitable than Prais and Houthakker's for applied work, but it contains an important insight that I shall use again in the next subsection, so that it is worth a brief statement. Barten built the idea of commodity-specific scales into the frame- work of utility theory, writing the household utility function—best thought of as the utility of each member of the household—in the form

$$(4.40) \qquad u = \upsilon(q_1/m_1,\ldots,q_n/m_n)$$

where the m's have essentially the same commodity-specific scale interpretation as in Prais and Houthakker's model. The maximization of (4.40) subject to the usual budget constraint $p.q = x$, can be conveniently rewritten by defining the scaled quantities $q_i^* = q_i/m_i$ and scaled prices $p_i^* = p_i m_i$, so that the consumer's problem can be rewritten as the maximization of $\upsilon(q^*)$ subject to the budget constraint that $p^*.q^* = x$. This problem immediately generates standard-form demand functions in which q_i^* is a function of the prices p_i^*, so that

$$(4.41) \qquad q_i/m_i = g_i(x, m_1 p_1,\ldots,m_n p_n).$$

Note first that if all the m_i were identical and equal to household size, (4.41) would give the sensible result that consumption per head is equal to the standard Marshallian demand function of outlay per head and prices. (Recall that demand functions are homogeneous of degree zero.) More generally, when the scaling factors differ from one commodity to another, the income reduction effects will still be present, working by scaling up each price by a greater or lesser amount. However, and this is the central insight of the Barten model, there are also substitution effects. Goods that are child-intensive are relatively expensive in a household with many children, and family decisionmakers will substitute against them.

While the recognition of the possibility of such substitution is an important contribution of the Barten model, the model is clearly incomplete as it stands. The fundamental identification of equivalence scales comes from the assumption that household composition acts entirely analogously to prices, so that, not surprisingly, the model cannot be estimated without data with price variation (see again Muellbauer 1980 and Deaton and Muellbauer 1980a, pp. 202–5). But the analogy with price, while conceivably a part of the story, is surely not all of it. For example, as pointed out by Deaton and Muellbauer (1980a, p. 200) and forcefully argued by Nelson (1993), there is no reason to suppose that a child-intensive good, such as milk, could not be highly price elastic in families without children;

for adults, beer or soda may be good substitutes for milk, though one might hesitate to make the same substitutions for children. Within the Barten model, if the substitution effect is large enough, this situation can lead to a reduction in milk demand when a child is added to the family, a result that compromises the empirical usefulness of the model as well as any claim that the model might have to represent the welfare of children as well as adults. It is possible to extend the model to improve the situation, for example by following Gorman's (1976) suggestion to make allowance for fixed costs of children, but the empirical implementation of such models is cumbersome out of all proportion to their advantages over the simpler Rothbarth methodology.

Economies of scale within the household

It is an old and plausible idea that two can live more cheaply together than two can live separately, yet there has been relatively little serious empirical analysis of the phenomenon, and our understanding of the topic is even less complete than that of child costs. One good approach to the issue is through the recognition that there are public goods within the household, goods that can be shared by several people without affecting the enjoyment of each. In this last subsection, I discuss some of the literature—which is again dominated by Engel's method—and then sketch out an approach to economies of scale based on the existence of public goods that can be shared within the household. The public good approach reveals serious flaws in the Engel methodology, and suggests an alternative approach. Attempts to implement this alternative founder on an empirical paradox that is currently unresolved.

I start by dismissing children, and thinking only about households containing n identical adults. The conceptual issues with which I am concerned are not affected by the presence of children, and if children are to be included, we can suppose that they have already been converted to adults using a child equivalence scale. Consider the direct utility function $\upsilon(q_1,q_2,\ldots,q_m)$, which we think of as the utility of a single individual who consumes q_1 of good 1, q_2 of good 2, up to q_m of good m. For a household of n individuals who share consumption equally, the utility of each is given by the utility function applied to an nth of the household's consumption, so that total household utility is written

$$(4.42) \qquad u_h = n\upsilon(q_1/n,\ldots,q_m/n).$$

But this equation assumes that there are no economies of scale, and that a household of n people generates no more welfare than n households of one person each. Suppose instead that, by some process that is left implicit, the needs for each good do not expand with the number of people, but less rapidly, for example in proportion to n^θ for some quantity $0 < \theta \le 1$. (This isoelastic form is easily generalized, but little is gained by doing so.) If $\theta = 1$, there are no economies of scale, and each person gets an nth of the total; for $\theta < 1$, there are economies of scale, and each person receives more than his or her share of the total. The quantity $1 - \theta$ is therefore a measure of the extent of economies of scale. With this specification, household utility (4.42) is modified to

$$(4.43) \qquad u_h = n\upsilon(q_1/n^\theta, \ldots, q_m/n^\theta).$$

It is a straightforward exercise to show that the maximization of (4.43) subject to the budget constraint that the total cost of purchases be equal to x, gives demand functions

$$(4.44) \qquad \frac{p_i q_i}{x} = \frac{p_i q_i/n}{x/n} = \phi_i\left(\frac{x}{n^\theta}, p_1, \ldots, p_m\right)$$

so that the budget share of good i, for all goods $i = 1, \ldots, m$, is a function of prices and of total expenditure deflated by household size to the power of θ. The indirect utility function corresponding to (4.43) and (4.44) is

$$(4.45) \qquad u_h = n\psi(x/n^\theta, p_1, \ldots, p_m)$$

where $\psi(x, p_1, \ldots, p_n)$ is the indirect utility of a single individual with outlay x. Because both the budget shares and indirect utility depend on family size only through the term x/n^θ, welfare is correctly indicated by the budget share of any good, and two households of different size are equally well-off when their patterns of budget shares are the same. There is an empirical restriction—that we get the same answer whichever budget share we use—but I ignore it for the moment

Instead consider one particular budget share, that of food. As before, I use the subscript f for food, and rewrite (4.44) as

$$(4.46) \qquad w_f = \phi_f\left(\frac{x}{n^\theta}, p_1, \ldots, p_m\right)$$

an equation that provides a formal justification of using Engel's method—see Figure 4.7—not for measuring child costs, but for measuring economies of scale. In particular, if we adopt the same functional form as before, (4.14), the general form (4.46) becomes

$$(4.47) \qquad w_f = \alpha_f + \beta_f \ln(x/n) + \beta_f(1-\theta)\ln n$$

so that the economies of scale parameter θ can be obtained by regressing the food share on the logarithm of PCE and the logarithm of household size, computing the ratio of coefficients, and subtracting the result from unity. If we want to pursue the utility interpretation, we could then estimate θ from other goods and compare, or we might simply wish to accept Engel's assertion that the food share indicates welfare, and not concern ourselves with its possible theoretical foundations.

Table 4.5 above provides estimates of (4.47) for the Indian and Pakistani data. As predicted by (4.47), the coefficients on the logarithm of household size are negative; with PCE held constant, larger households are better-off and reveal the fact by spending a smaller fraction of their budget on food. The θ parameter is estimated to be 0.72 in the Indian data, and 0.87 in the Pakistani data, so that if we double household size and double household resources, the Maharashtran (Pakistani) households have effectively had a 28 (13) percent increase in per capita resources. Using the 1991 Living Standards Survey from Pakistan, Lanjouw and Ravallion (1995) find even larger economies of scale, with θ estimated to be 0.6, so that doubling size and resources would increase effective resources by 40 percent.

This Engel method is currently the only simple method for measuring economies of scale. There is no equivalent to the Rothbarth method, which focusses explicitly on children. This is unfortunate, since Engel's method is just as unsatisfactory for measuring economies of scale as it is for measuring child costs. There are two problems. The first is the lack of an answer to Pollak and Wales' identification result. Even if (4.47) is an accurate representation of the data, by what assumption are we allowed to interpret θ, or better $1 - \theta$, as a measure of economies of scale? In the technical note at the end of this subsection, I show that the identification problem is real by providing an example. In particular, if the utility function (4.43) is modified to make the economies of scale parameter differ for different levels of living, the demand functions (4.47) are unaffected. As a result, the true economies of scale are not captured by our estimates.

The second problem is the lack of an explicit justification for the mysterious process whereby sharing prevents the effective per capita consumption of all goods falling in proportion to the number of sharers. The remainder of this section shows that attempts to model this process lead to a discrediting of Engel's assertion. If we replace Engel—or (4.43)—by a more appropriate model in which economies of scale are attributed to public goods, we are led to a different scheme for measurement that is much closer to Rothbarth's child cost procedure than it is to Engel's. Unfortunately, this promising and sensible strategy is confounded when we turn to the data, which show behavior that is difficult to interpret in any coherent manner. The following is based on Deaton and Paxson (1996); the Rothbarth-like procedure for measuring economies of scale was suggested to the author by Jean Drèze.

In the simplest case, suppose that there are two goods, one private, and one public. For the private good, if the household buys 10 kilos, and there are ten people, each gets one kilo; no one benefits from anyone else's consumption, and if one uses the good, another cannot. For the public good, by contrast, everyone consumes the total that is purchased; no one person's consumption precludes the consumption of anyone else. Works of art are a good example, although housing, cooking, and toilet facilities may be approximately so described up to the point of congestion. If q is household consumption of the private good, and z household consumption of the public good, each member of the household obtains utility

$$(4.48) \qquad\qquad u = \upsilon(q/n, z)$$

and the household maximizes this—or equivalently n times this—subject to the budget constraint. Note that this problem is precisely analogous to Barten's formulation of compositional effects, or more precisely, it is a special case of Barten's formulation (see also Nelson 1988, 1992 for discussions of economies of scale along these lines). The demand functions from (4.48) are, for the private good

$$(4.49) \qquad \frac{q}{n} = g(x, np, p_z) = g\left(\frac{x}{n}, p, \frac{p_z}{n}\right)$$

where p and p_z are the prices of the private and public good, and for the public good

$$(4.50) \qquad z = g_z\left(\frac{x}{n}, p, \frac{p_z}{n}\right).$$

Suppose first that all goods are private. Then (4.49) gives the obvious and obviously sensible result that in a household with n identical individuals, per capita demand is the same as individual demand, provided we replace total outlay by per capita outlay. In this situation, the household is simply a collection of identical individuals, and their aggregate behavior is the replication of what would be the behavior of each individual in isolation. The presence of the public good affects this purely private allocation because additional people reduce the price of the public good. Compared with the private good, the public good is n-times blessed, and its price is reduced in proportion to the number of people in the household. As usual, this price reduction will have income effects, increasing the demand for all normal goods compared with the purely private solution, and substitution effects, which tip consumption towards the public goods.

This account of public and private goods can be used as a basis for measuring economies of scale. Suppose that we can identify in advance a private good that is not easily substituted for other goods. (Note the analogy with the Rothbarth method, which requires the identification of an adult good that is not affected by substitution effects associated with children, and with the sharing-rule approach, which requires exclusive or assignable goods). When we increase the number of household members holding PCE constant, resources are progressively released from the public good—the income effect of the price decrease—and consumption of the private good will increase. If there are no substitution effects on consumption of the private good, its additional consumption can be used to measure economies of scale. In particular, we can calculate the reduction in PCE that would restore the per capita consumption of the private good to its level prior to the increase in size.

Figure 4.9 illustrates. On the vertical axis is consumption per head of the private good which, for the purpose of the argument, I shall refer to as "food." In poor countries, with people close to subsistence, food has few substitutes, and food eaten by one household member cannot be eaten by another. The horizontal axis is PCE, and the diagram illustrates an increase in household size, from n_1 to n_2, with PCE held constant. Given that total resources have increased in line with household size, the household could keep its demand pattern unchanged if it

Figure 4.9. Drèze's method for measuring economies of scale

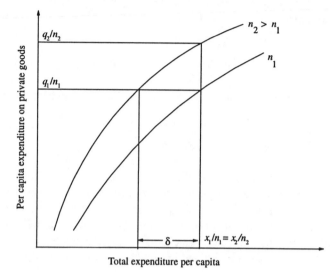

Total expenditure per capita

wished. But because there are public goods that do not need to be fully replicated, members of the household can typically do better than this. Provided the price elasticity of food is low—which is equivalent to low substitution out of food in favor of the now effectively cheaper public goods—food consumption per capita will increase as shown. Although the result depends on the assumption of limited substitution, it is clearly robust, at least for poor households. The (over)compensated increase in household size makes the household better-off, and in poor, near-subsistence economies, better-off households spend more on food.

The diagram also shows δ, the amount by which PCE of the larger household could be decreased to reduce per capita food consumption to its original level. If the compensated own-price elasticity of food is exactly zero, food expenditure per head is an exact indicator of welfare, and δ is the per capita money value of the economies of scale. Even when substitution effects are nonzero, food is likely to be a good indicator of welfare, a case that has been well argued by Anand and Harris (1990, 1994). In any case, δ sets a lower bound on the value of the scale economies. After a reduction in PCE of δ, the large household has the same per capita food consumption as the small household. But it faces a higher relative price for food and a lower relative price for the public good so that, given some possibility of substitution, it could be as well-off with rather less food and rather more public good. In consequence, a precisely compensated larger household will have less food consumption per head than the smaller household, which implies that δ is an understatement of the value of the scale economies.

All that remains is to implement the method on the data and to fill in the ideas of Figure 4.9 with real numbers. But as is perhaps already apparent, there is a serious problem. The results in Table 4.5 are not consistent with the figure. Because the coefficients on the logarithm of household size are negative, the curve for the larger household lies below that for the smaller household. In these Indian and Pakistani examples, the budget share of food falls with household size with PCE held constant. Because the budget share is the ratio of per capita food expenditure to per capita total expenditure, the budget share can only decline with household size at constant PCE if food expenditure per head also declines. That the same result holds more widely is documented by Deaton and Paxson (1996), not only for households of Pakistan in 1991, in South Africa in 1993, and in Thailand in 1992, but also in the much richer economies of Taiwan (China), Britain, France, and the United States. Their evidence shows that, in all these economies, among households with the same level of PCE, larger households spend less per capita on food. Furthermore, the declines are largest where they are hardest to explain, among households in the poorest economies, Pakistan, Thailand, and South Africa.

That food consumption per capita declines with household size at constant PCE is a prediction of the Engel model, so that the empirical evidence might be interpreted as evidence in favor of that model, and against the story of public goods and economies of scale. But to argue in favor of the Engel assertion is not credible. It makes apparent (but only apparent) sense to argue that a larger household with the same PCE as a smaller household is better-off, and so should have a lower food share because better-off households generally have lower food shares. But once it is recognized that we are holding PCE constant, so that a lower food share means lower consumption per head, the implausibility of the argument is revealed. In poor countries, making people better-off causes them to buy more food, not less. Recall that Lanjouw and Ravallion (1995) estimate that θ is 0.6 for Pakistan in 1991. According to this, two adults can attain the same welfare level as two single adults for only $2^{0.6} = 1.52$ times as much money (see equation 4.45). For a society where the food accounts for more than half of the budget, this estimate seems low. But what is truly incredible is the implication that the couple can each reduce their food consumption by a quarter and be as well-off as they were as individuals.

When it comes to the measurement of economies of scale, we are therefore in a most unsatisfactory predicament. We have a model that works, and fits the data, but makes no sense, and a model that makes sense, but whose most elementary implications are contradicted by the data. It is hard to see how we can make much progress until we can understand the paradoxical relationship between food consumption and household size. On this, there has been little or no progress so far. Deaton and Paxson list a number of possible explanations, none of which is very convincing. Only one is worth noting here, because the issue will arise again in the next chapter. Not everyone pays the same price for their food (or other goods), and it is easy to imagine that larger households obtain discounts by buying in bulk, that they buy lower-quality food, or that they buy more of the cheaper foods. If so, it is possible that, although larger households spend less per head on food at the same level of PCE, they consume larger quantities. The evidence on this question is limited by the number of surveys that collect data on both expenditures and quantities. However, what evidence there is—some of which appears in the next chapter—shows the opposite of what would be required; at a constant level of PCE, larger households spend more per unit on food, not less. Indeed, exactly this result was treated as evidence of economies of scale and used to measure their extent by Prais and Houthakker (1972, ch. 10). In consequence, the paradox is only deepened; people who must surely be better-off are switching to higher-quality foods—which makes perfect sense—while at the same time cutting consumption—which makes none.

Utility theory and the identification of economies of scale

Suppose that we are prepared to assert that economies of scale operate by multiplying the cost of living by a concave function of household size. Provided the utility function is not homothetic, so that the pattern of demand is a function of real income, the scaling function can be identified from the data, so that it is possible to test the implications of the model and to use the parameters to estimate the extent of economies of scale. Under the assumption that the scaling function is isoelastic, n^{θ}, this is exactly what is done by the Engel method as outlined in equations (4.43) through (4.47) above. But what then of the underidentification of demographic effects in the utility function? By working through a simple example, I show that the problem is still present. Indeed, the scaling model, although identified on the data once specified, has the same empirical implications as other models in which the economies of scale are clearly different. As a result, whatever it is that the Engel method measures, there are no grounds for claiming that it is economies of scale.

In order to examine the effects of changing household size, we need to start from the preferences of a household with only one member. Consider the case where the cost of living is related to utility by

$$(4.51) \qquad c(u,p) = \alpha(p) u^{\beta(p)}$$

where $\alpha(p)$ is linearly homogeneous and $\beta(p)$ zero-degree homogeneous in prices. One convenient specification for cross-sectional work is

$$(4.52) \qquad \ln\alpha(p) = \Sigma\alpha_k\ln p_k; \quad \ln\beta(p) = \Sigma\beta_k\ln p_k.$$

The budget shares are the elasticities of the cost function with respect to prices, so that using these two equations and the fact that cost equals total expenditure x, the system of demand patterns takes Working's form

$$(4.53) \qquad w_i = (\alpha_i - \Sigma\alpha_k\ln p_k) + \beta_i\ln x = \alpha_i^* + \beta_i\ln x.$$

We can now introduce household size and economies of scale by multiplying the cost function by an isoelastic function of n, so that (4.51) becomes

(4.54) $$\tilde{c}(u, p, n) = n^{\theta} \alpha(p) u^{\beta(p)}$$

where θ is, as before, the parameter controlling economies of scale. If we derive the budget share equations as before, we get, in place of (4.53), *cf.* (4.47) above,

(4.55)
$$w_i = \alpha_i^* + \beta_i \ln(x/n^{\theta}) = \alpha_i^* + \beta_i \ln x - \beta_i \theta \ln n$$
$$= \alpha_i^* + \beta_i \ln(x/n) + \beta_i (1-\theta) \ln n$$

which is the equation that I have been using to interpret the data.

To see the identification problem, suppose that, instead of (4.54), we also make the economies of scale parameter θ, not a constant, but a function of the utility level u, in the form $\theta + \theta_1 \ln u$. This is plausible enough and certainly cannot be ruled out in advance; additional people may not affect costs proportionately, but have larger or smaller effects the better-off is the household. Substitution gives our last cost function

(4.56) $$\tilde{c}(u, p, n) = n^{\theta + \theta_1 \ln u} \alpha(p) u^{\beta(p)} = n^{\theta} \alpha(p) u^{\beta(p) + \theta_1 \ln n}.$$

If we follow through the calculations for a third time, we simply come back to (4.55); the incorporation of the household size function into the elasticity has had no effect on behavior, and so we cannot tell (4.54) and (4.56) apart on the data. But the two cost functions have different implications for household welfare. The indirect utility function for (4.56) is

(4.57) $$\ln u = [\beta(p) + \theta_1 \ln n]^{-1} [\ln x - \theta \ln n - \ln \alpha(p)]$$

which contains the term $\theta_1 \ln n$ in the denominator. Welfare levels, unlike the demand functions, are affected by the presence of this term so that, once again, we cannot infer welfare from behavior.

4.4 Guide to further reading

There is an enormous background literature on the topics covered in this chapter, and it is probably best approached through surveys. The recent book by Dasgupta (1993) is much concerned with gender discrimination (Chapter 11) and nutrition (Chapters 14 through 17). Dasgupta argues the case for the nutritional wage hypothesis as the root cause of destitution, but one does not have to accept all his arguments to benefit from his extensive reviews of the literatures in economics and in nutrition. Drèze and Sen (1989) is also concerned with undernutrition, its causes, and the design of public policy for its alleviation; it also provides extensive references to the literature. At the narrower and more technical level, both Bouis and Haddad (1992) and Strauss and Thomas (1995) provide reviews of earlier literature as well as their own contributions to measurement. The reports of the *International Food Policy Research Institute* in Washington are frequently concerned with nutritional issues in a range of countries. On equivalence scales, the easiest place to begin is with Chapter 8 of Deaton and Muellbauer (1980a), and to update with Deaton and Muellbauer (1986). Buhmann et al. (1988) provide a review of some of the equivalence scales that have been used in the academic literature as well as in government programs, and show how different scales affect poverty and inequality measurement for the (developed) countries in the Luxembourg Income Study. There is also a literature on "subjective" approaches to the construction of equivalence scales that parallels attempts to measure poverty lines by direct questioning (see, for example, Rainwater 1974; Danziger et al. 1984; and van Praag, Hagenaars, and van Weerden 1982). The issue of economies of scale that is sketched in the penultimate subsection is dealt with much more fully in Deaton and Paxson (1996).

5 *Looking at price and tax reform*

In a world of *laissez-faire*, prices set in free competitive markets guarantee economic efficiency. As has long been recognized, such efficiency is of a limited nature; its achievement requires strong assumptions and takes no account of the distribution of income, even to the extent of being consistent with some individuals being unable to survive. *Laissez-faire* pricing also leaves little room for the government to collect revenue, whether to influence the distribution of resources or to finance its own activities. The lump sum taxes that would (by definition) leave behavior unaffected generate little revenue if they exist at all, and the limited range of tax instruments on which governments in poor countries must rely are often quite distortionary. As a result, the best that can be hoped for is a price system that is efficient in the sense of minimizing distortion for any given amount of revenue. The design of such systems is the topic of optimal tax theory, starting from Mirrlees (1971) and Diamond and Mirrlees (1971), a brief account of which is given in the first section below.

In recent years, public economics has been greatly influenced by what is now referred to as "political economy," a branch of economics and political science that uses the tools of economic analysis, particularly the typical economic assumptions of rationality and greed, to help explain the behavior of political actors. These models often seem relevant to poor countries, where the empirical reality is often in stark contrast to the assumptions of a previous generation of models in which the government was seen as a benevolent dictator acting in the public interest. As a result, there has been a good deal of suspicion—and in some cases rejection—of optimal tax models in which prices are set to maximize a social welfare function subject to budgetary and behavioral constraints. These criticisms are justified in that it is absurd to regard the optimal models as descriptions of the social and political equilibria that actually exist in developing countries. Even when the motivation of a given government is clear, existing taxes are likely to be a web of only partially consistent levies and subsidies, the fossilized traces of long-dead administrations of differing purposes and philosophies.

Even so, it is important to think rationally about what system of prices would be desirable, at least to the extent of meeting the legitimate needs of government for revenue and redistribution while minimizing the costs of collection and distor-

271

tion. Indeed, international organizations such as the World Bank and the International Monetary Fund are required to make proposals for reform, sometimes in opposition to what governments would choose left to themselves. Although optimal tax theory is unlikely to predict the tax structure in any given situation, it provides a systematic and indispensable framework for thinking about the standard issues of distribution and economic efficiency that are the basis for any intelligent discussion of price and tax reform.

My main concern in this chapter is not with the theory itself, but with its implementation, and with the use of household survey data to make the calculations. In Chapter 3, I showed how the surveys could be used to see who gets what and who produces what, so that we could calculate who benefits and who loses from price changes, and thus assess the distributional consequences of a change in pricing policy. That analysis is an important part of the analysis of price reform, but to go further, we must also know something about efficiency, which means finding out how behavior responds to the incentives provided by price changes. Traditionally, such evidence has been obtained by examining the historical experience, linking demand and production decisions to historical variations in price. What I shall mostly be concerned with here is a different approach that uses variation in prices across space to identify behavioral responses. This line of work has been developed in a series of papers over recent years (Deaton 1987a, 1988, 1990a and Deaton and Grimard 1992), and the account in this chapter is intended to be more complete and comprehensible than is possible within the confines of a journal article. It also aims to show how the results of the calculations can be used to look at price reform in practice, with examples from India and Pakistan using the data sets introduced in previous chapters.

Section 5.1 presents a brief review of the theory that is required for practical implementation in poor countries. It also provides a first discussion of how the formulas might be used, and reviews the various procedures that have been adopted in the literature. I argue that, without using the data from the surveys, it is almost impossible to derive policy recommendations that are firmly based on the empirical evidence. While it is certainly possible to make policy based on prior reasoning, on the results of computable general equilibrium (CGE) models, or on econometric evidence from historical data, such recommendations—sensible though they may be—are largely grounded in prior assumption, and are not much affected by empirical evidence. Section 5.2 is a first look at the evidence on spatial price variation from the Pakistani and Maharashtran data, with a particular focus on whether the unit value data that come from the surveys can be trusted for an econometric analysis of behavioral responses to price. This section also considers some of the difficulties that lie in the way of a straightforward use of spatial price variation to estimate demand responses. Section 5.3 presents a model of consumer behavior that is designed to accommodate the behavior we see in the surveys, particularly the fact that better-off households pay more for each unit of even quite narrowly defined commodities. I show how to derive a simple econometric model that is based on this theory. Section 5.4 works through the stages of the estimation using the Indian and Pakistani data. Section 5.5 uses the results to examine price reform, and highlight the differences that come from using the data-based methodology. In particular, I emphasize interaction effects; because there are important substitution effects between goods, it is important not to consider price reform one good at a time. The final Section 5.6 considers a number of directions for future research, and in particular the possible use of nonparametric estimation.

5.1 The theory of price and tax reform for developing countries

The theory of taxation for developing countries is extensively treated in the monograph by Newbery and Stern (1987), which is not only a collection of applications from several countries, but which also contains introductory chapters that review the underlying theory. Interested readers are strongly advised to consult that source for a fuller account than given here; my purpose is to provide only those results that are required for practical analysis of reform, and to identify those quantities for which empirical evidence is required. The analysis will be concerned almost exclusively with indirect taxes (and subsidies). Although income taxes provide a large share of government revenue in developed countries, they are less important in poorer countries, for obvious administrative reasons. Most poor countries do indeed have income taxes, but it is difficult to collect revenue from the self-employed, particularly in agriculture, or from those employed in small businesses or informal enterprises. As a result, most income taxes come from the relatively small formal sectors, or from the government paying income taxes to itself on the incomes of its own employees. A simple linear income tax can be effectively replicated (except in its treatment of saving) by an indirect tax system that taxes all goods at the same rate and that uses a poll tax or subsidy that is identical for all individuals. However, the practical usefulness of this identity is limited by the impossibility of taxing all consumer goods in most countries; in particular, it is not possible to drive a tax wedge between producer and consumer when the producer and consumer are one and the same, as is the case for farm households. And although many countries provide food subsidies for urban residents, arbitrage places limits on differences in prices between urban and rural areas. For these (and other) reasons, the tax instruments that are available to governments in developing countries are typically much more limited than is the case in richer countries with their more elaborate distribution networks, and the fact must always be kept in mind when discussing reforms.

Tax reform

The theory of tax reform is concerned with small departures from an existing tax structure. This is in contrast to the theory of optimal taxes, which is concerned with characterizing the (constrained) optimum in which taxes and subsidies are set at their socially desirable level. The differences are sometimes blurred in both theory and practice; the formulas for tax reform often have obvious implications for the optimum, and any practical reform will involve a discrete change in price.

However, the empirical burdens of calculating tax reforms are much lighter than those of calculating optima. The former asks us to evaluate the current position, and to calculate the desirability of various directions of reform, for which we need information about supply and demand and behavioral responses calculated at the current position of the economy. The calculation of an optimal tax system, by contrast, will require us to know the same quantities at the hypothetical welfare optimum, a position that is most likely far from the current one, or from anything in the historical record.

We begin by specifying the accounting apparatus for judging prices, as well as the rules that govern the behavioral responses. This is done in exactly the same way as in Chapter 3, by specifying a social welfare function and its determinants. As in Chapter 3, the social welfare function should be regarded as an accounting device that keeps track of who gets what, and that is used to consider alternative distributions of real resources among individuals or households. In Chapter 3, equation (3.1), social welfare was defined over the "living standards" x of each member of the population, where x was later equated with real expenditure levels. Here, because we are interested in the effects of changes in prices, we need to be more explicit about the link between prices and welfare. To do so, rewrite social welfare as a function of the individual welfare levels u, which are in turn given by the values of the indirect utility functions that give the maximum attainable welfare in terms of prices and outlays. Hence,

$$(5.1) \qquad\qquad W = V(u_1, u_2, \ldots, u_N)$$

where N is the number of people in the economy and the welfare levels are given by

$$(5.2) \qquad\qquad u_h = \psi(x_h, p)$$

for household h's indirect utility function $\psi(x_h, p)$, where x_h is total outlay, and p the vector of prices. The indirect utility function defines not only the way that welfare is affected by prices, but also encapsulates the behavioral responses of individuals; given the indirect utility function $\psi(x_h, p)$, demand functions can be derived by Roy's identity, (3.46).

I am using the subscript h to identify individuals or households, and I shall deal with the difference between them later. I also assume that everyone faces the same price, an assumption that will be relaxed below, but which simplifies the initial exposition. Note finally that I am avoiding dealing either with labor supply, or with intertemporal choice and saving. Because there is no income tax in this model, there is no need to model earnings, not because labor supply is unaffected by commodity taxes and subsidies, but because with an untaxed wage, the induced changes in labor supply have no affect on tax collections. A similar argument applies to saving, and I interpret (5.2) as the single period utility associated with an additively intertemporal utility function of the kind to be discussed in Chapter 6. Even so, the current approach fails to recognize or account for differences between the distribution of welfare over lifetimes and over single periods.

We can also begin with a simplistic model of price determination whereby the consumer price is the sum of a fixed (for example, world) price and the tax or subsidy, so that

$$(5.3) \qquad\qquad p_i = p_i^0 + t_i$$

where t_i is the tax (if positive) or subsidy (if negative) on good i. The simplest (and best) justification of (5.3) is in the case where the good is imported, there is a domestic tax (or import tariff), and the country is small enough so that changes in domestic demand have no effect on the world price. Another possible justification runs in terms of a production technology displaying constant returns to scale, with a single nonproduced factor, and no joint products, in which case the non-substitution theorem holds, and producer prices are unaffected by the pattern of demand (see, for example, the text by Mas-Colell, Whinston, and Green 1995, pp. 157–60). The assumptions required for this are overly strong, even for a modern industrialized economy, and make less sense in a poor one with a large agricultural sector. We shall see how to dispense with them in the next subsection.

Government revenue is the last character in the cast. It is simply the sum over all goods and all households of tax payments less subsidy costs:

$$(5.4) \qquad\qquad R = \sum_{i=1}^{M} \sum_{h=1}^{H} t_i q_{ih}$$

where q_{ih} is the amount of good i purchased by household h and there are M goods in all. We can think of this revenue as being spent in a number of ways. One is administration and other public goods that generate either no utility, or generate utilities that are separable in preferences, while the other is to generate lump sum subsidies (poll subsidies) that are paid to everyone equally, for example through a limited inframarginal food ration to which everyone is entitled. Both of these will affect the distribution of welfare over individuals, the latter explicitly through the x's in (5.2). I need not make them explicit here because I shall not be considering varying them. However—and I shall come back to the point—the structure of optimal tax systems are quite sensitive to the amount and design of these lump sum subsidies (see Deaton 1979 and Deaton and Stern 1986).

We are now in a position to consider the effects of a small change in a single tax. Given the simplistic price assumption, the price change will be the same as the tax change and will have two effects, one on government revenue (5.4), and one on individual welfare levels through (5.2) and thus on social welfare (5.1). The derivative of revenue with respect to the tax change is

$$(5.5) \qquad\qquad \partial R / \partial t_i = \sum_{h=1}^{H} q_{ih} + \sum_{h=1}^{H} \sum_{j=1}^{M} t_j \partial q_{jh} / \partial p_i.$$

The effect on social welfare is obtained from (5.1) and (5.2) using the chain rule

$$(5.6) \qquad\qquad \partial W / \partial t_i = \sum_{h=1}^{H} \frac{\partial V}{\partial u_h} \cdot \frac{\partial u_h}{\partial p_i}$$

an expression that is conveniently written using Roy's identity as

$$(5.7) \qquad \partial W / \partial t_i = - \sum_{h=1}^{H} \eta_h q_{ih}$$

where η_h, the social marginal utility of money in the hands of h, is

$$(5.8) \qquad \eta_h = \frac{\partial V}{\partial u_h} \cdot \frac{\partial \psi_h}{\partial x_h} = \frac{\partial W}{\partial x_h}.$$

For future reference, it is important to note that these formulas do not require that the purchase levels q_{ih} be positive. If individual h does not purchase good i, he or she is not harmed by a price increase, as in (5.7), and the effects of price changes on government revenue in (5.5) depend on the derivatives of aggregate demand, and are unaffected by whether or not individual consumers make purchases.

The quantities η_h in (5.7) and (5.8) are the only route through which the social welfare function has any influence on the calculations, and it is here that the distribution of real income comes into the analysis. If part of the object of the price reform is distributional, which could happen because we want the price change to help the poor more than the rich or hurt them less, or because other instruments (including preexisting taxes and subsidies) have not eliminated the distributional concern, the differential effects of price changes across real income groups must be taken into account. It is sometimes argued that price systems (or projects) are not the most appropriate way to handle distributional issues, with the implication that everyone should be treated equally in these calculations. But this only makes sense if alternative instruments are in place to take care of the distribution of income, something that is often not the case in poor countries, where subsidies on basic foods may be one of the few methods for helping the poor and are likely to be an important element in any social safety net.

The two equations (5.5) and (5.7) represent the social benefits and (minus) the social costs of a tax increase. The benefit is the additional government revenue, the social value of which comes from the uses to which that government revenue is put. The costs are born by any individual who purchases the good. The money equivalent cost to each unit price change is the quantity that he or she purchases, and these costs are aggregated into a social cost by weighting each cost by the social weight for the individual. The social weights can be derived explicitly from a social welfare function, for example the Atkinson social welfare function (3.4), although we will also sometimes wish to recognize regional or sectoral priorities. The ratio of cost—the negative of the marginal social benefit in (5.7)—to benefit is usually denoted by λ_i and is defined by

$$(5.9) \qquad \lambda_i = \frac{\displaystyle\sum_{h=1}^{H} \eta_h q_{ih}}{\displaystyle\sum_{h=1}^{H} q_{ih} + \sum_{h=1}^{H} \sum_{j=1}^{M} t_j \partial q_{jh} / \partial p_i}$$

so that λ_i is the social cost of raising one unit of government revenue by increasing the tax (reducing the subsidy) on good i. If the ratio is large, social welfare would be improved by decreasing the price of the ith good, either because the good is hurting those whose real incomes are especially socially valuable, or because the taxation of the good is distortionary, or both. Goods with low λ_i ratios are those that are candidates for a tax increase or subsidy reduction. When all the ratios are the same, taxes are optimally set and there is no scope for beneficial reform.

Equation (5.9) is consistent with and generalizes standard notions about distortion and about the avoidance of taxes that are particularly distortionary. Suppose, for the sake of argument, that the only good with a nonzero tax is good i, so that the second term in the denominator involves only the own-price response $\partial q_{ih}/\partial p_i$. If this is large and negative, which is the case where a tax is causing distortion, and if the tax is positive, the last term will be negative, so that other things being equal, the larger the price responses, the larger the λ_i ratios and the less attractive it would be to try to raise further revenue by this means. If the good is subsidized, large price responses will make the denominator large and positive, yielding a small λ_i ratio, with the implication that the tax ought to be raised. In this special case, we get the familiar result that highly price-elastic goods are poor candidates for taxation or subsidy because of the resulting distortion. Of course, price elasticity is not the whole story in (5.9). The numerator will be large for necessities and small for luxuries if the social weights favor the poor. If it is also the case that necessities have low price elasticities—necessities are hard to do without and have few substitutes—then the equity and efficiency effects of commodity taxes will offset one another, favoring the taxation of necessities on efficiency grounds, and of luxuries on equity grounds. Note also the potential importance of cross-price effects; changing the price of one good affects the demand for others through income and substitution effects, and if these goods bear taxes or subsidies, there will be "second-round" efficiency effects that must be taken into account in the calculations.

Generalizations using shadow prices

The cost-benefit ratios can be rewritten in a form that allows a substantial generalization of the analysis, and that permits us to relax the assumption that producer prices are fixed.

Start from the budget constraint of household h, which using (5.3) can be written in the form

$$(5.10) \qquad x_h = \sum_{k=1}^{M} p_k q_{kh} = \sum_{k=1}^{M} (p_k^0 + t_k) q_{kh}.$$

Since the total expenditure of each household is unaffected by the tax increase, we can differentiate (5.10) with respect to t_i holding p_i^0 constant to give

$$(5.11) \qquad q_{ih} + \sum_{k=1}^{M} t_k \partial q_{kh}/\partial p_i = -\sum_{i=1}^{M} p_k^0 \partial q_{kh}/\partial p_i.$$

If (5.11) is substituted into the revenue equation (5.5) and thence into the formula for the cost-benefit ratios, we can rewrite the latter as

$$(5.12) \qquad \lambda_i = \frac{\sum_{h=1}^{H} \eta_h q_{ih}}{-\sum_{h=1}^{H} \sum_{j=1}^{M} p_j^0 \partial q_{jh} / \partial p_i}.$$

So far, (5.12) is simply a rewritten form of (5.9). That it can be more than this has been shown by Drèze and Stern (1987) and Stern (1987, pp. 63–6) who prove that under appropriate but standard assumptions, the prices p_i^0 can be reinterpreted as *shadow prices*, defined (as usual) as the marginal social resource costs of each good. Under this interpretation, (5.12) is valid whether or not producer prices are fixed, and thus so is (5.9), provided that the t_j are interpreted as "shadow taxes," defined as the difference between shadow and domestic prices. In some cases, such as when the p_i^0 are world prices and therefore shadow prices, (5.12) and (5.9) coincide. But the shadow price interpretation of (5.12) makes intuitive sense. The denominator is simply minus the resources costs of a change in price, with resources valued—as they should be—at shadow prices, so that (5.12) is the social cost per unit of the socially valued resources that are released by an increase in a price.

In practical applications in developing countries, (5.12) is useful in exactly the same way that shadow prices are useful in project evaluation. Instead of having to account for all the distortions in the economy by tracing through and accounting for all the general equilibrium effects of a price change, we can use shadow prices as a shortcut and to give us a relatively quick—if necessarily approximate—evaluation of the effects of a price change.

Evaluation of nonbehavioral terms

The cost-benefit ratios in (5.9) and (5.12) require knowledge of quantities, of social weights, and of the responses of quantities to price. Of these it is only the behavioral responses that pose any difficulty, and most of this chapter is concerned with their estimation. The first term in the denominator, the aggregate quantity consumed, can be estimated either from the survey data, or from administrative records. If the commodity is being taxed or subsidized, the amounts involved are typically known by the taxing authority, and these figures provide a useful—if occasionally humbling—check on the survey results.

The evaluation of the numerator will require survey data if the social weights vary from household to household. The weights themselves depend on the degree of inequality aversion that is to be built into the calculation, as well as on possible sectoral or regional preference. To illustrate how this works in practice, suppose that we use the Atkinson social welfare function (3.4), extended to recognize that there are n_h individuals in household h,

$$(5.13) \qquad W = \frac{1}{H} \sum_{h=1}^{H} \frac{n_h}{1-\epsilon} \left(\frac{x_h}{n_h} \right)^{1-\epsilon}.$$

According to (5.13), each member of the household receives household per capita consumption, and the resulting social welfare contributions are multiplied by the number of people in the household. Given this, the numerator of (5.12) is

$$(5.14) \qquad \sum_{h=1}^{H} \eta_h q_{ih} = H^{-1} \sum_{h=1}^{H} (x_h/n_h)^{-\epsilon} q_{ih}$$

which can be thought of as a weighted average of the demands for good i, with weights depending (inversely) on PCE. Given a value for the inequality aversion parameter ϵ, this expression can be evaluated from the survey, using the sample data and the appropriate inflation factors. The usual practice, which will be followed in this chapter, is to evaluate (5.14) and the cost-benefit ratios (5.12) for a range of values of ϵ. When ϵ is small—in the limit zero—(5.14) will be close to average consumption of good i, and as ϵ increases will be increasingly weighted towards the consumption of the poor.

Because the right-hand side of (5.14) can be evaluated directly from the data, its evaluation does not require parametric modeling. Although it would be possible to specify and estimate an Engel curve for each good and to use the results to calculate (5.14), there are no obvious advantages compared with a direct appeal to the data. The actual relationship between the consumption of individual goods and total expenditure may be quite complicated in the data, and there is no need to simplify (and possibly to oversimplify) by enforcing a specific functional form.

Alternative approaches to measuring behavioral responses

Almost all of the difficulty in evaluating the cost-benefit ratios comes from the final term in the denominator, which summarizes the behavioral responses to price changes. The remaining sections of this chapter document my own approach to the estimation of this term, based on the use of spatial variation in prices, but it is useful to review alternative strategies, some of which have been implemented in the previous literature.

The standard data source for estimates of price responses is the historical record. Variations over time in relative prices permit the econometric analysis of aggregate demand functions in which average quantities are related to average outlays and prices. The aggregate nature of these exercises is not a problem in the current context since, as is easily checked from (5.9) and (5.12), the cost-benefit formulas depend only on the response of aggregate demand to prices. The difficulty lies rather in the typical paucity of the relevant data and the consequent effects on the precision of estimation as well as on the number of explanatory variables that can reasonably be modeled. The latter limitation is particularly damaging when it comes to the estimation of cross-price effects. In practical policy exercises, where we need to separately distinguish goods that are taxed—or that might be taxed—at different rates, a detailed disaggregation if often required, and we require estimates of all the own- and cross-price responses for each good in the disaggregation. With an annual time series that is nearly always shorter than 40 years, say, such calculations are close to impossible. Even for developed countries, where in a few cases there is nearly a 100-year span of data, it has not proved possible to estimate demand responses with any degree of conviction for disaggregations of more than a very few commodities (see Barten 1969 for a classic attempt using Dutch data, and Deaton 1974a for a much smaller (although not much more successful) attempt for Britain). If we have to rely on historical data, and if we are not prepared to restrict the problem in any way, it is effectively impossible to obtain reliable estimates of own- and cross-price elasticities for disaggregated systems of demand equations.

It is possible to do a good deal better by using prior restrictions on behavior, especially restrictions that limit the interactions between goods. Perhaps the crudest type of restrictions are those that simply ignore cross-price effects. But crude remedies are often effective, and if (5.9) is rewritten under the assumption that the derivatives $\partial q_{ih} / \partial p_j$ are zero when i is not equal to j, at least on average over all households, we reach the much simpler expression

$$(5.15) \qquad \lambda_i = \frac{\sum\limits_{h=1}^{N} \eta_h q_{ih}}{Q_i(1 + \tau_i e_{ii})}$$

where Q_i is aggregate consumption of good i, τ_i is the tax rate t_i/p_i, and e_{ii} is the own-price elasticity of aggregate demand. This expression contains only one magnitude that does not come directly from the data, the own-price elasticity, which can be estimated using a simple model, guessed, or "calibrated" from other studies in the literature. The disadvantages of such a procedure are as obvious as its advantages. There is no reason to suppose that all the cross-price effects are small, especially when close substitutes are taxed at different rates. Even when own-price effects can be expected to dominate over individual cross-price effects, that is far from the same as assuming that the total effect of all cross-price effects on tax revenue is small enough to ignore. Finally, economic theory teaches us that there are both income and substitution effects of price changes, so that even when substitution effects are small or zero, income effects will still be present.

Instead of restricting price effects by arbitrary zero restrictions, it is possible to use standard restrictions from economic theory. One particularly convenient assumption is that preferences are additive, meaning that the utility function is (a monotone increasing transformation of) a sum of M functions, each with a single good as its argument. By far the most popular case of additive preferences is the linear expenditure system—sometimes referred to as the Stone-Geary demand system—which has the utility function

$$(5.16) \qquad \upsilon(q) = \sum_{i=1}^{M} \beta_i \ln(q_i - \gamma_i)$$

and associated demand functions

$$(5.17) \qquad q_i = \gamma_i + p_i^{-1}\beta_i(x - p.\gamma)$$

where the $2M - 1$ parameters (the β's must add to 1) are to be estimated. The system (5.17) is readily estimated on short time-series data; indeed the β's are identified from the Engel curves in a single cross section, as are the γ's up to a constant. Once estimates have been obtained, (5.17) can be used to calculate the complete set of own- and cross-price responses, so that (5.9) or (5.12) can be evaluated without need for further assumptions.

The convenience of the linear expenditure system has led to its extensive use in the applied policy literature, including work on tax reform in developing countries (see Ahmad and Stern 1991, or Sadoulet and de Janvry 1995). The model is certainly superior to that based on the crude assumption that cross-price effects are zero; it is based on an explicit utility function and thus satisfies all theoretical requirements. However, the linear expenditure system still offers a relatively limited role for measurement, relying instead on the assumptions built into its functional form. Of course, that is the point. Without much data, there is little alternative but to use prior restrictions to aid estimation, and there is much to be said for using restrictions that are consistent with economic theory. But having done so, it is important to investigate which of our results come from the measurement, and which from the assumptions.

In the case of the linear expenditure system, much is known about the effects of its supporting assumptions. As shown in Deaton (1974b), additive preferences imply that own-price elasticities are approximately proportional to total expenditure elasticities, so that the efficiency effects of the taxes, which work through the price elasticities, tend to be offset by the equity effects, which work through the total expenditure elasticities. Indeed, Atkinson (1977) showed that if all preferences are given by the Stone-Geary form (5.16), and if the government has available to it a lump sum polltax or subsidy that is the same for everyone in the economy and that is optimally set, then the optimal solution is to tax all commodities at the same rate. This result can be generalized somewhat; Deaton (1979) shows that the result holds provided only that the Engel curves are linear and there is separability between goods and leisure. Furthermore, if to these requirements is added the assumption that preferences are additive—as in the linear expenditure system—then not only are uniform taxes optimal, but any move toward uniform taxes is welfare improving (see Deaton 1987b). It is even possible to allow for variation in tastes across individuals, provided that the optimal poll taxes or subsidies are set to take such variation into account (see Deaton and Stern 1986). In all these cases, the tax reform exercise does not require any econometric estimation at all! The answer is known before we start, and the analysis of the data adds nothing to the policy recommendations.

If the linear expenditure system is plausible, then these results are very useful, since they tell us what sort of price reforms to recommend. Unfortunately, the model is much too restrictive to be credible, especially in the context of price reform in poor countries. Demand functions from additive preferences do not permit inferior goods, and the substitution effects between commodities are of a simple and restrictive kind that do not permit complementarities between goods, nor any specific kinds of substitutability (see Deaton and Muellbauer 1980a, ch. 5, for a more precise discussion). When we are thinking about tax and subsidy policy in poor countries, many of the commodities involved are foods, some of which may be close substitutes, such as different types of cereals, and some of which are complements, such as cooking oil and the foods with which it is used. In several countries, there are also important inferior goods, such as cassava in Indonesia, the consumption of which is largely confined to members of the poorest households. Neither the linear expenditure system nor any other model of additive preferences can handle this sort of consumption pattern.

A somewhat different approach to tax and price reform in developing countries is to use CGE models. These (often quite elaborate) representations of the economy usually conform to the standard textbook representations of a general equilibrium system, with specifications for consumer preferences, for the technology of production, and for the process by which supply and demand are brought into equilibrium, usually by setting prices at their market clearing levels. The parameters of these models are not estimated using standard statistical methods; instead, the models are "calibrated" by choosing the parameters of preferences and technology so as to match the historical record (if only roughly) as well as to bring key responses into line with estimates in the literature. Many of these models use the linear expenditure system, or one of its variants; the parameters of (5.16) could be calibrated from (5.17) by looking at a set of expenditure Engel curves, which would yield the β's and the intercepts $\gamma_i - \gamma.p$; the individual γ parameters can be solved out given one more piece of information, for example the own-price elasticity of food, for which there exist many estimates in the literature. Alternatively, parameters can be taken from the many estimates of the linear expenditure system for developing countries, such as those assembled in the World Bank study by Lluch, Powell, and Williams (1977).

While such models can be useful as spreadsheets for exploring alternative policies and futures, the incorporation of the linear expenditure system has exactly the same consequences as it does in the more explicitly econometric framework. The results of tax reform exercises in CGE models are entirely determined by the assumptions that go into them. When a CGE model incorporates the linear expenditure system—or the even more restrictive Cobb-Douglas or constant elasticity of substitution preferences—a prescription for uniform taxes or for a move towards uniform taxes is a prescription that comes directly from the assumptions about functional form, and is unaffected by the values of the parameters attached to those forms. The finding cannot therefore be shown to be robust by calculating alternative outcomes with different parameter values; it is guaranteed to be robust provided the functional forms are not changed. It is also guaranteed not to be robust with respect to changes in those functional forms. Atkinson and Stiglitz (1976) and Deaton (1981) provide examples of cases where major changes in optimal tax structure, for example between regressive and nonregressive taxation, can be brought about by minor variations in separability assumptions, variations that would be hard to detect in an econometric analysis.

If we are to make recommendations about tax reform that recognize the actual structure of demand in developing countries, there is no alternative to the estimation of a model of demand that is sufficiently general to allow for that structure.

5.2 The analysis of spatial price variation

In the literature on demand analysis in developed countries, almost all of the identifying price variation has come from price changes over time, with little attention paid to variation in prices over space (although see Lluch 1971 for an exception). The reason for this is obvious enough; in countries like the United States, where transport and distribution systems are highly developed, and where transport costs are relatively low, there is little price variation between localities at any given time. In developing countries, transport is often more difficult, markets are not always well integrated, and even the presence of potential arbitrage cannot equalize prices between different geographical locations. In consequence, when we are trying to identify behavioral responses in demand, we have in developing countries a source of price variation that is not usually available in developed economies.

Regional price data

Data on regional price differences are often available from the statistical offices responsible for constructing consumer price indexes; even when national estimates are the main focus of interest, standardized bundles of goods are priced in a number of (usually urban) locations around the country. These price data can be merged with the household survey data by associating with each household the prices in the nearest collection center at the time closest to the reporting period for that household. The combined data can then be used to estimate a demand system with individual households as the units of analysis. Alderman (1988) uses such a procedure to estimate a demand system for Pakistan. However, there are a number of difficulties. One is that with only a few sites where prices are collected, the data may give inaccurate estimates of the prices faced by at least some households. In particular, urban prices may be a poor guide to rural prices, especially when there are price controls that are more effective in urban areas. The paucity of collection sites may also leave us in much the same situation as with the historical record, with too many responses to estimate from too few data points. The situation is made worse by the fact that it is often desirable to allow for the effects of regional and seasonal taste variation in the pattern of demand by entering regional and seasonal dummies into the regression, so that the price effects on demand are only identified to the degree that there are multiple observations within regions or that regional prices do not move in parallel across seasons.

Household price data

The individual household responses often provide a useful source of price data. In many surveys, although not in all and in particular not in the original LSMS surveys, households are asked to report, not only their expenditures on each good, but also the physical amount that they bought, so that we get one observation in kilos and one in currency. The ratio of these two observations is a measurement of price, or more accurately, of unit value. The attraction of such measures is the amount of data so provided. If the current Indian NSS were available on a nation-wide basis, we would have upwards of a quarter of a million observations on prices, a data set that would certainly permit the estimation of a much richer pattern of responses than could ever be obtained from a few dozen years of the historical record. Other surveys are not so large, but a typical comparison would still be between many thousands of observations from a survey and less than 50 from time series. As always, there is a price to be paid. Unit values are not the same thing as prices, and are affected by the choice of quality as well as by the actual prices that the consumer faces in the market. Not every household in each survey reports expenditures on every good, and no unit values can be obtained from those that do not. And when there are measurement errors in the data—which means always—there are obvious risks in dividing expenditure by quantity and using the result to "explain" quantity. These problems and others have to be dealt with if the analysis is to be convincing.

Even so, it is worth beginning by looking at the unit values, and trying to see whether they give us useful information about prices. I do this using (once again) the Pakistani data from the 1984–85 Household Income and Expenditure Survey and the Maharashtran state sample from the 38th round of the Indian NSS. The results summarized here are reported in full in Deaton and Grimard (1992) for Pakistan, and in Deaton, Parikh, and Subramanian (1994) for Maharashtra.

Table 5.1 for Pakistan and Figures 5.1 and 5.2 for Maharashtra provide differ-ent ways of looking at the spatial variation in the unit values. Table 5.1 reports two different sets of calculations for the Pakistani data. In the first, reported in the top panel, the logarithms of the unit values are regressed against a set of dummies for each of the four provinces in the survey—Punjab, Sindh, North West Frontier Province (NWFP), and Baluchistan (the omitted category)—and for each of the four quarters (omitting the fourth) of the calendar year during which the survey was conducted. These regressions are intended to capture broad regional and seasonal patterns. The bottom half of the table looks at variation from village to village within each province, and uses analysis of variance to decompose price variation into its within-village and between-village components.

The unit values for all goods but the last come directly from the survey, al-though the wheat category includes bread and flour converted to wheat content. The unit value for the final category, other food, is computed from a set of weights—here the average budget share for each component over all households in the survey—that are used to construct a weighted geometric index from the unit values for each of the individual foods in the other food category. Although the same weights are applied to all households, they are rescaled in each case to account for goods not purchased to ensure that the weights add to one for the cal-culated unit value for each household. If a unit value were calculated for such a heterogeneous category by adding up expenditures and dividing by the sum of the physical weights, the result would be as much determined by the composition of demand between items in the category as by any variation in prices. The rescaling by fixed weights has some of the same effect since households that buy only ex-

Table 5.1. Variation in log unit values of foods by provinces and villages, rural Pakistan, 1984–85

Regression (top panel — coefficients; absolute *t*-values in brackets)

Provinces and quarters	Wheat	Rice	Dairy products	Meat	Oils & fats	Sugar	Other foods
Punjab	-7.2 (6.0)	-8.0 (4.5)	-68.7 (15.8)	-22.1 (16.4)	-2.0 (8.5)	-6.6 (21.9)	-9.7 (11.8)
Sindh	7.3 (5.2)	-43.1 (22.3)	-78.3 (15.5)	-13.8 (9.5)	-2.6 (10.4)	-2.9 (9.0)	-11.8 (13.3)
NWFP	6.3 (4.7)	-2.8 (1.4)	-26.0 (5.4)	-31.1 (20.8)	-1.3 (5.0)	-3.7 (10.9)	-6.3 (6.9)
Jul–Sep 1984	-2.1 (2.6)	0.4 (0.4)	2.0 (0.7)	-1.4 (1.6)	-0.2 (1.4)	0.3 (1.7)	0.9 (1.7)
Oct–Dec 1984	-2.4 (3.0)	-1.0 (0.8)	-1.5 (0.5)	-3.4 (4.1)	-0.5 (2.9)	-0.2 (1.1)	-4.3 (8.4)
Jan–Mar 1985	0.0 (0.0)	-2.0 (1.6)	-3.0 (1.1)	-1.9 (2.2)	-0.3 (1.8)	0.3 (1.5)	-6.9 (13.3)

Analysis of variance (bottom panel)

	Wheat		Rice		Dairy products		Meat		Oils & fats		Sugar		Other foods	
	F	R^2	F	R^2	F	R^2	F	R^2	F	R^2	F	R^2	F	R^2
Punjab	4.02	0.33	9.14	0.59	3.07	0.39	7.85	0.45	13.7	0.61	7.2	0.42	12.8	0.53
Sindh	5.42	4.40	4.40	0.44	9.44	0.78	8.61	0.48	10.4	0.51	19.9	0.66	14.1	0.57
NWFP	6.06	7.12	7.12	0.57	10.63	0.67	4.46	0.30	13.5	0.54	13.9	0.59	10.8	0.48
Baluchistan	9.14	8.52	8.52	0.61	17.70	0.80	10.97	0.61	7.74	0.50	18.0	0.70	17.9	0.69

Note: The top panel shows coefficients from a regression of the logarithms of unit values on province and quarter dummies. The figures in brackets are absolute *t*-values. The bottom panel shows F- and R^2-statistics for cluster (village) dummies within each of the five regions. Regressions and analyses of variance use data from only those households that report expenditures on the good in question.

Source: Deaton and Grimard (1992, Table 3).

pensive items will have higher unit values, but there is no way of completely avoiding the difficulty, and the effect will have to be taken into account in the analysis.

The top panel of Table 5.1 shows that interprovincial price differences are much larger than are seasonal differences, though the latter are statistically significant for most of the categories. Apart from wheat, which is more expensive in Sindh and in NWFP than in Baluchistan, all province means are lower than those in Baluchistan. For oils and fats and for sugar, there is a good deal of state price control, and there is relatively little variation in price across the provinces, and the same holds to a lesser extent for wheat. Rice is very much cheaper in Sindh than elsewhere.

The bottom panel reports, not parameter estimates, but the F-tests and R^2-statistics from what can be thought of as a regression of the logarithm of unit value on dummies for each village, of which there are 440 in Punjab, 152 in Sindh, 110 in NWFP, and 55 in Baluchistan, although not all villages appear in each regression since the village is excluded if no household reports that type of expenditure. It is impossible (and unnecessary) to include seasonal dummies in these regressions because all the members of a village are interviewed within a few days of one another in the same calendar quarter. What we are looking for here is evidence that unit values are informative about prices, and since prices should not vary by much within villages over a short period of time, there should be significant F-statistics for the village effects, or put differently, the village dummies should explain a large share of the total variance in the logarithms of the unit values. While it is not clear how much is enough, all the F-statistics are significant at conventional values, and the village effects explain around a half of the total variance. Given that unit values are contaminated by measurement error, and given that there is variation within villages as richer households buy higher-quality goods, the results in the table seem sufficient to justify the suppositions both that there is spatial price variation and that variation in unit values provides a (noisy) guide to it.

Figures 5.1 and 5.2 show the behavior of the unit values for rice and for *jowar* in the Maharashtran data; similar graphs can be drawn for other foods, but these illustrate the point and the commodities are important in their own right. Instead of looking at the unit values at the village level, these diagrams display averages over households by district and quarter, so that each panel shows the seasonal pattern for that district in 1983, while a comparison of different panels reveals the differences in prices from one district to another. As for Pakistan, there is variation in unit values, both across space and over the seasons of the year. Both diagrams show pronounced seasonal patterns that are correlated—although far from perfectly so—between the districts. For rice, the logarithm of the unit value rose on average by 15 percent from the first to the third quarter, and by a further 2 percent between the third and fourth quarters. There is also substantial variation by district, both in levels and in the nature of the seasonal pattern. For example, in Dhule and Jalgaon, the average unit value of rice peaked in the second quarter, at which point the price of rice was nearly a third higher than in Chandrapur, for ex-

Figure 5.1. Log unit price of rice by district and subround, Maharashtra, 1983

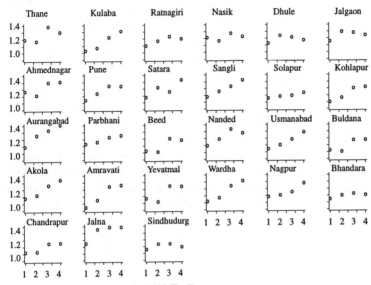

Source: Deaton, Parikh, and Subramanian (1995, Fig. 1).

Figure 5.2. Log unit price of *jowar* by district and subround, Maharashtra, 1983

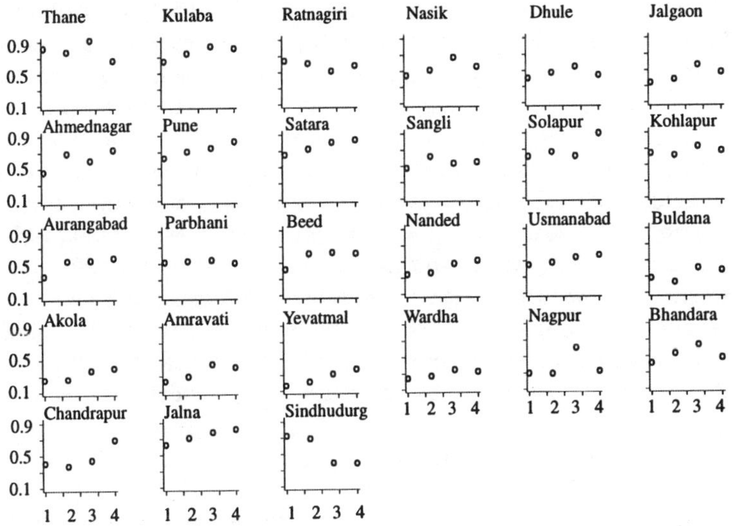

Source: Deaton, Parikh, and Subramanian (1995, Table 2).

ample. *Jowar* prices also rise through the year, by 13 percent from the first to the third quarter, falling by 2 percent in the final quarter. Interdistrict variation in *jowar* prices is much larger than for rice. In the inland eastern districts, Buldana, Akola, Amravati, Yevatmal, Wardha, and Nagpur, which are also the main producing districts, prices are lower throughout the year, by a half or 50 paise per kilogram, than in the coastal districts where no *jowar* is grown. Of course, these figures come from only the 1983 survey, but the spatial and seasonal patterns appear to be typical of other years.

For Maharashtra, it is also possible to compare the unit values from the survey with other price information. Government of India (1987) publishes monthly data on market prices in selected locations for a number of foodstuffs and crops. In cases where these prices can be matched by district, the two sets of numbers correspond very closely (see Deaton, Parikh, and Subramanian for details). Although the market price data are not sufficiently complete to serve as an alternative for estimating price responses, they are nevertheless useful as a check on the unit values that are reported by individual households in the NSS survey data.

While the examination of the unit value data cannot establish that they can be treated as if they were prices, the results here indicate that unit values are at the very least useful as an indicator of seasonal and spatial price variation.

Unit values and the choice of quality

One reason why unit values are not the same thing as prices is that unit values are affected by the choice of quality. A kilo of the best steak costs a great deal more than does a kilo of stewing beef, Roquefort costs more than cheddar, and even for relatively homogeneous commodities such as rice, there are many different grades and types. Unit values are computed by dividing expenditures by physical quantities, and high-quality items, or mixtures that have a relatively large share of high-quality items, will have higher unit prices. As a consequence, and in contrast to a market price, over which the consumer has no control, a unit value is chosen, at least to some extent. In particular, since better-off households tend to buy higher-quality goods, unit values will be positively related to incomes or total outlays. Because unit values are choice variables, there is a risk of simultaneity bias in any attempt to use them to "explain" the patterns of demand. Hence, instead of explaining the demand for rice by the price of rice, we are in effect regressing two aspects of the demand for rice on one another, with results that are unlikely to give what we want, which is the response of demand to price.

The size of quality effects can be assessed by running regressions of the logarithm of unit value on the logarithm of total expenditure and the usual list of household demographics and other characteristics. Such a model is written

$$(5.18) \qquad \ln v = \alpha^1 + \beta^1 \ln x + \gamma^1 \ln n + \sum_{1}^{K-1} \zeta_j (n_j/n) + u_1$$

where v is the unit value, x is total household expenditure, and the demographic terms are as in equation (4.14), the logarithm of household size and household structure as represented by the ratios to household size of persons in various age and sex categories. Although we might expect income (or total expenditure) to be the most important variable in explaining the choice of quality and thus the unit value, there is no reason to rule out other household characteristics; some groups within the household may choose particular items within a food category, and religious dietary preferences will also affect quality. Regressions like (5.18) were first examined by Prais and Houthakker (1955), who used a 1937–39 survey of British households to estimate values of β^1, a parameter that they referred to as the "quality elasticity," or more precisely as the expenditure elasticity of quality. For working-class households, they estimated quality elasticities ranging from 0.02 for onions, cocoa, and lard, to as high as 0.28 for sausages, 0.29 for fresh fish, and 0.33 for cake mixes (Prais and Houthakker 1972, Table 27, p. 124). They also emphasized local variations in the range of varieties; for example, the quality elasticity of cheese in Holland is 0.20 as compared with only 0.05 in Britain—British working-class households in the 1930s ate only cheddar—and the quality elasticity of tea in Bombay was 0.25 as against 0.06 in Britain.

Because unit values will vary not only with the choice of quality, but also with actual market prices, (5.18) should ideally be estimated with price data included on the right-hand side. This is impossible from the data that we have, but it is nevertheless possible to estimate the nonprice parameters of (5.18) consistently, provided that we are prepared to make the assumption that market prices do not vary within each village over the relevant reporting period. In rural areas in most developing countries, this is a reasonable assumption. Most villages have only a single market, and prices are likely to be much the same for a group of households that are in the same location and surveyed at the same time. Hence, equation (5.18) can be extended to include prices simply by adding dummy variables for each village. With large surveys, there may be several thousand villages, so the regression must usually be run, not by asking the computer to calculate it directly, but by first calculating village means for all variables, and then running a regression using as left- and right-hand-side variables the deviations from village means. By the Frisch-Waugh (1933) theorem, the regression of deviations from village means gives identical parameter estimates to those that would have been obtained from the regression containing the village dummies.

Two practical points are worth noting. First, the removal of village means must be done on exactly the same data that are to be used in the regressions. This seems obvious enough, but in the case of (5.18), where different subsets of households purchase different goods so that the samples with usable unit values are different for each good, the village means for variables such as $\ln x$, which are available for all households, will have to be different for each good. One simple way of checking that the demeaning has been done correctly is to check that the estimated intercept in the demeaned regression is zero, at least up to the accuracy of the machine. Second, the standard errors given by the usual OLS formula will not be correct, although the error will typically be small, and is in any case easily corrected. If there are n households in the survey, grouped into C clusters, the hypothetical regression with all the dummies would have $n-k-C-1$ degrees of freedom when there are k other regressors (such as those listed in (5.18) above). But the regression using the demeaned data includes all n observations, and has k regressors, so that when the equation standard error is estimated, the computer will divide the sum of squares of the residuals not by $n-k-C-1$, as it should, but by $n-k$. The correct standard errors can be calculated by scaling the calculated standard errors by the square root of the ratio of $n-k-C-1$ to $n-k$, which with (say) 10 households per cluster, amounts to inflating the standard errors by the square root of 0.9, or by 5.4 percent. (All of these issues can be avoided by using the "areg" command in STATA, which when used with the option "absorb (cluster)" will estimate the regression with implicit dummies for each cluster.)

Tables 5.2 and 5.3 present parameter estimates of (5.18) for the two data sets using the methodology of the previous paragraph. Only the coefficients on the logarithms of total expenditure and household size are shown, although the regressions contain a full range of compositional and socioeconomic variables in addition to the village dummies. Apart from the case of sugar in urban Pakistan, where the coefficient is zero, all the expenditure elasticities of quality are positive, and most are statistically significant. The heterogeneous meat commodity has the highest quality elasticities, and the elasticity of 0.242 in urban Pakistan is the highest in either table. The important cereal categories—rice, wheat, and coarse cereals—have modest quality elasticities, from 3 to 11 percent. Price control for sugar and oil in Pakistan is reflected in very low quality elasticities, although the estimate of 0.006 for sugar in the rural sector is significantly different from zero. The response of quality to household size is negative, except for the intriguing case of fruit in Maharashtra, where both rural and urban estimates are positive. As

Table 5.2. Within-village regressions for unit values, Pakistan, 1984–85

Food	Rural		Urban	
	lnx	lnn	lnx	lnn
Wheat	0.095	−0.033	0.027	−0.028
	(14.7)	(4.3)	(7.6)	(6.7)
Rice	0.107	−0.062	0.111	−0.075
	(12.4)	(6.3)	(16.5)	(9.7)
Dairy products	0.139	−0.031	0.010	−0.023
	(6.4)	(1.3)	(0.9)	(1.9)
Meat	0.154	−0.099	0.242	−0.156
	(23.7)	(13.5)	(34.0)	(19.0)
Oils & fats	0.000	0.000	0.003	−0.002
	(0.4)	(0.0)	(2.6)	(2.1)
Sugar	0.006	−0.004	−0.000	−0.000
	(4.6)	(2.8)	(0.3)	(0.1)
Other foods	0.076	−0.033	0.129	−0.076
	(21.2)	(7.9)	(25.9)	(13.1)

Note: The dependent variable is the logarithm of unit value. Included, but not shown, are demographic ratios by age and sex. Absolute values of t-values are shown in brackets.
Source: Deaton and Grimard (1992, Table 4).

**Table 5.3. Within-village regressions for unit values,
rural Maharashtra, 1983**

Food	*ln*x	*abs* t	*ln*n	*abs* t
Rice	0.058	(8.8)	−0.041	(5.7)
Wheat	0.047	(6.3)	−0.026	(3.2)
Coarse cereals	0.042	(7.1)	−0.042	(6.5)
Other cereals	0.123	(5.6)	−0.011	(0.5)
Pulses & gram	0.022	(3.9)	−0.026	(4.2)
Dairy products	0.109	(7.2)	−0.034	(2.1)
Oils & fats	0.034	(7.6)	−0.022	(4.4)
Meat	0.179	(11.4)	−0.085	(5.2)
Vegetables	0.037	(7.6)	−0.015	(2.9)
Fruit & nuts	0.097	(3.6)	−0.046	(1.6)
Sugar & *gur*	0.052	(10.6)	−0.046	(8.7)

Note: Regressions also include demographic ratios by sex and age, as well as dummies for scheduled caste, religion, and worker type.
Source: Deaton, Parikh, and Subramanian (1994, Table 5).

was the case for the Engel curves in Chapter 4, the elasticity with respect to household size tends to be large and negative when the elasticity on total expenditure is large and positive, suggesting that increases in household size act like reductions in income. The estimated coefficients on household size are mostly smaller in absolute size than the coefficients on total expenditure, a result that once again suggests the presence of economies of scale (see the discussion in the final subsection of Section 4.3).

The demographic composition of the household exerts little or no influence on the reported unit values. However, some of the other variables are occasionally important. In Maharashtra, households headed by agricultural laborers buy lower-quality cereals than do others, presumably because of their greater need for calories. Hindu, Jain, Parsi, and Buddhist households spend more per unit of meat than do Muslim or Christian households, not because they get charged more for meat, but because they rarely consume meat, but when they do so, will purchase only the relatively expensive chicken and lamb.

These results, and those from similar regressions in Deaton (1988, 1990a) for Côte d'Ivoire and Indonesia, respectively, show that the quality effects in unit values are real, that they work as expected with better-off households paying more per unit, but that the size of the effects is modest. That they should be so makes good intuitive sense. Although it is true that it is possible to find very expensive and very cheap varieties within any commodity group, most people will buy a range of qualities, so that it would be a large difference if rich households were to spend twice as much (say) per kilo as poor households, even for a heterogeneous commodity like meat. It is a rough but useful rule of thumb that rich households spend about six times as much as poor households, so that we have an upper limit on the quality elasticity of 15 percent, close to what is observed in practice.

Even though the quality effects on unit values are modest, it is wise to be cautious about treating unit values as if they were prices. Any positive effect of incomes on unit values will cause price responses to be (absolutely) overstated. The argument is straightforward and depends on higher prices causing consumers to shade down quality. Suppose that when there is a price increase, consumers adapt, not only by buying less, but also by buying lower-quality items, thus spreading the consequences of the price increase over more than one dimension. We want to measure the price elasticity of quantity, which in an idealized environment would be calculated as the percentage reduction in quantity divided by the percentage increase in price. However, we observe not the price but the unit value. With quality shading, the unit value increases along with the price, but not by the full amount. As a result, if we divide the percentage decrease in quantity by the percentage increase in unit value, we are dividing by something that is too small, and the result of the calculation will be too large. If the response of quality to income is close to zero, it is also plausible that quality shading in response to price increases will also be negligible, but such a result needs to be established more formally, which is one of the objects of the model in the next section.

Measurement error in unit values

Quality effects in unit values are not the only reason why they cannot be treated as prices, and may not even be the most important. Because unit values are derived from reported expenditures and quantities, measurement error in quantity will be transmitted to measurement error in the unit value, inducing a spurious negative correlation. To see how this works, consider the simplest possible model in which the logarithm of demand depends on the logarithm of price, and where there are no quality effects, so that the ratio of expenditure to quantity is price, but expenditure and quantity are each measured with error. The substantive equation can therefore be written as

$$(5.19) \qquad \ln q_h = \mu + \epsilon_p \ln p_h + u_h$$

where the subscript h denotes a household, and where ϵ_p is the price elasticity that we wish to estimate. The magnitudes in (5.19) are measured with error, and are not observed; instead, households report

$$(5.20) \qquad \ln p_h^* = \ln p_h + v_{1h}$$

$$(5.21) \qquad \ln q_h^* = \ln q_h + v_{2h}$$

for measurement errors v_{1h} and v_{2h} with variances σ_1^2 and σ_2^2, and covariance σ_{12}. Note that (5.20) and (5.21) do not imply that households either recall or report price and quantity; the two equations are entirely consistent with perhaps the most obvious recall strategy, where households report expenditures and quantities, and the analyst calculates the price. What is important is that the covariance σ_{12} be allowed to take on any value. If households recall expenditures correctly, but have difficulty in recalling quantities, then the covariance will be negative, as it will be in the more general case where there are measurement errors in expenditures that are independent of the errors in the quantities. But we cannot be sure how households do their reporting. For example, even if they are asked to report expenditures and quantities, they may calculate the latter from the former by recalling a price. This and other possibilities are consistent with (5.20) and (5.21) provided that the covariance is not restricted.

If the measurement equations (5.20) and (5.21) are used to substitute for the unobservable quantities in (5.19), and the resulting equation is estimated by OLS, then straightforward algebra shows that the probability limit of the estimate of the price elasticity is given by a special case of (2.62)

$$(5.22) \qquad \text{plim} \, \hat{\epsilon}_p = \epsilon_p + m_*^{-1}(\sigma_{12} - \epsilon_p \sigma_1^2)$$

where m_* is the large sample variance of the mismeasured price. The important thing to note about this formula is that, even in the "standard" case where the covariance σ_{12} is negative, it is not necessarily the case that the spurious negative correlation between mismeasured price and mismeasured quantity will lead to a downward bias. Instead, (5.22) is a generalization of the standard attenuation result. Indeed, if the covariance is zero, (5.22) is exactly the attenuation formula, and the mismeasurement of price has the usual effect of biasing the elasticity towards zero, which since the elasticity is negative, means an upward bias. Adding in the effect of the covariance will give a downward bias if the covariance is negative, but taking the two effects together, we cannot sign the net effect. Even so, in the special but leading case where the measurement errors in the logarithm of expenditure and the logarithm of unit value are independent, the covariance σ_{12} is equal to minus the variance σ_1^2. If in addition, $\epsilon_p > -1$, so that demand is price inelastic, the estimate of the price elasticity will be biased downward, with the spurious negative correlation dominating the attenuation bias. More generally, but still on the assumption that $\sigma_{12} = -\sigma_1^2$, the estimated price elasticity will be biased toward -1.

In the next section, I propose a methodology that permits consistent estimation of the price elasticities in the presence of both measurement errors and quality contamination of unit values.

5.3 Modeling the choice of quality and quantity

The purpose of this section is to construct an empirical model that can be used with the survey data, including the unit value information, to provide consistent estimates of price elasticities of demand. The basic ideas that underlie the model are straightforward, but the application involves a certain amount of detail, and the final model can appear to be complex if encountered all at once. To avoid unnecessary complexity, I proceed in stages, introducing a very simple version of the model first, and using it to explain the basic principles. I then introduce the various complications one at a time. For the reader only interested in the empirical results, only the first few subsections need be read, leaving the more technical material to be consulted only by those who wish to use the methods.

A stripped-down model of demand and unit values

In the simplest possible model of demand, the quantities consumed are related to total outlay (or income) and to price. To that basic model, we must add the special features of the current problem, notably that we observe not price but unit value, and that prices do not vary within villages (clusters) but only between them. One version of such a model has a demand function and a unit value function

$$(5.23) \qquad \ln q_{hc} = \alpha^0 + \epsilon_x \ln x_{hc} + \epsilon_p \ln \pi_c + f_c + u_{hc}^0$$

$$(5.24) \qquad \ln v_{hc} = \alpha^1 + \beta^1 \ln x_{hc} + \psi \ln \pi_c + u_{hc}^1.$$

In these two equations, h is a household (or observation) and c is the cluster or village where it lives. The reported quantity demanded is q_{hc} and recorded unit value is v_{hc}. Total outlay is x_{hc} and is the only household-specific variable introduced at this stage; I shall bring in demographics and other household characteristics later. The logarithms of both demand and unit value depend on the logarithm of the price of the good, written here as $\ln \pi_c$; I shall introduce cross-price effects later but, for the moment, $\ln \pi_c$ is a scalar. Price is not observed—so that (5.23) and (5.24) are not standard regressions—and does not vary within clusters; hence the c subscript and the absence of the h subscript. The total expenditure elasticity ϵ_x and price elasticity ϵ_p are treated as constants by (5.23), and the latter is the main parameter of interest.

The quantity equation has two error terms. The first, f_c, is a village-level effect that is the same for all households in the village, and that should be thought of either as a "random effect" or as a "fixed effect." The choice is largely a matter of taste, but the important point is that the f_c, while possibly correlated with household outlays—and with other sociodemographic characteristics—must be uncorrelated with the prices. Since both fixed effects and prices are unobserved, we cannot hope to measure the influence of the latter if they are allowed to be arbitrarily correlated. The reason that the f_c are required at all is clear if we think about average demand over villages, where even with identical village incomes, prices, and other variables that we can measure, we should still expect random variation from one village to another. Individuals within villages will often be more like one another than people in different villages, even when we have controlled for all the obvious determinants of demand.

The second error term in the demand equation, u_{hc}^0, is more standard, but it incorporates not only the usual unobservables, but also any measurement error in the logarithms of recorded quantities. It therefore includes the measurement error in (5.21), and will be correlated with the error term in the unit value equation, u_{hc}^1, which includes measurement error in unit values as in (5.20). If the number of households in each village is sufficiently large, the means of u^0 and u^1 will be approximately zero, although there is no reason to expect either measurement error or behavioral errors to average to zero for each village in the usual samples where there are only a few households in each.

The unit value equation is essentially the same as (5.18) above although, for expository purposes, I have removed the demographics and have explicitly included the unobservable prices. The coefficient ψ would be unity if unit values were equal to prices up to measurement error—in which case α^1 and β^1 would be zero—but quality shading in response to prices will make ψ less than unity. Unlike the quantity equation, the unit value equation contains no village fixed effects. Prices certainly vary from village to village, but, conditional on price, unit value depends only on the quality effects and measurement error. The introduction of an additional fixed effect would break the link between prices and unit values, would prevent the latter giving any useful information about the former, and would thus remove any possibility of identification.

In the next two subsections, I present the economic and econometric background for identifying the parameters in (5.23) and (5.24), after which I shall discuss complications. These are concerned with the introduction of the sociodemographics, with allowing for cross-price as well as own-price elasticities, and with the adoption of a more appropriate functional form than is provided by the logarithmic formulation. However, the simple structure avoids notational clutter, and the logarithmic specification is one in which the subsequent analysis is the most transparent.

It is clear from inspection of (5.23) and (5.24) that, without further information, and in the presence of the unobservable price terms, not all of the parameters can be estimated. That any parameters can be identified may seem surprising at first. However, in the previous section we saw how the parameters of total expenditure and the sociodemographics in the unit value equation could be consistently estimated by including cluster dummies on the assumption that prices are constant within villages. This result clearly also extends to the quantity as well as the unit value equation, and will allow estimation of the effect of any variable that is not constant within villages.

The immediate issue is how to identify the coefficients on the price terms. As written in (5.23) and (5.24), the situation looks hopeless. Since we know nothing about prices, there is no way of pinning down either ϵ_p or ψ. However, it is possible to say something about their ratio. In particular, if we use (5.24) to write $\ln \pi_c$ in terms of the logarithm of unit value, total outlay, and the error term, and substitute the result into (5.23), we obtain a linear relationship between the logarithm of quantity, the logarithm of outlay, and the logarithm of unit value, plus various error terms. The coefficient on the logarithm of unit value in this equation is $\psi^{-1}\epsilon_p$, which can be estimated, not by OLS, since the measurement errors will make the unit values correlated with the compound error term, but by (say) instrumental variables provided a suitable instrument can be found. If such is the case, the relationship between the logarithm of quantity and the logarithm of unit value identifies not the price elasticity ϵ_p, but the hybrid parameter $\psi^{-1}\epsilon_p$, an amount that will be larger than ϵ_p if there is quality shading and ψ is less than unity. This is simply the formalization in terms of (5.23) and (5.24) of the general argument given at the end of the previous section, that the existence of quality effects in unit values will tend to bias downward estimates of price elasticities that are obtained by comparing quantities with unit values on the false supposition that the latter can be treated as if they were prices.

To disentangle ϵ_p from estimates of $\psi^{-1}\epsilon_p$ requires more information, which can be obtained from a model of quality shading. I do this in the next subsection, where I define quality more precisely, and then model it in a way that is specific enough to circumvent the identification problem. The basic idea is that quality shading in response to price increases is not likely to be very large if the elasticity of quantity with respect to income is not very large. More precisely, if the parameters β^1 in (5.24) are close to zero—as we have already seen they are in practice—then the parameter ψ should be close to unity, so that $\psi^{-1}\epsilon_p$ is close to ϵ_p. If so, we can more or less ignore the quality issue and treat the unit values as prices, except for measurement error. The next subsection can therefore be skipped by readers prepared to take the result on trust and to accept that the quality corrections in the next section are more for completeness than for substance.

Modeling quality

In textbook consumer theory, there are quantities and prices, and their product is expenditure. When quality is introduced into the picture, there are three players, quantity, quality, and price. Expenditure is the product of quantity and unit value, and unit value is part price and part quality. Indeed, we can define quality in such a way that unit value is price multiplied by quality, so that the textbook identity is extended to become expenditure is equal to the product of quantity, quality, and price. There are several different ways of thinking about quality, but the one that is most suitable for my purposes is to define quality as a property of commodity aggregates. At the finest possible level of disaggregation, there exist perfectly homogeneous goods, rice defined in terms of purity, variety, and number of broken grains, or a car defined by make, year, and fittings. The actual categories used in the survey are collections or bundles of such goods, rice or cars. However, two rice bundles with the same physical weight may be made up of different compositions of the varieties, and we can think of the higher-quality bundle as that which contains the higher proportion of relatively expensive varieties, where expensive and cheap are defined relative to some reference price vector.

To make these notions precise, think of a group of goods (rice, or meat) denoted by the subscript G. If q_G denotes the household's vector of consumption levels of each item within the group, I define a group quantity index Q_G by

$$(5.25) \qquad Q_G = k_G.q_G$$

where k_G is a vector used to add together the possibly incommensurate items in the group. If physical weight is a sensible measure, and if the quantities are reported as weights, then each element of k_G will be unity. More generally, the vector can be used, for example, to add together flour, wheat, and bread, in wheat equivalent units, or to measure quantities in terms of calories, in which case k_G would be a vector of calorie conversion coefficients. Corresponding to the quantity vector is a vector of prices, p_G, and since each commodity that makes up the vector is perfectly homogeneous by definition, these prices contain no quality effects. They are genuine prices, not unit values. Write this price vector in the form

$$(5.26) \qquad\qquad p_G = \pi_G p_G^0$$

where π_G is a scalar measure of the level of prices in the group, and p_G^0 is a reference price vector. Equation (5.26) is introduced in order to give us a simple way of changing the level of prices while keeping fixed the structure of prices within the group. When I come to implement the model using data from households in different villages, I shall treat the π's as varying from one village to the next, and assume that relative prices are at least approximately constant across villages.

If expenditure on the group $p_G \cdot q_G$ is denoted x_G, we can use the two equations (5.25) and (5.26) to give the identity

$$(5.27) \qquad x_G = p_G \cdot q_G = Q_G(p_G \cdot q_G / k_G \cdot q_G) = Q_G \pi_G (p_G^0 \cdot q_G / k_G \cdot q_G)$$

so that, if we define quality ξ_G by

$$(5.28) \qquad\qquad \xi_G = p_G^0 \cdot q_G / k_G \cdot q_G$$

(5.27) implies that expenditure is the product of quantity, price, and quality. In logarithms

$$(5.29) \qquad\qquad \ln x_G = \ln Q_G + \ln \pi_G + \ln \xi_G.$$

The definition of quality in (5.28) is clearly the only one that will allow (5.29) to hold given the definition of group price and group quantity. But it also corresponds to the ideas sketched in the first paragraph of this subsection. Quality is defined as the value of a bundle of goods at fixed reference prices relative to its physical volume. It is a function of the consumption bundle q_G, and any change in this bundle towards relatively expensive goods and away from relatively cheap goods will increase the quality of the bundle as a whole.

Having settled definitional matters, we can now address the issue of quality shading in response to price, and whether we can say anything about what happens to quality ξ_G when there is a change in the price π_G. The definitions allow us to tie the price elasticity of quality to the usual price and quantity elasticities, but without further restriction, there is no straightforward link between the income and price elasticities of quality. However, such a link can be constructed if the goods in G form a separable group in household preferences. Provided the marginal rates of substitution between different goods in the group are independent of quantities consumed outside of the group, there will always exist subgroup demand functions for the goods inside the group in which the only arguments are total group expenditure and within-group prices (see for example Deaton and Muellbauer 1980a, pp. 120–26). When preferences are separable over a group, overall utility depends on the consumption of goods within the group through a group subutility function, so that maximization of overall utility requires that subutility be maximized subject to whatever is spent on the group. We therefore have subgroup demand functions

$$(5.30) \qquad q_G = f_G(x_G, p_G) = f_G(x_G / \pi_G, p_G^0)$$

where the last step comes from using (5.26) and the fact that demand functions are homogeneous of degree zero.

Equation (5.30) shows that separability delivers the restriction that we need. According to (5.28), and given the reference price vector, quality depends only on the composition of demand within the group. But according to (5.30), the group demands depend only on the ratio of group expenditure to group price, so that changes in group price must work in very much the same way as do changes in total expenditure. This links the price elasticity of quality (shading) to the income elasticity of quality. By (5.28), ξ_G depends on p_G^0, k_G, and q_G, the first two of which are fixed constants. Thus the effect on quality of changes in price π_G works only through q_G, which by (5.30), depends only on the ratio of x_G to π_G. As a result, ξ_G depends only on $\ln x_G - \ln \pi_G$ and not on each separately, so that

$$(5.31) \qquad \frac{\partial \ln \xi_G}{\partial \ln \pi_G} = \frac{\partial \ln \xi_G}{\partial \ln x_G} \left(\frac{\partial \ln x_G}{\partial \ln \pi_G} - 1 \right).$$

The term in brackets on the right-hand side is the price elasticity of Q_G with respect to π_G, or ϵ_p, say. The first term is closely related to the Prais-Houthakker (income) elasticity of quality which is β^1 in (5.24). In particular, by the chain rule,

$$(5.32) \qquad \beta^1 = \frac{\partial \ln \xi_G}{\partial \ln x} = \frac{\partial \ln \xi_G}{\partial \ln x_G} \cdot \frac{\partial \ln x_G}{\partial \ln x}.$$

The last term on the right-hand side of (5.32) is the total expenditure elasticity of the group, ϵ_x, say, so that, combining (5.31) and (5.32), we have

$$(5.33) \qquad \frac{\partial \ln \xi_G}{\partial \ln \pi_G} = \beta^1 \epsilon_p / \epsilon_x.$$

The elasticity of unit value with respect to price, or the parameter ψ in (5.24) is one plus the elasticity of quality to price, so that we have finally that

$$(5.34) \qquad \psi = 1 + \beta^1 \epsilon_p / \epsilon_x.$$

According to (5.33), separability implies that quality shading in response to price is determined by the price, income, and quality elasticities of the commodity group. When prices rise holding relative prices constant, there is a reduction in demand for the group as a whole, and the size of the reduction is controlled by the price elasticity ϵ_p. When less is bought, there is a quality effect whose magnitude depends on the elasticity of quality with respect to expenditure on the group, an elasticity that is the quality elasticity with respect to total expenditure divided by the expenditure elasticity of the group. As a result, there will be no quality shading if either the price elasticity or the quality elasticity is zero. The parameter ψ, the elasticity of unit value with respect to price in the unit value equation (5.24), is one if there is no quality shading, and will be less than one by an amount that is larger the larger are the price and quality elasticities. The separability assumption thus provides the basis for quantifying (and correcting) the bias that would arise if quality effects are ignored, and unit values treated as prices.

Because (5.34) provides an additional relationship between the quantity and unit value elasticities ϵ_p and ψ, it can be used to identify the two elasticities separately from estimates of the ratio $\psi^{-1}\epsilon_p$, which as we have seen is all that can be identified from the quantity and unit value data. If we write ϕ for the ratio of ϵ_p to ψ, equation (5.34) implies that

$$(5.35) \qquad \phi = \frac{\epsilon_p}{\psi} = \frac{\epsilon_p}{(1 + \beta^1 \epsilon_p / \epsilon_x)}$$

so that, upon rearrangement, we have

$$(5.36) \qquad \epsilon_p = \frac{\phi}{1 - \phi \beta^1 / \epsilon_x}.$$

As a result, if we know the ratio ϕ and the quantity and quality elasticities ϵ_x and β^0, we can use (5.36) to calculate the price elasticity ϵ_p. Since all of the magnitudes on the right-hand side of (5.36) can be estimated from the data, the separability-based model of quality shading provides the basis for identifying the price elasticity.

Equation (5.36) can also be thought of as a correction formula, where the uncorrected (for the effects of quality) price elasticity is ϕ, and where the correction will be small if β^1, the total expenditure elasticity of quality, is small. In the next subsection, I show how the data can be used to give consistent estimates of all of the identified parameters up to and including the ratio ϕ. Once this is done, a final correction is made by applying equation (5.36) to the estimated parameters to obtain an estimate of the price elasticity.

Estimating the stripped-down model

We are now in a position to estimate all of the parameters of the two-equation quantity and unit value model (5.23) and (5.24). There are two stages. The first, which we have already seen—uses within-village information to estimate the total expenditure elasticities, and the second, discussed here, uses between-village information to estimate the price elasticities.

Suppose that the first-stage estimates of ϵ_x and β^1 have been obtained. Use these estimates to construct the two variables

$$(5.37) \qquad \hat{y}_{hc}^0 = \ln q_{hc} - \hat{\epsilon}_x \ln x_{hc}$$

$$(5.38) \qquad \hat{y}_{hc}^1 = \ln v_{hc} - \hat{\beta}^1 \ln x_{hc}.$$

Note that these are not the residuals from the first-stage regressions; these regressions contain village dummies, and in (5.37) and (5.38), it is only the effects of total expenditure that are being netted out, and the price information contained in the village dummies must be left in. The residuals from the first-stage regressions play a different role, which is to estimate the variances and covariances of the residuals in the quantity and unit value equations. Let e^0 and e^1 be the residuals from the quantity and unit value regressions, respectively, and write $n-k-C-1$ for the number of degrees of freedom in these regressions; recall n is the total number of observations, C the number of clusters, and k—which is one here—is the number of other right-hand-side variables. Then we can estimate the variance of u_{ch}^1 and the covariance of u_{ch}^1 and u_{ch}^0 using

$$(5.39) \qquad \hat{\sigma}^{11} = e^{1\prime}e^1/(n-k-C-1) \qquad \hat{\sigma}^{01} = e^{0\prime}e^1/(n-k-C-1).$$

We shall shortly see how these estimates are to be used.

Since the second stage uses the between-village information, it begins from (5.37) and (5.38), the quantities and unit values purged of the effects of total expenditure, averaging them by cluster. Denote these averages $\hat{y}_c^0$ and $\hat{y}_c^1$, respectively, the absence of the household subscript h denoting village averages. Corresponding to these estimates are the underlying "true" values y_c^0 and y_c^1, which we would have obtained had the first-stage parameters been known rather than estimated. From (5.23) and (5.24), these can be written as

$$(5.40) \qquad y_c^0 = \alpha^0 + \epsilon_p \ln \pi_c + f_c + u_c^0$$

$$(5.41) \qquad y_c^1 = \alpha^1 + \psi \ln \pi_c + u_c^1$$

where, once again, the u's have been averaged over villages. For a large enough sample of villages, we would therefore have

$$(5.42) \qquad \text{cov}(y_c^0, y_c^1) = \epsilon_p \psi m + \sigma^{01}/n_c$$

where m is the large-sample intervillage variance of log prices, and n_c is the number of households per village. The last term comes from noting that u_c^0 and u_c^1 in (5.40) and (5.41) are averages over the n_c households in each cluster. (When I come to deal with the complications, I shall return to these formulas and to what happens when there are different numbers of households in different clusters, as well as when there are different numbers of observations on quantities and unit values.) Corresponding to (5.42), we can also write the variance of the corrected unit values as

$$(5.43) \qquad \text{var } y_c^1 = \psi^2 m + \sigma^{11}/n_c.$$

The comparison of (5.42) and (5.43) yields

$$(5.44) \qquad \phi = \frac{\epsilon_p}{\psi} = \frac{\text{cov}(y_c^0 y_c^1) - \sigma^{01}/n_c}{\text{var}(y_c^1) - \sigma^{11}/n_c}$$

so that, by replacing theoretical magnitudes by their first-stage estimates, we can obtain a consistent estimate of the ratio $\psi^{-1}\epsilon_p$. For reference, I record the formula:

$$(5.45) \qquad \hat{\phi} = \frac{\text{cov}(\hat{y}_c^0 \hat{y}_c^1) - \hat{\sigma}^{01}/n_c}{\text{var}(\hat{y}_c^1) - \hat{\sigma}^{11}/n_c}$$

where the terms on the right-hand side come from (5.37), (5.38), and (5.39).

Equations (5.44) and (5.45) look somewhat unfamiliar at first sight, but they are readily related to standard estimators, especially errors-in-variables estimators. Note first that the bivariate OLS estimator of the regression of y on x is the ratio of the covariance of x and y to the variance of x. In the absence of σ^{01} and σ^{11}, the error variances and covariances from the first stage, (5.45) is simply the OLS regression of average village demand on the village average unit value, where both right-hand and left-hand variables have been purged of the effects of household total expenditure. The σ^{01} and σ^{11} terms, which would vanish if each village were large enough, are designed to correct for the part of the between-village variances and covariances that comes from measurement and econometric error in the underlying first-stage equations. Indeed, (5.45) is a standard errors-in-variables estimator in which the $X'X$ matrix and $X'y$ vector are purged of the contributions of measurement error (see 2.66). That the estimator is relatively unfamiliar in practice is because it is not feasible in the absence of information about the moments of the measurement error, information that is rarely available, at least in economics. In the current case, because of the two-stage structure of the problem, the information can be obtained from the residuals of the first-stage within-village regressions.

That (5.45) reduces to OLS when the number of households in each village is infinite, gives a useful insight into the nature of the estimation procedure. It is designed to give a consistent estimate of the ratio ϕ as the number of villages tends to infinity, holding fixed the number of households in each village. Although the first stage of estimation uses only the within-village information, it pools such data over many villages so that, provided the fixed effects are the only form of village heterogeneity, the first-stage parameters will converge to their true values as the number of villages increases, even if there are only a few households per village. But even if the first-stage parameters were known, so that the "hats" in (5.45) could be removed, the correction for the first-stage errors would still have to be made if there are not enough households in each village to average them away. Apart from this correction, (5.45) is simply a least squares estimate of the price elasticity using the variation in quantities and prices across the villages.

In the case where y's and σ's are known, the asymptotic variance of ϕ is given by the delta method, or from Fuller (1987, p. 108)

$$(5.46) \qquad v(\hat{\phi}) = C^{-1}(m^{11} - \sigma^{11}/n_c)^{-2}[\mu^0 m^{11} + (m^{01} - \phi m^{11})]$$

where

$$(5.47) \qquad \mu^0 = m^{00} - 2m^{01}\phi + m^{11}\phi^2$$

and m^{00}, m^{11}, and m^{01} are the variance of y^0, the variance of y^1, and the co-variance of y^0 and y^1, respectively. This formula will generally understate the variance because it ignores the estimation uncertainty from the first-stage estimates. The formula given by Fuller also covers the case where the σ's are estimated, but it does not allow for the fact that the y's are also estimated here, nor for the resulting lack of independence between the estimates of the y's and the σ's. But because the first-stage estimates are based on many more data points than the second-stage estimates—there are more households than there are villages—the contribution to the variance of the estimate from the first stage is small relative to that captured by (5.46) and (5.47). As a result, these formulas will often be adequate without further modification. Variance estimates can also be obtained by bootstrapping, which I shall use for the final estimates below.

An example from Côte d'Ivoire

Although the methodology outlined here requires modification before use, it is useful to work through a simple example of this version of the model to see how the numbers fit into the formulas. The data come from the 1979 *Enquête Budget Consommation* from Côte d'Ivoire, and the full set of calculations are reported in Deaton (1987a). I illustrate with the example of beef using the numbers in Table 5.4. The top panel, of "crude" elasticities, shows the results of yielding to the temptation of regressing the logarithm of quantity on the logarithm of unit value and other variables. With no allowance for taste variation across households, the regression generates an estimate of the "price elasticity" of -0.560, which is robust to the inclusion of broad regional and seasonal dummies, but increases to -0.796 when cluster-level and seasonal dummies are included. In these data, clusters were visited on multiple occasions, so that it is possible to include both seasonal and village effects, or, as in the last row of the top panel, to interact the village and quarterly dummies so as to calculate the within-estimator, which has the value of -0.940. If it is true that there is no genuine price variation within villages at a given visit, and if unit values were truly prices and were measured without error, the within-estimator would not be identified. As it is, the model interprets this estimate as the covariance-to-variance ratio of the error terms in the quantity and unit value equations, a quantity that has nothing to do with the price elasticity.

The second panel, labeled "improved elasticities," follows the calculations of this subsection. The intervillage covariance of the village averages of corrected log unit value and corrected log quantity is -0.083, so that compared to the intervillage variance of the former of 0.138, we would get an intervillage OLS estimate of the price elasticity of -0.600. According to the model, this estimate is contaminated by the effects of the measurement error because the cluster size is insufficiently large to average it away. Indeed, the average cluster size in this case is only 1.97 households—see the next subsection and equation (5.55) below for an explanation of how this is measured—and the estimates of the error covariance and variance are -0.049 and 0.052, respectively. The sign of the covariance con-

Table 5.4. Estimates of the price elasticity of beef, Côte d'Ivoire, 1979

	Estimate	*t-value*
"Crude" elasticities		
No taste variation	−0.560	(5.0)
Regional and seasonal taste variation	−0.547	(4.4)
Village and seasonal taste variation	−0.796	(4.6)
Within-estimator σ^{10}/σ^{11}	−0.940	
"Improved" elasticities		
Intervillage covariance	−0.083	
Intervillage price variance	0.138	
Estimate of σ^{01}	−0.049	
Estimate of σ^{11}	0.052	
"Average" village size	1.97	
Covariance to variance ratio	−0.600	
With measurement error correction	−0.512	(2.5)
With quality correction	−0.504	(2.6)

Source: Deaton (1987a).

firms what might be expected, that measurement errors in quantity and unit value are negatively correlated. Correction for measurement errors using (5.45) leads to an estimate of the price elasticity of −0.512 with an asymptotic *t*-value of 2.5. The estimated expenditure elasticity of quality for beef is only 0.025, so that the final quality correction (5.36) exerts little further change, leaving us with a final estimate of −0.504 with an asymptotic *t*-value of 2.6. In this example, the final estimate is close to the initial estimate, which is an accident of these particular data; in general, the "crude" elasticity estimates will not be consistent.

*Functional form

The logarithmic model (5.23) and (5.24) is analytically tractable and has the advantage that its parameters are elasticities which provide a simple, convenient, and dimensionless way to measure price responses. However, not all households consume all the goods, and because we cannot take the logarithm of zero, the logarithmic model can only be used to describe the behavior of those households who purchase positive amounts. For narrowly defined commodities, such a restriction can eliminate a large fraction of the sample, and when we come to extend the model to many goods, the restriction that all households purchase all the goods can result in an unacceptable loss of households from the sample. The fundamental issue here is whether we wish to model demand conditional on making purchases, or whether we want an unconditional formulation, covering nonconsumers as well as consumers. For some purposes, the former would be correct, for example if the factors leading to purchase are different from the factors that determine the amount once the decision to purchase has been taken. However, it is equally clear that for purposes of tax and price reform, we need to include all households, whether they purchase or not. We are ultimately trying to calculate the change in government revenue associated with a change in price, see (5.5), and the derivative in the denominator of (5.9) is a sum over all households, whether they make purchases or not. The model must therefore be one that includes all households, which is not possible for the logarithmic formulation.

A simple alternative is provided by modifying (5.23) to make the dependent variable the budget share rather than the logarithm of quantity consumed. This is Working's model that I used as an Engel curve in Section 4.2, although now with the addition of price terms. If we make the change to (5.23) and at the same time add a vector of demographic and other variables z_{hc}, we can write

$$(5.48) \qquad w_{hc} = \alpha^0 + \beta^0 \ln x_{hc} + \gamma^0 . z_{hc} + \theta \ln \pi_c + f_c + u_{ch}^0$$

where w_{hc} is the share of the good in the budget of household h in cluster c. This equation is paired with the unit value equation (5.24), which need only be supplemented with demographic terms to read

$$(5.49) \qquad \ln v_{hc} = \alpha^1 + \beta^1 \ln x_{hc} + \gamma^1 . z_{hc} + \psi \ln \pi_c + u_{hc}^1.$$

Although the same right-hand-side variables appear in (5.48) as in the logarithmic model (5.23), their coefficients are no longer elasticities, so that the model needs reinterpretation and the quality correction formulas must also be reworked. I shall turn to this below, but first it is worth thinking briefly about what kind of demand function is represented by (5.48) and what, if any, is its relationship to standard demand theory.

At a superficial level, (5.48) is closely related to standard demand models like the "almost ideal demand system" in which the budget share is a linear function of the logarithms of total expenditure and prices. However, the analogy is at best incomplete. First, this is a model where utility depends, not only on quantity, but also on quality, so that, at the very least it has to be shown that (5.48) is consistent with the appropriately augmented utility theory. I shall examine this question below, but even when the model is utility-consistent, the fact may be largely irrelevant in practice. Standard empirical demand systems, such as the almost ideal system, are derived under the assumption that all goods are purchased, so that the budget shares are strictly positive. While choice theory certainly permits "corner solutions" in which nothing is bought of some goods, the formal incorporation of corners into tractable empirical demand functions remains a largely unsolved problem. For a one-good model, the presence of corners generates a Tobit model which, as we have seen in Chapter 2, is problematic enough in practical situations. However, when several goods are considered at once, as will be the case in the real applications below, there are a large number of possible regimes depending on which combination of goods is being bought. As a result, equation (5.48) can at best be thought of as a linear approximation to the regression function of the budget share conditional on the right-hand-side variables, averaging over zero and nonzero purchases alike. While this may be more or less satisfactory for the purpose at hand—the modeling of average behavior—the averaging will remove any direct link between (5.48) and utility theory. In this respect, the model is on much the same footing as an *aggregate* demand system where the averaging over agents almost never permits an interpretation in terms of a representative agent.

Consider now what (5.48) and (5.49) imply for the elasticities and how the estimation of the previous section must be modified to deal with the new functional form. In (5.48) the elasticity of the budget share with respect to total expenditure is β^0/w, but since the budget share is unit value times quantity divided by total expenditure, we have

$$(5.50) \qquad \epsilon_x + \beta^1 = (\beta^0/w) + 1$$

where β^1 is, as before, the total expenditure elasticity of quality from the (unchanged) unit value equation (5.24) or (5.49). Similarly, for the price elasticity ϵ_p we have

$$(5.51) \qquad \epsilon_p + \psi = (\theta/w).$$

Because both total expenditure and price elasticities depend on the budget share, neither will be constant but will vary from household to household.

The two-stage estimation technique works in the same general way as before. At the first stage, the budget shares and the logarithms of the unit values are each regressed on the household demographics and the logarithms of total expenditure. The "corrected" y_c^0 and y_c^1 are formed as before, although the former is now a corrected budget share rather than a log quantity. As before the residuals from the first-stage regressions are used to estimate the covariance and variance σ^{01} and σ^{11}, and the results used to calculate $\hat{\phi}$ in (5.45), although given the budget share equation (5.48), what is being estimated is now the ratio $\psi^{-1}\theta$. Again as before, we use the simple quality theory to allow the separate recovery of both parameters, although the formulas are now different. The theoretical relationship between the quality, price and expenditure elasticities in (5.34) gives, on substitution from (5.50) and (5.51) and rearrangement

$$(5.52) \qquad \psi = 1 - \frac{\beta^1(w-\theta)}{\beta^0 + w}.$$

Given $\phi = \psi^{-1}\theta$ and (5.52), θ can therefore be recovered from

$$(5.53) \qquad \theta = \frac{\phi}{1 + (w-\phi)\zeta}$$

where

$$(5.54) \qquad \zeta = \frac{\beta^1}{\beta^0 + w(1-\beta^1)}.$$

If β^1 is small, ζ will be small, and so will be the correction to θ in (5.53); when the income elasticity of quality is small, there will be little shading of unit value in response to price.

With the parameters recovered, the elasticities can be calculated from (5.50) and (5.51). Equations (5.46) and (5.47) remain correct for the variance of $\hat{\phi}$ and the variances and covariances of the other parameters can be obtained using the delta method (see Deaton 1988 for the formulas).

One other practical detail is worth noting. Since not every household reports a purchase, and since unit values are only reported for those who do, there will be unequal numbers of observations for the budget share equation (5.48) and the unit value equation (5.49). Suppose that in cluster c there are n_c households of which n_c^+ record purchases. At the first stage of the estimation, the imbalance in numbers makes no difference. At the second stage, however, when the corrected budget shares and unit values are averaged by cluster, there are different numbers in the budget share average than in the unit value average, and the numbers will differ from village to village. The difference is important when we compute the variances and covariance of the averaged residuals u_c^0 and u_c^1. Since the former is averaged over n_c observations, its variance is σ^{00}/n_c, while the variance for the latter is clearly σ^{11}/n_c^+. Straightforward algebra shows that the covariance is σ^{01}/n_c. As a result, the n_c in equations (5.42) through (5.46) must be replaced by τ and τ^+, respectively, where

$$(5.55) \qquad \tau^{-1} = \lim_{C \to \infty} C^{-1} \Sigma n_c^{-1}; \quad (\tau^+)^{-1} = \lim_{C \to \infty} C^{-1} \Sigma (n_c^+)^{-1}.$$

In practice, these magnitudes are unknown, but estimates of τ^{-1} and $(\tau^+)^{-1}$ can be calculated from the averages in (5.55) ignoring the limits.

Rewriting the model in terms of budget shares, (5.48) and (5.49), takes us close to what we require for implementation. What remains is an exploration of the welfare foundations of the model, of how quality and quantity interact in utility. This analysis will also show how to embed the demand for each good in a system of demand equations. Although the general model is the one that should be used in practice, the simpler case in this subsection is useful for investigating practical econometric issues. In Deaton (1990a), I report a number of Monte Carlo experiments using (5.48) and (5.49). The experiments yield estimates that are correctly centered, in contrast to estimates that do not allow for village fixed effects, or that ignore measurement error. As usual, the price of consistency is an increase in variance. However, the experiments show that the estimator performs adequately even when there are as few as two observations in each village. Increasing the number of villages or clusters is much more important than increasing the number of observations in each. The asymptotic variance formulas worked well and accurately predicted the variance across experiments.

Quality, quantity, and welfare: cross-price effects

In this subsection, I show how quality and quantity can be interpreted within the standard model of utility maximization. At the same time, we shall see how to incorporate cross-price effects. For price and tax reform, where subsidies and taxes are frequently levied on closely related goods, some knowledge of cross-

price effects is essential, and as I argued in Section 5.1, it is one of the main advantages of household survey data that they provide some hope of estimating
these effects. The extension of the model from a single equation to a system of
demand equations is conceptually straightforward, and consists of little more than
adding additional price terms to the budget share equation (5.48). Even so, there
are some theoretical issues that must also be taken care of, particularly the extension of the model of quality under separability to the multigood case, so that we
can handle the effects of changes in the price of one good on the quality choice of
another. These theoretical issues are the topic of this subsection. In the econometric analysis, which is discussed in the next subsection, there is a good deal of what
is essentially book-keeping, and the resulting algebra is a good deal more complex than that required so far. Readers who are willing to take this material on
trust can safely omit the details and move on to Section 5.4 where the empirical
results are presented.

The theoretical basis for a multigood model with quality effects is a utility
function that is separable in each of M commodity groups. Write this as

$$(5.56) \qquad u = V[v_1(q_1),\ldots,v_G(q_G),\ldots,v_M(q_M)]$$

where each q_G is a vector of goods, each element of which is perfectly homogeneous. The group utility functions, which are sometimes referred to as subutility
or felicity functions, have all the properties of the usual utility functions, and I
shall denote the value of each by u_G. Since overall utility is increasing in each of
the subutilities, and since consumption in each group, q_G, affects overall utility
only in so far as it affects group subutility, the consumer will maximize each
$v_G(q_G)$ subject to the amount spent on the group, an amount that I denote by
$x_G = p_G \cdot q_G$. For this subutility maximization problem, define the cost function
$c_G(u_G, p_G)$, the minimum amount of money needed to attain u_G at prices p_G. For
a utility-maximizing consumer, money is spent efficiently, so that

$$(5.57) \qquad x_G = c_G(u_G, p_G).$$

I can now set up the definitions of quality and quantity. Physical quantity is
defined as before, equation (5.25) repeated here for convenience

$$(5.58) \qquad Q_G = k_G \cdot q_G.$$

The utility from the consumption of group G is conveniently measured using
"money-metric utility," the minimum cost need to reach u_G at a reference price
vector p_G^0. Define quality ξ_G implicitly by the identity

$$(5.59) \qquad c_G(u_G, p_G^0) = \xi_G Q_G.$$

According to (5.59), the utility from group G consumption can be expressed as
the product of quality and quantity; in the special case where there is only one

way of attaining utility u_G, which is to buy the quantity q_G, (5.59) reduces to (5.28). We also define the price index π_G as the ratio of costs at actual prices to costs at the reference prices,

$$(5.60) \qquad \pi_G = \frac{c_G(u_G, p_G)}{c_G(u_G, p_G^0)}$$

so that, as before, we have

$$(5.61) \qquad x_G = \pi_G \xi_G Q_G.$$

Expenditure is the product of quantity, quality, and price. In general, the price indexes, π_G, are functions of the utility levels u_G; this will not be so when preferences are homothetic within the group, in which case the pattern of demand in the group is independent of the level of living, and there are no quality effects!

In this formulation, group utility u_G is a monotone increasing function of the product of quality and quantity, (5.59), so that we can write overall utility as

$$(5.62) \qquad u = V^*(\xi_1 Q_1, \ldots, \xi_G Q_G, \ldots, \xi_M Q_M),$$

which, given (5.61), is maximized subject to the budget constraint

$$(5.63) \qquad \sum_1^M \pi_G \xi_G Q_G = x.$$

This is a standard-form utility maximization problem, and will have standard demand functions as solutions. I write these

$$(5.64) \qquad \xi_G Q_G = g_G(x, \pi_1, \ldots, \pi_G, \ldots, \pi_M)$$

which will satisfy all of the standard properties of demand functions: homogeneity, Slutsky symmetry, and negative definiteness of the Slutsky matrix. Provided we treat the product of quality and quantity as the object of preference, the standard apparatus of demand analysis applies as usual.

The demand functions (5.64) are somewhat more complicated than they look. The prices of the composite goods, π_G, defined by (5.60), are each a function of u_G, or equivalently, of $\xi_G Q_G$, so that (5.64) is not an explicit set of demand functions, but a set of equations that has to hold when choices are made optimally. The dependence of the π's on the u's vanishes under the conditions of the Hicks' composite commodity theorem which, in the current context, means that the relative prices of the goods within each group are the same in each cluster. If the constant of proportionality in cluster c is π_{Gc}^*, so that the price vector in the cluster is $p_{Gc} = \pi_{Gc}^* p_G^0$, (5.60) gives $\pi_{Gc} = \pi_{Gc}^*$, which is independent of u_G. In practice, we will not usually want to assume the constancy of relative prices—in areas by water, fish will be cheap, while in arid areas, fish will be dear—and we need only the higher-level assumption that the dependence of π_G on u_G is negligible, for which constant relative prices is a sufficient, but not necessary, condition.

For the empirical work, we draw from the literature and adopt a standard flexible functional form for the demand system (5.64). One suitable form is the almost ideal demand system of Deaton and Muellbauer (1980b), whereby (5.64) takes the form

$$(5.65) \qquad w_G = \alpha_G^0 + \beta_G^0 \ln(x/\pi) + \sum_{H=1}^{M} \theta_{GH}^* \ln\pi_H$$

where (the unsubscripted) π is a linearly homogeneous price index formed from all the prices (see Deaton and Muellbauer for the theoretical definition). Here I follow their practical suggestion of using a Stone index for π whereby

$$(5.66) \qquad \ln\pi = \sum_{H=1}^{M} \bar{w}_H \ln\pi_H$$

and $\bar{w}_H$ is the sample average of the budget share of H. If (5.66) is substituted into (5.65), we have

$$(5.67) \qquad w_G = \alpha_G^0 + \beta_G^0 \ln x + \sum_{H=1}^{M} \theta_{GH} \ln\pi_H$$
$$= \alpha_G^0 + \beta_G^0 \ln x + \sum_{H=1}^{M} (\theta_{GH}^* - \beta_G^0 \bar{w}_H) \ln\pi_H.$$

The unit values $v_G = \xi_G \pi_G$ are themselves functions of total expenditure and the prices, and for lack of any theoretical guidance on functional form, I use the generalization of (5.49),

$$(5.68) \qquad \ln v_G = \alpha_G^1 + \beta_G^1 \ln x + \sum_{H=1}^{M} \psi_{GH} \ln\pi_H$$

where the original scalar quality shading elasticity ψ is replaced by a matrix of elasticities ψ_{GH}. In the absence of quality shading, unit value would be equal to price, the Ψ matrix would be the identity matrix, and α^1 and β^1 would be zero.

Because the budget shares add to unity, the vector α^0 in (5.65) must sum to unity, while the vector β^0, and each column of the θ-matrix, must add to zero. The system should also be homogeneous of degree zero in total expenditure and prices; a doubling of both should double unit values and leave the budget shares unchanged. This will occur if, and only if, the rows of θ_{GH}^* add to zero, or equivalently that, for all G,

$$(5.69) \qquad \Sigma_H \theta_{GH} + \beta_G^0 = 0.$$

Similarly, linear homogeneity of the unit value equation (5.68) requires that, for all groups G,

$$(5.70) \qquad \Sigma_H \psi_{GH} + \beta_G^1 = 1.$$

The adding-up and homogeneity restrictions enable us to "complete" the demand system by adding another commodity defined as "all other goods," and to infer its own- and cross-price elasticities from the adding-up and homogeneity restrictions.

When using unit values to indicate prices, which is the methodological basis for this work, we will never obtain prices for a complete enumeration of consumers' expenditures, since there are many goods that do not have obvious quantity units, and for which only expenditure data are collected. For these goods, we can do no better than an "other goods" category.

The Slutsky (or substitution) matrix of the demand system will be symmetric if, and only if, $\theta_{GH}^* = \theta_{HG}^*$, or equivalently,

$$(5.71) \qquad \theta_{GH} + \beta_G^0 \bar{w}_H = \theta_{HG} + \beta_H^0 \bar{w}_G.$$

It is common in demand analysis to use the symmetry restrictions to add to the precision of the parameter estimates. In the context of price reform it might be thought that such considerations would carry less weight, partly because there are so many observations in the survey data, and partly because the existence of corner solutions—zero purchases—for many households precludes a clean relationship between the theory and its empirical application. Unless we build different models for the different "regimes" comprising different combinations of purchased goods, and then link these regimes within a general statistical model of selection, we cannot follow the parameters of the theory through into the empirical specification. As a result, even though the utility restrictions hold for a single agent who buys all of the goods, they will not hold in the survey data.

However, there are also some arguments for using the restrictions. First, although there are many observations, there is not always a great deal of price variation. In the Pakistani data, there are at least partially successful controls on the prices of sugar and of edible oil, so that even with nearly 10,000 observations, it will be difficult to estimate price elasticities involving these goods. Indeed, the interest in price reform is often at its most intense in countries with a history of price control and we are frequently faced with using survey data with little price variation to try to predict what will happen when markets are liberalized. Second, not all of the restrictions from the theory have the same status, and we might be much more willing to impose absence of money illusion on the empirical demand functions than to impose Slutsky symmetry. Unfortunately, it is the latter that is likely to be the most helpful when we are trying to infer the price elasticities involving a controlled good. In such a situation, we need restrictions from somewhere, and we might use the utility restrictions for want of better ones, just as symmetry and homogeneity are frequently imposed on aggregate data without rigorous justification.

One task remains, to generalize the quality model so as to link the matrices Θ and Ψ, so that they can be separately identified. The multigood treatment of this section permits a direct generalization of equation (5.34). From the definitions of quality and quantity, equations (5.58) and (5.59), we have

$$(5.72) \qquad \ln \xi_G = \ln c(u_G, p_G^0) - \ln(k_G \cdot q_G).$$

As before, note that $q_G = f_G(x_G / \pi_G, p_G^0)$, so that (5.31) generalizes to

$$(5.73) \qquad \frac{\partial \ln \xi_G}{\partial \ln \pi_H} = \frac{\partial \ln \xi_G}{\partial \ln x_G} \left(\frac{\partial \ln x_G}{\partial \ln \pi_H} - 1 \right).$$

Equation (5.32) remains unchanged, so that

$$(5.74) \qquad \frac{\partial \ln \xi_G}{\partial \ln \pi_H} = \frac{\beta_G^1 e_{GH}}{e_G}.$$

In consequence, we have

$$(5.75) \qquad \psi_{GH} = \frac{\partial \ln v_G}{\partial \ln \pi_H} = \delta_{GH} + \frac{\beta_G^1 e_{GH}}{e_G}$$

where δ_{GH} is the Kronecker delta, equal to unity when $G = H$ and zero otherwise. When $G = H$, (5.75) and (5.34) are identical. Otherwise, when the price of one commodity increases, the effects on quality of another are controlled by how much the price increase affects quantity, i.e. by the cross-price elasticity.

Cross-price effects: estimation

A good place to begin is with a final statement of the two equations for the budget share and for the logarithm of unit value. With demographics, fixed effects, and errors included, (5.67) and (5.68) become, for good G, household h, in cluster c

$$(5.76) \qquad w_{Ghc} = \alpha_G^0 + \beta_G^0 \ln x_{hc} + \gamma_G^0 \cdot z_{hc} + \sum_{H=1}^{M} \theta_{GH} \ln \pi_{Hc} + (f_{Gc} + u_{Ghc}^0)$$

$$(5.77) \qquad \ln v_{Ghc} = \alpha_G^1 + \beta_G^1 \ln x_{hc} + \gamma_G^1 \cdot z_{hc} + \sum_{H=1}^{M} \psi_{GH} \ln \pi_{Hc} + u_{Ghc}^1$$

and our task is to estimate the parameters. The first stage is exactly as before; the budget shares, the logarithms of the unit values, the z's, and the logarithms of the x's are demeaned by their cluster means, and the two regressions run using the demeaned variables. Because all of the prices are constant within clusters, the demeaning removes all the prices as well as the fixed effects and so allows consistent estimation of the α's, β's, and γ's. The first-stage estimates are used to compute the village averages

$$(5.78) \qquad \tilde{y}_{Gc}^0 = n_c^{-1} \sum_{i \in c} (w_{Gic} - \tilde{\beta}_G^0 \ln x_{ic} - \tilde{\gamma}_G^0 \cdot z_{ic})$$

$$(5.79) \qquad \tilde{y}_{Gc}^1 = n_{Gc}^{+ -1} \sum_{i \in c} (\ln v_{Gic} - \tilde{\beta}_G^1 \ln x_{ic} - \tilde{\gamma}_G^1 \cdot z_{ic})$$

where n_c is the number of households in cluster c, n_{Gc}^+ is the number of households in the cluster who purchase good G (and thus report unit values), and superimposed tildes indicate estimates from the first, within-cluster stage.

As before, the first-stage regressions are also used to estimate the variances and covariances of the u^0 and u^1 in (5.76) and (5.77), although in place of the original two variances and a covariance there are now $2M$ variances and $M(2M-1)$ covariances. Suppose that Σ, typical element σ_{GH}, is the variance-covariance matrix of the u^0's, that Ω, typical element ω_{GH}, is the variance-covariance matrix of the u^1's, and that X, typical element χ_{GH}, is the covariance matrix of u^1 (on the rows) and u^0 (on the columns). Estimators of these matrices are constructed from

$$(5.80) \qquad \tilde{\sigma}_{GH} = (n-C-k)^{-1} \sum_c \sum_{h \in c} e^0_{Ghc} e^0_{Hhc}$$

$$(5.81) \qquad \tilde{\omega}_{GH} = (n-C-k)^{-1} \sum_c \sum_{h \in c} e^1_{Ghc} e^1_{Hhc}$$

$$(5.82) \qquad \tilde{\chi}_{GH} = (n-C-k)^{-1} \sum_c \sum_{h \in c} e^1_{Ghc} e^0_{Hhc}$$

where e^1 and e^0 are the residuals from the first-stage, within-village unit value and budget share regressions, respectively. In practice, it will often be too much to expect the data to deliver good estimates of all elements of these three matrices, in which case only the diagonal elements need be calculated, and the off-diagonals set to zero. The empirical results in the next section are constructed in this way.

The between-village variance-covariance matrix of the (theoretical, not estimated) y^0_G is written Q, that of the y^1_G is S, their covariance is R, and the elements of these matrices are estimated from (5.78) and (5.79),

$$(5.83) \qquad \tilde{q}_{GH} = \mathrm{cov}(\hat{y}^0_{Gc}, \hat{y}^0_{Hc}), \quad \tilde{s}_{GH} = \mathrm{cov}(\hat{y}^1_{Gc}, \hat{y}^1_{Hc}),$$
$$\tilde{t}_{GH} = \mathrm{cov}(\hat{y}^1_{Gc}, \hat{y}^0_{Hc}).$$

If we were to use the $\hat{y}^0$ and $\hat{y}^1$ to run a between-village multivariate ordinary least squares regression, we would obtain

$$(5.84) \qquad B_{OLS} = \tilde{S}^{-1} \tilde{T}$$

where the Gth column of B_{OLS} is the vector of OLS coefficients of $\hat{y}^0_G$ regressed on all the $\hat{y}^1$'s as explanatory variables. However, as in the univariate case, this estimator takes no account of the influence of u^0 and u^1 when the cluster size is finite. The corrected estimator is written

$$(5.85) \qquad \tilde{B} = (\tilde{S} - \tilde{\Omega}\, \tilde{N}_+^{-1})^{-1} (\tilde{T} - \tilde{X}\tilde{N}^{-1})$$

where $\tilde{N}_+^{-1} = C^{-1}\sum_c D(n_c^+)^{-1}$, $D(n_c^+)$ is a diagonal matrix formed from the elements of n_{Gc}^+, and the matrix $\tilde{N}^{-1}$ is the corresponding quantity formed from the n_c's. The estimator (5.85) is the multivariate generalization of (5.45) in the univariate case, so that the matrix B now plays the role previously played by the scalar ϕ. As in that case, its probability limit in the presence of the quality effects is not Θ, but the matrix generalization of the ratio of Θ to Ψ,

$$(5.86) \qquad \mathrm{plim}\, \tilde{B} = B = (\Psi')^{-1}\Theta'.$$

The transposition is because $\tilde{B}$ has the estimates for each equation down the columns, whereas in Θ they are arranged along the rows.

As before, the Θ matrix is not identified without further information, here supplied by the separability theory of quality. The quality theory delivered equation (5.75) above, which in matrix notation is

$$(5.87) \qquad \Psi = I + D(\beta^1)D(e)^{-1}E.$$

E is the matrix of price elasticities, and the diagonalization operator $D(.)$ converts its vector argument into a diagonal matrix. The matrix of price elasticities and the vector of total expenditure elasticities are linked to the model parameters by

$$(5.88) \qquad E = -\Psi + D(\bar{w})^{-1}\Theta$$

$$(5.89) \qquad e = \iota - \beta^1 + \beta^0 D(\bar{w})^{-1}.$$

Equations (5.87) through (5.89) can be combined with (5.86) so as to retrieve Θ and thus E from B,

$$(5.90) \qquad \Theta = B'\Psi = B'[I - D(\zeta)B' + D(\zeta)D(\bar{w})]^{-1}$$

$$(5.91) \qquad E = [D(\bar{w})^{-1}B' - I]\Psi = [D(\bar{w})^{-1}B' - I][I - D(\zeta)B' + D(\zeta)D(\bar{w})]^{-1}$$

where the elements of ζ are defined by

$$(5.92) \qquad \zeta_G = [(1-\beta_G^1)\bar{w}_G + \beta_G^0]^{-1}\beta_G^1.$$

This completes the estimation stage; the first-stage parameters and residuals are used to make the covariance matrices in (5.80) through (5.83), the results are used to calculate the matrix $\tilde{B}$ in (5.85), an estimate that is corrected using the first-stage estimates to give the Θ parameters or elasticity matrix using (5.90) or (5.91).

Variance-covariance matrices for the estimated parameters and elasticities can be obtained by bootstrapping—which is the approach used for the results reported here—or analytical formulas can be derived that are valid in large samples. The algebra for the latter requires the introduction of a good deal of new notation, and is not given here. Intrepid readers can use the results in Deaton and Grimard (1992) and Deaton (1990a) as templates for the slightly different expressions here. The main value of such an exercise would be to provide asymptotic approximations that could be used to improve the bootstrap calculations, as described in Section 1.4. However, I suspect that a straightforward application of the bootstrap is adequate, and it certainly delivers standard errors that are close to those from the asymptotic formulas. In practice, I have adopted a further shortcut, which is to bootstrap only the second stage of the estimation. The first-stage, within-cluster, estimates are calculated—with standard errors routinely provided by STATA—and (5.78) and (5.79) are used to calculate estimates of the cluster averages of the "purged" unit values and budget shares. This cluster-level data set is then treated as the base data from which bootstrap samples are drawn. This shortcut saves a large amount of computer time because the first-stage estimation is much more time-consuming than the second stage. It is justified by inspection of the asymptotic variance formulas, which show that it is the contribution from the second stage that dominates, and from practical experience which shows that the first-stage contribution to the variance is negligible.

Technical note: completing the system

This note, which is intended only for those who wish to pursue their own calculations, and need to understand the code, lays out the calculations needed to complete the system by adding a single composite commodity, "nonfood." I also explain how to impose symmetry, at least approximately. The calculations start from the $M \times M$ matrix Θ defined in (5.67) and calculated from (5.90). Write the corresponding $(M+1) \times (M+1)$ matrix for the complete system Θ^x, which differs from Θ by having an additional row and column. Using the homogeneity restriction (5.69), the final column of Θ^x is given by

$$(5.93) \qquad \theta^x_{GM+1} = -\beta^0_G - \sum_{H=1}^{M} \theta_{GH}.$$

The final row of Θ^x is computed from the adding-up restriction, so that

$$(5.94) \qquad \theta^x_{M+1G} = -\sum_{H=1}^{M} \theta^x_{HG}.$$

In the same way, the adding-up restrictions are used to extend the vectors α^0, β^0, and $\bar{w}$ to α^{0x}, β^{0x}, and $\bar{w}^x$. The vector of quality elasticities β^1 cannot be extended in the same way; instead it is necessary to assume some plausible quality elasticity for the nonfood category. That done, (5.92) is used to calculate the extended vector ζ^x. From (5.90) applied to the complete system, we have

$$(5.95) \qquad \Theta^x = B^{x\prime} \Psi^x$$

$$(5.96) \qquad \Psi^x = I + D(\zeta^x) D(\bar{w}^x) - D(\zeta^x) B^{x\prime}$$

so that, eliminating B^x,

$$(5.97) \qquad \Psi^x = [I + D(\zeta^x) D(\bar{w}^x)]^{-1} [I + D(\zeta^x) \Theta^x].$$

The full-system matrix of price elasticities and of total expenditure elasticities are then calculated from (5.88) and (5.89).

Satisfying the symmetry condition (5.71) requires the imposition of a nonlinear restriction on the matrix B. Rather than attempt this, I have fallen back on an approximation that relies on the validity of the empirical finding that the quality elasticities are small. In this case, Ψ is approximately equal to the identity matrix, so that Θ and B' are approximately equal. In view of this, the symmetry condition used in the code is that the matrix

(5.98) $$B + \bar{w}\,\beta^{0\prime}$$

be symmetric. (An alternative would be simply to require that B be symmetric.) To see how the restricted estimate is obtained, we need some notation; a good introduction to the concepts used here is provided by Magnus and Neudecker (1988). The "vec" operator converts a matrix into a vector by stacking its columns vertically. The Kronecker product of two matrices, as in $A \otimes B$, is the matrix formed by multiplying each element of A by the whole matrix B, and arranging the results into a matrix patterned after A, so that the top left-hand submatrix is $a_{11}B$, with $a_{12}B$ to its right, and $a_{21}B$ underneath, and so on. The "commutation" matrix K is defined by what it does, which is to rearrange the vec of a matrix B so that it becomes the vec of the transpose of B,

(5.99) $$K\,\text{vec}B = \text{vec}B'.$$

Finally, we require the matrix L, a "selection" matrix which picks out from the vec of a square matrix the elements that lie below the diagonal in the original matrix.

Given these definitions, the restriction (5.98) can be rewritten as

(5.100) $$L(I-K)(\text{vec}B + \beta^0 \otimes \bar{w}) = 0$$

where I have used the fact that $\text{vec}(ab') = b \otimes a$. The selection matrix L is required here in order to prevent each symmetry restriction being applied twice. Without it, we would be trying to impose that element $\{1,2\}$ should equal element $\{2,1\}$ as well as that element $\{2,1\}$ should equal element $\{1,2\}$, a redundancy that will lead to singularities in the matrices to be inverted. If we write b for $\text{vec}B$, (5.100) can be written in the familiar linear form

(5.101) $$Rb = r$$

with R and r defined from (5.100). We already have an unrestricted estimate from (5.85). Write A for the matrix $\tilde{S} - \tilde{\Omega}\tilde{N}_+^{-1}$ in (5.85), and define the restricted estimate of B, by

(5.102) $$\text{vec}\tilde{B}_R = \text{vec}\tilde{B} + (I \otimes A)^{-1}[R(I \otimes A)^{-1}R']^{-1}(r - R\,\text{vec}\tilde{B}).$$

5.4 Empirical results for India and Pakistan

In this section, I take the technical apparatus for granted and return to my main purpose of deriving demand parameters for the analysis of price reform. I begin with a preliminary subsection on data issues and the selection of goods, and then turn to the first- and second-stage results.

Preparatory analysis

The first choice in any demand analysis is the choice of goods to be included. Because we are interested in price and tax reform, the analysis must distinguish goods with different (actual or potential) tax rates. In some cases, there are goods of particular concern, for example those whose nutrient content is important, or goods that are substitutes or complements for the goods whose prices might be altered. There are also data limitations. We cannot estimate the demand for a good whose price is constant across the sample, and it will be difficult to obtain reliable estimates of goods that are purchased by only a few households. Larger demand systems are also harder to deal with than small ones; the more goods, the greater the computational problem, and the harder it is to report the results.

It is of the greatest importance to subject the data to close scrutiny before undertaking the formal analysis. In addition to outliers or incorrectly coded data, there are special problems associated with the unit values which must be carefully checked for plausibility. We have already seen one way of doing so, by checking the reported unit values against other price data, by looking at seasonal and spatial patterns, and by an analysis of variance. Univariate analysis of the unit values is also important in order to expose difficulties that can arise if spatial variation in tastes causes spatial differences in unit values. The problem arises in its most acute form when the commodity group consists of a single good that comes in different forms. Consider, for example, the category "fish." The main components of the group will usually be "dried fish" and "fresh fish," with different unit values per kilo; suppose that, allowing for transport and processing margins (the cost of drying the fish), a dried fish costs a little more than the same fish fresh, but weighs less because it contains less water. Suppose also that the country has a coastline but no lakes or rivers, and that the proportion of dried fish rises with the distance from the sea. Even if everyone consumes exactly the same number of fish, some fresh and some dried but with added water, there will be a negative spatial correlation between the weight of fish purchased and their unit values, a correlation that we are in danger of interpreting as the price elasticity of demand.

The first-stage estimates

The first-stage estimates of the unit value equations are presented in Tables 5.2 and 5.3, and have already been discussed in Section 5.2 above. Tables 5.5 and 5.6 present a selection of coefficients from the corresponding within-village regressions for the budget shares. The last column of each table lists the sample averages of the budget shares for each good. Wheat, including bread and flour, is the basic staple in most of Pakistan, and accounts for 12.8 percent of the budget of rural households. In rural Maharashtra, wheat accounts for only 3.7 percent of the budget, and the most important single category is *jowar*, which accounts for 12.3 percent of the total, and is followed in importance by rice, with 8.2 percent. All of these basic foodstuffs attract negative β^0 coefficients, and thus have total expenditure elasticities that are less than unity. The total expenditure elasticity of

Table 5.5. Within-village regressions for budget shares, rural Pakistan, 1984–85

Food	ln x	ln n	e_x	$\bar{w}$
Wheat	−0.068	0.070	0.37	0.128
	(53.4)	(47.0)		
Rice	−0.006	0.007	0.68	0.027
	(7.3)	(8.4)		
Dairy products	0.024	−0.007	1.05	0.127
	(12.0)	(3.1)		
Meat	0.009	−0.006	1.10	0.037
	(13.1)	(7.6)		
Oils and fats	−0.024	0.013	0.42	0.041
	(39.9)	(17.7)		
Sugar	−0.004	0.002	0.86	0.029
	(7.9)	(3.9)		
Other foods	−0.040	0.020	0.59	0.122
	(38.3)	(16.1)		

Note: Absolute values of *t*-values are shown in brackets.
Source: Deaton and Grimard (1992).

wheat in Pakistan is 0.37, that of *jowar* in Maharashtra is 0.29. The elasticity of rice, which is the secondary cereal in both surveys, is 0.68 in Pakistan and 0.67 in Maharashtra. Meat and dairy products have greater than unity elasticities in both countries, and edible oil and sugar are necessities in both. These results suggest two similar populations, but with different cereals playing the primary and secondary roles in each.

The relationship between the coefficients on total expenditure and household size conform to the by now familiar pattern where the estimate for $\ln n$ has the opposite sign to that for $\ln x$, but is smaller in absolute magnitude. For the basic cereals, wheat in Pakistan and coarse cereals and rice in Maharashtra, the coefficients on household size are close to (minus) the coefficients on total expenditure, so that the per capita consumption is approximately determined by PCE independently of household size.

Price responses: the second-stage estimates for Pakistan

The top panel of Table 5.7 presents the first set of own- and cross-price elasticities for rural Pakistan together with bootstrapped estimates of "standard errors." The numbers are arrayed so that the elasticity in row i and column j is the response of consumption of good i to the price of good j. The bootstrapped "standard errors" are calculated by making 1,000 draws from the cluster (second-stage) data, recalculating the estimates for each, and then finding (half) the length of the interval that is symmetric around the bootstrapped mean, and that contains 68.3 percent of the bootstrapped estimates. If the distribution of estimates were normal, this interval would be one standard deviation on either side of the mean,

Table 5.6. Within-village regressions for budget shares, rural Maharashtra, 1983

Food	ln x	ln n	e_x	$\bar{w}$
Rice	−0.023	0.020	0.67	0.082
	(11.5)	(9.6)		
Wheat	0.006	0.003	1.12	0.037
	(4.2)	(2.1)		
Jowar	−0.082	0.084	0.29	0.123
	(33.2)	(7.5)		
Other cereals	−0.015	0.017	0.46	0.035
	(9.3)	(9.6)		
Pulses and gram	−0.018	0.011	0.67	0.060
	(20.8)	(11.8)		
Dairy products	0.012	−0.006	1.11	0.053
	(7.6)	(3.4)		
Oils and fats	−0.011	0.008	0.79	0.060
	(12.7)	(8.3)		
Meat, eggs, and fish	0.008	0.000	1.05	0.034
	(6.3)	(0.1)		
Vegetables	−0.018	0.007	0.59	0.047
	(26.5)	(10.3)		
Fruit and nuts	0.002	−0.001	0.98	0.023
	(3.0)	(0.9)		
Sugar and *gur*	−0.013	0.008	0.65	0.043
	(20.2)	(11.9)		

Note: Absolute values of *t*-values are shown in brackets.

Source: Deaton, Parikh, and Subramanian (1994, Tables 2, 5, and 6).

which is why I refer to the numbers as "standard errors" but, in general, there is no reason to suppose that the distributions have finite moments. In the top panel of the table, I have completed the system, but have not imposed symmetry. Province and quarter effects in demands are allowed for by regressing the corrected cluster averages of budget shares and unit values on quarterly and province dummies and then using the residuals in the second-stage calculations. The rationale for this will be discussed in the next subsection.

The estimates are relatively well determined, at least in comparison to similar estimates from time-series data. Apart from sugar—on which more below—all of the diagonal terms—the own-price elasticities—are negative, and that for rice is less than −1. Only a minority of the cross-price effects is significantly different from zero; several of these involve the two goods rice and meat. According to these estimates, increases in the price of rice increase the demand for all other goods except other foods, and there are statistically significant effects for oils and fats and for sugar. Similarly, an increase in the price of meat has significantly positive effects on the demand for rice and for oils and fats. The estimated elasticities in the sugar and oils and fats columns are poorly determined; this is because there is little variance of sugar and oil prices in the sample. Although the estimated

Table 5.7. Unconstrained and symmetry-constrained estimates of price elasticities, rural Pakistan, 1984–85

Food	Wheat	Rice	Dairy	Meat	Oils & fats	Sugar	Other foods	Nonfoods
Unconstrained estimates								
Wheat	−0.61 (0.10)	0.16 (0.07)	0.02 (0.04)	−0.06 (0.07)	0.30 (0.31)	−0.14 (0.27)	−0.09 (0.10)	−0.03 (0.39)
Rice	−0.06 (0.45)	−2.16 (0.25)	−0.25 (0.12)	0.66 (0.32)	−1.20 (1.00)	−0.59 (1.10)	−0.14 (0.37)	2.95 (1.58)
Dairy	0.13 (0.14)	0.09 (0.07)	−0.89 (0.04)	−0.13 (0.09)	0.10 (0.39)	0.72 (0.34)	−0.24 (0.14)	−0.84 (0.46)
Meat	−0.58 (0.22)	0.18 (0.14)	−0.05 (0.08)	−0.57 (0.18)	−1.57 (0.70)	−0.75 (0.60)	0.82 (0.20)	1.29 (0.81)
Oils and fats	0.09 (0.05)	0.12 (0.03)	0.01 (0.02)	0.09 (0.04)	−0.80 (0.18)	−0.12 (0.14)	−0.01 (0.05)	0.46 (0.23)
Sugar	0.02 (0.17)	0.34 (0.09)	0.07 (0.05)	0.15 (0.10)	−0.16 (0.51)	0.11 (0.53)	0.05 (0.15)	−1.36 (0.75)
Other foods	0.22 (0.09)	−0.12 (0.05)	0.02 (0.03)	0.08 (0.06)	0.24 (0.41)	0.09 (0.25)	−0.51 (0.10)	−0.62 (0.40)
Nonfoods	0.09 (0.03)	0.02 (0.01)	0.00 (0.01)	0.03 (0.02)	−0.06 (0.07)	0.08 (0.06)	0.03 (0.02)	−0.60 (0.09)
Symmetry-constrained estimates								
Wheat	−0.63 (0.10)	0.11 (0.05)	0.03 (0.04)	−0.08 (0.05)	0.08 (0.05)	−0.01 (0.05)	0.10 (0.07)	−0.04 (0.15)
Rice	0.49 (0.27)	−2.04 (0.22)	−0.14 (0.11)	0.47 (0.17)	0.44 (0.13)	0.36 (0.12)	−0.58 (0.18)	0.20 (0.38)
Dairy	−0.05 (0.03)	−0.04 (0.02)	−0.90 (0.04)	−0.03 (0.02)	−0.02 (0.01)	0.02 (0.01)	−0.05 (0.03)	0.00 (0.05)
Meat	−0.40 (0.20)	0.33 (0.13)	−0.10 (0.08)	−0.54 (0.18)	0.14 (0.10)	0.04 (0.09)	0.40 (0.16)	−1.11 (0.32)
Oils and fats	0.10 (0.06)	0.11 (0.03)	0.01 (0.02)	0.06 (0.03)	−0.81 (0.18)	−0.10 (0.10)	0.02 (0.07)	0.44 (0.23)
Sugar	−0.08 (0.21)	0.29 (0.10)	0.11 (0.06)	0.06 (0.11)	−0.34 (0.34)	0.09 (0.53)	0.12 (0.18)	−1.04 (0.72)
Other food	0.07 (0.07)	−0.11 (0.10)	0.01 (0.03)	0.13 (0.04)	0.01 (0.06)	0.03 (0.04)	−0.50 (0.09)	−0.24 (0.12)
Nonfoods	0.05 (0.02)	0.00 (0.01)	0.00 (0.01)	0.04 (0.01)	−0.03 (0.03)	0.04 (0.03)	0.07 (0.02)	−0.58 (0.06)

Note: The rows show the commodity being affected and the columns the commodity whose price is changing. The figures in brackets are obtained from 1,000 replications of the bootstrap using the cluster-level data and are defined as half the length of the interval around the bootstrap mean that contains 0.638 (the fraction of a normal random variable within two standard deviations of the mean) of the bootstrap replications.

Source: Author's calculations using Household Income and Expenditure Survey, 1984–85.

own-price elasticity of sugar is positive, it has a large standard error, and is not significantly different from zero. Indeed, the standard errors in these two columns are two to three times larger than those elsewhere in the table.

Given the lack of information in the survey on sugar and oil prices, the symmetry-constrained estimates deserve attention. Although the theoretical restriction cannot be rigorously defended, it offers us the choice between some answers and no answers, and will guarantee that the estimates satisfy unique substitution–complementarity patterns, ruling out the possibility that good a is a substitute for good b when good b is a complement for good a.

The restricted estimates for the full system are given in the bottom panel of the table. In those cases where the previous estimates were well determined, which are the goods whose unit values show substantial variation in the data, there is little change in the estimates, although the restrictions bring some increase in estimated precision. However, there are large reductions in the standard errors in the sugar and oil columns, because symmetry allows us to use the effect of (say) rice on sugar, something that is well determined because of the variability in rice prices, to "fill in" the estimate of the effect of sugar on rice. Of course, symmetry cannot help with the own-price elasticities, nor can adding up and homogeneity, which are being used to complete the system, not to impose cross-equation restrictions. As a result, the own-price elasticities for both sugar and oil still have large standard errors, and the estimate for the former remains (insignificantly) positive.

The symmetry restriction also helps pin down some of the other estimates. The substitutability between rice and wheat—an effect that is of considerable importance for price reform in an economy where both are subsidized—is similar in the top and bottom panels, but is more precise in the latter. The pattern of elasticities shows that meat, oils, and sugar are also substitutes for rice. The final row and column relates to the "ghost" category of nonfood, where we have no price data, but where the elasticities are determined by the theoretical restrictions. Appropriately enough, the standard errors in the last column are large.

The configuration of these elasticities is very different from what would be the case if we had used a demand model based on additive preferences, such as the linear expenditure system. Such models not only restrict the cross-price elasticities to be small, as is mostly the case here, but also enforces an approximate proportionality that has dramatic effects for tax policy. The estimates in Tables 5.5 and 5.7 show no such proportionality. Table 5.5 estimates that meat and dairy products are luxuries and rice a necessity, and yet Table 5.7 estimates that rice is more price elastic than is either dairy products or meat. Taxing rice is therefore doubly unattractive compared with taxing either of the other two goods. I shall turn to these issues in more detail in the next and final section.

Price estimates and taste variation: Maharashtra

Table 5.8 provides a first look at the price elasticities for Maharashtra, but is primarily designed to explore another issue, which is the extent to which we should

Table 5.8. The effects of alternative specification on own-price elasticities, rural Maharashtra, 1983

Food	Quarters & regions	Neither quarters nor regions	Quarters only	Regions only
Rice	−1.19	−2.38	−2.31	−1.10
Wheat	−1.29	−1.17	−1.25	−1.22
Jowar	−0.52	−0.80	−0.81	−0.55
Other cereals	−3.31	−3.39	−3.65	−3.17
Pulses	−0.53	−0.76	−0.77	−0.53
Dairy products	−0.15	−0.61	−0.53	−0.22
Edible oils	−0.40	−0.48	−0.42	−0.49
Meat	−1.08	−1.84	−1.85	−1.05
Vegetables	−0.73	−0.74	−0.82	−0.71
Fruit	−1.09	−1.04	−1.02	−1.12
Sugar and *gur*	−0.20	−0.29	−0.33	−0.18
All cereals	−0.28	−0.38	−0.38	−0.22
All foods	−0.27	−0.32	−0.30	−0.26

Source: Deaton, Parikh, and Subramanian (1994 Table 7).

make separate allowance for regional and temporal taste variation that is unre lated to price, and whether we wish to require that demand respond to seasonal price differences in the same way as it responds to spatial price differences. Rice may usually be 10 percent cheaper at the beginning of the year than in the summer, and it may generally be 10 percent cheaper in one district than another. But seasonal and regional differences in tastes may result in differences in demands not being the same in the two situations, even once we have controlled for incomes, demographics, and other observable covariates. Of course, if we imposed no structure on tastes, and allow demands to vary arbitrarily from village to village, it would be impossible to estimate any parameters. My preferred procedure is to allow quarterly and regional dummies, and the (unconstrained) own-price elasticities from this specification are reported in the first column of Table 5.8, together with aggregate elasticities for cereals and the sum of the foods, calculated on the assumption that prices change proportionally for all components of the aggregate.

Columns two through four show the effects on these own-price elasticities of excluding both sets of dummies, of including only quarterly dummies, and of including only regional dummies. The important issue turns out to be whether or not regional dummies are included. The estimates in the first and last columns, where regions are included, are close to one another, as are the estimates in the second and third columns, where regions are excluded. In most but not all cases, the estimates in the central columns are absolutely larger than those in the outer columns. One interpretation runs in terms of the long-run effects of prices. Some interregional price differences are of very long standing, and it is plausible on

Table 5.9. Symmetry-constrained estimates of price elasticities, rural Maharashtra, 1983

Food	Rice	Wheat	Jowar	Other cereals	Pulses	Dairy products	Edible oils	Meat	Vegetables	Fruit	Sugar	Other goods
Rice	**-1.05**	0.28	0.37	**-0.46**	**-0.71**	**-0.33**	-0.19	-0.30	-0.02	-0.14	0.24	**1.13**
Wheat	0.63	**-1.32**	-0.18	**0.42**	0.40	0.28	-0.05	-0.09	-0.03	0.02	-0.27	-0.94
Jowar	**0.27**	-0.02	**-0.45**	**0.54**	0.04	0.12	0.08	**0.22**	0.06	0.03	**-0.26**	**-0.94**
Other cereals	**-1.15**	**0.47**	**2.04**	**-3.29**	-0.12	0.16	0.21	**-0.33**	0.14	0.07	**0.21**	**1.02**
Pulses	**-0.95**	**0.25**	0.04	-0.07	**-0.57**	0.04	0.10	-0.03	**0.22**	**0.11**	**0.29**	-0.04
Dairy products	**-0.57**	0.19	0.18	0.08	0.02	-0.13	0.17	-0.01	-0.09	-0.05	**0.21**	**-1.18**
Edible oils	-0.27	-0.01	0.12	0.11	0.09	**0.16**	**-0.28**	0.06	0.03	0.04	**0.32**	**-1.11**
Meat	**-0.81**	-0.10	**0.73**	**-0.37**	-0.10	-0.01	0.09	**-1.12**	0.16	-0.02	0.15	0.18
Vegetables	-0.03	-0.00	0.12	0.10	**0.31**	-0.08	0.05	0.13	**-0.66**	0.05	-0.15	-0.44
Fruit	**-0.57**	0.04	0.11	0.09	**0.29**	-0.12	0.09	-0.03	0.09	**-1.09**	-0.02	0.04
Sugar and *gur*	0.48	-0.22	**-0.82**	**0.16**	**0.44**	**0.28**	**0.47**	0.13	-0.17	-0.00	-0.33	**-1.12**
Other goods	**-0.18**	0.06	**0.26**	-0.04	0.03	**0.10**	**0.12**	-0.01	**0.05**	0.00	**0.09**	**-0.85**

Note: Estimates shown in boldface are greater in absolute value than twice their bootstrapped standard errors. For the description of bootstrapped standard errors, see the note to Table 5.7.

Source: Deaton, Parikh, and Subramanian (1994 Table 8).

general theoretical grounds that long-run price elasticities are absolutely larger than short-term elasticities. In consequence, regional dummies may capture some of the long-run price effects, and estimated price elasticities will be lower when regional dummies are included. When we consider price reform proposals, we are probably not greatly interested in effects that take many years, perhaps even centuries, to be established, so that the relevant estimates are the generally lower figures that come from inclusion of the dummies.

Table 5.9 gives the final set of results, obtained by completing the system and by imposing the symmetry restriction; the patterns in this table are not very different from the unconstrained estimates which are therefore not shown here. With 12 goods, the inclusion of standard errors makes it very hard to read the table, so I have highlighted those estimates that are more than twice their (bootstrapped) standard errors. As in the Pakistani case, the credibility and usefulness of symmetry is enhanced by the fact that the important and well-determined elasticities in the table, particularly the own-price elasticities, are changed very little by the imposition of the restriction.

The results show a number of important patterns, particularly of substitutability between the various foods. Rice, wheat, and *jowar* are substitutes, as are *jowar* and other coarse cereals. Sensibly enough, pulses and dairy products are complements with rice, but pulses are substitutes for vegetables, fruit and nuts, and sugar and *gur*. Sugar is a substitute for other cereals, edible oils, and dairy products, as well as for pulses, but is complementary with *jowar*. The substitutability between edible oils and sugar is important because the former is taxed—implicitly through protection of domestic processing—and the latter subsidized, so that we need to look at both together when thinking about reform.

It is instructive to compare these estimates with those for Pakistan. In Pakistan, the staple food is wheat, rather than *jowar*, and as incomes rise, the movement is towards rice, as opposed to towards rice and then wheat in Maharashtra. As was the case for the total expenditure elasticities, and with allowance for the different roles of the different foods, the elasticities are similar. The own-price elasticity for wheat in rural Pakistan is estimated to be –0.63, while that for the "superior" rice is –2.04. In Table 5.9, *jowar* has a price elasticity of –0.45, while the estimates for rice and wheat are –1.05 and –1.32, respectively. In both cases rice and wheat are substitutes, in Pakistan the elasticity of rice with respect to the wheat price is 0.49, compared with 0.63 for the estimated elasticity of wheat with respect to the rice price in Maharashtra.

5.5 Looking at price and tax reform

I am now in a position to return to the main purpose of the chapter, the analysis of price and tax reform. Spatial price variation has been investigated, a model proposed, and parameters estimated. It is now time to use the results to investigate the consequences of various kinds of price reform in India and Pakistan. A good deal of the work in such exercises is concerned with the description of the environment, with how actual taxes and subsidies work, and with the derivation of shadow prices. Given the length of this chapter, and the fact that I have nothing new to add to these topics, I content myself with a brief description of the background in each country, and with a description of how the results of Section 5.4 can be combined with the theoretical formulas in Section 5.1. I start with the descriptions of each country, then discuss how to adapt the formulas of Section 5.1 to accommodate the empirical results, and conclude with the policy evaluation.

Shadow taxes and subsidies in Pakistan

The implementation of the tax reform formula (5.9) or (5.12) requires information on the consumption of the various commodities, which we have from the survey, the price derivatives, which have been estimated in the previous section, social income weights, which are discussed below, and shadow prices. Ahmad, Coady, and Stern (1988) have estimated a complete set of shadow prices for Pakistan based on an 86 × 86 input-output table for 1976, and Ahmad and Stern (1990, 1991) use these shadow prices in their tax reform experiments. However, these prices embody a large number of assumptions, about shadow prices for land, labor, and assets as well as, most crucially, judgments about which goods are tradeable (further divided into importables and exportables) and which goods are nontraded. These assumptions all have a role in determining the shadow prices, and while the procedure itself is unimpeachable, the use of their prices for the current exercise makes it very difficult to isolate the role played in the reform proposals by each of the different elements in the story. Instead, I shall work here with an illustrative set of shadow prices for the eight goods in the demand analysis. These prices are illustrative only in the sense that they do not claim to take into account all the ingredients that should ideally be included in shadow prices. However, they are based on the actual situation in Pakistan, and they are simple and transparent enough so that we can see how features of that situation enter into the analysis of price reform.

The crucial commodities are wheat, rice, and sugar. Rice and wheat sell at domestic prices that are substantially lower than their world prices at the official exchange rate. According to the *Pakistan Economic Survey* (Government of Pakistan, annual), the border price for both rice and wheat was approximately 40 percent above the domestic price in the mid-80s. Both are tradeable, and for both I work with accounting ratios (shadow prices divided by consumer prices) of 1.4. In the case of sugar, there is a heavily protected domestic refining industry, and the border price of refined sugar is some 60 percent of the domestic price. Oils and fats are also protected by a system of taxes and subsidies with the result that the border price is perhaps 95 percent of the domestic price. For the other four goods in the system, I work with accounting ratios of unity. Although there are tariffs and taxes on many nonfood items, which would call for accounting ratios less than unity, many other items are nontraded, so that their shadow prices depend on the shadow price or conversion factor for labor, which, given the pricing of wheat and rice, is likely greater than unity. The experiments are therefore conducted under the supposition that the ratio of shadow prices to consumer prices for the eight goods (wheat, rice, dairy, meat, oils and fats, sugar, other food, nonfood) are given by the vector (1.4, 1.4, 1.0, 1.0, 0.95, 0.6, 1.0, 1.0).

It is important to be precise about exactly which policy experiments are being considered, and which are not. The instruments that are being considered here are instruments that increase or decrease the consumer price of the good, as would be the case, for example, if there were a value-added tax, or if the good had a fixed world price and were imported over a tariff. Such instruments may be available in Pakistan for sugar or for oils. However, to the extent that the rice and wheat subsidies are maintained by export taxes, the experiments described here do not correspond to what would happen if the export tax were changed. An increase in an export tax increases consumer welfare at the same time as it increases government revenue, so that if only these two effects were considered, as is the case in (5.9) and (5.12), it would be desirable to increase the tax indefinitely. Of course, export taxes are limited by the supply responses of farmers, as well as by international demand when the country has some monopoly power, as is the case for Pakistan with *basmati*. An export tax is an instrument that alters not only consumer prices but also producer prices, and it cannot be fully analyzed without looking at the supply responses. The calculations here, which look only at the demand side, correspond to a different hypothetical experiment, in which producer and consumer prices are separated. This would suppose that the government procures the total output of rice and wheat at one set of prices, that it sells the commodities either to foreigners at world prices, or to domestic consumers at a third set of prices. It is the consequences of changing these domestic prices that can be examined using the apparatus described above. Of course, these are artificial experiments which are not feasible in practice. Farmers who grow wheat or rice cannot be charged one price for consumption and paid another for procurement. However, more realistic policies will have the same effects as those described here, plus additional effects that work through the supply side. What I have to say here is only a part of the story, but it is a part that has to be understood if well-informed policy decisions are to be made.

Shadow taxes and subsidies in India

The Indian reform exercise is rendered somewhat artificial by the fact that the survey data come from Maharashtra, rather than all India. In consequence, I focus only on the major distortions in Indian agricultural policy, and once again make no attempt to derive a full set of shadow prices; for an example of the latter for 1979/80 based on the data used in the Technical Note to the Sixth Indian Plan (see Ahmad, Coady, and Stern 1986). Indian domestic prices of rice and of wheat are held below their world prices by the Public Distribution System (PDS) which procures and stockpiles cereals, and which sells them to consumers through "fair-price" shops. While purchases in fair-price shops are rationed, so that above the ration, the marginal price is the free-market price—which is presumably higher than it would be in the absence of PDS—we simplify by treating the PDS as if it straightforwardly subsidized rice and wheat. The other important distortion that we incorporate is the effective taxation of edible oils. The government protects the domestic groundnut processing industry, and in consequence the prices of edible oils are above the world prices. Gulati, Hansen, and Pursell (1990) calculate that, on average from 1980 to 1987, the domestic price of rice was 67 percent of its world price, that of wheat was 80 percent of the world price, and that of groundnuts was 150 percent of the world price. These translate into tax factors, the (shadow) tax share in the domestic price $\tau_i / (1 + \tau_i)$ of –0.50, –0.25, and 0.33 for rice, wheat and groundnut oil, so that the accounting ratios for the 12 goods (rice, wheat, *jowar*, other cereals, pulses, dairy products, edible oils, meat, vegetables, fruit, sugar, other goods) are (1.5, 1.25, 1.00, 1.00, 1.00, 1.00, 0.67, 1.00, 1.00, 1.00, 1.00, 1.00). While these are stylized figures, and ignore other price distortions in food prices, like the Pakistani figures, they are based on the reality of the 1980s, and will serve to illustrate the general points of the analysis.

Adapting the price reform formulas

Before using the formulas of Section 5.5, I need to match them to the empirical model, and more substantively, I need to adapt the theory to a world in which prices are not the same for everyone and where both quality and quantity adapts to price. To do the latter requires an assumption about how tax changes affect the different prices that people pay, and the simplest such assumption is that changes in taxes affect all prices proportionately within a commodity group. This makes most sense when taxes are *ad valorem*, and may fail in some cases, for example if a good is taxed through an import tariff, if spatial price variation reflects transport costs, and if transport costs depend on volume rather than value.

Suppose that the (shadow) tax rate on good i is τ_i, so that the price paid, π_i, is $\bar{\pi}_i (1 + \tau_i)$, where $\bar{\pi}_i$ is taken to be fixed as the tax rate changes. When utility depends on quality as well as quantity as in equation (5.62), the derivative of the cost of living with respect to price changes is the product of quality and quantity. A change in the tax rate $\Delta\tau_i$ induces a price change $\bar{\pi}_i \Delta\tau_i$, so that if h buys $\xi_{ih} Q_{ih}$, the compensation required is $\bar{\pi}_i \xi_{ih} Q_{ih} \Delta\tau_i = x_h w_{ih} \Delta\tau_i (1 + \tau_i)^{-1}$ where, as before, x_h is total expenditure and w_{ih} is the budget share of good i. I adopt the standard Atkinson social welfare function (5.13), so that

$$(5.103) \qquad \eta_h = \frac{\partial W}{\partial x_h} = \left(\frac{x_h}{n_h}\right)^{-\epsilon}.$$

The numerator of the λ_i ratio in (5.9) is therefore replaced by

$$(5.104) \qquad \frac{\partial W}{\partial \tau_i} = (1+\tau_i)^{-1} \Sigma_h \eta_h \pi_{ih} \xi_{ih} Q_{ih} = (1+\tau_i)^{-1} \Sigma_h (x_h/n_h)^{-\epsilon} x_h w_{ih}.$$

A value of ϵ of unity implies that additional income is twice as valuable to someone with half the income, with higher values implying a greater focus on the poor. Note that, by (5.103), social welfare accounting is done for individuals, not households, but under the assumptions that each person in the household receives the same, and that PCE is an adequate measure of the welfare of each.

Tax revenue collected from household h is

(5.105) $$R_h = \sum_{k=1}^{M} \tau_k \bar{\pi}_k \xi_{kh} Q_{kh} = \sum_{k=1}^{M} (\tau_k/1+\tau_k) x_h w_{kh}.$$

The derivative of revenue with respect to a change in the rate can be related to the empirical model by looking first at the derivative of the budget shares with respect to the tax rate,

(5.106) $$\frac{\partial w_k^h}{\partial \tau_i} = \frac{\partial w_{kh}}{\partial \ln \pi_i} \cdot \frac{\partial \ln \pi_i}{\partial \tau_i} = \frac{\theta_{ki}}{1+\tau_i}.$$

Substituting into (5.105) and averaging over all households, we have

(5.107) $$(1+\tau_i)\frac{\partial \bar{R}}{\partial \tau_i} = \bar{x} \tilde{w}_i \left[1 - \frac{\tau_i}{1+\tau_i} + \sum_{k=1}^{M} \frac{\tau_k}{1+\tau_k} \frac{\theta_{ki}}{\tilde{w}_i}\right]$$

where $\bar{x}$ is the mean of x_h and $\tilde{w}_i$ is the "plutocratic" average budget share,

(5.108) $$\tilde{w}_i = \sum_{h=1}^{H} x_h w_{ih} / \sum_{h=1}^{H} x_h.$$

Finally, if we define the "socially representative budget share" w_i^ϵ by

(5.109) $$w_i^\epsilon = \left[\sum_{h=1}^{H} (x_h/n_h)^{-\epsilon} x_h w_{ih}\right] / \sum_{h=1}^{H} x_h$$

the marginal cost-benefit ratio of a tax increase λ_i can be written

(5.110) $$\lambda_i = \frac{w_i^\epsilon/\tilde{w}_i}{1 + \frac{\tau_i}{1+\tau_i}\left(\frac{\theta_{ii}}{\tilde{w}_i}-1\right) + \sum_{k\neq i} \frac{\tau_k}{1+\tau_k} \frac{\theta_{ki}}{\tilde{w}_i}}.$$

The numerator of (5.110) is a pure distributional measure for good i; it can be interpreted as the relative shares of the market-representative individual (the representative agent) and the socially representative individual, whose income is lower the higher is the inequality aversion parameter ϵ. This measure is modified by the action of the terms in the denominator. The first of these (apart from 1) is the (shadow) tax factor multiplied by the elasticity of expenditure on good i with respect to its price, quality and quantity effects taken together. This term measures the own-price distortionary effect of the tax. If it is large and negative, as would be the case for a heavily taxed and price-elastic good, the term will contribute to a large λ_i-ratio and would indicate the costliness of raising further revenue by that route. The last term is the sum of the tax factors multiplied by the cross-price elasticities, and captures the effects on other goods of the change in the tax on good i, again with quantity and quality effects included. From a theoretical point of view, this decomposition is trivial, but when we look at the results, it is useful to separate the own- and cross-price effects, because the former are likely to be more reliably measured than the latter, and because the latter are often omitted or handled by assumption in more restrictive systems. (In the calculations below, the term $\tilde{w}_i^\epsilon$ is arbitrarily scaled to sum to unity across goods. Changes in social welfare are not measured in money units, and for any given value of ϵ, we are concerned only with the relative values of the λ's across different goods.)

Equity and efficiency in price reform in Pakistan

Table 5.10 shows the efficiency effects of raising taxes on each of the goods, distinguishing between the terms in the denominator of (5.110). The first column shows the tax factors $\tau_i/(1+\tau_i)$ calculated from the accounting ratios discussed above; these are the shadow taxes calculated from comparison of the world and domestic prices. Wheat and rice carry shadow subsidies, oils and sugar, shadow taxes. The second column shows the own-price elasticities of quantity times quality; these are the own-good contributions to the tax distortion. Because the quality elasticities are small, the combined elasticities are approximately equal to the own-price elasticities (see equations (5.90) and (5.91) above), but they are conceptually distinct. Taxes are *ad valorem*, so that quality shading in response to tax increases depresses revenue just as do decreases in quantity. The third column shows the own-price distortions and corresponds to the middle term in the denominator of (5.110). Goods that bear no shadow taxes do not appear in this column since there are no distortionary effects of small tax increases at zero tax rates. The large effects are on wheat and rice, with the latter much larger because its own-price elasticity is much larger. By themselves, these own-price terms will generate small cost-benefit ratios, particularly for rice. Subsidies are being paid, they are distortionary, particularly for rice, and it is desirable to reduce them, at least from this limited perspective.

The cross terms in the next column are typically smaller, the exception being oils and fats, where the negative term acts so as to decrease the attractiveness of raising those prices. By checking back through the matrix of price elasticities in the lower half of Table 5.8, we can see that the cross-price elasticity responsible is that between the price of sugar and the demand for rice. An increase in the price of edible oil causes the demand for rice to rise—the elasticity is 0.44—which is distortionary because rice subsidized, an effect which is enhanced by a smaller but still positive cross-price elasticity with wheat, which is also subsidized. The final column in the table presents the sum of both effects, plus 1 according to (5.110). According to these—and bearing in mind that nothing has yet been said about distributional issues—rice is the commodity whose price should be raised, and oils and fats the commodity whose price should be lowered. The wheat subsidy too is distortionary, and there is an efficiency case for raising the price.

Equity effects are incorporated in Table 5.11 for a range of values of the distributional parameter ϵ. The first panel corresponds to $c = 0$ where there are no distributional concerns, and the cost-benefit ratios are simply the reciprocals of the last column in Table 5.10. Rice is a good candidate for a price increase, and edible oils for a price decrease. As we move through the table to the right, the distributional effects modify this picture to some extent. The first column in each

Table 5.10. Efficiency aspects of price reform in Pakistan

Food	$\dfrac{\tau_i}{1+\tau_i}$	$\dfrac{\theta_i}{\bar{w}_i} - 1$	Own effect	Cross effects	Total
Wheat	−0.40	−0.64	0.25	−0.05	1.20
Rice	−0.40	−2.08	0.83	−0.05	1.78
Dairy products	0.00	−1.01	0.00	0.01	1.01
Meat	0.00	−0.57	0.00	0.01	1.01
Oils and fats	0.05	−2.33	−0.12	−0.38	0.51
Sugar	0.40	0.13	0.05	−0.14	0.91
Other foods	0.00	−0.53	0.00	0.02	1.02
Nonfoods	0.00	−1.11	0.00	−0.02	0.98

Note: The columns correspond to the elements in the denominator of (5.110). Column 3 is the product of columns 1 and 2; column 4 is the last term in the denominator; and column 5 is 1 plus the sum of columns 3 and 4.
Source: Author's calculations using Household Income and Expenditure Survey, 1984–85.

case, which shows the relative budget shares of an increasingly poor individual relative to the market-representative individual, moves away from luxuries and towards necessities as the distributional parameter increases. Wheat, the basic staple, attracts a larger weight as we move down the income distribution, as do oils and fats. Other food, which contains pulses, also has a weight that increases with ϵ. Wheat is a target for price increases on efficiency grounds, although not as much as is rice, but the equity effects tend to make it less attractive, and its λ-value becomes relatively large as we move to the right in the table. However, for oils and fats, which were the main candidates for price decreases, the equity effects only strengthen the conclusions. Oils and fats figure relatively heavily in the budgets of low-income consumers, and reducing their price is desirable for both equity and efficiency reasons. Rice remains the best candidate for consumer tax increases; it is not consumed by the very poor, and its subsidy is the most distortionary.

Table 5.11. Equity effects and cost-benefit ratios for price increases, Pakistan

Food	$\epsilon = 0$		$\epsilon = 0.5$		$\epsilon = 1.0$		$\epsilon = 2.0$	
	$w^\epsilon/\bar{w}$	λ	$w^\epsilon/\bar{w}$	λ	$w^\epsilon/\bar{w}$	λ	$w^\epsilon/\bar{w}$	λ
Wheat	1.00	0.83	1.09	0.90	1.16	0.97	1.28	1.06
Rice	1.00	0.56	1.04	0.58	1.06	0.59	1.06	0.59
Dairy prod.	1.00	0.99	1.01	1.00	1.01	1.00	0.97	0.96
Meat	1.00	0.99	0.98	0.97	0.95	0.94	0.88	0.87
Oils and fats	1.00	1.97	1.07	2.12	1.13	2.24	1.22	2.41
Sugar	1.00	1.10	1.01	1.10	1.00	1.10	0.97	1.06
Other foods	1.00	0.98	1.04	1.01	1.06	1.04	1.10	1.08
Nonfoods	1.00	1.02	0.96	0.99	0.94	0.96	0.92	0.94

Note: The two columns for each value of ϵ are the numerator of (5.110) and (5.110) itself.
Source: Author's calculations using Household Income and Expendiutre Survey, 1984–85.

In conclusion, I emphasize once again that these policy implications do not apply directly to the tax instruments currently in use in Pakistan. The findings suggest that raising revenue from an increase in the price of rice to consumers would be desirable on grounds of efficiency and equity. But the main instrument for controlling the price of rice is the export tax, a decrease in which would certainly increase the consumer price of rice, but it would also decrease rather than increase government revenue, and it would change supplies of rice, effects which we are in no position to consider here. Nevertheless, the fact that rice and wheat are substitutes in consumption, and that there are further substitution effects between rice, wheat, and edible oils, would have to be taken into account in a reform of any export tax, just as they are taken into account here. Indeed, perhaps the most useful lesson of this analysis is how important it is to measure the way in which price changes affect the pattern of demand. The Pakistani substitution patterns between rice, wheat, and edible oils are not consistent with additive preferences, and so cannot be accommodated within a model like the linear expenditure system. In countries where some prices are far from opportunity cost, cross-price effects of tax changes will often be as important as the effects on the good itself, and these effects must be measured in a flexible way. Nor could additive preferences accommodate the pattern of total expenditure and own-price elasticities that characterize demand patterns in Pakistan. Oils and fats are a necessity, but have a high own-price elasticity, so that the ratio of the own-price to income elasticity is many times greater than for a rice, which has high own-price and income elasticities. Additive preferences require that this ratio be (approximately) the same for all goods. Yet it is this ratio that is the principal determinant of how the balance between equity and efficiency ought to be struck.

Equity and efficiency in price reform in India

Table 5.12 shows the calculated efficiency effects for the Indian case, and corresponds to Table 5.10 for Pakistan. As before, the first column shows the factors $\tau_i/(1+\tau_i)$ calculated from the accounting ratios, while the second column shows the own-price elasticities of quality and quantity together. The product of the first and second columns, which is shown as the third column, gives the contribution of the own-price effects to the measure of the distortion that would be caused by a marginal increase in price. These are nonzero only for the goods that bear taxes or subsidies, rice, wheat, and oils. Wheat is more price elastic than rice, but its subsidy is less, and the own-price distortion effect is also less. However, as the next column shows, the distortion caused by the wheat subsidy is alleviated by the cross-price effects, largely because a lower wheat price draws demand away from rice, which is even more heavily subsidized. There are also important cross-price effects for other cereals, pulses, dairy products, meat, and fruit. Increases in the price of any of these goods decreases the demand for rice, and helps reduce the costs of the rice subsidy. On efficiency grounds alone, the prices of rice, other cereals, pulses, dairy products, and meat should be increased, and those of *jowar* and nonfoods decreased.

Table 5.12. Efficiency aspects of price reform in India

Food	$\dfrac{\tau_i}{1+\tau_i}$	$\dfrac{\theta_i}{\bar{w}_i} - 1$	Own effect	Cross effects	Total
Rice	−0.50	−1.13	0.57	−0.15	1.42
Wheat	−0.25	−1.33	0.33	−0.32	1.01
Jowar	0.00	−0.39	0.00	−0.12	0.88
Other cereals	0.00	−3.51	0.00	0.58	1.58
Pulses	0.00	−0.60	0.00	0.55	1.55
Dairy products	0.00	−0.21	0.00	0.26	1.26
Edible oils	0.33	−0.27	−0.09	0.16	1.07
Meat	0.00	−1.13	0.00	0.43	1.43
Vegetables	0.00	−0.66	0.00	0.04	1.04
Fruit	0.00	−1.08	0.00	0.27	1.27
Sugar and *gur*	0.00	−0.28	0.00	−0.03	0.97
All other	0.00	−1.43	0.00	−0.20	0.80

Note: The columns correspond to the elements of the denominator of (5.110). Column 3 is the product of columns 1 and 2; column 4 is the last term in the denominator; and column 5 is 1 plus the sum of columns 3 and 4.
Source: Deaton, Parikh, and Subramanian, (1994 Table 9).

Table 5.13 brings in the equity effects, and computes the cost-benefit ratios that trade off both equity and efficiency. In the first pair of columns, the Atkinson inequality aversion parameter is zero, so that all individuals are treated alike, no matter how much their household spends. In this case, the λ-ratios are simply the reciprocals of the last column in Table 5.12, and we get the same ranking of relative tax costs. As we move to the right, and the ϵ parameter increases, the equity

Table 5.13. Equity effects and cost-benefit ratios for price increases, India

Food	$\epsilon = 0$		$\epsilon = 0.5$		$\epsilon = 1.0$		$\epsilon = 2.0$	
	$w^\epsilon/\bar{w}$	λ	$w^\epsilon/\bar{w}$	λ	$w^\epsilon/\bar{w}$	λ	$v^\epsilon/\bar{w}$	λ
Rice	1.00	0.71	1.02	0.72	1.03	0.73	1.02	0.72
Wheat	1.00	0.99	0.98	0.97	0.96	0.95	0.91	0.90
Jowar	1.00	1.14	1.11	1.27	1.21	1.38	1.39	1.58
Other cereals	1.00	0.63	1.09	0.69	1.16	0.73	1.24	0.78
Pulses	1.00	0.65	1.05	0.68	1.09	0.70	1.15	0.75
Dairy prod.	1.00	0.79	0.97	0.77	0.94	0.74	0.87	0.69
Edible oils	1.00	0.94	1.02	0.96	1.04	0.98	1.07	1.01
Meat	1.00	0.70	1.00	0.70	0.98	0.69	0.94	0.66
Vegetables	1.00	0.96	1.04	1.00	1.06	1.02	1.09	1.05
Fruit	1.00	0.79	0.96	0.76	0.93	0.73	0.84	0.66
Sugar & *gur*	1.00	1.03	1.03	1.07	1.07	1.10	1.12	1.16
All other	1.00	1.25	0.96	1.20	0.92	1.15	0.88	1.10

Note: The two columns for each value of ϵ are the numerator of (5.110) and (5.110) itself.
Source: Deaton, Parikh, and Subramanian (1994 Table 10).

column gives larger values to the goods most heavily consumed by the poor, and relatively smaller values to those that are most heavily consumed by those who live in households that are better-off. For $\epsilon = 0.5$, *jowar* receives the highest weight, with other cereals, pulses, vegetables, sugar, rice, and edible oils all showing equity effects greater than unity. These are the goods most heavily consumed by the poor. As ϵ increases further, the importance of these goods for distribution increases further. Of the two subsidized cereals, the equity case is stronger for rice than wheat—which is indeed why rice carries the larger subsidy—and the difference between them increases with the degree of inequality aversion. Neither cereal is consumed as heavily by the poor as are the coarse cereals, although there are limitations on the extent to which the government could intervene in that market.

The cost-benefit ratios λ bring together the equity and efficiency effects. Because of the subsidy, and because it is less heavily consumed by the poor than coarse cereals, rice is always a candidate for a price increase. But when concern for the poor is relatively low, increases in the prices of pulses and of other cereals are less socially costly, because of the large cross-price elasticities with rice. Given any positive degree of equity preference, the most attractive candidate for a price decrease is *jowar*. When equity preference is large, the efficiency case for raising prices of pulses and other cereals is outweighed by equity criteria, and meat and fruit become the best candidates for tax increases.

5.6 Price reform: parametric and nonparametric analysis

This has been a long chapter, and although the topic has been the same throughout, we have followed it from the theory through the data problems to the econometric implementation and policy evaluation. Although the methodology is inevitably complex in parts, it has been successfully applied in a number of countries, there is standardized software which is included in the Code Appendix, and the real difficulties lie, as always, not in the econometric sophistication, but in setting up the problem in a sensible way, picking the right goods for the analysis, and in the crucial preliminary analysis of the data, looking for outliers, interpreting and examining the unit value data, and making whatever adaptations are necessary for local conditions or institutions. It is rarely possible to do satisfactory policy analysis with "off-the-shelf" econometrics. Even so, the procedures of this chapter should be helpful as a basis for analysis of tax reform and pricing issues. In this brief final section, I want to draw attention to areas where the methodology is weakest, and where there is likely to be the greatest payoff to further research.

A major contrast between the analysis of this chapter and that in Chapters 3 and 4 is that the absence of nonparametric methods. Instead, I have used a parametric model of demand to deliver the price responses, and this is in sharp contrast to exercises like that in Chapter 3, where I looked at the distributional effects of rice pricing in Thailand without having to resort to a specific functional form. The reason for the difference is the difficulty in estimating price responses; even with thousands of observations, there is often limited price variation, so that there is little hope of direct measurement without imposing prior structure. Although the model in this chapter also used a parametric form to specify the effects of total expenditure and sociodemographics, this is only necessary to allow isolation of the price responses, and no use of the results is made in the policy exercises in Section 5.5; the survey data themselves are used directly to calculate the average and socially representative budget shares in the cost-benefit formulas.

An important topic for research is whether it is possible to do better, and bring a nonparametric element to the estimation of the price responses. The hope comes from the fact that the cost-benefit formula (5.9) does not require an estimate of the price derivative at every point in the sample, or even for different values of total expenditure or the socio-demographics. Instead, all that appears in (5.9) is the aggregate of each household's response, or equivalently, since we can divide top and bottom of (5.9) by the number of households, the average price response for all households. Among recent developments in econometrics have been methods for estimating such average derivatives without requiring the specification of a functional form (see Härdle and Stoker 1989; Stoker 1991; and Powell, Stock, and Stoker 1989, for the basic techniques, and Deaton 1995, for a discussion in the context of pricing policy in developing countries). These "semiparametric" methods deliver only averages, not estimates for each household, but in large enough samples they do so almost as efficiently as does parametric regression.

A preliminary investigation of average derivative techniques using the Pakistani data is provided by Deaton and Ng (1996). The method has both advantages and disadvantages. Among the former is the removal of any need to write down a theoretically consistent model of demand. Even more importantly, the absence of a functional form provides a clean solution to the problems associated with some households buying the good, and some not. The average derivative methods estimate the derivative of the regression function, the expectation of demand conditional on prices, total expenditure, and sociodemographics, but unconditional on whether or not the household buys the good. This is exactly what the cost-benefit formulas require, and so the method avoids the conventional detour through the complexity of utility theory and switching regression models.

There are equally serious disadvantages. First, there is no apparent way of allowing for either quality effects or measurement error. The former is perhaps not too serious, but there are many examples where the neglect of the latter could produce serious biases. Second, although we can do without a functional form, it remains necessary to specify which are the conditioning variables, and the omission of relevant variables will lead to inconsistent estimates of price derivatives when the omitted variables are correlated with prices, in exactly the same way that OLS is biased by omitted variables. Third, although the average derivative method finesses the problem of zero observations in the unit values, it provides no assistance with the fact that unit value observations are missing for such households. Because the missing households are unlikely to be randomly selected—more households will buy nothing where prices are high than where they are low—there is a risk of selectivity bias, and that risk is present whether we use parametric or semiparametric methods. In the methods of this chapter, the effects of selectivity are moderated by the averaging over clusters, so that a village is included as long as one of its households purchases the good. Such averaging is much less attractive once the parametric framework is abandoned, since although the average derivative estimation is asymptotically as efficient as ordinary least squares, it requires a good many more observations in practice.

The final disadvantage, at least for the present, is the time required to compute the estimates. The formulas are not complex, and the estimators can be written in closed form, so that there is no need for iterative solution, but with realistic sample sizes, the calculations are slow even with very fast machines. Although this problem will inevitably diminish over time, the methods are difficult to recommend now, partly because many researchers in developing countries have access to fast machines with only a considerable lag, and because the computational costs have limited the experience with the methods in real applications, so that we cannot be sure that there are not hidden difficulties that will only become apparent through use.

5.7 Guide to further reading

The World Bank volume edited by Newbery and Stern (1987) contains the theoretical background for this chapter, as well as a number of applied essays that discuss applications to specific countries. The introductory essays by Stern, Chapters 2 and 3, as well as Chapters 7 and 13 on taxation and development, and on agricultural taxation by Newbery are worth special attention. Newbery's Chapter 18 on agricultural price reform in the Republic of Korea is a model for how such studies should be done. The book by Ahmad and Stern (1991) also reviews the theory and, like this chapter, applies it to tax reform in Pakistan. Sah and Stiglitz (1992) develop the theory of pricing in the context of a conflict between agricultural producers and urban consumers. The theory of price reform is closely related to the theory of cost-benefit analysis, the former dealing with the effect on social welfare of small changes in prices, the latter with the effects of small changes in quantities—projects. Survey papers that emphasize this link are Drèze and Stern (1987, 1990) as well as the splendid review by Squire (1989). Quite different insights into pricing policy are obtained from the perspective of political economy; this literature is more concerned with why prices and taxes come to be what they are, and less with prescriptions based on equity and efficiency (see the World Bank volumes by Krueger, Schiff, and Valdes 1991–92, the early political analysis by Bates 1981, Grossman and Helpman 1994, and the immensely readable monograph by Dixit 1996).

6 Saving and consumption smoothing

There are many reasons to be interested in the saving behavior of households in developing countries. One is to understand the link between saving and growth, between saving and economic development itself. Although economists are still far from a generally accepted understanding of the process of development, saving plays an important role in all the theoretical accounts and the data show a strong positive correlation between saving and growth, both over time in individual countries, and in international comparisons across countries. If we believe that saving generates growth, and since there is a close link between household and national saving rates, both over time and over countries—see Figure 6.1 for evidence from a number of developing countries—then it is to the determinants of household saving that we must look if we are to understand economic growth. If instead we suppose that saving rates are a by-product of economic growth generated in some other way—for example by government-directed investment programs, or by the dynamic gains from trade—our understanding is not complete unless we can explain why it is that economic growth causes households to save a larger fraction of their incomes.

The second reason for examining household saving is to understand how people deal with fluctuations in their incomes. The majority of people in poor countries are engaged in agriculture, and their livelihoods are often subject to great uncertainty, from weather and natural calamities, from sickness, and from fluctuations in the prices of their crops. Individuals close to subsistence need to free consumption from income, so that they are not driven to extremities simply because their incomes are temporarily low. These "smoothing" or "insurance" mechanisms can take a number of forms, of which saving is one. By laying aside some income in good times, people can accumulate balances for use in bad times, a procedure that would be available even to Robinson Crusoe, provided that he had some commodity that could be stored. In a society with many people, risks can be pooled, either through formal financial intermediaries or through more informal networks of personal credit or social insurance, at the local or national levels.

One useful way of classifying saving behavior is by the length of the time period over which households can detach consumption from income. We would

Figure 6.1. National and household saving, selected countries
(percent)

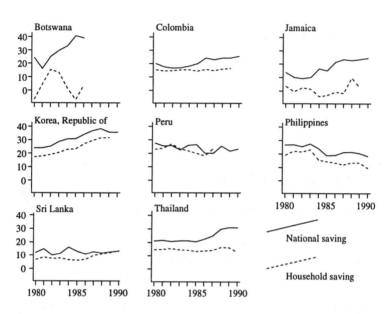

Source: UN *Statistical Yearbook*, various years.

normally expect even the poorest households to be able to consume on days on which they received no income, but it is more of an issue whether or not consumption is at risk from seasonal fluctuations in income, and there is a substantial literature in development economics on the risks associated with seasonal shortages and fluctuations in prices. Another literature, often couched in terms of the permanent income hypothesis, looks at whether farmers set something aside in good years and so detach their annual consumption levels from their annual incomes. Beyond this, people may smooth their consumption over their lifetimes, saving when they are young to make provision for their old age. Whether and how well individuals undertake these various kinds of saving has implications not only for welfare, but also for the behavior of the macroeconomy and for the relationship between saving and growth. In particular, the life-cycle hypothesis, that households successfully undertake lifetime consumption smoothing, has the famous implication that changes in the rate of economic growth will cause changes in saving rates in the same direction (Modigliani 1966, 1970, 1986).

Paralleling the taxonomy of consumption smoothing over different time periods is a taxonomy of consumption smoothing over different groups of people. At one extreme, every individual is an island, and must deal alone with income fluctuations and other threats to consumption by saving and dissaving. At the other extreme, we can imagine social insurance schemes, spanning large groups of agents, in which individual risk is diversified away by being spread over everyone, leaving consumption subject only to economy-wide risk. Intermediate cases are of the greatest practical interest. We usually suppose that consumption risk is pooled within families, and the anthropological literature gives many examples of risk pooling in agricultural villages. Social security exists in one form or another, but rarely provides more than partial protection.

My concern in this book is with the analysis of household survey data, and the main task of this chapter is to present evidence from surveys that helps us understand the determinants of household saving. This is a difficult and speculative undertaking, and one that is a good deal more provisional than anything else in the book. First, for the reasons discussed in Chapter 1, the measurement of saving in household surveys is subject to large margins of error, so that especially where household saving rates are low, it may be almost impossible to obtain any useful measure of household saving. Second, there are several different theoretical explanations of household saving, and there is no general agreement on which (if any) is correct. We are not yet at the stage where the policy prescriptions are clear, and where the only remaining task for empirical analysis is to provide the magnitudes necessary to set the controls. Instead, new empirical evidence and theoretical insights are still coming in, and we remain at the stage where there coexist different models and different interpretations with quite different policy implications

In the main sections of this chapter, I present some of the most important models of household consumption, and discuss methods and results for using them to interpret the survey data. As always, my aim is not to provide a comprehensive treatment of the topic, nor to survey previous research in the area, but to provide template examples of empirical analyses that cast light on the topic in question. I consider in turn the life-cycle hypothesis (Section 6.1) and the shorter-term smoothing over years and seasons that is predicted by various versions of the permanent income hypothesis (Section 6.2). Section 6.3 develops the theory of intertemporal choice and uses the results to consider extensions beyond the permanent income and life-cycle models, extensions where households have a precautionary motive for saving, or where households have no access to credit markets, but use assets as a buffer to help smooth their consumption. Section 6.4 reviews recent work on insurance mechanisms, on whether households are able to stabilize their consumption by pooling risks across individuals instead of by saving and dissaving over time. Section 6.5 is about the relationship between saving, age, and inequality. Section 6.6 tries to bring all of the material together and to summarize its implications for a number of policy questions. In particular, I draw some tentative conclusions about the relationship between saving and growth.

6.1 Life-cycle interpretations of saving

The life-cycle model, originally proposed by Modigliani and Brumberg (1954, 1979) sees individuals (or couples) smoothing their consumption over their lifetimes. In the simplest "stripped-down" model, people receive labor income (earnings) only until the retirement age, but hold their consumption constant over their lives. As a result, they are net savers during their working years, and dissavers during retirement. The assets that are sold by the elderly to finance their consumption are accumulated by the young, and provided there is neither population nor income growth, the provision for old age will support a constant ratio of wealth to earnings in the economy as a whole, and there will be no net saving. With either population growth or per capita earnings growth, the total amount of saving by the young will be magnified relative to the total amount of dissaving by the elderly, who are fewer in number and have less lifetime wealth, so that increases in either type of growth will increase the saving rate. Simplified versions of the model predict that the saving ratio should increase by about 2 percentage points for each percentage point increase in the growth rate, a prediction that is consistent both with the cross-country relationship between saving and growth as well as with the declines in saving rates that have accompanied the productivity slowdown in the industrialized countries (Modigliani 1993).

The positive causality from growth to saving is qualitatively robust to changes in assumptions about the shapes of lifetime profiles of consumption, earnings, and saving, provided only that the average age at which saving takes place is lower than the average age of dissaving. This may not be the case if the rate of economic growth is expected to be very high, because the young may wish to dissave in anticipation of higher earnings in the future. Even so, it is plausible that these groups will be unable to borrow the resources needed to finance such spending, so that a presumption remains that growth will increase saving rates for the economy as a whole. A fuller account of this summary can be found in many sources, for example in Modigliani's (1986) Nobel address; a review by the author is Deaton (1992c, Chapter 2).

The validity of the life-cycle description of saving has been the subject of a great deal of debate and research, mostly in the context of developed economies. Although there is still room for differences of opinion, my own belief, argued more fully in Deaton (1992c), is that the life-cycle model overstates the degree to which consumption is in fact detached from income over the life cycle, and that aside from institutionalized employer or national pension schemes, relatively few households undertake the long-term saving and dissaving that is predicted by the model. There are also questions about applying the model to developing countries. In the poorest economies, where family size is large, and life expectancy relatively low, the fraction of old people is small and very few of them live alone. In the LSMS for Côte d'Ivoire in 1986, less than 1 (10) percent of females (males) aged 70 or over live alone or with their spouse. Even in Thailand, where the demographic transition is much further advanced, the corresponding figures for men and women in rural areas in the 1986 Socioeconomic Survey were 15 and 25 percent (see Deaton and Paxson 1992, Table 6.4). When the elderly live with their children, they can be provided for directly and personally; there is no need for the accumulation and decumulation of marketable assets that is done in developed economies through anonymous and impersonal financial markets.

Nevertheless, there is a wide range of income levels, demographic structures and customary living arrangements among developing countries. For those countries where economic development and the demographic transition have proceeded the furthest, living arrangements are already changing, and provision for consumption by the elderly is moving into the forefront of public policy. These changes are at their most rapid in the fast-growing economies of East and South East Asia, countries which also have national and household saving rates that are very high by historical and international standards. The mechanisms that produce this conjunction are far from clear. Is the high saving a consequence of the rapid growth, or its cause? Are the high saving rates generated by demographic change and the fact that many current savers will have to fend for themselves in their old age? Does the political pressure for social security spring from the same concerns, and will its introduction cut saving rates and threaten economic growth? Indeed, will the aging of the population that is already underway mean lower saving rates as the fraction of dissavers increases? One key to many of these questions is whether or not the life-cycle hypothesis provides an adequate description of the behavior of saving.

In this section, I look at life-cycle saving behavior in the data from Côte d'Ivoire, Thailand, and Taiwan (China), starting with simple age profiles of consumption, and moving on to a more sophisticated analysis based on the cohort methods of Section 2.6 to interpret the data in terms of the life-cycle model.

Age profiles of consumption

Perhaps the most obvious way to examine the life-cycle behavior of consumption from survey data is to plot consumption and saving against age. But as soon as we try to do so, we encounter the difficulty of measuring income and thus saving, as well as the fact that much income data and almost all consumption data relate to households and not individuals. It is far from clear that the large households that exist in many rural areas around the world, and that often contain subunits of several families, can be adequately described in terms of the simple life cycle of the nuclear family. Even so, we have little choice but to classify households by the age of the head, to measure income as best we can, and to see whether the results make sense.

Figure 6.2, taken from Deaton (1992c, p. 55), shows age profiles of consumption and income for 1,600 or so households in the Côte d'Ivoire Living Standards Surveys for 1985 and 1986, as well as profiles for 3,589 urban and 5,012 rural households from the 1986 Thai Socioeconomic Survey. In order to keep the profiles relatively smooth, I have used the averages for each age to calculate the five-year moving averages shown in the figures; five-year smoothing also eliminates problems of "age-heaping" when some people report their age rounded to the nearest five years.

The graphs do not look much like the stylized life-cycle profiles of the textbook; there is little evidence of either "hump saving" among the young or of dissaving among the elderly. Instead, and with the exception of urban Thailand, there is very little saving (or dissaving) at any age, with the consumption profile very close to the income profile. Even in urban Thailand, where there is positive

Figure 6.2. Age profiles of income and consumption, Côte d'Ivoire, 1985–86, and Thailand, 1986

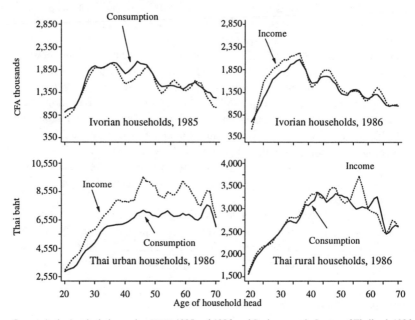

Source: Author's calculations using CILSS 1985 and 1986, and Socioeconomic Survey of Thailand, 1986.

saving, the consumption profile is similar to the income profile, and most saving takes place after age 40. There is also no sign of the predicted dissaving among older households. This close co-ordination between consumption and income has been encountered in several other cross-sectional data sets. For example, Carroll and Summers (1991) find a close correlation in the United States between consumption and income profiles for different educational and occupational groups, and conclude that consumption "tracks" income more closely than would be expected from life-cycle models whose essence is that consumption and income need bear no relationship to one another. Similarly, Attanasio and Davis (1993) use cohort data from the United States to find a close relationship between five-year consumption and income changes, although the relationship is much weaker between one-year changes. More comprehensively, Paxson (1996) uses cohort data from the United States, Britain, Thailand, and Taiwan (China) to document consumption and income tracking. While it is possible that the age profiles of consumption are simply those that people like, and just happen to match the shape of income profiles, it stretches belief that the coincidence should happen for every educational and occupational group as well as for a wide range of countries, the preferences of each just happening to look like its income path, even though the income profiles differ from case to case.

Even so, the evidence in Figure 6.2 has to be treated with a great deal of caution and is subject to several interpretations. In spite of positive saving among urban Thai households, the household saving rate from the 1986 survey is much lower than that reported in the National Income and Product Accounts (NIPA). Although NIPA measures of saving should never be automatically credited over measures from household surveys—NIPA measures of household saving are frequently derived as residuals—the discrepancies serve to remind us of the general difficulty of measuring saving, whether by surveys or other means. In this particular case, Paxson (1992) has pointed out that in the presence of inflation, the practice of comparing money income reported for the last year with twelve times the money consumption reported for the last month will depress estimates of saving. However, her corrections for 1986 are not large, and she reports negative total savings on average for all nonurban households; among the latter, total saving is less than ten percent of their total income. These figures are not consistent with the national accounts data shown in Figure 6.1.

Even in the absence of measurement error, there are a number of difficulties with age profiles of consumption such as those in Figure 6.2. First, these profiles are simply the cross sections for the households in the surveys, and there is no reason to suppose that the profiles represent the typical or expected experience for any individual household or group of households. We are not looking across ages for the same household or same cohort of households, but at the experience at different ages of different groups of households, whose members were born at different dates and have had quite different lifetime experiences of education, wealth, and earnings. Without controlling for these other variables, many of which are likely to affect the level and shape of the age profiles, we cannot isolate the pure effect of age on consumption and saving. In the examples in Figure 6.2, these problems are likely to be most serious for Thailand, where there has been more than 3 percent annual growth in per capita income over the past quarter-century. As a result, the 20-year-olds at the left of the graphs are four to five times better-off over their lifetimes than are the 70-year-olds on the right. Lifetime resources are diminishing as we move from left to right in the diagrams, and since, according to the life-cycle hypothesis it is lifetime resources that determine the level of the consumption path, the cross-sectional consumption trajectories will be raised among the young and pulled down among the older households, so that the cross-sectional profiles will be rotated clockwise relative to the genuine lifetime profiles. The Thai panels are therefore consistent with an interpretation in which consumption grows steadily with age, and in which the hump shape comes from the lower lifetime wealth of the elderly.

The second problem with these simple age profiles of consumption is that they take no account of variation in household size with the age of the head. Without a good procedure for counting adult equivalents, there is no ideal correction, but even a crude conversion to a per capita basis does a great deal to flatten out the profiles in Figure 6.2. The age profile of household size has much the same shape as the age profile of household income. If we were to discover the lifetime profiles of individual consumption were strongly correlated with age profiles of individual income, there would be cause for concern about the individual's apparent lack of ability to protect consumption from swings in income, and in particular to make adequate provision for old age when earnings capacity is low. However, it is less clear that we should be concerned when household consumption tracks household income, and when household numbers and composition are changing as children are born, grow up, and leave home, and as elderly parents and relations move in. Indeed, since decisions about household division and augmentation are not made in a vacuum, household size may itself respond to the earnings opportunities available to the household, not only through fertility, but also by migration and the splitting and joining of family subgroups. But even if there were no consequences for individual welfare of household consumption tracking household income, the lack of "hump" saving and subsequent dissaving removes the supposition of a link between growth and saving in the aggregate economy.

A third difficulty with the age profiles is selection as households age, a difficulty that is particularly serious when looking at saving or dissaving among the old. For example, the bottom left panel of Figure 6.2 shows positive saving at all ages, including households headed by people to age 70. But many households cease to exist as independent units even before the head reaches age 70, because of death, or because old people tend to live with their children. Although there is little evidence on the subject, it is easy to imagine that high-saving households are more likely to survive as independent units, in which case the profiles will show saving rates that are upward biased to a degree that increases with age. (See Shorrocks 1975 for a similar analysis of the relationship between age and wealth holdings, where a correction for differential mortality by wealth converts upward-sloping age profiles of wealth into downward-sloping profiles, at least among the elderly.)

Consumption and saving by cohorts

Where there exists a time series of household surveys with information on consumption and income, it is possible to track the behavior of cohorts over time, and thus to avoid one of the major difficulties associated with a single cross section of consumption and income. Such data also have a direct interpretation in terms of the life-cycle hypothesis, with the age effects, which come from tastes, separated from the wealth effects, which come from the lifetime budget constraint, and which differ between cohorts by an amount that depends on how fast the economy is growing. In this subsection, I show how to fit the life-cycle model to cohort data using the results of the study of saving in Taiwan (China) by Deaton and Paxson (1994a); similar analyses for Britain, Thailand, and the United States are reported by Paxson (1996).

The Taiwanese surveys, which have already been used in Chapters 1 and 2, begin in 1976, so that with data up to 1990, there are 15 successive surveys that can be used to track cohorts over time. The surveys collect data on the various components of both consumption and income over the past year, and although the annual savings estimates are far from identical to—and are usually lower than—those in the national accounts, both sources show that households save between a fifth and a quarter of their incomes. By the standards of most countries, this is an unusually close correspondence, perhaps because saving rates are so high in Taiwan (China).

Figures 6.3 and 6.4 present the consumption data in two different ways. Figure 6.3 shows the cross-sectional age profiles of (constant-price) consumption for every second year from 1976 through 1990. Each graph plots against head's age the average consumption (in 1986 prices) of all households with heads of that age. The growth of real consumption is raising these profiles through time, although the second oil shock had the effect of slowing growth, and the 1980 and 1982 consumption profiles are not far apart. As was the case for Thailand in Figure 6.2, the age profiles rise somewhat from age 20 through 50, and decline thereafter. Note the sampling effects in these graphs. The averages are for a single year of age in each year, and are not smoothed by combining adjacent years into moving averages. As a result, the profiles for the youngest and oldest heads are relatively imprecisely estimated. The rapid growth of consumption in Taiwan (China) means that these profiles bear no relation to the experience of any given cohort. Someone who is 25 years old in 1976 is 27 years old, not in 1976 but in 1978, so that to trace the average consumption of such people, the points should be connected, not within years as in Figure 6.3, but within cohorts, linking up the behavior, if not of the same individuals, at least of the randomly selected representatives of the same cohort over time.

Figure 6.4 shows the cohort consumption experience for every fifth cohort, beginning with those born in 1966, and then moving back (increasing in age) five years at a time until we reach the cohort of those born in 1911. The first line segment connects the average consumption of those who were 20 years old in 1976 to the average consumption of 21-year-olds in 1977, of 22-year-olds in 1978, until the last observation of the cohort in 1990, when they were 34 years old. The second line segment repeats the exercise for those who were five years older, and so on. Figures 6.3 and 6.4 use exactly the same data on average consumption by age of head, and if Figure 6.3 showed every year, and Figure 6.4 showed every cohort, the two figures would contain exactly the same points but connected differently.

Figure 6.4, which shows a marked resemblance to the cohort earnings profiles in the first panel of Figure 2.5—a similarity to which I shall return—shows just how misleading are the cross-section age profiles when what we are interested in is the life-cycle profiles. Far from consumption first rising gently then declining with age, as in Figure 6.3, consumption rose with age for all cohorts, except possibly the very oldest. For the youngest cohorts, consumption rose very rapidly with age, and the rate of growth was slower the older the cohort, so that it was young households who gained the most from consumption growth in this period. (Of course, old people may have gained too, since many presumably relocated into younger households.) The decline in consumption after age 45 in the cross-section age profiles in Figure 6.3 is entirely due to the fact that, at any given date, older people have lower consumption, and not to any tendency for consumption to decline with age for anyone. (This effect presumably also applies to the Thai figures in the lower half of Figure 6.2.) According to the life-cycle model, the

Figure 6.3. Cross-sectional consumption profiles, alternate years, Taiwan (China), 1976–90

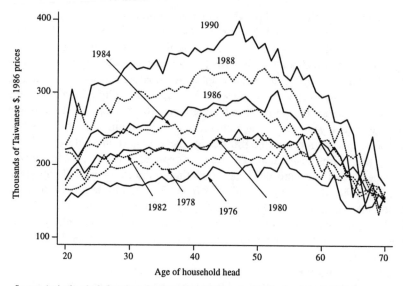

Source: Author's calculations from Surveys of Personal Income Distribution, Taiwan (China).

Figure 6.4. Consumption profiles, selected cohorts, Taiwan (China)

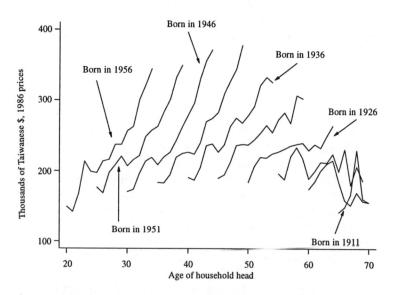

Source: Author's calculations from Surveys of Income Distribution, Taiwan (China).

lower consumption of older cohorts is attributed to their lower lifetime wealth, so that Figure 6.4 would be interpreted as showing a preference for consumption to rise with age, albeit more slowly at higher ages. This interpretation can be precisely quantified using the cohort decomposition techniques of Section 2.6.

Estimating a life-cycle model for Taiwan (China)

Suppose that individual i is born in year b and is observed in year t. If the life-cycle hypothesis is correct and if uncertainty is not important, the individual's consumption level is proportional to lifetime resources with a factor of proportionality that depends on age, so that

$$(6.1) \qquad\qquad c_{ibt} = g_i(t-b)W_{ib}$$

where W is lifetime wealth—the sum of financial wealth and the discounted present value of expected future earnings—and $t-b$, the difference between today's date and the year of birth, is age. In this simple model with no uncertainty, lifetime wealth does not vary over time, and we can think of the individual—or at least the household—having its lifetime resources set at birth (or at incorporation) and then choosing how to allocate consumption over time according to its preferences as represented by the function g. In general, this function will also depend on the real rate of interest, with higher rates causing the age profile to tip counterclockwise, but I ignore this dependence for the moment.

If we first take logarithms of equation (6.1) and then average over all households in the cohort born at time b and observed at t, we obtain

$$(6.2) \qquad\qquad \overline{\ln c}_{bt} = \overline{\ln g}(t-b) + \overline{\ln W}_b$$

so that the average of the logarithms of individual consumptions is the sum of two components, one of which depends only on age, and one of which depends only on cohort. As a result, we can estimate (6.2) using the methods of Section 2.6, regressing the average log of cohort consumption on a set of age and cohort dummies. The former recovers preferences about intertemporal choice and the latter the lifetime wealth levels of each cohort. There is no need to assume a functional form for preferences nor to measure lifetime wealth levels. Equation (6.2) is even consistent with some uncertainty; as long as the members of the cohort can estimate their future earnings correctly on average, there is no need to suppose that each can do so. While this is a better assumption than is complete certainty, it still rules out the sort of macroeconomic shocks that would provide "surprises" for all members of the cohort. We are effectively assuming that, at least by 1976, members of each of these Taiwanese cohorts neither systematically over- nor underestimated the growth in consumption that was to come in the next decade and a half.

Although there is no general theoretical framework to support such a construction, we can treat income in exactly the same way as consumption in (6.2), taking logarithms, averaging, and regressing on age and cohort dummies. The validity of the decomposition requires that incomes follow an unchanging lifetime profile, but that the position of the profile moves up from older to younger cohorts as economic growth raises earnings. The difference between the logarithm of income and the logarithm of consumption is a monotone increasing function of the saving-to-income ratio, and is approximately equal to the saving ratio when the saving ratio is small, so that the cohort-age decomposition of log consumption and log income automatically delivers a cohort-age decomposition of the saving ratio.

The results of the calculations are shown in Figures 6.5 and 6.6, and come from two regressions. In the first, the average of the logarithm of consumption for each cohort in each year is regressed on age and cohort dummies, and on the average numbers of adults and children in each cohort, the last two being included to make allowance for the differential consumption requirements of adults and children; family composition can be thought of as an argument of the preference function g in (6.1). The second regression does the same for the averages of log income. Year effects are not included, although the results are very much the same when they are, provided they are restricted to average to zero and to be orthogonal to time (see Section 2.7). The cohort effects for both regressions, as well as the difference between the two sets of age effects, which I am interpreting as the cohort effects in the ratio of saving to income, are plotted as a function of cohort age (age of the household head in 1976) in Figure 6.5. Figure 6.6 shows the age effects as a function of the age of the household head; the three graphs are the age structure of log income in the absence of growth, the preferred age profile of log consumption, and the resulting age profile of the saving ratio. Each point on each graph corresponds to a coefficient from one or other regression; the curves are not constrained to take on any particular shape, so that the relatively smooth curves in the figures come directly from the data.

What do Figures 6.5 and 6.6 tell us about the usefulness of the life-cycle model for explaining saving behavior among Taiwanese households? Figure 6.5 shows that the cohort effects in both log consumption and log income are declining with age in 1976, so that the younger the household, the higher is its lifetime profile of both real income and real consumption. The cohort effects increase at about 5 percent per annum for income and at about 3.5 percent per annum for consumption, rates that are considerably lower than the rate of growth of per capita GDP. The difference between the cohort income and consumption growth rates means that the saving rate is growing from older to younger cohorts. A household headed by a 25-year-old in 1990 is saving 20 percent more of its income than was a 25-year-old household 35 years before, in 1955.

According to the life-cycle model, consumption profiles can only grow less rapidly than lifetime wealth profiles if bequests are a luxury good, so that the share of lifetime consumption in lifetime resources, including inherited bequests, is falling over time. Put differently, pure accumulation is an important motive for saving, accumulation that is not simply designed to be run down in old age. This is entirely plausible in Taiwan (China), where many families are accumulating

Figure 6.5. Cohort effects in consumption, income, and saving, Taiwan (China)

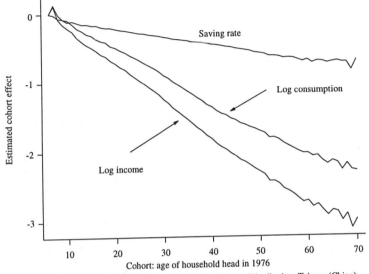

Source: Author's calculations from Surveys of Personal Income Distribution, Taiwan (China), and Deaton and Paxson (1994a).

Figure 6.6. Age effects in consumption, income, and saving, Taiwan (China)

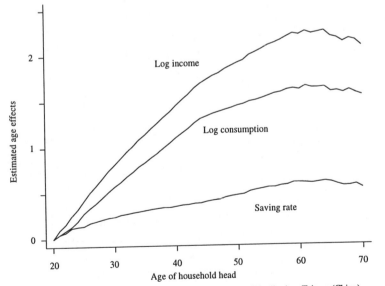

Source: Author's calculations from Surveys of Personal Income Distribution, Taiwan (China), and Deaton and Paxson (1994a).

Figure 6.7. Averages of log consumption and log income, by year and cohort, Taiwan (China)

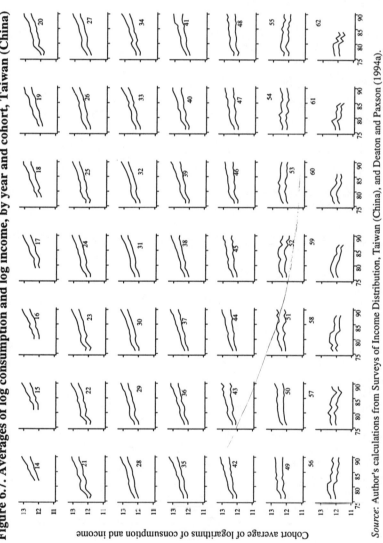

Cohort average of logarithms of consumption and income

Source: Author's calculations from Surveys of Income Distribution, Taiwan (China), and Deaton and Paxson (1994a).

property—housing and small businesses—which they intend to leave to their children, but it remains unclear why this motive should have become so much stronger over time unless bequests are luxury goods. It is also possible that Taiwanese of working age, who are wealthier and have fewer children than did their parents, are saving more to support themselves in a retirement that ever fewer can expect to spend with their children. Such a change should not cause consumption to grow less rapidly than income in the long run, since there will be additional dissaving when these people retire. However, it is possible that, with few of these people retired to date, the analysis could mistake the phenomenon for an increase in the demand for bequests.

The age profiles of consumption and saving in Figure 6.6 also present problems for a life-cycle interpretation of the data. In particular, there is no evidence of dissaving among the old; indeed, the saving rate increases with age at least up to age 60. It is possible that age selectivity is responsible for this finding, and that the potential dissavers are those who have already exhausted their assets, are living with their children, or are dead. While it seems impossible to rule out such an explanation, the lack of saving among the elderly is a common finding in other countries (see for example Mirer 1979 for the United States, Börsch-Supan and Stahl 1991 for Germany, Attanasio and Weber 1992 for Britain—though see also Shorrocks 1975) and the selectivity explanation is no more plausible than a number of other stories, for example that the elderly have little need for consumption at the margin, or that they feel a duty to pass on their assets to their heirs.

The rapidly rising age profile of consumption, although very far from the flat profile that is often assumed in the textbooks, is not in itself inconsistent with the theory. There is no reason why people should not choose a consumption profile that increases with age, and the high real interest rates in Taiwan (China) certainly provide an incentive to postpone consumption until late in life. However, there must be at least a suspicion that the similarity between the income and consumption profiles in Figure 6.6 is not entirely coincidental, and that consumption might be determined by income. Such a suspicion is reinforced by looking at the same data in yet another way. Figure 6.7 plots the averages of log consumption and log income for each cohort starting with those who were 14 in 1976 (in the top left panel) and finishing with those who were 62 in 1976 (in the bottom right panel). For most of these cohorts, the income and consumption lines move apart over time, restating the fact that the saving ratio is rising, but there is a very marked similarity in the two lines for each cohort. Whatever is the time profile of income, so too is the time profile of consumption. According to the life-cycle model, such tracking could come about through a coincidence of the age profiles of preferences and incomes; the desired life-cycle profile of consumption happens to match the actual life-cycle profile of income. Alternatively, the data are consistent with people saving a fraction of their incomes, a fraction that drifts upward over time. To say so is not much more than a description of the data, and it is far from clear why people should behave in this way. For people who have no interest in accumulation, and who would like to borrow but cannot, consumption would move closely with income because consumption is equal to income. But for these

Taiwanese households, who save a great deal and have consequently accumulated assets that are several multiples of their income, there is no obvious reason why consumption and income should be so closely tied. Nor is this phenomenon confined to Taiwan (China); Paxson (1996) finds similar close links between consumption and income for cohort data from Thailand, Britain, and the United States, and Carroll and Summers (1991) find the same across occupational and educational groups in the United States.

In summary, the Taiwanese data permit a life-cycle interpretation but there are uncomfortable anomalies. The saving rate rises with age, which may be a selection effect, and there is secular increase in saving rates across cohorts, which is perhaps attributable to bequest motives, or to changes in living arrangements. But neither phenomenon has a natural interpretation in the life-cycle model, and both need to be explained away.

It is worth recalling from Section 2.7 that the identification of the cohort and age effects in Figures 6.5 and 6.6 rests on the assumption that there is no trend in year effects. In consequence, if we were to extend the model to include an upward time trend in the saving rate, it would be possible to eliminate both the downward trend in the cohort saving rates—Figure 6.5—and the upward trend in the age saving rates—Figure 6.6—after which both figures would be closer to the predictions of the theory. But this is just another way of admitting that the theory cannot explain the data. Aggregate saving rates rose in Taiwan (China) between 1976 and 1990, and the rise is not explained by any simple version of the life-cycle model, but by a residual time-trend. Life-cycle theory is supposed to explain aggregate saving in terms of changes in cohort size—demographics—and changes in cohort lifetime resources—wealth effects. Instead, we are left with the uninformative conclusion that, for some unknown and unmodeled reason, saving rates went up. Paxson (1996) encounters the same failures of the life-cycle model in trying to explain trends in the saving rates in Britain, the United States, and Thailand; indeed, in her calculations, the Taiwanese case is the most favorable for the life-cycle story!

6.2 Short-term consumption smoothing and permanent income

The evidence in Section 6.1 shows that consumption moves parallel to income over the life cycle and indeed, that they are tied together over periods longer than a few years. Such a finding does not imply that consumption and income are closely related at shorter frequencies of days, months, seasons, or years. Such short-term or "high-frequency" smoothing reveals the extent to which households can maintain their consumption and living standards in the face of short-term fluctuations in their incomes, fluctuations that can be frequent and large for agricultural households. Short-term consumption smoothing is one way that households insure their consumption in the presence of risky and variable incomes.

The extent to which consumption is smoothed is important for a number of policy issues in developing countries. If agricultural households are somehow incapable of suitable intertemporal allocation, then there is a possible custodial role for the government to make the allocation on their behalf. Indeed, the supposed inability of poor households to save lies at the heart of the once-standard project evaluation guidelines (Dasgupta, Marglin, and Sen 1972; Little and Mirrlees 1974; and Squire and van der Tak 1975). The supposition that consumption is constrained by current income, even in the short run, is also frequently used as a justification for commodity-price stabilization schemes, or marketing boards for crops that pay farmers fixed prices for their crops and "protect" them from the fluctuations in market prices. For example, in an early discussion, Bauer and Paish (1952) argued that marketing boards should make payments to farmers based on a moving average of world prices, on the grounds that "Small producers are unlikely to have the self-restraint and foresight to set aside in good times sufficient reserves to cushion the effects of worse ones, or, even if they have, may be debarred from doing so by social customs and obligations." (p. 766). The link with saving was made in a reply by Friedman (1954), who emphasized that the scheme forced farmers to save, and who doubted whether marketing boards were a suitable substitute for education and the development of credit markets. (Of course, the question of a custodial saving policy depends not only on the extent to which peasants can make good intertemporal decisions, but also on whether the government can do better.)

Just as low-frequency smoothing is associated with the life-cycle hypothesis, so can high-frequency smoothing be associated with the at least some versions of Friedman's (1957) permanent income hypothesis. According to Friedman's theory, consumption is determined not by current income, but by permanent income, where permanent income can be defined over various possible time horizons. If the horizon is the lifetime, the permanent income model coincides with the life-cycle model, but we can also consider an infinite horizon, which would be appropriate for a dynastic or long-lived extended family, and which has been much used in the macroeconomic literature for a "representative" agent, or a short horizon of just a few years.

It is not straightforward to use household survey data to discover the extent to which consumption is smoothed over time. Looking at changes in income and consumption requires panel data, and as we have seen, such changes are typically very poorly measured in the few examples of panel data that we have. However, our understanding of these issues has been enhanced by a number of valuable studies based on household survey data, and in this section, I look at some of the methods that are available, and some of the results.

Saving and weather variability

A convenient way to state the permanent income model for empirical analysis is to write consumption as a function of permanent and transitory income, together with other variables, for example the demographic structure of the household. Write this in the form:

$$(6.3) \qquad c_{ht} = \alpha + \beta y_{ht}^{P} + \gamma y_{ht}^{T} + \theta.z_{ht} + u_{ht}$$

where the subscripts h and t refer to households and time periods, the superscripts P and T denote permanent and transitory, respectively, and total measured income is the sum of its transitory and permanent components. In a "strict" version of the permanent income hypothesis, the parameters β and γ would be one and zero, respectively, but if we can find evidence that β is greater than γ, that a greater fraction of what is seen as transitory income is saved, it would suggest that households are acting so as to smooth their consumption relative to income.

The estimation of (6.3) requires additional assumptions about what is transitory and what is permanent. Suppose that we substitute $y^P = y - y^T$ so that (6.3) can be written as

$$(6.4) \qquad c_{ht} = \alpha + \beta y_{ht} + \theta . z_{ht} + (\gamma - \beta) y_{ht}^T + u_{ht}.$$

If transitory income is absorbed into the error term, this equation can be estimated from a single cross section provided that we have at least one instrumental variable that is correlated with permanent income, but that is orthogonal to transitory income. Variants of this technique have been used by a number of authors: Musgrove (1978, 1979) for urban households in Colombia, Ecuador, and Peru, and Bhalla (1979, 1980) and Wolpin (1982) for India; instruments have included assets and education (Musgrove), lagged income, averages of income over previous years (Bhalla), and long-run averages of rainfall (Wolpin). These studies have rarely found that the propensity to spend out of permanent income is as large as unity, but have nearly all found that it is larger than the propensity to consume out of transitory income, suggesting at least some smoothing.

A number of difficulties with this methodology should be noted. There is the familiar difficulty of finding convincing instruments, and it is usually easier to justify the role of instruments such as assets and lagged income as predictors of permanent income than it is to defend their absence from the direct determination of consumption in the equation of interest. For example, education may make people less myopic and more willing to substitute future for current consumption, landholdings might enhance the demand for calories for agricultural work, and so on. Second, it is always difficult to distinguish genuine transitory income from measurement error. Indeed, Friedman's original formulation was built on a precise (and complete) analogy between transitory income and measurement error, with permanent income analogous to correctly measured income. Given this correspondence, it is always difficult to distinguish genuine measurement error from transitory income. Hence, for example, if we ignore the transitory income term in (6.4) and use OLS to obtain an estimate of β that is smaller than when we instrument by assets, landholding, or education, then we have no way of knowing whether the result is what we are interested in, that people are smoothing their consumption, or whether we are seeing the effects of the omnipresent measurement error in income, measurement error with which assets, landholding, or education are only partially correlated.

These issues can be illustrated with the LSS data from Côte d'Ivoire. For example, if we use the 688 households in the 1986–87 panel and regress household consumption on household total income, household size, and dummies for four of the five zones (Abidjan, Other urban, East Forest, West Forest, and Savannah), the marginal propensity to consume is estimated to be 0.209 with a *t*-value of 22. If the same regression is estimated by IV using income in 1986 as an instrument (together with household size and regional dummies) the marginal propensity to consume, instead of rising, falls to 0.187 with a *t*-value of 18. According to (6.4), since $\beta > \gamma$ and the covariance of total and transitory income is positive, β will be biased down by the omission of transitory income, so that we would expect the estimate of β to be larger under IV than OLS if households are smoothing their consumption. Of course, lagged income might not be a valid instrument, either because there are dynamics in consumption patterns so that consumption is directly affected by both current and lagged income, or because transitory income is correlated from one year to the next. If lagged income is negatively correlated with current transitory income, which would be true if unusually high incomes are followed by unusually low ones, as is the case for some tree crops, then the IV estimates using lagged income will be biased down just as the OLS estimates are biased up. If instead of lagged income, we use as instruments the head's education and the beginning of period values of assets—personal, business, and agricultural assets are separately distinguished—the estimate of β rises to 0.516 ($t = 13$), this time in accord with the permanent income model in which education and assets are correlated with permanent but not transitory income.

However, we know how difficult it was to calculate income estimates for these data, and that the margin of error is large. So it is possible that the increase in the coefficient has nothing to do with permanent income, but comes from the fact that assets and education are uncorrelated with the measurement errors in income. Business and agricultural income are also by far the most difficult to measure, and income from earnings the easiest, so we could construct an instrumental variables estimate using current (1987) earnings to instrument total income, not on permanent income grounds, but simply to control the measurement error. This estimate is 0.410 ($t = 17$) and takes us most of the way from the OLS to the IV estimates using assets and education. Of course, it can also be argued that earnings are less variable than either agricultural or business income, so that these results too are consistent with a permanent income interpretation. Measurement error and transitory income are essentially indistinguishable in these models, and it is hopeless to try to test hypotheses that depend on the distinction between them.

Paxson's (1992) study of rice farmers in Thailand circumvents these problems an provides convincing evidence that farmers respond differently to transitory and permanent income. Most rice farms in Thailand are not irrigated, so that crop sizes depend on the amount of rainfall, with more rainfall resulting in more income over the relevant range. Although average rainfall is predictably different from place to place, the deviation of each year's rainfall from its local mean is serially uncorrelated and thus unpredictable. Hence income associated with good rainfall is transitory, with close to no direct effect on future or permanent income. Paxson uses data on farmers' incomes from the Thai Socioeconomic Surveys of 1975–76, 1980–81, and 1986, and matches the geographical location of each household to 21 local rainfall stations, from which monthly rainfall data are available over 35 years. She then regresses measured income on the rainfall and other variables, which allows a transitory component of income to be isolated. Entered into a consumption regression, this component attracts a lower coefficient than does the remainder of income. These Thai rice farmers appear to recognize that it is wise to lay aside a substantial fraction of the rain-induced income.

Paxson (1993) has also used the Thai data to investigate consumption smoothing over seasonal frequencies. One would perhaps expect even the most myopic of agricultural consumers to understand the implications of seasonal income fluctuations, and the need to make adequate provision in good seasons for the lean times to come. Nevertheless, there is a literature in economic development (see for example the papers in Sahn 1989), that argues that poor households are sometimes unable to make adequate provision for seasonal fluctuations. Paxson's idea is to compare the seasonal consumption patterns of groups whose seasonal income patterns are very different. If consumption is constrained by seasonal income patterns, the seasonal patterns of consumption will be different across the different groups, while if seasonal patterns of consumption are determined purely by seasonal variations in prices or tastes, they should plausibly be the same across groups. Paxson compares the seasonal consumption patterns of rural versus urban consumers, of farm versus nonfarm households, and of single-cropping rice farmers versus double-cropping rice farmers. Even though the Thai surveys do not track individuals over even a whole year, seasonals can be computed by averaging over different members of each group. The results show that consumption patterns of the different groups are very similar, even for those groups with large differences in their income patterns. At least for these data, consumption seasonality is a matter of choice, not of constraint.

Saving as a predictor of income change?

Another method for testing whether people make provision for the future is to test whether their saving predicts future changes in their incomes. That this is a consequence of the permanent income hypothesis was first stated and investigated by Campbell (1987) using American macroeconomic data, but the idea is even more appropriate for microeconomic analysis, particularly for farm households. Consider the case of a tree-crop farmer, say a cocoa or coffee smallholder in Côte d'Ivoire. If trees are destroyed by bush fires or by infestation by pests, the farmer knows that his harvest will be low for the next year or two. Similarly, even within the harvest year, the state of a tree provides substantial information about its yield long before the harvest is collected, and even longer before the farmer receives payment. Farmers thus have a good deal of advance information about their future incomes, information that they should use when deciding how much to consume and how much to save in the present. A farmer who discovers that his trees have been destroyed in the previous night should cut consumption immediately rather than waiting for the misfortune to be turned into hard cash.

When people look to the future in setting their behavior, there are important econometric implications. In particular, if people use information about the future that is not available to the econometrician, the existence of the information will show up in their current behavior, which can thus be used to predict the future, even though there is no causal link. If we know that someone has checked the weather forecast, and observe her carrying an umbrella, we can use the umbrella to "predict" the rain, even though the causality runs from rain to umbrellas, not the other way around. In the same way, the saving behavior of the Ivorian small-holders, who can read something of their future income in their trees, can tell us what they expect to happen to their incomes. Of course, if the survey data collected all the information relevant for predicting income, the health of the trees, rainfall to date, and myriad other factors, and if we conditioned our forecasts on all of these things, then saving would not add additional information. But in practice, there is no hope that the econometrician could know as much as the farmer, so that, if farmers are deliberately smoothing their consumption, saving should predict future income. More specifically, bad news should engender a cut in consumption and good news an increase, so that saving should negatively predict changes in income.

The prediction that saving predicts a fall in income can be tested if we have panel data with several observations on income, consumption, and saving, and this is the case for the two successive panels (1985–86 and 1986–87) of the Côte d'Ivoire LSS. However, it is necessary to be careful when constructing a test. Given a long enough panel, we could simply test for each household whether saving in year t helped predict income in year $t+1$ using, for example, a standard Granger causality test. However, panels are typically short—in the Ivorian case only two years—so that we have to use the cross-sectional dimension of the data, and test whether people who saved a great deal in one year were also those whose income was lowest in the next. But different individuals have different average income levels, and we do not want to contaminate the test with the cross-section relationship between saving and income levels. However, if each household's income varies around its own individual (constant) mean—a household fixed effect—then the change in income will be purged of the fixed effect, and we can test whether saving in one year is negatively correlated with the change in income from that year to the next. Under the permanent income hypothesis, households with stationary income streams use saving to smooth consumption, not to accumulate, so that saving itself will be stationary and, over a long enough period of time, will average to zero. Hence, if all that households are doing is smoothing their consumption, and if income is a stationary process for each, the cross-section regression of income change on lagged saving is free of household-specific fixed effects and can be used to test the proposition that saving helps predict income change.

Table 6.1 shows the results of regressing the change in income for the Ivorian panel households on their saving in the previous year. (The data used here and in subsequent tables in this chapter come from an earlier release than those used in Chapter 1, and are therefore not strictly comparable with them.) The left-hand side of the table shows the regressions for the 1985–86 panel households, and the right-hand side those for the 1986–87 panel. Each of the five regions is shown

Table 6.1. The effects of saving on the next period's income, Côte d'Ivoire, 1985–86 and 1986–87

Region	1985–86		1986–87	
Abidjan	−0.439	(1.9)	−0.022	(2.0)
Other urban	−0.627	(3.6)	−0.465	(3.6)
West Forest	−0.694	(10.8)	−0.781	(4.0)
East Forest	−0.868	(14.7)	−0.761	(5.4)
Savannah	−0.625	(3.5)	−0.792	(11.9)

Note: The numbers are the regression coefficients (and absolute t-values, corrected for cluster effects) of year t's saving in a regression where the dependent variable is the change in income from year t to $t+1$. Source: Author's calculations using CILSS data.

separately. It is reasonable to expect that the degree of private information will vary from region to region, that it will probably be larger for farmers than wage earners, and larger for tree-crop farmers than for cultivators of perennials like cotton. The coefficients appear to confirm the hypothesis. All are negative and all except for Abidjan are significantly different from zero. The households who saved the most were those whose income fell the most in the next period.

Unfortunately, this evidence is far from convincing. The culprit, as so often, is measurement error in income. Suppose, for example, that income in period t is overstated. As a result, saving in t will be overstated while the increase in income from t to $t+1$ will be understated and there will be a spurious negative correlation between lagged saving and income change, a correlation that might account for the OLS results in the table. Of course, since saving is mismeasured and since saving is the explanatory variable, there will also be an attenuation bias, but if we suppose that there is no true relation between saving and future income, zero will be attenuated to zero, and the spurious negative correlation will generate a negative probability limit for the OLS estimator. Formally, if the true relationship is

$$(6.5) \qquad \Delta y^*_{it+1} = \alpha + \beta s^*_{it} + u_{it}$$

where asterisks denote correctly measured variables, then the probability limit of the OLS estimator is, cf. (2.62)

$$(6.6) \qquad \text{plim}\,\beta = \beta\frac{\text{var}\,s^*}{\text{var}\,s^* + \text{var}\,\epsilon_s} + \frac{\text{cov}(\epsilon_s \epsilon_{\Delta y})}{\text{var}\,s^* + \text{var}\,\epsilon_s}$$

where the variances and covariances are taken over observations in the cross section, and ϵ_s and $\epsilon_{\Delta y}$ are the (unobserved) measurement errors in saving and the income change, respectively. The first term shows the standard attenuation effects of the measurement error, and the second is the effect of the spurious correlation. If the mismeasurement of income is the dominant component in the mismeasurement of saving, which is itself small, (6.6) could yield a number close to −1, even if the true β is zero.

Unfortunately, it is difficult to do much about the measurement error with the Ivorian data. Instruments for saving are hard to come by, not because there are no plausible candidates, but because it is hard to find any valid instrument that predicts saving in the first-stage regression. It is hard not to interpret this finding as further evidence that the saving data are mostly measurement error. If some households had been followed for a third year, it would be possible to test whether saving in year t predicted the income change from $t+1$ to $t+2$, and since the income measure used in constructing saving would be a year away from the income measure used to construct the income change, the spurious correlation would be eliminated. With only two years of panel data, I have found no way to construct a test without making arbitrary—and fundamentally indefensible—identification assumptions. An attempt is in Deaton (1992a), where the theory underlying the analysis of this subsection is elaborated.

6.3 Models of saving for poor households

I have already discussed simple versions of the permanent income and life-cycle models of consumption, but these do not exhaust the theoretical possibilities for households in poor countries. In this section, I review the basic theoretical apparatus of intertemporal choice, and discuss the variants that appear to be most suited to describing behavior in developing countries. All of these models are concerned with the allocation of resources over time, which is the essence of saving behavior, but differ in their detailed assumptions and institutional description.

The basic model of intertemporal choice

In order to discuss intertemporal choice, we need to specify preferences and a budget constraint. A standard intertemporal utility function is written in the form

(6.7)
$$u = E_t \sum_{k=t}^{T} \upsilon_k(c_k)$$

where c_k is consumption in period k, T is the time-horizon or date of death, $\upsilon_k(.)$ is the instantaneous subutility function for period k, and E_t is the expectation conditional on information available at time t. In general, we need to recognize that the subutility functions will change with time, if only because needs change with age, and because we shall usually have to work with household-level data, and the structure of households changes over time. The budget constraint within which utility is to be maximized is partly characterized by the equation that governs the evolution of assets over time, written here as

(6.8)
$$A_{t+1} = (1+r_{t+1})(A_t+y_t-c_t)$$

where A_t is the real value at t of a single real asset, r_{t+1} is the real interest rate from period t to $t+1$, and y_t is earnings in period t. Earnings and real interest rates are typically treated as stochastic. To complete the model, there has to be some terminal asset condition, for example that assets at time T are zero or at least non-negative.

This specification of intertemporal choice ignores labor supply, something that might be hard to justify for (say) a farm household in India. According to (6.8), earnings are outside the control of the individual, and there is a clear separation between labor income (earnings) and capital income which here is the increment to assets when the real interest rate is nonzero. For a farmer, or indeed any self-employed person, hours worked can be varied, and asset income and labor income are practically impossible to separate. To make sense of the saving decisions of such people, the model must be extended. For some simple cases, such as when farm income is largely determined by the weather and where capital accumulation is unimportant, the simple model can still be useful.

There are a number of ways of characterizing the solution of the intertemporal optimization problem. Perhaps the simplest is to rewrite the problem as a dynamic program. Write $V_t(A_t)$ for the value of the program at time t for a person with assets A_t, where the value is simply the expected utility at t according to (6.7). Then (6.7) can be rewritten as

$$(6.9) \qquad V_t(A_t) = \max_\omega \{v_t(A_t + y_t - \omega) + E_t V_{t+1}[(1 + r_{t+1})\omega]\}$$

where ω is the amount from total resources $A_t + y_t$ (or "cash on hand") that is withheld for future consumption, and which will be augmented in the next period by the stochastic real rate of interest.

If we differentiate (6.9) with respect to real assets A_t, we have

$$(6.10) \qquad V_t'(A_t) = v_t'(c_t) \equiv \lambda_t(c_t), \text{ say.}$$

This equation is an immediate consequence of the envelope theorem, that when differentiating the right-hand side of (6.9), we can ignore the implicit dependence of ω on A_t (see for example Dixit 1976, ch. 3). The expression $\lambda_t(c_t)$ is introduced to denote the marginal utility of consumption, a quantity with which we shall be much concerned. The other condition that we need from (6.9) is the first-order condition associated with the optimal choice of ω. Provided that there are no restrictions on borrowing or lending, so that current consumption can be set independently of current resources, this is

$$(6.11) \qquad v_t'(c_t) = E_t[(1 + r_{t+1}) V_{t+1}'(A_{t+1})].$$

If we use the definition of $\lambda_t(c_t)$ on the left-hand side, and equation (6.10) to substitute for the right-hand side, we obtain

$$(6.12) \qquad \lambda_t(c_t) = E_t[(1 + r_{t+1}) \lambda_{t+1}(c_{t+1})].$$

Equation (6.12), often referred to as the Euler equation of intertemporal optimization, ensures that, up to a discount factor, money is expected to be equally valuable at the margin in all periods, or more loosely, that the marginal rate of substitution between consumption in any two periods should reflect the relative opportunity cost of funds in the two periods. It provides a number of useful insights about saving behavior, as well as serving as a basis for empirical analysis.

Special cases: the permanent income and life-cycle models

Under special assumptions, the Euler equation (6.12) is consistent with the permanent income hypothesis and with the simplest form of the life-cycle model. In particular, suppose that each period's subutility function is identical up to a discounting factor, so that

$$(6.13) \qquad v_t(c_t) = (1+\delta)^{-t} v(c_t)$$

for time-invariant function $v(.)$. The parameter δ controls the rate at which subutility tomorrow is discounted relative to subutility today, and is thus the rate of time preference. Suppose also that the rate of interest is a constant r, so that if $\lambda(c)$ is the derivative of $v(c)$, (6.12) takes the special form

$$(6.14) \qquad \lambda(c_t) = \frac{1+r}{1+\delta} E_t \lambda(c_{t+1}).$$

If we make two further assumptions, (i) that the rate of time preference is equal to the rate of interest, and (ii) that the subutility functions are quadratic so that the marginal utility functions are linear in consumption, then (6.14) implies that

$$(6.15) \qquad c_t = E_t c_{t+1}.$$

This equation says that consumption is a "martingale," a stochastic process whose expected future value is its current value; indeed, by successive substitution in (6.15), current consumption is also the expected value of consumption in any future period. (6.15) also can be rewritten as

$$(6.16) \qquad c_{t+1} = c_t + u_{t+1}$$

where u_{t+1} is a stochastic shock or "innovation" whose expectation at time t is zero.

Equations (6.15) and (6.16), which trace back to the seminal work of Hall (1978), are often referred to as the "random walk" property of consumption. However, a random walk is a special case of a martingale, when the variance of the innovations u_{t+1} is constant over time, something that is not implied by (6.15). Note too that (6.15) is itself obtained from (6.14) under very special—and very implausible—assumptions, and that even (6.14) is a specialization of the Euler equation (6.12). Substantively, the transition from (6.12) to (6.15) rules out variations in real interest rates and imposes a quite unreasonable homogeneity on household structure, something that would have to be modified in practice. As we shall see in the next subsection, the specialization from (6.14) to (6.15) rules out a type of precautionary behavior that is plausible for poor people in developing countries. And all of these special assumptions are added to the basic assumption underlying the Euler equation (6.12), that consumers have access to as much borrowing as they need when they need it, and that they pay the same rate for loans as they get on their savings.

If we accept all the assumptions, (6.15) provides a formal justification for models in which planned consumption is constant. In a life-cycle interpretation, where the focus is less on uncertainty than on the age profiles of consumption, earnings, and savings, the martingale property becomes the constant consumption property of the simplest "stripped-down" life-cycle model. The permanent income hypothesis is essentially the same, though it tends to be stated, not that consumption is constant, but that consumption is equal to permanent income, defined as the annuity value of the sum of current assets and the discounted present value of expected future earnings. In the absence of uncertainty, permanent income will be constant, and so will be consumption. With stochastic earnings, permanent income is revised as expectations about income are revised, but since permanent income is itself an expected value, its expected change is zero, and it is itself a martingale. Although constant consumption, or constant expected consumption, is an attractive and simple baseline against which to compare more elaborate models of intertemporal allocation, its derivation requires very strong assumptions that we cannot reasonably expect to hold for poor households in developing countries.

A richer version of the life-cycle model can be derived by recognizing the dependence of the marginal utility of consumption on factors other than consumption, such as age or household composition. Suppose that there is no uncertainty, but that (6.14) is extended to include household characteristics z_t, sometimes referred to as "taste shifters,"

$$(6.17) \qquad \lambda(c_t, z_t) = \frac{1+r}{1+\delta} \lambda(c_{t+1}, z_{t+1}) = \left(\frac{1+r}{1+\delta}\right)^k \lambda(c_{t+k}, z_{t+k})$$

so that, since the last equality holds for all k, we have the result that the age profile of consumption is determined by household characteristics, or tastes, and by the relationship between the real rate of interest and the rate of time preference (see Ghez and Becker 1975 for one of the first derivations along such lines).

If $r > \delta$, so that the rewards for waiting are sufficient to overcome impatience, the marginal utility of consumption will be falling with age, and consumption will be rising. Conversely, if impatience overcomes the incentives to wait, marginal utility will be rising, and consumption falling. The level of consumption, as opposed to its profile with age, is determined by the intertemporal budget constraint, which in the absence of uncertainty is summarized by lifetime resources. If the marginal utility functions in (6.17) are homogeneous—for example if they are of the standard isoelastic constant relative risk aversion type—then the ratio of consumption levels in different periods will be independent of the level of lifetime resources, so that changes in lifetime resources will simply move the profile up or down in parallel, without altering its shape. Such a model provides a formal basis for the life-cycle model that was applied to Taiwan (China) in Section 6.1 (see equation 6.1).

Further analysis of the basic model: precautionary saving

Although the permanent income and life-cycle models are perhaps the two leading examples that are consistent with the general theory of intertemporal choice,
they are by no means the only ones. Each simplifies in a different direction, the
permanent income model downplaying the effects of age and family composition
to focus on the way in which consumption responds to new information, and the
life-cycle model abstracting from uncertainty in order to derive simple forms for
the age profiles of consumption and saving. As we have seen in the first two
sections, each of these simplifications is potentially useful for thinking about
different aspects of consumption smoothing in developing countries, the permanent income model for thinking about fluctuations in seasonal or annual incomes,
and the life-cycle model for examining relationships between saving and age.
However, there are important cases that are covered by neither one, perhaps the
most important of which is behavior when there is uncertainty, and when the
marginal utility of consumption is not linear.

The marginal utility of consumption function $\lambda(c)$ can usefully be thought of
as determining a "shadow-price" for consumption; because there is diminishing
marginal utility of consumption, this price is higher when consumption is low
than when it is high. Additional consumption is more urgent in the lean season
than in the fat season, and consumers will be prepared to give up more for it when
they have little, for example by paying higher interest rates for loans to tide them
over. It is also possible—perhaps even reasonable—to suppose that the marginal
utility of consumption rises more rapidly when consumption is low than when
consumption is high. For example, if there is a subsistence level of consumption,
then the marginal value of consumption might well tend to infinity as consumption falls to that level. Based on such arguments, we might want to suppose that
the marginal utility of consumption function is (strictly) convex.

Consider the implications of equation (6.14) in the case where the marginal
utility of consumption function is convex. Suppose that, for some unspecified
reason, future consumption becomes more uncertain, in that its mean remains unchanged but its spread around the mean is larger. Because the marginal utility
function is convex, the increase in spread will increase its expected future value,
and so the current marginal utility of consumption must also increase to preserve
the equality in (6.14). Since marginal utility is diminishing, this means that current consumption will fall and saving increase. Since (6.14) also implies that the
marginal utility of current consumption is the appropriately discounted expectation of the marginal utility of consumption in any future period, the same argument shows that an increase in uncertainty about consumption in any future period will also increase current saving. When the marginal utility function is convex, increases in future uncertainty in the sense defined lead to an increase in
current saving, something that can be thought of as precautionary saving.

This argument is limited by the fact that it does not specify the cause of the
mean-preserving spread in future consumption, and the proposition cannot be
readily translated into statements about the effects of increased uncertainty in the

more fundamental underlying variables, such as earnings and interest rates. For example, it is not true without further assumptions that a farmer with convex marginal utility will increase current saving in response to a mean-preserving spread in next period's harvest (see for example the discussion and references in Dasgupta 1993, pp. 260–64). However, the convexity of marginal utility has proved to be a useful way of characterizing the precautionary motive, and seems particularly promising for analyzing the behavior of people for whom subsistence or worse is a real possibility.

It should be noted that the convexity of the marginal utility of consumption—which characterizes how prudent or cautious people are—is not at all the same thing as the concavity of the utility function—which characterizes the degree of risk aversion. Declining marginal utility, as in the permanent income hypothesis, implies risk aversion, but it does not necessarily imply the existence of a precautionary motive. Risk aversion relates to the second derivative of the utility function, and prudence to the third, a fact that has been used by Kimball (1990) to provide simple measures of prudence that parallel—but differ from—the standard measures of risk aversion. Of course, for specific utility functions, prudence and risk aversion may be related. For example, in the standard isoelastic utility function with marginal utility $c^{-\rho}$, where ρ is the coefficient of relative risk aversion, prudence is also controlled by the single parameter ρ, so that consumers who are more risk averse are automatically also more prudent.

One reason that the permanent income and life-cycle models have dominated discussion is that they are easy to work with, and it is possible to provide closed-form solutions that characterize consumption and saving. This is not possible with precautionary motives, and apart from a few special cases of limited interest, there are no closed-form solutions to (6.14) when there is uncertainty and when $\lambda(c)$ is nonlinear. As a result, we understand less about precautionary savers than we do about permanent income or life-cycle savers. Even so, much recent progress has been made using approximations by letting computers solve sample dynamic programs and then simulating behavior (see Skinner 1988; Zeldes 1989a; Carroll forthcoming, and Hubbard, Skinner, and Zeldes 1994, 1995). Several points are worth noting.

When there is a precautionary motive for saving, intertemporal transfers of funds that are actuarially neutral are capable of affecting behavior. In the life-cycle or permanent income models, where consumption depends on expected lifetime resources or on permanent income, a fully funded but compulsory social security system that accumulates contributions with interest cannot affect consumption because it does not affect the discounted present value of lifetime resources. If the contributions leave the consumer short of liquidity, loans can be negotiated with the accumulated contributions as collateral. However, if consumers are prudent, and like to have precautionary balances on hand, the compulsory contributions will generate an addition to saving. Savings that are accumulated for retirement can perfectly well double as a reserve for emergencies, but if direct access to them is removed, or if they cannot be used as collateral for loans, they must be replaced.

The obvious question is why such consumers do not borrow, and why the availability of loans does not remove the need for precautionary balances. The answer is that prudent consumers may be reluctant to borrow, even when loans are available, so that in the absence of precautionary balances, consumption may have to be cut when income is low. Although a loan may protect consumption now, it has to be repaid in the future, and if the consumer is unlucky enough, may have to be repaid when things are even worse than they are at present. In the limit, if utility is infinitely low at subsistence, and if income can fall as low as subsistence levels, consumers will never borrow (see Skinner 1988 and Carroll forthcoming). A plan that involves entering the last period of life with nonpositive assets involves a finite risk of subsistence, and thus cannot be optimal. But a consumer with non-positive assets in the second to last period also has a finite risk of exiting the period with non-positive assets, so such a plan cannot be optimal either, and so on back to the present. Such an argument raises more questions than it answers—about the support from friends or relatives that might be available in extreme circumstances, and about incentives to provide, accept, or exploit such support—but it provides an illustration of why credit availability might be of limited value to consumers for whom precautionary motives are important.

Even when consumers are not completely unwilling to borrow, the computer analyses show that prudent consumers smooth their consumption less than do permanent income consumers. When income is low, at the beginning of life, or because of a poor harvest, consumption is also lowered at least to some extent, because to maintain consumption would run down precautionary balances or run up loans, either of which would expose the consumer to possible low consumption in a future in which low incomes might occur again. As a result, if incomes are sufficiently uncertain, if marginal utility functions sufficiently convex, and if the rate of time preference is sufficiently high to prevent people wanting to accumulate, the consumption of prudent consumers may track their incomes quite closely (see particularly Carroll forthcoming).

Restrictions on borrowing

The other major challenge to the permanent income and life-cycle accounts of consumption comes from models that explicitly impose a borrowing constraint. Although it is clear that most consumers in developing countries have access to credit on some terms, many people do not have access to the low borrowing rates of formal credit markets, and must rely when necessary on the very high rates charged by moneylenders. Such a situation could be modeled by assuming that borrowing rates are much higher than lending rates, but a simpler way to start is to make the borrowing rate infinite, i.e. to prohibit borrowing altogether. This extreme assumption is also an important baseline, because it allows us to investigate the extent to which it is possible for consumption to be smoothed in "autarky" when agents have no one to rely on but themselves, when there are no friends, relatives, or social systems to pool risks and provide insurance, and when there are no credit markets to provide loans when resources are low.

A consumer with a borrowing constraint can be modeled in the same way as in the basic case, maximizing (6.7) subject to (6.8) but with the additional constraint that assets are nonnegative, so that

$$(6.18) \qquad\qquad A_t \geq 0.$$

The asymmetry in (6.18) is important; consumers cannot borrow, but nothing prevents them from accumulating assets. This may seem obvious, but for many poor people around the world, even this may be difficult. Savings institutions may not exist, or may not be trusted, and there may be no safe place to store cash. As a result, people may be forced to save by stockpiling grain, or by hoarding jewelry or gold, assets that may have low or even negative returns.

For those people whose original plan does not call for negative assets, the restriction will have no effect on their intertemporal allocation between t and $t+1$, so that the original Euler equation (6.12) will hold as before. For others, or for the same people in different circumstances, the Euler equation might represent behavior in the absence of borrowing, but its satisfaction calls for higher consumption than is available out of current income or assets, something that is impossible in the absence of borrowing. Indeed, the borrowing restriction (6.18) implies that consumption is also limited, and must satisfy

$$(6.19) \qquad\qquad c_t \leq A_t + y_t.$$

By (6.19), the marginal utility of money (which is lower the higher is consumption) cannot be less than $\lambda(A_t + y_t)$, so that the effect of the borrowing restriction is to replace the original Euler equation (6.12) by

$$(6.20) \qquad \lambda_t(c_t) = \max\!\big(\lambda(A_t + y_t), E_t[(1 + r_{t+1})\lambda_{t+1}(c_{t+1})]\big).$$

The solution of (6.20) appears to be even less readily accessible than the solution to the precautionary saving problem without the credit constraint but, in fact, the problem is rather better understood, and yields insights that seem useful for describing what we see for at least some poor, agricultural households.

Consider the special case of (6.20) that ignores taste shifters, and that assumes constant rates of interest and time preference; this is the modification of (6.14) that incorporates the borrowing constraint:

$$(6.21) \qquad \lambda(c_t) = \max\!\left(\lambda(A_t + y_t), \frac{1+r}{1+\delta} E_t \lambda(c_{t+1}) \right).$$

What (6.21) implies for behavior depends on how income behaves or is expected to behave, as well as on the relationship between r and δ. If the consumer wishes to save rather than borrow, the constraint will not bind, and behavior will be the same as in the standard case. This will be so if people are relatively patient, with low enough rates of time preference, or if income is not expected to rise too much. Much can be learned from examining the special case where income y_t is stationary, and where impatience outweighs the reward for waiting, so that $\delta > r$.

Consider a farmer whose income is determined by the weather, who has no access to credit, who has no wish to accumulate, but who needs assets to provide a cushion in bad years. In the absence of uncertainty, his income would be the same every year. If the farmer could borrow, he would do so. According to the unconstrained solution (6.14) with $\delta > r$, the marginal utility of consumption is rising through time, so that consumption is falling. This relatively impatient consumer wants consumption to be higher than income in the short run, and will pay off the resulting debts by having consumption lower than income in the future. If borrowing is not permitted, he will first run down any assets that he has, and then consume his income in every period thereafter. However, as soon as we introduce uncertainty, this may not be the best strategy. Setting consumption equal to income will introduce variations in consumption that can at least partially be avoided, not by accumulating assets over the long run, which is never desirable for this impatient individual, but by putting something aside in good years that can be drawn on in the bad years that will sooner or later inevitably follow.

The simplest case is when income is independently and identically distributed, so that each harvest tells the farmer nothing about harvests in the future. Provided his horizon is long enough, the optimal solution to (6.21) is for the farmer to determine his consumption in relation to $A_t + y_t$, his stock of "cash on hand" after each harvest (see Schechtman 1976 and Schechtman and Escudero 1977, for the original analysis, and Deaton 1990b, 1991, for a fuller exposition in the current context). The relationship between consumption and cash on hand has the property that when cash on hand is low, because the harvest has been poor, or because previous harvests were poor so that few assets were carried over from previous years, or both, everything should be consumed. This is the situation in which the farmer would borrow if he could, but since that option is not available, he does the next best thing, and consumes everything. And while it is true that the harvest may be poor again next year, the risk has to be taken if things are bad enough in the present; even when everything is spent, the marginal utility of consumption is higher now than it is expected to be in the future. When cash on hand is above the critical level, something should be put aside as a precautionary reserve for future consumption, and the more cash is available, the larger is the fraction that ought to be saved.

This optimal behavior takes into account not only the inability to borrow today, and the tradeoff between consumption today and consumption tomorrow, but also the farmer's knowledge that he will not be able to borrow in the future. Indeed, the fact that future consumption is limited by future income will enhance the precautionary motive, since it makes the marginal utility of consumption higher than it would otherwise have been when income is low, and thus strengthens the effect of uncertainty on raising the expected marginal utility of future consumption. The model can also be extended to handle the case where harvests are not serially independent. Once again tree crops provide a natural example. Suppose that once damage to trees has been inflicted, it lasts more than one season, so that low income in one year usually means that income will also be low in the following year. The farmer must now take into account, not only his cash on hand, but also his expectations about next year's harvest. He will then be less likely than before to spend everything in bad years, because he knows that next year is also likely to be bad. But in good years, he can spend more than he otherwise could have done, because a good harvest now also means that the trees are in good shape for next year.

The formal mechanism for recovering the farmer's consumption rule from (6.21) is discussed in the references given above. It is not possible to derive an analytical solution, but given a specification for the utility function, for the stochastic process characterizing income, and for the values of the rates of real interest and time preference, the rule can be calculated numerically. But it turns out that most of the properties of the optimal rule can be captured by relatively simple rules of thumb according to which the farmer spends everything if cash on hand is below a critical value close to mean income, and then saves a fixed fraction of anything above that level (see Deaton 1992b, from which the following example is taken).

Suppose that the farmer's income y_t is an independent and identically distributed (i.i.d.) normal variable with mean 100 and standard deviation 10. Write x_t for cash on hand $A_t + y_t$, and consider the consumption rule of the form

$$(6.22) \qquad\qquad c_t = x_t - 0.7(x_t - 100)1(x_t > 100)$$

where $1(.)$ takes the values of 1 or 0 depending on whether its argument is true or not. By (6.22), consumption is equal to cash on hand whenever cash on hand is less than 100, which is the mean harvest, while 70 percent of any excess is saved. The choice of mean income for the critical value and of 70 percent for the saving parameter comes from roughly matching (6.22) to the optimal nonlinear rule (which is not discussed here), but the choice can also be justified directly in a way that will be described below. But first it is useful to examine what happens to consumption and assets for a consumer who behaves according to (6.22). This can be done by assuming that initial assets (at the end of period 0) are zero, so that $x_1 = y_1$, then randomly generating a time series for "income" from independent drawings from $N(100, 10^2)$. Consumption in the first period is given by applying (6.22) to x_1, and the next period's cash on hand using (6.8) to update x,

$$(6.23) \qquad\qquad x_{t+1} = (1+r)(x_t - c_t) + y_{t+1}$$

so that we get a simulated series for income, consumption, and assets.

Results for one particular 100-period horizon are shown in Figure 6.8 where I have chosen a real interest rate of 5 percent. The top line of the graph shows the simulated income series, the middle line (the scale for which appears on the right) is consumption, and the bottom series assets. The most obvious feature of these simulations is how much smoother is consumption than income, a result that is achieved purely by the smoothing rule (6.22) and in the absence of any ability to borrow. In Figure 6.8, the standard deviation of consumption is 65 percent of the standard deviation of income; the average over a larger number of simulations is

Figure 6.8. Simulation of income, consumption, and assets

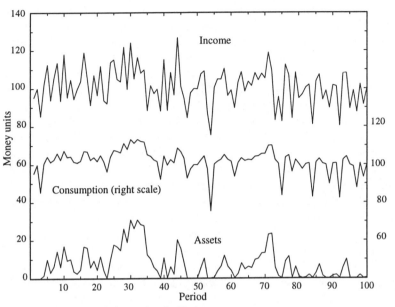

Source: Author's calculations as described in the text.

62 percent. This relative smoothness is made possible by the existence of assets that are usually available to buffer the effects of poor harvests. The bottom line on the graph shows that the amount of assets required to achieve the smoothing is quite small; the average value of assets in the figure is 7.3, less than 10 percent of average income or one standard deviation of income.

The bottom line in the figure shows how assets are built up when income is good and drawn down when income is poor, and although there are long periods when assets are positive—for example in the long series of good harvests around period 30 or near period 70—there comes a time when assets are exhausted, a period when cash on hand is low enough to make it desirable to spend everything now rather than to hold something for a future that is likely to be better. This periodic—but random—exhaustion of assets is a general feature of these models; although assets will run out more or less frequently depending on the nature of harvest uncertainty and on the preferences of the individual, sooner or later they will always do so. Once assets are zero, and since the harvest process is i.i.d., there will eventually come a poor harvest without assets, and the consumer will have no choice but to cut consumption by the shortfall in income. There are several such episodes in Figure 6.8: in period 3 before the consumer has had time to build up any assets, and in period 54 where assets were already exhausted so that consumption had to bear the consequence of the poor harvest. As a result, this sort of buffering leaves consumers vulnerable to a succession of poor harvests, or to poor harvests that are close to one another. For example, there are two poor harvests in periods 72 and 74 in the figure. In the first, consumption is protected by assets, but in the second it is not, partly because assets were low after the first shock. The figure also shows that the distribution of consumption is negatively skewed. It is always possible for the farmer to stop consumption becoming too high, by building up assets, but consumption can only be protected from falling when there are assets, which is usually but not invariably the case.

Figure 6.8 illustrates the consequences of only one particular rule, and we might ask what are the effects of changing the parameters—the cutoff point and the fraction saved—and how we should choose between the various possible rules. Figure 6.9 shows what would have happened in Figure 6.8 if the farmer had been more conservative and had saved 85 percent of the excess of cash on hand above mean income. The income series in the top lines of the two figures are the same, so that we can isolate the effects of changes in the saving rule. As is to be expected from the more cautious behavior, consumption is now much smoother than before, although there are still occasional downward spikes; while the frequency of these spikes can be affected by the policy, they cannot be eliminated entirely and will occur from time to time however conservative the policy. The price of the additional smoothness is that assets are much higher on average, and for an impatient consumer whose rate of time preference is higher than the rate of interest, these assets are unwelcome because they represent missed consumption opportunities. The choice between the two figures therefore depends on the trade-off between security and impatience, something that can only be settled by appeal

Figure 6.9. The effects of a conservative saving policy

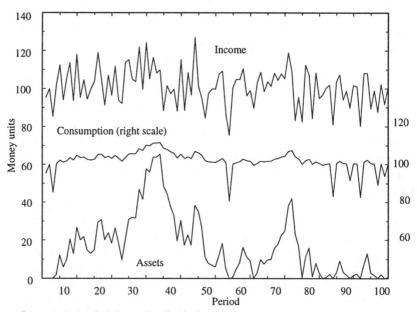

Source: Author's calculations as described in the text.

to a specific utility function. For the commonly used isoelastic single-period utility function c_t^{-3} and rate of time preference of 10 percent, the less conservative rule in the top figure is superior.

Such utility comparisons also offer a straightforward way of computing optimal parameters for a piecewise linear policy rule like (6.22). For any combination of cutoff and saving propensity, run a simulation like those described here, and calculate the average per period utility value over a long enough simulation to approximate expected utility. The parameters that maximize this value—found by grid search or some other method—are the optimal ones within this class of rules. In general, the propensity to save will be larger and the cutoff lower the more cautious is the consumer, and the more variable is income, both of which increase the value of a conservative saving policy.

Borrowing restrictions and the empirical evidence

It is far from straightforward to construct a direct test of the buffering model. We would require accurate data on consumption and income that tracked households over several years, and it is hard to see how to use one or two cross sections to substitute for the lack of such a panel. Nevertheless, it is worth emphasizing the consistency between the buffering model and the evidence on saving that I have already reviewed in this chapter.

First, the evidence from the permanent income literature, while far from establishing that the permanent income hypothesis is an accurate description of consumption behavior by poor households, has convincingly established that the propensity to save out of transitory income is relatively high so that consumption is smoother than income. Such behavior is also predicted by the buffering model; consumption is smoothed over the random time horizon defined by the time between "stockouts" of assets. Second, as we saw in Section 6.1 above, there is a good deal of evidence against the life-cycle proposition that people smooth consumption over their lifetimes, with the data showing a fairly close "tracking" between consumption and income. Once again, this is consistent with the buffering model which predicts that consumption is smoothed relative to income in the short run, but is tied to income in the longer run, because assets are not accumulated over long periods of time. However, I should note that the buffering model does not offer any clear explanation for why consumption tracks income in Taiwan (China). Taiwanese households own very substantial assets, and are clearly not in a position where they would like to borrow but cannot.

Households who follow the buffering rule accumulate no assets in the long run, and dissave as often as they save. The model is therefore consistent with data showing a large fraction of households with consumption greater than income in any given year, although because some income shocks are common to all households, we would not expect to see half of households saving in each year, but more in one year and less in another. As was discussed in Chapter 1, household surveys from developing countries frequently do record dissaving by substantial fractions of households. There is no doubt that some of this is due to underestimation of income relative to consumption, but the observation may have more truth to it than is often credited.

Like the permanent income hypothesis, the buffering model implies that saving will predict declines in income. Farmers who see that their incomes will be low next period can accumulate assets in advance, and those who see good times coming can run down their assets. It is only those people who receive advance notice of good fortune, but who have no assets, who will be prevented from borrowing to turn their anticipations into consumption now. This last has been used to construct formal tests for the presence of liquidity constraints, tests that can also be regarded as attempts to distinguish between the two Euler equations (6.14)—with no borrowing restrictions—and (6.21)—where borrowing is prohibited (see Hayashi 1985a, 1985b, and Zeldes 1989b). To see how these work, rewrite (6.21) in the form

$$(6.24) \qquad \lambda(c_t) = \frac{1+r}{1+\delta} E_t \lambda(c_{t+1}) + \xi_t$$

where ξ_t is positive if the credit restrictions are binding—which requires that assets are zero—and will be zero otherwise. If ξ_t is positive, marginal utility of consumption is higher than the consumer would wish, and so consumption is lower; without assets and without access to borrowing, it is not possible to raise consumption above the amount of cash on hand.

Suppose that we can isolate a group of consumers for whom we are sure that the borrowing constraints are not binding, for example those with assets, landholdings, or regularly high incomes. For them, ξ_t will be zero, so that if we select a specific utility function, we can estimate (6.24) ignoring the last term. Using the estimated parameters, we can then estimate ξ_t for a group of possibly constrained consumers and see whether, as predicted by the theory, it tends to be positive.

To take a concrete example, suppose that utility is isoelastic, so that the marginal utility of consumption is $c^{-\rho}$, in which case (6.24) can be written for the unconstrained households as

$$(6.25) \qquad \frac{1+r}{1+\delta} c_{t+1}^{-\rho} - c_t^{-\rho} = u_{t+1}.$$

u_{t+1} is a zero-mean shock that is the difference between the realization and its expectation and, as such, is orthogonal to any variable known to the consumer at time t or earlier. In particular, the mean of the left-hand side of (6.25) should be zero for a large enough group of unconstrained consumers, as should be the mean of the left-hand side multiplied by any variable known at time t or earlier. Suppose that we have data on J such variables, and that z_{tj} is the realization of the jth in period t. Then the sample means,

$$(6.26) \qquad s_j = n^{-1} \sum_1^n z_{tj} \left(\frac{1+r}{1+\delta} c_{t+1}^{-\rho} - c_t^{-\rho} \right)$$

should converge to zero as the number of unconstrained households becomes large. Choosing the parameters to make the s_j as small as possible is the generalized methods of moments (GMM) estimation method first applied in a closely related context by Hansen and Singleton (1982). Once the parameters have been estimated, the average (6.26) can be recalculated for the supposedly constrained households with z_{jt} replaced by unity, and the result checked to see if it is positive. This general framework has been applied to developed economies by Hayashi (1985a, 1985b) and Zeldes (1989b) with results that supported the supposition that households are credit constrained.

A closely related but perhaps somewhat simpler methodology is to note that the unconstrained Euler equation (6.25) can be thought of as determining the rate of growth of consumption between t and $t+1$. In the absence of credit restrictions, consumption growth will reflect the different needs in the two periods, for example associated with changes in family size, as well as the rate of interest and the rate of time preference. Such a rate of growth equation can be estimated for unconstrained households, and the average residual from the equation calculated for possible constrained households. If some of these households are credit constrained, and are being forced to postpone consumption from t to $t+1$, their consumption growth should be higher than predicted, and the average residual positive. Put differently, if low income and low or zero assets are a sign of being credit constrained, consumption growth should be negatively related to initial assets and income in the presence of credit restrictions. This appears to be the case in Zeldes' (1989b) work for the United States, and a similar result has been discovered for the ICRISAT households in southwestern India by Morduch (1990), who also investigates the impact of the borrowing restrictions on these farmers' production decisions.

That poor people in developing countries face limits on the amount that they can borrow is a plausible conclusion, and one that is supported by a good deal of less formal observation and description. However, there are some serious problems with these tests. First, there are difficulties with "macro" shocks, unpredictable changes in income that affect all households in common (see Hayashi 1985a, 1985b, whose tests are constructed to be immune to the problem). If there is an unexpectedly good harvest in a region as a whole, consumption growth will be unexpectedly high for everyone, the shocks in (6.25) will be correlated across individuals, and neither their average shock over households nor (6.26) will be zero, even though there are no borrowing restrictions. Simple macro shocks that are the same for everyone can readily be dealt with by allowing year dummies in the growth rate regressions, but there is no guarantee that macro shocks work in this way—for example high rainfall is good for some crops and bad for others. The basic problem here is that tests of the various models require time-series data on individual households, and that cross sections or short panels are not an adequate substitute.

The second problem has been pointed out by Carroll (forthcoming). He constructs a model of precautionary saving without borrowing restrictions, in which people are impatient but choose not to borrow (because they fear the possible consequences) and where assets buffer consumption in very much the same way as in the model with borrowing restrictions in the previous subsection. In such a model, households with low initial income and assets are households with little protection against a poor harvest next year, and so must save more than households with more income or assets. As a result, consumption growth will be larger for households with lower income and assets, not because of borrowing restrictions, but because of precautionary saving.

The third and final problem is possible lack of power of tests based on violations of the unconstrained Euler equation (6.14). Consider once again Figures 6.8 and 6.9, which illustrate the behavior of consumers who cannot borrow at all, and whose rule-of-thumb behavior delivers a close approximation to the optimal behavior in such circumstances. These consumers have rates of time preference greater than the real rate of interest, and would have declining consumption trajectories based on initial borrowing if loans were available to them. As a result of their inability to borrow, their behavior is quite different, with each person's consumption following a stationary process. For these people, the borrowing restrictions change consumption in a fundamental way, replacing a downward-trending series with a stationary one. In spite of this radical change in behavior, the liquidity constrained consumers in these figures usually hold assets, and so satisfy the unrestricted Euler equation in most periods. As a result, tests for borrowing constraints that look for zero assets and violation of Euler equations may have few observations to work with, even when consumers are never allowed to borrow. Once again, the tests are only likely to be powerful when we have long time series on individual households.

Given the wealth of informal observation on rural credit markets in developing countries, almost no one would suppose that the typical household can lend and borrow unlimited amounts at a common real interest rate. Even so, we have made surprisingly little progress in detecting the effects on consumption and welfare of these less than perfect credit markets. Data quality is responsible for a good number of the difficulties, but there is also room for imaginative new research that finds new ways of examining the issue.

6.4 Social insurance and consumption

Saving is only one of the ways that people can protect their consumption against fluctuations in their incomes. An alternative is to rely on other people, to share risk with friends and kin, with neighbors, or with anonymous other participants through private or government insurance schemes, or through participation in financial markets. Imagine a group of rural cultivators who live in the same village, but whose plots are scattered around the village, are sown to a range of different crops, and are subject to different risks. Some farmers will be richer than others by virtue of their larger or more productive landholdings and from assets accumulated in the past, but suppose that all are risk averse, and would sacrifice some of their average income for greater income stability. Each has diminishing marginal utility of consumption, so that the welfare loss associated with a poor harvest is greater than the welfare gain associated with a good one. If there are enough farmers and their risks are uncorrelated so that their average income is nonstochastic, then before each farmer knows how good his or her harvest will be, they would agree to a pact whereby each agrees to pool the surpluses above (or shortfalls from) their individual means, so that each would be guaranteed their own mean income. When risks are correlated—as we would expect them to be in an agricultural village—it is not possible to guarantee a nonstochastic income for everyone, but it will still be advantageous to pool individual deviations from the average outcome, so that each farmer's consumption is smoothed as much possible. Members of the village will also have incentives to seek partnerships with people outside the village.

The problems of implementing such schemes are as obvious as their advantages. Although individuals have an incentive to join the pact ex ante, the lucky ones will want to renege ex post. They will also wish to conceal income if it is possible to do so. The schemes also reduce individual incentives for effort and to avoid risk—the good husbandry that minimizes losses from pests, diseases, and fires—so that complete consumption insurance may be neither desirable nor possible. As a result, the schemes are more likely to exist among groups of people among whom information is good, where income is difficult to hide, and where behavior can be monitored and influenced by the group. Families, kin groups, or villages are the obvious examples. And indeed, there are various local institutions that provide this sort of insurance to a greater or lesser extent (see the excellent review by Platteau 1991). The mutual insurance schemes that are common among certain occupations are one example; "tithes" paid to the church and used for poor relief are another. Some villages have extensive sharing systems. In traditional Indian villages each occupation or caste within the village receives a prespecified share of the harvest in exchange for labor or other services; the blacksmith, the fisherman, and the basket-maker is each entitled to some share of the harvest for goods or services rendered earlier in the year (see Srinivas 1976). Similar institutions in Thailand are described by Townsend (1993a, 1993b, 1995), by Platteau (1991) for fishing communities in Kerala, and by Udry (1990), who details how villagers in northern Nigeria have evolved schemes to punish participants who renege or otherwise do not abide by the rules.

Risk sharing among individuals can also be accomplished anonymously through financial and insurance markets. Formal insurance is available for some well-defined and easily observed events, such as death, injury, flooding, or hail, but its scope is limited by the same moral hazard and information problems that limit the provision of local personalized insurance. Risky assets whose values fluctuate with events can also provide some coverage, but few poor agricultural households in developing countries hold financial assets. Forward sales of agricultural crops can be thought of in this way, as can crops in the ground if market price fluctuates inversely with output.

While it is hard to believe that any of these mechanisms could provide complete consumption insurance for poor households, the very multiplicity of existing mechanisms makes it likely that there is at least partial insurance through financial or social institutions, and that such risk sharing adds to the possibilities for autarkic consumption smoothing through intertemporal transfers of money or goods. There has also been an increased interest in the possibility that local groups can deal with some of the externalities between people that arise in administering schemes that are potentially beneficial (see for example Wade's 1988 discussion of water rights in India). There has therefore arisen a line of research that examines consumption behavior to find the extent of insurance, if any. Although it is also possible to examine the mechanisms, the insurance contracts, tithes, and transfers, their multiplicity makes it attractive to look directly at the magnitude that is supposed to be smoothed, namely consumption. In the United States, there is now overwhelming evidence against complete consumption insurance at the national level (see Cochrane 1991 and Attanasio and Davis 1993 as well as Attanasio and Weber's 1992 and Nelson's 1994 refutations of Mace's 1991 earlier, apparently positive, results). More interesting is the hypothesis that there is risk sharing within extended families, but Altonji, Hayashi, and Kotlikoff (1992) found no evidence for complete risk sharing between parents and their grown-up children in the U.S. Panel Study of Income Dynamics. But none of this evidence denies the existence of partial risk sharing, nor is it directly relevant to the extent of risk sharing in the very different environments of high-risk, low-income villages in developing countries.

The evidence on transfers in poor countries is quite extensive and almost all of it is consistent with a risk-sharing and consumption-smoothing interpretation. For example, Lucas and Stark (1985) find that transfers in Botswana are responsive to drought, and Rosenzweig (1988) shows how transfers in the ICRISAT villages in India are sensitive to shortfalls in income. There is also some evidence that more than money is involved. Rosenzweig and Stark (1989) investigate the extent to which marriage decisions are influenced by the desirability of constructing a risk-sharing network, and Ainsworth (1992) documents the relationship between child-fostering and risk in Côte d'Ivoire.

There is an impressive series of papers by Cox and Jimenez (1991a, 1991b, 1992a, 1992b, 1992c, 1993) who use survey data—including several Living Standards Surveys—to investigate the correlates of private transfers in Peru, Ghana, Côte d'Ivoire, Colombia, and the Philippines. Although the details vary from country to country, there is a remarkably consistent picture overall. Transfers are typically from better-off households to poorer households, so that they equalize the distribution of income, and households are more likely to receive transfers when they are headed by a woman, or when their members are ill or unemployed. The data also show a remarkable inverse correlation between the age profile of consumption and the age profile of the fraction of households receiving transfers, evidence which suggests that transfers even play a role in smoothing consumption over the life cycle. In most of these studies, the transfers do not appear to be very large, except in the Philippines, where remittances from abroad are important, and where transfers averaged nearly one-fifth of income for urban recipients. In the other surveys, transfers of only a few percentage points of consumption are more common, although there is some evidence that standard surveys understate the size of transfers, perhaps by a large amount. Even so, the extent to which transfers stabilize consumption remains more at issue than the fact that they do so.

In this section, I discuss first the theoretical framework that justifies the claims made at the beginning of this section, that insurance is socially desirable and can be brought about by an appropriate system of state-contingent assets. This theory also delivers predictions that can be tested on the consumption data. I then look at some of the empirical results.

Consumption insurance in theory

Start from the social problem for the agricultural village. Suppose that each household h has an intertemporal utility function

$$(6.27) \qquad u^h = \sum_t \sum_s \pi_{st} v_t^h(c_{st}^h)$$

where s indicates states of nature, t time periods, and π_{st} is the probability of state s in time period t. This is the expected utility function as in (6.7) above, but with a finite number of states of nature with explicit probabilities. If the farmers are to cooperate in a village pact to provide mutual insurance in an optimal fashion, they will have to decide who gets what share of the total—presumably by some process of initial bargaining that takes into account relative wealth and thus the utility of each member without the scheme—and then maximize an appropriately weighted sum of utilities subject to an overall constraint on total consumption in each state in each time period. The Lagrangean of this problem can be written

$$(6.28) \qquad \Phi = \sum_h \mu^h \sum_t \sum_s \pi_{st} v_t^h(c_{st}^h) + \sum_s \sum_t \xi_{st}(C_{st} - \sum_h c_{st}^h)$$

where μ^h is the social weight for household h that controls the share obtained by that household, C_{st} is aggregate village consumption in state s and time t, c_{st}^h is consumption of h in s and t, and ξ_{st} are the Lagrange multipliers associated with the resource constraints. Note that this formulation simplifies, not only by ruling out any transactions between the villagers and outsiders, but by also assuming away saving, borrowing, or buffering activities by each villager on his or her own account. The village council is assumed to control the consumption level of each member. Allowing for autarkic consumption smoothing as well as risk sharing makes the problem a great deal more complex.

If the individual consumption levels are the controls, the first-order condition for (6.28) can be written in logarithms as

$$(6.29) \qquad \ln \lambda_t^h(c_{st}^h) = \ln \xi_{st} - \ln \mu^h - \ln \pi_{st}$$

where, as before, $\lambda(c)$ is the marginal utility function of consumption. Since only one state is actually realized in period t, the s subscript in (6.29) can be dropped, and the equation will hold for each time period. In particular, we can take first differences, which will eliminate the individual fixed effect $\ln \mu^h$ to yield

$$(6.30) \qquad \Delta \ln \lambda_t^h(c_t^h) = \Delta \ln \xi_t - \Delta \ln \pi_t = \Delta \ln \xi_t^*$$

so that, with complete consumption insurance, the rate of growth of each partici-
pant's marginal utility of consumption is the same.

The implications of (6.30) for consumption depend on the shape of the marginal utility functions, as well as on other factors that affect marginal utility and
contribute to interpersonal differences in tastes. For example, suppose that household utility functions take the form

$$(6.31) \qquad v_t^h(c_t^h) = \theta_t^h n_t^h v(c_t^h/n_t^h) = (1-\rho)^{-1}\theta_t^h n_t^h (c_t^h/n_t^h)^{1-\rho}$$

so that household utility is the utility of consumption per head multiplied by the
number of people, and where I have further specialized to the isoelastic form. The
quantity θ_t^h is an unobservable "taste shifter" that accounts for intertemporal and
interpersonal variations in needs that are not captured by the household size.
Given this specification, (6.30) becomes

$$(6.32) \qquad \Delta \ln(c_t^h/n_t^h) = -\rho^{-1}(\Delta \ln \xi_t^* - \Delta \ln \theta_t^h) = -\rho^{-1}\Delta \ln \xi_t^* + \epsilon_t^h$$

so that, up to taste shifters that can be treated as mean-zero error terms, the
growth of per capita consumption is the same for all households. More generally,
we might suppose that the growth of consumption depends on any factors that
alter needs from period to period. However, and this is the main empirical prediction of complete insurance, the growth of each household's consumption should
not depend on the change in that household's resources once the change in aggregate resources has been taken into account. The individual harvests are all pooled
in the insurance scheme, and while the aggregate village harvest affects each
person's consumption outcome, there is no further influence of individual circum-
stance.

While I have presented the analysis in terms of a village insurance scheme,
exactly the same result can be obtained by using financial markets, provided there
is a complete set of assets, meaning that for each state and time period there exists
an asset that will pay one unit if that state occurs in that time period, and zero
otherwise. These securities are then freely traded among the participants and their
prices competitively set, and will enable each person to achieve exactly the same
outcomes as those described above (see Deaton 1992c, pp. 34–37, for an exposition in this context). This market outcome is simply the decentralized version of
the "central planner's" problem that here is handled by the village mutual insurance scheme.

Empirical evidence on consumption insurance

Empirical evidence on consumption insurance in developing countries comes
from Townsend (1994), who looks at the ICRISAT villages in southwestern India,
and from Townsend (1995), who looks at *amphoes* (roughly, counties) in Thailand. The ICRISAT data track individual households over a number of years, and
their consumption streams appear to move more closely together than do their

income streams, something that is certainly consistent with (6.32), although also with standard autarkic intertemporal smoothing, with or without borrowing constraints. However, Townsend finds that the growth of household consumption is positively influenced by household income flows, which should not happen if consumption is completely insured. There are no similar panel data for Thailand, but Townsend uses successive surveys to trace income and consumption changes at the *amphoe* level, and once again finds that the change in *amphoe* consumption less the average national consumption change is affected by the change in *amphoe* income. Of course, the absence of consumption insurance over such wide areas does not imply that there is not perfect insurance at the village or lower level.

The Ivorian Living Standards Survey data can be used to look at consumption insurance at the village level, and the following results are based on the (early release version of the) data from 1985, 1986, and 1987, which between them contain two two-year panels each intended to cover 800 households. Each survey has 100 sample clusters, 43 of which are in urban areas, so that there are 57 clusters corresponding to rural villages, each of which is designed to contain 16 households. There are 31 village clusters that are common to the 1985 and 1986 surveys, and which comprise the first panel. In 1986 and 1987 there are 26 common panel clusters; these are not the same villages as made up the first panel. The structure of the sample is shown in Table 6.2. These figures are for the households actually used in the analysis below; inevitably, some households have been excluded. The majority are households that produced no useable data but a few others were excluded because the data on income or consumption were implausible either in levels or in changes. Consumption and income totals are the sums of a large number of components, more than a hundred for consumption, and several hundred for income, and for all but a very few cases it was possible to repair the estimates by identifying and replacing a component. There are three regions of the country shown in the table. The West and East Forest comprise the tropical south of the country. Both areas derive much of their incomes from cocoa and coffee production, while the northern Savannah depends on rainfed agriculture, with cotton and rice the main cash crops.

Table 6.2. Structure of the samples, Côte d'Ivoire, 1985–86 and 1986–87
(numbers of households and clusters)

Region	1985–86		1986–87	
	Clusters	*Households*	*Clusters*	*Households*
West Forest	11	150	5	77
East Forest	12	181	11	165
Savannah	8	123	10	150
All rural	31	454	26	392

Note: One cluster in the West Forest contains only a single household.

Table 6.3 shows estimates of income and consumption for the panel households in each of the years covered by the surveys. There are two sets of estimates for 1986 because that year appears in both of the panels, but the two estimates come from different households in different clusters. As always, and for the reasons discussed in Chapter 1, the consumption estimates are almost certainly a good deal more reliable than those for income. Even so, for the purposes of this analysis, it is less important that income be precisely measured than that it capture at least some of the idiosyncratic resource flows to the household. Income from sales of cocoa and coffee, which is an important component of agricultural income in the Forest, is almost certainly well measured; the crop is acquired by a parastatal marketing board at a predetermined price—a price confirmed by the survey data—and the quantities are carefully measured and credibly reported.

Table 6.3. Income and consumption estimates, 1985, 1986, and 1987
(thousands of CFAs, annual rates, household averages)

Region	1985		1986(1)		1986(2)		1987	
	c	*y*	*c*	*y*	*c*	*y*	*c*	*y*
West Forest	1,188	1,098	903	790	1,026	1,225	893	1,151
East Forest	1,005	896	1,042	1,056	1,147	1,283	1,048	1,151
Savannah	671	630	828	788	770	742	659	716
All rural	975	891	938	896	977	1,061	867	1,011

Note: *c* is consumption and *y* is income. The two sets of numbers for 1986 are for the panel households held over from the first year (1) and for the new panel households that were carried forward into 1987 (2).

Changes in incomes and consumption are shown in Table 6.4, together with F-tests for the significance of cluster effects. These F-tests, which can be obtained straightforwardly in STATA by regressing consumption and income changes on village dummies, or by the use of the "anova" command, measure the extent to which changes in income and consumption are more similar within villages than between villages. Statistically insignificant values of the tests indicate that changes in household income or consumption within the same village are no more similar than changes in income and consumption from households in different villages. Large F-values for income change would tend to indicate the presence of covariant risk, most plausibly coming from the similarity of weather for households located in the same village. We would also expect large F-values for consumption changes in the presence of consumption insurance at the village but not national level. Village insurance schemes will induce a stronger comovement in consumption within villages than is observed between villages, and we would expect the F-statistics to be larger for consumption, which is smoothed over households, than for income, which is not.

The statistics for income changes are generally low; common village components explain very little of the variation in individual income changes. In the 1985–86 panel, the F-statistic for the West Forest has an associated p-value of

Table 6.4. Income and consumption changes, 1985–86 and 1986–87
(thousands of CFAs, household averages)

	1985–86				1986–87			
Income	Δy	F	df_1	df_2	Δy	F	df_1	df_2
West Forest	−308	2.04	10	139	−74	1.93	4	72
East Forest	160	1.28	11	169	−64	2.05	10	154
Savannah	159	1.52	7	115	−26	1.17	9	144
All rural	5	2.30	30	423	−51	1.65	25	370
Consumption	Δc	F	df_1	df_2	Δc	F	df_1	df_2
West Forest	−285	4.10	10	139	−133	4.04	4	72
East Forest	37	4.15	11	169	−99	2.16	10	154
Savannah	157	1.35	7	115	−111	0.70	9	114
All rural	−37	4.62	30	423	−110	2.14	25	370

Source: Author's calculations using CILSS data.

0.03, and that for the rural areas as a whole one of 0.0002, albeit from a much larger sample size. Clearly, a few of the West Forest villages did worse than others in 1986, and it is those same income falls in one region that generate the *F*-statistic for all regions. But these effects, as well as those for 1986–87, are much smaller than might be expected if we think that covariant agricultural risk is important. None of the *F*-statistics are close to the log(sample size) critical value of the Schwarz test. Nor is it easy to explain these results by appealing to measurement error. If, for example, the observed within-village variation in income changes is composed of equal parts of measurement error and "real" change, then it is easy to show that the observed *F*-statistics would be a little more than half what they ought to be. But doubling the figures in the top half of the table still does not generate very impressive values.

The literature on agricultural risk in developing countries places great emphasis on the covariation between income risks for different farmers in the same location, and the consequent desirability of risk-pooling schemes that link the village to different agricultural zones or to urban areas. There is little evidence of such covariation in these data, even though they span at least two quite distinct agricultural zones, the Forest and the Savannah. Côte d'Ivoire may be an exception to the general pattern, or these two years may be atypical in some ways. One possibility is that there is little covariance in normal years, but that there are infrequent but important events, such as fires or droughts, that affect everyone together, and that it is these rare events that shape risk-bearing strategy. Some risks can be an ever-present threat without occurring often. Even so, crops in Côte d'Ivoire are certainly affected by weather conditions, and fires in the cocoa- and coffee-growing areas are frequent occurrences, so that the absence of significant village-level effects remains something of a puzzle. It is also possible that village effects do indeed exist, but are swamped by intravillage variation from one household to another.

Inspection of the lower half of Table 6.4 reveals that the *F*-tests for village effects in consumption changes are typically much larger than those for income changes. Although there is little evidence of village effects in the Savannah, there are strong effects in the East and West Forest regions in 1985–86, and in the West Forest in 1986–87. Some factor is causing consumption levels within each village to move more closely together than do income levels. Risk pooling is certainly one possibility. Another is that consumption is measured more accurately than income, and that for correctly measured magnitudes, the *F*-statistics would be closer. Nor is it difficult to think of explanations for intravillage comovement in consumption that do not involve risk sharing; the effective real rate of interest may vary between but not within villages, or there may simply be village taste effects related to the geographical distribution of tribal groups in Côte d'Ivoire. Whatever its cause, the comovement does indeed exist; consumption changes are more similar within villages than between them, and are more similar than are income changes.

Table 6.4 shows a close relationship across regions and over time between consumption change and income change. Table 6.5 explores these connections more closely. The top panel of the Table gives estimates for 1985–86, and the bottom panel for 1986–87. The first row in each case shows that for each of the regions the ordinary least squares regression of the change on consumption on the change in income generates a significant positive coefficient. These values differ a good deal from region to region, and from the first panel to the second, but the coefficient is always positive and the *t*-values are large, ranging from 3.2 to 8.8. Of course, this finding is consistent with complete risk sharing; consumption changes are determined by the village average change in resources, which—by construction—is positively correlated with the individual changes. However, if consumption insurance is complete, the coefficients on income change should fall to zero when the change in village average income is introduced into the regression, or when village dummies are included, since the average change is a linear combination of the village dummies. Indeed, given the difficulties in measuring incomes, and given that there may be village resources that are not counted in individual incomes, the test is more convincing if village dummies are used.

The second rows for each of the panels show that the introduction of village dummies makes little difference to the original income coefficients. The dummies themselves are often jointly significant, but their presence does not affect the estimates of the income coefficients, something that effectively follows from the result in Table 6.3 that the village dummies do not predict of income change. The coefficients on individual income changes remain significantly positive as before, in contradiction to the complete insurance story which would require them to be zero.

One possible explanation for the results could be an upward bias in the income coefficients that comes about as follows. For many of these rural households a significant share of income and consumption is accounted for by food that is produced and consumed by the household and neither sold nor bought in the market. A value is imputed to this home-produced food and the figure is included in both

Table 6.5. OLS **and** IV **estimates of the effects of income on consumption**

	West Forest		East Forest		Savannah		All rural	
	OLS 1985–86							
No dummies	0.290	(6.2)	0.153	(3.2)	0.368	(5.8)	0.259	(8.8)
Village dummies	0.265	(5.7)	0.155	(3.5)	0.373	(5.7)	0.223	(7.7)
Own income	0.265	(5.3)	0.155	(3.2)	0.373	(5.6)	0.223	(7.1)
Village income	0.199	(1.4)	–0.031	(0.2)	–0.050	(0.2)	0.252	(3.0)
	IVE 1985–86							
No dummies	0.192	(3.9)	–0.003	(0.1)	0.271	(4.0)	0.126	(4.0)
Village dummies	0.171	(3.5)	0.029	(0.6)	0.270	(3.8)	0.107	(3.4)
Own income	0.171	(3.2)	0.029	(0.5)	0.270	(3.7)	0.107	(3.1)
Village income	0.161	(1.1)	–0.417	(2.0)	0.020	(0.1)	0.144	(1.6)
	OLS 1986–87							
No dummies	0.458	(8.8)	0.162	(5.3)	0.168	(4.0)	0.239	(10.4)
Village dummies	0.424	(8.1)	0.173	(5.6)	0.164	(3.8)	0.235	(10.1)
Own income	0.424	(7.9)	0.173	(5.3)	0.164	(3.8)	0.235	(9.7)
Village income	0.350	(2.0)	–0.094	(1.0)	0.061	(0.4)	0.039	(0.5)
	IVE 1986–87							
No dummies	0.418	(7.8)	0.090	(2.8)	0.088	(2.0)	0.177	(7.4)
Village dummies	0.388	(7.3)	0.105	(3.2)	0.087	(1.9)	0.177	(7.3)
Own income	0.388	(7.1)	0.105	(3.1)	0.087	(1.9)	0.177	(7.0)
Village income	0.353	(2.0)	–0.127	(1.3)	0.015	(0.1)	–0.002	(0.0)

Note: Absolute values of *t*-values are shown in brackets The first row of each panel shows the coefficient on income change of a regression of consumption changes on income changes. The second row reports the same result when village dummies are included in the regression. The third and fourth rows show the estimates from a regression of consumption changes on individual household and village average changes in income. The IV regressions use the change in the value of cash income, individual and village average, as instruments for total income including imputations; the *t*-values on these instruments in the first-stage regressions are large, typically larger than 30. Because village dummies "sweep out" the village means, the coefficients—but not the standard errors—are identical in the second and third rows in each panel.

income and consumption. In consequence, any errors in this imputation—and finding the correct price for the imputation is an obvious source of difficulty—will add a common error component to whatever other errors of measurement are present in the income and consumption totals. Positively correlated measurement errors do not necessarily generate an upward bias in the regressions in Table 6.5. For positive coefficients, the upward bias works in the opposite direction to the standard downward attenuation bias produced by the income errors alone, and the net effect cannot be signed in advance. To try to correct for these problems, I have calculated IV estimators using as an instrument income changes excluding changes in the imputed value of home-produced food and other income in kind. This quantity is a major component of the income change, and is therefore strongly positively correlated with it, but by excluding the imputations, the spurious correlation is avoided. Note that I am not challenging the appropriateness of including these imputations in both income and consumption. Rather the IV technique is an attempt to correct for the consequences of measurement error given the imputation procedures.

The IV estimates in the lower second and fourth panels show that these concerns have some foundation, especially for the East Forest and the Savannah, where the estimated marginal propensities to consume are a good deal lower. Indeed for the East Forest in 1985–86 and for the Savannah in 1986–87, there is no longer any significant relationship between consumption and income changes. However, the instrumentation makes no difference to the relationship between the estimates with and without the village effects. As was the case for OLS, the introduction of the village dummies does not shift the estimates, and for the West Forest in both panels, the East Forest in the second panel, and the Savannah in the first, there remains a strong positive relationship between consumption change and income change that is robust to the inclusion of the village dummies.

These results seem to provide fairly firm evidence against the most extreme hypothesis, that there is complete consumption insurance within each of these villages in Côte d'Ivoire. But given the moral hazard, incentive, and information difficulties associated with complete consumption insurance, it is hardly surprising that there should exist at least some link between individual effort and its consumption reward. What would be more interesting would be evidence on whether there is partial insurance between households in the same village. One possibility is that the change in consumption for each household is partly determined by its own income change, and partly determined by the change in average village income, so that

$$(6.33) \qquad \Delta c_t^h = \alpha + \beta \Delta y_t^h + \gamma \Delta \bar{y}_t + \epsilon_t^h$$

where $\Delta \bar{y}_t$ is the change in average village income. If there is no saving in the village as a whole, so that the average income change is equal to the average consumption change, then $\alpha = 0$ and $\gamma + \beta = 1$, but it is not necessary to impose such a restriction, especially given the measurement errors in income changes, and the fact that the average village income changes will be more accurately measured than the individual income changes. Our concern here is simply whether, conditional on individual income change, there is a role for the village average income change in explaining individual consumption changes. This test, which is the converse of the test for complete consumption insurance, is a test for whether there is any role for village-level insurance in an otherwise autarkic world.

The results are shown in the third and fourth rows of each of the four panels of Table 6.5; the third row shows the coefficient of individual income, which is (mechanically) identical to the coefficient in the presence of dummy variables, and the fourth row shows the coefficient on the change in the village averages. As before, the second and fourth sets of results are estimated by IV; by analogy, I have used the change in average village *cash* income as an instrument for the change in average village income. In the East Forest and in the Savannah, there is no effect of the village averages on individual consumption. However, the consumption changes of households in the West Forest show some effect of average income, especially in the second panel from 1986–87. This effect is robust to instrumentation, and in this single case, the effect of average village income is almost as large as the effect of individual income. But given the failure of this effect to appear in the other case, as well as the possibility that the average income change is simply better measured than the individual income change, these estimates from the West Forest provide no more than a tantalizing suggestion that there is some risk sharing taking place at the village level.

6.5 Saving, consumption, and inequality

This section describes research by Deaton and Paxson (1994b, 1995) on the relationship between saving, inequality, and population growth. If consumption insurance is not perfect, as the empirical evidence shows, then, at least under some circumstances, the process whereby a group of individuals save and dissave in order to smooth their consumption will lead to widening consumption disparities within the group. Even if everyone gets the same luck on average, the accumulation of assets and ultimately the level of consumption will depend on their accumulated luck. A group of people flipping unbiased coins will each throw heads half the time if they throw for long enough, but there will be steadily increasing inequality in the total numbers of heads accumulated by each member of the group. In the same way, a group of farmers who are not co-insured, and who borrow and lend to smooth their consumption as in the permanent income model, will show gradually expanding inequality of assets and consumption over time. An implication of the analysis is that the inequality of income and consumption within any given cohort should be increasing with the age of the cohort. In consequence, the decline in the rate of population growth that comes with the demographic transition, and which expands the numbers of older relative to younger people, will also tend to increase aggregate inequality, as population weights are shifted from relatively equal young cohorts to relatively unequal older cohorts.

In this section, I explain the theory behind these mechanisms and use the Taiwanese household survey data to show that the predictions are indeed supported by the evidence. I also explain how the aging of the population that accompanies a slowing of population growth acts so as to increase inequality, again with illustrations from the Taiwanese case. Taiwan (China) is one of the leading cases of "growth with equity" in economic development, and has experienced rapid rates of economic growth while maintaining low measures of inequality. However, there has been some upward drift in measures of inequality over the last decade, and at least some of this can be attributed to the mechanisms described here. The increase in inequality, far from being a problem, is a concomitant of the essentially welcome decrease in rates of population growth.

Consumption, permanent income, and inequality

The simplest relationship between intertemporal choice and inequality is for the permanent income hypothesis with uncertainty. Recall from Section 6.3 that the permanent income hypothesis extends the constant lifetime consumption rule to one in which consumption does not change except when the consumer receives new information, so that today's expectation of consumption in any future period is the same as today's consumption, equation (6.15) above. If we write this in the form (6.16), and add an i suffix to distinguish each individual, we have

$$(6.34) \qquad c_{it+1} = c_{it} + u_{it+1}$$

so that u_{it+1} is the component of consumption in period $t+1$ that comes from new information received by i after period t. Given what is known in period t, this innovation has a zero expectation.

Take variances of both sides of (6.34) over the cross section of individuals that are present at both t and $t+1$, and assume that the cross-sectional covariance of c_{it} and u_{it+1} is zero, so that

$$(6.35) \qquad \text{var} \, c_{t+1} = \text{var} \, c_t + \sigma_{t+1}$$

where the variances are taken across the cross section of individuals, and σ_{t+1} is the cross-sectional variance of consumption innovations. If we measure consumption inequality by the variance, inequality is increasing through time. The result can be made a good deal stronger if we are prepared to assume that the innovations are independent of the previous level of consumption. Given this assumption, (6.34) says that the distribution of consumption at $t+1$ is the distribution of consumption at time t with the addition of mean-zero random variation, so that the Lorenz curve of consumption in t will lie everywhere within the Lorenz curve of consumption in any later period. In consequence, any measure of inequality that respects the principle of transfers will show increasing inequality over time (see Section 3.1).

What is the intuition behind the result, and how robust is it to relaxation of the various assumptions necessary to derive it? A useful way of looking at (6.34) is to write consumption at time t as original consumption at time zero plus the sum of all the subsequent innovations:

$$(6.36) \qquad c_{it} = c_{i0} + \sum_{\tau=1}^{t} u_{i\tau}.$$

Each of the individual innovations $u_{i\tau}$ has zero mean, and their average will converge to zero given a long enough period of time. But consumption does not depend on the average, but on the sum, and the variance of the sum is increasing with time. While good luck and bad luck can be expected to average out over time, consumption depends on cumulated luck, and the cumulated histories of fortune for different individuals can be expected to diverge with the passage of time. Note the crucial role of uncertainty in driving the expanding inequality. Without uncertainty, the permanent income hypothesis predicts constant consumption streams over time, inequality is set by the distribution of lifetime resources, and once set, remains constant over time. In the presence of uncertainty, forward-looking permanent-income consumers adjust their consumption only when they get new information, so that provided everyone does not get the same news, the flow of new information will constantly act to widen the distribution of consumption. The consumption streams of any group of people will be "fanning out" over time.

The reasoning requires no assumption about what is happening to earnings of different people, and it is perfectly possible for the permanent income hypothesis to hold for a group of people for whom the distribution of earnings is constant over time. For such a group, the expanding distribution of consumption is supported by an expansion in the distribution of assets. The lucky consumers, those who have a positive run of innovations, will accumulate assets, and the income from those assets permits higher consumption. As a result, not only is the distribution of consumption becoming more dispersed with time, but so is the distribution of *income*, provided that income is (properly) taken to include both earnings and asset income. Formally establishing this result takes some algebra, and the interested reader is referred to Deaton and Paxson (1994b).

The fact that the inequality of consumption and income is increasing over time for any group of people does not necessarily imply that inequality is increasing for society as a whole. For any given cohort, consumption and income inequality will increase as the cohort ages, so that inequality is increasing over time for any given group. What happens to aggregate inequality will depend on whether old generations pass on their inequality to their children, so that each new generation has a higher level of inequality at the start of their lives, and overall inequality is increasing, or whether there is no inheritance of inequality, so that each generation begins with the same starting level of inequality, and aggregate inequality is constant. The analysis here casts no light on these questions, and so is consistent with any pattern of aggregate inequality.

The simple story of within-cohort inequality growth that comes from the permanent income hypothesis has to be modified in various ways once the assumptions are made more relaxed, and more realistic versions of the model are discussed in Deaton and Paxson (1994b). In summary: in the presence of covariant risk, consumption innovations will be correlated across individuals, and it is possible for there to be a nonzero cross-sectional covariance between the innovations and lagged consumption. However, there are plausible assumptions under which this covariance has to average to zero over a run of years, so that even if inequality does not increase year by year, it must increase on average. It is also necessary to recognize that consumption will change from year to year, not only when there is new information as in (6.34), but also when needs change, for example as people age, or as household size and composition changes. The "taste shifters" are certainly capable of destroying the relationship between inequality and cohort age. For example, the dispersion of household size tends to contract during late middle age of household heads, and there is likely to be an associated contraction in the dispersion of household consumption and income. Even so, the spread of inequality associated with good and poor fortune will still be present, and will be superimposed on whatever changes are wrought by changes in household size or tastes. Finally, if we move away from the permanent income hypothesis, and allow for precautionary motives in saving, the spread of inequality can be slowed down or even halted. Consumption becomes more unequal because people respond to the opportunities that fortune lays before them. Extreme precautionary behavior makes people reluctant to respond to opportunities, and a cohort of savers can be prudent enough to choke off the inequality-promoting effects of uncertainty.

In spite of all the qualifications, there remains a presumption that intertemporal choice in the presence of uncertainty will generate increases in inequality within a group of people. This presumption does not extend to all other models of consumption. In particular, consider the buffering model in Section 6.3 and the model of complete consumption insurance in Section 6.4. In the former, where consumers are relatively impatient but cannot borrow, the consumption of each household follows a stochastic process like those described in Figures 6.8 and 6.9. As the figures illustrate, and as can be formally demonstrated, the stochastic processes for consumption are stationary so that if we look at a group of consumers, all of whom are buffering their consumption, the distribution of consumption among them will not be spreading out over time, and there will be no trend in inequality. Because all of these consumers are impatient, none are accumulating assets in the long term, and since borrowing is ruled out by assumption, none are accumulating debts, so that in all but the short run, consumption moves with earnings. In consequence, there will be growing consumption inequality if and only if the inequality of earnings is growing.

The case of complete consumption insurance, although very different from autarkic buffering behavior by individual households, has the same implications for the development of inequality. The operation of the insurance scheme will cause the marginal utilities of individual consumption levels to move in lockstep, so that unless there are systematic divergences in tastes over time, there is no scope for an increase in the dispersion of consumption. Indeed, it is precisely to prevent the dispersion of consumption that the insurance scheme exists.

It is possible for there to be increasing consumption inequality for reasons different than those given above. In particular, if the distribution of earnings within a cohort is dispersing with the age of the cohort, and if households are liquidity constrained so that consumption is tied to income over all but the short run, then consumption inequality will be driven by the rising inequality in earnings and will also increase. That the inequality of earnings should rise with age is predicted by standard models of education and earnings in which different people have different amounts of education (see Mincer 1974 and Dooley and Gottschalk 1984). Even within a homogenous education group, earnings inequality could increase if different individuals experience different rates of return to human capital.

Inequality and age: empirical evidence

In order to test the prediction that inequality increases with time within any given group of people, we need either panel data, in which the members of the group are tracked over a period of time, or a time series of cross sections through which we can follow the randomly selected representatives of a number of cohorts as in Section 2.6. I look first at the latter, using the repeated cross sections from Taiwan (China), and then briefly consider evidence from the ICRISAT panel of households in India.

Figures 6.10 and 6.11 are reproduced from Deaton and Paxson (1994b) and show how consumption inequality evolves with the age of the household head in Taiwan (China) from 1976 through 1990. Figure 6.10 shows the variance of the logarithm of consumption for every fifth cohort, as measured by tracking the cohort through the surveys. For example, the top left graph in the figure shows the cohort born in 1961, whose members were 15 years old in the first survey year, 1976. Of course, there are no 15-year-old household heads, so that the first time we observe the cohort is in 1981, when they are 20, and when at least a few show up as heads. The subsequent points in the graph show the variance of logarithms of household consumption for households headed by 21-year-olds in 1982, 22-year-olds in 1983, through to 29-year-olds in 1990. The series of graphs show that there is little increase in inequality at young ages, but once household heads reach age 40, the inequality lines begin to turn upward, rising quite rapidly through the 40s and 50s, with dispersion ceasing or reversing after age 60. The final panel of the figure shows the variance of log consumption for all households in Taiwan (China) tracking through each of the 15 surveys. As documented elsewhere (Republic of China 1989), there has been a mild increase in consumption

Figure 6.10. Variances of log household consumption, selected cohorts, Taiwan (China), 1976–90

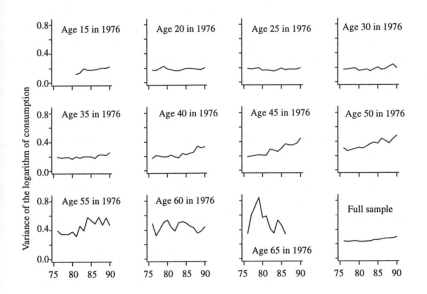

Source: Deaton and Paxson (1994b).

Figure 6.11. Age effects in (log) consumption inequality, Taiwan (China)

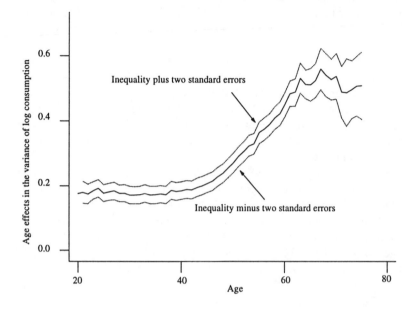

Source: Deaton and Paxson (1994b).

inequality over the period, but it is dwarfed by the changes within the middle-aged cohorts.

Figure 6.11 graphs the age effects from a regression of the variance of logs on age and cohort dummies as described in Section 2.6, and extracts the relationship between inequality and age from the multiple graphs in the previous figure. Inequality does not change very much until age 40, and then increases until age 60, after which there is no further dispersion. This is what is to be expected from the theory if dispersion is being driven by innovations in earnings, and if people either retire or have only predictable changes in earnings after age 60. The broken lines in the graph are drawn at two estimated standard errors from the age inequality lines, and show that the results are not being driven by the fact that the cohort inequality measures are based on sample data.

Deaton and Paxson (1994b, 1997b) provide similar analyses for Britain, the United States, and Thailand, with similar results. The shapes of the age inequality profiles are somewhat different. Taiwan (China) is the only country of the three to show the convex profile displayed in Figure 6.11, but the increase in inequality from age 20 to age 70 is the same in the four economies. In all four countries, the inequality profiles of earnings and income also increase with age, so that the results on consumption inequality are consistent, not only with the permanent income story of the previous subsection, but also with an explanation in which the fundamental cause of expanding inequality lies in dispersion of earnings with age, with consumption tied to earnings through borrowing restrictions.

A very different context for examining inequality is provided by the household panel data from three of the ICRISAT villages in Maharashtra and Karnataka in southwestern India. These households are followed over time, so there is no need to create cohort data, and we can look directly at the individual consumption trajectories. Figure 6.12 presents the evidence. Each panel comes from a separate village, and shows the deviation of each household's consumption from the mean logarithm of consumption taken over the sample households in the relevant village. The trajectories are thus centered around zero, and add to zero in each agricultural year (June to May). In none of these villages is there any apparent tendency for the bundle of consumption trajectories to fan out over time. Nor do corrections to the consumption data for household size in the form of division by the number of adult equivalents yield different results. These households are apparently not setting their consumption according to the permanent income hypothesis or one of the other models of intertemporal choice that predicts increasing inequality in consumption. Although complete consumption insurance is consistent with constant inequality, we already know from Townsend's (1994) work on these data that household consumption levels respond to changes in individual incomes, so that insurance is at best imperfect. Figure 6.12 is more obviously consistent with the buffering model, in which households are not insured, but accumulate assets only in the short run. Household incomes in these villages also show no increase in inequality over time, so that both income and consumption data are consistent with the autarkic behavior of impatient and liquidity-cons-

Figure 6.12. Consumption trajectories for households in the Indian ICRISAT villages, 1976–91

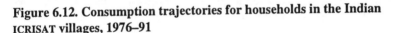

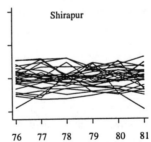

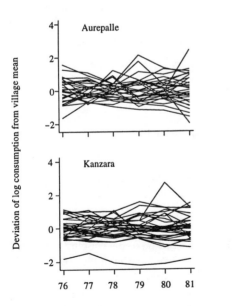

Source: Author's calculations from ICRISAT data.

trained consumers, who smooth their consumption as best they can without help from their neighbors.

Aging and inequality

In economies where inequality rises with age, as in Taiwan (China), the United States, and Britain, changes in the age structure of the population will affect overall levels of inequality. In particular, declines in the rate of population growth will tip the structure of the population towards the elderly, so that the older, more unequal generations will become more heavily represented and the younger, more equal generations will be less heavily represented, a process that will tend to increase overall inequality. The age-sex pyramids for Taiwan (China) in Figure 1.2 become steadily more top-heavy over time as the population ages, and Taiwan (China) is only one of many developing countries in Asia where there have been similar declines in population growth rates, and similar increases in the average age of the population. If aging in these economies has an automatic tendency to increase inequality, it is important that the mechanism be understood and quantified, so that the process is not misinterpreted, and inappropriate policy action taken to try to correct a non-problem.

The relationship between population aging and inequality is not as straightforward as this summary might suggest, but a number of results can be proved under the appropriate assumptions. One approach that requires strong assumptions about economic growth and the inequality process but only very weak assumptions about population structure is based on the analysis of inequality in Chapter 3, and is adapted from a related analysis by Anand and Kanbur (1992). Suppose that $F(x)$ is the cumulative distribution function of consumption (or income) in the population as a whole, and that $F_i(x)$ is the corresponding cumulative distribution function for age group i. These functions are then related by the identity

$$(6.37) \qquad F(x) = \sum_{i=0}^{T} \pi_i F_i(x)$$

where T is the age of the oldest group and π_i is the proportion of the population aged i. We might then consider social welfare and inequality in this society through the function

$$(6.38) \qquad W = \int \upsilon(x) dF(x) = \sum_{i=0}^{T} \pi_i \int \upsilon(x) dF_i(x)$$

where $\upsilon(x)$ is a monotone increasing concave function, which can be thought of as an individual or social evaluation function for the welfare of each individual.

Suppose that inequality is being generated according to the simplest version of the permanent income hypothesis described at the beginning of the previous subsection, so that consumption inequality is fanning out with age, and that the distribution of consumption at any age is second-order stochastically dominated by the distribution of consumption at any earlier age. Suppose too that the distribution of consumption within the economy is stationary over time, so that the distributions of consumption for each age group in the cross section are the same as the distributions of consumption for each cohort as it ages. This means that the distribution of consumption among the old now is the same as the distribution of consumption will be among those who are young now when they are old, so that economic growth (or decline) is ruled out by assumption. Given these assumptions, any aging of the population will unambiguously increase inequality.

To see the result, imagine a new age distribution $\tilde{\pi}_i$ that is the same as the old, but with a transfer from a younger to an older age group, so that for some $j > k$, and $\delta > 0$

(6.39)
$$\begin{aligned} \tilde{\pi}_i &= \pi_i - \delta, \quad i = k \\ \tilde{\pi}_i &= \pi_i + \delta, \quad i = j \\ \tilde{\pi}_i &= \pi_i, \quad i \neq j, k. \end{aligned}$$

From (6.38), we then have at once that

(6.40)
$$W - \tilde{W} = \delta \left(\int \upsilon(x) dF_k(x) - \int \upsilon(x) dF_j(x) \right) > 0$$

where the inequality follows from the fact that when $k < j$, F_k second-order stochastically dominates F_j so that, by the definition of second-order stochastic dominance, for any concave function $\upsilon(x)$

(6.41)
$$\int \upsilon(x) dF_k(x) > \int \upsilon(x) dF_j(x).$$

The result (6.40) shows that, under the assumptions, any transfer of population from younger to older age groups will result in a distribution that is stochastically dominated by the original distribution. Since the assumptions guarantee that the mean of the distribution is unchanged, population aging shifts out the Lorenz curve, with an unambiguous increase in inequality according to any measure that respects the principle of transfers.

Once we allow for economic growth, it is no longer possible to establish such general results on the relationship between aging and inequality. When consumption is growing from one generation to the next, older cohorts are poorer over their lifetimes than the younger cohorts, so that the lifetime experience of each cohort will be quite different from the cross-section relationship between consumption and age at any given moment of time. Aggregate inequality depends, not only on inequality within cohorts, as in the analysis above, but also on the distribution of consumption between cohorts. In consequence, even if we suppose that age profiles of consumption are unchanged in the face of changes in the age structure of the population, such changes will change not only inequality, but also means. Even so, it is possible to make some fairly general statements provided that we restrict ourselves to stable demographic equilibria associated with constant rates of population growth, and provided we work with a specific inequality measure, the variance of logs.

Deaton and Paxson (1995, 1997b) show that in demographic equilibrium, the variance of log consumption is a decreasing function of the rate of population growth provided that the lifetime consumption profile for each cohort displays steady growth, steady decline, or is flat. The most important practical case where the result fails is when the cross-sectional consumption to age profile is increasing with age, but is concave, so that the lowest levels of consumption are found among the youngest households, either because they have low income and face borrowing restrictions, or because they contain a large proportion of children. If these households show the lowest levels of consumption, and are the major contributors to the cross-cohort component of inequality, aging the population by redistributing people from these groups to older groups will decrease cross-cohort inequality, and the effect is potentially large enough to overcome the increase in the weight attached to the within-cohort inequality of the older groups. Under the life-cycle model, higher rates of economic growth make such effects less likely, because the higher the rate of growth, the higher are the lifetime wealth levels of younger relative to older consumers, which will tend to tip the cross-sectional consumption-to-age profile in a clockwise direction, raising the consumption of the young relative to that of the old. As we shall see below, there is not much evidence that this effect exists in the data; instead, the age profile of consumption is determined by the age profile of earnings.

Table 6.6 provides some illustrative calculations based on Taiwanese parameters. They are based on the validity of the life-cycle model, with the consumption-age effects taken from the calculations reported in Section 6.2 above. These age effects determine the age profile of consumption for any given cohort, and the assumed rates of economic growth determine the relative lifetime wealth levels for each cohort. Higher economic growth rotates clockwise the cross-sectional consumption-age profile, and thus changes the intercohort component of inequality. The estimated age effects, shown in Figure 6.6, rise sharply with age, so that we are in the situation described in the previous paragraph where increases in the rate of population growth increase intercohort inequality when economic growth is low and the cross-section consumption profiles are steeply upward sloping, but decrease intercohort inequality when economic growth is high and the cross-sectional age profiles are flatter. In these calculations, the middle figure in each row is increasing to the right when economic growth is 0 or 2 percent, is non-monotonic at 4 percent, and is decreasing at 6 percent. Increased rates of population growth always decrease the intracohort component of inequality, a component that is unaffected by the rate of economic growth, and is shown in the first row of each panel of the table. In these particular calculations, the effects of population growth on intercohort inequality is larger than the effect on intracohort inequality, and it is the former that dominates the overall result. However, the large intercohort effects come from the assumption that economic growth does in fact tip the cross-sectional consumption profile—something that probably does not happen in reality—and are thus likely to be overstated.

Although it will take a good deal more research to refine these sort of calculations, the table illustrates plausible magnitudes for the effects of economic and

Table 6.6. The relationship between inequality and growth
(Taiwan (China), hypothetical calculations: variances of logarithms)

	Percentage rate of population growth		
	0	2	4
Consumption growth = 0			
Within-cohort inequality	0.289	0.262	0.240
Between-cohort inequality	0.261	0.309	0.347
Total inequality	0.550	0.572	0.588
Consumption growth = 2 percent			
Within-cohort inequality	0.289	0.262	0.240
Between-cohort inequality	0.082	0.112	0.142
Total inequality	0.371	0.374	0.382
Consumption growth = 4 percent			
Within-cohort inequality	0.289	0.262	0.240
Between-cohort inequality	0.037	0.035	0.042
Total inequality	0.326	0.297	0.283
Consumption growth = 6 percent			
Within-cohort inequality	0.289	0.262	0.240
Between-cohort inequality	0.126	0.080	0.049
Total inequality	0.416	0.342	0.289

Source: Deaton and Paxson (1995, Table 2).

population growth on aggregate consumption inequality. Given that aggregate inequality is usually rather insensitive to economic change, with inequality measures changing little over long periods of time, the effects shown in the table are large. For example, if we assume the distributions of consumption are (at least approximately) lognormal, the variances of logarithms can be converted into Gini coefficients (see Aitchison and Brown 1969, pp. 12–13 for the formula and its derivation). Table 6.6 then shows that, at a 6 percent annual rate of growth of consumption per head, the difference between 3 and 1 percent annual population growth rate is the difference between a Gini coefficient of 0.309 and 0.352, a difference that would typically be sufficient to cause concern if not correctly interpreted as a composition effect.

6.6 Household saving and policy: a tentative review

This chapter, like the research it has reported, has inevitably been fragmentary; there is no coherent story in which the fragments can be set, and that tells us what is the role of saving in economic development and in the lives of people in developing countries. In this final section, I try to pull together, not a complete account, but some themes that have appeared in different places in the chapter, and to address the issues that are most important for policy.

Motives, consequences, and policy

Some people save to accumulate wealth, for themselves or for their heirs. Others save so as to have something for a "rainy day," a rainy year, or a rainy retirement, and yet others save because they fear the consequences of facing an uncertain future with no assets. Saving may even reflect the lack of suitable consumption opportunities, or simply the inability of a traditionally poor people to adjust their habits quickly to their newfound prosperity. Where credit markets are poorly developed, people need to save in anticipation of large purchases of items such as houses or cars. Different motives generate different patterns of saving, among individuals and in the aggregate economy, and imply different responses of individual welfare and of aggregate saving to policies such as interest rates, direct saving incentives such as tax deductions, or the provision of state-sponsored social security. Empirical research to date has found at least some support for several different interpretations of saving behavior, but failures of measurement, and perhaps of imagination, have prevented economists from coming to the solid understanding that could serve as a basis for policy.

Recent research has focussed on interpretations of saving that are associated with smoothing consumption, whereby individuals free their consumption from earnings in either (or both) the short run (seasons, years) or long run (lifetimes). The results reviewed in this chapter provide good evidence that households in poor countries are capable of purposeful intertemporal allocation of resources, at least sufficient to help protect their consumption against seasonal and year-to-year fluctuations in incomes. The evidence that individuals or households in developing countries make effective provision for retirement by saving is weaker or nonexistent, nor is it even clear that it makes sense for them to try given traditional social and family arrangements. I shall return in the next section to the implications of this failure of the life-cycle model, but the success of short-term smoothing is itself of major importance for thinking about policy.

Many countries operate tax and pricing schemes, the ostensible purpose of which is to stabilize farmers' incomes; for example, many countries in Africa pay their farmers a price for cash crops that is both more stable and a good deal lower than world prices. Although there are undoubtedly cases where price stabilization is used as a screen for taxation, there is an arguable case for the state attempting to stabilize farmers' incomes, though it is far from clear that price stabilization is the best way to do so (see Newbery and Stiglitz 1981). The arguments for stabilization typically assume a close relationship between farm incomes and consumption. When incomes are low, and credit markets are absent or imperfect, consumption will also be low, while high incomes will generate conspicuous and wasteful consumption or investment, since uneducated farmers cannot be expected to make adequate provision for the future (see for example the statement quoted on p. 351 above). As a result, farmers need to be protected against their own fecklessness by the stabilization board. Not only do the empirical results suggest that these concerns are exaggerated, but there is also a considerable body of historical and contemporary evidence that governments find it very difficult to deal with the fluctuations in government revenues that are generated by the stabilization and taxation schemes (see for example Hirschman 1977; Bauer 1984; Bevan, Collier, and Gunning 1989; Deaton and Miller 1995; and Collier and Gunning 1997 for discussion and evidence). Of course, none of this should be taken to mean that poor agricultural communities are capable of costlessly dealing with all fluctuations in their incomes, nor that outside help should be denied in time of need, only that policy should not be based on a presumption that rural households are incapable of making sensible intertemporal choices, nor on the presumption that the state can do better.

Section 6.4 discussed some of the recent research concerned with consumption insurance. This work is relatively new and the results are both controversial and unclear. Some of the empirical work appears to show evidence of the operation of local insurance schemes, although there is increasing agreement that such schemes cannot and do not provide the complete pooling of resources that would maximize the degree of insurance cover. This is a topic that deserves a great deal more research, in more and in different contexts, and with attention to the links with other literatures on risk sharing, credit markets, and sharecropping contracts. We need to know, not only whether and to what extent consumption is insured, but what mechanisms are involved. The understanding of this topic is once again a prerequisite for sensible policy design, particularly as the process of development inevitably brings greater demands for formal and state-sponsored insurance schemes.

Saving and growth

What have we learned from the household data about the macroeconomics of saving, and particularly about one of the longest-standing questions in economic development, the relationship between saving and growth? Is it true, as the classical economists believed, and as has become credible once again, that higher saving is the precursor of economic growth, so that the key to raising growth rates is to design incentives to encourage saving, almost certainly in conjunction with educational expansion so that physical and human capital formation are expanded together? Or are high savings rates simply a symptom of rapid growth, whose wellsprings lie elsewhere?

One of the great attractions of the life-cycle hypothesis is that it offers a coherent microeconomic theory of individual saving that is capable of delivering important macroeconomic conclusions through a process of explicit aggregation over households. Instead of simply invoking the anthropomorphic fallacy of aggregation, imputing human motives to the behavior of national averages, aggregate saving is explicitly linked to the rates of growth of income and of population. Faster growth, whether of population or of per capita income, expands the total scale of saving among the young relative to the scale of dissaving among the old and so raises the average saving rate. In a stationary population with constant per capita incomes, saving would be zero, even though each household saves at some point during its existence. On the surface, the empirical evidence supports this account. There is a strong positive relationship between per capita growth and saving rates across the cross section of countries. Countries like Hong Kong, Indonesia, Korea, Taiwan (China), and Thailand, that have increased their growth rates, have also increased their saving rates, and in the industrialized countries where growth rates have been lower in the 80s than in the 70s, and lower in the 70s than in the 60s, there has been a corresponding and almost universal decline in national saving rates. Moreover, the magnitude of these effects is very close to that predicted by straightforward "back-of-the-envelope" calculations using the life-cycle model.

Unfortunately, recent evidence has not been kind to this elegant and apparently satisfactory account. First, the simple cross-sectional age profiles of consumption tend to be similar to those illustrated in Figure 6.2 for Thailand and Côte d'Ivoire; there is some evidence of hump saving in middle age, but it is limited in extent, and apparently unmatched by dissaving among the elderly. As discussed in Section 6.1 above, there are arguments that help reconcile these findings with the life-cycle model, but the extent of saving among the young and dissaving among the old (if it exists) is not sufficient to support an account in which growth is responsible for the increase in saving rates that appears in the data. Second, detailed analysis of the experience using repeated cross-sectional surveys does not support the life-cycle interpretation of secular changes in the saving ratio. Bosworth, Burtless, and Sabelhaus (1991) and Attanasio and Weber (1992) for the United States, Blundell and Banks (1992) for Britain, and particularly Paxson (1996) for the United States, Britain, Taiwan (China) and Thailand, show that changes in national saving rates are not aggregation effects associated with the relative wealth and size of different cohorts, but come from secular changes of saving rates within cohorts. Paxson's work, like the earlier work of Carroll and Summers (1991) also establishes that the cross-country correlation of saving with growth cannot be attributed to the life-cycle model.

If the correlation between saving and growth does not come from life-cycle behavior, how can we explain it? The obvious possibility is that the causation runs in reverse, not from growth to saving, but from saving to growth. Such an explanation has always had its adherents among development economists, and Lewis (1954) was probably expressing no more than the then widely accepted view when he saw the problem of raising the saving rate as the central problem of economic development. The supposition that increases in saving rates could increase the steady-state rate of growth was (perhaps only) temporarily discredited by the Solow (1956) model, which showed that in a neoclassical framework, increases in the saving rate would increase the level of per capita income, but would raise the rate of growth only along the transition from one growth path to the other, not permanently. But as has long been known from the early work of Atkinson (1969), the transitions can last for a long period, and more recent empirical work by Mankiw, Romer, and Weil (1992) has shown that the Solow model is capable of giving a surprisingly good account of the data, with the ratio of investment to GDP an important determinant of growth. In a world of perfect international capital markets, there is no obvious reason why there should be a relationship between investment and saving ratios at the country level, but the correlation is nevertheless strong and positive—Feldstein and Horioka (1980)— even if weakening over time. Recent research on economic growth has also given a good deal of attention to models in which there are constant returns to scale to some broadly defined concept of capital—typically including human as well as physical capital—and such models clearly have the ability to generate permanent increases in growth rates in response to increases in the (broadly defined) saving ratio.

Attributing differences in growth rates to differences in saving rates leaves aside the question of what determines international differences in saving rates. Treating saving rates as determined by tastes (the Confucian ethic) is hardly satisfactory and does a poor job (for example) of explaining why Korean and Taiwanese saving rates should only recently have become so high. Nevertheless, if the life-cycle explanation is ruled out, we are left with only partial and incomplete explanations.

Determinants of saving

One popular explanation of the rate of saving looks to interest rates, and sees the high real interest rates that accompany economic growth—in unofficial if not official markets—as promoting saving and providing the fuel for growth. In many countries, governments have attempted to keep interest rates low (once thought to be the recipe for high investment and growth) in order to keep down the costs of their own borrowing. The accompanying physical controls on rates—financial repression—are seen as discouraging saving, diverting what saving there is to the finance of government deficits, and stifling economic growth by limiting private investment. I have written elsewhere about the theoretical and empirical support for this argument (see Deaton 1990b but also Balassa 1990 and Fry 1988 for more sympathetic treatments). The arguments may be summarized briefly as follows. First, in spite of stubborn beliefs to the contrary, the economic theory of intertemporal choice does not predict that higher interest rates raise saving, but is ambiguous about the direction of the effect. Both the life-cycle hypothesis and the buffering model described in Section 6.3 are consistent with modest positive effects of interest rates on saving, but it is hard to make an argument for anything other than small effects. Second, the lack of interest rate effects on saving should not be confused with the existence of possibly large interest rate effects on portfolio allocation. Where households have been forced to buffer their consumption with expensive assets such as stocks of grain, or hard-to-protect assets like cash, the introduction of sound financial intermediation is likely to be welcome, and to generate a flow of "saving" into the institutions. But this is a portfolio reallocation effect, and does not represent a cut in consumption in response to the higher interest rate.

Third, of the econometric work that shows strong interest rate effects, much is nonreplicable, and very little is credible. Most careful econometric work is consistent with the theoretical prediction, that interest rate effects are small or nonexistent. Fourth, most households do not hold interest-bearing assets, in either rich or poor countries. Nonsmokers are not much affected by the price of tobacco, and people who hold no interest-bearing assets are not much affected by the price of assets. Even in the United States, where financial intermediation is as sophisticated as anywhere in the world, around a quarter of total household consumption is located in households where no one possesses any financial assets whatever, not even a bank or savings account. In the Ivorian LSS, there are no rural households that admit to holding financial assets. It is certainly true that these people, like their counterparts in the United States, are not thereby absolved from making intertemporal choices, but the returns that they face, on loans from moneylenders or on their own physical investments, bear little or no relationship to the interest rates that are influenced by the government.

A second avenue of research is to recognize that saving may be prompted more by motives of accumulation than by the need to transfer resources from youth to old age. Such an explanation is perhaps consistent with the evidence from Taiwan (China) in Section 6.1, where the elasticity of consumption with respect to lifetime resources is estimated to be substantially less than unity, so that, as people become better-off, they commit a larger fraction of their lifetime resources to accumulating bequests. It is also consistent with the recent upward reevaluation of the contribution of bequests to national wealth in the United States and other developed economies (see Kotlikoff and Summers 1981, Modigliani 1988, and Kotlikoff 1988). However, if it is true that bequests are a luxury good, saving rates will be positively correlated with the level of economic development, rather than with the rate of growth, which is what the data appear to show.

A third promising research topic is the relationship between saving and housing, an account that potentially combines life-cycle and accumulation motives. Saving for house purchase is an explanation that is frequently offered by high savers in Hong Kong, Korea, and Taiwan (China), countries where house prices are also extremely high relative to incomes, at least judged by similar ratios in the United States. High house prices are also cited as an explanation for the high saving ratios, though given limited land in these relatively small countries, it would make just as much sense to attribute the high land prices to the high saving ratios. Older people also emphasize the desirability of bequeathing housing to their heirs. As far as I am aware, no one has combined these sort of considerations into a coherent account of growth, land prices, and saving, let alone tested such a model against the data, but the topic deserves a good deal further investigation.

A fourth explanation of saving is that consumption is subject to habits or "ratchet effects." According to such models—which date back at least to Duesenberry (1949)—it hurts more to reduce consumption than to increase it, so consumers respond to growth in their incomes only slowly, and attempt not to reduce their consumption when incomes fall. Alternatively, it might be supposed that tastes and technology of consumption respond slowly to growth, so that it takes time for Korean and Taiwanese entrepreneurs to construct the leisure and service industries that would facilitate the increase in consumption. According to such models, saving rates should be highest among those consumers who have recently experienced the most rapid rates of real income growth. As reported above, there is some support for this idea in the Taiwanese data, but the effect is much too small to explain much of Taiwanese saving rates, or to account for the cross-country relationship between saving and growth.

The simple buffer-stock model of Section 6.3 also predicts a positive relationship between saving and growth, but as in the case of the habit model, the effect is too small. When households hold assets only for precautionary purposes, the amount will depend on the variance of earnings, rather than on its level or its expected rate of growth. Suppose that in equilibrium, and for whatever reason, assets are a constant multiple of income. If income is growing at rate g, so must be assets, and since saving is the rate of increase of assets, we have

$$(6.42) \qquad g = \frac{\Delta A}{A} = \frac{s}{A} = \frac{s}{y}\frac{y}{A}.$$

From the first and last equalities, we have immediately that

$$(6.43) \qquad \frac{s}{y} = g\frac{A}{y}.$$

The ratio of assets to income for buffering households will depend on how much smoothness people want, and how much they are prepared to pay for it. However, the ratio is only 0.075 in the simulation in Figure 6.8, and could hardly be more than a third, so that, according to (6.43), buffering cannot account for the cross-country relationship. For the equation to match the data requires an asset to income ratio of two to three, which is roughly in accord with actual national magnitudes, which are also much the same as those predicted by stripped-down versions of the life-cycle model. All of which would suggest that the life-cycle model might do a good job of explaining the cross-country results. The difficulty, of course, is that the evidence is not consistent with the supposition that saving for retirement is such a large multiple of income.

Disentangling these various explanations from one another and confronting them with the evidence is a major research task, and one on which we can expect progress in the near future. Progress to date has been hampered by data quality, especially in household surveys where saving rates are very low, and by the limited information to be obtained from short aggregate time series, either for individual countries or from international comparisons. But there exist good household surveys from many of the high-saving nations of East and South-East Asia, and as the information in these is sifted, our knowledge should greatly increase.

6.7 Guide to further reading

There is an immense literature on saving in both developing and developed economies, and only a few of the topics are discussed in this chapter. Gersovitz (1988) provides a comprehensive review of the literature on saving and development and deals with many of the topics that are not covered here. My own review for the

World Bank's first Annual Conference on Development Economics, Deaton (1990b), builds on Gersovitz's survey and also focusses on some of the same topics covered here. Besley's (1995a) review takes a broader perspective and is more up to date. Deaton (1992c) is a fuller treatment that contains some development material, but is more concerned with the American literature, much of which focusses on macroeconomic time-series issues (see also Browning and Lusardi 1996, for an update). Nevertheless, it provides an up-to-date treatment of the theory of intertemporal choice, and a review of the most important empirical results. There is much to be learned from going back to the classics, to Lewis (1954) and to Modigliani and Brumberg's (1954, 1979) original account of the life-cycle model. Modigliani's (1986) Nobel address is a particularly useful statement of the achievements of the life-cycle model, achievements that have been the basis for almost all subsequent work. Some recent work on social insurance and consumption smoothing, which also provides a further introduction to the literature, is contained in a symposium in the *Journal of Economic Perspectives*, Townsend (1995), Morduch (1995), and Besley (1995b).

Code appendix

This appendix provides the STATA code used to produce the results in the text. These are *not* intended to be self-contained; they cannot be run as they stand without modification and, at the very least, the addition of the user's own data set. The idea is not to supply a software package that will replicate the analyses in the text, but to provide the code to serve as a template for the user's own analysis. I have not provided code for straightforward cases such as tabulations or standard regressions. I have tried to add enough comments to the code to make it broadly comprehensible and to aid those who wish to translate it into languages other than STATA; in most cases, the translation should not be difficult. Apart from some later addition of comments, the code given here is the code that was actually used to produce the results in the text. I have taken a good deal of care to check the code, but I give no guarantee that it is error free, let alone that it will automatically work on different data sets and different machines. The code listed here should be available from mid-1997 on the LSMS site on the Web at the address

http://www.worldbank.org/html/prdph/lsms/lsmshome.html

A.1 Chapter 1

There are three examples. The first is for the saving, expenditure, and income tabulation for Thailand in Table 1.3, the second for the alternative estimates of standard errors for mean PCE in Pakistan in Table 1.4, and the third for the bootstrap estimates of standard errors, also for Pakistan, discussed on pp. 57–58.

Example 1.1. Saving, expenditure, and income in Thailand

The program, which was used to calculate Table 1.3, takes data on income, expenditure, and weights from a file thaicy.dta, creates a measure of saving, sorts by income and by expenditure, and creates deciles for each, taking into account the weights. Income, expenditure, and saving are then summarized by decile.

```
version 4.0
#delimit ;
```

```
cap log close;
log using table13, replace;
drop _all;
set more 1;
* data with income, expenditure, and weights;
use thaicy;
* remove missing values;
drop if inc1==.;
drop if exp1==.;
* getting the sum of the weights for normalization;
qui summ weight;
global bigw=_N*_result(3);

*first sorting by household total income;
sort inc1;
gen sumwt=sum(weight)/$bigw;
gen dec=int(sumwt*10)+1;
* puts the richest household in the top decile, not the 11th;
replace dec=10 if dec==11;

sort dec;
*average saving by deciles of total household income;
by dec: summ sav1 [aweight=weight];
*all;
summ sav1 [aweight=weight];
*average income by deciles of total household income;
by dec: summ inc1 [aweight=weight];
*all;
summ inc1 [aweight=weight];
drop dec sumwt;

*now repeating by household total expenditure;
sort exp1;
gen sumwt=sum(weight)/$bigw;
gen dec=int(sumwt*10)+1;
replace dec=10 if dec==11;

sort dec;
*average saving by deciles of total household expenditure;
by dec: summ sav1 [aweight=weight];
summ sav1 [aweight=weight];
*average expenditure by deciles of total household expenditure;
by dec: summ exp1 [aweight=weight];
summ exp1 [aweight=weight];

log close;
```

Example 1.2. Estimating standard errors for average PCE in Pakistan

The program takes data from a file consdata.dta, which contains information on total expenditure, household size, and survey design variables, that were taken from the expenditure files of the PIHS. It then computes weighted and unweighted means, together with various correct and incorrect variances and standard errors. This program should not be used in preference to the complex survey design procedures that became available in Version 5.0 of STATA.

```
version 4.0
#delimit ;
cap log close;
log using table15, replace;
drop _all;
set more 1;
```

```
use consdata;
*per capita household expenditure;
gen pce=totmexp/hhsize;
*stratum identifiers;
gen strat=int(hhid/1000000);
*cluster identifiers;
gen clust=int(hhid/1000);
*province identifiers;
gen prov=int(hhid/100000000);
tab prov;
keep pce strat clust weight prov;
save temp, replace;

*defining the program to do the work;
cap program drop surv;
program def surv;
dis("first the ordinary unweighted mean");
*ci provides a standard error of the estimate, col 2;
ci pce;
dis("now the weighted mean");
summ pce [aweight=weight];
local xw=_result(3);
*xw is the correct, weighted mean;
qui summ weight;
local nhat=_result(1)*_result(3);
gen dx2=(pce-`xw')^2;
qui summ dx2 [aweight=weight];
*this is a weighted variance estimate;
local varx1=_result(3)/_result(1);
display("first incorrect variance");
dis `varx1';
display("standard error for col 4");
dis sqrt(`varx1');
dis("allowing weights but no stratification or clusters");
*this corresponds to (1.28);
gen vi2dx2=(weight/`nhat')^2*dx2;
qui summ vi2dx2;
local varx2=_result(1)*_result(3);
display("second incorrect variance");
dis `varx2';
display("standard error");
dis sqrt(`varx2');
dis("allowing weights and stratification, but no clusters");
*this uses (1.28) and adds over strata using (1.36);
egen svarx2=mean(vi2dx2), by(strat);
egen ns=count(pce), by(strat);
gen fac=ns/(ns-1);
replace svarx2=svarx2*fac;
qui summ svarx2;
local varx3=_result(1)*_result(3);
display("third incorrect variance");
dis `varx3';
display("standard error");
dis sqrt(`varx3');
dis("now allowing for everything");
*this is evaluated according to (1.63);
gen z=weight*pce;
egen zcs=sum(z), by(clust);
egen wcs=sum(weight), by(clust);
sort clust;
qui by clust: keep if _n==1;
egen zs=mean(zcs), by(strat);
egen ws=mean(wcs), by(strat);
gen dall=((zcs-zs)-`xw'*(wcs-ws))^2;
egen tm=sum(dall), by(strat);
sort strat;
qui by strat: keep if _n==1;
qui replace tm=tm*fac;
qui summ tm;
```

```
local varok=_result(1)*_result(3)/(`nhat'^2);
display("correct variance");
dis `varok';
display("standard error");
dis sqrt(`varok');
end;

surv;

**Now doing the provinces;
cap program drop cont;
program def cont;
        local pno=1;
        while `pno' <= 4 {;
        drop _all;
        use temp;
        keep if prov==`pno';
        surv;
        local pno=`pno'+1;
        };
end;

cont;

log close;
```

Example 1.3. Bootstrapping weighted means and medians

The program uses the same data as in Example 1.2 to construct bootstrap samples
with the same stratified and clustered structure as the original. In each bootstrap
replication, weighted and unweighted means and medians are calculated and saved
in a data set. The standard deviations over the bootstrap replications are used to indicate the sampling variability of the original estimates.

```
version 4.0
#delimit ;
cap log close;
log using ex13, replace;
set more 1;
drop _all;
use consdata;
gen clust=int(hhid/1000);
gen strat=int(hhid/1000000);
gen pce=totmexp/hhsize;
keep clust strat pce weight;
egen newstrat=group(strat);
*egen numbers the strata 1,2, etc;
drop strat;
save tempbase, replace;

**Bootstrapping for srs and weighted mean;
**Using strata and clusters;
cap program drop sbsmean;
program def sbsmean;
        tempname sim;
        tempfile bsres samp ssamp;
         postfile `sim' x xw xmed xmedw using `bsres', replace;
        local ic=1;
        while `ic' <= 100 {;
            display "replication no. " `ic';
            /* at each replication build up bs sample
            ** stratum by stratum: `is' is stratum counter */
            local is=1;
             while `is' <= 22 {;
```

```
            use tempbase, clear;
            qui keep if newstrat==`is';
            sort clust;
            qui save `ssamp', replace;
            keep clust;
            qui by clust: drop if _n ~= 1;
            /* bs sampling of clusters */
            bsample _N;
            sort clust;
            qui by clust: gen dum=_N;
            qui by clust: drop if _n ~= 1;
            merge clust using `ssamp';
            qui drop if _merge ~= 3;
            qui expand dum;
            drop _merge dum;
            if `is'==1 {;
                qui save `samp', replace; };
                else {;
                append using `samp';
                qui save `samp', replace;};
                local is=`is'+1;
            };
            use `samp', clear;
            /* the unweighted estimate */
            qui summ pce, d;
            local md=_result(10);
            local mn=_result(3);
            /* the weighted estimate */
            qui summ pce [aweight=weight],d;
            local mnw=_result(3);
            local mdw=_result(10);
            post `sim' `mn' `mnw' `md' `mdw';
            local ic=`ic'+1;
        };
        postclose `sim';
        drop _all;
        use `bsres';
        summ;
        save ex13, replace;
end;

sbsmean;

log close;
```

A.2 Chapter 2

There are two examples. The first concerns the heteroskedastic censored regression model and the second, the decomposition of data from a time series of cross-sections into age, cohort, and year effects.

Example 2.1. Comparing OLS, Tobit, and Powell's censored LAD estimators

The heteroskedastic censored regression model is discussed on pp. 85–90. I give the code for the Monte Carlo experiment comparing Powell's censored LAD estimator with OLS and MLE Tobit, the results of which are discussed on p. 90.

```
version 4.0
#delimit ;
set more 1;
/* control program */
/* number of observations, either 100 or 1000 */
```

```
global nobs=100;

cap program drop doit;
program define doit;
local ct = 1;
while `ct' < `1' {;
dis ("Experiment number `ct'");
runtest;
append using temp;
qui save temp, replace;
local ct=`ct'+1;
};
end;

cap program drop runtest;
program define runtest;
drop _all;
qui set obs $nobs;
gen x=_n/($nobs/100);
gen u=invnorm(uniform());
qui replace u=u*20;
gen ytrue=max(0,x-40);
/* this is the heteroskedasticity   */
qui replace u=u*(1+0.03*ytrue);
gen ystar=-40+x+u;
qui replace ystar=0 if ystar < 0;
qui regress ystar x;
/* ols regression */
global bols=_coef[x];
qui tobit ystar x, ll;
/* mle tobit estimation */
mac def btob=_coef[x];
/* censored LAD estimation: 10 loops */
qui qreg ystar x, qu(0.5);
predict xb1;
local iloop=2;
while `iloop' <=10 {;
qui qreg ystar x, qu(0.5), if xb1 > 0;
predict xb2;
qui replace xb1=xb2;
drop xb2;
local iloop=`iloop'+1;
};
/* powell estimate coefficient */
mac def bpow=_coef[x];
drop _all;
qui set obs 1;
gen zols=$bols;
gen ztob=$btob;
gen zpow=$bpow;
list;
end;

drop _all;
set obs 1;
gen zols=999;
gen ztob=999;
gen zpow=999;
cap save temp, replace;
doit 100;
drop if zols==999;
gen absols=abs(zols-1);
gen abstob=abs(ztob-1);
gen abspow=abs(zpow-1);
gen powbest=0;
replace powbest=1 if (abspow <=abstob) & (abspow < absols);

summ;
```

Example 2.2. Decompositions into age, cohort, and year effects

The second example presents the code for the decomposition of earnings in Taiwan
(China) into age, cohort, and year effects; the methods are discussed on pp.
116–27, and the results are shown in Figure 2.5.

```
version 4.0
#delimit ;
set more 1;
drop _all;
use finp;
/*
**finp is a data set that is constructed from the
**original surveys from 1975-1990. For the individual-
**level data, in each survey, the average earnings at
**each year is calculated, and this is saved, so that
**for each year from 1975 to 1990, finp contains age,
**average earnings of individuals of that age, and
**the survey year
**/
keep age yr iearn;
gen cohort=age-yr+65;
drop if age < 25;
drop if age > 65;
/* generating dummies for each age, cohort and year */
tab age, gen(aged);
tab cohort, gen(cohd);
tab yr, gen(yrd);
drop aged1;
drop cohd1;
/*
**constructing variables so that the year effects
**add to zero, and are orthogonal to a time trend */
replace yrd15=yrd15-14*yrd2-13*yrd1;
replace yrd14=yrd14-13*yrd2-12*yrd1;
replace yrd13=yrd13-12*yrd2-11*yrd1;
replace yrd12=yrd12-11*yrd2-10*yrd1;
replace yrd11=yrd11-10*yrd2-9*yrd1;
replace yrd10=yrd10-9*yrd2-8*yrd1;
replace yrd9=yrd9-8*yrd2-7*yrd1;
replace yrd8=yrd8-7*yrd2-6*yrd1;
replace yrd7=yrd7-6*yrd2-5*yrd1;
replace yrd6=yrd6-5*yrd2-4*yrd1;
replace yrd5=yrd5-4*yrd2-3*yrd1;
replace yrd4=yrd4-3*yrd2-2*yrd1;
replace yrd3=yrd3-2*yrd2-1*yrd1;
drop yrd2;
drop yrd1;

regress iearn aged* cohd* yrd*;
/* calculating & storing the year in variable yreff */
gen yreff=_b[yrd3] if yr==67;
replace yreff=_b[yrd4] if yr==68;
replace yreff=_b[yrd5] if yr==69;
replace yreff=_b[yrd6] if yr==70;
replace yreff=_b[yrd7] if yr==71;
replace yreff=_b[yrd8] if yr==72;
replace yreff=_b[yrd9] if yr==73;
replace yreff=_b[yrd10] if yr==74;
replace yreff=_b[yrd11] if yr==75;
replace yreff=_b[yrd12] if yr==76;
replace yreff=_b[yrd13] if yr==77;
replace yreff=_b[yrd14] if yr==78;
replace yreff=_b[yrd15] if yr==79;
global tem = -2*_b[yrd3]-3*_b[yrd4]-4*_b[yrd5]-5*_b[yrd6]-6*_b[yrd7]
        -7*_b[yrd8]-8*_b[yrd9]-9*_b[yrd10]-10*_b[yrd11]-11*_b[yrd12]
        -12*_b[yrd13]-13*_b[yrd14]-14*_b[yrd15];
```

```
replace yreff=$tem if yr==66;
global alpha1= -$tem-_b[yrd3]-_b[yrd4]-_b[yrd5]-_b[yrd6]-_b[yrd7]
        -_b[yrd8]-_b[yrd9]-_b[yrd10]-_b[yrd11]-_b[yrd12]
        -_b[yrd13]-_b[yrd14]-_b[yrd15];
replace yreff=$alpha1 if yr==65;
replace yr=yr+11;
/* calculating and storing cohort effects in coheff */
global nc=2;
global ic=12;
gen coheff=0 if cohort==11;
cap program drop doit;
program def doit;
        while $ic < 66 {;
        global ix="cohd$nc";
        replace coheff=_b[$ix] if cohort==$ic;
        global ic=$ic+1;
        global nc=$nc+1;
        };
end;
doit;
/* calculating and storing age effects */
mac def nc=2;
mac def ic=26;
gen ageff=0 if age==25;
cap program drop doit;
program def doit;
        while $ic < 66 {;
        mac def ix="aged$nc";
        replace ageff=_b[$ix] if age==$ic;
        mac def ic=$ic+1;
        mac def nc=$nc+1;
        };
end;
doit;
* Look at the results;
set more 0;
graph yreff yr, c(l) s(p) xlabel ylabel sort;
graph ageff age, c(l) s(.) xlabel ylabel sort;
graph coheff cohort, c(l) s(.) xlabel ylabel sort;
```

A.3 Chapter 3

The examples provide code for the summary measures of living standards, inequality, and poverty in Côte d'Ivoire and South Africa shown in Tables 3.1–3.4
and Figures 3.5 and 3.6. Figures 3.7–3.12 were calculated using the functions
provided by STATA and do not require special coding. The GAUSS code for Figures
3.13 and 3.14 is given as Example 3.7. I have not provided the code for the Thai
rice calculations; Figures 3.15 and 3.16 are calculated in the same way as Figures
3.13 and 3.14. The nonparametric regressions shown in Figures 3.17 and 3.18 are
kernel regressions, a method that has been superceded by the locally weighted
regressions shown in Figure 3.20 and the code for which is given in Example 3.8.

Example 3.1. Consumption measures for Côte d'Ivoire (Table 3.1)

The code uses data on household expenditures, prices, and weights to calculate
means for households and individuals, as well as their standard errors taking into
account the survey design.

```
version 4.0
/* NB the code uses the survey commands incoporated into the main
        code from version 5.0 of STATA  */
#delimit ;
drop _all;
cap log close;
log using table31.log, replace;
use c:\cdi1996\1985dta\hhexp85;
matrix prices=(100,107.3,107.75,115.31\92.84,100.45,98.58,106.74\
        87.01,93.36,94.95,99.84\78.25,80.11,81.50,83.51\
        75.97,85.97,88.20,94.42);
/*
**These are the prices reported on p 49 of the CLISS documentation
**Rows are regions, Abidjan, Other Cities, EForest, WForest, Savannah
** Columns are 1985, 1986, 1987, 1988
*/
matrix prices=prices*.01;
gen hhid=clust*100+nh;
ren reg region;
ren hhsize5 hhs;
keep hhid region hhexp hhs clust;
replace hhexp=hhexp/1000;
replace hhexp=hhexp/prices[1,1] if region==1;
replace hhexp=hhexp/prices[2,1] if region==2;
replace hhexp=hhexp/prices[3,1] if region==3;
replace hhexp=hhexp/prices[4,1] if region==4;
replace hhexp=hhexp/prices[5,1] if region==5;
gen year=1985;
sort hhid;
save temp, replace;
use c:\cdi1996\1985dta\weight85;
gen hhid=clust*100+nh;
keep hhid allwaitn;
sort hhid;
merge hhid using temp;
tab _m; drop _m;
gen pce=hhexp/hhs;
sort hhid;
save temp, replace;
drop _all;

use c:\cdi1996\1986dta\hhexp86;
gen hhid=clust*100+nh;
ren reg region;
ren hhsize6 hhs;
keep hhid region hhexp hhs clust;
replace hhexp=hhexp/1000;
replace hhexp=hhexp/prices[1,2] if region==1;
replace hhexp=hhexp/prices[2,2] if region==2;
replace hhexp=hhexp/prices[3,2] if region==3;
replace hhexp=hhexp/prices[4,2] if region==4;
replace hhexp=hhexp/prices[5,2] if region==5;
gen year=1986;
sort hhid;
save tempa, replace;
use c:\cdi1996\1986dta\weight86;
gen hhid=clust*100+nh;
keep hhid allwaitn;
sort hhid;
merge hhid using tempa;
tab _m; drop _m;
gen pce=hhexp/hhs;
append using temp;
save temp, replace;

use c:\cdi1996\1987dta\hhexp87;
gen hhid=clust*100+nh;
ren reg region;
ren hhsize7 hhs;
```

```
keep hhid region hhexp hhs clust;
replace hhexp=hhexp/1000;
replace hhexp=hhexp/prices[1,3] if region==1;
replace hhexp=hhexp/prices[2,3] if region==2;
replace hhexp=hhexp/prices[3,3] if region==3;
replace hhexp=hhexp/prices[4,3] if region==4;
replace hhexp=hhexp/prices[5,3] if region==5;
gen year=1987;
sort hhid;
save tempa, replace;
use c:\cdi1996\1987dta\weight87;
gen hhid=clust*100+nh;
keep hhid allwaitn;
sort hhid;
merge hhid using tempa;
tab _m; drop _m;
gen pce=hhexp/hhs;
append using temp;
save temp, replace;

use c:\cdi1996\1988dta\hhexp88;
gen hhid=clust*100+nh;
ren reg region;
ren hhsize8 hhs;
keep hhid region hhexp hhs clust;
replace hhexp=hhexp/1000;
replace hhexp=hhexp/prices[1,4] if region==1;
replace hhexp=hhexp/prices[2,4] if region==2;
replace hhexp=hhexp/prices[3,4] if region==3;
replace hhexp=hhexp/prices[4,4] if region==4;
replace hhexp=hhexp/prices[5,4] if region==5;
gen year=1988;
sort hhid;
save tempa, replace;
use c:\cdi1996\1988dta\weight88;
gen hhid=clust*100+nh;
keep hhid allwaitn;
sort hhid;
merge hhid using tempa;
tab _m; drop _m;
gen pce=hhexp/hhs;
append using temp;
save cdi85_88, replace;

tab year;

varset strata region;
varset psu clust;
varset pweight allwaitn;

svymean hhexp if year==1985;
svymean hhexp if year==1986;
svymean hhexp if year==1987;
svymean hhexp if year==1988;

svymean hhs if year==1985;
svymean hhs if year==1986;
svymean hhs if year==1987;
svymean hhs if year==1988;

svymean pce if year==1985;
svymean pce if year==1986;
svymean pce if year==1987;
svymean pce if year==1988;

svyratio hhexp/hhs if year==1985;
svyratio hhexp/hhs if year==1986;
svyratio hhexp/hhs if year==1987;
svyratio hhexp/hhs if year==1988;
```

```
gen combwt=allwaitn*hhs;
varset pweight combwt;
svymean pce if year==1985;
svymean pce if year==1986;
svymean pce if year==1987;
svymean pce if year==1988;


log close;
```

Example 3.2. Inequality measures for Côte d'Ivoire (Table 3.2)

The code calculates each of the inequality measures in Table 3.2, with and without weights.

```
version 4.0
#delimit ;
drop _all;
cap log close;
log using table32, replace;
/* defining program to calculate gini without weights */
cap program drop giniu;
program def giniu;
        local yr=1985;
        while `yr' <= 1988 {;
                drop _all;
                use cdi85_88;
                keep if year==`yr';
                gsort - pce;
                gen hrnk=sum(hhs);
                gen hhrnk=hrnk[_n-1]+1;
                replace hhrnk=1 in 1;
                qui summ hhs;
                local bign=_result(1)*_result(3);
                qui summ pce [aweight=hhs];
                local mn=_result(3);
                gen rnkx=pce*(hhrnk+0.5*(hhs-1));
                qui summ rnkx [aweight=hhs];
                local g=(`bign'+1)-(2/`mn')*_result(3);
                local g=`g'/(`bign'-1);
                dis("Gini coefficient `yr' =`g'");
                local yr=`yr'+1;
        };
end;

/* defining program to calculate gini with weights */
cap program drop giniw;
program def giniw;
        local yr=1985;
        while `yr' <= 1988 {;
                drop _all;
                use cdi85_88;
                keep if year==`yr';
                gsort - pce;
                replace hhs=hhs*allwaitn;
                gen hrnk=sum(hhs);
                gen hhrnk=hrnk[_n-1]+1;
                replace hhrnk=1 in 1;
                qui summ hhs;
                local bign=_result(1)*_result(3);
                qui summ pce [aweight=hhs];
                local mn=_result(3);
                gen rnkx=pce*(hhrnk+0.5*(hhs-1));
                qui summ rnkx [aweight=hhs];
                local g=(`bign'+1)-(2/`mn')*_result(3);
                local g=`g'/(`bign'-1);
```

```
                        dis("Gini coefficient `yr' =`g'");
                        local yr=`yr'+1;
                };
        end;
        **Unweighted ginis;
        giniu;
        **Weighted ginis;
        giniw;

        /* program for Atkinson measures */
        /* argument `1' is the inequality aversion */
        cap program drop aba;
        program def aba;
                local yr=1985;
                while `yr' <= 1988 {;
                        drop _all;
                        use cdi85_88;
                        keep if year==`yr';
                        replace hhs=hhs*allwaitn;
                        qui summ pce [aweight=hhs];
                        local mn=_result(3);
                        gen pcerat=pce/`mn';
                        if `1' ==1 {;
                                gen tm=ln(pce/`mn');
                                qui summ tm [aweight=hhs];
                                local ineq=1-exp(_result(3));};
                        else {;
                                gen tm=(pce/`mn')^`1';
                                qui summ tm [aweight=hhs];
                                local ineq=1-(_result(3))^(1/(1-`1'));};
                        dis("`yr' Atkinson coefficient, eps=`1' =`ineq'");
                        local yr=`yr'+1;
                };
        end;

        aba 0.5;
        aba 1;
        aba 2;

        /* program for standard deviation of logs */
        cap program drop sdlogs;
        program define sdlogs;
                local yr=1985;
                while `yr' <= 1988 {;
                        drop _all;
                        use cdi85_88;
                        keep if year==`yr';
                        replace hhs=hhs*allwaitn;
                        gen lnpce=ln(pce);
                        qui summ lnpce [aweight=hhs];
                        local sdln=sqrt(_result(4));
                        dis("`yr' s.d. of lnpce, = `sdln'");
                        local yr=`yr'+1;
                };
        end;

        sdlogs;

        /* program for coefficient of variation */
        cap program drop coefvar;
        program define coefvar;
                local yr=1985;
                while `yr' <= 1988 {;
                        drop _all;
                        use cdi85_88;
                        keep if year==`yr';
                        replace hhs=hhs*allwaitn;
                        qui summ pce [aweight=hhs];
                        local cv=sqrt(_result(4))/_result(3);
```

```
                      dis("`yr' c.o.v. of pce, = `cv'");
                      local yr=`yr'+1;
            };
end;

coefvar;

log close;
```

Example 3.3. Poverty measures for Côte d'Ivoire (Table 3.3)

The code calculates the four poverty measures, together with their bootstrapped standard errors.

```
version 4.0
#delimit ;
drop _all;
cap log close;
log using table33,replace;
/* setting the poverty line */
global pline=128.6;

/* program for various poverty measures */
/* this iterates over the four years */
cap program drop peas;
program def peas;
        local yr=1985;
        while `yr' <= 1988 {;
                use cdi85_88;
                keep if year==`yr';
                gen wt=hhs*allwaitn;
                gen pind=pce <= $pline;
                qui summ pind [aweight=wt];
                local p0=_result(3);
                gen df=(1-pce/$pline)*pind;
                qui summ df [aweight=wt];
                local p1=_result(3);
                gen dfa=(1-pce/$pline)^2*pind;
                qui summ dfa [aweight=wt];
                local p2=_result(3);
                drop if pce > $pline;
                giniw;
                local psen=`p0'*$g+`p1'*(1-$g);
                dis("P0=`p0',P1=`p1',P2=`p2',Psen=`psen'");
                drop _all;
                local yr=`yr'+1;
                };
end;

/* we need this for the gini among the poor */
cap program drop giniw;
program def giniw;
        gsort - pce;
        qui {;
        gen hrnk=sum(wt);
        gen hhrnk=hrnk[_n-1]+1;
        replace hhrnk=1 in 1;};
        qui summ wt;
        local bign=_result(1)*_result(3);
        qui summ pce [aweight=wt];
        local mn=_result(3);
        gen rnkx=pce*(hhrnk+0.5*(wt-1));
        qui summ rnkx [aweight=wt];
        global g=(`bign'+1)-(2/`mn')*_result(3);
        global g=$g/(`bign'-1);
end;
```

```
peas;


/* bootstrapping the measures*/

drop _all;
set more 1;
cap log close;
log using t33boot, replace;

/* program for creating clustered bootstrap sample */
/* and calculating poverty measures */
cap program drop bootit;
program def bootit;
        use tempclus;
        bsample _N;
        sort clus;
        qui {;
        by clus: gen nreps=_N;
        by clus: keep if _n==1;
        merge clus using tempall;
        keep if _merge==3;
        expand nreps;
        drop nreps;};
        weepeas;
        drop _all;
end;

/* control program */

cap program drop runit;
cap program def runit;
        local yr=1985;
        while `yr' <= 1988 {;
                use cdi85_88;
                keep if year==`yr';
                gen wt=hhs*allwaitn;
                keep clus hhid pce wt;
                sort clus;
                save tempall, replace;
                keep clus;
                qui by clus: keep if _n==1;
                save tempclus, replace;
                drop _all;
                local mcrep=1;
                while `mcrep' <= 100 {;
                        dis ("Year `yr', Replication `mcrep'");
                        bootit;
                        drop _all;
                        qui set obs 1;
                        gen year=`yr';
                        gen p0=$p0;
                        gen p1=$p1;
                        gen p2=$p2;
                        gen psen=$psen;
                        if `mcrep' != 1 | `yr' != 1985 {;
                                append using t33boot;
                        };
                        qui save t33boot, replace;
                        drop _all;
                        local mcrep=`mcrep'+1;
                };
        local yr=`yr'+1;
        };
end;

/* calculates the various measures */
cap program drop weepeas;
program def weepeas;
```

```
              global pline=128.6;
              qui {;
              gen pind=pce <= $pline;
              qui summ pind [aweight=wt];
              global p0=_result(3);
              gen df=(1-pce/$pline)*pind;
              qui summ df [aweight=wt];
              global p1=_result(3);
              gen dfa=(1-pce/$pline)^2*pind;
              qui summ dfa [aweight=wt];
              global p2=_result(3);
              drop if pce > $pline;
              giniw;
              global psen=$p0*$g+$p1*(1-$g);
              drop _all;
              };
end;

runit;
drop _all;
use t33boot;
sort year;
by year: summ;

log close;
```

Example 3.4. Welfare measures for South Africa (Table 3.4)

The code is similar to that for Côte d'Ivoire but is adapted to the South African
data.

```
version 4.0
#delimit ;
drop _all;
cap log close;
log using sastats, replace;
/* household roster file */
use c:\safrica\work\m6_hrost;
/* keeping only members */
keep if mcode==1;
drop if gender_n==1;
drop if age==.;
drop if age <= 0;
keep hhid;
sort hhid;
qui by hhid: gen hhs=_N;
qui by hhid: keep if _n==1;
/* picking up the weights */
merge hhid using c:\safrica\work\strata2;
tab _m; drop _m;
keep hhid hhs race rsweight;
sort hhid;
/* picking up household expenditures */
merge hhid using c:\safrica\work\hhexptl;
keep hhid hhs race rsweight totmexp;
gen pce=totmexp/hhs;
gen wt=rsweight*hhs;
gen clus=int(hhid/1000);
sort race;
summ totmexp hhs pce [aweight=rsweight];
summ pce [aweight=wt];
by race: summ totmexp hhs pce [aweight=rsweight];
by race: summ pce [aweight=wt];
varset pweight wt;
varset psu clus;
svymean pce;
svymean pce, subpop(race==1);
```

```
svymean pce, subpop(race==2);
svymean pce, subpop(race==3);
svymean pce, subpop(race==4);
varset pweight rsweight;
svyratio totmexp/hhs;
svyratio totmexp/hhs, subpop(race==1);
svyratio totmexp/hhs, subpop(race==2);
svyratio totmexp/hhs, subpop(race==3);
svyratio totmexp/hhs, subpop(race==4);
save sastats, replace;
drop _all;
cap program drop ginisa;
program def ginisa;
        local rg=0;
        while `rg' <= 4 {;
                drop _all;
                use sastats;
                if `rg' > 0 {;keep if race==`rg';};
                giniw;
                dis("Gini coefficient race =`rg' =$g");
                local rg=`rg'+1;
        };
end;

cap program drop abasa;
program def abasa;
        local rg=0;
        while `rg' <= 4 {;
                drop _all;
                use sastats;
                if `rg' > 0 {;keep if race==`rg';};
                qui summ pce [aweight=wt];
                local mn=_result(3);
                gen pcerat=pce/`mn';
                if `1' ==1 {;
                        gen tm=ln(pce/`mn');
                        qui summ tm [aweight=wt];
                        local ineq=1-exp(_result(3));};
                else {;
                        gen tm=(pce/`mn')^`1';
                        qui summ tm [aweight=wt];
                        local ineq=1-(_result(3))^(1/(1-`1'));};
                        dis("race `rg' Atkinson coefficient, eps=`1'
=`ineq'");
                local rg=`rg'+1;
        };
end;

cap program drop sdlogssa;
program define sdlogssa;
        local rg=0;
        while `rg' <= 4 {;
                drop _all;
                use sastats;
                if `rg' > 0 {;keep if race==`rg';};
                gen lnpce=ln(pce);
                qui summ lnpce [aweight=wt];
                local sdln=sqrt(_result(4));
                dis("Race `rg' s.d. of lnpce, = `sdln'");
                local rg=`rg'+1;
        };
end;

cap program drop coefvar;
program define coefvar;
        local rg=0;
        while `rg' <= 4 {;
                drop _all;
                use sastats;
```

```
                     if `rg' > 0 {;keep if race==`rg';};
                     qui summ pce [aweight=wt];
                     local cv=sqrt(_result(4))/_result(3);
                     dis("Race `rg' c.o.v. of pce, = `cv'");
                     local rg=`rg'+1;
                };
end;

cap program drop peassa;
program def peassa;
        local rg=0;
        while `rg' <= 4 {;
                drop _all;
                use sastats;
                if `rg' > 0 {;keep if race==`rg';};
                gen pind=pce <= $pline;
                qui summ pind [aweight=wt];
                local p0=_result(3);
                gen df=(1-pce/$pline)*pind;
                qui summ df [aweight=wt];
                local p1=_result(3);
                gen dfa=(1-pce/$pline)^2*pind;
                qui summ dfa [aweight=wt];
                local p2=_result(3);
                drop if pce > $pline;
                if _N > 0 {;
                giniw;};
                else {;global g=1;};
                local psen=`p0'*$g+`p1'*(1-$g);
                dis("P0=`p0',P1=`p1',P2=`p2',Psen=`psen'");
                drop _all;
                local rg=`rg'+1;
                };end;

cap program drop giniw;
program def giniw;
        gsort - pce;
        qui {;
        gen hrnk=sum(wt);
        gen hhrnk=hrnk[_n-1]+1;
        replace hhrnk=1 in 1;};
        qui summ wt;
        local bign=_result(1)*_result(3);
        qui summ pce [aweight=wt];
        local mn=_result(3);
        gen rnkx=pce*(hhrnk+0.5*(wt-1));
        qui summ rnkx [aweight=wt];
        global g=(`bign'+1)-(2/`mn')*_result(3);
        global g=$g/(`bign'-1);
end;

ginisa;
abasa 0.5;
abasa 1;
abasa 2;
sdlogssa;
coefvar;
global pline=105;
peassa;

log close;
```

Example 3.5. Lorenz curves for South Africa (Figure 3.5)

The code shows how to calculate the cumulative fractions of population and of PCE and uses the results to draw the standard Lorenz curves.

```
version 4.0
#delimit ;
drop _all;
cap log close;
log using lorenz, replace;

cap program drop lc;
program def lc;
        drop _all;
        /* data saved from code in Ex3.4 above */
        use sastats;
        drop if pce==.;
        if `1' > 0 {; keep if race==`1';};
        sort pce;
        gen cumpop=sum(wt);
        gen cumpce=sum(pce);
        qui summ wt;
        replace cumpop=cumpop/(_result(1)*_result(3));
        qui summ pce;
        replace cumpce=cumpce/(_result(1)*_result(3));
        local gg=int(_N/100);
        keep if ((`gg'*int(_n/`gg')-_n)==0)|_n==1|_n==_N;
        sort pce;
        graph cumpce cumpop cumpop,
                c(ll) s(..) xlabel(0,0.2,0.4,0.6,0.8,1.0)
                ylabel(0, 0.2,0.4,0.6,0.8,1.0) border;
        gen rcode=`1';
        keep cumpce cumpop rcode;
        if `1' > 0 {; append using temp; };
        save temp, replace;
end;

lc 0;
lc 1;
lc 4;
drop _all;
use temp;

gen cumpce0=cumpce if rcode==0;
gen cumpce1=cumpce if rcode==1;
gen cumpce4=cumpce if rcode==4;
drop cumpce;
graph cumpce* cumpop cumpop,
      c(llll) s(....) xlabel(0,0.2,0.4,0.6,0.8,1.0)
         ylabel(0, 0.2,0.4,0.6,0.8,1.0) saving(lorenz, replace) border;
log close;
```

Example 3.6. Transformed Lorenz curves for Côte d'Ivoire (Figure 3.6)

This example adapts the code for the standard Lorenz curves so as to plot the distance between the Lorenz curve and the 45-degree line.

```
version 4.0
#delimit ;
drop _all;
cap log close;
log using lorenzic, replace;

cap program drop lcic;
program def lcic;
        drop _all;
        use cdi85_88;
        drop if pce==.;
        if `1' > 0 {; keep if year==`1';};
        sort pce;
```

```
            gen wt=hhs*allwaitn;
            gen cumpop=sum(wt);
            gen cumpce=sum(pce);
            qui summ wt;
            replace cumpop=cumpop/(_result(1)*_result(3));
            qui summ pce;
            replace cumpce=cumpce/(_result(1)*_result(3));
            local gg=int(_N/100);
            keep if ((`gg'*int(_n/`gg')-_n)==0)|_n==1|_n==_N;
            sort pce;
            graph cumpce cumpop cumpop,
                c(ll) s(..) xlabel(0,0.2,0.4,0.6,0.8,1.0)
                ylabel(0, 0.2,0.4,0.6,0.8,1.0);
            gen ycode=`1';
            keep cumpce cumpop ycode;
            if `1' > 1985 {; append using temp; };
            save temp, replace;
end;

lcic 1985;
lcic 1986;
lcic 1987;
lcic 1988;
drop _all;
use temp;

gen cumpce5=cumpce if ycode==1985;
gen cumpce6=cumpce if ycode==1986;
gen cumpce7=cumpce if ycode==1987;
gen cumpce8=cumpce if ycode==1988;
drop cumpce;
graph cumpce* cumpop cumpop,
            c(lllll) s(.....) xlabel(0,0.2,0.4,0.6,0.8,1.0)
            ylabel(0, 0.2,0.4,0.6,0.8,1.0) saving(lorenzic, replace);
/* defining the complementary lorenz curves as graphed */
gen compce5=cumpop-cumpce5;
gen compce6=cumpop-cumpce6;
gen compce7=cumpop-cumpce7;
gen compce8=cumpop-cumpce8;
graph compce* cumpop, c(ll111) s(.....) xlabel(0,0.2,0.4,0.6,0.8,1.0)
            ylabel(0, 0.1,0.2,0.3,0.4) saving(complc,replace);

log close;
```

Example 3.7. Contours and netmaps (Figures 3.13 and 3.14)

The code for the contours and netmaps is given in GAUSS because these facilities do not exist in STATA. I have also calculated the kernel estimates in GAUSS, though it would also have been possible to go to this stage in STATA.

```
/* GAUSS program for contouring joint density of log pce for first
two years of CDI data, results shown in Figures 3.13 and 3.14 */

/* the data pan8586 of log pce in the two years was
            created in STATA and converted to GAUSS format */

library pgraph;
open f1="pan8586";
x=readr(f1,10000);
f1=close(f1);
x=packr(x);
n=rows(x);
v=(x-meanc(x)')'*(x-meanc(x)')/n;
dt=det(v);
v_1=invpd(v);
```

```
/* the inverse variance-covariance matrix of the data */
xmin=3;
xmax=8;
ymin=3;
ymax=8;
grid=99;
stx=(xmax-xmin)/(grid-1);
sty=(ymax-ymin)/(grid-1);
ans=zeros(grid,grid);
ggx=seqa(xmin,stx,grid);
ggy=seqa(ymin,sty,grid);

/* setting the bandwidth */
h=1.0;
/* doing the density estimation */
ic=1;
do until ic==grid+1;
        ic;
        jc=1;
        do until jc==grid+1;
                locate 10,1; ic;;jc;
                xx=ggx[ic,1]|ggy[jc,1];
                df=(x-xx')/h;
                t2=v_1[1,1]*df[.,1]^2+2*v_1[1,2]*df[.,1].*df[.,2]
                        +v_1[2,2]*df[.,2]^2;
                ans[ic,jc]=sumc(selif((1-t2),t2 .lt 1));
                jc=jc+1;
        endo;
        ic=ic+1;
endo;

ans=ans*2/(pi*n*h^2*sqrt(dt));
ans=missrv(ans,0);
/* save for future use */
save ansp1h1=ans;

/* making Figure 3.13 */
graphset;
begwind;
xtics(3,8,1.0,2);
ytics(3,8,1.0,2);
_pdate="";
_plctrl=-1;
_pstype=4;
_psymsiz=1;
_plev={0,0.01,0.02,0.03,0.05,0.1,0.2,0.4,0.6,0.8,1.0,1.2,1.4};
makewind(10,8,0,0,1);
contour(ggx',ggy,ans');
makewind(10,8,0,0,1);
xy(x[.,1],x[.,2]);
endwind;
gkp=seqa(1,2,50);
graphset;
xtics(3,8,1.0,2);
ytics(3,8,1.0,2);
ztics(0,0.4,0.1,1);
_pdate="";
_pticout=1;
begwind;
window(1,2,0);
surface(ggx[gkp,.]',ggy[gkp,.],ans[gkp,gkp]');
nextwind;
_pview={1,10,-3,4};
surface(ggx[gkp,.]',ggy[gkp,.],ans[gkp,gkp]');
endwind;
end;
```

Example 3.8. Locally weighted regression (Figure 3.20)

Figure 3.20 shows plots of expected actual and potential pension receipts against the logarithm of household per capita income. These are calculated using locally weighted regressions, the code for which is given below.

```
/* this is for Africans, i.e., left panel of Figure 3.20 */

version 4.0
#delimit ;
cap log close;
log using fanpen, replace;
set more 1;
drop _all;
use socpenh;
keep if race==1;
/* prepinc is total income less pension income */
gen prepinc=totminc-socpen1;
drop if prepinc <= 0;
gen ppens=n60f+n65m;
gen lnpcy=log(prepinc/hhsizem);
gen incpc=prepinc/hhsizem;
global penamt=370;
gen psocpen=ppens*$penamt;
keep psocpen socpen1 lnpcy;
/*
** psocpen is potential pension receipts
** socpen1 is receipts of social pensions
** lnpcy is the log of nonpension income
*/
/*
** lowrex does the locally weighted regression
** argument 1 is the regressand (input)
** argument 2 is the regressor (input)
** argument 3 is the estimated regression function (output)
** argument 4 is the derivative of the regression function (output)
** argument 5 is the bandwidth (input)
** argument 6 is the grid over the regressor for evaluation (input)
*/

cap program drop lowrex;
program def lowrex;
        local ic=1;
        gen `3'=.;
        gen `4'=.;
        while `ic' <= $gsize {;
        dis `ic';
        quietly {;
        local xx=`6'[`ic'];
        gen z=abs((`2'-`xx')/`5');
        gen kz=(15/16)*(1-z^2)^2 if z <= 1;
        reg `1' `2' =kz if kz ~= .;
        replace `4'=_b[`2'] in `ic';
  *     replace `3'=_b[_cons]+_b[`2']*`xx' in `ic';
        drop z kz;
        };
        local ic=`ic'+1;
        };
end;

global xmin=0;
global xmax=9;
global gsize=50;
global st=($xmax-$xmin)/($gsize-1);
global h=1.0;
gen xgrid=$xmin+(_n-1)*$st in 1/$gsize;
lowrex psocpen lnpcy smthp dsmth $h xgrid;
```

```
drop dsmth;
lowrex socpen1 lnpcy smtha dsmth $h xgrid;
sort xgrid;
keep in 1/$gsize;
graph smthp smtha xgrid, c(11) s(ii) ylabel xlabel(0,2,4,6,8,10)
    xline(4.654) saving(fanaf, replace);
log close;
```

A.4 Chapter 4

The programs below were used to generate Figures 4.4 and 4.5 in the text. The code for the contour maps in Figures 4.2 and 4.3 is a straightforward application of Example 3.7 above. The results in Section 4.2 are obtained from straightforward regression analysis, and the code is not given here.

Example 4.1. Locally weighted regressions for calorie Engel curves

There are three sections of code which, for logical transparency, are presented in the reverse order in which they should be run. The first section calculates the estimated regression function and its derivatives and then picks up the bootstrap replications from the second and third sections of the code to construct Figures 4.4 and 4.5.

```
/*
** This is Section 1 of the code and calulates the main results
*/

version 4.0
# delimit ;
drop _all;
set more 1;
capture log close;
capture log using ex41a.log, replace;
/* setting up the data */
use ..\feb95\working;
gen lnpce=log(totexp/nmems);
gen lncal=log(tcal1/nmems);
drop if lncal == .;
drop if lnpce == .;
keep lnpce lncal;

/* the locally weighted regression code */
cap program drop lowrex;
program def lowrex;
        local ic=1;
        gen `3'=.;
        gen `4'=.;
        while `ic' <= 100 {;
        dis `ic';
        quietly {;
        local xx=`6'[`ic'];
        gen z=abs((`2'-`xx')/`5');
        gen kz=(15/16)*(1-z^2)^2 if z <= 1;
        reg `1' `2' =kz if kz ~= .;
        replace `4'=_b[`2'] in `ic';
        replace `3'=_b[_cons]+_b[`2']*`xx' in `ic';
        drop z kz;
        };
        local ic=`ic'+1;
        };end;
```

```
global xmin=3.5;
global xmax=6.0;
global st=($xmax-$xmin)/99;
global h=0.5;
gen xgrid=$xmin+(_n-1)*$st in 1/100;
lowrex lncal lnpce smth dsmth $h xgrid;
set more 0;
/* graphing the estimated regression function */
graph smth xgrid, c(l) s(i) xlabel ylabel;
/* graphing the slope */
graph dsmth xgrid, c(l) s(i) xlabel ylabel;
keep smth dsmth xgrid;
sort xgrid;
save temp, replace;
/* bringing in the bootstrap results (w/o clustering) */
use ..\feb95\lowboot;
drop if replic==0;
egen sdsmth=sd(smth), by(xgrid);
egen sddsmth=sd(dsmth), by(xgrid);
sort xgrid;
qui by xgrid: drop if _n ~= 1;
keep xgrid sdsmth sddsmth;
merge xgrid using temp;
tab _merge;
drop _merge;
sort xgrid;
/* bands for the smooth and its slope */
gen smthu=smth+2*sdsmth;
gen smthd=smth-2*sdsmth;
gen dsmthu=dsmth+2*sddsmth;
gen dsmthd=dsmth-2*sddsmth;
save temp, replace;
/* repeating with clustered bootstrap */
use clusam;    /* clustered version of lowboot */
drop if replic==0;
egen sdsmthc=sd(smth), by(xgrid);
egen sddsmthc=sd(dsmth), by(xgrid);
sort xgrid;
qui by xgrid: drop if _n ~= 1;
keep xgrid sdsmthc sddsmthc;
merge xgrid using temp;
tab _merge;
drop _merge;
sort xgrid;
gen smthuc=smth+2*sdsmthc;
gen smthdc=smth-2*sdsmthc;
gen dsmthuc=dsmth+2*sddsmthc;
gen dsmthdc=dsmth-2*sddsmthc;
graph smth* xgrid, c(lllll) pen(22222) s(iiiii)
        xlabel(3.4,3.8,4.2,4.6,5.0,5.4,5.8,6.2)
        ylabel(7,7.2,7.4,7.6,7.8,8.0,8.2)saving(lowregx1, replace);
graph dsmth* xgrid, c(lllll) pen(22222) s(iiiii)
        xlabel(3.4,3.8,4.2,4.6,5.0,5.4,5.8,6.2)
        ylabel(0.0,0.1,0.2,0.3,0.4,0.5,0.6,0.7,0.8,0.9,1)
        saving(lowregx2, replace);
log close;


/* Section 2: Bootstraps the locally weighted regression
** Without any allowance for cluster design */

version 4.0
#delimit ;
drop _all;
set more 1;
cap log close;
log using ex41b, replace;
use ..\feb95\working;
gen lnpce=log(totexp/nmems);
```

```
gen lncal=log(tcal1/nmems);
drop if lncal == .;
drop if lnpce == .;
keep lnpce lncal;

save temp, replace;

ren lncal smth;
ren lnpce xgrid;
gen dsmth=.;
gen replic=0;
save lowboot, replace;
/* this program controls the bootstrap */
cap program drop lowrxit;
program def lowrxit;
        local jc=1;
        while `jc' <= 50 {;
        dis `jc';
        drop _all;
        use temp;
        bsample _N;
        local xmin=3.5;
        local xmax=6.0;
        local st=(`xmax'-`xmin')/99;
        local h=0.5;
        qui gen xgrid=`xmin'+(_n-1)*`st' in 1/100;
        qui lowregx lncal lnpce smth dsmth `h' xgrid;
        drop lncal lnpce;
        keep in 1/100;
        gen replic=`jc';
        append using lowboot;
        save lowboot, replace;
        local jc=`jc'+1;
        };
end;

lowrxit;
/* plotting bunches of regression functions and derivatives */
set more 0;
gen lnc=smth if replic==0;
replace smth=. if replic==0;
sort replic xgrid;
graph lnc smth xgrid, c(.L) s(oi) xlabel ylabel;
graph smth xgrid if replic > 0, c(L) s(i) xlabel(3.5,4,4.5,5,5.5,6)
        ylabel saving(lowboot1, replace);
graph dsmth xgrid if replic > 0, c(L) s(i) xlabel(3.5,4,4.5,5,5.5,6)
        ylabel saving(lowboot2, replace);
log close;


/* Section 3: Bootstrapping the locally weighted regression
** With allowance for cluster design */

version 4.0
#delimit;
cap log close;
log using ex41c, replace;
set more 1;
drop _all;

use ..\feb95\working;
gen lnpce=log(totexp/nmems);
gen lncal=log(tcal1/nmems);
drop if lncal == .;
drop if lnpce == .;
keep lnpce lncal hid;
gen long cluster=int(hid/100);
sort cluster;
save tempwork, replace;
```

```
keep cluster;
qui by cluster: drop if _n ~= 1;
save tempclus, replace;

cap program drop csampl;
program define csampl;
        use tempclus;
        bsample _N;
        sort cluster;
        qui by cluster: gen dum=_N;
        qui by cluster: drop if _n ~= 1;
        merge cluster using tempwork;
        qui drop if _merge ~= 3;
        drop _merge;
        qui expand dum;
        drop dum;
        sort cluster;
end;

use tempwork;
ren lncal smth;
ren lnpce xgrid;
gen dsmth=.;
gen replic=0;
save clusam, replace;

cap program drop loxit;
program def loxit;
        local jc=1;
        while `jc' <= 50 {;
        dis `jc';
        drop _all;
        csampl;
        local xmin=3.5;
        local xmax=6.0;
        local st=(`xmax'-`xmin')/99;
        local h=0.5;
        qui gen xgrid=`xmin'+(_n-1)*`st' in 1/100;
        qui lowregx lncal lnpce smth dsmth `h' xgrid;
        drop lncal lnpce;
        keep in 1/100;
        gen replic=`jc';
        append using clusam;
        save clusam, replace;
        local jc=`jc'+1;
        };end;

loxit;
/* plotting bunches of regression functions and derivatives */
set more 0;
gen lnc=smth if replic==0;
replace smth=. if replic==0;
sort replic xgrid;
graph lnc smth xgrid, c(.L) s(.i) xlabel ylabel;
graph smth xgrid if replic > 0, c(L) s(i) xlabel(3.5,4,4.5,5,5.5,6)
        ylabel saving(clusam1, replace);
graph dsmth xgrid if replic > 0, c(L) s(i) xlabel(3.5,4,4.5,5,5.5,6)
        ylabel saving(clusam2, replace);

log close;
```

A.5 Chapter 5

I provide the code for calculating the system of demand equations, including the own- and cross-price elasticities, for completing the system, and for calculating the symmetry-constrained estimates. The code here is for the Maharashtran case; except for minor details—the number and names of the goods, and the definition of the other variables—the Pakistani code is the same. There are four separate programs: the first, allindia.do, is for estimating the demand system. Appended to it is a program mkmats.do, that calculates the commutation and selection matrices required for the symmetry-constrained estimates, as well as procedures for making the "vec" of a matrix, and for reversing the operation. The code in bootall.do bootstraps the procedure in order to obtain measures of sampling variability. Finally, the program policy.do calculates the efficiency and equity components of the cost-benefit ratios for price reform and was used to give the results in Tables 5.12 and 5.13.

```
program allindia.do
* program for doing eveything in one shot
* requires a data set indinr on log unit values
* budget shares, lnx, and lnn, as well as subrounds
* and regions and household characteristics
*
version 4.0
#delimit ;
drop _all;
set matsize 400;
set maxvar 1724 width 1832;
set more 1;
capture log close;
log using allindia, replace;
*The log unit values begin with luv, e.g. luvwhe;
*The budget shares begin with w, e.g. wric;
*lnexp is log of outlay, lnhhs log of household size;
*regional and subround (seasonal) variables;
*Demographics and other variables to taste;
*Here they are rm1-rm5 and rf1-rf4, age-sex ratios;
*Caste, religion, and labor types;
use indinr;
*These are the commodity identifiers: used as three-letter prefixes;
global goods "ric whe jow oce pul dai oil mea veg fru sug";
*Number of goods in the system;
global ngds=11;

matrix define sig=J($ngds,1,0);
matrix define ome=J($ngds,1,0);
matrix define lam=J($ngds,1,0);
matrix define wbar=J($ngds,1,0);
matrix define b1=J($ngds,1,0);
matrix define b0=J($ngds,1,0);

*Average budget shares;
cap program drop mkwbar;
program def mkwbar;
local ig=1;
while "`1'" ~= ""{;
qui summ w`1';
matrix wbar[`ig',1]=_result(3);
local ig=`ig'+1;
mac shift};
end;

mkwbar $goods;

*First stage regressions: within village;
cap program drop st1reg;
program def st1reg;
local ig=1;
```

```
while "`1'" ~= ""{;
*Cluster fixed-effect regression;
areg luv`1' rm* rf* lnexp lhhs
        schcaste hindu buddhist labtyp*, absorb(cluster);
*Measurement error variance;
matrix ome[`ig',1]=$S_E_sse/$S_E_tdf;
*Quality elasticity;
matrix b1[`ig',1]=_coef[lnexp];
*These residuals still have cluster effects in;
predict ruv`1', resid;
*Purged y's for next stage;
gen y1`1'=luv`1'-_coef[lnexp]*lnexp-_coef[lhhs]*lhhs-_coef[rm1]*
        rm1-_coef[rm2]*rm2-_coef[rm3]*rm3-_coef[rm4]*rm4-_coef[rm5]*

rm5-_coef[rf1]*rf1-_coef[rf2]*rf2-_coef[rf3]*rf3-_coef[rf4]*rf4
        -_coef[schcaste]*schcaste-_coef[hindu]*hindu-_coef[buddhist]*
        buddhist-_coef[labtyp1]*labtyp1-_coef[labtyp2]*labtyp2
        -_coef[labtyp3]*labtyp3-_coef[labtyp4]*labtyp4;
drop luv`1';
*Repeat for budget shares;
areg w`1' rm* rf* lnexp lhhs
        schcaste hindu buddhist labtyp*, absorb(cluster);
predict rw`1', resid;
matrix sig[`ig',1]=$S_E_sse/$S_E_tdf;
matrix b0[`ig',1]=_coef[lnexp];
gen y0`1'=w`1'-_coef[lnexp]*lnexp-_coef[lhhs]*lhhs-_coef[rm1]*
        rm1-_coef[rm2]*rm2-_coef[rm3]*rm3-_coef[rm4]*rm4-_coef[rm5]*

rm5-_coef[rf1]*rf1-_coef[rf2]*rf2-_coef[rf3]*rf3-_coef[rf4]*rf4
        -_coef[schcaste]*schcaste-_coef[hindu]*hindu-_coef[buddhist]*
        buddhist-_coef[labtyp1]*labtyp1-_coef[labtyp2]*labtyp2
        -_coef[labtyp3]*labtyp3-_coef[labtyp4]*labtyp4;
*This next regression is necessary to get covariance of residuals;
qui areg ruv`1' rw`1' lnexp lhhs rm* rf*
        schcaste hindu buddhist labtyp*, absorb(cluster);
matrix lam[`ig',1]=_coef[rw`1']*sig[`ig',1];
drop w`1' rw`1' ruv`1';
local ig=`ig'+1;
mac shift};
end;

st1reg $goods;

matrix list sig;
matrix list ome;
matrix list lam;
matrix list b0;
matrix list b1;

drop lnexp rm* rf*;
drop labtyp* schcaste hindu buddhist lhhs;
*Saving so far as a protection;
save tempa, replace;

drop _all;
use tempa;

*Averaging by cluster;
*Counting numbers of obs in each cluster for n and n+;
cap program drop clustit;
program def clustit;
local ig=1;
while "`1'" ~= ""{;
        egen y0c`ig'=mean(y0`1'), by(cluster);
        egen n0c`ig'=count(y0`1'), by(cluster);
        egen y1c`ig'=mean(y1`1'), by(cluster);
        egen n1c`ig'=count(y1`1'), by(cluster);
        drop y0`1' y1`1';
        local ig=`ig'+1;
```

```
mac shift };
end;

clustit $goods;
sort cluster;
*keeping one obs per cluster;
*NB subround and region are constant within cluster;
qui by cluster: keep if _n==1;

*Saving cluster-level information;
*Use this for shortcut bootstrapping;
save tempclus, replace;

*Removing province and quarter effects;
qui tab region, gen(regiond);
qui tab subround, gen(quard);
drop regiond6 quard4;
cap program drop purge;
program define purge;
        local ig=1;
        while `ig' <= $ngds {;
                qui regress y0c`ig' quard* regiond*;
                predict tm, resid;
                replace y0c`ig'=tm;
                drop tm;
                qui regress y1c`ig' quard* regiond*;
                predict tm, resid;
                replace y1c`ig'=tm;
                drop tm;
                local ig=`ig'+1;
        };
end;

purge;
drop regiond* quard*;

matrix define n0=J($ngds,1,0);
matrix define n1=J($ngds,1,0);

*Averaging (harmonically) numbers of obs over clusters;
cap program drop mkns;
program define mkns;
        local ig=1;
        while `ig' <= $ngds {;
                replace n0c`ig'=1/n0c`ig';
                replace n1c`ig'=1/n1c`ig';
                qui summ n0c`ig';
                matrix n0[`ig',1]=(_result(3))^(-1);
                qui summ n1c`ig';
                matrix n1[`ig',1]=(_result(3))^(-1);
                drop n0c`ig' n1c`ig';
                local ig=`ig'+1;
        };
end;

mkns;

*Making the intercluster variance and covariance matrices;
*This is done in pairs because of the missing values;

matrix s=J($ngds,$ngds,0);
matrix r=J($ngds,$ngds,0);
cap program drop mkcov;
program def mkcov;
local ir=1;
while `ir' <= $ngds {;
        local ic=1;
        while `ic' <= $ngds {;
                qui corr y1c`ir' y1c`ic', cov;
```

```
                  matrix s[`ir',`ic']=_result(4);
                  qui corr y1c`ir' y0c`ic', cov;
                  matrix r[`ir',`ic']=_result(4);
                  local ic=`ic'+1;
          };
          local ir=`ir'+1;
  };
end;

mkcov;

*We don't need the data any more;
drop _all;

matrix list s;
matrix list r;

*Making OLS estimates;
matrix bols=syminv(s);
matrix bols=bols*r;
display("Second-stage OLS estimates: B-matrix");
matrix list bols;
display("Column 1 is coefficients from 1st regression, etc");


*Corrections for measurement error;
cap program drop fixmat;
program def fixmat;
matrix def sf=s;
matrix def rf=r;
local ig=1;
        while `ig' <= $ngds {;
        matrix sf[`ig',`ig']=sf[`ig',`ig']-ome[`ig',1]/n1[`ig',1];
        matrix rf[`ig',`ig']=rf[`ig',`ig']-lam[`ig',1]/n0[`ig',1];
        local ig=`ig'+1;
};
end;

fixmat;

matrix invs=syminv(sf);
matrix bhat=invs*rf;
*Estimated B matrix without restrictions;
matrix list bhat;

*Housekeeping matrices, including elasticities;

cap program drop mormat;
program def mormat;
matrix def xi=J($ngds,1,0);
matrix def el=J($ngds,1,0);
local ig=1;
        while `ig' <= $ngds {;
        matrix xi[`ig',1]=b1[`ig',1]/(b0[`ig',1]+
                (1-b1[`ig',1]*wbar[`ig',1]));
        matrix el[`ig',1]=1-b1[`ig',1]+b0[`ig',1]/wbar[`ig',1];
        local ig=`ig'+1;
};
end;

mormat;

global ng1=$ngds+1;
matrix iden=I($ngds);
matrix iden1=I($ng1);
matrix itm=J($ngds,1,1);
matrix itm1=J($ng1,1,1);
matrix dxi=diag(xi);
matrix dwbar=diag(wbar);
```

```
matrix idwbar=syminv(dwbar);
display("Average budget shares");
matrix tm=wbar';
matrix list tm;
display("Expenditure elasticities");
matrix tm=el';
matrix list tm;
display("Quality elasticities");
matrix tm=b1';
matrix list tm;

*This all has to go in a program to use it again later;
*Basically uses the b matrix to form price elasticity matrix;
cap program drop mkels;
program define mkels;
        matrix cmx=bhat';
        matrix cmx=dxi*cmx;
        matrix cmx1=dxi*dwbar;
        matrix cmx=iden-cmx;
        matrix cmx=cmx+cmx1;
        matrix psi=inv(cmx);
        matrix theta=bhat'*psi;
        display("Theta matrix");
        matrix list theta;
        matrix ep=bhat';
        matrix ep=idwbar*ep;
        matrix ep=ep-iden;
        matrix ep=ep*psi;
        display("Matrix of price elasticities");
        matrix list ep;
end;

mkels;

**Completing the system by filling out the matrices;


cap program drop complet;
program define complet;
        *First extending theta;
        matrix atm=theta*itm;
        matrix atm=-1*atm;
        matrix atm=atm-b0;
        matrix xtheta=theta,atm;
        matrix atm=xtheta';
        matrix atm=atm*itm;
        matrix atm=atm';
        matrix xtheta=xtheta\atm;
        *Extending the diagonal matrices;
        matrix wlast=wbar'*itm;
        matrix won=(1);
        matrix wlast=won-wlast;
        matrix xwbar=wbar\wlast;
        matrix dxwbar=diag(xwbar);
        matrix idxwbar=syminv(dxwbar);
        matrix b1last=(0.25);
        matrix xb1=b1\b1last;
        matrix b0last=b0'*itm;
        matrix b0last=-1*b0last;
        matrix xb0=b0\b0last;
        matrix xe=itm1-xb1;
        matrix tm=idxwbar*xb0;
        matrix xe=xe+tm;
        matrix tm=xe';
        display("extended outlay elasticities");
        matrix list tm;
        matrix xxi=itm1-xb1;
        matrix xxi=dxwbar*xxi;
        matrix xxi=xxi+xb0;
```

```
        matrix tm=diag(xb1);
        matrix tm=syminv(tm);
        matrix xxi=tm*xxi;
        matrix dxxi=diag(xxi);
        *Extending psi;
        matrix xpsi=dxxi*xtheta;
        matrix xpsi=xpsi+iden1;
        matrix atm=dxxi*dxwbar;
        matrix atm=atm+iden1;
        matrix atm=syminv(atm);
        matrix xpsi=atm*xpsi;
        matrix ixpsi=inv(xpsi);
        *Extending bhat & elasticity matrix;
        matrix xbhatp=xtheta*ixpsi;
        matrix xep=idxwbar*xbhatp;
        matrix xep=xep-iden1;
        matrix xep=xep*xpsi;
        display("extended matrix of elasticities");
        matrix list xep;
end;

complet;

**Calculating symmetry-restricted estimators;
**These are only approximately valid & assume no quality effects;
run mkmats;
vecmx bhat vbhat;
** R matrix for restrictions;
lmx $ngds llx;
commx $ngds k;
global ng2=$ngds*$ngds;
matrix bigi=I($ng2);
matrix k=bigi-k;
matrix r=llx*k;
matrix drop k;
matrix drop bigi;
matrix drop llx;
** r vector for restrictions, called rh;
matrix rh=b0#wbar;
matrix rh=r*rh;
matrix rh=-1*rh;
**doing the constrained estimation;
matrix iss=iden#invs;
matrix rp=r';
matrix iss=iss*rp;
matrix inn=r*iss;
matrix inn=syminv(inn);
matrix inn=iss*inn;
matrix dis=r*vbhat;
matrix dis=rh-dis;
matrix dis=inn*dis;
matrix vbtild=vbhat+dis;
unvecmx vbtild btild;

**the following matrix should be symmetric;
matrix atm=b0';
matrix atm=wbar*atm;
matrix atm=btild+atm;
matrix list atm;

**going back to get elasticities and complete sytem;
matrix bhat=btild;
mkels;
complet;

log close;


program mkmats.do
```

```
**calculates two matrices, the commutation matrix and
**the lower diagonal selection matrix that are needed
**in the main calculations; these are valid only for
**square matrices
**also a routine for taking the vec of a matrix
**and a matching unvec routine

**for calculating the commutation matrix k
**the matrix is defined by K*vec(A)=vec(A')

cap program drop commx
program define commx
local n2=`1'^2
matrix `2'=J(`n2',`n2',0)
local i=1
local ik=0
while `i' <= `1'{
        local j=1
        local ij=`i'
        while `j' <= `1'{
                local ir=`j'+`ik'
                matrix `2'[`ir',`ij']=1
                local ij=`ij'+`1'
                local j=`j'+1
        }
        local i=`i'+1
        local ik=`ik'+`1'
}
end

**for vecing a matrix, i.e., stacking it into a column vector

cap program drop vecmx
program def vecmx
local n=rowsof(`1')
local n2=`n'^2
matrix def `2'=J(`n2',1,0)
local j=1
while `j' <= `n' {
        local i=1
        while `i' <= `n' {
                local vcel=(`j'-1)*`n'+`i'
                matrix `2'[`vcel',1]=`1'[`i',`j']
                local i=`i'+1
        }
local j=`j'+1
}
end

*program for calculating the matrix that extracts
*from vec(A) the lower left triangle of the matrix A

cap program drop lmx
program define lmx
local ng2=`1'^2
local nr=0.5*`1'*(`1'-1)
matrix def `2'=J(`nr',`ng2',0)
local ia=2
local ij=1
while `ij' <= `nr'{
        local ik=0
        local klim=`1'-`ia'
        while `ik' <= `klim' {
                local ip=`ia'+(`ia'-2)*`1'+`ik'
                matrix `2'[`ij',`ip']=1
                local ij=`ij'+1
                local ik=`ik'+1
        }
local ia=`ia'+1
```

```
}
end

**program for unvecing the vec of a square matrix;

cap program drop unvecmx
program def unvecmx
local n2=rowsof(`1')
local n=sqrt(`n2')
matrix def `2'=J(`n',`n',0)
local i=1
while `i' <= `n' {
        local j=1
        while `j' <= `n' {
                local vcel=(`j'-1)*`n'+`i'
                matrix `2'[`i',`j']=`1'[`vcel',1]
                local j=`j'+1
        }
local i=`i'+1
}
end

program bootall.do
**for bootstrapping Indian demand estimates

version 4.0
#delimit ;
capture log close;
set more 1;
drop _all;
do allindia;
log using bootall, replace;
drop _all;
set maxvar 300;
vecmx xep vxep;
set obs 1;
gen reps=0;
global nels=$ng1*$ng1;
global nmc=1000;
cap program drop vtodat;
program define vtodat;
local ic=1;
while `ic' <= $nels {;
        gen e`ic'=vxep[`ic',1];
        local ic=`ic'+1;
};
end;
vtodat;
save bootall, replace;
drop _all;

cap program drop purge;
program define purge;
        local ig=1;
        while `ig' <= $ngds {;
                qui regress y0c`ig' quard* regiond*;
                predict tm, resid;
                replace y0c`ig'=tm;
                drop tm;
                qui regress y1c`ig' quard* regiond*;
                predict tm, resid;
                replace y1c`ig'=tm;
                drop tm;
                local ig=`ig'+1;
        };
end;

cap program drop mkns;
program define mkns;
```

```
            local ig=1;
            while `ig' <= $ngds {;
                    replace n0c`ig'=1/n0c`ig';
                    replace n1c`ig'=1/n1c`ig';
                    qui summ n0c`ig';
                    matrix n0[`ig',1]=(_result(3))^(-1);
                    qui summ n1c`ig';
                    matrix n1[`ig',1]=(_result(3))^(-1);
                    drop n0c`ig' n1c`ig';
                    local ig=`ig'+1;
            };
    end;

    cap program drop mkcov;
    program def mkcov;
    local ir=1;
    while `ir' <= $ngds {;
            local ic=1;
            while `ic' <= $ngds {;
                    qui corr y1c`ir' y1c`ic', cov;
                    matrix s[`ir',`ic']=_result(4);
                    qui corr y1c`ir' y0c`ic', cov;
                    matrix r[`ir',`ic']=_result(4);
                    local ic=`ic'+1;
            };
            local ir=`ir'+1;
    };
    end;

    cap program drop fixmat;
    program def fixmat;
    matrix def sf=s;
    matrix def rf=r;
    local ig=1;
            while `ig' <= $ngds {;
            matrix sf[`ig',`ig']=sf[`ig',`ig']-ome[`ig',1]/n1[`ig',1];
            matrix rf[`ig',`ig']=rf[`ig',`ig']-lam[`ig',1]/n0[`ig',1];
            local ig=`ig'+1;
    };
    end;

    cap program drop mkels;
    program define mkels;
            matrix cmx=bhat';
            matrix cmx=dxi*cmx;
            matrix cmx1=dxi*dwbar;
            matrix cmx=iden-cmx;
            matrix cmx=cmx+cmx1;
            matrix psi=inv(cmx);
            matrix theta=bhat'*psi;
            display("Theta matrix");
            matrix list theta;
            matrix ep=bhat';
            matrix ep=idwbar*ep;
            matrix ep=ep-iden;
            matrix ep=ep*psi;
    end;

    cap program drop complet;
    program define complet;
            *First extending theta;
            matrix atm=theta*itm;
            matrix atm=-1*atm;
            matrix atm=atm-b0;
            matrix xtheta=theta,atm;
            matrix atm=xtheta';
            matrix atm=atm*itm;
            matrix atm=atm';
            matrix xtheta=xtheta\atm;
```

```
        *Extending the diagonal matrices;
        matrix wlast=wbar'*itm;
        matrix won=(1);
        matrix wlast=won-wlast;
        matrix xwbar=wbar\wlast;
        matrix dxwbar=diag(xwbar);
        matrix idxwbar=syminv(dxwbar);
        matrix bllast=(0.25);
        matrix xb1=b1\bllast;
        matrix b0last=b0'*itm;
        matrix b0last=-1*b0last;
        matrix xb0=b0\b0last;
        matrix xe=itm1-xb1;
        matrix tm=idxwbar*xb0;
        matrix xe=xe+tm;
        matrix tm=xe';
        matrix xxi=itm1-xb1;
        matrix xxi=dxwbar*xxi;
        matrix xxi=xxi+xb0;
        matrix tm=diag(xb1);
        matrix tm=syminv(tm);
        matrix xxi=tm*xxi;
        matrix dxxi=diag(xxi);
        *Extending psi;
        matrix xpsi=dxxi*xtheta;
        matrix xpsi=xpsi+iden1;
        matrix atm=dxxi*dxwbar;
        matrix atm=atm+iden1;
        matrix atm=syminv(atm);
        matrix xpsi=atm*xpsi;
        matrix ixpsi=inv(xpsi);
        *Extending bhat & elasticity matrix;
        matrix xbhatp=xtheta*ixpsi;
        matrix xep=idxwbar*xbhatp;
        matrix xep=xep-iden1;
        matrix xep=xep*xpsi;
end;

cap program drop bootindi;
program define bootindi;
local expno=1;
while `expno' <= $nmc {;
display("Experiment number `expno'");
quietly {;
use tempclus;
bsample _N;
qui tab region, gen(regiond);
qui tab subround, gen(quard);
drop regiond6 quard4;
purge;
drop regiond* quard*;
matrix define n0=J($ngds,1,0);
matrix define n1=J($ngds,1,0);
*Averaging (harmonically) numbers of obs over clusters;
mkns;
*Making the intercluster variance and covariance matrices;
*This is done in pairs because of the missing values;
matrix s=J($ngds,$ngds,0);
matrix r=J($ngds,$ngds,0);
mkcov;
*We don't need the data any more;
drop _all;
*Making OLS estimates;
matrix bols=syminv(s);
matrix bols=bols*r;
*Corrections for measurement error;
fixmat;
matrix invs=syminv(sf);
matrix bhat=invs*rf;
```

```
global ng1=$ngds+1;
matrix iden=I($ngds);
matrix iden1=I($ng1);
matrix itm=J($ngds,1,1);
matrix itm1=J($ng1,1,1);
matrix dxi=diag(xi);
matrix dwbar=diag(wbar);
matrix idwbar=syminv(dwbar);
mkels;
**Completing the system by filling out the matrices;
complet;
**Calculating symmetry restricted estimators;
vecmx bhat vbhat;
** R matrix for restrictions;
lmx $ngds llx;
commx $ngds k;
global ng2=$ngds*$ngds;
matrix bigi=I($ng2);
matrix k=bigi-k;
matrix r=llx*k;
matrix drop k;
matrix drop bigi;
matrix drop llx;
** r vector for restrictions, called rh;
matrix rh=b0#wbar;
matrix rh=r*rh;
matrix rh=-1*rh;
**doing the constrained estimation;
matrix iss=iden#invs;
matrix rp=r';
matrix iss=iss*rp;
matrix inn=r*iss;
matrix inn=syminv(inn);
matrix inn=iss*inn;
matrix dis=r*vbhat;
matrix dis=rh-dis;
matrix dis=inn*dis;
matrix vbtild=vbhat+dis;
unvecmx vbtild btild;
**going back to get elasticities and complete sytem;
matrix bhat=btild;
mkels;
complet;
vecmx xep vxep;
set obs 1;
gen reps=`expno';
vtodat;
append using bootall;
save bootall, replace;
drop _all;
local expno=`expno'+1;
};};
end;

bootindi;
use bootall;
display("Monte Carlo results");
summ;

log close;


program policy.do
** Does the policy analysis tables starting by running allindia
** and then processes to produce the two tables, Table 5.12 and 5.13
**

version 4.0
#delimit ;
```

```
set more 1;
drop _all;   /*
do allindia;   */
capture log close;
log using policy, replace;

drop _all;
global xgoods "ric whe jow oce pul dai oil mea veg fru sug oth";
matrix ap=(1.5\1.25\1.0\1.0\1.0\1.0\0.67\1.0\1.0\1.0\1.0\1.0);

cap program drop mkws;
program def mkws;
use indinr;
keep lnexp lhhs w*;
gen xh=exp(lnexp);
gen nh=exp(lhhs);
gen woth=1-wwhe-wric-wjow-woce-wpul-wdai-wmea-woil-wsug-wveg-wfru;
matrix wtild=J(12,1,0);
matrix weps=J(12,4,0);
*Plutocratic and soc rep budget shares;
local ig=1;
while "`1'" ~= ""{;
qui summ w`1' [aweight=xh];
matrix wtild[`ig',1]=_result(3);
matrix weps[`ig',1]=_result(3);
gen tem=w`1'*(xh/nh)^(-0.5);
qui summ tem [aweight=xh];
matrix weps[`ig',2]=_result(3);
drop tem;
gen tem=w`1'*(xh/nh)^(-1);
qui summ tem [aweight=xh];
matrix weps[`ig',3]=_result(3);
drop tem;
gen tem=w`1'*(xh/nh)^(-2);
qui summ tem [aweight=xh];
matrix weps[`ig',4]=_result(3);
drop tem;
local ig=`ig'+1;
mac shift};
*Scaling the matrices;
matrix itm1t=itm1';
matrix wsum=itm1t*weps;
local ic=1;
while `ic'<=$ng1 {;
local id=1;
while `id' <=4 {;
        local stmp=1/wsum[1,`id'];
        matrix weps[`ic',`id']=`stmp'*weps[`ic',`id'];
        local id=`id'+1;
};
local ic=`ic'+1;
};
end;


mkws $xgoods;

cap program drop equi;
program def equi;
local ic=1;
while `ic' <= 4 {;
matrix wtmp=weps[.,`ic'];
matrix tmp=mxw*wtmp;
matrix tmp1=dtot*tmp;
display("equity effect");
matrix list tmp;
display("Cost-benefit ratio");
matrix list tmp1;
local ic=`ic'+1;
```

```
end;

cap program drop calpol;
program def calpol;
matrix tauotau=itml-ap;
display("Column one");
matrix list tauotau;
matrix dth=vecdiag(xtheta);
matrix dth=dth';
matrix mxw=diag(wtild);
matrix mxw=syminv(mxw);
matrix midt=mxw*dth;
matrix col2=midt-itml;
display("second column");
matrix list col2;
matrix dtau=diag(tauotau);
matrix col3=dtau*col2;
display("third column");
matrix list col3;
matrix col4=xtheta';;
matrix col4=col4*tauotau;
matrix col4=mxw*col4;
matrix tmp=dtau*midt;
matrix col4=col4-tmp;
display("fourth column");
matrix list col4;
matrix tot=itml+col3;
matrix tot=tot+col4;
display("totals");
matrix list tot;
display("Going on to next Table");
matrix dtot=diag(tot);
matrix dtot=syminv(dtot);
equi;
end;

calpol;

log close;
```

A.6 Chapter 6

None of the calculations in Chapter 6 require new or nonstandard coding. The decomposition of the logarithms of income, the logarithm of consumption, and the saving ratio into age and cohort effects in Figures 6.5 and 6.6, as well as the age effects in inequality in Figure 6.11, were calculated in the same way as in Example 2.2 above.

Bibliography

The word "processed" describes informally reproduced works that may not be commonly available through libraries.

Ahluwalia, Montek S., 1978, "Rural poverty and agricultural performance in India," *Journal of Development Studies*, **14**, 298–323.

——, 1985, "Rural poverty, agricultural production, and prices: a re-examination," in John W. Mellor and Guvunt Desai, eds., *Agricultural change and rural poverty: variations on a theme by Dharm Narain*, Baltimore, Md., Johns Hopkins for International Food Policy Research Institute, 59–75.

Ahluwahlia, Montek S., John H. Duloy, Graham Pyatt, and T. N. Srinivasan, 1980, "Who benefits from economic development? Comment," *American Economic Review*, **70**, 242–45.

Ahmad, Asif, and Jonathan Morduch, 1993, "Identifying sex bias in the allocation of household resources: evidence from limited household surveys from Bangladesh," Harvard University, processed.

Ahmad, S. Ehtisham, David Coady, and Nicholas H. Stern, 1986, "Shadow prices and commercial policy in India 1979/80," London School of Economics, processed.

——, 1988, "A complete set of shadow prices for Pakistan," *Pakistan Development Review*, **27**, 7–43.

Ahmad, S. Ehtisham, and Nicholas H. Stern, 1990, "Tax reform and shadow prices for Pakistan," *Oxford Economic Papers*, **42**, 135–59.

——, 1991, *The theory and practice of tax reform in developing countries*, Cambridge University Press.

Ainsworth, Martha, 1992, *Economic aspects of child fostering in Côte d'Ivoire*, LSMS Working Paper 92, Washington, D.C., World Bank.

Ainsworth, Martha, and Juan Muñoz, 1986, *The Côte d'Ivoire living standards study*, LSMS Working Paper 26, Washington, D.C., World Bank.

Aitchison, J., and J. A. C. Brown, 1969, *The lognormal distribution*, Cambridge. Cambridge University Press.

Alderman, Harold, 1988, "Estimates of consumer price response in Pakistan using market prices as data," *Pakistan Development Review*, **27**, 89–107.

Alonso-Borrego, César, and Manuel Arellano, 1996, "Symmetrically normalized instrumental-variable estimation using panel data," CEMFI, Madrid, processed.

Altonji, Joseph, Fumio Hayashi, and Laurence J. Kotlikoff, 1992, "Is the extended family altruistically linked? Direct tests using micro data," *American Economic Review*, **82**, 1177–98.

Anand, Sudhir, and Christopher J. Harris, 1990, "Food and standard of living: an analysis based on Sri Lankan data," in Jean Drèze and Amartya Sen, eds., *The political economy of hunger: Vol. 1: Entitlement and well-being*, Oxford. Clarendon.

_____, 1994, "Choosing a welfare indicator," *American Economic Review*, **84**, (*papers and proceedings*), 226–31.

Anand, Sudhir, and S. M. Ravi Kanbur, 1992, "The Kuznets process and the inequality-development relationship," *Journal of Development Economics*, **40**, 25–52.

Anderson, Gordon , 1996, "Nonparametric tests of stochastic dominance in income distributions," *Econometrica*, **64**, 1183–93.

Anderson, Theodore W., and Takemitsu Sawa, 1979, "Evaluation of the distribution function of the two-stage least-squares estimate," *Econometrica*, **47**, 163–82.

Angrist, Joshua D., 1990, "Lifetime earnings and the Vietnam era draft lottery: evidence from social security administrative records," *American Economic Review*, **80**, 313–36.

Angrist, Joshua D., and Alan B. Krueger, 1991, "Does compulsory school attendance affect schooling and earnings?" *Quarterly Journal of Economics*, **106**, 979–1014.

_____, 1994, "Why do World War II veterans earn more?" *Journal of Labor Economics*, **12**, 74–97.

Apps, Patricia F., and Ray Rees, 1996, "Labour supply, household production and intrafamily welfare distribution," *Journal of Public Economics*, **60**, 199–219.

Arabmazar, Abbas, and Peter Schmidt, 1981, "Further evidence on the robustness of the Tobit estimator to heteroskedasticity," *Journal of Econometrics*, **17**, 253–58.

_____, 1982, "An investigation of the robustness of the Tobit estimator to non-normality," *Econometrica*, **50**, 1055–63.

Arellano, Manuel, 1987, "Computing robust standard errors for within-groups estimators," *Oxford Bulletin of Economics and Statistics*, **49**, 431–34.

Arellano, Manuel, and S. R. Bond, 1991, "Some tests of specification for panel data: Monte Carlo evidence and an application to employment equations," *Review of Economic Studies*, **58**, 277–97.

Arellano, Manuel, and Olympia Bover, 1993, "Another look at the instrumental variable estimation of error-components models," CEMFI and Bank of Spain, Madrid, processed.

Ashenfelter, Orley, Angus Deaton, and Gary Solon, 1986, *Collecting panel data in developing countries: does it make sense?* LSMS Working Paper 23, Washington, D.C., World Bank.

Atkinson, Anthony B., 1969, "On the timescale of economic models: how long is the long run?" *Review of Economic Studies*, **36**, 137–52.

_____, 1970, "On the measurement of inequality," *Journal of Economic Theory*, **2**, 244–63.

_____, 1977, "Optimal taxation and the direct versus indirect tax controversy," *Canadian Journal of Economics*, **10**, 590–606.

_____, 1987, "On the measurement of poverty," *Econometrica*, **55**, 749–64.

_____, 1992, "Measuring inequality and differing social judgments," *Research on Economic Inequality*, **3**, 29–56.

Atkinson, Anthony B., and François Bourguignon, 1982, "The comparison of multi-dimensioned distribution of economic status," *Review of Economic Studies*, **49**, 183–201.

_____, 1987, "Income distribution and differences in needs," in George R. Feiwel, ed., *Arrow and the foundations of the theory of economic policy,* New York University Press, 350–70.

_____, 1989, "The design of direct taxation and family benefits," *Journal of Public Economics*, **41**, 3–29.

Atkinson, Anthony B., and Joseph E. Stiglitz, 1976, "The design of tax structure: direct versus indirect taxation," *Journal of Public Economics*, **6**, 55–75.

Attanasio, Orazio, 1994, "Personal saving in the United States," in James M. Poterba, ed., *International comparisons of household saving,* Chicago University Press for the National Bureau of Economic Research, 57–123.

Attanasio, Orazio, and Steven Davis, 1993, "Relative wage movements and the distribution of consumption," Department of Economics, Stanford University, and Graduate School of Business, University of Chicago, processed.

Attanasio, Orazio, and Guglielmo Weber, 1992, "Consumption growth and excess sensitivity to income: evidence from U.S. micro data," Departments of Economics, Stanford University and University College, London, processed.

Balassa, Bela, 1990, "The effects of interest rates on savings in developing countries," *Banco Nazionale del Lavoro Quarterly Review,* **172,** 101–18.

Banks, James, and Richard Blundell, 1994, "Household saving behaviour in the United Kingdom," in James M. Poterba, ed., *International comparisons of household saving,* Chicago University Press for the National Bureau of Economic Research, 169–205.

Bardhan, Pranab K., 1973, "The incidence of rural poverty in the sixties," *Economic and Political Weekly,* **8,** 245–54.

——, 1974, "The pattern of income distribution in India: a review," in Bardhan and Srinivasan, eds., 1974, 103–38.

Bardhan, Pranab K., and T. N. Srinivasan, eds., 1974, *Poverty and income distribution in India,* Calcutta, Statistical Publishing Society.

Barten, Anton P., 1964, "Family composition, prices, and expenditure patterns," in Peter E. Hart, Gordon Mills, and John K. Whitaker, eds., *Economic analysis for national economic planning,* London, Butterworth.

——, 1969, "Maximum likelihood estimation of a complete system of demand equations," *European Economic Review,* **1,** 7–73.

Bates, Robert H., 1981, *Markets and states in tropical Africa: the political basis of agricultural policies,* Berkeley, University of California Press.

Bauer, Peter, 1984, "Remembrance of studies past: retracing first steps," in Gerald M. Meier and Dudley Seers, eds., *Pioneers in Development,* New York, Oxford University Press, 27–43.

Bauer, Peter, and Frank Paish, 1952, "The reduction of fluctuations in the incomes of primary producers," *Economic Journal,* **62,** 750–80.

Becker, Gary, 1981, *A treatise on the family,* Cambridge, Mass., Harvard University Press.

Becketti, Sean, William Gould, Lee Lillard, and Finis Welch, 1988, "The panel study of income dynamics after fourteen years: an evaluation," *Journal of Labor Economics,* **6,** 472–92.

Behrman, Jere R., 1987, "Intrahousehold allocation of nutrients and gender effects," Department of Economics, University of Pennsylvania, Philadelphia, processed.

Behrman, Jere R., and Anil B. Deolalikar, 1987, "Will developing country nutrition improve with income? A case study for rural south India," *Journal of Political Economy,* **95,** 108–38.

Benjamin, Dwayne, 1992, "Household composition, labor markets, and labor demand: testing for separation in agricultural household models," *Econometrica,* **60,** 287–322.

——, 1993, "Can unobserved land quality explain the inverse productivity relationship?" Department of Economics, University of Toronto, processed.

Benjamin, Dwayne, and Angus Deaton, 1993, "Household welfare and the pricing of cocoa and coffee in Côte d'Ivoire: Lessons from the Living Standards Surveys," *The*

World Bank Economic Review, **7**, 293–318.

Berry, Albert R., and William R. Cline, 1979, *Agrarian structure and productivity in developing countries*, Baltimore, Md., Johns Hopkins University Press.

Besley, Timothy, 1995a, "Savings, credit, and insurance," in Jere Behrman and T. N. Srinivasan, eds., *Handbook of development economics*, **3a**, Amsterdam, Elsevier, 2123–207.

———, 1995b, "Nonmarket institutions for credit and risk sharing in low-income countries," *Journal of Economic Perspectives*, **9**, 115–127.

Besley, Timothy, and Anne C. Case, 1994, "Unnatural experiments? Estimating the incidence of endogenous policies," NBER Working Paper 4956, NBER, Cambridge, Mass., processed.

Bevan, David, Paul Collier, and Jan Willem Gunning, 1989, *Peasants and government: an economic analysis*, Oxford, Clarendon.

Bhalla, Surjit S., 1979, "Measurement errors and the permanent income hypothesis: evidence from rural India," *American Economic Review*, **69**, 295–307.

———, 1980, "The measurement of permanent income and its application to saving behavior," *Journal of Political Economy*, **88**, 722–43.

Bhalla, Surjit S., and Prannoy Roy, 1988, "Mis-specification in farm productivity analysis: the role of land quality," *Oxford Economic Papers*, **40**, 55–73.

Bidani, Benu, and Martin Ravallion, 1994, "How robust is a poverty profile?" *The World Bank Economic Review*, **8**, 75–102.

Bierens, Herman J., and Hettie A. Pott-Buter, 1990, "Specification of household Engel curves by nonparametric regression," *Econometric Reviews*, **9**, 123–84.

Blackorby, Charles, and David Donaldson, 1978, "Measures of equality and their meaning in terms of social welfare," *Journal of Economic Theory*, **18**, 59–80.

Bliss, Christopher J., and Nicholas H. Stern, 1981, "Productivity, wages, and nutrition," *Journal of Development Economics*, **5**, 331–98.

Börsch-Supan, Axel, and Konrad Stahl, 1991, "Life cycle savings and consumption constraints: theory, empirical evidence, and fiscal implications," *Journal of Population Economics*, **4**, 233–55.

Bosworth, Barry, Gary Burtless, and John Sabelhaus, 1991, "The decline in saving: some microeconomic evidence," *Brookings Papers on Economic Activity*, 183–241.

Bouis, Howarth E., 1994, "The effect of income on demand for food in poor countries: are our databases giving us reliable estimates?" *Journal of Development Economics*, **44**, 199–226.

Bouis, Howarth E., and Lawrence J. Haddad, 1992, "Are estimates of calorie-income elasticities too high? A recalibration of the plausible range," *Journal of Development Economics*, **39**, 333–64.

Bound, John and Alan B. Krueger, 1991, "The extent of measurement error in longitudinal earnings data: do two wrongs make a right?" *Journal of Labor Economics*, **9**, 1–24.

Bound, John, David A. Jaeger, and Regina Baker, 1993, "The cure can be worse than the disease: a cautionary tale regarding instrumental variables," NBER Technical Paper 137, NBER, Cambridge, Mass., processed.

Bourguignon, François, and Pierre-André Chiappori, 1992, "Collective models of household behavior: an introduction," *European Economic Review*, **36**, 355–64.

Bourguignon, François, Martin J. Browning, Pierre-André Chiappori, and Valérie Lechene, 1993, "Intra-household allocation of consumption: a model and some evidence from French data," *Annales d'Économie et de Statistique*, **29**, 137–56.

Bowley, Arthur L., 1926, "The measurement of the precision attained in sampling," *Bulletin of the Institute of International Statistics*, **22**, 440.

Breusch, Trevor S., and Adrian R. Pagan, 1979, "A simple test for heteroskedasticity and random coefficient variation," *Review of Economic Studies*, **47**, 1287–94.

Browning, Martin, François Bourguignon, Pierre-André Chiappori, and Valérie Lechene, 1994, "Income and outcomes: a structural model of intrahousehold allocation," *Journal of Political Economy*, **102**, 1067–96.

Browning, Martin J., and Annamaria Lusardi, 1996, "Household saving: micro theories and macro facts," *Journal of Economic Literature*, **34**, 1797–855.

Buchinsky, Moshe, 1994, "Changes in the U.S. wage structure 1963–1987: application of quantile regression," *Econometrica*, **62**, 405–58.

Budd, John W., 1993, "Changing food prices and rural welfare: a nonparametric examination of the Côte d'Ivoire," *Economic Development and Cultural Change*, **41**, 587–603.

Buhmann, Brigitte, Lee Rainwater, Guenther Schmaus, and Timothy M. Smeeding, 1988, "Equivalence scales, well-being, inequality, and poverty: sensitivity estimates across ten countries using the Luxembourg Income Study (LIS) Database," *Review of Income and Wealth*, **34**, 115–42.

Buse, Adolf, 1992, "The bias of instrumental variable estimation," *Econometrica*, **60**, 173–80.

Campbell, John Y., 1987, "Does saving anticipate declining labor income? An alternative test of the permanent income hypothesis," *Econometrica*, **55**, 1249–73.

Card, David E., 1989, "The impact of the Mariel boatlift on the Miami labor market," NBER Working Paper 3069, NBER, Cambridge, Mass., processed.

Card, David E., and Alan B. Krueger, 1994, "Minimum wages and employment: a case study of the fast-food industry in New Jersey and Pennsylvania," *American Economic Review*, **84**, 772–93.

Carroll, Christopher D., forthcoming, "Buffer stock saving and the permanent income hypothesis," *Quarterly Journal of Economics*.

Carroll, Christopher D., and Lawrence J. Summers, 1991, "Consumption growth parallels income growth: some new evidence," in B. Douglas Bernheim and John B. Shoven, eds., *National saving and economic performance*, Chicago University Press for National Bureau of Economic Research, 305–43.

Case, Anne C., and Angus Deaton, 1996, "Large cash transfers to the elderly in South Africa," Research Program in Development Studies, Princeton University, processed

Casley, D. J., and D. A. Lury, 1981, *Data collection in developing countries*, Oxford, Clarendon.

Chamberlain, Gary, 1984, "Panel data," in Zvi Griliches and Michael D. Intriligator, eds., *Handbook of Econometrics*, **2**, Amsterdam, Elsevier, 1247–322.

——, 1986, "Asymptotic efficiency in semiparametric models with censoring," *Journal of Econometrics*, **32**, 189–92.

Chayanov, Aleksander V., 1966, *The theory of peasant economy*, Homewood, Il., Irwin. (First published in Russian, Moscow, 1925.)

Chesher, Andrew, 1984, "Testing for neglected heterogeneity," *Econometrica*, **52**, 865–72.

Chiappori, Pierre-André, 1988, "Rational household labor supply," *Econometrica*, **56**, 63–89.

——, 1992, "Collective labor supply and welfare," *Journal of Political Economy*, **100**, 437–67.

China, Republic of, *Report on the survey of personal income distribution in Taiwan area of the Republic of China*, Tapei, Directorate General of Budget, Accounting and Statistics Executive Yuan.

———, 1992, *Monthly statistics of Republic of China, Taipei,* Directorate General of Budget, Accounting and Statistics Executive Yuan. (data diskette)

Christensen, Laurits R., Dale W. Jorgenson, and Laurence J. Lau, 1975, "Transcendental logarithmic utility functions," *American Economic Review,* **65**, 367–83.

Chow, Gregory C., 1983, *Econometrics,* New York, McGraw-Hill.

Cleveland, William S., 1979, "Robust locally weighted regression and smoothing scatter plots," *Journal of the American Statistical Association,* **74**, 829–36.

Coale, Ansley, 1991, "Excess female mortality and the balance of the sexes: an estimate of the number of 'missing females'," *Population and Development Review,* **17**, 517–23.

Cochrane, John, H., 1991, "A simple test of consumption insurance," *Journal of Political Economy,* **99**, 957–76.

Cochrane, William G., 1977, *Sampling techniques,* New York, Wiley.

Coder, John, 1991, "Exploring nonsampling errors in the wage and salary income data from the March current population survey," Household and Household Economic Statistics Division, Bureau of the Census, Washington, D.C., processed.

Collier, Paul, and Jan Gunning, 1997, *Trade shocks in developing countries,* Oxford, Clarendon.

Cosslett, Stephen R., 1993, "Estimation from endogenously stratified samples," in G. S. Maddala, C. R. Rao, and H. D. Vinod, eds., *Handbook of statistics,* **11**, Amsterdam, Elsevier, 1–43.

Coulombe, Harold, and Lionel Demery, 1993, *Household size in Côte d'Ivoire: sampling bias in the CILSS,* LSMS Working Paper 97, Washington, D.C., World Bank.

Coulombe, Harold, Andrew McKay, and Graham Pyatt, 1993, "Has household size really been declining in the Côte d'Ivoire?" Department of Economics, University of Warwick, and Institute of Social Studies, The Hague, processed.

Cowell, Frank A., 1995, *Measuring inequality,* (2nd edition), London. Prentice Hall.

Cowgill, Donald O., 1986, *Aging around the world,* Belmont, Ca., Wadsworth.

Cox, Donald, and Emmanuel Jimenez, 1991a, "The relationship between community characteristics and private transfers: evidence for Ghana," Department of Economics, Boston College and Policy Research Department, World Bank, Washington, D.C., processed.

———, 1991b, "A study of motivation for private transfers in Côte d'Ivoire," Department of Economics, Boston College and Policy Research Department, World Bank, Washington, D.C., processed.

———, 1992a, "Household networks and risk-sharing in urban Colombia," Department of Economics, Boston College and Policy Research Department, World Bank, Washington, D.C., processed.

———, 1992b, "Motives for private transfers over the life-cycle: an analytical framework and evidence for Peru," Department of Economics, Boston College and Policy Research Department, World Bank, Washington, D.C., processed.

———, 1992c, "Social security and private transfers in developing countries: the case of Peru." *The World Bank Economic Review,* **6**, 155–69.

———, 1993,"Private transfers and the effectiveness of public income redistribution in the Philippines," Department of Economics, Boston College and Policy Research Department, World Bank, Washington, D.C., processed.

Cramer, Jan S., 1969, *Empirical econometrics*, Amsterdam, North-Holland.

Crooks, Edmund, 1989, *Alcohol consumption and taxation*, Report Series 34, London, Institute for Fiscal Studies.

Dalton, Hugh, 1920, "The measurement of the inequality of incomes," *Economic Journal*, **30**, 384–61.

Dandekar, V. M., and N. Rath, 1971a, "Poverty in India: dimensions and trends," *Economic and Political Weekly*, **6**, 25–48.

———, 1971b, *Poverty in India*, Pune, Indian School of Political Economy.

Danziger, Sheldon, Jacques van der Gaag, Michael K. Taussig, and Eugene Smolensky, 1984, "The direct measurement of welfare levels: how much does it cost to make ends meet?" *Review of Economics and Statistics*, **66**, 500–05.

Das Gupta, Monica, 1987, "Selective discrimination against female children in rural Punjab, India," *Population and Development Review*, **13**, 77–100.

Dasgupta, Partha, 1993, *An inquiry into well-being and destitution*, Oxford, Clarendon Press.

Dasgupta, Partha, Stephen A. Marglin, and Amartya K. Sen, 1972, *Guidelines for project evaluation*, New York, United Nations.

Dasgupta, Partha, and Debraj Ray, 1986, "Inequality as a determinant of malnutrition and unemployment: theory," *Economic Journal*, **96**, 1011–34.

———, 1987, "Inequality as determinant of malnutrition and unemployment: policy," *Economic Journal*, **97**, 177–88.

Davidson, Russell, and James G. MacKinnon, 1993, *Estimation and inference in econometrics*, Oxford, Oxford University Press.

Davies, David, 1795, *The case of labourers in husbandry*, Bath.

Deaton, Angus, 1974a, "The analysis of consumer demand in the United Kingdom, 1900–1970," *Econometrica*, **42**, 341–67.

———, 1974b, "A reconsideration of the implications of additive preferences," *Economic Journal*, **84**, 338–48.

———, 1979, "Optimally uniform commodity taxes," *Economics Letters*, **2**, 357–61.

———, 1981, "Optimal taxes and the structure of preferences," *Econometrica*, **49**, 1245–60.

———, 1985, "Panel data from time series of cross-sections," *Journal of Econometrics*, **30**, 109–26.

———, 1987a, *Quality, quantity, and spatial variation of price: estimating price elasticities from cross-sectional data*, LSMS Working Paper 30, Washington, D.C., World Bank.

———, 1987b, "Econometric issues for tax design in developing countries," in Newbery and Stern, 1987, 92–113.

———, 1988, "Quality, quantity, and spatial variation of price," *American Economic Review*, **78**, 418–30.

———, 1989a, "Rice prices and income distribution in Thailand: a non-parametric analysis, *Economic Journal*, **99** (Supplement), 1–37.

———, 1989b, "Looking for boy-girl discrimination in household expenditure data," *The World Bank Economic Review*, **3**, 1–15.

———, 1989c, "Household survey data and pricing policies in developing countries," *The World Bank Economic Review*, **3**, 183–210.

———, 1990a, "Price elasticities from survey data: extensions and Indonesian results," *Journal of Econometrics*, **44**, 281–309.

_____, 1990b, "Saving in developing countries: theory and review," *Proceedings of the First Annual World Bank Conference on Development Economics,* Washington D.C., 61–96.

_____, 1991, "Saving and liquidity constraints," *Econometrica,* **59,** 1221–48.

_____, 1992a, "Saving and income smoothing in the Côte d'Ivoire," *Journal of African Economies,* **1,** 1–24.

_____, 1992b, "Household saving in LDCs: credit markets, insurance, and welfare," *Scandinavian Journal of Economics,* **94,** 253–73.

_____, 1992c, *Understanding consumption,* Oxford, Clarendon Press.

_____, 1995, "Data and econometric tools for development analysis," in Jere Behrman and T. N. Srinivasan, eds., *Handbook of development economics,* **3a,** Amsterdam, Elsevier, 1785–882.

Deaton, Angus, and Dwayne Benjamin, 1988, *The living standards survey and price policy reform: a study of cocoa and coffee production in the Côte d'Ivoire,"* LSMS Working Paper 44, Washington D.C., World Bank.

Deaton, Angus, and Eric V. Edmonds, 1996, "Measuring consumption and price in LSMS surveys," Research Program in Development Studies, Princeton University, Princeton, N.J., processed.

Deaton, Angus, and Franque Grimard, 1992, *Demand analysis for tax reform in Pakistan,"*LSMS Working Paper 85, Washington, D.C., World Bank.

Deaton, Angus, and Ronald I. Miller, 1995, *International commodity prices, macroeconomic performance, and politics in sub-Saharan Africa,* Princeton Studies in International Finance, No. 79, International Finance Section. Princeton University.

Deaton, Angus, and John Muellbauer, 1980a, *Economics and consumer behavior,* New York, Cambridge University Press.

_____, 1980b, "An almost ideal demand system," *American Economic Review,* **70,** 312–26.

_____, 1986, "On measuring child costs: with applications to poor countries," *Journal of Political Economy,* **94,** 720–44

Deaton, Angus, and Serena Ng, 1996, "Parametric and non-parametric approaches to tax reform," Princeton University Research Program in Development Studies, processed.

Deaton, Angus, Kirit Parikh, and Shankar Subramanian, 1994, "Food demand patterns and pricing policy in Maharashtra: an analysis using household-level survey data," *Sarvekshana,* **17,.** 11–34.

Deaton, Angus, and Christina H. Paxson, 1992, "Patterns of aging in Thailand and Côte d'Ivoire," in David A. Wise, ed., *Topics in the economics of aging,* Chicago University Press for the National Bureau of Economic Research.

_____, 1994a, "Saving, growth, and aging in Taiwan," in David A. Wise, ed., *Studies in the economics of aging,* Chicago University Press for the National Bureau of Economic Research.

_____, 1994b, "Intertemporal choice and inequality," *Journal of Political Economy,* **102,** 437–67.

_____, 1995, "Saving, inequality, and aging: an East Asian perspective," *Asia-Pacific Economic Review,* **1,** 7–19.

_____, 1996, "Economies of scale, household size, and the demand for food," Research Program in Development Studies, Princeton University, processed.

_____, 1997a, "Poverty among the elderly," in David Wise, ed., *Inquiriesin the economics of aging,* Chicago, Il., Chicago University Press for the National Bureau of Economic

Research, forthcoming.

_____, 1997b, "The effects of economic and population growth on national saving and inequality," *Demography*, forthcoming.

Deaton, Angus, Javier Ruiz-Castillo, and Duncan Thomas, 1989, "The influence of household composition on household expenditure patterns: theory and Spanish evidence," *Journal of Political Economy*, **97**, 179–200.

Deaton, Angus, and Nicholas H. Stern, 1986, "Optimally uniform commodity taxes, taste differences, and lump-sum grants," *Economics Letters*, **20**, 263-66.

Demery, Lionel and Christiaan Grootaert, 1993, "Correcting for sampling errors in the measurement of welfare and poverty: the case of the Côte d'Ivoire Living Standard Survey," *The World Bank Economic Review*, **7**, 263–92.

Diamond, Peter A., and James A. Mirrlees, 1971, "Optimal taxation and public production, Part I: production efficiency," and "Part II: tax rules," *American Economic Review*, **61**, 8–27 and 261–78.

Dixit, Avinash K., 1976, *Optimization in economic theory*, Oxford, Oxford University Press.

_____, 1996, *The making of economic policy: a transaction-cost politics perspective*, Cambridge, Mass., MIT Press.

Dooley, Martin D., and Peter Gottschalk, 1984, "Earnings inequality among males in the United States: trends and the effects of labor force growth," *Journal of Political Economy*, **92**, 59–89.

Dorfman, Robert, Paul A. Samuelson, and Robert Solow, 1958, *Linear programming and economic analysis*, New York, McGraw-Hill.

Drèze, Jean, and Amartya K. Sen, 1989, *Hunger and public action*, Oxford, Clarendon Press.

Drèze, Jean, and Nicholas H. Stern, 1987, "The theory of cost-benefit analysis," in Alan Auerbach and Martin Feldstein, eds., *Handbook of public economics*, Amsterdam, Elsevier.

_____, 1990, "Policy reform, shadow prices, and market prices," *Journal of Public Economics*, 42, 1–45.

Dublin, Louis I., and Alfred J. Lotka, 1930, *The money value of a man*, New York, Ronald.

Ducpétiaux, Edouard, 1855, *Budgets économiques des classes ouvrières en Belgique*, Brussels, M. Hayez imp. de la Commission Centrale de Statistique.

Duesenberry, James S., 1949, *Income, saving, and the theory of consumer behavior*, Cambridge, Mass., Harvard University Press.

Dumouchel, W. H., and Greg J. Duncan, 1983, "Using sample survey weights in multiple regression analysis of stratified samples," *Journal of the American Statistical Association*, **78**, 535–43.

Eden, Frederick M., 1797, *The state of the poor*, London, Davis.

Efron, Bradley, 1979, "Bootstrap methods: another look at the jackknife," *Annals of Statistics*, **7**, 1–26.

Efron, Bradley, and Robert J. Tibshirani, 1993, *An introduction to the bootstrap*, London, Chapman and Hall.

Eicker, F., 1967, "Limit theorems for regressions with unequal and dependent errors," in L. M. Le Cam and J. Neyman, eds., *Fifth Berkeley Symposium on Mathematical Statistics and Probability*, **1**, Berkeley, University of California Press, 59–82.

El-Badawi, Ibrahim, A. Ronald Gallant, and Geraldo Souza, 1983, "An elasticity can be estimated consistently without knowledge of functional form," *Econometrica*, **51**, 1731–51.

Engel, Ernst, 1857, "Die productions- und consumtionsverhältnisse des Königreichs Sachsen," in Ernst Engel, *Die lebenkosten belgischer arbeiter-familien*, Dresden, 1895, C. Heinrich.

Engle, Robert F., Clive W. J. Granger, J. Rice, and A. Weiss, 1986, "Semiparametric estimates of the relation between weather and electricity sales," *Journal of the American Statistical Association*, **81**, 310–20.

Espenshade, Thomas J., 1973, *The cost of children in urban United States*, Population Monograph Series 14, Berkeley, University of California Institute of International Studies.

Estes, Eugena and Bo Honoré, 1996, "Partial regression using one nearest neighbor," Department of Economics, Princeton University, in preparation.

Fan, Jianqing, 1992, "Design-adaptive nonparametric regression," *Journal of the American Statistical Association*, **87**, 998–1004.

Feder, Gershon, 1985, "The relation between farm size and farm productivity," *Journal of Development Economics*, **18**, 297–313.

Feldstein, Martin, and Charles Horioka, 1980, "Domestic saving and international capital flows," *Economic Journal*, **90**, 314–29.

Fields, Gary S., 1977, "Who benefits from economic development? A re-examination of Brazilian growth in the 60s," *American Economic Review*, **67**, 570–82.

Fisher, Gordon M., 1992, "The development and history of the poverty thresholds," *Social Security Bulletin*, **55**, 3–14.

Fisher, Ronald A., 1925, *Statistical methods for research workers*, London, Oliver & Boyd.

Fogel, Robert W., 1994, "Economic growth, population theory, and physiology: the bearing of long-term processes on the making of economic policy," *American Economic Review*, **84**, 369–95.

Foster, James, 1984, "On economic poverty: a survey of aggregate measures," *Advances in Econometrics*, **3**, 215–51.

Foster, James, J. Greer, and Eric Thorbecke, 1984, "A class of decomposable poverty measures," *Econometrica*, **52**, 761–65.

Foster, James, and Amartya K. Sen, 1997, "*On economic inequality* after a quarter of a century," annexe to Amartya K. Sen, *On economic inequality* (enlarged edition), Oxford. Clarendon.

Freedman, David A., 1991, "Statistical models and shoe leather," *Sociological Methodology* **21**, 291–313.

Friedman, Milton, 1954, "The reduction of fluctuations in the incomes of primary producers: a critical comment," *Economic Journal*, **64**, 698–703.

——, 1957, *A theory of the consumption function*, Princeton University Press.

Frisch, Ragnar and F. V. Waugh, 1933, "Partial time regressions as compared with individual trends," *Econometrica*, **1**, 387–401.

Fry, Maxwell J., 1988, *Money, interest, and banking in economic development*, Baltimore, Md., Johns Hopkins University Press.

Fuller, Wayne A., 1987, *Measurement error models*, New York, John Wiley.

Gallant, A. Ronald, 1981, "On the bias in flexible functional forms and an essentially unbiased form: the Fourier flexible form," *Journal of Econometrics*, **15**, 211–45.

Gallant, A. Ronald, and Geraldo Souza, 1991, "On the asymptotic normality of Fourier flexible form estimation," *Journal of Econometrics*, **50**, 329–53.

Geiseman, Raymond, 1987, "The consumer expenditure survey: quality control by comparative analysis," *Monthly Labor Review*, March, 8–14.

Gersovitz, Mark, 1988, "Saving and development," in Hollis Chenery and T. N. Srinivasan, eds., *Handbook of development economics*, Amsterdam, Elsevier, 381–424.

Gertler, Paul, and Jacques van der Gaag, 1990, *The willingness to pay for medical care: evidence from two developing countries*, Baltimore, Md., Johns Hopkins University Press.

Ghez, Gilbert R., and Gary S. Becker, 1975, "The allocation of time and goods over the life-cycle," New York, Columbia University Press for NBER.

Glewwe, Paul, and Gillette Hall, 1995, *Who is most vulnerable to macroeconomic shocks? Hypothesis tests using panel data from Peru*, LSMS Working Paper 117. Washington, D.C., World Bank.

Goldberger, Arthur S., 1964, *Econometric theory*, New York, John Wiley.

———, 1983, "Abnormal selection bias," in S. Karlin et al., eds., *Studies in econometrics, time series, and multivariate statistics*, New York, Academic Press, 67–84.

Gopalan, C., B. Sastri, V. Rama, and S. C. Balasubramanian, 1971, *Nutritive value of Indian foods*, Hyderabad, National Institute of Nutrition.

Gorman, William M., 1976, "Tricks with utility functions," in Michael J. Artis and Robert A. Nobay, eds., *Essays in economic analysis*, Cambridge University Press.

Graaff, Jan de-Villiers, 1977, "Equity and efficiency as components of the general welfare," *South African Journal of Economics*, **45**, 362–75.

Greenhalgh, Susan, 1985, "Sexual stratification: the other side of 'growth with equity' in East Asia," *Population and Development Review*, **11**, 265–314.

Gregory, A. W., and M. R. Veall, 1985, "On formulating Wald tests for nonlinear restrictions," *Econometrica*, **53**, 1465–68.

Griffin, Keith, and A. K. Ghose, 1979, "Growth and impoverishment in the rural areas of Asia," *World Development*, **7**, 361–83.

Griliches, Zvi, and Jerry A. Hausman, 1986, "Errors in variables in panel data," *Journal of Econometrics*, **31**, 93–118.

Gronau, Rueben, 1973, "The effects of children on the housewife's value of time," *Journal of Political Economy*, **81**, S168–99.

Grootaert, Christiaan, 1993, "How useful are integrated household survey data for policy-oriented analyses of poverty?: lessons from the Côte d'Ivoire Living Standards Survey," Working Paper WPS 1079, Africa Technical Department, World Bank, Washington, D.C., processed.

Grootaert, Christiaan, and Ravi Kanbur, 1992, "A new regional price index for Côte d'Ivoire using data from the international comparisons project," Poverty and Social Policy Division,World Bank, Washington, D.C.

Grosh, Margaret E., 1994, *Administering targeted social programs in Latin America: from platitudes to practice*, Washington, D.C., World Bank.

Grosh, Margaret, and Paul Glewwe, 1992, "Using large, nationally representative household surveys for food policy analysis: an examination of the World Bank's LSMS surveys," Policy Research Department, World Bank, Washington, D.C., processed.

———, 1995, *A guide to living standrads measurement study surveys and their data sets*,

LSMS Working Paper 120, Washington, D.C., World Bank.

Grosh, Margaret E., and Juan Muñoz, 1996, *A manual for planning and implementing the LSMS survey*, LSMS Working Paper 126, Washington, D.C., World Bank.

Grosh, Margaret E., Qing-hua Zhao, and Henri-Pierre Jeancard, 1995, "The sensitivity of consumption aggregates to questionnaire formulation: some preliminary evidence from the Jamaican and Ghanaian LSMS surveys," Poverty and Human Resources Division, Policy Research Department, World Bank, Washington, D.C., processed.

Grossman, Gene M., and Elhanan Helpman, 1994, "Protection for sale," *American Economic Review*, **84**, 833–50.

Grossman, Jean Baldwin, 1994, "Evaluating social policies: principles and U.S. experience" *The World Bank Research Observer*, **9**, 159–80.

Groves, Robert M., 1989, *Survey errors and survey costs*, New York, Wiley.

Gulati, Ashok, James Hansen, and Gary Pursell, 1990, "Effective incentives in India's agriculture: cotton, groundnuts, wheat, and rice," WPS 332, Country Economics Department, World Bank, Washington, D.C., processed.

Haaga, John, Julie DaVanzo, Christine Peterson, and Tey Nai Peng, 1994, "Twelve-year follow-up of respondents in a sample survey in Peninsular Malaysia," *Asia-Pacific Population Journal*, **9**, 61–72.

Haddad, Lawrence, and S. M. Ravi Kanbur, 1990, "How serious is the neglect of intra-household inequality," *Economic Journal,* **100**, 866–81.

Hall, Peter, 1995, "Methodology and theory for the bootstrap," in Robert F. Engle and Daniel L. McFadden, eds., *Handbook of econometrics*, **4**, Amsterdam, Elsevier, 2341–81.

Hall, Robert E., 1971, "The measurement of quality change from vintage price data," in Zvi Griliches, ed., *Price indexes and quality change*, Cambridge, Mass., Harvard University Press.

——, 1978, "Stochastic implications of the life cycle–permanent income hypothesis: theory and evidence," *Journal of Political Economy*, **96**, 971–87.

Hammond, R. J., 1951, *Food Vol. 1: the growth of policy*, London, Longmans. (History of the Second World War: United Kingdom Civil Series, ed. W. K. Hancock.)

Hansen, Lars Peter, and Kenneth J. Singleton, 1982, "Generalized instrumental variables estimation of nonlinear rational expectations models," *Econometrica*, **50**, 1269–86.

Hansen, M. H., W. N. Hurwitz, and W. G. Madow, 1953, *Sample survey methods and theory*, **1** and **2**, New York, Wiley.

Härdle, Wolfgang, 1991, *Applied non-parametric regression*, Cambridge University Press.

Härdle, Wolfgang, and Oliver Linton, 1994, "Applied nonparametric methods," in R. F. Engle, and D. McFadden, eds., *Handbook of econometrics*, **4**, Amsterdam, Elsevier, 2295–381.

Härdle, Wolfgang, and Thomas M. Stoker, 1989, "Investigating smooth multiple regression by the method of average derivatives," *Journal of the American Statistical Association*, **84**, 986–95.

Harriss, Barbara, 1990, "The intrahousehold distribution of hunger," in Jean Drèze and Amartya K. Sen, eds., *The political economy of hunger*, Oxford, Clarendon Press.

Hastie, Trevor, and Clive Loader, 1993, "Locally weighted regression," *Statistical Science*, **8**, 120–43.

Hausman, Jerry A., 1978, "Specification tests in econometrics," *Econometrica*, **46**, 1251–72.

_____, 1981, "Exact consumer surplus and deadweight loss," *American Economic Review*, **71**, 662–76.

Hausman, Jerry A., and Whitney K. Newey, 1995, "Nonparametric estimation of exact consumers' surplus and deadweight loss," *Econometrica*, **63**, 1445–76.

Hausman, Jerry A., and David A. Wise, 1977, "Social experimentation, truncated distributions, and efficient estimation," *Econometrica*, **45**, 919–38.

_____, 1981, "Stratification on endogenous variables and estimation: the Gary income maintenance experiment," in C. F. Manski and D. McFadden, eds., *Structural analysis of discrete data with econometric applications*, Cambridge, Mass., MIT Press.

Hayashi, Fumio 1985a, "The effect of liquidity constraints on consumption: a cross-sectional analysis," *Quarterly Journal of Economics*, **100**, 183–206.

_____, 1985b, "The permanent income hypothesis and consumption durability: analysis based on Japanese panel data," *Quarterly Journal of Economics*, **100**, 1083–113.

Heckman, James J., 1974, "Shadow prices, market wages, and labor supply," *Econometrica*, **42**, 679–93.

_____, 1976, "The common structure of statistical models of truncation, sample selection, and limited dependent variables and a simple estimator for such models, *Annals of Economic and Social Measurement*, **5**, 475–92.

_____, 1990, "Varieties of selection bias," American Economic Review (papers and proceedings.), **80**, 313–18.

Henderson, A. M., 1949–50a, "The cost of children," Parts I–III, *Population Studies*, **3**, 130–50, **4**, 267–98.

_____, 1949–50b, "The cost of a family," *Review of Economic Studies*, **17**, 127–48.

Hirschman, Albert O., 1977, "A generalized linkage approach to development, with special reference to staples," *Economic Development and Cultural Change*, **25** (Supplement), 67–98.

Hoch, Irving, 1955, "Estimation of production function parameters and testing for efficiency," *Econometrica*, **23**, 325–26, (abstract).

Hoddinott, John, and Lawrence Haddad, 1992, "Does female income share influence household expenditure patterns?" Centre for the Study of African Economies, Oxford, and International Food Policy Research Institute, Washington, D.C., processed.

Holtz-Eakin, Doug, Whitney Newey, and Harvey Rosen, 1988, "Estimating vector auto-regressions with panel data," *Econometrica*, **56**, 1371–95.

Hotelling, Harold, 1932, "Edgeworth's taxation paradox and the nature of demand and supply functions," *Journal of Political Economy*, **40**, 577–616.

Howes, Stephen, and Jean Olson Lanjouw, 1995, "Making poverty comparisons taking into account survey design: how and why," Policy Research Department, World Bank, Washington, D.C., and Yale University, New Haven, processed.

Hubbard, R. Glenn, Jonathan Skinner, and Stephen P. Zeldes, 1994. "The importance of precautionary motives in explaining individual and aggregate saving," *Carnegie Rochester Conference Series in Public Policy*, **40**, 59–125.

_____, 1995, "Precautionary saving and social insurance," *Journal of Political Economy*, **103**, 360–99.

Huber, Peter J., 1967, "The behavior of maximum likelihood estimates under non-standard conditions," *Proceedings of the fifth Berkeley symposium on mathematical statistics and probability*, **1**, 221–33.

Hurd, Michael, 1979, "Estimation in truncated samples when there is heteroskedasticity,"

Journal of Econometrics, **11**, 247–58.

India, Government of, 1987, *Agricultural prices in India, 1982–85*, New Delhi, Directorate of Economics and Statistics.

_____, 1988, *Child mortality estimates of India, 1981*, Occasional Paper 5 of 1988, Demography Division, Office of the Registrar General, New Delhi.

_____, 1993, *Report of the expert group on estimation of proportion and number of poor*, Perspective Planning Division, Planning Commission, New Delhi.

Jensen, Robert T., 1996, "Public transfers, private transfers and the 'crowding out' hypothesis: theory and evidence from South Africa," Research Program in Development Studies, Princeton University, processed.

Jeong, Jinook, and G. S. Maddala, 1993, "A perspective on application of bootstrap methods in econometrics," in G. S. Maddala, C. R. Rao, and H. D. Vinod, eds., *Handbook of statistics,* **11**, Amsterdam, Elsevier, 573–610.

Jimenez, Emmanuel, 1987, *Pricing policy in the social sectors: cost recovery for education and health in developing countries*, Baltimore, Md., Johns Hopkins University Press.

Johnson, Nancy L., and Vernon W. Ruttan, 1994, "Why are farms so small?" *World Development*, **22**, 691–706.

Johnston, John, 1972, *Econometric methods*, New York, McGraw-Hill (second edition).

Johnston, John, and John DiNardo, 1997, *Econometric methods*, New York, McGraw-Hill (fourth edition).

Jolliffe, Dean, and Kinnon Scott, 1995, "The sensitivity of measures of household consumption to survey design: results from an experiment in El Salvador," Policy Research Dept., World Bank, Washington, D.C., processed.

Jorgenson, Dale W., 1990, "Aggregate consumer behavior and the measurement of social welfare," *Econometrica*, **58**, 1007–40.

Jorgenson, Dale W., and Daniel T. Slesnick, 1984, "Aggregate consumer behavior and the measurement of inequality," *Review of Economic Studies*, **51**, 369–92.

Kakwani, Nanak C., 1980, *Income inequality and poverty: methods of estimating and policy applications*, Oxford University Press.

Kemsley, W. F. F., 1975, "Family expenditure survey: a study of differential response based on a comparison of the 1971 sample with the census," *Statistical News*, **31**, 16–21.

Kemsley, W. F. F., R. V. Redpath, and M. Holmes, 1980, *Family expenditure survey handbook*, London, Her Majesty's Stationery Office.

Kennan, John, 1989, "Simultaneous equations bias in disaggregated econometric models," *Review of Economic Studies*, 56, 151–56.

Kimball, Miles S., 1990, "Precautionary saving in the small and in the large," *Econometrica*, **58**, 53–73.

Kish, Leslie, 1965, *Survey sampling*, New York, John Wiley.

Kish, Leslie, and Martin R. Frankel, 1974, "Inference from complex samples (with discussion), *Journal of the Royal Statistical Society, Series B*, **36**, 1–37.

Kloek, Tenn, 1981, "OLS estimation in a model where a microvariable is explained by aggregates and contemporaneous disturbances are equicorrelated," *Econometrica*, **49**, 205–07.

Koenker, Roger, and Gilbert Bassett, 1978, "Regression quantiles," *Econometrica*, **46**, 33–50.

_____, 1982, "Robust tests for heteroskedasticity based on regression quantiles," *Econometrica*, **50**, 43–61.

Kolm, Serge Christophe, 1976, "Unequal inequalities, Parts 1 and 2" *Journal of Economic Theory*, **12**, 416–42, and **13**, 82–111.

Konüs, A. A., 1924, "The problem of the true index of the cost of living," (in Russian) *The Economic Bulletin of the Institute of Economic Conjuncture*, Moscow, Nos 9–10, 64–71. (English translation, *Econometrica*, **7**, 10–29,1939).

Kotlikoff, Laurence J., 1988, "Intergenerational transfers and savings," *Journal of Economic Perspectives*, **2**, 41–58.

Kotlikoff, Laurence J., and Lawrence H. Summers, 1981, "The role of intergenerational transfers in aggregate capital formation," *Journal of Political Economy*, **89**, 706–32.

Krueger, Anne O., Maurice Schiff, and Alberto Valdes, 1991–92, *The political economy of agricultural pricing policy*, Baltimore, Md., Johns Hopkins University Press. (5 vols.)

Kuznets, Simon, 1962, "Quantitative aspects of the economic growth of nations: VII: The share and structure of consumption," *Economic Development and Cultural Change*, **10**, 1–92.

_____, 1966, *Modern economic growth: rate, structure and spread*, New Haven, Yale University Press.

_____, 1979, *Growth, population, and income distribution: selected essays*, New York, Norton.

Lal, Deepak, 1976, "Agricultural growth, real wages, and the rural poor in India," *Economic and Political Weekly*, Review of Agriculture.

Lanjouw, Peter, and Martin Ravallion, 1995, "Poverty and household size" *Economic Journal*, **105**, 1415–34.

Lazear, Edward P., and Robert T. Michael, 1988, *Allocation of income within the household*, University of Chicago Press.

Leamer, Edward E., 1978, *Specification searches: ad hoc inference with nonexperimental data*, New York, Wiley.

Leibenstein, Harvey, 1957, *Economic backwardness and economic growth*, New York, Wiley.

Levy, Paul S., and Stanley Lemenshow, 1991, *Sampling of populations: methods and applications*, New York, Wiley.

Lewis, Sir W. Arthur, 1954, "Economic development with unlimited supplies of labor," *The Manchester School*, **22**, 139–91.

Lindert, Peter H., 1978, *Fertility and scarcity in America*, Princeton University Press.

_____, 1980, "Child costs and economic development," in Richard A. Easterlin, ed., *Population and economic change in developing countries*, Chicago University Press for NBER.

Lipton, Michael, and Martin Ravallion, 1995, "Poverty and policy," in Jere Behrman and T. N. Srinivasan, eds., *Handbook of development economics*, **3b**, Amsterdam, Elsevier, 2551–657.

Little, Ian M. D., and James A. Mirrlees, 1974, *Project appraisal and planning for developing countries*, London, Heinemann.

Lluch, Constantino, 1971, "Consumer demand functions, Spain, 1958–64," *European Economic Review*, **2**, 277–302.

Lluch, Constantino, Alan A. Powell, and Ross A. Williams, 1977, *Patterns in household demand and saving*, Oxford University Press.

Lucas, Robert E. B., and Oded Stark, 1985, "Motivations to remit: evidence from Botswana," *Journal of Political Economy*, **93**, 901–18.

Lundberg, Shelley, and Robert A. Pollak, 1993, "Separate spheres bargaining and the marriage market," *Journal of Political Economy*, **101**, 988–1010.

Mace, Barbara J., 1991, "Full insurance in the presence of aggregate uncertainty," *Journal of Political Economy*, **99**, 928–56.

Maddala, G. S., and Jinook Jeong, "On the exact small sample distribution of the instrumental variable estimator," *Econometrica*, **60**, 181–83.

Magnus, Jan R., and Heinz Neudecker, 1988, *Matrix differential calculus with applications in statistics and econometrics*, New York, Wiley.

Mahalanobis, P. C., 1944, "On large-scale sample surveys," *Philosophical Transactions of the Royal Society, Series B*, **231**, 329–451.

——, 1946, "Recent experiments in statistical sampling in the Indian Statistical Institute," *Journal of the Royal Statistical Society*, **109**, 325–78.

——, 1960, "The method of fractile graphical analysis," *Econometrica*, **28**, 325–51.

Mangahas, Mahar, 1979, "Poverty in the Philippines: some measurement problems," *The Philippine Economic Journal*, **18**, 630–40.

——, 1982, "What happened to the poor on the way to the next development plan?" *The Philippine Economic Journal*, **21**, 126–46.

——, 1985, "Rural poverty and operation land transfer in the Philippines," in Rizwanul Islam, ed., *Strategies for alleviating poverty in rural Asia*, Dhaka, Bangladesh Institute of Development Studies, 201–41.

Mankiw, N. Greg, David Romer, and David Weil, 1992, "A contribution to the empirics of economic growth," *Quarterly Journal of Economics*, **107**, 407–37.

Manser, Marilyn, and Murray Brown, 1980, "Marriage and household decision-making: a bargaining analysis," *International Economic Review*, **21**, 31–44.

Manski, Charles F., 1988, "Identification of binary response models," *Journal of the American Statistical Association*, **83**, 729–38.

Manski, Charles F., and Steven Lerman, 1977, "The estimation of choice probabilities from choice-based samples," *Econometrica*, **45**, 1977–88.

Marschak, Jacob, and William H. Andrews, 1944, "Random simultaneous equations and the theory of production," *Econometrica*, **12**, 143–205.

Mas-Colell, Andreu, Michael D. Whinston, and Jerry R. Green, 1995, *Microeconomic Theory*, Oxford, Oxford University Press.

McElroy, Marjorie, 1990, "The empirical content of Nash-bargained household behavior," *Journal of Human Resources*, **25**, 559–83.

McElroy, Marjorie, and Mary Jean Horney, 1981, "Nash-bargained household decisions: towards a generalization of the theory of demand," *International Economic Review*, **22**, 333–49.

McKay, Andrew, 1996, "Collection of data on household incomes in LSMS surveys," Department of Economics, University of Nottingham, processed.

Mincer, Jacob A., 1974, *Schooling, experience, and earnings*, New York, Columbia University Press.

Minhas, B. S., 1988,"Validation of large-scale sample survey data: case of NSS household consumption expenditure," *Sankhya, Series B*, **50**, (Supplement) 1–63.

——, 1991, "On estimating the inadequacy of energy intakes: revealed food consumption behavior versus nutritional norms (Nutritional status of Indian people in 1983)," *Jour-*

nal of Development Studies, **28**, 1–38.

Minhas, B. S., and S. M. Kansal, 1989, "Comparison of NSS and CSO estimates of private consumption: some observations based on 1983 data," *The Journal of Income and Wealth*, **11**, 7–24.

Mirer, Thad W., 1979, "The wealth-age relationship among the aged," *American Economic Review*, **69**, 435–43.

Mirrlees, James A., 1975, "A pure theory of underdeveloped economies," in Lloyd A. Reynolds, ed., *Agriculture in development theory*, New Haven, Yale University Press.

____, 1971, "An exploration in the theory of optimum income taxation," *Review of Economic Studies*, **38**, 175–208.

Modigliani, Franco, 1966, "The life-cycle hypothesis of saving, the demand for wealth, and the supply of capital," *Social Research*, **33**, 160–217.

____, 1970, "The life-cycle hypothesis of saving and intercountry differences in the saving ratio," in W. A. Eltis, M. FG. Scott and J. N. Wolfe, eds., *Induction, trade, and growth: Essays in honour of Sir Roy Harrod*, Oxford, Clarendon Press, 197–225.

____, 1986, "Life cycle, individual thrift, and the wealth of nations," *American Economic Review*, **76**, 297–313.

____, 1988, "The role of intergenerational transfers and life cycle saving in the accumulation of wealth," *Journal of Economic Perspectives*, **2**, 15–40.

____, 1993, "Recent declines in the savings rate: a life cycle perspective," in Mario Baldassarri et al., eds., *World saving, prosperity, and growth*, New York, St. Martin's Press, 249–86.

Modigliani, Franco, and Richard Brumberg, 1954, "Utility analysis and the consumption function: an interpretation of cross-section data," in Kenneth K. Kurihara, ed., *Post-Keynesian economics*, New Brunswick, N.J., Rutgers University Press, 388–436.

____, 1979, "Utility analysis and the consumption function: an attempt at integration," in Andrew Abel , ed., *The collected papers of Franco Modigliani*, Vol. 2, Cambridge, Mass., MIT Press, 128–97.

Morduch, Jonathan, 1990, "Risk, production, and saving: theory and evidence from Indian households," Department of Economics, Harvard University, Cambridge, Mass., processed.

____, 1995, "Income smoothing and consumption smoothing," *Journal of Economic Perspectives*, **9**, 103–14.

Moulton, Brent R., 1986, "Random group effects and the precision of regression estimates," *Journal of Econometrics*, **32**, 385–97.

____, 1990, "An illustration of a pitfall in estimating the effects of aggregate variables on micro units," *Review of Economics and Statistics*, **72**, 334–38.

Muellbauer, John N. J., 1980, "The estimation of the Prais-Houthakker model of equivalence scales," *Econometrica*, **48**, 153–76.

Mundlak, Yair, 1961, "Empirical production function free of management bias," *Journal of Farm Economics*, **43**, 44–56.

Murthy, M. N., 1977, *Sampling theory and methods*, Calcutta, Statistical Publishing Co. (2nd ed.).

Musgrove, Philip, 1978, *Consumer behavior in Latin America*, Washington, D.C., Brookings Institution.

____, 1979, "Permanent household income and consumption in urban South America," *American Economic Review*, **69**, 355–68.

Mwabu, Germano, and T. Paul Schultz, 1995, "Wage premia for education and location by gender and race in South Africa," Economic Growth Center, Yale University, New Haven, processed.

———, 1996, "Education returns across quantiles of the wage function: alternative explanations for returns to education in South Africa," *American Economic Review*, **86**, 335–39.

Nagar, A. L., 1959, "The bias and moment matrix of the general k-class estimators of the parameters in simultaneous equations," *Econometrica*, **27**, 575–95.

Nelson, Charles, and Richard Startz, 1990a, "The distribution of the instrumental variable estimator and its *t*-ratio when the instrument is a poor one," *Journal of Business*, **63**, S125–40.

———, 1990b, "Some further results on the exact small sample properties of the instrumental variable estimator," *Econometrica*, **58**, 967–76.

Nelson, Forrest D., 1981, "A test for misspecification in the censored normal model," *Econometrica*, **49**, 1317–29.

Nelson, Julie A., 1988, "Household economies of scale in consumption: theory and evidence," *Econometrica*, **56**, 1301–14.

———, 1992, "Methods of estimating household equivalence scales: theory and policy," *Review of Income and Wealth*, **38**, 295–310.

———, 1993, "Household equivalence scales: theory and policy," *Journal of Labor Economics*, **11**, 471–93.

———, 1994, "On testing full insurance using consumer expenditure survey data," *Journal of Political Economy*, **102**, 384–94.

Newbery, David M. G., and Nicholas H. Stern, eds., 1987, *The theory of taxation for developing countries*, New York, Oxford University Press.

Newbery, David M. G., and Joseph E. Stiglitz, 1981, *The theory of commodity price stabilization: a study in the economics of risk*, Oxford, Clarendon Press.

Newey, Whitney K., 1987, "Specification tests for distributional assumptions in the Tobit model," *Journal of Econometrics*, **34**, 125–45.

Newey, Whitney K., James L. Powell, and James R. Walker, 1990, "Semiparametric estimation of selection models: some empirical results," *American Economic Review*, **80**, 324–28.

Newman, John, Laura Rawlings, and Paul Gertler, 1994, "Using randomized control designs in evaluating social sector programs in developing countries," *The World Bank Research Observer*, **9**, 181–201.

Neyman, Jerzy, 1934, "On the two different aspects of the representation method: the method of stratified sampling and the method of purposive selection," *Journal of the Royal Statistical Society*, **97**, 558–625.

Nicholson, J. Leonard, 1949, "Variations in working class family expenditure," *Journal of the Royal Statistical Association, Series A*, **112**, 359–411.

———, 1976, "Appraisal of different methods of estimating equivalence scales and their results," *Review of Income and Wealth*, **22**, 1–11.

Nickell, Stephen, 1981, "Biases in dynamic models with fixed effects," *Econometrica*, **49**, 1417–26.

Orshansky, Mollie, 1963, "Children of the poor," *Social Security Bulletin*, **26**, 3–5.

———, 1965, "Counting the poor: another look at the poverty profile, *Social Security Bulletin*, **28**, 3–29.

Otsuka, Keijiro, Hiroyuki Chuma, and Yujiro Hayami, 1992, "Land and labor contracts in agrarian economies," *Journal of Economic Literature*, **30**, 1965–2018.

Pakistan, Government of, (annual), *Pakistan Economic Survey*, Islamabad, Ministry of Finance.

Parrish, William L., and Robert J. Willis, 1992, "Daughters, education, and family budgets: Taiwan experiences," National Opinion Research Center, Chicago, Il., processed.

Paxson, Christina H., 1992, "Using weather variability to estimate the response of savings to transitory income in Thailand," *American Economic Review*, **82**, 15–33.

———, 1993, "Consumption and income seasonality in Thailand," *Journal of Political Economy*, **101**, 39–72.

———, 1996, "Saving and growth: evidence from micro data," *European Economic Review*, **40**, 255–88.

Pfefferman, D., and T. M. F. Smith, 1985, "Regression models for grouped populations in cross-section surveys," *International Statistical Review*, **53**, 37–59.

Pindyck, Robert S., and Daniel L. Rubinfeld, 1991, *Econometric models and economic forecasts*, New York, McGraw-Hill. (3rd ed.).

Pischke, Jörn-Steffen, 1995, "Measurement error and earnings dynamics: some estimates from the PSID validation study," *Journal of Business and Economic Statistics*, **13**, 305–14.

Pitt, Mark M., and Mark R. Rosenzweig, 1986, "Agricultural prices, food consumption, and the health and productivity of farmers," in Inderjit Singh, Lyn Squire, and John Strauss, eds., *Agricultural household models: extensions and applications*, Baltimore, Md., Johns Hopkins University Press.

Pitt, Mark M., Mark R. Rosenzweig, and Donna M. Gibbons, 1993, "The determinants and consequences of the placement of government programs in Indonesia," *The World Bank Economic Review*, **7**, 319–48.

Pitt, Mark M., Mark R. Rosenzweig, and M. Nazmul Hassan, 1990, "Productivity, health, and inequality in the intrahousehold distribution of food in low-income countries," *American Economic Review*, **80**, 1139–56.

Platteau, Jean-Phillipe, 1991, "Traditional systems of social security and hunger insurance: some lessons from the evidence pertaining to third world village societies," in Ehtisham Ahmad et al., eds., *Social security in developing countries*, Oxford, Clarendon Press.

Pollak, Robert A., and Terence J. Wales, 1979, "Welfare comparisons and equivalent scales," *American Economic Review*, **69**, (*papers and proceedings*), 216–21.

Powell, James L., 1984, "Least absolute deviations estimation for the censored regression model," *Journal of Econometrics*, **25**, 303–25.

———, 1986, "Symmetrically trimmed least squares estimation for Tobit models," *Econometrica*, **54**, 1435–60.

———, 1989, "Semiparametric estimation of censored selection models," Department of Economics, University of Wisconsin–Madison, processed.

Powell, James L., James H. Stock, and Thomas M. Stoker, 1989, "Semiparametric estimation of index coefficients," *Econometrica*, **57**, 1403–30.

Prais, Sigbert J., and Hendrik S. Houthakker, 1955, *The analysis of family budgets*, Cambridge University Press, 2nd ed. 1972.

Pudney, Stephen, 1989, *Modelling individual choice: the econometrics of corners, kinks, and holes*, Oxford, Blackwell.

Pyatt, Graham, 1976, "On the interpretation and disaggregation of gini coefficients," *Economic Journal*, **76**, 243–55.

Rainwater, Lee, 1974, *What money buys: inequality and the social meanings of income*, New York, Basic Books.

Rao, J. N. K., and C. F. J. Wu, 1988, "Resampling inference with complex survey data," *Journal of the American Statistical Association*, **83**, 231–41.

Ravallion, Martin, 1993, *Poverty comparisons: a guide to concepts and methods*, LSMS Working Paper 88, Washington, D.C., World Bank.

Rawls, John, 1972, *A theory of justice*, Oxford University Press.

Reutlinger, Shlomo, and Marcelo Selowsky, 1976, *Malnutrition and poverty: magnitude and policy options*, Baltimore, Md., Johns Hopkins University Press.

Robinson, Peter M., 1988, "Root-N-consistent semiparametric regression," *Econometrica*, **56**, 931–54.

Rosenzweig, Mark R., 1988, "Risk, implicit contracts and the family in rural areas of low-income countries, *Economic Journal*, **98**, 1148–70.

Rosenzweig, Mark R., and T. Paul Schultz, 1982, "Market opportunities, genetic endowments, and intrafamily resource distribution: child survival in rural India," *American Economic Review*, **72**, 803–15.

Rosenzweig, Mark R., and Oded Stark, 1989, "Consumption smoothing, migration, and marriage: evidence from rural India," *Journal of Political Economy*, **97**, 905–27.

Rosenzweig, Mark R., and Kenneth I. Wolpin, 1986, "Evaluating the effects of optimally distributed public programs," *American Economic Review*, **76**, 470–82.

Rothbarth, Erwin, 1943, "Note on a method of determining equivalent income for families of different composition," appendix 4 of C. Madge, ed., *War time pattern of saving and spending*, Occasional Paper No. 4, London, National Income of Economic and Social Research.

Rowntree, B. Seebohm, 1985, *Poverty and progress*, New York and London. Garland. (originally published in 1941).

Roy, René, 1942, *De l'utilité: contribution à la théorie des choix*, Paris, Hermann.

Rudd, Jeremy B., 1993, "Boy-girl discrimination in Taiwan: evidence from expenditure data," Research Program in Development Studies, Princeton University, processed.

Rudra, Ashok, 1974, "Minimal level of living: a statistical examination," in Bardhan and Srinivasan, eds., 1974, 281–90.

Sadoulet, Elisabeth, and Alain de Janvry, 1995, *Quantitative development policy analysis*, Baltimore and London, Johns Hopkins University Press.

Sah, Raaj, and Joseph E. Stiglitz, 1992, *Peasants versus city-dwellers: taxation and the burden of development*, Oxford, Clarendon.

Sahn, David, 1989, *Seasonal variation in third world agriculture: the consequences for food security*, Baltimore, Md., Johns Hopkins University Press for the International Food Policy Research Institute.

Schechtman, Jack, 1976, "An income fluctuation problem," *Journal of Economic Theory*, **12**, 218–41.

Schechtman, Jack, and Vera Escudero, 1977, "Some results on 'An income fluctuation problem'," *Journal of Economic Theory*, **16**, 151–66.

Schultz, T. Paul, 1989, "Women and development: objectives, framework, and policy interventions," Population and Human Resources Department, World Bank,

Washington, D.C., processed.

Schwarz, Gideon, 1978, "Estimating the dimension of a model," *Annals of Statistics*, **6**, 461–64.

Scott, A. J., and D. Holt, 1982, "The effect of two-stage sampling on ordinary least squares methods," *Journal of the American Statistical Association*, **77**, 848–54.

Scott, Christopher, 1992, "Estimation of annual expenditure from one-month cross-sectional data in a household survey," *Inter-Stat Bulletin*, **8**, 57–65.

Scott, Christopher, and Ben Amenuvegbe, 1990, *Effect of recall duration on reporting of household expenditures: an experimental study in Ghana*, Social Dimensions of Adjustment in Sub-Saharan Africa Working Paper 6, Washington, D.C., World Bank.

Sen, Amartya K., 1962, "An aspect of Indian agriculture," *Economic Weekly*, **14**, Annual Number.

_____, 1966, "Peasants and dualism with and without surplus labor," *Journal of Political Economy*, **74**, 425–50.

_____, 1975, *Employment, technology, and development*, Oxford, Clarendon Press.

_____, 1976a, "Real national income," *Review of Economic Studies*, **43**, 19–39.

_____, 1976b, "Poverty: an ordinal approach to measurement," *Econometrica*, **46**, 437–46.

_____, 1985, *Commodities and capabilities*, Amsterdam, North-Holland.

_____, 1989, "Women's survival as a development problem," *Bulletin of the American Academy of Arts and Sciences*, **43**, 2.

_____, 1992, *Inequality re-examined*, Oxford, Clarendon Press.

Seng, You Poh, 1951, "Historical survey of the development of sampling theory and practice," *Journal of the Royal Statistical Society* (A), **114**, 214–31.

Shorrocks, Anthony F., 1975, "The age-wealth relationship: a cross-section and cohort analysis," *Review of Economics and Statistics*, **57**, 155–63.

_____, 1983, "Ranking income distributions," *Economica*, **50**, 3–17.

Siamwalla, Ammar, and S. Setboongsarng, 1991, "Agricultural pricing policies in Thailand 1960–84," in Anne O. Krueger, Maurice Schiff, and Alberto Valdes, eds., *The political economy of agricultural pricing policy*, Baltimore, Md., Johns Hopkins University Press.

Silverman, Bernard W., 1986, *Density estimation for statistics and data analysis*, London and New York, Chapman and Hall.

Singh, Inderjit, Lyn Squire, and John Strauss, 1986, *Agricultural household models: extensions and applications*, Baltimore, Md., Johns Hopkins University Press.

Sitter, R. R., 1992, "Comparing three bootstrap methods for survey data," *Canadian Journal of Statistics*, **20**, 135–54.

Skinner, C. J., D. Holt, and T. M. F. Smith, 1989, *Analysis of complex surveys*, New York, Wiley.

Skinner, Jonathan, 1988, "Risky income, life-cycle consumption, and precautionary saving," *Journal of Monetary Economics*, **22**, 237–55.

Smith, James P., Lynn A. Karoly, and Duncan Thomas, 1992, "Migration in retrospect: differences between men and women," Santa Monica, Ca., Rand Corporation, processed.

Smith, James P., and Duncan Thomas, 1993, "On the road: marriage and mobility in Malaysia," Santa Monica, Ca., Rand Corporation, Labor and Population Program Working Paper Series 93–11, processed.

Snow, John, 1965, *On the mode of communication of cholera*, reprint ed. New York,

Hafner (originally published 1855).

Solow, Robert M., 1956, "A contribution to the theory of economic growth," *Quarterly Journal of Economics*, **70**, 65–94.

Som, Ranjan Kumar, 1973, *A manual of sampling techniques*, London, Heinemann.

Squire, Lyn, 1989, "Project evaluation in theory and practice," in Hollis Chenery and T. N. Srinivasan, eds., *Handbook of development economics*, **2**, Amsterdam, Elsevier, 1093–137.

Squire, Lyn, and Hermann van der Tak, 1975, *Economic analysis of projects*, Baltimore, Md., Johns Hopkins University Press.

Srinivas, M. N. 1976, *The remembered village*, Delhi, Oxford University Press.

Srinivasan, T. N., 1972, "Farm size and productivity: implications of choice under uncertainty," *Sankhya, Series B*, **34**, 409–20.

Staiger, Douglas, and James H. Stock, 1993, "Instrumental variables regression with weak instruments," NBER Technical Paper 151, NBER, Cambridge, Mass., processed.

Stata Corporation, 1993, *Stata reference manual: release 3.1, 6th edition*, College Station, Tex. (3 vols).

Statistical Institute and Planning Instiute of Jamaica, 1996, *Jamaica survey of living conditions 1994*, Kingston.

Stern, Nicholas H., 1987, "Aspects of the general theory of tax reform," in Newbery and Stern, eds., 1987, 60–91.

Stigler, George J., 1945, "The cost of subsistence," *Journal of Farm Economics*, **27**, 303–14.

———, 1954, "The early history of empirical studies of consumer behavior," *Journal of Political Economy*, **42**, 95–113.

Stiglitz, Joseph E., 1976, "The efficiency wage hypothesis, surplus labor, and the distribution of income in LDCs," *Oxford Economic Papers*, **28**, 185–207.

Stoker, Thomas M., 1991, *Lectures on semi-parametric econometrics*, Louvain-la-Neuve, Belgium, CORE Foundation.

Strauss, John, 1982, "Determinants of food consumption in rural Sierra Leone," *Journal of Development Economics*, **11**, 327–53.

———, 1986, "Does better nutrition raise farm productivity?" *Journal of Political Economy*, **94**, 297–320.

Strauss, John, and Duncan Thomas, 1990, "The shape of the calorie-expenditure curve," Rand Corporation, Santa Monica, and Yale University, New Haven, processed .

———, 1995,"Human resources: empirical modeling of household and family decisions," in Jere Behrman and T. N. Srinivasan, eds., *Handbook of development economics*, **3a**, Amsterdam, Elsevier, 1883–2023.

Streeten, Paul, Shahid Javed Burki, Mahbub Ul Haq, Norman Hicks, and Frances Stewart, 1981, *First things first: meeting basic human needs in developing countries*, Oxford University Press.

Subramanian, Shankar, 1994, "Gender discrimination in intra-household allocation in India," Department of Economics, Cornell, and Indira Gandhi Institute of Development Research, Bombay, processed.

Subramanian, Shankar, and Angus Deaton, 1991, "Gender effects in Indian consumption patterns," *Sarvekshana*, **14**, 1–12.

———, 1996, "The demand for food and calories," *Journal of Political Economy*, **104**, 133–62.

Sundrum, R. M., 1990, *Income distribution in less developed countries*, London and New York, Routledge.

Sydenstricker, E., and W. I. King, 1921, "The measurement of the relative economic status of families," *Quarterly Publication of the American Statistical Association*, **17**, 842–57.

Thomas, Duncan, 1991, *Gender differences in household resource allocation*, LSMS Working Paper 79, Washington, D.C., World Bank.

———, 1994, "Like father, like son; like mother, like daughter: parental resources and child height," *Journal of Human Resources*, **29**, 950–88.

Timmer, C. Peter, 1981, "Is there 'curvature' in the Slutsky matrix?" *Review of Economics and Statistics*, **63**, 395–402.

Timmer, C. Peter, and Harold Alderman, 1979, "Estimating consumption patterns for food policy analysis," *American Journal of Agricultural Economics*, **61**, 982–87.

Tobin, James, 1958, "Estimation of relationships for limited dependent variables," *Econometrica*, **26**, 24–36.

Townsend, Robert M., 1993a, "Intra-regional risk sharing in Thailand, an uneven but growing economy," Institute for Policy Reform, Washington, D.C., processed.

———, 1993b, "Financial systems in northern Thai villages," Department of Economics, University of Chicago, processed.

———, 1994, "Risk and insurance in village India," *Econometrica*, **62**, 539–91.

———, 1995, "Consumption insurance: an evaluation of risk-bearing systems in low-income economies," *Journal of Economic Perspectives*, **9**, 83–102.

Trairatvorakul, Prasarn, 1984, *The effects on income distribution and nutrition of alternative rice price policies in Thailand*, Washington, D.C., International Food Policy Research Institute.

Udry, Christopher, 1990, "Credit markets in northern Nigeria: credit as insurance in a rural economy," *The World Bank Economic Review*, **4**, 251–69.

United Nations, 1991, *National accounts statistics: main aggregates and detailed tables, 1989*, Part II, New York.

van der Gaag, Jacques, Morton Stelcner, and Wim Vijverberg, 1989, "Wage differentials and moonlighting by civil servants: evidence from Côte d'Ivoire and Peru," *The World Bank Economic Review*, **3**, 67–95.

van Praag, Bernard M. S., Aldi J. Hagenaars, and H. van Weerden, 1982, "Poverty in Europe," *Review of Income and Wealth*, **28**, 345–59.

Vartia, Yrjö O., 1983, "Efficient methods of measuring welfare change and compensated income in terms of market demand functions," *Econometrica*, **51**, 79–98.

Vaughan, Denton R., 1992, "Exploring the use of the public's views to set income poverty thresholds and adjust them over time," *Social Security Bulletin*, **56**, 22–46.

Visaria, Pravin, and Shyamalendu Pal, 1980, *Poverty and living standards in Asia: an overview of the main results and lessons of selected household surveys*, LSMS Working Paper 2, Washington, D.C., World Bank.

Wade, Robert, 1988, *Village republics: economic conditions for collective action in South India*, Cambridge University Press.

Weiss, Yoram, and Lee A. Lillard, 1978, "Experience, vintage, and time effects in the growth of earnings: American scientists, 1960–1970," *Journal of Political Economy*, **86**, 427–47.

White, Halbert, 1980, "A heteroskedasticity-consistent covariance matrix estimator and a direct test for heteroskedasticity," *Econometrica,* **48,** 817–38.

——, 1984, *Asymptotic theory for econometricians,* New York, Academic Press.

Wilkinson, Richard G., 1986, "Socio-economic differences in mortality: interpreting the data on their size and trends," in Richard G. Wilkinson, ed., *Class and health: research and longitudinal data,* London and New York, Tavistock.

Wolfson, Michael C., 1994, "When inequalities diverge," *American Economic Review* (*paps. & procs.*), **84,** 353–58.

Wolpin, Kenneth I., 1982, "A new test of the permanent income hypothesis: the impact of weather on the income and consumption of farm households in India," *International Economic Review,* **23,** 583–94.

Wolter, Kirk M., 1985, *Introduction to variance estimation,* New York and Berlin, Springer-Verlag.

Working, Holbrook, 1943, "Statistical laws of family expenditure," *Journal of the American Statistical Association,* **38,** 43–56.

World Bank, 1992, "Indonesia: public expenditures, prices, and the poor," Indonesia Resident Mission 11293–IND, Jakarta, processed.

Yule, George Udny, 1899, "An investigation into the causes of changes in pauperism in England, chiefly during the last two intercensal decades," *Journal of the Royal Statistical Society,* **62,** 249–95.

Zeldes, Stephen P., 1989a, "Consumption and liquidity constraints: an empirical investigation," *Journal of Political Economy,* **97,** 305–46.

——, 1989b, "Optimal consumption with stochastic income: deviations from certainty equivalence," *Quarterly Journal of Economics,* **104,** 275–98.

Subject index

Author index